Studies in Jewish and Christian Literature

Messiah and the Throne, Timo Eskola
Defilement and Purgation in the Book of Hebrews, William G. Johnsson
Father, Son, and Spirit in Romans 8, Ron C. Fay
Within the Veil, Félix H. Cortez

Within the Veil

Within the Veil

The Ascension of the Son in the Letter to the Hebrews

Félix H. Cortez

Fontes

Within the Veil:
The Ascension of the Son in the Letter to the Hebrews

Copyright © 2020 by Félix H. Cortez

ISBN-13: 978-1-948048-36-1 (hardback)
ISBN-13: 978-1-948048-37-8 (paperback)

All rights reserved. No part of this publication may be reproduced, stored in a retrieval system, or transmitted in any form or by any means—electronic, mechanical, photocopy, recording, or any other—except for brief quotations in printed reviews, without the prior permission of the publisher.

Scripture quotations unless otherwise noted are from New Revised Standard Version Bible, copyright © 1989 National Council of the Churches of Christ in the United States of America. Used by permission. All rights reserved worldwide.

FONTES PRESS
DALLAS, TX
www.fontespress.com

For Alma Gloria Alvarez-Yanes

Contents

Chapter 1: Introduction.. 1
    Statement of the Problem... 4
    State of Affairs: The Day of Atonement Ritual Provides the Analogy to Jesus's
    Ascension... 6
        Critique of the State of Affairs: A More Limited Role for the Day of
        Atonement Imagery? 13
            There Is Absence of "Affliction of the Soul" in Relation to Jesus's
            Entrance into the Heavenly Sanctuary................................. 13
            The Azazel Ritual Is Omitted.. 15
            The Sprinkling of Jesus's Blood in Heaven Does Not Refer to the
            Day of Atonement Ritual 17
            The Day of Atonement Provides Only Secondary Imagery to Jesus's
            Sacrifice 19
            Summary... 20
    Alternative Suggestion: Moses's Inauguration of the Sanctuary Provides
    the Analogy to Jesus's Ascension 21
        Critique of the Analogy to Moses's Inauguration of the Sanctuary.......... 24
    A Third Way: The Enthronement of the Ideal Davidic King Provides
    the Analogy to Jesus's Ascension 27
    Delimitations and Methodology.. 33

Chapter 2: The Davidic Covenant and the Expectation of an Ideal King in the Hebrew Bible and Early Judaism.................................... 35
    The Institution of the Davidic Covenant 37
        Is the Davidic Covenant Unconditional? 39
        What Is the Relationship between the Davidic and the Mosaic Covenants? ... 41
            The Davidic King as Covenant Mediator: He Renews the Mosaic
            Covenant under "Better Promises".................................... 43
            The Davidic King as Reformer of the Cult: He Reorganizes the
            Priesthood and the Service of the Temple 46
            The Davidic King Is Confirmed in God's House and Kingdom:
            The Davidic Covenant in 1 Chronicles 17 49
        Summary... 51
    Righteous Kings and the Davidic Covenant in Monarchic Israel 51
        Solomon.. 52
        Asa 55
        Joash... 57
        Hezekiah 60
            Covenant Renewal.. 60
            Re-Consecration of the Priests and Temple 61
            Re-Inauguration of the Service of the Temple 64
            Re-Consecration of the Nation 64
            Celebration of Passover 65

Rest from Their Enemies	67
Josiah	67
Cleansing of the Land	68
Repair of the Temple	69
The Book of the Law Is Found	69
Renewal of the Covenant	70
Reorganization of the Cult	70
Summary	72
The Davidic Covenant in the Rest of the Hebrew Bible	73
The Psalms	73
Psalm 89	74
Psalm 132	74
Other Psalms	75
The Pre-exilic Prophets and the Davidic Covenant	76
Amos	76
Hosea	77
Micah	78
Isaiah	80
Exilic Interpretation of the Davidic Covenant	88
Jeremiah	88
Ezekiel	95
The Post-Exilic Prophets and the Davidic Covenant	100
Haggai	100
Zechariah	102
Summary	108
The Davidic Covenant in Early Judaism	110
Wisdom of Ben Sira	110
First Maccabees	117
Psalms of Solomon 17	119
Dead Sea Scrolls	123
Words of the Luminaries (4Q504)	123
Commentary on Genesis A (4Q252)	126
Florilegium (4Q174)	127
Commentary on Isaiah (4Q161)	130
Sefer Hamilḥama (4Q285)	131
Apocryphon of Daniel or "Son of God" Document (4Q246)	133
Summary	136
4 Ezra	136
Josephus	137
Summary	140
Conclusion	141
CHAPTER 3: ASCENSION AND INAUGURATION OF THE RULE OF THE "SON" IN THE LETTER TO THE HEBREWS	145

"... When He Brings the Firstborn into the World" (Heb 1:6): Ascension
and the Enthronement of the Son 146
    Does This Passage Refer to the Ascension of Jesus? 146
        The Case for the Incarnation 146
        The Case for the Parousia 148
        The Case for the Exaltation 150
    The Enthronement of the Firstborn over the World to Come 153
        The Catena Describes the Enthronement Ceremony of the Son 153
        The Enthronement of the Son Culminates His Victory over Death 160
    *Enthronement as the Basis for Exhortation: The Son's Exaltation
    Prefigures and Makes Possible the Glorification of the Sons* 168
        Jesus as "Son" in Hebrews 169
        The Son and the Sons in the Argument of Hebrews 180
    Summary 185
" ... A Great High Priest Who Has Passed through the Heavens"
(Heb 4:14–16): Ascension and Entrance into God's Rest 185
    High Priesthood and Ascension "through the Heavens" 186
    Jesus Leads Believers into the Rest 191
        Hebrews 4:14–16 in the Argument of the Letter 192
        The Exalted High Priest Helps the People to Enter the Rest 195
    Summary 202
"A Hope That Enters the Inner Shrine behind the Curtain" (Heb 6:19–20):
Ascension and the Appointment of a Faithful Priest 202
    Ascension as Entering behind the Curtain 202
    The Ascension Shows the Unchangeable Character of God's Promises 206
        The Role of the Ascension in Hebrews 6:19–20 206
        Jesus Is the Hope That Enters "within the Veil" 209
        *Jesus Embodies God's Oath Which Confirms God's Promises to the
        Believers* 210
        When Did Jesus Become a High Priest? 213
    Summary 217
"When Christ Came as a High priest of the Good Things That Have
Come" (9:11–14, 24; 10:19–25): Ascension and the Inauguration of the
New Covenant 218
    The Ascension Inaugurates the New Covenant (Hebrews 9:11–14) 218
        *Hebrews 9:11–14 Describes Jesus's Entrance into the (Heavenly)
        Sanctuary of the New Covenant* 219
        *Hebrews 9:11–14 Understands the Ascension as the Inauguration
        of the Ministry of the New Covenant* 240
        Summary 258
    *The Ascension Inaugurates the Fulfillment of the New Covenant
    Promises (Hebrews 9:24–28)* 258
        Ascension as an Act of Appearance before God on Our Behalf 260
        *The Ascension Has the Purpose of Removing Sin and Executing
        Judgment* 261

  Ascension as the Basis for Exhortation (Hebrews 10:19–25)..............277
   Jesus's Ascension Is Described as Providing Full Access to the
    Presence of God 277
   The Ascension Is the Basis for the Exhortation to Approach God........281
  Summary..284
 "You Have Come to Mount Zion" (12:18–29): The Ascension of the
 Believers to the Heavenly Jerusalem 285
  The Believers Have Ascended to the Heavenly Jerusalem in the World of the
   Scriptures 287
   Hebrews' Use of the Old Testament Creates a World in Which the Readers
    Stand in the Presence of God......................................292
   God Performs the Events at Mount Zion through His Word............296
  The Audience's Participation at Mount Zion Is What Provides Compelling Force
   to the Exhortation of Hebrews 298
 Conclusion 301

CHAPTER 4: CONCLUSION: JESUS'S ASCENSION INAUGURATES HIS RULE AS THE ESCHATOLOGICAL "SON" OF GOD, FULFILLING THE EXPECTATIONS OF A DAVIDIC RIGHTEOUS RULER IN THE OT 305

BIBLIOGRAPHY 311

INDEX 357

Abbreviations

AB	Anchor Bible
ABRL	Anchor Bible Reference Library
ACCS	Ancient Christian Commentary on Scripture
ACNT	Augsburg Commentaries on the New Testament
AIPHOS	*Annuaire de l'Institut de philologie et d'histoire orientales et slaves*
ALGHJ	Arbeiten zur Literatur und Geschichte des hellenistischen Judentums
AnBib	Analecta biblica
ANF	*Ante-Nicene Fathers*
ANRW	*Aufstieg und Niedergang der römischen Welt: Geschichte und Kultur Roms im Spiegel der neueren Forschung.* Edited by H. Temporini and W. Haase. Berlin, 1972–
ANTC	Abingdon New Testament Commentaries
AOAT	Alter Orient und Altes Testament
AOTC	Abingdon Old Testament Commentaries
AR	*Archiv für Religionswissenschaft*
AS	Assyriological Studies
AsJT	*Asia Journal of Theology*
AUSDDS	Andrews University Seminary Doctoral Dissertation Series
AUSS	*Andrews University Seminary Studies*
AUSTR	American University Studies, Series 7: Theology and Religion

BBB	Bonner biblische Beiträge
BBR	*Bulletin for Biblical Research*
BDAG	Bauer, W., F. W. Danker, W. F. Arndt, and F. W. Gingrich. *Greek-English Lexicon of the New Testament and Other Early Christian Literature*. 3d ed. Chicago, 2000
BDB	Brown, F., S. R. Driver, and C. A. Briggs. *A Hebrew and English Lexicon of the Old Testament*. Oxford, 1907.
BDF	Blass F., A. Debrunner, and R. W. Funk. *A Greek Grammar of the New Testament and Other Early Christian Literature*. Chicago, 1961
BGBE	Beiträge zur Geschichte der biblischen Exegese
Bib	*Biblica*
BibInt	*Biblical Interpretation*
BibInt	Biblical Interpretation Series
BibSem	The Biblical Seminar
BiPa	*Biblia Patristica: Index des citations et allusions bibliques dans la littérature*. Paris: CNRS, 2000
BJS	Brown Judaic Studies
BLS	Bible and Literature Series
BN	*Biblische Notizen*
BNTC	Black's New Testament Commentaries
BNP	*Brill's New Pauly: Encyclopaedia of the Ancient World*. Edited by Hubert Cancik. 22 vols. Leiden: Brill, 2002–2011
BR	*Biblical Research*
BRLA	Brill Reference Library of Judaism
BSac	*Bibliotheca Sacra*
BZ	*Biblische Zeitschrift*
BZAW	Beihefte zur Zeitschrift für die alttestamentliche Wissenchaft
BZNW	Beihefte zur Zeitschrift für die neutestamentliche Wissenschaft und die Kunde der älteren Kirche
CBC	Cambridge Bible Commentary
CBET	Contributions to Biblical Exegesis and Theology
CBQ	*Catholic Biblical Quarterly*
CBQMS	Catholic Biblical Quarterly Monograph Series

CJT	*Canadian Journal of Theology*
Cmio	*Communio: Commentarii internationales de ecclesia et theología*
ConBOT	Coniectanea biblica: Old Testament Series
ConBNT	Coniectanea biblica: New Testament Series
CRBR	*Critical Review of Books in Religion*
CRINT	Compendia rerum iudaicarum ad Novum Testamentum
CSHJ	Chicago Studies in the History of Judaism
CTQ	*Concordia Theological Quarterly*
CurBR	*Currents in Biblical Research (formerly Currents in Research: Biblical Studies)*
DA	Day of Atonement
DARCOM	Daniel and Revelation Committee Series
DJD	Discoveries in the Judaean Desert
DJG	*Dictionary of Jesus and the Gospels.* Edited by Joel B. Green, Jeannine K. Brown, and Nicholas Perrin. 2nd ed. Downers Grove, IL: InterVarsity Press, 2013
DLNT	*Dictionary of the Later New Testament and Its Developments.* Edited by R. P. Martin and P. H. Davids. Downers Grove, IL: InterVarsity Press, 1997
DNTB	*Dictionary of New Testament Background.* Edited by Craig A. Evans and Stanley E. Porter. Downers Grove, IL: InterVarsity Press, 2000
DOTHB	*Dictionary of the Old Testament: Historical Books.* Edited by Bill T. Arnold and H. G. M. Williamson. IVP Academic; InterVarsity Press, 2005.
DOTP	*Dictionary of the Old Testament: Pentateuch.* Edited by T. Desmond Alexander and David W. Baker. InterVarsity Press, 2003.
DSD	*Dead Sea Discoveries*
EBib	*Études bibliques*
EdF	Erträge der Forschung
EKKNT	Evangelisch-Katholischer Kommentar zum Neuen Testament
EncJud	*Encyclopaedia Judaica.* 16 vols. Jerusalem, 1972
ER	*Encyclopedia of Religion.* Edited by Lindsay Jones. 2nd ed. 15 vols. Detroit: Macmillan Reference USA, 2005.

ESEC	Emory Studies in Early Christianity
EstAg	*Estudio Agustiniano*
EstBib	*Estudios bíblicos*
ETR	*Études théologiques et religieuses*
EvQ	*Evangelical Quarterly*
ExpTim	*Expository Times*
FoiVie	*Foi et vie*
FRLANT	Forschungen zur Religion und Literatur des Alten und Neuen Testaments
GNS	*Good News Studies*
HALOT	Koehler, L., and W. Baumgartner, and J. J. Stamm, *The Hebrew and Aramaic Lexicon of the Old Testament*, Translated and edited under the supervision of M. E. J. Richardson. 4 vols. Leiden, 1994–1999
HB	Hebrew Bible
HDR	Harvard Dissertations in Religion
Hermeneia	Hermeneia: A Critical and Historical Commentary on the Bible
Hex.	*Hexapla*
HeyJ	*Heythrop Journal*
HNT	Handbuch zum Neuen Testament
HNTC	Harper's New Testament Commentaries
Hok	*Hokhma*
HSM	Harvard Semitic Monographs
HSS	Harvard Semitic Studies
HTR	*Harvard Theological Review*
HTS	Harvard Theological Studies
IBC	Interpretation: A Bible Commentary for Teaching and Preaching
IDB	*The Interpreter's Dictionary of the Bible*. Edited by George A. Buttrick. 4 vols. New York: Abingdon, 1962
IBS	*Irish Biblical Studies*
ICC	International Critical Commentary
Imm	*Immanuel*

Int	*Interpretation*
ISBL	Indiana Studies in Biblical Literature
JAOS	*Journal of the American Oriental Society*
JETS	*Journal of the Evangelical Theological Society*
JJS	*Journal of Jewish Studies*
JNSL	*Journal of Northwest Semitic Languages*
JOTT	*Journal of Translation and Textlinguistics*
JPS	Jewish Publication Society
JSJSup	Supplements to the Journal for the Study of Judaism
JSNT	*Journal for the Study of the New Testament*
JSNTSup	Journal for the Study of the New Testament: Supplement Series
JSOT	*Journal for the Study of the Old Testament*
JSOTSup	Journal for the Study of the Old Testament: Supplement Series
JSPSup	Journal for the Study of the Pseudepigrapha: Supplement Series
JTS	*Journal of Theological Studies*
KEK	Kritisch-exegetischer Kommentar über das Neue Testament (Meyer-Kommentar)
LCL	Loeb Classical Library
LD	Lectio divina
LHBOTS	The Library of Hebrew Bible/Old Testament Studies
L&N	*Greek English Lexicon of the New Testament: Based on Semantic Domains.* Edited by J. P. Louw and E. A. Nida. 2d ed. New York, 1989
LSJ	Liddell, H. G., R. Scott, and H. S. Jones, *A Greek-English Lexicon.* 9th ed. with revised supplement. Oxford, 1996
LSTS	The Library of Second Temple Studies
LumVie	*Lumière et vie*
LXX	Septuagint (the Greek OT)
MS(S)	manuscript(s)
NA[28]	*Novum Testamentum Graece*, Nestle-Aland, 28th ed.
NAB	New American Bible

NAC	New American Commentary
NCBCom	New Century Bible Commentary
NCE	*New Catholic Encyclopedia*. Edited by William J. McDonald et al. 15 vols. New York: McGraw-Hill, 1967
NEchtB	Neue Echter Bibel
Neot	*Neotestamentica*
NIB	*The New Interpreter's Bible*. Edited by Leander E. Keck. 12 vols. Nashville: Abingdon, 1994–2004
NIBC	New International Biblical Commentary
NICNT	New International Commentary on the New Testament
NICOT	New International Commentary on the Old Testament
NIDNTT	*New International Dictionary of New Testament Theology*. Edited by C. Brown. 4 vols. Grand Rapids, 1975–1985
NIGTC	New International Greek Testament Commentary
NIVAC	NIV Application Commentary
NovT	*Novum Testamentum*
NovTSup	Supplements to Novum Testamentum
NPNF[1]	*Nicene and Post-Nicene Fathers*, Series 1
NPNF[2]	*Nicene and Post-Nicene Fathers*, Series 2
NRSV	New Revised Standard Version
NSBT	New Studies in Biblical Theology
NT	New Testament
NTD	Das Neue Testament Deutsch
NTL	New Testament Library
NTM	New Testament Message: A Biblical-Theological Commentary
NTS	*New Testament Studies*
NTTS	New Testament Tools and Studies
OBO	Orbis biblicus et orientalis
OLZ	*Orientalistische Literaturzeitung*
OT	Old Testament
OTM	Oxford Theological Monographs
OTL	Old Testament Library

OTP	*Old Testament Pseudepigrapha.* Edited by J. H. Charlesworth. 2 vols. New York, 1983
PG	Patrologia graeca [= Patrologiae cursus completus: Series graeca]. Edited by J.-P. Migne. 162 vols. Paris, 1857–1886
PW	Pauly, A. F. *Paulys Realencyclopädie der Classischen Altertumswissenschaft.* New edition G. Wissowa. 49 vols. Stuttgart, 1901.
RB	*Revue biblique*
ResQ	*Restoration Quarterly*
RevExp	*Review and Expositor*
RevistB	*Revista bíblica*
RevQ	*Revue de Qumran*
RevScRel	*Revue des sciences religieuses*
RivB	*Rivista biblica italiana*
RRef	La revue réformée
RSMS	Religious Studies Monograph Series
RTR	*Reformed Theological Review*
SANT	Studien zum Alten und Neuen Testaments
SBFA	Studium Biblicum Franciscanum Analecta
SBLAcBib	Society of Biblical Literature Academia Biblica
SBLBMI	Society of Biblical Literature The Bible and Its Modern Interpreters
SBLDS	Society of Biblical Literature Dissertation Series
SBLEJL	Society of Biblical Literature Early Judaism and Its Literature
SBLMS	Society of Biblical Literature Monograph Series
SBLSBS	Society of Biblical Literature Sources for Biblical Study
SBLSCS	Society of Biblical Literature Septuagint and Cognate Studies
SBLSPS	Society of Biblical Literature Seminar Paper Series
SBLWAW	Society of Biblical Literature Writings from the Ancient World
SC	Sources chrétiennes. Paris: Cerf, 1943–
ScEs	*Science et Esprit*
ScrHier	Scripta hierosolymitana
ScrB	*Scripture Bulletin*
SHR	Studies in the History of Religions (supplement to *Numen*)

SJud	Studies in Judaism
SJLA	Studies in Judaism in Late Antiquity
SJT	*Scottish Journal of Theology*
SNT	Studien zum Neuen Testament
SNTSMS	Society for New Testament Studies Monograph Series
SR	*Studies in Religion*
SSEJC	Studies in Scripture in Early Judaism and Christianity
SSS	Semitic Studies Series
STDJ	Studies on the Texts of the Desert of Judah
StPB	Studia post-biblica
Str–B	Strack, H. L., and P. Billerbeck. *Kommentar zum Neuen Testament aus Talmud und Midrasch*. 6 vols. Munich, 1922–1961
StuBibLit	Studies in Biblical Literature (Lang)
SubBi	*Subsidia biblica*
SwJT	*Southwestern Journal of Theology*
TBT	*The Bible Today*
TDNT	*Theological Dictionary of the New Testament*. Edited by G. Kittel and G. Friedrich. Translated by G. W. Bromiley. 10 vols. Grand Rapids, 1964–1976
TDOT	*Theological Dictionary of the Old Testament*. Edited by G. J. Botterweck and H. Ringgren. Translated by J. T. Willis, G. W. Bromiley, and D. E. Green. 15 vols. Grand Rapids, 1974–2006
Theo	*Theologika*
THKNT	Theologischer Handkommentar zum Neuen Testament
ThTo	*Theology Today*
TJ	*Trinity Journal*
TLNT	*Theological Lexicon of the New Testament*. C. Spicq. Translated and edited by J. D. Ernest. 3 vols. Peabody, Mass., 1994
TLOT	*Theological Lexicon of the Old Testament*. Edited by E. Jenni, with assistance from C. Westermann. Translated by M. E. Biddle. 3 vols. Peabody, Mass., 1997
TLZ	*Theologische Literaturzeitung*
TNTC	Tyndale New Testament Commentaries
TQ	*Theologische Quartalschrift*

TRu	*Theologische Rundschau*
TS	*Theological Studies*
TynBul	*Tyndale Bulletin*
UCOP	University of Cambridge Oriental Publications
VT	*Vetus Testamentum*
VTSup	Supplements to Vetus Testamentum
WBC	Word Biblical Commentary
WMANT	Wissenschaftliche Monographien zum Alten und Neuen Testament
WTJ	*Westminster Theological Journal*
WUNT	Wissenschaftliche Untersuchungen zum Neuen Testament
ZAW	Zeitschrift für die alttestamentliche Wissenschaft
ZNW	Zeitschrift für die neutestamentliche Wissenschaft und die Kunde der älteren Kirche

Tables

Table 1: King and House in 2 Samuel 7:16 and 1 Chronicles 17:14 49

Table 2. Pattern of Rule of Righteous Davidic Kings in Monarchic Israel 74

Table 3. The New Covenant and the Covenants with David and Phinehas in Jeremiah 95

Table 4. Literary Relationship between Hebrews 4:14–16 and 10:19–23 193

Table 5. Literary Relationship between Hebrews 3:1 and 4:14 194

Table 6. Transition from the Daily to the Yearly Ritual in the Israelite Cult (the Day of Atonement) and the Transition between the Old and New Covenants in Hebrews 228

Table 7. Literary Relationship between Hebrews 9:9–10 and 8:13 228

Table 8. The First Covenant and the Day of Atonement in the Argument of the Letter to the Hebrews 269

Table 9. Jesus's Sacrifice and the Sacrifices of the Day of Atonement and First Covenant in the Argument of the Letter to the Hebrews 271

Table 10. Patterns and Foils That Explain the New Covenant Realities. ... 273

Table 11. The Enthronement of the "Son" in Hebrews as an Eschatological Amplification of the Achievements of Righteous Davidic Rulers 310

Chapter 1

Introduction

Ascension to heaven played an important role in ancient Mediterranean religions. The journey to heaven served different purposes and could be divided into four basic types or categories: invasion of heaven, revelation, entrance into immortal heavenly life, and foretaste of the heavenly world.[1]

In the Bible, ascension into heaven is also an important theme. Five persons are reported to have ascended to heaven: Enoch (Gen 5:24; Heb 11:5); Elijah (2 Kgs 2:1–12); Jesus (Luke 24:51; Acts 1:9); Paul (2 Cor 12:2–4); and John (Rev 4:1). There are also four other accounts in which a vision of the heavenly court is granted to humans: Moses, Aaron, and the elders of Israel (Exod 24:9–11); Micaiah (1 Kgs 22:19–23; 2 Chr 18:18–21); Isaiah (Isa 6:1–13); and Ezekiel (Ezek 1, 10).[2]

Of all the heavenly journeys attested in the Bible, however, Jesus's ascension is the most important and, arguably, the pivotal event in salvation history. J. G. Davies has claimed that "the witness of the New Testament writings to the Ascension of Christ is remarkable in its universality."[3] In fact, Jesus's ascension stands at the foundational core of NT theology. Jesus's heavenly intercession and parousia cannot be explained apart from it, and the doctrine

---

[1] James D. Tabor, "Ascent to Heaven," *ABD* 3:91–94. See also, Hans Bietenhard, *Die himmlische Welt im Urchristentum un Spätjudentum*, WUNT I/2 (Mohr Siebeck, 1951); A. F. Segal, "Heavenly Ascent in Hellenistic Judaism, Early Christianity and Their Environment," in *ANRW* 23.2:1333–94; J. Edward Wright, *The Early History of Heaven* (Oxford University Press, 2000); Nicolas Wyatt, *Space and Time in the Religious Life of the Near East*, Biblical Seminar 85 (Sheffield Academic, 2001), 192–207.

[2] Tabor, "Ascent to Heaven," 91.

[3] *He Ascended into Heaven: A Study in the History of Doctrine*, Bampton Lectures 1958 (Association, 1958), 45. See also John F. Jansen, "The Ascension, the Church, and Theology," *ThTo* 16 (1959): 18–25.

of God makes no sense without it.⁴ It is not a surprise, then, that "belief in the ascension was universal in the early church, both East and West."⁵

The state of affairs has changed in the meantime, however. In 2001, James D. G. Dunn noted that "the impression is easily given that the ascension is closer to the embarrassing end of Christian belief."⁶ Presumably, the reason is that the historical nature of the event is highly troubling for the modern mind. The idea of ascending into heaven itself is puzzling for a generation that no longer considers heaven as "above."⁷ Melanchthon was the first to attempt to harmonize the ascension with science in the 16th century, but after him theologians and biblical scholars have mostly shunned it.⁸ From the 19th century on, most biographies of Jesus omit it and systematic theologians barely mention it. Friedrich Schleiermacher rejected it as not belonging to the doctrine of Jesus's person—together with the resurrection and the prediction of his return to judge.⁹ Karl Barth, in his *Church Dogmatics*, opposed visualizing the ascension as a "literal event."¹⁰ In his work on Christology, Wolfhart Pannenberg refers to the ascension only incidentally.¹¹

---

4   Brian K. Donne, "The Significance of the Ascension of Jesus Christ in the New Testament," *SJT* 30 (1977): 567; Joseph Haroutunian, "The Doctrine of the Ascension," *Int* 10 (1956): 280. Furthermore, note that the ascension is intimately connected to four aspects of NT Christology: the enthronement of the seed of David, the Prince of Life's conquer of death, the entrance of the high priest into the holy of holies, and the eschatological entrance of the messianic judge, Timo Eskola, *Messiah and the Throne: Jewish Merkabah Mysticism and Early Christian Exaltation Discourse*, WUNT II/142 (Mohr Siebeck, 2001), 347–361.

5   A. B. Swete, *The Ascended Christ* (London: 1910), 1, quoted in Norman R. Gulley, "Ascension of Christ," *ABD* 1:473. Critics of this belief may be found through the centuries, however. For a brief analysis of the nature of the different allusions to the ascension of Jesus Christ in the New Testament, see Joseph A. Fitzmyer, "The Ascension of Christ and Pentecost," *TS* 45 (1984): 409. Brian K. Donne closes his study on the ascension with the affirmation that, "theologically, the Ascension of Jesus Christ is at the very heart of the New Testament" ("The Significance of the Ascension," 568).

6   "The Ascension of Jesus: A Test Case for Hermeneutics," in *Auferstehung –Resurrection*, ed. Friedrich Avemarie and Hermann Lichtenberger, WUNT I/135 (Mohr Siebeck, 2001), 302. Yet, Chiara Ombretta Tommasi notes that the ascension, understood as "a journey into divine realms where the soul, living or dead, reaps many rewards," remains an important element of the majority of religious traditions, "Ascension," *Encyclopedia of Religion* (Thomson, 2005), 1:518.

7   Dunn, "The Ascension of Jesus," 301.

8   For an analysis of the different ideas regarding the ascension after the Reformation, see Victorien Larrañaga, *L'ascension de Notre-Seigneur dans le Nouveau Testament*, Scripta pontificii instituti biblici (Pontifical Biblical Institute, 1938).

9   *The Christian Faith*, ed. H. R. Mackintosh and J. S. Stewart (T&T Clark, 1928), 417–424.

10   "There is no sense in trying to visualize the ascension as a literal event, like going up in a balloon," *Doctrine of Creation*, ed. Geoffrey W. Bromiley and Thomas F. Torrance, vol. 3/2, *Church Dogmatics* (T&T Clark, 1960), 453. Barth also noted, "This does not mean, however, that He ceased to be a creature, man" (*Doctrine of Creation*, 454).

11   *Jesus: God and Man*, trans. Lewis L. Wilkins and Duane A. Priebe, 2nd ed. (Westminster, 1977), 91, 151, 153, 299. He subsumed the study of the ascension under that of the resurrection.

There is also the problem of the complexity of the NT's and the Church Fathers' witness to the ascension. Both mostly assume it rather than describe it or discuss it. The only three descriptions of the event itself in the NT are problematic: Luke 24:51 and Acts 1:9 seem to differ in their account regarding the circumstances of the ascension, and Mark 16:19 is mostly considered not to be part of the original text.[12] In the Apostolic Fathers it is referred to directly—but not discussed—only in Barn. 15:9.[13]

In summary, though ancient Christianity seemed to embrace the doctrine without further discussion, today, cosmological questions, biblical criticism, and secularization have reduced interest in it.[14] John F. Jansen may be right when he claims that "no part [of the Christian faith] has suffered such neglect and oblivion, as has the doctrine of the ascension."[15] It is not surprising to find out, then, that no major work has been devoted to the study of the ascension in the Letter to the Hebrews.[16]

See Wolfhart Pannenberg, *The Apostles' Creed: In the Light of Today's Questions*, trans. Margaret Kohl (Westminster, 1972), 96–115.

12   In the NA[28], Mark's ascension account appears in a section enclosed in double brackets. See, Bruce M. Metzger, *A Textual Commentary on the Greek New Testament*, 2nd. ed. (Deutsche Bibelgesellschaft, 2002), 102–106.

13   See Davies, *He Ascended into Heaven*, 69–94.

14   Gulley, "Ascension of Christ," 473.

15   Jansen, "The Ascension, the Church, and Theology," 17. Several books have been written on the topic since; for example, Peter Atkins, *Ascension Now: Implications of Christ's Ascension for Today's Church* (Liturgical, 2001); Andrew Burgess, *The Ascension in Karl Barth*, Barth Studies (Ashgate, 2004); Gerrit Scott Dawson, *Jesus Ascended: The Meaning of Christ's Continuing Incarnation* (P&R; T&T Clark, 2004); Douglas Farrow, *Ascension and Ecclesia: On the Significance of the Doctrine of the Ascension for Ecclesiology and Christian Cosmology* (Eerdmans, 1999); Douglas Farrow, "Ascension and Atonement," in *The Theology of Reconciliation*, ed. Colin E. Gunton (T&T Clark, 2003); Gerhard Lohfink, *Die Himmelfahrt Jesu: Untersuchungen zu den Himmelfahrts- und Erhöhungstexten bei Lukas*, SANT 26 (Kösel, 1971); Mikeal C. Parsons, *The Departure of Jesus in Luke–Acts*, JSNTSup 21 (JSOT Press, 1987); Peter Toon, *The Ascension of Our Lord* (Thomas Nelson, 1984); Thomas F. Torrance, *Space, Time and Resurrection* (Handsel, 1976); A. W. Zwiep, *The Ascension of the Messiah in Lukan Christology*, NovTSup 87 (Brill, 1997). Yet, in 2001, James D. G. Dunn still considered that the ascension "has attracted relatively little attention from scholars over the years" ("The Ascension of Jesus," 301). Joseph A. Fitzmyer, however, considers that "literature on the NT accounts of the ascension is vast" but it has not been discussed with the requisite distinctions; namely, those who only allude to the ascension and those who describe it in "time and space" ("The Ascension of Christ and Pentecost," 410, n. 3, 414).

16   Mostly, studies of the ascension in Hebrews are limited to a section in wider works dealing with the ascension in the NT or Christianity; e.g., Davies, *He Ascended into Heaven*, 65–67; Donne, "The Significance of the Ascension," 562–563; Farrow, "Ascension and Atonement," 67–92; Lohfink, *Die Himmelfahrt Jesu*, 91–93; William Milligan, *The Ascension and Heavenly Priesthood of Our Lord* (Mcmillan, 1892); Toon, *The Ascension of Our Lord*, 53–72.

The only major work of which I am aware is Robert David Kaylor, "The Ascension Motif in Luke–Acts, the Epistle to the Hebrews, and the Fourth Gospel" (Ph.D. diss., Duke University, 1964), 83–125. He notes how the ascension appears at "strategic points" and is essential to the

Statement of the Problem

More than any other book in the NT, Hebrews brings out the theological meaning of Jesus's ascension.[17] Hans Windisch claimed that "Die originellste und bedeutsamste Lehre des Hebr ist die von der Himmelfahrt Christi."[18] Hebrews itself asserts that a main point of the document is the fact that Jesus has ascended and been exalted to the right hand of God:[19]

> Since, then, we have a great high priest *who has passed through the heavens*, Jesus, the Son of God, let us hold fast to our confession. For we do not have a high priest who is unable to sympathize with our weaknesses, but we have one who in every respect has been tested as we are, yet without sin. Let us therefore approach the throne of grace with boldness, so that we may receive mercy and find grace to help in time of need. (Heb 4:14–16, emphasis mine)

> Now the main point in what we are saying is this: we have such a high priest, one who is seated at the right hand of the throne of the Majesty *in the heavens*, a minister in the sanctuary and the true tent that the Lord, and not any mortal, has set up. (Heb 8:1–2, emphasis mine)

Nevertheless, the reason that the study of Jesus's ascension in Hebrews has been neglected may not only be due to the unpopularity of this belief. The main reason seems to be of a different nature.

Hebrews asserts prominently three things about Jesus that are intimately related to each other: Jesus offered himself as a sacrifice, entered heaven, and sat at the right hand of God (session).[20] Hebrews scholarship has focused

---

idea of Jesus's superiority, his high-priestly ministry, and the paraenetical purpose of the Letter ("The Ascension Motif," 124–125). The ascension is preliminary to the session or glorification of Christ at the right hand of the Father: "The session is the state which has resulted from the accomplished deed of Jesus's ascension; it is the imagery of the session, however, that defines the meaning and content of the image of the ascension for the author of Hebrews" ("The Ascension Motif," 90).

17 William J. Larkin Jr., "Ascension," *DLNT* 98; also, Davies, *He Ascended into Heaven*, 44–45. The ascension also has an important paraenetical significance for Hebrews because it is the basis for the call to endure suffering (e.g., Heb 12:1–4).

18 (The most original and significant teaching of Hebrews is that of Christ's ascension to heaven.) *Der Hebräerbrief*, 2nd. ed., HNT 14 (Mohr Siebeck, 1931), 70.

19 Note that κεφάλαιον in Heb 8:1 lacks the definite article.

20 J. G. Davies is correct when he asserts that "as in the fourth Gospel the glorification of Christ is a single process consisting of three components, viz. Crucifixion, Resurrection and Ascension, so in the Epistle to the Hebrews the entrance of Christ upon His Priesthood [in the heavenly sanctuary] is a single process consisting of these same three elements" (*He Ascend-*

on the first and the third elements, while the second (ascension) has been considered mostly a *precondition* to or *subsumed* under the third. In other words, the fact itself that Jesus entered heaven is implicitly considered void of theological significance. Had Hebrews not mentioned Jesus's ascension, no theological datum would be lost and Hebrews would be among those passages that jump directly from the cross to the session (e.g., Acts 2:32–33; 5:30–31; Phil 2:8–11; 1 Thess 1:10; 4:16; Rev 3:21; 6:1–7; 7:17) or fuse them (e.g., John 3:14; 12:32, 34). In fact, Robert David Kaylor—and others—states that when Hebrews speaks of the ascension, it really means session (or, glorification).[21] Thus, it could be argued that Hebrews' scholarship has given attention to the topic from the perspective of the session and no further attention is necessary.

Franz Laub holds a different view. He argues that Hebrews assigns theological significance to the ascension itself. In his evaluation, Jesus's entrance into heaven is the high point of Hebrews' Christology and not what happens afterwards: "Ohne hier auf die schwierige Einzelexegese dieser Texte einzugehen, dürfte doch von vornherein soviel deutlich sein, daß gerade im Zusammenhang der für Hebr zentralen καταπέτασμα-Vorstellung das εἰσέρχεσθαι selbst und nicht, was danach geschieht, als das heilsentscheidende hohepriesterliche Handeln Jesu erscheint."[22] Thomas Aquinas, likewise, assigns theological significance to the ascension:

> Just as the high priest in the Old Testament entered the sanctuary into God's presence to represent the people, Christ entered heaven to intercede for us. The presence of his human nature in heaven is itself an intercession for us, for God, who exalted the human nature in Christ, will also show mercy towards those for whose sake this nature was assumed.[23]

---

ed into Heaven, 66; also Milligan, *The Ascension and Heavenly Priesthood of Our Lord*, 72–83). Both make their remarks in the context of Hebrews' ambiguity regarding "when" Jesus began his work as high priest. Some texts would imply that Jesus was a priest here on earth (e.g., Heb 5:1–10), while others that Jesus's priesthood begins at the ascension (Heb 9:11).

21 Kaylor, "The Ascension Motif," 90. Also Fitzmyer, "The Ascension of Christ and Pentecost," 414; Davies, *He Ascended into Heaven*, 66; Torrance, *Space, Time and Resurrection*, 139; Lohfink, *Die Himmelfahrt Jesu*, 91.

22 (Without entering into the difficult detailed exegesis of this text, it should be clear from the beginning, especially in the context of Hebrews' central idea of the καταπέτασμα, that εἰσέρχεσθαι itself and not what happens afterwards appears as Jesus's high priestly act crucial for salvation.) " 'Ein für allemal hineingegangen in das Allerheiligste' (Heb 9,12)—Zum Verständnis des Kreuzestodes im Hebräerbrief," *BZ* 35 (1991): 68.

23 *Summa Theologiae* III.57 (art. 6). Translation from St. Thomas Aquinas, *The Resurrection of the Lord (3a. 53–59)*, trans. C. Thomas Moore, vol. 55, *Summa Theologiae* (Blackfriars, 1976), 97.

It seems to me, then, that there are two main reasons that call for a fuller study of the ascension in Hebrews. First, Jesus's entrance into heaven itself is emphasized in Hebrews and related—or equated, as Laub and Aquinas argue—to the achievement of salvation. Hebrews 9:11–14 affirms that Jesus "entered once for all into the holy place ... thus obtaining eternal redemption." Hebrews 6:19 defines Christian hope as Jesus's entrance into "the inner shrine behind the curtain." This idea is repeated in 7:19 and 10:19–23 (cf. Heb 9:24). Hebrews 4:14–16 refers to Jesus's passing "through the heavens" as the basis for the exhortation to hold fast to the confession.

The second reason is the cosmology of Hebrews. The Letter emphasizes a clear distinction between earthly and heavenly realities.[24] This emphasis enhances the importance of Jesus's ascension because it involves an overcoming of that separation.

The focus of this study is on the purpose of Jesus's ascension and its role in the argument of Hebrews. It is concerned with the theology of the ascension and not its historicity or the elucidation of its circumstances, because Hebrews itself is not troubled by such matters. It consists, instead, of an analysis of those passages in which Jesus's ascension is referred to and a study of the imagery Hebrews uses to couch its theology, giving special attention to the role of this imagery in the progression of the argument. This study, then, is both exegetical and theological in nature, seeking to provide an analysis of specific passages as well as systematization of their import.

State of Affairs: The Day of Atonement Ritual Provides the Analogy to Jesus's Ascension

A great majority of scholars hold that the author of Hebrews uses Day of Atonement imagery to describe Jesus's ascension and that a typological relationship exists between them. In this sense, the annual entrance of the high

---

24 For a study of the cosmological language of Hebrews and its use of sanctuary imagery, see Paul Ellingworth, "Jesus and the Universe in Hebrews," *EvQ* 58 (1986): 337–50. He concludes that Hebrews juxtaposes "two distinct pictures of the one universe in which Christ is supreme" and uses sanctuary imagery for both. One is vertical and presupposes an intermediate sphere populated by angels. The other is horizontal and contrasts simply heaven and earth (no intermediate sphere). Therefore, the author's terminology is "fluid, imprecise, and sometimes confusing; yet it is not incoherent" ("Jesus and the Universe in Hebrews," 350). See also Edward Adams, "The Cosmology of Hebrews," in *The Epistle to the Hebrews and Christian Theology*, ed. Richard Bauckham et al., (Eerdmans, 2009), 122–139.

priest into the holy of holies explains the nature of Jesus's entrance into heaven.²⁵ Marie Isaacs is explicit:

> In his book, *The Epistle of Priesthood* (Edinburgh: T. and T. Clark, 2nd ed., 1915), Alexander Nairne suggested that the main message of Hebrews was, 'Think of our Lord as a priest, and I will make you understand' (p. 136). We need to be more precise than that, however. It is not to priests in general, but to ancient Judaism's high priest in particular, and even more particularly, to his part in the Day of Atonement ritual, that our author turns his thought.²⁶

There is no doubt that the Day of Atonement plays an important role in the argument of Hebrews. It is referenced directly in three passages (Heb 9:6–7; 9:24–25; 10:1–4) and possibly alluded to in several others (Heb 1:3; 3:2, 5, 6; 2:11, 14, 15; 4:14; 5:3; 6:19, 20; 9:5, 23, 28; 13:9–16).²⁷ The Day of Atonement was important for early Christians (Acts 27:9; Barn. 7:3–11) and many have sug-

---

25 E.g., "Nel mistero della sua morte e risurrezione Cristo ha quindi realizzato in pienezza tutti gli effetti che l'AT si proponeva con il suo complesso sistema sacrificale e con i solenni riti del Giorno dell'Espiazione" (In the mystery of his death and resurrection Christ has, therefore, carried out in fullness to all intents and purposes what the OT intended with its complex sacrificial system and with the solemn rite of the Day of Atonement), Fulvio Di Giovambattista, *Il Giorno dell'Espiazione nella Lettera agli Ebrei*, Tesi Gregoriana Serie Teologia (Pontificio Istituto Biblico, 2000), 199.

26 "Priesthood and the Epistle to the Hebrews," *HeyJ* 38 (1997): 55. Similarly, "In Hebrews, the ritual of the Day of Atonement metaphorically describes Jesus's work of salvation as a Day of Atonement ceremony performed in heaven (Heb 6–9). Jesus is the high priest of a heavenly sanctuary. He enters into the most holy place with his own blood to achieve eternal redemption for the people," Edgar V. McKnight and Christopher Church, *Hebrews–James*, Smyth & Helwys Bible Commentary (Smyth & Helwys, 2004), 115.

27 For a brief evaluation of the allusions to the Day of Atonement identified by scholars of Hebrews, see William G. Johnsson, "Day of Atonement Allusions," in *Issues in the Book of Hebrews*, ed. Frank B. Holbrook, DARCOM 4 (Biblical Research Institute General Conference of Seventh-day Adventists, 1989), 112–115.

Hebrews 1:3: We cannot be sure that the phrase "purification of sins" alludes necessarily to the Day of Atonement ritual because in the argument of Hebrews the complex of sacrifices related to the inauguration of the covenant (Heb 9:15–23) have also an expiatory function. See, Susan Haber, "From Priestly Torah to Christ Cultus: The Re-Vision of Covenant and Cult in Hebrews," *JSNT* 28 (2005): 109. See, Scott W. Hahn, "A Broken Covenant and the Curse of Death: A Study of Hebrews 9:15–22," *CBQ* 66 (2004): 416–36.

Hebrews 3:2, 5, 6: The phrase οἶκος αὐτοῦ might be a veiled reference to Lev 16:6, 11, 17, 24 (LXX), Di Giovambattista, *Il Giorno dell'Espiazione*, 146–147.

Heb 2:11: There was a purification and consecration (sanctification) of the altar of holocaust on the Day of Atonement (Lev 16:19). See, James Patrick Scullion, "A Traditio-Historical Study of the Day of Atonement" (Ph.D. diss., Catholic University of America, 1990; UMI, 1991), 210–211. Heb 2:11 refers, though, to the consecration of Jesus and the believers.

Hebrews 2:14, 15: It refers to the victory over the forces of evil, a motif associated with Yom Kippur in Second Temple Judaism, Daniel Stökl Ben Ezra, *The Impact of Yom Kippur on Early*

gested that it was used in other NT writings beside Hebrews to describe and interpret Jesus's death on the cross.[28]

It has been argued that the Day of Atonement motif dominates the thinking of the author of Hebrews to the extent that it shapes the form of his argument. For example, Aelred Cody, whose work on Hebrews has had a strong influence on later scholarship, considers that Hebrews' emphasis on the ascension rather than the resurrection of Jesus is the result of the dominance of the Day of Atonement motif.[29] Paul Ellingworth claims that the author of

---

Christianity: The Day of Atonement from Second Temple Judaism to the Fifth Century, WUNT I/163 (Mohr Siebeck, 2003), 185, cf. 122.

Hebrews 4:14: The "throne of grace" is said to be the antitype of the mercy seat of the old cultus before which the blood was sprinkled on the Day of Atonement. See, Johnsson, "Day of Atonement Allusions," 114.

Hebrews 5:3: The high priest was required to offer sacrifices "for his house" in the Day of Atonement (Lev 16:6, 11, 17). Johnsson argues, however, that the inclusion of *daily* in the same phrase in Heb 7:26–27 "seriously weakens the case" for 3:2 and 5:3 ("Day of Atonement Allusions," 114).

Hebrews 6:19, 20: It is commonly held that the phrase τὸ ἐσώτερον τοῦ καταπετάσματος refers to the holy of holies (i.e., "within the [second] veil") which was entered only on the Day of Atonement (Lev 16:2). George E. Rice challenged this view arguing that in the context of the argument of Hebrews it could refer to the (first) veil that provides access to the sanctuary as a whole ("Hebrews 6:19: Analysis of Some Assumptions Concerning *Katapetasma*," AUSS 25 [1987]: 65–71). Later on, Roy E. Gane responded that though Rice's view is still "theoretically possible" .... The LXX tends to support rather than undermine this view [that it refers to the holy of holies]." ("Re-Opening *Katapetasma* ['Veil'] in Hebrews 6:19," AUSS 38 [2000]: 8).

Hebrews 9:5: The mercy seat is mentioned, but is not clear if this is an allusion to the Day of Atonement ritual. See, Johnsson, "Day of Atonement Allusions," 114.

Hebrews 9:28: For a critique of the view that the author refers to the Parousia here, see César Augusto Franco Martínez, *Jesucristo, su persona y su obra, en la Carta a los Hebreos: Lengua y cristología en Heb 2, 9–10; 5, 1–10; 4, 14 y 9, 27–28*, Studia Semitica Novi Testamenti 1 (Ciudad Nueva, 1992), 317–384.

Hebrews 13:9–16: "On the Day of Atonement the carcasses of the bullock and Lord's goat were burned outside the camp (Lev 16:27). But the point is not clear-cut because this procedure was also followed for some sin offerings, apart from the Day of Atonement (Exod 29:14; Lev 4:12; 8:17; 9:11)." See, Johnsson, "Day of Atonement Allusions," 115.

28   E.g., Rom 3:25, 26; Gal 3:10, 13; Matt 27:15–23; John 1:29; 17:19; 1 Pet 2:22–24; 1 John 2:2, 4:10; Rev 8:1–5; 11:15–19; 15:1–8. See, Stökl Ben Ezra, *Impact of Yom Kippur*, 145–257. Regarding John 17:19, see Farrow, "Ascension and Atonement," 71. For references to Revelation, see G. B. Caird, *The Revelation of Saint John*, BNTC (Black, 1966; reprint, Hendrickson), 103–111, 140–46; Farrow, "Ascension and Atonement," 90–91. Jon Paulien accepts that Rev 11:15–19 points to the Day of Atonement, but considers that 8:1–5 and 15:1–8 refer to the inauguration (and de-inauguration) of the sanctuary instead ("The Role of the Hebrew Cultus, Sanctuary, and Temple in the Plot and Structure of the Book of Revelation," AUSS 33 [1995]: 252–253).

29   "If Hebrews has emphasized the Ascension rather than the Resurrection, it is because in the Epistle's typological exposition Our Lord's crossing over into the new, spiritual, divine world of ultimate reality fits very well into the type-complex of the Day of Atonement's sin-expiating ritual, while the Resurrection from the dead does not" (*Heavenly Sanctuary and Liturgy in the Epistle to the Hebrews: The Achievement of Salvation in the Epistle's Perspective* [Grail, 1960], 174). On the dominance of the Day of Atonement motif, Marie Isaacs adds: "So much does the model of this particular ceremony dominate Hebrews, that even when he appeals to

Hebrews concentrates "in the Day of Atonement, as the lesser counterpart of Christ's sacrifice, all his thinking about sin and forgiveness under the old covenant."[30] Emile Guers calls Hebrews "[le] divin commentaire" of Lev 16.[31]

A majority of expositors consider that Jesus's ascension in Hebrews is structured in three stages that correspond to the Day of Atonement ritual: (1) the passion and death of Jesus correspond to the immolation of the victim (Heb 9:13, 14), (2) the ascension to heaven corresponds to the entrance of the high priest into the holy of holies (9:11–12), (3) and Jesus's purification of believers corresponds to the purification of the heavenly sanctuary (9:23).[32]

---

a wholly different sacrifice, that offered to ratify the covenant, the author makes that expiatory as well" ("Priesthood and the Epistle to the Hebrews," 55).

30 Paul Ellingworth, *The Epistle to the Hebrews: A Commentary on the Greek Text*, NIGTC (Eerdmans, 1993), 435–436.

31 Quoted by F. Dunkel, "Expiation et Jour des Expiations dans L'épître aux Hebreux, " *RRef* 33, no. 2 (1982): 63. Timo Eskola refers to the cultic argument of Hebrews as a "christological pesher on the cultic text of Leviticus (16:15)" (*Messiah and the Throne*, 357). Gabriella Gelardini has recently suggested that Hebrews is an ancient synagogue homily for *Tisha be-Av*. This was the most important day of mourning in Jewish Tradition and was intimately related to the Day of Atonement. These two days are the only ones in which the most rigorous fasting is required in the liturgical year, "Hebrews, an Ancient Synagogue Homily for *Tisha be-Av*: Its Function, Its Basis, Its Theological Interpretation," in *Hebrews: Contemporary Methods—New Insights*, ed. Gabriella Gelardini, BibInt 75 (Brill, 2005), 107–127.

32 Aelred Cody, *Heavenly Sanctuary and Liturgy in the Epistle to the Hebrews: The Achievement of Salvation in the Epistle's Perspective* (Grail, 1960), 170–202. Also, Christian A. Eberhart, "Characteristics of Sacrificial Metaphors in Hebrews," in *Hebrews: Contemporary Methods—New Insights*, ed. Gabriella Gelardini, BibInt 75 (Brill, 2005), 62–64; Haber, "From Priestly Torah to Christ Cultus," 117–124; Donald A. Hagner, "The Son of God as Unique High Priest: The Christology of the Epistle to the Hebrews," in *Contours of Christology in the New Testament*, ed. Richard N. Longenecker, McMaster New Testament Studies (Eerdmans, 2005), 259–260; Craig R. Koester, "God's Purposes and Christ's Saving Work According to Hebrews," in *Salvation in the New Testament: Perspectives on Soteriology*, ed. Jan G. van der Watt, NovTSup 121 (Brill, 2005), 373; McKnight and Church, *Hebrews-James,* 115; N. T. Wright, *Hebrews for Everyone*, 2d ed. (SPCK; Westminster John Knox, 2004), 103–104; Ellen Bradshaw Aitken, "The Hero in the Epistle to the Hebrews: Jesus as an Ascetic Model," in *Early Christian Voices: In Texts, Traditions, and Symbols: Essays in Honor of François Bovon*, ed. David H. Warren, Ann Graham Brock, and David W. Pao, BibInt 66 (Brill, 2003), 183; Margaret Barker, *The Great High Priest: The Temple Roots of Christian Liturgy* (T&T Clark, 2003), 26–54; Richard D. Nelson, " 'He Offered Himself': Sacrifice in Hebrews," *Int* 57 (2003): 252–257; Kenneth L. Schenck, *Understanding the Book of Hebrews: The Story Behind the Sermon* (Westminster John Knox, 2003), 14–15, 72; Stökl Ben Ezra, *Impact of Yom Kippur,* 225, 180–197; Daniel J. Brege, "Eucharistic Overtones Created by Sacrificial Concepts in the Epistle to the Hebrews," *CTQ* 66 (2002): 66–70; Norman H. Young, "The Day of Dedication or the Day of Atonement? The Old Testament Background to Hebrews 6:19–20 Revisited," *AUSS* 40 (2002): 61–68; Gareth Lee Cockerill, "Structure and Interpretation in Hebrews 8:1–10:18: A Symphony in Three Movements," *BBR* 11 (2001): 188, 192; David A. deSilva, *Perseverance in Gratitude: A Socio-Rhetorical Commentary on the Epistle "to the Hebrews"* (Eerdmans, 2000), 291; Di Giovambattista, *Il Giorno dell'Espiazione*, 196; C. K. Barrett, "The Christology of Hebrews," in *Who Do You Say That I Am: Essays on Christology*, ed. Mark Allan Powell and David R. Bauer (Westminster John Knox, 1999), 124–125; J. C. O'Neill, "Jesus in Hebrews," *JHC* 6 (1999): 71; Fred B. Craddock, "The Letter to the Hebrews," in *The New Interpreter's Bible*, ed. Leander E. Keck and others (Abingdon, 1998), 12:106–13; Mary Rose D'Angelo, "He-

Some add a fourth stage, Jesus's second coming corresponds to the exit of the

---

brews," in *Women's Bible Commentary*, ed. Carol A. Newsom and Sharon H. Ringe (Westminster John Knox, 1998), 455; George H. Guthrie, *Hebrews*, NIVAC (Zondervan, 1998), 310; Bernhard Heininger, "Sündenreinigung (Heb 1,3): Christologische Anmerkungen zum Exordium des Hebräerbriefs," *BZ* 41 (1997): 62; Daniel L. Segraves, *Hebrews: Better Things* (Word Aflame, 1997), 2:25; D. Álvarez Cineira, "Los Sacrificios en la Carta a los Hebreos 10,1–18," *EstAg* 30 (1995): 237; John T. Carroll and Joel B. Green, *The Death of Jesus in Early Christianity* (Hendrickson, 1995), 135–136; Steve Stanley, "Hebrews 9:6–10: The 'Parable' of the Tabernacle," *NovT* 37 (1995): 398; J. C. McCullough, "Hebrews in Recent Scholarship," *IBS* 16 (1994): 81; Michèle Morgen, "Christ venu une fois pour toutes," *LumVie* 43, no. 2 (1994): 41; Morna D. Hooker, *Not Ashamed of the Gospel: New Testament Interpretations of the Death of Christ* (Eerdmans, 1994), 118; Ellingworth, *The Epistle to the Hebrews*, 445–448; Erich Gräßer, *An die Hebräer*, EKKNT 17 (Benziger Neukirchener, 1990–1997), 142, 143; Darrell J. Pursiful, *The Cultic Motif in the Spirituality of the Book of Hebrews* (Mellen Biblical, 1993), 62–72; Marie E. Isaacs, *Sacred Space: An Approach to the Theology of the Epistle to the Hebrews*, JSNTSup 73 (Sheffield: JSOT Press, 1992), 89–90; William L. Lane, *Hebrews 1–8*, WBC 47a (Word, 1991), cxxiv; Laub, "Ein für allemal hineingegangen in das Allerheiligste," 69; Barnabas Lindars, *The Theology of the Letter to the Hebrews*, New Testament Theology (Cambridge University Press, 1991), 84; David J. MacLeod, "The Present Work of Christ in Hebrews," *BSac* 148 (1991): 188–189; John M. Scholer, *Proleptic Priests: Priesthood in the Epistle to the Hebrews*, JSNTSup 49 (JSOT Press, 1991), 163; Hans-Friedrich Weiß, *Der Brief an die Hebräer*, KEK 13 (Vandenhoeck & Ruprecht, 1991), 463; F. F. Bruce, *The Epistle to the Hebrews*, rev. ed., NICNT (Eerdmans, 1990), 214; Harold W. Attridge, *The Epistle to the Hebrews*, ed. Helmut Koester, Hermeneia (Fortress, 1989), 245; Samuel Bénétreau, "La mort du Christ selon L'épître aux Hébreux," *Hok* 39 (1989): 32, 37, 39; Mathias Rissi, *Die Theologie des Hebräerbriefs: Ihre Verankerung in der Situation des Verfassers und seiner Leser*, WUNT I/41 (Mohr Siebeck, 1987), 80; James Swetnam, "Christology and the Eucharist in the Epistle to the Hebrews," *Bib* 70 (1989): 92; R. McL. Wilson, *Hebrews*, NCBCom (Eerdmans, 1987), 149–53; Philip Edgcumbe Hughes, "The Christology of Hebrews," *SwJT* 28, no. 1 (1985): 26; Donald Guthrie, *The Letter to the Hebrews: An Introduction and Commentary*, TNTC (Inter-Varsity, 1983), 187; Kenneth Grayston, "Salvation Proclaimed: III Hebrews 9:11–14," *ExpTim* 93, no. 6 (1982): 167; David Peterson, *Hebrews and Perfection: An Examination of the Concept of Perfection in the 'Epistle to the Hebrews,'* SNTSMS 47 (Cambridge University Press, 1982), 143–144; William R. G. Loader, *Sohn und Hoherpriester: Eine traditionsgeschichtliche Untersuchung zur Christologie des Hebräerbriefes*, WMANT 53 (Neukirchener, 1981), 182–91; Norman H. Young, "The Gospel according to Hebrews 9," *NTS* 27 (1981): 208; Robert J. Daly, *Christian Sacrifice: The Judaeo-Christian Background before Origen*, Catholic University of America Studies in Christian Antiquity 18 (Catholic University of America Press, 1978), 268–73; Frances M. Young, *Sacrifice and the Death of Christ* (SPCK, 1975), 65, 66, 69–70; Walter Edward Brooks, "The Perpetuity of Christ's Sacrifice," *JBL* 89 (1970): 208–209; Otto Michel, *Der Brief and die Hebräer*, KEK 13 (Vandenhoeck & Ruprecht, 1966), 309; Hugh Montefiore, *A Commentary on the Epistle to the Hebrews*, HNTC (Harper & Row, 1964), 153; H. H. Meeter, *The Heavenly High Priesthood of Christ: An Exegetico-Dogmatic Study* (Eerdmans, n.d.), 118; Franz Delitzsch, *Commentary on the Epistle to the Hebrews*, trans. Thomas L. Kingsbury (Eerdmans, 1952), 123; Ceslas Spicq, *L'épître aux Hébreux*, EBib (Gabalda, 1952), 2:257; Windisch, *Der Hebräerbrief*, 75; Brooke Foss Westcott, *The Epistle to the Hebrews: The Greek Text with Notes and Essays* (Mcmillan, 1892; repr., Eerdmans, 1984), 260.

Others consider that the Day of Atonement is used in Hebrews to explain Jesus's ascension but not his death as a sacrifice; for example, Ina Willi-Plein, "Some Remarks on Hebrews From the Viewpoint of Old Testament Exegesis," in *Hebrews: Contemporary Methods—New Insights*, ed. Gabriella Gelardini, BibInt 75 (Brill, 2005), 28; Joseph Moingt, "La fin du sacrifice," *LumVie* 43, no. 2 (1994): 24–25. Or, that "the intent of the apostolic writer is not to show that Calvary is the antitype of the Day of Atonement, but that Calvary is the antitype of all the sacrifices of the OT," William G. Johnsson, "Defilement/Purification and Hebrews 9:23," in *Issues in the Book*

high priest from the holy of holies on the Day of Atonement (9:28).[33]

The strength of this view lies in the rigorous antithetical parallelism (μὲν ... δὲ) that exists between 9:1–10 and vv. 11–14, which has been considered the heart of the argument of Hebrews' central section.[34] Hebrews 9:1–10 explains the regulations of the Mosaic covenant (see the *inclusio* in vv. 1, 10) by describing the two rooms of the sanctuary (vv. 1–5) and the ministries carried in each (vv. 6–10). This section places a clear emphasis on the holy of holies and the Day of Atonement liturgy.[35] Hebrews 9:11–14 describes in contrast the priestly work of Jesus in the heavenly sanctuary. The argument seems clear: Jesus's heavenly ministry achievements are superior to those of the high priest on the Day of Atonement because they provide for cleansing of the conscience.

This antithetical parallelism also appears in other passages. Hebrews 9:24–25 again compares the Day of Atonement with Jesus's heavenly ministry. The contrast emphasizes the superiority of Jesus's ministry because it is carried on in heaven (versus the Day of Atonement liturgy in the "sanctuary made by human hands") and offers a unique sacrifice (versus the Day of Atonement multiple "year after year" sacrifices).

A final explicit comparison is found in Heb 10:1–4 and vv. 5–10.[36] Verses 1–4 focus on the inability of the Day of Atonement "to take away sins" (v. 4) arguing that, in fact, the Day of Atonement does the opposite: it is "a reminder of sin year after year" (v. 3). Verses 5–10 oppose the sacrifice of Jesus's body and will, which provides forgiveness of sins (vv. 10, 18), to the Day of Atonement sacrifices of "bulls and goats." Once again, the contrast emphasizes the superiority of Jesus's achievements.

---

of Hebrews, ed. Frank B. Holbrook, DARCOM 4 (Biblical Research Institute General Conference of Seventh-day Adventists, 1989), 80.

33   E.g., Craig R. Koester, *Hebrews: A New Translation with Introduction and Commentary*, AB 36 (Doubleday, 2001), 423. Against, Johnsson, "Day of Atonement Allusions," 115. César Augusto Franco Martínez has challenged the view that this passage refers to the Parousia, arguing that it refers to the "revelación del Resucitado, de la que sólo los que le acogen como Salvador son beneficiarios" (revelation of the Risen One, of which only those who embrace him as Savior are beneficiaries), (*Jesucristo, su persona y su obra*, 383).

34   Albert Vanhoye argues that Hebrews has a chiastic structure in which Heb 9:11 is at the center, *Structure and Message of the Epistle to the Hebrews*, SubBi (Editrice Pontificio Istituto Biblico, 1989), 40a–40b. Regarding the antithetical parallelism between vv. 1–10 and 11–14 see, for example, Koester, *Hebrews*, 412.

35   Laub, "Ein für allemal hineingegangen in das Allerheiligste," 69–70.

36   Most commentators consider that Heb 13:10–13 compares Calvary with the Day of Atonement in the fact that sacrificed animals on this day were "burned outside the camp" (Lev 16:27; e.g., Attridge, *The Epistle to the Hebrews*, 397; Ellingworth, *The Epistle to the Hebrews*, 708–10; Gräßer, *An die Hebräer*, 3:382–383; Marie E. Isaacs, "Hebrews 13:9–16 Revisited," *NTS* 43 (1997): 268–284; Koester, *Hebrews*, 576). The issue is not clear-cut, however, because the same procedure was followed for other sin offerings apart from the Day of Atonement (Exod 29:14; Lev 4:12; 8:17; 9:11), Johnsson, "Day of Atonement Allusions," 115.

It is also argued that Hebrews not only compares Jesus's sacrifice to the Day of Atonement sacrifices, but also uses Day of Atonement imagery to describe Jesus's ascension. Norman Young, for example, provides in table form a comparison of Hebrews' descriptions of the entrance of the high priest into the holy of holies on the Day of Atonement and Jesus's entrance into heaven:

> The terms in Heb 9.11–12 and in 9.25 [which describe Jesus's sacrifice and ascension] follow an identical pattern to those in 9.7 [which describe the Day of Atonement], as the table below demonstrates:

Heb 9.7	Heb 9.11–12	Heb 9.25
ὁ ἀρχιερεύς	[ὁ] ἀρχιερεύς	ὁ ἀρχιερεύς
[εἴσεισι]	εἰσῆλθεν εἰς τὰ ἅγια	εἰσέρχεται
εἰς δὲ τὴν δευτέραν	ἐφάπαξ	εἰς τὰ ἅγια
ἅπαξ τοῦ ἐνιαυτοῦ	οὐδὲ δι' αἵματος ... διὰ	κατ' ἐνιαυτὸν
οὐ χωρὶς αἵματος	δὲ τοῦ ἰδίου αἵματος	ἐν αἵματι ἀλλοτρίῳ

In summary, it is argued that Day of Atonement imagery is the quarry where Hebrews obtains the construction materials for its theology of Jesus's heavenly ministry.

Nevertheless, the issue is not as straightforward as it seems. Harold W. Attridge has warned that "the application of the model of the Yom Kippur ritual to the death of Christ in Hebrews is a complex and subtle hermeneutical effort."[37] The discussion regarding Hebrews's use of the Day of Atonement liturgy as a typological counterpart of Jesus's ascension has gravitated around two questions: "(1) how detailed is the application of the OT data to the author's picture (*Bildhäfte*) of Christ's exaltation? and (2) what are the heavenly realities (*Sachhäfte*) to which, in our author's view, the OT data point?"[38] The second question has baffled several interpreters and drawn most of the attention: Does a heavenly sanctuary require purification?[39] It is the first question, however, that interests us now: "How detailed is the application of the

---

37 Harold W. Attridge, "The Uses of Antithesis in Hebrews 8–10," *HTR* 79 (1986): 9.
38 Ellingworth, *The Epistle to the Hebrews*, 445–446.
39 The difficulty of the second question relates prominently to the meaning of Heb 9:23: "Thus it was necessary for the sketches of the heavenly things to be purified with these rites, but the heavenly things themselves need better sacrifices than these." First, what are these "heavenly things" that need purification? Answers fall mainly along two lines of interpretation: heaven itself or human beings (see, Koester, *Hebrews*, 421). Second, do heavenly things need purification? The mere idea of a purification of heaven is perplexing to many and "almost fantastic" for others, e.g., James Moffatt, *A Critical and Exegetical Commentary on the Epistle to the Hebrews*, ICC (T&T Clark, 1924), 132. C. Spicq says: "L'idée d'impureté antérieure est un nonsens pour le sanctuarie céleste" (The idea of previous impurity is a nonsense for the heavenly sanctuary, *L'épître aux Hébreux*, 267).

OT data [—Day of Atonement imagery in this case—] to the author's picture (*Bildhäfte*) of Christ's exaltation?"⁴⁰

Critique of the State of Affairs: A More Limited Role for the Day of Atonement Imagery?

Several inconsistencies between Day of Atonement liturgy and the imagery of Jesus's ascension in Hebrews have been identified by scholars. Mostly, it has been considered that this is because Hebrews is not concerned with "cultic minutiae."⁴¹ A closer look may suggest, however, that it was not carelessness but that the author envisioned a more restricted use of Day of Atonement imagery for Jesus's ascension than has been allowed by contemporary scholarship.

There Is Absence of "Affliction of the Soul" in Relation to Jesus's Entrance into the Heavenly Sanctuary

F. F. Bruce notes that affliction of the soul, an important element of the celebration of Yom Kippur, is absent.⁴² Leviticus 23:29 says regarding the Day of Atonement: "For anyone who does not practice self-denial during that entire day shall be cut off from the people" (also 16:29, 31; 23:27, 32).

In the Second Temple period, "self-denial" was interpreted as fasting and assigned atoning power: "[The righteous] atones for (sins of) ignorance by fasting and humbling his soul, and the Lord will cleanse every devout person and his house" (Pss. Sol. 3:8 [*OTP* 2:655]).⁴³ By New Testament times, Yom Kippur could be referred to simply as "the fast" (e.g., Acts 27:9; Philo, *Spec. Laws* 1.188; 2.193–201; *Moses* 2.23–24; *Aleg. Interp.* 2.52; *Embassy* 306; Josephus *J.W.* 236; cf. Barn. 7.3). The Mishnah lists six prohibitions for this festival: "On the Day of Atonement it is forbidden to (1) eat, (2) drink, (3) bathe, (4) put on any sort of oil, (5) put on a sandal, (6) or engage in sexual relations" (m. Yoma 8:1 [Neusner, *Mishnah*]).⁴⁴ In addition, others may wear sackcloth and put ashes on their heads (m. Ta'an. 2:1), abstain from sleep (b. Yoma 19b), induce tears and cry, and other more extreme afflictions.⁴⁵

---

40 Ellingworth, *The Epistle to the Hebrews*, 445–446.
41 Ibid., 452. Ellingworth's conclusion is representative of the view of many others.
42 F. F. Bruce, *The Epistle to the Hebrews*, 212.
43 Psalms of Solomon have been dated to approximately 70–45 BCE. R. B. Wright, "Psalms of Solomon: A New Translation and Introduction," *OTP* 2:640–641.
44 Jacob Neusner, *The Mishnah: A New Translation* (Yale University Press, 1988), 277.
45 Stökl Ben Ezra, *Impact of Yom Kippur*, 34.

In Hebrews, however, the atmosphere that surrounds Jesus's entrance into the heavenly sanctuary is that of feasting and rejoicing: "What used to be 'the good things to come' are now 'the good things that have come' [Heb 9:11]."[46]

It is true that there are evidences of joy and celebration on the Day of Atonement:

> Said Rabban Simeon b. Gamaliel, "There were no days better for Israelites than the fifteenth of Ab and the Day of Atonement." For on these days Jerusalemite girls go out in borrowed white dresses—so as not to shame those who owned none. All the dresses had to be immersed. And the Jerusalemite girls go out and dance in vineyards. What did they say? "Fellow, look around and see—choose what you want! "Don't look for beauty, look for family." (m. Ta'an. 4:8 [Neusner, *Mishnah*])

These celebrations, however, came after the end of the solemnities. *Mishnah Yoma* 7:4 mentions that the high priest celebrated with his friends the fact that he had come forth whole from the sanctuary.[47] Rabi Aqiba also considered forgiveness provided in this day a reason for celebration: "Happy are you, O Israel. Before whom are you made clean, and who makes you clean? It is your Father who is in heaven" (m. Yoma 8:9 [Neusner, *Mishnah*]).[48]

Likewise, the atmosphere of celebration in Hebrews is due to the fact that Jesus has provided expiation for sins perfecting the believers and obtaining "eternal redemption" (Heb 9:11–14). This does not fit, however, with Hebrews' use of Day of Atonement imagery. If scholars are correct in their reading, Jesus has not come out yet from the "most holy place" (9:28).[49] Thus, if Jesus's "Day of Atonement" has not finished yet, it is probably too soon for Christians to celebrate.

---

46 Bruce, *The Epistle to the Hebrews*, 212. Cf. the great scene of joy in Heb 12:22–24. Also, Wilson, *Hebrews*, 149.

47 Cf. Sir 50:5–21 that describes Ben Sira's joy at the exit of Simon Son of Onias from the sanctuary. Most commentators consider the ceremonies described as those of the Day of Atonement. F. Ó Fearghail has argued, however, that it refers to the daily whole offering, "Sir 50,5–21: Yom Kippur or the Daily Whole-Offering?" *Bib* 59 (1978): 301–316. See, Patrick W. Skehan, Translation and Notes and Alexander A. Di Lella, Introduction and Commentary, *The Wisdom of Ben Sira*, AB 39 (Doubleday, 1987), 550–551.

48 See also, Roy E. Gane, *Leviticus, Numbers*, NIVAC (Zondervan, 2004), 403–404.

49 In fact, Jesus has arrived to stay. He has been enthroned in heaven over a kingdom that will not be shaken (Heb 12:28) and his priestly intercession is meant to last forever (7:25)

The Azazel Ritual Is Omitted

Hebrews does not mention Azazel.[50] This is an intriguing omission. The rite of Azazel's goat was the culmination of the ritual expiation on the Day of Atonement (Lev 16:7–10, 20–22). It was not until the sins of the people were placed on the goat for Azazel and sent to the desert that the sanctuary's cleansing was achieved (Lev 16:20–22). The announcement that the goat had been pushed over a cliff, according to rabbinic tradition, was "relayed to the temple by the stations along the route. However, according to legend, a scarlet thread tied to the door of the sanctuary turned white at the very moment the goat was pushed over the precipice, as a sign that the people were cleansed of their sins (Yom. 6.8; cf. Isa. 1:18)."[51]

If Hebrews follows a Day of Atonement typology relating the cleansing of the conscience (9:14) with the purification of the sanctuary (v. 23),[52] we have the problem that Jesus has not come out of the most holy place yet (heaven). As mentioned above, several scholars believe that this exit of the most holy place is described in Heb 9:28, which lies still in the future.[53] If this is the case, then, Azazel's rite lies still in the future, and the purification of sins has not been accomplished yet; but, for Hebrews purification of sin has been accomplished (Heb 10:10–13, 18).

It could be argued that this omission is due to the fact that Hebrews emphasizes the blood ritual of the Day of Atonement (goat and bull, Lev 16:6, 9; cf. Heb 9:12) as a counterpart to the cross and that no further eschatological events as a counterpart to the rite of Azazel are in view.[54]

This is possible but does not explain satisfactorily the absence of Azazel. The cross does not have only an expiatory function in the argument of Hebrews, but a hortatory function as well. Jesus is the forerunner who has gone through rejection, shame, and abuse to glory and Christians are invited to follow him, enduring patiently the rejection, shame, and abuse he suffered (Heb 12:1–4; 13:13, 14; cf. 10:32–39). Early Christian writers commonly considered

---

50 Bruce, *The Epistle to the Hebrews*, 207; Barnabas Lindars, "Hebrews and the Second Temple," in *Templum amicitiae: Essays on the Second Temple Presented to Ernst Bammel*, ed. William Horbury, JSNTSup 48 (JSOT Press, 1991), 420.

51 J. Coert Rylaarsdam, "Day of Atonement," *IDB* 1:315. See also, Gane, *Leviticus, Numbers*, 274.

52 See e.g., Attridge, *The Epistle to the Hebrews*, 262.

53 Page 15, n. 33.

54 Notwithstanding, the author is interested in events that will take place in the future as well (e.g., 9:28; 10:13 [cf. 1:13]; 12:26–28).

the rejection and abuse of the goat for Azazel a type of Jesus's sufferings.[55] In the *Letter of Barnabas*, the goat for Azazel, accursed, abused, and sent to the desert with his head encircled "with scarlet wool" serves as a type of Christ who is accursed and "despised, and pierced, and mocked," yet crowned (Barn. 7 [*ANF* 1:141]).[56] Justin Martyr, in his *Dialogue with Trypho* (ca. 155 ce), also considers the rite of Azazel as "declarative" of Jesus's sufferings: "in which the elders of your people, and the priests, having laid hands on Him and put Him to death, sent Him away as the scape [goat]" (Justin, *Dial.* 40 [*ANF* 1:215]).[57] Yet, Hebrews does not mention the goat for Azazel on the Day of Atonement as a type of Christ. Instead, the author of Hebrews chooses the minor aspect of the ritual that "the bodies of those animals whose blood is brought into the sanctuary by the high priest as a sacrifice for sin are burned outside the camp" (13:11) to encourage the readers to "go to him [Jesus] outside the camp and bear the abuse he endured" (v. 13). In fact, the burning of the bodies of sacrificed animals outside the camp is not exclusive to the Day of Atonement and does not imply rejection and shaming.[58]

---

55   "Increasingly the people participated in the goat's departure, pulling out its wool, pricking it, spitting on it, and urging it to be gone" (Barn. 7.8; Yom. 6:4), Rylaarsdam, "Day of Atonement," 315. See also, Daniel Stökl Ben Ezra, "The Christian Exegesis of the Scapegoat Between Jews and Pagans," in *Sacrifice in Religious Experience*, ed. Albert I. Baumgarten, SHR 93 (Brill, 2002), 207–232.

56   The *Letter of Barnabas* is an important witness of early Christian traditions and could have been written before the end of the 1st century ce. Since Barn. 16.3 refers to the destruction of the temple and is first quoted by Clement of Alexandria (ca. 190), the range of dates possible for Barnabas go from 70 ce to the end of the 2nd century. The application of the prophecy of Dan (7:7–14) to the contemporary situation (Barn. 4.4), the hope of the reconstruction of the temple, the separation of Christianity from Judaism, and an ecclesiastic organization in embryonic stages have been used as internal evidence for a more precise date, mostly in the times of Vespasian (69–79), Nerva (97–98), or Hadrian (118–138).

Helmut Koester argues for a date toward the end of the 1st century: "The date of its composition is problematic. Other New Testament writings are never used in *Barnabas*, neither explicitly nor tacitly, which would suggest an early date, perhaps even before the end of the 1st century" (*History and Literature of Early Christianity, Introduction to the New Testament*, 2nd. ed. [Walter de Gruyter, 2000], 2:280). Recently, Ferdinand R. Prostmeier has argued for 130–131 ce as the time of composition on the basis of the Author's non-mention of Hadrian's prohibition of circumcision for Jews (*Der Barnabasbrief*, Kommentar zu den Apostolischen Vätern 8 [Vandenhoeck & Ruprecht, 1999], 118–119). The increasing tendency has been to say, however, that "the internal evidence is inconclusive," Reidar Hvalvik, *The Struggle for Scripture and Covenant: The Purpose of the Epistle of Barnabas and Jewish-Christian Competition in the Second Century*, WUNT II/82 (Mohr [Siebeck], 1996), 17. See also Pierre Prigent and Robert A. Kraft, Épître de Barnabé, SC 172 (Cerf, 1971), 26–27; James Carleton Paget, *The Epistle of Barnabas: Outlook and Background*, WUNT II/64 (Mohr [Siebeck], 1994), 9–27.

57   Justin Martyr is considered the most significant apologist for Christianity of the 2nd century ce Robert M. Grant, "Justin Martyr," *ABD* 3:1133. See also, Ruth Majercik, "Dialogue," *ABD* 2:187.

58   For the burning of bodies "outside the camp," see page 7 n. 27.

Why is it, then, that Hebrews does not employ the Azazel rite? While Hebrews can and does elect imagery from a variety of OT rituals, election of the image of burning of the bodies "outside the camp" instead of the rite of Azazel for the paraenetic function of Jesus's sacrifice undermines the idea that Day of Atonement imagery dominates the thinking of Hebrews.

The Sprinkling of Jesus's Blood in Heaven Does Not Refer to the Day of Atonement Ritual

Hebrews emphasizes the cultic image of the sprinkling of Jesus's blood in heaven but not in the context of the Day of Atonement.[59] Instead, it describes this sprinkling as part of the inauguration of the new covenant (10:19, 29; 12:24; 13:20; cf. 9:15–23). Hebrews typologizes a conflation of three rituals or events: the institution of the covenant, the ordination of priests, and the inauguration of the sanctuary (Heb 9:15–23).[60] In this conflated event, the sprinkling of Jesus's blood as the ratification of the new covenant (not an eschatological Day of Atonement) purifies the worshipers, providing for the forgiveness of their sins.[61]

Hebrews 9:15 explains that Jesus's sacrifice has the purpose of redeeming believers from "the transgressions that were *committed* under the first covenant" (Heb 9:15 NASB, emphasis original). As Scott W. Hahn has shown, these transgressions provide the context for the discussion of Jesus's death as a forgiveness of sin in Heb 9:15–22.[62] The debt incurred in these transgressions needed to be settled in order that believers could enter into a second or new covenant. In other words, where there is a [broken] covenant, "it is necessary that the death of the covenant maker be carried out" (Heb 9:16, translation mine).[63] Thus, Jesus died in order to provide forgiveness of sin and establish a new covenant between God and the believers (9:15).

---

59 The high point of the ritual of the Day of Atonement came when the high priest sprinkled the blood of the sacrifices upon the mercy seat and in front of it to purify the sanctuary (Lev 16:15–16). Interestingly, Hebrews departs from the language of the LXX to describe the manipulation of blood by the High Priest on the Day of Atonement: the blood is not "sprinkled" on the sanctuary but "offered" (9:7). See William L. Lane, *Hebrews 9–13*, WBC 47b (Word, 1991), 223. Also Pursiful, *The Cultic Motif*, 70.

60 See, Mary Rose D'Angelo, *Moses in the Letter to the Hebrews*, SBLDS 42 (Scholars Press, 1979), 243–249. Also, Stökl Ben Ezra, *Impact of Yom Kippur*, 187.

61 D'Angelo, *Moses in the Letter to the Hebrews*, 246; Haber, "From Priestly Torah to Christ Cultus," 109–10. Also, Hahn, "A Broken Covenant," 416–36.

62 Hahn, "A Broken Covenant," 416–36. Also, Scott W. Hahn, "Covenant, Cult, and the Curse of Death: Διαθήκη in Heb 9:15–22," in *Hebrews: Contemporary Methods—New Insights*, ed. Gabriella Gelardini, BibInt 75 (Brill, 2005), 65–88.

63 This is based on the analysis of Hahn, "A Broken Covenant," 432–433. See the section below on "Hebrews 9:15–23 describes Jesus's sacrifice and ascension as the inauguration of a

The cleansing of the sanctuary in Heb 9:23 should probably also be understood in the context of the inauguration of the new covenant and not of the Day of Atonement. Hebrews 9:23 says: "Thus it was necessary for the sketches of the heavenly things to be purified with these rites, but the heavenly things themselves need better sacrifices than these." The expression "these rites" in 9:23 refers back to the description of the cleansing of the sanctuary in its inauguration (9:21) and not in the Day of Atonement (9:7, 25).[64]

It is commonly agreed that both Day of Atonement and inauguration of covenant imageries are used in Hebrews to describe Jesus's sacrifice.[65] But, in this and subsequent sections, the ratification of the covenant (which in Hebrews conflates the inauguration of the sanctuary and the ordination of priests) becomes the primary typology for Jesus's death. Jesus is described mainly as the mediator of a new covenant (7:22; 8:6; 9:15) and his sacrifice is referred to primarily as the "blood of the covenant" (10:29; 12:24; 13:20). In his study of Yom Kippur, James P. Scullion agrees: "It should be noted that the key to this central section is not Yom Kippur itself, but the connection that the author makes between the cult and the new covenant."[66] William R. G. Loader concurs:

> Einerseits muß klar gesehen werden, daß diese Typology [Yom Kippur] eine wichtige Rolle in den Gedanken des Vf in 9,1–10,18 spielt; andererseits darf ihre Besonderheit nicht so weit hervorgehoben werden, daß sie als eigentliches Thema oder vorherrschender Gedanke dieses Abschnittes bezeichnet wird.[67]

In summary, the sprinkling of Jesus's blood in Hebrews has the primary intention of creating an analogy to the sacrifice for the ratification of the covenant.

---

new covenant. The interpretation of Jesus's death as the sacrifice for the inauguration of the new covenant in 9:15–23 is the subject of debate. Most commentators see a semantic shift in the use of the word διαθήκη from the sense "covenant" to the sense "will/testament" in vv. 16–17 and back to the sense "covenant" in vv. 18–22. This view, however, faces several crippling difficulties." See on page 242, "Heb 9:15–23 describes Jesus's sacrifice and ascension as the inauguration of a new covenant."

64 Ellingworth, *The Epistle to the Hebrews*, 477.

65 E.g., Álvarez Cineira, "Los Sacrificios," 237; Haber, "From Priestly Torah to Christ Cultus," 105–24; Nelson, "He Offered Himself," 252.

66 Scullion, "the Day of Atonement," 252.

67 (On the one hand it must clearly be seen, that this typology [Yom Kippur] plays an important role in the thinking of the author in 9:1–10:18; on the other hand, its peculiarity must not be stressed so much, that it is described as the essential theme or predominant thought of this section) *Sohn und Hoherpriester*, 172.

If there is an analogy between Jesus's sacrifice and the sacrifice of the Day of Atonement, it seems to be secondary.

The Day of Atonement Provides Only Secondary Imagery to Jesus's Sacrifice

Finally, Hebrews' argument seems not to rest on those things Jesus's sacrifice and the Day of Atonement had in common.

Several characteristics of Jesus's sacrifice are emphasized in the argument of Hebrews. First, Jesus's sacrifice is a one-time event. He offered himself "once for all" for our sins (7:27; 9:12, 26, 28; 10:10). Second, Jesus's sacrifice provides forgiveness. Jesus "offered himself ... [to] purify our conscience from dead works to worship the living God!" (9:14). And third, Jesus's sacrifice provides access to the presence of God. The author testifies that "we have confidence to enter the sanctuary by the blood of Jesus" (10:19–22).

Hebrews emphasizes, however, the opposite characteristics in the Day of Atonement ritual. The Day of Atonement is described not as a "once a year" event but as a repetitive, "year after year" event (9:25; 10:1, 3).[68] The Day of Atonement functions as a proof that the "way of the sanctuary" is not yet open (9:8). Finally, the Day of Atonement sacrifices do not provide forgiveness; instead, they function as a "reminder of sin" (10:3). The Day of Atonement seems to function in Hebrews, then, as an epitome of what was defective and imperfect in the old covenant system rather than as a type of what Jesus's sacrifice would be.[69]

On the other hand, Jesus is compared positively to the sacrifice for the ratification of the covenant. The comparison is explicit in Heb 9:15–22. First, Jesus's sacrifice like that of Moses is unique (Exod 24)—that is, not meant to be repeated (Heb 9:15–18).[70] Second, Jesus's sacrifice for the inauguration of the covenant provides forgiveness. His death "redeems them from the trans-

---

68 The exception is 9:7 where the Day of Atonement is described as a "once a year" event. For the purpose of Day of Atonement imagery in this passage, see Félix H. Cortez, "From the Holy to the Most Holy Place: The Period of Heb 9:6–10 and the Day of Atonement as a Metaphor of Transition," *JBL* 125 (2006): 527–547. He argues that the Day of Atonement illustrates in this passage the transition from the first to the second covenant and not specifically Jesus's ascension to heaven.

69 The selection by the author of the Day of Atonement ritual as an epitome for the old system is apposite. For Max L. Margolis, "The Day of Atonement is the keystone of the sacrificial system of post-exilic Judaism" ("Day of Atonement," *The Jewish Encyclopedia*, ed. Isidore Singer [Funk and Wagnalls, 1902], 2:286). See on page 266, "Jesus's ascension and the Day of Atonement."

70 The sacrifice for the inauguration of a covenant is by nature non-repeatable. The renewal of the covenant at Moab, for example, did not include the repetition of the sacrifice Moses performed at Sinai forty years before; it included only the repetition of its laws for the new generation (Deut 29–31).

gressions under the first covenant" (9:15, cf. 22). By means of his blood Jesus inaugurated [ἐνεκαίνισεν] a "new and living way" into the presence of God (10:19–22), just as Moses inaugurated the first covenant with the blood of "calves and goats" (9:18–19; see the section below on "The sacrifice of "goats and calves" does not refer particularly to the sacrifices of the Day of Atonement. Hebrews 9:12 contrasts Jesus's sacrifice to those "of goats and calves." The expression "goats and calves" (τράγων καὶ μόσχων), however, does not refer specifically to the animals sacrificed on the Day of Atonement (Lev 16). Richard M. Davidson notes correctly that, according to the LXX, τράγοι (he-goats) were not offered on the Day of Atonement. The LXX refers, instead, to χίμαροι (young male goats, Lev 16:5, 7–10). In fact, τράγοι and χίμαροι translate different Hebrew nouns: עַתּוּד and שָׂעִיר respectively. The sacrifices of τράγοι appear in cultic contexts in the Pentateuch only in Num 7 as part of the sacrifices for the inauguration of the tabernacle. Richard M. Davidson suggests, then, that the phrase "with the blood of goats and calves" (δι' αἵματος τράγων καὶ μόσχων) is an allusion to the complex of events related to the inauguration of the covenant and not to the Day of Atonement. This seems to be confirmed by the fact that Heb 9:19 refers to the sacrifice of τράγοι and μόσχοι as part of the ritual for the inauguration of the Mosaic covenant." See on page 238, "The sacrifice of 'Goats and calves' does not refer particularly to the sacrifices of the Day of Atonement.").

This observation suggests that the Day of Atonement imagery provides only part of the elements of the comparison to Jesus's sacrifice and that in this comparison it fulfills not a primary but a secondary function. We must not forget that the only explicit references to the Day of Atonement are found in Heb 8–10 (see page 7 n. 27), but it is in these chapters where the institution of the new covenant dominates the argument. Consequently, Jesus is primarily referred to throughout the work as the mediator of the new covenant (8:6; 9:15; 12:24; cf. 7:22), and his blood identified as the "blood of the covenant" (10:29; 13:20; cf. 12:24). Therefore, an analysis of the ascension of Jesus that considers the Day of Atonement ritual as its primary reference runs the risk of providing a skewed vision of the argument of Hebrews.

Summary

One question has ruled the discussion thus far. How detailed is the application of the Day of Atonement imagery to Hebrews' picture of Christ's ascension?

I have pointed out some limitations in Hebrews' usage of Day of Atonement imagery as an analogy for Jesus's ascension. First, several aspects of the Day of Atonement ritual are not part of the analogy. For example, the character of the Day of Atonement festival does not correspond to the character of Jesus's ascension in Hebrews. Jesus's entrance into the heavenly sanctuary is not a time of fasting for believers, but of rejoicing. Azazel, the culmination of the ritual, is not mentioned either. Second, the analogy for the sprinkling of Jesus's blood in heaven does not refer to the Day of Atonement ritual but to a complex of events in which Moses inaugurated God's covenant with Israel. Moreover, the primary analogy for Jesus's sacrifice as a forgiveness for sin is not the Day of Atonement ritual but the rituals for the inauguration of the covenant.

These limitations suggest that the imagery of the inauguration of the covenant plays a more important role for Hebrews' exposition of Jesus's ascension than the imagery of the Day of Atonement; yet few scholars allow for this connection.

Alternative Suggestion: Moses's Inauguration of the Sanctuary Provides the Analogy to Jesus's Ascension

Though often unmentioned, it also has been suggested that Jesus's ascension follows the analogy of the inauguration of the tabernacle by Moses in the context of the inauguration of the covenant.[71]

A recent advocate of this view is Richard M. Davidson. He suggests that Moses's inauguration of the sanctuary is the OT background for Jesus's entrance into the heavenly sanctuary in Hebrews. Following Albert Vanhoye's

---

71 E. E. Andross, *A More Excellent Ministry* (Pacific Press, 1912), 42–54; Gregory K. Beale, *The Temple and the Church's Mission: A Biblical Theology of the Dwelling Place of God*, NSBT 17 (Apollos, InterVarsity, 2004), 293–312; Nils A. Dahl, "A New and Living Way: The Approach to God According to Hebrews 10:19–25," *Int* 5 (1951): 401–412; D'Angelo, *Moses*, 233–234; Richard M. Davidson, "Christ's Entry 'Within the Veil' in Hebrews 6:19–20: The Old Testament Background," *AUSS* 39 (2001): 175–90; "Inauguration or Day of Atonement? A Response to Norman Young's 'Old Testament Background to Hebrews 6:19–20 Revisited'," *AUSS* 40 (2002): 69–88; J. H. Davies, *A Letter to Hebrews*, CBC (Cambridge University Press, 1967), 91; Ellingworth, *The Epistle to the Hebrews*, 477; Lincoln D. Hurst, *The Epistle to the Hebrews: Its Background of Thought*, SNTSMS 65 (Cambridge University Press, 1990), 38–39; Spicq, *L'épître aux Hébreux*, 2:267; Gregory E. Sterling, "Ontology versus Eschatology: Tensions between Author and Community in Hebrews," in *In the Spirit of Faith: Studies in Philo and Early Christianity in Honor of David Hay*, ed. David T. Runia and Gregory E. Sterling, SPhiloA 13, Brown Judaic Studies 331 ([Brown University], 2001), 198. Several of these scholars allow for a double analogy of Jesus's ascension that would include the Day of Atonement and Moses's inauguration of the sanctuary (e.g., Paul Ellingworth). For previous commentators who held this position, see John H. A. Ebrard, *Biblical Commentary on the Epistle to the Hebrews*, trans. John Fulton, Clark's Foreign Theological Library 32 (T&T Clark, 1853), 299; Spicq, *L'épître aux Hébreux*, 267.

and William H. Shea's literary analysis of the structure of Hebrews, he notes that Heb 6:19–20; 9:11–14, 24; and 10:19–22 are parallel passages that refer to the same event and should explain one another.[72] He presents four main arguments:

1. Jesus is king and high priest.[73] The fact that he is described in Hebrews as being a high priest "according to the order of Melchizedek" makes clear that Hebrews does not wish to establish an Aaron-Jesus typology. Aaron is not king. Moses, instead, functions in Hebrews as a type of Jesus (3:1–6; 9:15–24). Moses functions as a king high priest, particularly in his role of inaugurator of the covenant, which includes the inauguration of the sanctuary. Moses entered the inner room of the sanctuary as part of the inauguration rites (Exod 26:33; 40:1–9; Lev 8:10–12; and Num 7:1).[74]

2. Hebrews 10:19–22 refers to the "new and living way which He [Jesus] inaugurated [ἐνεκαίνισεν] for us through the veil" (NASB). It is argued that the verb ἐγκαινίζω is used here in a cultic sense just as in Heb 9:18 where it refers to the inauguration of the first covenant—which includes the inauguration of the Mosaic tabernacle (vv. 19–21).[75] Therefore, the "new and living way" denotes the heavenly sanctuary which is inaugurated by Christ.[76]

3. Hebrews 9:12 refers to the sacrifices "of goats and calves" (τράγων καὶ μόσχων). The word for goats (τράγων) does not appear in the sacrifices of the Day of Atonement in Lev 16 (LXX) but appears only in Num 7 where the inauguration rites of the sanctuary are described. There, the sacrifices of calves (μόσχων) also appear.[77] Thus Num 7–8 is the only place in the LXX where there is reference to the sacrifices of goats and calves (τράγων

---

72 Davidson, "Christ's Entry," 175–190; Davidson, "Inauguration," 69–88.

73 For a study of the notions of Moses as king and high priest in Jewish religion, see John Lierman, *The New Testament Moses: Christian Perceptions of Moses and Israel in the Setting of Jewish Religion*, WUNT II/173 (Mohr Siebeck, 2004), 65–123. For example, Scripture says: "Moses and Aaron were among his priests" (Ps 99:6). See also, Jacob Milgrom, *Leviticus 1–16: A New Translation with Commentary*, AB 3 (Doubleday, 1991), 555–558.

74 Davidson, "Christ's Entry," 176–177.

75 Ἐγκαινίζω means "renew, ratify, inaugurate, dedicate." BDAG, 272. This verb, and its derivatives, is used for the inauguration of the tabernacle (Num 7:10, 11, 84, 88), Solomon's temple (2 Chr 7:9; Ps 30:1; 2 Macc 2:9), the temple after the exile (Ezra 6:16, 17; 1 Esd 7:7), and the rededication of the altar in the time of the Maccabees (1 Macc 4:36, 56, 59; 2 Macc 2:19). In fact, this rededication in the time of the Maccabees had become an important festival by New Testament times and was known as Hanukkah or τὰ ἐγκαίνια (see John 10:22).

76 Davidson, "Christ's Entry," 180–81. Also, Dahl, "A New and Living Way," 403.

77 Davidson, "Christ's Entry," 182–5.

καὶ μόσχων). Hebrews 9:19 mentions both kinds of animals for the sacrifice of the inauguration of the covenant.⁷⁸

4. Hebrews 9:24 describes Jesus's entrance into the heavenly sanctuary in the context of the inauguration of the new covenant and the tabernacle as described in 9:15–22. Richard M. Davidson concedes, however, that in this case the cleansing of the heavenly sanctuary remains ambiguous and refers to the inauguration of the sanctuary (9:15–22) as well as the Day of Atonement (9:25).⁷⁹

Thus, Heb 6:19–20, which is a parallel passage to 9:11–14, 24; 10:19–22, should be understood in the context of an analogy to Moses's inauguration of the sanctuary and not to the annual ritual of the Day of Atonement.

Other scholars present further arguments in favor of this position.

Nils A. Dahl notes that the juxtaposition of sprinkling and ritual washing in 10:22 closely parallels the ceremony of the initiation of priests performed by Moses. Note that this ceremony was carried out together with the inauguration of the sanctuary (Exod 29:1–37; 30:22–33; 40:1–15; Lev 8–9). Likewise, Hebrews conflates the inauguration of the sanctuary with the consecration of the priesthood in a single event (Heb 9:18–21).⁸⁰ The import of this analogy is that just as the sanctuary and priests were consecrated by Moses so they could have access to the sanctuary, Jesus consecrates believers by virtue of his sacrifice and ascension so they might approach God (10:19–22; cf., 9:11–14).

Mary Rose D'Angelo argues that the term ἐπιτελεῖν in Heb 8:5 should be translated as "complete" or "consecrate" and not "build" as normally translated.⁸¹ She notes that the sanctuary was completed only when it was consecrated (Exod 40:33; Num 7:1). She also argues that Heb 8:5 quotes Num 7:1 and not Exod 25:40 and, therefore,

> the *typos* of the cult which Moses saw was a *typos* which instructed him precisely for the consecration.... The explication of the *typos* as especially the *typos* of the inauguration (ἐνκαίνωσις) of the tent and the ordination of the priests helps to explain Hebrews' definition of the purpose of the service as to perfect or ordain the worshipper (τελειῶσαι τὸν λατρεύοντα).⁸²

---

78 The text without "καὶ τῶν τράγων" is supported by important mss.; e.g., 𝔓46, ℵ², K, L, Y, 181, 1241, 1739, syrp, h, pal. It is probable, however, that the words were omitted either "accidentally (through homoteleuton) or deliberately (to conform the statement to Ex 24.5)" (Metzger, 599).
79 "Christ's Entry," 185–188.
80 Also, D'Angelo, *Moses*, 244.
81 Ibid., 233.
82 Ibid., 235.

Ceslas Spicq also considers that 9:23 refers to the inauguration of the heavenly sanctuary. He argues that the omission of the verb in the last clause of Heb 9:23 is important. He suggests that the verb to be supplied there is ἐγκαινίζεσθαι and not καθαρίζεσθαι. In his opinion, this helps to resolve the problem of the purification of the heavenly sanctuary, which for him is a "non sens": it is not purification, but consecration that Hebrews is talking about in this passage.[83] His explanation is unnecessary, however. The terms ἐγκαινίζεσθαι and καθαρίζεσθαι appear intimately related in the context of the inauguration or re-dedication of the sanctuary in Jewish thinking (1 Macc 4:36–59; 2 Macc 2:19; 2 Chr 29:15; Neh 13:9, 30).[84]

Gregory K. Beale calls attention to the quotation of Hag 2:6 in Heb 12:26–27.[85] That prophecy was given in the context of the construction of Zerubbabel's temple. It promises that God "will shake the heavens and the earth" and the glory of that house would be greater than that of Solomon's temple. In his view, Hebrews interprets this prophecy as being fulfilled in the ratification of the new covenant and inauguration of a "greater and more perfect tabernacle" (9:11 NASB; cf. v. 24).

The strength of the inauguration view is that it seems to follow the straightforward argument of the text, at least of 9:11–23. Hebrews interprets Jesus's sacrifice and ascension of 9:11–14 as the inauguration of the new covenant in 9:15–22.[86] Hebrews also correlates Moses's consecration of the tabernacle (v. 21) with the purification of the heavenly sanctuary in 9:23.[87] Thus, Philip E. Hughes considers that "there is much to attract in this proposal, which has both simplicity and strength."[88]

Critique of the Analogy to Moses's Inauguration of the Sanctuary

There are, however, several criticisms that have been leveled against this view.

---

83 Spicq, *L'épître aux Hébreux*, 267. Also, Ebrard, *The Epistle to the Hebrews* 299. Note the significant number of previous commentators he mentions who held the same opinion.

84 James C. Vanderkam notes: "One noteworthy case in point is the fact that the account in 1 Macc 4:36–61 centers on the dedication or restoration of the altar, while the various references in 2 Maccabees (1:18; 2:16, 19; 10:3, 5, 7) focus on the cleansing of the temple" ("Feast of Dedication," *ADB* 2:124).

85 Beale, *The Temple and the Church's Mission*, 303–309.

86 Note that the διὰ τοῦτο of 9:15 creates a causal relationship between both sections.

87 When Heb 9:23 says that "the heavenly things themselves need better sacrifices than these," the demonstrative pronoun ταύτας refers to the sacrifices of the inauguration of the covenant (vv. 19–21). Ellingworth, *The Epistle to the Hebrews*, 477–478; Attridge, *The Epistle to the Hebrews*, 261.

88 Philip Edgcumbe Hughes, *A Commentary on the Epistle to the Hebrews* (Eerdmans, 1977), 380.

First, several expressions in the ascension passages of Hebrews privilege an analogy to the Day of Atonement. For example, the only passage in the OT that speaks about the *high priest* going "within the veil"—the expression used in Heb 6:19 (cf. 10:20)—is Lev 16 (vv. 2, 12, 15) where the Day of Atonement is described.[89] The idea that Moses went "within the veil" in order to consecrate the sanctuary is *inferred* from the consecration passages (Exod 40; Lev 8, Num 7) but not directly mentioned.[90] Similarly, while Jesus is designated a high priest, none of the passages of the consecration of the sanctuary (Exod 40; Lev 8, Num 7) refer to Moses as a high priest.[91] Also, Hebrews consistently draws a contrast between the Melchizedek order to which Jesus belongs and the Aaronic order to which Moses did not belong.[92] Therefore, it is argued that there is no typological relationship between Moses and Jesus *as far as* Jesus's entrance and cleansing of the heavenly sanctuary are concerned.[93]

Second, the reference to τράγοι in connection to μόσχοι in Heb 9:12 does not necessarily imply the sacrifices for the consecration of the sanctuary. In Num 7 (thirteen passages in total), the term τράγος forms part of the animal sacrifices for whole burnt offerings. The blood of these sacrifices was not brought into the sanctuary (Lev 1:10–13) and thus may not refer to the blood that is brought into the sanctuary according to Hebrews.[94] Note as well, that the context of Heb 10:4 implicates that the author uses the term τράγος to refer to the he-goat sacrificed on the Day of Atonement. Likewise, the Greek versions of Aquila (early 2d c. ce) and Symmachus (late 2d–early 3d c. ce) use the term τράγος instead of χίμαρος for the he-goat of Lev 16.[95] Philo and Pseudo-Barnabas also prefer τράγος over χίμαρος in their description of Day of Atonement sacrifices.[96] Thus—it is argued—it is more correct to say that

---

89 Norman H. Young, " 'Where Jesus Has Gone as a Forerunner on Our Behalf' (Hebrews 6:20)," *AUSS* 39 (2001): 171.

90 Young, "Day of Dedication," 62. Note, however, that Philo refers to Moses's entrance into the sanctuary to anoint the holy furniture explicitly, including the ark of the covenant (*Moses* 2.146, 152–154).

91 Note, again, that Philo refers to Moses as high priest (*Moses* 2.3).

92 Young, "Day of Dedication," 62.

93 Note, however, that there is an explicit comparison between Moses and Jesus in their relation to "God's house" (Heb 3:1–6).

94 Young, "Day of Dedication," 65.

95 Fridericus Field, ed., *Origens hexaplorum: Quae supersunt sive veterum interpretum graecorum in totum vetus testamentum*, 2 vols. (Georg Olms, 1964), 2:194. See also, Westcott, *The Epistle to the Hebrews*, 258; Moffatt, *The Epistle to the Hebrews* 121; Spicq, *L'épître aux Hébreux*, 257. On the versions of Aquila and Symmachus, see Stanley E. Porter, "Septuagint/Greek Old Testament," *DNTB* 1102.

96 Philo, *Spec.* 1.188 (χίμαρος); *Leg.* 2.52; *Post.* 70; *Plant.* 61; *Heres* 179. Pseudo-Barnabas, 7.4, 6, 8, 10. Josephus (37 – post 93 ce) is another first-century example of how fluid Jewish writers were in their choice of words for the sacrifices. He uses ἔριφος (kid, he-goat) and ταῦρος

the phrase "blood of goats and calves" in Heb 9:12 is a generic expression that refers to the sacrifice of animals in general and not specifically to the inauguration of the sanctuary.

Third, Heb 9:23 may not parallel vv. 19–21. It has been argued that v. 22 functions as a "contextual break" and v. 23 is connected, instead, to vv. 24–28 that deal with mediation and not consecration.[97] Another view is that the parallel to v. 23 is vv. 11–14 where reference is made to the cleansing of the conscience.[98]

Finally, Heb 9:23 does not say that the heavenly sanctuary is "inaugurated" but "cleansed," and these terms are not synonymous.[99] It is argued that the cleansing of the heavenly sanctuary has to do with the remission of sins mentioned immediately before (v. 22), and the consecration of the sanctuary did not accomplish this.[100]

The consecration of the heavenly sanctuary as an alternative for the interpretation of Heb 9:23 is hardly mentioned in recent commentaries though we have reason to believe that serious scholars are acquainted with it. This view meets the same fate in other passages as well (4:14–16; 6:19–20; 9:11–14; 10:19–22). Apparently, the view of a Day of Atonement typology for Jesus's ascension is so widely accepted among scholars today that it is difficult for another idea even to be entertained.[101]

I will argue below, in my analysis of these passages, that the critiques raised against this view are not compelling and that a study of the relationship between the inauguration of the covenant and Jesus's ascension merits more attention than it has received thus far.

In my opinion, the principal shortcoming of both views introduced above is that neither of them explains adequately the interrelationship between the allusions to the Day of Atonement and the inauguration of the covenant in the Letter to the Hebrews. Both rituals are referred to explicitly in the text and both are related to Jesus's sacrifice and ascension. The question is, why did the author choose to integrate allusions to two different rituals in the exposi-

---

(bull, ox) for the sin-offerings of the Day of Atonement (*Ant.* 3.239–240, Young, "Day of Dedication," 65).

97 Johnsson, "Defilement/Purification," 95–96.

98 Attridge, *The Epistle to the Hebrews*, 261.

99 Johnsson, "Defilement/Purification," 96. See, David J. MacLeod, "The Cleansing of the True Tabernacle," *BSac* 152 (1995): 69.

100 Attridge, *The Epistle to the Hebrews*, 261. Note, however, that Lev 8:15 mentions the purification of the altar after the priests laid their hands on the victim. See also Lev 9:7, where there were expiatory sacrifices for the people in the context of the inauguration of the tabernacle.

101 Young, "Where Jesus Has Gone," 166.

tion of Jesus's sacrifice and ascension instead of taking the more simple route of alluding to only one ritual? Is it possible to find coherence in Hebrews' use of allusions to the rituals of the Old Testament? Until now, scholars have neglected one set of allusions or the other in their analyses.

A Third Way: The Enthronement of the Ideal Davidic King Provides the Analogy to Jesus's Ascension

I want to suggest a third perspective that may better explain Hebrews' exposition of Jesus's ascension into heaven.

The author of Hebrews refers to the ascension of Jesus not only in chs. 8–10, but throughout the work; therefore, we should study the ascension in the context of the general thrust of the document. The six passages that refer explicitly to Jesus's ascension in Hebrews (1:6; 4:14–16; 6:19–20; 9:11–14, 24; 10:19–22) associate the ascension with different aspects of Jesus's achievements. Hebrews 1:6 relates the ascension with Jesus's enthronement (also 4:14–16); 6:19–20, with his appointment as high priest; 9:11–14, 24; and 10:19–22, with the inauguration of the new covenant. It seems clear, however, that all of these events form part of Jesus's exaltation at the right hand of God (1:3, 13; 8:1; 10:12; 12:2) and contribute to his identity as "Son." I will argue that the title "Son"—or "Son of God"—is used in Hebrews eminently as a royal title. Note that Jesus is the "Son" enthroned as king (1:3, 8), consecrated as high priest (4:14; 5:5, 8; 7:28), and mediator of the new covenant (10:29; cf. 6:6). In other words, I suggest that Hebrews conceives the ascension as the inauguration of his office as "Son" at the "right hand of God" (Heb 1:3, 13; 4:14–16; 8:1–2; 10:12–13; 12:1–2) and that it understands the title "Son" as the fulfillment of the promise made to David which is claimed for Jesus explicitly in Heb 1:5. Thus, all the other achievements related to Jesus's ascension are a function of, or derive from, his installation as Israel's promised Davidic king.

In this sense, Jesus fulfills the expectations raised in the Old Testament regarding the rule of a future righteous Davidic king. The rule of righteous Davidic kings in Jewish history was characterized by seven actions—not always in the same order—that are intriguingly familiar to the argument of Hebrews. After ascending the throne, the king would (1) renew the covenant between God and the nation, (2) cleanse the land, (3) build or repair the temple, (4) reform the cult and reorganize the priests and Levites, (5) promote the reunification of Israel, and (6) achieve rest by defeating the enemies. The rise to power of the Davidic king often coincides as well with (7) the emergence of a faithful priest.

Thus, Jesus is the "Son" enthroned at the right hand of God (1:3, 5–6). He has defeated "death," the enemy (2:14–16), built the "house of God" (3:1–6; 8:1–5), and provided "rest" for his people (4:1–10). His ascension to the throne implies as well the emergence of a new faithful priest of the order of Melchizedek (chs. 5–7) and a reformation of the cult—specifically of the law of sacrifices (9:24–10:18) and priesthood (7:13–28). The new king cleanses his people (9:11–14), mediates a new covenant (9:15–23), and reforms the cult by establishing one sacrifice that is effective "once for all" (9:24–10:18) and multiple spiritual sacrifices (13:10–16), all of which conclude in a joyous celebration at Mount Zion (12:22–29)—as the reforms of ancient Jewish kings did.

It is important to note, however, that the main thrust of Hebrews is not to prove that Jesus is the "Son" enthroned at the right hand of God; instead, the author of Hebrews refers to Jesus's exaltation—and what it implies—as the basis for a call to the readers—or exhortation—to remain faithful to him (e.g., 2:1–4; 4:14–16; 10:19–25, 35–39; 12:1–4).

Although Hebrews does not explicitly call Jesus the "son of David," the fact that it recognizes his descent from the tribe of Judah (7:14), applies to him the promises of the Davidic covenant (Heb 1:5; quoting Ps 2:7 and 2 Sam 7:14; par. 1 Chr 17:13), and refers to his enthronement as "Son" "at the right hand of God" (1:3, 13; 5:6; 7:17, 21; 10:13; 12:2; quoting Ps 110:1, 4) makes it highly probable that Davidic traditions function as a subtext of the letter.[102]

Traditions and expectations often provided powerful rhetorical subtexts in the ancient Mediterranean world. Here is an important example from close to the time when the book of Hebrews was written. In his fascinating work *Nero*, Edward Champlin gives us a glimpse of the power and role subtexts had in the political discourse of first-century-ce Rome.[103]

Historians inform us that after 59 CE Nero began to appear on stage at the theater, assuming a diversity of roles. (Nero considered himself a poet and lyre player as well.) Tradition has seen in these "inordinate artistic pretensions" irresponsibility and "puerile ambitions."[104] Edward Champlin, however, in a *tour de force*, attempts to subvert the received opinion suggesting that it was not sheer insanity that drove Nero's sponsorship of and participation in the theater, but a rational delusion, a brilliant act of his artistic genius. He

---

[102] Subtext refers to "any meaning or set of meanings which is implied rather than explicitly stated in a literary work," Chris Baldick, *The Concise Oxford Dictionary of Literary Terms* (Oxford University Press, 1990), s.v. "Subtext." See also, J. A. Cuddon, *A Dictionary of Literary Terms and Literary Theory*, 3d ed. (Blackwell, 1991); Edward Quinn, *A Dictionary of Literary and Thematic Terms* (Facts on File, 1999).

[103] Edward Champlin, *Nero* (Belknap, 2003).

[104] *Encyclopaedia Britannica Standard Edition*, 2005 ed., CD-ROM, s.v. "Nero."

notes that the afterlife of Nero's image was unique in antiquity.[105] He suggests that the reason for the fascination he exerted on the masses and history was that "he staged his life as a mythological enactment to shock and amuse his people."[106]

In late March 59 CE, Nero killed his mother, alleging she craved power and posed a threat to his reign.[107] It was also rumored that he had committed incest with her.[108] Nero, however, did not successfully cover up his crime, and soon the popular view of Nero's guilt was expressed in pasquinades (lampoons) posted anonymously in public places. In fact, a cynic philosopher and an actor rebuked the emperor in public with oblique references to his crime. The remarkable fact is that Nero was exceptionally lenient in his dealing with them and others who dared to attack him in speech, verse, or other forms. He banished the actor and the philosopher but did not take action against a senator, and refused to allow such kind of accusations to be brought to court.[109] Instead, Nero decided to stage his defense at the theater using the power of imagery and myth to his advantage. He chose what roles he would play with care and modified the imagery (e.g., masks, wardrobe, and probably lyrics too) to produce a calculated effect on the audience.

Cassius Dio and Suetonius recorded several details of Nero's theatrical performances:

> In putting on the mask [he] threw off the dignity of his sovereignty to beg in the guise of a runaway slave, to be led about as a blind man, to be heavy with child, to be in labour, to be a madman, or to wander an outcast, his favourite rôles being those of Oedipus, Thyestes, Heracles, Alcmeon, and Orestes[.] The masks that he wore were sometimes made to resemble the characters he was portraying and sometimes bore his own likeness; but the women's masks were all fashioned after the features of Sabina, in order that, though dead, she might still take part in the spectacle. All the situations that ordinary actors simulate in their acting he, too, would portray in speech or action or in submitting to the action of others—save

---

105 Champlin, *Nero*, 9.
106 Kathleen Coleman, review of *Nero*, by Edward Champlin, *Roman Archaeology* 18 (2005): 545.
107 Champlin, *Nero*, 88–89.
108 About the incest, historians differ regarding who was the seducer and if in fact it was consummated (Suetonius 28.2; Tacitus 14.2; Dio 61.11.3–4). Edward Champlin concludes: "Whatever the truth, the common version appears to be that Agrippina offered herself to Nero in 58 or 59 but was circumvented by her enemies; and that he himself did nothing either to prevent her or to suppress the rumor" (*Nero*, 88).
109 Ibid., 92.

only that golden chains were used to bind him; for apparently it was not thought proper for a Roman emperor to be bound in iron shackles. All this behaviour, nevertheless, was witnessed, endured, and approved, not only by the crowd in general, but also by the soldiers. (Dio 62.9.4–10.1 [Cary, LCL])

He also put on the mask and sang tragedies representing gods and heroes and even heroines and goddesses, having the masks fashioned in the likeness of his own features or those of the women of whom he chanced to be enamoured. Among other themes he sang "Canace in Labor," "Orestes the Matricide," "Oedipus Blinded," and the "Hercules Mad." (Suetonius, *Nero* 21.3 [Rolfe, LCL])

Edward Champlin emphasizes two aspects of these accounts. First, Nero used to wear a mask at the stage that "bore his own likeness." Second, he infers that Nero's "favourite rôles" had a political purpose: Nero *was* Orestes and Alcmeon the matricides, Oedipus who killed his father and married his own mother, and Hercules who killed his wife and children in a fit of madness.

The tale of Orestes was well known in antiquity. Orestes is ordered by Apollo's oracle at Delphi to avenge his father's death (Agamemnon) by killing the murderers: Clytemnestra (wife of Agamemnon and mother of Orestes) and Aegisthus (her lover). After being tormented by the furies, Orestes is acquitted at a great murder trial at Athens by one vote, that of Athena. The key for Nero was that Orestes is "a *justified* matricide." Orestes kills Clytemnestra not only because of Apollos' command, but also because she had stolen his inheritance from him, and the people of Mycenae were suffering under the tyranny of a woman. Likewise, Nero avenges his adoptive father's death (Claudius) by killing Agrippina, who had poisoned him, liberating also the people from her power-craving tyranny.[110]

Nero pursues a similar objective in his assumption of the roles of Oedipus and Hercules. In "Oedipus Blinded" he described himself as one certainly guilty of incest, but only as an act of ignorance. In "Hercules Mad," Nero reenacted his inadvertent killing of Poppaea Sabina, who was pregnant with his son, in the summer of 65. Like Hercules, in a flash of temper, he lashed out in blind ferocity killing the object of his love and his heir. Nero thus portrayed himself not as a murderer, but as the victim of divine madness.

Whether Edward Champlin is accurate in his interpretation of Nero's artistic deeds is open to debate. Kathleen Coleman points out that several aspects of Champlin's argument are not convincing; for example, Champlin's

---

110 Ibid., 97–98. The tale of Alcmeon is virtually a double to that of Orestes. For an analysis of it, see Champlin, *Nero*, 98–99.

argument that Nero did not suffer what scholars call *damnatio memoriae*, or his defense of the tradition that Nero started Rome's fire. She concludes that the grand scheme in which Edward Champlin fits almost all of Nero's actions as mythological enactments is more logical than reality probably was and perhaps more the result of Champlin's dexterity than Nero's own genius.[111]

The important thing for us, however, is the forcefulness with which Edward Champlin portrays the power of subtext in ancient Rome. He concludes that "audiences *expected* to find contemporary relevance in the productions [and] performers *expected* to have their pointed remarks and actions caught, interpreted, and appreciated" to the extent that "the audience sometimes saw an allusion where none was intended."[112]

Joseph P. Wilson shows that this phenomenon is based on a tradition that can be traced back to the 5th century BCE.[113] He argues that Sophocles' *Oedipus at Colonus* played a political role "for the troubled Athenian *polis* in the last decade of the tumultuous 5th century" and that "it was understood that the messages of a play should be oblique, opaque, and apprehensible by inference and implication ... [and], at the conclusion of the play, the audience was expected to retain images rather than dialogue."[114]

Alan Cameron provides several examples of the same phenomenon in the times of imperial Rome:

> On one occasion the line 'Videsne ut cinaedus orbem digito temperat' (in fact referring to a priest of the Magna Mater striking a tambourine) was taken—and no doubt intended by the actor—as a homosexual allegation about Augustus. A reference to an 'old goat licking the does (*capreae*)' was taken to denote Tiberius' supposed debaucheries on Capri. Galba's ill-omened entry in Rome in 69 was hit at by a line in a farce, and the people sang the whole song with one voice, to the accompaniment of suitable gestures. The unlettered Maximin was (perhaps fortunately) unable to understand a *risqué* song addressed to him in Greek by a bold actor.[115]

He agrees with Cicero that in fact the theater—as well as the gladiatorial shows—became the only venue where popular opinion was truly expressed.

---

111 Coleman, review of *Nero*, 550.
112 R. W. Reynolds, "Criticism of Individuals in Roman Popular Comedy," *CQ* 37 (1943): 40, as quoted in Champlin, *Nero*, 95.
113 *The Hero and the City: An Interpretation of Sophocles' Oedipus at Colonus* (University of Michigan Press, 1997), 187–99.
114 Ibid., 189.
115 Alan Cameron, *Circus Factions: Blues and Greens at Rome and Byzantium* (Clarendon, 1976), 160.

There is ample evidence that politicians usually traced their pedigrees to ancient heroes and used them as weapons, weaving myth into contemporary Roman political life.[116] Paul Zanker aptly describes the role that images played in the struggle between Octavian and Marc Antony.[117] Antony adopted the figure of Dionysus, favored in Asia Minor and previously adopted by Alexander the Great as appropriate for him as the "giver [of] joy and beneficent" (Plutarch, *Ant.* 24.3 [Perrin, LCL]). Octavian shrewdly took advantage of Antony's disregard of the kind of impact these images could have in Rome and Italy and used them as a ready supply of ammunition in his attack of Antony as advocating revelry, luxury, and decadence. Instead, Octavian appropriated the image of Apollos who "stood first of all for discipline and morality."[118]

It is clear, then, that literary subtexts were a powerful element of political discourse in Nero's Rome and audiences were ready to discern every allusion and find a deeper meaning in them. A majority of scholars have suggested that Hebrews was probably written to Christians in Rome around this time (between 60 CE and 90 CE).[119] Others consider that it was more likely that

---

116 Paul Zanker, *The Power of Images in the Age of Augustus*, trans. Alan Shapiro, Jerome Lectures (University of Michigan Press, 1988), 44.

117 Ibid., 33–77.

118 Ibid., 52.

119 Hebrews itself does not identify its addressees; therefore, many places have been suggested as the destination of Hebrews. Since at least the 4th century interpreters have suggested Jerusalem. For example, Chrysostom, most medieval authors, Delitzsch, *The Epistle to the Hebrews*, 1:20–21; Westcott, *The Epistle to the Hebrews*, xl; George Wesley Buchanan, *To the Hebrews: Translation, Comment and Conclusions*, AB 36 (Doubleday, 1972), 256. A Jerusalem destination is not likely, however. The title "to the Hebrews" was added by a later hand. It is unlikely that the author would have written in an elegant Greek style to people in Jerusalem, or used the LXX as a basis for his argument (especially in those places where it differs from the MT), or that the readers had not heard Jesus preach (Heb 2:3, see Koester, *Hebrews*, 48–49). Others have suggested Spain, Palestine or Syria, Colossae, Ephesus, Galatia, Cyprus, Berea, Corinth and Asia Minor (see Spicq, *L'épître aux Hébreux*, 1:220–252; Donald Guthrie, *New Testament Introduction*, 4th ed. [InterVarsity, 1990], 700–701; Koester, *Hebrews*, 48, n. 104).

Rome has found growing support among modern interpreters on the basis of the following evidence: (1) the phrase "Those from Italy send you greetings" (Ἀσπάζονται ὑμᾶς οἱ ἀπὸ τῆς Ἰταλίας; Heb 13:24) probably means that some Italians who are away from Italy are sending greetings back home (cf. Acts 18:2), (2) Timothy (mentioned in 13:24) was known to the Roman Christians (Col 1:1; Phlm 1), (3) the use of the term ἡγούμενοι for the leaders (Heb 13:7, 17, 24) is similar to 1 Clem. 1:3 (cf. 21:6) which was written from Rome, (4) Hebrews is first attested in 1 Clem. 36:1–5 which was written from Rome (ca. 96 ce), (5) the allusion to the generosity of the readers (Heb 6:10; 10:32) fits well with the known history of the Roman church from other sources, (6) reference to ceremonial food (Heb 13:9) is similar to the tendency seen in Rom 14, and (7) the spoliations of goods referred to in 10:32 could be explained by Claudius's edict (49 ce) or Nero's persecution (Guthrie, *New Testament Introduction*, 698–699). Those who propose a Roman destination include, Koester, *Hebrews*, 49–51; Lane, *Hebrews 1–8*, lviii–lx; "Social Perspectives on Roman Christianity during the Formative Years from Nero to Nerva: Romans, Hebrews, 1 Clement," in *Judaism and Christianity in First-Century Rome*, ed. Karl P. Donfried and Peter Richardson (Eerdmans, 1998), 214–224; Ellingworth, *The Epistle to the Hebrews*, 28–29;

Hebrews was written from Rome.¹²⁰ In any case, the audience probably participated in this culture where imagery introduced a deeper meaning of discourse. Therefore, a correct interpretation of the cultic imagery that couches Jesus's ascension is crucial for the interpretation of its message.

I want to suggest that the same rhetorical function that the literary traditions of Orestes and Alcmeon (the matricides), Oedipus (who killed his father and married his own mother), and Hercules (who killed his wife and children in a fit of madness) had for the interpretation of Nero is the function the author of Hebrews assigns to the Davidic traditions for the interpretation of Jesus's rule. In both cases the traditions are applied tacitly, but this does not lessen their impact.

Delimitations and Methodology

The present work is structured in three sections, which amount to three chapters of the book. The present chapter introduced the state of affairs regarding the theology of the ascension in Hebrews. It explored how Hebrews' scholarship has associated the ascension to the rituals of the Day of Atonement and/or the rituals for the consecration of the Mosaic tabernacle and the problems of both approaches.

Chapter 2 analyzes the elements associated with the rule of a righteous Davidic king in the Hebrew Bible and early Judaism. The purpose of this chapter is to explore the traditions concerning the rule of the ideal Davidic king as it is attested in the Hebrew Bible and writings from the early Judaism period.

Attridge, *The Epistle to the Hebrews*, 9–10; Nello Casalini, *Agli Ebrei: Discorso di esortazione*, Studium Biblicum Franciscanum Analecta 34 (Franciscan, 1992), 53–55; Weiß, *Der Brief an die Hebräer*, 76; Bruce, *The Epistle to the Hebrews*, 13–14.

It is difficult to set a precise date for Hebrews. The latest date is set by Clement's epistle to the Corinthians (ca. 96 CE), which is the first to use Hebrews. Timothy is mentioned in Heb 13:23. If this Timothy is the companion of Paul, the letter should have been written after 49 CE (Acts 16:1–3). The persecution mentioned in Heb 10:32–34 was probably not instigated by Nero because no reference is made to Christians being killed (Heb 12:4; Tacitus, *Ann.* 15.44.6). If Rome is the destination, Claudius's expulsion of the Jews from Rome in 49 CE better fits the evidence (Koester, *Hebrews*, 52). Several recent scholars believe that the absence of any reference to the destruction of the temple favors a date before 70 CE. Others favor a date in the 80s or 90s on the basis that the text deals with the fatigue of second-generation Christians or the sense of loss over the destruction of Jerusalem. For a list of scholars and the dates they propose, see Ellingworth, *The Epistle to the Hebrews*, 33, n. 105; Koester, *Hebrews*, 54, nn. 114, 115.

120 See Carl Mosser, "No Lasting City: Rome, Jerusalem and the Place of Hebrews in the History of Earliest 'Christianity' " (PhD diss., The University of St Andrews, 2005); David L. Allen, *Hebrews*, NAC (Broadman & Holman, 2010); Félix H. Cortez, *The Letter to the Hebrews*, Seventh-day Adventist International Bible Commentary (Nampa, ID: Pacific Press, forthcoming).

Chapter 3 analyzes every passage in the Letter to the Hebrews that refers to Jesus's entrance into heaven.[121] The passages are Heb 1:6; 4:14–16; 6:19; 9:11–14, 24; 10:19–22. Those passages that implicate Jesus's ascension by referring to his session at the right hand but not referring to it explicitly are studied in the context of the explicit passages mentioned above.[122] I explain in this section, as well, my understanding of the function of the rituals of the Day of Atonement and the inauguration of the covenant in relation to the ascension of Jesus.

Finally, the conclusion summarizes and systematizes the findings of chapters 1–3.

---

121 I will also refer throughout this chapter to the results of several monographs and articles that have been devoted to the concept of heavenly ascent in early Jewish writings and Greco-Roman literature. For example, Bietenhard, *Die himmlische Welt im Urchristentum un Spätjudentum*; John J. Collins, "A Throne in the Heavens: Apotheosis in Pre-Christian Judaism," in *Death, Ecstasy, and Other Worldly Journeys*, ed. John J. Collins and Michael Fishbane (State University of New York Press, 1995), 43–58; Mary Dean-Otting, *Heavenly Journeys: A Study of the Motif in Hellenistic Jewish Literature*, Judentum und Umwelt 8 (Lang, 1984); Ellingworth, "Jesus and the Universe," 337–350; Lohfink, *Die Himmelfahrt Jesu*; Segal, "Heavenly Ascent," 1333–94; James D. Tabor, *Things Unutterable: Paul's Ascent to Paradise in Its Greco-Roman, Judaic, and Early Christian Contexts*, SJud, ed. Jacob Neusner (University Press of America, 1986); Tabor, "Ascent"; Charles H. Talbert, "Myth of a Ascending-Descending Redeemer in Mediterranean Antiquity," *NTS* 22 (1976); Wright, *Heaven*.

122 E.g., Heb 1:1–4, 13; 2:9; 8:1–2; 10:12–13; 12:2.

CHAPTER 2

THE DAVIDIC COVENANT AND THE EXPECTATION OF AN
IDEAL KING IN THE HEBREW BIBLE AND EARLY JUDAISM

I have suggested that the Epistle to the Hebrews introduces Jesus to its audience as the ideal king-priest who ascended to heaven and has been enthroned at the "right hand of God" (Heb 1:3, 13; 2:9; 4:14–16; 8:1; 10:12–13; 12:2) and that the author invites his readers to interpret their historical situation in the light of this fact (2:1–4; 4:14–16; 10:19–25; 12:18–29). In this way, the author subscribes to the view—held by other NT authors as well—that Jesus is the "Son" in whom God's promises to David find fulfillment (1:2, 5; 3:6; 4:14; 5:5–6, 8, 7:28; 10:29; cf. 2 Sam 7:12; 1 Chr 17:11).[1]

The purpose of this chapter is to explore the range of beliefs regarding the Davidic covenant that existed toward the end of the early Judaic period (ca. 100 CE).[2] This will provide us with a conceptual map, a set of references, that

---

1 The literature on Jesus as the son of David in whom the Davidic promises are fulfilled is plentiful. See, for example, Raymond E. Brown, *The Birth of the Messiah: A Commentary on the Infancy Narratives in the Gospels of Matthew and Luke*, New updated ed., ABRL (Doubleday, 1993), 505–512; Christoph Burger, *Jesus Als Davidssohn: Eine traditionsgeschichtliche Untersuchung*, FRLANT 98 (Vandenhoeck & Ruprecht, 1970); Young S. Chae, *Jesus as the Eschatological Davidic Shepherd*, WUNT II/216 (Mohr Siebeck, 2006); Joseph A. Fitzmyer, "The Son of David Tradition in Mt 22:41–46 and Parallels," in *Essays on the Semitic Background of the New Testament*, SBLSBS 5 (Society of Biblical Literature and Scholars Press, 1974), 113–126; Ferdinand Hahn, *Christologische Hoheitstitel: Ihre Geschichte im Frühen Christentum*, 3d ed., FRLANT 83 (Vandenhoeck & Ruprecht, 1966), 242–279; David M. Hay, *Glory at the Right Hand: Psalm 110 in Early Christianity*, SBLMS 18 (Abingdon, 1973); Martin Karrer, *Der Gesalbte: Die Grundlagen des Christustitels*, FRLANT 151 (Vandenhoeck & Ruprecht, 1991); Eduard Lohse, "υἱὸς Δαυίδ" *TDNT* 8:478–488; Lidija Novakovic, *Messiah, the Healer of the Sick: A Study of Jesus as the Son of David in the Gospel of Matthew*, WUNT II/170 (Mohr Siebeck, 2003); Cleon L. Rogers, Jr, "The Davidic Covenant in the Gospels," *BSac* 150 (1993): 458–478; Cleon L. Rogers, Jr, "The Davidic Covenant in Acts–Revelation," *BSac* 151 (1994): 71–84. For example, Luke 1:32–33 is a free interpretation of 2 Sam 7:8–16. Brown, *The Birth of the Messiah*, 310–311.

2 It is difficult to establish clear-cut chronological boundaries in history. G. W. Nickelsburg and Robert A. Kraft have suggested that the early Judaic period goes from 330 BCE (Al-

will assist us in better understanding Hebrews' appropriation of the Davidic traditions and their application to Jesus.

This chapter does not attempt to provide a critical history of the Davidic traditions in early Judaism.³ It is not necessary—nor possible—to address the historical-critical problems related to these texts in order to understand how the writer of Hebrews in the second half of the 1st century CE understood them. Early Jewish authors perceived these texts synchronically; that is, as a group of writings belonging to the heritage of their nation. It is not difficult to recognize that, not being concerned with modern critical questions, "they perceived the Bible as a 'flat text.' "⁴ Thus, wherever possible, I will analyze each passage in the chronological order the passage claims for itself.

I will survey in this chapter the different expectations for the rule of the ideal Davidic king that existed in early Judaism. I will proceed in four stages. The first analyzes the institution of the Davidic covenant and the purposes

---

exander the Great's conquest of Palestine) to 130 CE (Roman Emperor Hadrian; see "Introduction: The Modern Study of Early Judaism," in *Early Judaism and Its Modern Interpreteters*, ed. Robert A. Kraft and George W. E. Nickelsburg, SBLBMI 2 [Fortress; Scholars Press, 1986], 1–2). This time limit seems appropriate since it is commonly believed that Hebrews was written towards the end of this period, no later than 96 CE (Lane, *Hebrews 1–8*, lxiii).

The traditional view that there was a uniform system of belief, or at least expectation, regarding a Davidic Messiah in early Judaism—e.g., Emil Schürer, *The History of the Jewish People in the Age of Jesus Christ*, ed. and rev. Geza Vermes, Fergus Millar, and Matthew Black (T&T Clark, 1979), 2:514; George Foot Moore, *Judaism in the First Centuries of the Christian Era: The Age of the Tannaim* (Harvard University Press, 1932), 2:323–376—has been impugned in recent years. Scholars have pointed out that such system is constructed from late sources and is heavily influenced by Christian theology. They also show that a Davidic messianic hope in Second Temple literature is strikingly scarce, incoherent, and seems to have arisen late only as a reaction to the faulty restoration of the Jewish monarchy by the non-Davidic Hasmoneans. See John J. Collins, *The Scepter and the Star: The Messiahs of the Dead Sea Scrolls and Other Ancient Literature*, ABRL (Doubleday, 1995), 3–4, 40–41; James H. Charlesworth, "From Jewish Messianology to Christian Christology: Some Caveats and Perspectives," in *Judaisms and Their Messiahs at the Turn of the Christian Era*, ed. Jacob Neusner, William Scott Green, and Ernest S. Frerichs (Cambridge University Press, 1987), 225–264; "From Messianology to Christology: Problems and Prospects," in *The Messiah: Developments in Earliest Judaism and Christianity*, ed. James H. Charlesworth (Fortress, 1992), 3–35; Kenneth E. Pomykala, *The Davidic Dynasty Tradition in Early Judaism: Its History and Significance for Messianism*, SBLEJL 7 (Scholars, 1995), 265–271. The pendulum, however, may have swung too far, according to John J. Collins, *The Scepter and the Star*, 4. William M. Schniedewind argues that the evidence suggests that there was in fact "a continuous and widespread discourse on the meaning of the Promise to David," though he admits that it led to a variety of interpretations (*Society and the Promise to David: A Reception History of 2 Samuel 7:1–17* [Oxford University Press, 1999], 168).

This study does not seek to understand Hebrews' appropriation of Davidic traditions in the context of an allegedly coherent view of such traditions in 1st century CE Judaism, but in the context of a scope of possibilities that Second Temple documents permit us to delineate.

3 This has been already done. See Pomykala, *The Davidic Dynasty Tradition,* and Schniedewind, *Society and the Promise to David.*
4 Pomykala, *The Davidic Dynasty Tradition*, 11.

for the Davidic dynasty established there (2 Sam 7; 1 Chr 17). The second stage surveys the story of righteous Davidic kings to find out how their actions expressed—in the mind of the biblical writers—the ideals established for the dynasty in the Davidic covenant. The third stage examines the references to the Davidic covenant in the rest of the Hebrew Bible. Special attention will be given to the reinterpretation of the Davidic covenant in the prophets as a reaction to the failure of the Davidic dynasty. Finally, the fourth stage studies the references to the Davidic covenant in the writings of early Judaism. This is a period characterized by the fragmentation or pluralism of Jewish religious beliefs. The intention of this section is to understand the different ways in which the Davidic covenant is referred to and how it is reinterpreted during this time.

The Institution of the Davidic Covenant

Second Samuel 7 is commonly considered among modern scholars as "the fountainhead of all texts dealing with the Davidic promise or covenant in the Hebrew Bible," a charter for the Davidic dynasty.[5] Coincidentally, it is also the first reference to the Davidic covenant in the Hebrew Bible. It contains the narrative of God's promises to David structured around a play on the word "house," which at different moments of the argument denotes David's house, God's temple, and the Davidic dynasty.[6]

This is the story: once God has given David "rest from all his enemies" and he "has settled in his house," David expresses to the prophet Nathan his intention to build a "house" for God. Nathan agrees immediately with him (vv. 1–3). God announces to Nathan, however, that David will not build a "house" for him but God himself will build a "house" for David—meaning a dynasty (v. 11).[7] God will accomplish this through a "son" who will be adopted by God

---

5 Steven L. McKenzie, "The Typology of the Davidic Covenant," in *The Land That I Will Show You: Essays on the History and Archaeology of the Ancient Near East in Honour of J. Maxwell Miller*, ed. J. Andrew Dearman and M. Patrick Graham, JSOTSup 343 (Sheffield Academic, 2001), 177. Also, Pomykala, *The Davidic Dynasty Tradition*, 13; Griphus Gakuru, *An Inner-Biblical Exegetical Study of the Davidic Covenant and the Dynastic Oracle*, Mellen Biblical Press Series 58 (Mellen, 2000), 93–94; Schniedewind, *Society and the Promise to David*, 29, cf. 30–34.

6 This word occurs 15 times in the chapter. Bill T. Arnold, *1 & 2 Samuel*, NIVAC (Zondervan, 2003), 473.

7 Verses 11c–16 form the theological and literary center of the oracle. This is signaled by a change of the verbal forms from the second person used elsewhere to the third person here (Bruce C. Birch, "The First and Second Books of Samuel," in *NIB* 2:1257). Some commentators consider that the phrase וְהִגִּיד לְךָ יְהוָה (the Lord declares to you) should not be read in sequence with those preceding it, but as "a perfect with the force of a solemn declaration" more accurately translated as "And hereby the Lord declares to you...." (Tryggve N. D. Mettinger, *King*

as his own. This "son" will build the temple for God and God will establish his throne forever (vv. 12–16).[8] Thus, God promises to David a house (dynasty) that is "made sure forever" (v. 16). This promise is understood by David and Judah as a covenant (2 Sam 23:5; 2 Chr 13:5; 21:7; Ps 89:28).

The Davidic covenant is divided in two sections, which include two different kinds of promises: those to be fulfilled during his lifetime (2 Sam 7:8–11a; par. 1 Chr 17:7–10a) and those to be fulfilled after his death (7:11b–16; par. 1 Chr 17:10b–14).[9] The first include the promises of (1) a "great name" (v. 9; cf. 8:13), (2) a place for the people of Israel (v. 10; cf. the catalogue of David's victories in chap. 8), (3) and rest (v. 11; cf. 1 Kgs 5:4).[10] The second include an eternal house (perpetual dynasty, vv. 12, 16), and an eternal throne and kingdom (vv. 13, 16). The promises of the first section make possible the fulfillment of the eternal promises of the second section by creating the conditions necessary for the building of God's temple and the creation of a dynasty (1 Kgs 5:3; 1 Chr 28).[11] On the other hand, they are a continuation of the blessings God has already given to David (vv. 8–9):[12] God has chosen David to be king over Israel (v. 8b), has been with him wherever he has gone (v. 9a), and cut off all his enemies (v. 9b).[13] God's promise to David implies, then, that God's favor shown

---

and Messiah: The Civil and Sacral Legitimation of the Israelite Kings, ConBOT 8 [Gleerup, 1976], 59, n. 29).

8   Note that 2 Sam 7:13a forms the real parallel to v. 5. God's answer to David is: "you" will not build a house for me but "he" (your son) will build a house for me. Both pronouns are placed in an emphatic position (Martin Noth, "David and Israel in II Samuel VII," in *The Laws in the Pentateuch and Other Studies*, trans. D. R. Ap-Thomas [Fortress, 1967], 251; also, W. J. Dumbrell, *Covenant and Creation: A Theology of Old Testament Covenants* [Thomas Nelson, 1984], 148).

9   The form of the first section is a first-person address; the second takes a third-person form. See, Bruce K. Waltke, "The Phenomenon of Conditionality within Unconditional Covenants," in *Israel's Apostasy and Restoration*, ed. Avraham Gileadi (Baker, 1988), 130. It has also been said that the first section introduces the promises of the covenant in general terms while the second does in specific ones (Arnold, *1 & 2 Samuel*, 474).

10   Birch, "The First and Second Books of Samuel," 1257; Walter Brueggemann, *First and Second Samuel*, IBC (John Knox, 1990), 255. The first aspect of the promise—a "great name" for David—is included in the old Greek among those things God has already accomplished for David (ἐποίησά σε ὀνομαστὸν ...), not something he will do in the future. See George J. Brooke, "The Ten Temples in the Dead Sea Scrolls," in *Temple and Worship in Biblical Israel*, ed. John Day, Library of Hebrew Bible/Old Testament Studies 422 (T&T Clark, 2005). Also A. A. Anderson, *2 Samuel*, WBC 11 (Word, 1989), 110, n. 9a, 120. For a discussion of the syntax, see P. Kyle McCarter, Jr., *II Samuel: A New Translation with Introduction, Notes and Commentary*, AB 9 (Doubleday, 1984), 202–203. The MT and the Syriac have the future (Alison Salvesen, *The Books of Samuel in the Syriac Version of Jacob of Edessa*, Monographs of the Peshitta Institute Leiden 10 [Brill, 1999], 84).

11   Dumbrell, *Covenant and Creation*, 148–149.

12   See Brueggemann, *First and Second Samuel*, 254–255.

13   Birch, "The First and Second Books of Samuel," 1257.

to David in the past is just a foreshadowing, or glimpse, of what he wants to do for him in the future.

Is the Davidic Covenant Unconditional?

What is striking about 2 Sam 7 is that God's promise to David is unconditional. Referring to the promised son, God declares:

> When he commits iniquity, I will punish him with a rod such as mortals use, with blows inflicted by human beings. *But I will not take my steadfast love from him*, as I took it from Saul, whom I put away from before you. Your house and your kingdom shall be made sure *forever* before me; your throne shall be established *forever.* (vv. 14b–16, emphasis mine)

According to this passage, God promises to David that his dynasty—house, kingdom, and throne—will be "forever" and that not even his scion's unfaithfulness can invalidate that promise.[14] Hebrews—as well as other NT writings—bases its claims regarding Jesus's kingship on the unconditional nature of this promise (Heb 1:5 quoting Ps 2:7 and 2 Sam 7:14; cf. Luke 1:31–33; Acts 2:29–36).

Nevertheless, later references to the Davidic covenant in the OT are ambivalent in this respect. Some passages seem to support the unconditional nature of the Davidic covenant (e.g., 2 Sam 23:1–7; Ps 89:19–37), while others

---

14 Surprisingly, 1 Chr 17:10b–14 does not include a parallel to the conditional clause of 2 Sam 7:14; yet, the promise is given "forever" as well.

The expression עַד־עוֹלָם (2 Sam 7:13, 16; 1 Chr 17:12, 14) can mean "perpetually, for always" and is translated "forever" in many cases. Yet, it is clear that in other cases it does not carry this sense but should be understood in the more limited sense of "long time" or "enduring" (cf. 1 Sam 2:30). See H. D. Preuss, "עוֹלָם," *TDOT* 10:535; also, the list of verses comparing both uses in Lyle Eslinger, *House of God or House of David: The Rhetoric of 2 Samuel 7*, JSOTSup 164 (JSOT Press, 1994), 46–48. The argument that the promise of David was not "eternal" but only for a "long time" does not solve the problem of the failure of the Davidic dynasty, however. The real puzzle is whether the promise was conditional or unconditional; whether human unfaithfulness could invalidate it or not.

It has been argued as well that this passage can be read in two ways. It could be understood as applying only to David's son, Solomon; that is, despite any wrongdoing on his part, God will not tear the kingdom out of his hands, though he may have to chastise him. Or, it could be understood to apply to all future Davidic kings, promising that a son of David would reign over the throne of Israel forever. See Pomykala, *The Davidic Dynasty Tradition*, 13, n. 3. Several passages in 1–2 Kgs, however, presuppose that the promise applies to Davidic kings beyond Solomon. For example, it is the rationale behind the fact that God did not tear the kingdom out completely from David's descendants Rehoboam (1 Kgs 11:12, 13, 32–36) and Abijam (15:4; cf. 2 Kgs 8:19), despite their—and Solomon's—apostasy.

seem to undermine it (e.g., Ps 132:11, 12).[15] The conundrum is painfully clear in the fact that when God confirms the Davidic, eternal, and *unconditional* promises to Solomon, he makes clear that their fulfillment is *conditional* on his obedience (1 Kgs 3:14; 6:12–13; 9:3–9). In fact, both David (1 Kgs 2:1–4) and Solomon (1 Kgs 8:25) express clearly their understanding of the conditionality of the promises.

Most scholars solve the problem by positing a diachronic development of this passage in one of two ways: the original text conveyed an unconditional promise and conditional elements were inserted later, or the opposite.[16] This solution, however, is unnecessary in my view. I agree with Bruce K. Waltke that when it comes to covenants "the terms *unconditional* and *conditional* may be misleading" (emphasis his).[17] He explains how both notions are not contradictory but complement each other in biblical covenantal thinking.

A close parallel to the unconditional language of 2 Sam 7 found in a Hittite text may shed light on the matter. This is a treaty between Hattusili III of Hatti and Ulmi-Teshshup of Tarhuntassa:

> I, My Majesty, will [not depose] your son. [I will accept] neither your brother nor anyone else. Later your son and grandson will hold [the land] which I have given [to you]. It may not be taken away from him. If any son or grandson of yours commits an offense, then the King of Hatti shall question him. And if an offense is proven against him, then the King of Hatti shall treat him as he pleases. *If he is deserving of death, he shall perish, but his household and land shall not be taken from him and given to the progeny of another. Only someone of the progeny of Ulmi-Teshshup shall take them.* Someone of the male line shall take them; those of the female line shall not take them. But if there is no male line of descent, and it is extinguished, then only someone of the female line of Ulmi-Teshshup shall be sought out. Even if he is in a foreign land, he shall be brought back from there and installed in authority in the land of Tarhuntassa [emphasis mine].[18]

---

15 See Eslinger, *House of David*, 90–94.

16 Unconventionally, Lyle Eslinger does not take a source-critical approach, but analyzes the passage in its final form in a rhetorical-critical approach (*House of David*, 95). On the other hand, both views regarding the conditional/unconditional nature of the Davidic covenant "need not be explained chronologically; they could just as easily be contemporary yet conflicting points of view" (J. J. M. Roberts, "Davidic Covenant," *DOTHB* 209).

The literature on 2 Sam 7 is just immense. For a succinct survey of research and bibliography on 2 Sam 7, see Schniedewind, *Society and the Promise to David*, 30–33.

17 Waltke, "The Phenomenon of Conditionality," 124.

18 Gary Beckman, *Hittite Diplomatic Texts*, ed. Harry A. Hoffner, Jr., 2d ed., SBLWAW 7 (Scholars, 1999), 109. M. Weinfeld calls this type of unconditional promise a "covenant of grant"

The promise to Ulmi-Theshshup that his descendants will rule the land of Tarhuntassa after him is unconditional; yet, the king of Hatti reserves the right to punish *individual* members of the dynasty, even unto death, if they rebel against him. Likewise, God's promise to David is unconditional; yet, he reserves the right to punish *individual* members of his dynasty.[19]

Therefore, it is possible to understand two dimensions in the Davidic covenant that explain the conditional elements in it: The Davidic covenant was unconditional when referring to David's progeny in *general*; but conditional, when referring to *individual* Davidic rulers.[20] That is to say, unfaithfulness may prevent an individual Davidic ruler from participating in the Davidic promises but this will not invalidate God's promises to David. God can choose another son of David to fulfill them. God's judgment on King Coniah (Jehoiachin) is a good example. Coniah and his children were barred from the throne because of their unfaithfulness (Jer 22:24–30); instead, God would fulfill his promises to David through another son of David, a righteous Branch (23:5–6).[21] Thus, there are conditional elements that belong in the unconditional Davidic covenant. This is important to correctly understand later references and allusions to the Davidic covenant in the Hebrew Bible which are apparently contradictory. This is so because they focus on one of these two aspects depending on the circumstances.

What Is the Relationship between the Davidic and the Mosaic Covenants?

What is the relationship between the Davidic and the Mosaic covenants?[22] It is clear, at least, that the Mosaic covenant does not become obsolete with the establishment of the Davidic covenant because its requirements continue to apply.[23] The king—and the people as well—continues to be bound by the regulations consecrated in the Mosaic legislation, especially regarding social justice (e.g., 1 Kgs 6:12–13). Though established with promises of eternal favor

---

and cites many examples from the ANE ("The Covenant of Grant in the Old Testament and in the Ancient Near East," *JAOS* 90 [1970]: 184–203).

19 See Weinfeld, "The Covenant of Grant," 189–196. Note as well that an eternal dynasty is offered in the *Temple Scroll* to all kings, not necessarily Davidic kings, who are faithful in obeying the law of the covenant (11QTemple LIX, 13–21).

20 "In general terms the line would not fail. Yet in particular terms, benefits might be withdrawn from individuals," Dumbrell, *Covenant and Creation*, 150.

21 See below section "Jeremiah" on page 88.

22 Some scholars, especially those committed to the documentary hypothesis, usually distinguish between the Sinaitic (the covenant made at Sinai) and the Deuteronomic covenants (the covenant made at Moab and comprised in Deuteronomy). I will bring here both together under the name "Mosaic covenant." See also, Waltke, "The Phenomenon of Conditionality," 124.

23 See Eslinger, *House of David*, vi, 89.

to the Davidic king, God explicitly preserves his right "to punish him with a rod" if the king forsakes his law (2 Sam 7:14; cf. Ps 89:30–32). Thus, the Mosaic covenant does not cease to exist; instead, God's covenant with David has the purpose of engrafting the monarchy into the existing (Mosaic) covenantal relationship between God and the nation.[24]

God grants his covenant to David and his house because of David's exceptional covenant loyalty. David is a man according to God's "own heart" and becomes the benchmark for the faithfulness of future kings (1 Sam 13:14; 16:7; 1 Kgs 3:6; 9:4; 14:8; etc.). His piety is especially evident in his wish to build a "house" for the "ark of God" (2 Sam 7:1) that represents God's covenant with the nation—mediated by Moses (1 Kgs 8:21; 2 Chr 6:11)—and enshrines its laws (1 Kgs 8:9; 2 Chr 5:10).

David's plan to build a temple for the ark is as well an act of legitimation of his rule and capital city by identifying them with the symbol of God's (Mosaic) covenant with Israel.[25] He wishes to establish a *permanent* relationship with and access to the God of Israel. The plan is rejected, however. The initiative must be God's not David's (2 Sam 7:4–7). Nonetheless, God legitimizes David's rule and dynasty by letting his son build the temple and choosing it as his resting place forever (1 Kgs 8:12–13, 29; 9:3; 2 Chr 6:1–2, 20, 41–42; 7:12, 16). The temple, then, becomes the new symbol of God's covenant with the nation. The permanent "house" (as opposed to "tent") symbolizes the permanence of God's presence (2 Sam 7:9, 14), the permanence of Israel in the land (v. 10), and the permanence of the dynasty (v. 16).[26] All of these testify to the permanence of the (Mosaic) laws enshrined in the temple. Therefore, God makes clear to Solomon after the dedication of the temple that unfaithfulness to the Mosaic covenant will result in the temple's destruction (1 Kgs 9:6–9; 2 Chr 7:19–22).[27] This is what finally happens. Because of the threat of

---

24 Dumbrell, *Covenant and Creation*, 127. Lyle Eslinger has argued that the Mosaic covenant was broken when Israel requested a king in order to be "like the other nations" (1 Sam 8:6): "The request of Yahweh's people (*'am yhwh*) to become like the nations (*kekol-haggôyim*) in political structure is, therefore, not only a rejection of theocracy and its judges, but even more it is a rejection of the covenant" (*Kingship of God in Crisis: A Close Reading of 1 Samuel 1–12*, BLS10 [JSOT Press, 1985], 257, quoted in Timo Eskola, *Messiah and the Throne: Jewish Merkabah Mysticism and Early Christian Exaltation Discourse*, WUNT II/142 [Mohr Siebeck, 2001], 58). This does not seem to be the case, however. Deuteronomy 17:14–20 (cf. 28:36) allows the possibility of a king over Israel in the context of the Mosaic covenant. Also, Israel suffers no covenant curses as a result of the establishment of the monarchy.

25 Regarding the building of the temple as an act of legitimation, see Brueggemann, *First and Second Samuel*, 254–261.

26 McCarter, *II Samuel*, 210.

27 Note that in both cases unfaithfulness is defined as an abandonment of the "LORD the God of their ancestors who brought them out of the land of Egypt" and gave them Canaan as their land.

Nebuchadnezzar, Zedekiah—the last Davidic king (597–586 BCE)—made a covenant with the people in the temple to proclaim liberty to their slaves according to the requirements of the Mosaic law (Jer 34:8–10; Lev 25:39–41). The people obeyed and God promised Zedekiah he would "die in peace" (v. 5). Later on, however, they forsook the covenant and "took back the male and female slaves they had set free" (v. 11) in open rebellion to the Mosaic law. This act seals the fate of the king and Jerusalem who will now endure the covenant curses (vv. 17–22).[28] Therefore, the Davidic king's participation in the eternal promises made to David and the permanence of Jerusalem are contingent on the king's obedience to the Mosaic laws.

The Davidic King as Covenant Mediator: He Renews the Mosaic Covenant under "Better Promises"

While it is true that Mosaic laws continue to apply, the Davidic covenant introduces a big change in the covenantal relationship between God and his people. The covenantal blessings are now contingent not on the nation's faithfulness, but on the faithfulness of the Davidic king (1 Kgs 6:12–13; cf. 9:4–7; 2 Chr 7:17–22). The Davidic king has become the mediator of the covenant.

The concept of the Davidic king as mediator goes beyond the idea of a person who "mediates between parties at variance."[29] Instead, the Davidic king is designated God's "son" and "firstborn" (2 Sam 7:14; Pss 2:6–7; 89:27) embodying Israel, the covenant people, which is also called "son" and "firstborn" (Exod 4:22–23; cf. Jer 3:19; 31:9). In this way God legitimizes the Davidic king as Israel's proxy.[30] Accordingly, God confirms to him—as the embodiment of the nation—the promises previously given Israel of a "place" where they would "rest" from their enemies (2 Sam 7:9–11a; cf. Deut 12:8–10) and his permanent presence in their midst by accepting a "house" to be built for his "name" (vv. 12a–16; Ps 132:11–14; cf. Exod 25:8; 33:12–23; Deut 12:5).[31]

---

28 Hans K. LaRondelle, *Our Creator Redeemer: An Introduction to Biblical Covenant Theology* (Andrews University Press, 2005), 48.

29 Frederick C. Mish, ed., *Merriam-Webster's Collegiate Dictionary*, 11th ed. (Merriam-Webster, 2003), s.v. "mediator." For the notion of the king as mediator between heaven and earth in the ANE, see Dale Launderville, *Piety and Politics: The Dynamics of Royal Authority in Homeric Greece, Biblical Israel, and Old Babylonian Mesopotamia* (Eerdmans, 2003), 292–304.

30 Avraham Gileadi, "The Davidic Covenant: A Theological Basis for Corporate Protection," in *Israel's Apostasy and Restoration*, ed. Avraham Gileadi (Baker, 1988), 160.

31 Second Samuel connects the fulfillment of the promise of rest of the Mosaic covenant to God's election of the place for his name to dwell (Deut 12:9–10) making Joshua's repartition of the land only a partial fulfillment of the promise (Josh 21:43–45; cf. 1:13, 15; 22:4; 23:1). See McCarter, *II Samuel*, 204.

This modification in the relationship between God and Israel by the insertion of a mediator makes possible the perpetuation of their covenantal relationship. The Mosaic covenant required the faithfulness of all Israel to receive God's protection. Joshua 7 registers a case in which the nation is imputed with the transgression of the covenant because of the sin of one man: Achan (vv. 1, 11–13). When the offender was punished, the covenantal relationship was restored (Josh 7:24–8:1).[32] The Davidic covenant, however, secures God's covenantal blessings upon Israel through the faithfulness of one person, the king. Note the promise to David and its relation to the nation:

> I will make for *you* [sg.] a great name, like the name of the great ones of the earth. And I will appoint a place for *my people Israel* and will plant *them*, so that *they* may live in *their* own place, and be disturbed no more; and evildoers shall afflict *them* no more, as formerly, from the time that I appointed judges over my people Israel; and I will give *you* [sg.] rest from all *your* [sg.] enemies. (2 Sam 7:9b–11a, emphasis mine; cf. 1 Chr 17:9–10b)

The connection between the faithfulness of the king and the perpetuation of God's covenant with the nation is particularly evident in God's confirmation of the covenant to Solomon:

> Concerning this house that you are building, *if you* [sg.] will walk in my statutes, obey my ordinances, and keep all my commandments by walking in them, then I will establish my promise *with you*, which I made to your father David. I will dwell among the children of Israel, and *will not forsake my people Israel.* (1 Kgs 6:12–13, emphasis mine; cf. 9:4–9; 2 Chr 7:17–22)

God explicitly informs Solomon that if he is faithful, God's covenantal relationship with the nation will remain. Avraham Gileadi's conclusion is apt: "The Davidic covenant did away with the necessity that all Israel—to a man—maintain loyalty to YHWH in order to merit his protection."[33]

As suggested above, however, the opposite is not true. The unfaithfulness of the king does not imply the revocation of the covenant. The apostasy of

---

32   Similarly, when the tribes of Reuben, Gad, and Manasseh built an altar beside the Jordan, the rest of the tribes considered that it was an act of rebellion against God and feared that God would be "angry with the whole congregation of Israel" (Josh 22:10–34, esp. v. 18). They in fact mentioned the case of Achan: "Did not Achan son of Zerah break faith in the matter of the devoted things, and wrath fell upon all the congregation of Israel? And *he did not perish alone for his iniquity!*" (v. 20; emphasis mine). A further example could be found in the apostasy concerning the Baal of Peor in Num 25.

33   Gileadi, "The Davidic Covenant," 160.

the Davidic scion does not make void God's promise to David of an eternal dynasty. It does disqualify, however, the apostate king from participating in the promises of the Davidic covenant and annuls God's covenantal protection over the people during his reign.[34] God will punish him "with a rod" (2 Sam 7:14). None of his children will rule and God will choose another Davidic faithful heir to continue his promise.

For example, when the king Ahaz sent tribute monies to Tiglath-pileser, king of Assyria, requesting his protection from Israel and Aram and called himself his "servant" and "son" (2 Kgs 16:7–8), he rejected his covenantal relationship with God (Isa 7:1–12). God's reaction is twofold. First, he announces the election of another "son"—Immanuel, "God with us" (v. 14). Second, he denies his protection to the apostate king and his people (v. 17). God punishes Ahaz through the king of Assyria whom he calls "the rod of my anger" (10:5).[35] Finally, the failure of the Davidic kings provokes the exile and God's decree regarding the Davidic dynasty: "Remove the turban, take off the crown; things shall not remain as they are. Exalt that which is low, abase that which is high. A ruin, a ruin, a ruin—I will make it! (Such has never occurred.) *Until he comes whose right it is; to him I will give it*" (Ezek 21:26–27, emphasis mine).[36] Note that this is not the end of the Davidic dynasty. The Davidic covenant makes possible the perpetuation of hope, as long as God may find or provide a faithful Davidic king to represent the nation.[37]

In summary, we could say that the Davidic covenant renews the Mosaic covenant—by confirming its laws and requirements—but under "better promises"—by providing a covenant mediator. Walter Brueggemann's dictum is highly appropriate here: "With David, however, the 'if' has disappeared.... In this astonishing promise, Yahweh has signed a blank check to the David enterprise and has radically shifted the theological foundations of Israel."[38]

As covenant mediator, the king also has the related responsibility of guaranteeing the observance of the covenant by the nation. In fact, Gerald Eddie Gerbrandt has argued that this constituted the ultimate responsibility of the

---

34 Note that because of David's transgression regarding the census of Israel (2 Sam 24:1), God's covenantal protection over Israel is annulled (v. 13). See ibid., 159.

35 Ibid., 161–162. I have mentioned above, as well, another example: God's judgment of the Davidic king Coniah (Jer 22:24–30).

36 LaRondelle, *Our Creator Redeemer*, 49.

37 In view of the evident human failure, Second Temple Judaism will debate the fate of the Davidic covenant (see below section "The Davidic Covenant in Early Judaism" on page 110). The New Testament will argue, however, that God decided to provide Jesus as a faithful "Son" to be a righteous king over Israel "forever" (Luke 1:30–33; Acts 2:29–36; Rom 1:3–5). See Robert D. Bergen, *1, 2 Samuel*, NAC 7 (Broadman & Holman, 1996), 340–41.

38 Brueggemann, *First and Second Samuel*, 257.

king according to the Deuteronomistic history: "Since Israel's continued existence as a people on the land was dependent on her obedience to the covenant, and since the king's ultimate responsibility was to insure this continued existence, the king's role was then to make sure that the covenant was observed in Israel. Practically, he could be called the *covenant administrator*" (emphasis his).[39] He notes in his survey of the records of good kings, especially Hezekiah and Josiah, that their enforcement of the covenant with God and their reforms to this end in the religious life of Israel were emphasized throughout this history. I believe this is true as well of the books of Chronicles (2 Chr 15:12; 23:16; 29:10; 34:30–32). Administrating the covenant included, then, calling people to repentance, when the covenant had been breached, and promoting faithfulness to it.

The Davidic King as Reformer of the Cult: He Reorganizes the Priesthood and the Service of the Temple

The institution of the Davidic covenant makes possible the realization of cultic changes that had been anticipated in the Mosaic legislation. The book of Deuteronomy instructed the nation that when they crossed "over the Jordan," lived in the "land," and God had given them "rest from … enemies all around" (12:10), God would choose "a place … out of all your tribes as his habitation to put his name there" (12:5, 11, 14, etc.). This election would implicate a change in the law of sacrifices, other offerings, and administration of justice, among others.[40]

---

39 Gerald Eddie Gerbrandt, *Kingship according to the Deuteronomistic History*, SBLDS 87 (Scholars, 1986), 99. Even the election of Saul as king and the institution of the monarchy by Samuel probably implicated the renewal of Israel's covenant with God. Note that 1 Sam 10:16, 26; 11:15 probably refer to the kingship of God more than to the kingship of Saul (Dumbrell, *Covenant and Creation*, 135).

40 One of the most conspicuous changes concerned the law of sacrifices. The reform consisted in the transition from the offering of sacrifices at multiple altars built "in every place where I cause my name to be remembered" (Exod 20:24) to one altar in the "place" chosen by God (Deut 12:6, 11): "You *shall* not act as we are acting here today, all of us according to our own desires" (Deut 12:8, emphasis mine). See R. E. Averbeck, "Sacrifices and Offerings," *DOTP* 729–732; McCarter, *II Samuel*, 217.

Additionally, the centralization of worship would make possible the non-sacrificial slaughter of domestic cattle for human consumption (Deut 12:15, 21; cf. Lev 17). See Duane L. Christensen, *Deuteronomy 1:1–21:9*, rev. ed., WBC 6A (Word, 2001), 257. Also, modification to the laws of offerings and their consumption (Deut 12:18; 14:22–27; 26:12; cf. Num 18:25–32).

The "place" chosen by God would become, as well, a kind of superior court for criminal cases particularly difficult to solve (Deut 17:8–10). See Christensen, *Deuteronomy 1:1–21:9*, 374–375.

The construction of the temple by Solomon, however, did not immediately centralize the cult. Time and again, the historian informs us that the people continued to worship in the high places (1 Kgs 14:23; 15:14; 22:43; 2 Kgs 12:3; 14:4; 15:4, etc.; 2 Chr 15:17; 20:33). These high places

The conditions for this reform were not in place until David had finished his wars and built the empire (2 Sam 8, 10; 21:15–22; 1 Chr 18–20). Joshua introduced the nation into the land and achieved a measure of "rest from all their enemies around" (23:1; cf. Josh 11:23; 14:15; 22:4); however, it is clear from Judg 1–2 that this rest was partial because there were still enemies and land to be conquered after the death of Joshua. Second Samuel 7:9b–11a has in mind Deut 11:24 which defines the "place" for Israel as going "from the wilderness to the Lebanon and from the River, the river Euphrates, to the Western Sea."[41] David's conquests achieved the rest anticipated in Deuteronomy, making it possible for Solomon to build the temple as the "place" for God to "put his name there" (2 Sam 7:1; 1 Kgs 5:4; 8:56; 1 Chr 23:25).[42] Thus, the inauguration of the temple, which confirms the Davidic covenant (1 Kgs 8:15–21, 66; 2 Chr 6:4–11), implicates not only the fulfillment of the promises in the Mosaic covenant, but also triggered a deep transformation of the "theological foundations of Israel" and a reform of the cult (see the section above "What Is the Relationship between the Davidic and the Mosaic Covenants?" on page 41).

Scholars have noted that the book of Chronicles portrays David as a founder of the cult together with Moses.[43] The Chronicler is careful to point

(בָּמָה) do not necessarily refer to pagan shrines. For example, Samuel used to offer sacrifices in them (1 Sam 9:12–27; cf. 10:5). Solomon offered sacrifices to the Lord at Gibeon, which is called a high place, and receives a divine vision there (1 Kgs 3:3–4; cf. 2 Kgs 18:22; 23:9; 1 Chr 16:39; 21:29). See also, A. Graeme Auld, *Kings without Privilege: David and Moses in the Story of the Bible's Kings* (T&T Clark, 1994), 87. These high places are removed until the time of Hezekiah and Josiah (since Manasseh had rebuilt them; 2 Kgs 18:22; 23:5–9; 2 Chr 31:1; 32:12; 34:3) and signal the culmination of the reformation of the cult anticipated by Deuteronomy.

41 Which is also the same territory God promises Abraham as the land for his descendants (Gen 15:18). The conquest of this territory would give David a "great name" which is also promised Abraham (12:2). See Dumbrell, *Covenant and Creation*, 149.

42 Ibid., 145–6; McCarter, *II Samuel*, 217–20. See also, Arnold, *1 & 2 Samuel*, 474–5. Note that Solomon's kingdom, built over David's victories (1 Chr 18–20), includes the ideal limits established in Deut 11:24 (1 Kgs 4:21–24). Note as well that 1 Kgs 5:3 claims that David was not able to build the temple because of his concern with conquests (cf. 1 Chr 22:8; 28:3).

43 David holds a dominant role in the Chronicler's account and is often mentioned in relation to the organization, provisions, or arrangements for the cult. David is mentioned 76 times apart from the genealogical material (1 Chr 2–3) and the narrative of his reign (chs. 11–29), William Riley, *King and Cultus in Chronicles: Worship and the Reinterpretation of History*, JSOTSup 160 (JSOT Press, 1993), 53. The following passages mention him in relation to the cult: 1 Chr 6:31; 9:22; 2 Chr 1:4; 2:7; 3:1; 5:1; 6:7, 42; 7:6; 23:9, 18; 29:25–27, 30; 33:7; 35:4, 15.

Simon J. de Vries has argued that the Chronicler presents David as founder of the cult together with Moses in order to substantiate the Levites' claim to "censorial oversight over the priests" in Judah's post-exilic cult ("Moses and David as Cult Founders in Chronicles," *JBL* 107 [1988]: 619–639). William Riley followed his lead with a fuller study arguing that, in fact, the overriding purpose of the Chronicler's work was to introduce David and his dynasty as institutors of the cult. Thus, David founded the cult, but his work was realized by Solomon and later monarchs and finally culminated in the reign of Josiah (2 Chr 35:20). Riley considers that the reason for this description of the Davidic dynasty is the Chronicler's wish to validate claims for

out that David and other righteous kings were careful to follow Moses's legislation for the cult (e.g., 1 Chr 22:12–13).[44] He also describes David, however, as one who *complements* Moses's legislation by introducing new elements into the cult. David gives to Solomon the תַּבְנִית (plan) for the temple to be built (1 Chr 28:11–19). This תַּבְנִית (pattern, figure) is by no means limited to the architectural design of the temple, its furniture, and vessels; it also includes stipulations regarding the priestly and Levitical courses and the service for the temple (1 Chr 28:13).[45] David's reforms are authoritative, then, because he receives them through revelation just as Moses did (1 Chr 28:19; Exod 25:9, 40).

David's תַּבְנִית, however, does not replace the Mosaic legislation but complements it. This is clear in 2 Chr 8:12–15:

> Then Solomon offered up burnt offerings to the LORD on the altar of the LORD that he had built in front of the vestibule, as the duty of each day required, offering *according to the commandment of Moses* for the sabbaths, the new moons, and the three annual festivals—the festival of unleavened bread, the festival of weeks, and the festival of booths. *According to the ordinance of his father David*, he appointed the divisions of the priests for their service, and the Levites for their offices of praise and ministry alongside the priests as the duty of each day required, and the gatekeepers in their divisions for the several gates; for so David the man of God had commanded. They did not turn away from what the king had commanded the priests and Levites regarding anything at all, or regarding the treasuries [emphasis mine].

This passage is programmatic for the later restorations of the cult by Joash (2 Chr 23:18), Hezekiah (chs. 29–30), and Josiah (35:1–9).

---

the cult in his post-exilic community (*King and Cultus in Chronicles*, 202–204). Both Riley and de Vries reject the view that the Chronicler understands the Davidic covenant as unconditional or that he holds a hope for the restoration of the Davidic dynasty; instead, the purpose of the Davidic dynasty was exhausted in its cultic function.

44 Also, 1 Chr 6:49; 15:15; 21:29; 2 Chr 1:3; 5:10; 8:13; 23:18; 24:6, 9; 25:4; 30:16; 33:8; 34:14; 35:6, 12. See de Vries, "Moses and David as Cult Founders," 619, n. 2.

45 The phrase וּלְכָל־מְלֶאכֶת עֲבוֹדַת בֵּית־יְהוָה "and all the work of the service in the house of the LORD" suggests that David's תַּבְנִית (pattern, figure) regulates the entire temple liturgy, Riley, *King and Cultus in Chronicles*, 63, n. 3; Sara Japhet, *I & II Chronicles: A Commentary*, OTL (SCM, 1993), 495. The reorganization of the priestly and Levitical courses and their function are explained in 1 Chr 23–26 (cf. 2 Chr 35:4; Neh 12:45).

The Davidic King Is Confirmed in God's House and Kingdom: The Davidic Covenant in 1 Chronicles 17

The Chronicler varies slightly from the account of the Davidic covenant in 2 Sam 7. This small variation, however, is significant because it highlights the special concern of the Chronicler for the temple, the cult, and the relationship of the king to them.[46] William M. Schniedewind has suggested that this modification attests to a trend in the post-exilic period towards bicephalic leadership which reached clear and full expression in the appointments of a king and a priest "with peaceful understanding between the two of them" in Zech 6:12–14 (cf. 4:2–3, 11–14; Hag 1:12–14).[47]

2 Sam 7:16	1 Chr 17:14
וְנֶאְמַן בֵּיתְךָ וּמַמְלַכְתְּךָ עַד־עוֹלָם לְפָנֶיךָ כִּסְאֲךָ יִהְיֶה נָכוֹן עַד־עוֹלָם׃	וְהַעֲמַדְתִּיהוּ בְּבֵיתִי וּבְמַלְכוּתִי עַד־הָעוֹלָם וְכִסְאוֹ יִהְיֶה נָכוֹן עַד־עוֹלָם׃
Your house and *your* kingdom shall be made sure forever before me; *your* throne shall be established forever.	... but I will confirm him in *my* house and in *my* kingdom forever, and *his* throne shall be established forever.

Table 1: King and House in 2 Samuel 7:16 and 1 Chronicles 17:14

This is most clear in a comparison of 1 Chr 17:14 to 2 Sam 7:16. (See Table 1.) The Chronicler changes the pronominal suffixes of the promise from the second to the first person and excludes the phrase "before me." These small modifications change the sense of the passage. Second Samuel 7:16 promised that *David's house* [בַּיִת], *Kingdom*, and *throne* would be established "forever" "before God." The focus, then, was on David's dynasty and rule. The Chronicler promises, instead, that *David's son* will be confirmed forever in *God's house* [בַּיִת] and *kingdom*.[48] The Chronicler focuses now on the eternity of God's temple and kingdom and promises the confirmation of David's son

---

46 Japhet, *I & II Chronicles*, 334–5; Gary N. Knoppers, *I Chronicles 10–29: A New Translation with Introduction and Commentary*, AB 12A (Doubleday, 2004), 672–3. It has been said that these "two verses are Chronicles in a nutshell," as referred to by J. A. Thompson, *1, 2 Chronicles*, NAC 9 (Broadman & Holman, 1994), 147.

47 William M. Schniedewind, "King and Priest in the Book of Chronicles and the Duality of Qumran Messianism," *JJS* 45 (1994): 71–78. According to Shemaryahou Talmon, the bicephalic pattern of the Qumran covenanteers reflects their dependence on this biblical pattern ("Waiting for the Messiah: The Spiritual Universe of the Qumran Covenanteers," in *Judaisms and Their Messiahs at the Turn of the Christian Era*, ed. Jacob Neusner, William Scott Green, and Ernest S. Frerichs [Cambridge University Press, 1987], 123–131).

48 The Chronicler refers in some places to the temple as God's house in connection to the palace as the king's house; e.g., 2 Chr 2:1, 12. See Schniedewind, "King and Priest," 73.

in relation to them. In the Chronicler's view, God's temple and kingdom are eternal. The Davidic covenant constitutes the Davidic dynasty and temple as an earthly expression of the eternal kingdom and house of God.[49] Brian E. Kelly concludes regarding the theology behind the Chronicler's account: "The closest links are ... forged between the two 'houses' of temple and dynasty, the twin foci of the Chronicler's work, and it is emphasized that both are brought into existence through the Davidic covenant."[50]

This close link between the temple and the dynasty in Chronicles implicates the close relationship between the offices of the king and the high priest. This comes to the surface also in the account of Solomon's anointing. According to 1 Kings, Zadok anointed Solomon as king at Gihon. The Chronicler's account is different, however. First Chronicles 29:22 says that the assembly anointed both Solomon as king *and* Zadok as priest together. This dual anointing brings to mind God's commission of Joshua (priest) and Branch (king) in Zech 6:9–13.

Notice, also, that several pairs of kings and priests beyond Solomon and Zadok are noteworthy in the story of Chronicles; for example, Jehoshaphat and Amariah (2 Chr 19:11), Joash and Jehoiada (chs. 23–24), Uzziah and Azariah (26:16–21); Hezekiah and Azariah (31:13); Josiah and Hilkiah (chs. 34–35).[51] Some have suggested that the Chronicler's account of their relationship reveals a tendency towards the views of the parity of offices, the predominance of the high priestly office, or even hierochracy that dominated Jewish politics in the Second Temple period.[52] A closer analysis shows, however, that as important as the high priest is for the cult, the Chronicler does not exalt the high priest over the Davidic king or treat him as his successor.[53] Only Jehoiada and

---

In what sense will David's son be confirmed in "my house and my kingdom"? According to Gary N. Knoppers, this phrase indicates that David's successor is to have an official role in the temple following the pattern of Ancient Near East royal ideology (*I Chronicles 10–29*, 672–673).

49 Brian E. Kelly, *Retribution and Eschatology in Chronicles*, JSOTSup 211 (Sheffield Academic, 1996), 156.

50 Ibid., 158.

51 The case of King Uzziah is significant. It focuses on the authority of the high priest vis-à-vis that of the king. Uzziah had been instructed in his youth by the priest Zechariah (2 Chr 26:5). The Chronicler registers that he was faithful to God and prospered marvelously and became strong (v. 15). He became arrogant, however, and tried to usurp the office of the priest (26:16–21) but the priest Azariah and fellow priests confronted him with these words: "It is not for you, Uzziah, to make offering to the LORD, but for the priests the descendants of Aaron, who are consecrated to make offering. Go out of the sanctuary; for you have done wrong, and it will bring you no honor from the LORD God" (2 Chr 26:18). This event is not registered in the story of Uzziah (Azariah) in 2 Kings (15:1–7). Its inclusion here underscores the Chronicler's concern for the relationship between these offices.

52 Schniedewind, "King and Priest," 76–78.

53 Kelly, *Retribution and Eschatology in Chronicles*, 204.

Hilkiah, because of the special circumstances in the beginning of the rules of Joash and Josiah, foreshadow the roles of later hierocratic rulers.

Summary

The Davidic covenant makes possible the engrafting of the Davidic dynasty into the existing (Mosaic) covenant relationship between YHWH and Israel. Its institution causes, however, a deep transformation of the theological foundations of Israel. God's relationship to the nation is now mediated through the Davidic king.

The Davidic covenant formalizes God's adoption of the Davidic king and assigns him the titles of "son"—and "firstborn"—that previously belonged to the nation. Therefore, he becomes the proxy of the nation in her relationship to God. Accordingly, he inherits the covenantal promises of a "place," and "rest from their enemies" given to Israel, making him the channel through which God's blessings will flow.

The promise of a dynasty, kingdom, and throne to David is unconditional and eternal. God reserves, however, the right to punish individual kings for their unfaithfulness. It is clear that God continues to expect the Davidic king's obedience to the Mosaic laws. His disobedience, however, does not invalidate the covenant. The eternal nature of the Davidic promise guarantees, then, the eternal validity of God's promises to Israel that had only been conditional under the Mosaic covenant. Thus, it is correct to say that the Davidic confirms the Mosaic covenant, but under "better promises."

The Davidic covenant implicates a deep transformation of God's relationship to the nation and the reformation of the cult. For example, it provides the necessary elements for the implementation of the centralization of the cult that had been anticipated in Deuteronomy. Regarding the relationship between God and the nation, just as God's election of the temple for his name to dwell centralizes Israel's cult in Jerusalem, God's election of the "son" of David centralizes his relationship with Israel in the person of the king.

I will proceed now to analyze how the Davidic covenant plays out in the history of monarchic Israel.

Righteous Kings and the Davidic Covenant in Monarchic Israel

The books 1 and 2 Kings consider that only five kings of Judah did what was "right in the sight of the Lord" *as* their "father David" had done. They are Solomon (1 Kgs 3:3 [though, see 11:4]), Asa (15:11), Joash (2 Kgs 12:2; cf. 14:3),

Hezekiah (18:3), and Josiah (22:2).[54] The books of Chronicles refer only to Hezekiah and Josiah in these terms (2 Chr 29:2; 34:2). The purpose of this section is to make a synoptic analysis of the rule of these kings that emulated the rule of David—the prototypical righteous king—and, thus, fulfilled more closely the ideal expressed in the Davidic covenant. This will help us determine the basic elements of the rule of the ideal Davidic king in the mind of the biblical historian.

Solomon

Solomon is a contradictory—yet foundational—figure of the Davidic monarchy. The evaluation of the first part of his rule is positive though not perfect: "Solomon loved the Lord, walking in the statutes of his father David; only he sacrificed and burnt incense on the high places" (1 Kgs 3:3). His later years of rule are evaluated rather negatively: "When Solomon was old, his wives turned away his heart after other gods; and his heart was not true to the LORD his God, as was the heart of his father David" (11:4). I will focus here on the

---

54   There are other Davidic kings who received qualified praise. The biblical historians considered that Amaziah (2 Kgs 14:3; cf. 2 Chr 25:2), and Jotham (2 Kgs 15:34; 2 Chr 27:2) also did "what was right in the sight of the Lord" but there is no explicit mention that they followed the example of their "father David"; therefore, I have decided not to include an analysis of their rules.

The case of Jehosaphat is more complicated. The MT of 2 Chr 17:3 (cf. 21:12) affirms that Jehoshaphat "followed the example of his father David's earlier days" (NASB; see also NIV). The LXX and a few Hebrew manuscripts omit, however, the mention of David: "he walked in the earlier ways of his father" (NRSV). They compare, then, Jehoshaphat's rule to that of Asa his immediate predecessor. I have decided not to include an analysis of Jehoshaphat's reign for two reasons. First, research suggests that the author of Hebrews dependeded on the LXX for his reading of the Hebrew Bible. See Martin Karrer, "The Epistle to the Hebrews and the Septuagint," in *Septuagint Research: Issues and Challenges in the Study of the Greek Jewish Scriptures,* ed. Wolfgang Kraus and R. Glenn Wooden, SBLSCS 53 (Society of Biblical Literature, 2006), 335–54; Radu Gheorghita, *The Role of the Septuagint in Hebrews: An Investigation of Its Influence with Special Consideration to the Use of Hab 2:3–4 in Heb 10:37–38,* WUNT II/160 (Mohr Siebeck, 2003). Second, it is probable that in this case the reading of the LXX is correct (e.g., NRSV). The books of Chronicles do not make a distinction between a good and an evil period in David's reign (1 and 2 Kings do). They do make a distinction, however, between a good and evil period in Asa's reign, who was the immediate predecessor of Jehoshaphat and most probably the object of comparison as in 1 Kgs 22:43. See Raymond B. Dillard, *2 Chronicles,* WBC 15 (Word, 1987), 132.

In any case, if I had decided to include Jehoshaphat among the Davidic righteous kings, a cursory review of his reign would tend to support the conclusions which I arrived at in this section. Jehoshaphat promoted covenant awareness and loyalty (2 Chr 17:9; 19:4), cleansed the land from idolatry (2 Chr 17:6; 19:3), dedicated votive offerings for the temple (2 Kgs 12:18), organized the Levites and priests (1 Chr 17:7–8; 19:8–10), promoted the reunification of Israel (2 Chr 19:4), had "rest" from his enemies (2 Chr 17:10; 20:1–30 [esp. v. 30]), and faithful priests emerged during his rule (2 Chr 19:11).

early years of his reign when he better fulfilled the expectations of an ideal Davidic king. The main actions of later righteous Davidic kings are found in Solomon's first years.

Solomon begins his rule by exterminating his enemies and, thus, securing the throne. (Only 1 Kings registers these actions.) He kills Adonijah (1 Kgs 2:13–25), Joab (vv. 28–35), and Shimei (vv. 36–46), and banishes Abiathar the priest, replacing him with Zadok (vv. 26–27). The book of Kings, however, does not negatively evaluate Solomon's actions.[55] Instead, by presenting them in the context of David's instruction to purge bloodguilt and curse from the house of David (2:1–9) and Solomon's assertion that "the throne of David shall be established before the LORD forever" (2:45–46; cf. 2 Sam 7:16), 1 Kings considers these actions constitutive of the fulfillment of God's promises to David.[56] In fact, 1 Kings attributes wisdom to Solomon in his dealings with his enemies (2:6, 9).[57] Therefore, from the perspective of the books of Kings, Solomon's first actions are conceived as an act of cleansing, a purge of the royal house from evil that makes possible the fulfillment of God's covenant for David and Israel.

Solomon's banishment and substitution of Abiathar—the priest—with Zadok marks the beginning of a new order in the priesthood of the Israelite cult according to the prophecy of Samuel (1 Kgs 2:26–27; cf. 1 Sam 2:27–36). The promotion of Zadok as high priest is considered the fulfillment of a prophecy proclaimed against the unfaithful house of Eli. Zadok is the promised "faithful priest" who "shall go in and out before my anointed one forever" (1 Sam 2:35).

The raising of a new "faithful priest" over Israel marks, as well, the beginning of a reformation in the cult of Israel (cf. Jer 7:1–15; 26:1–9).[58] Abiathar represented the cult centered around the tabernacle at Shiloh, the central sanctuary of the tribal confederacy (Josh 18:1), but the building of the temple by Solomon at Jerusalem represented the beginning of a new era for the Israelite cult. With the inauguration of the temple, Solomon implemented the major reorganization of the temple staff and duties that David had designed for the cult (2 Chr 7:6; cf. 8:14–15; 1 Chr 23–26).

John W. Wright has shown that David's reorganization of the cult in 1 Chr 23–27 functions in the narrative of the Chronicler as the description of "Da-

---

55 Simon J. de Vries, *1 Kings*, WBC 12 (Thomas Nelson, 2003), 42–44.
56 Paul R. House, *1, 2 Kings*, NAC 8 (Broadman & Holman, 1995), 103. Regarding bloodguilt, see Richard D. Nelson, *First and Second Kings*, IBC (John Knox, 1987), 24; de Vries, *1 Kings*, 40.
57 Nelson, *First and Second Kings*, 26.
58 Choon-Leong Seow, "The First and Second Books of Kings," *NIB* 3:33.

vid's chief legacy."⁵⁹ This cultic legacy will have a lasting influence on the history of monarchic Israel. The books of Chronicles will be especially interested in showing that righteous kings will be careful to implement David's reorganization of the cult. Thus, the Chronicler promotes David as a cult founder alongside Moses. The Chronicler clearly recognizes that the Mosaic laws continue to regulate the ritual, but he points out as well, time and again, that David's appointment of the Levites to their office has brought "the worship of Yahweh to its highest perfection and its true fulfillment."⁶⁰ It is Solomon's dedication of the temple that marks the implementation of David's reform of the Israelite cult (2 Chr 7:6; cf. 8:14).⁶¹

The reformation of the cult in connection with Solomon's dedication of the temple had been anticipated in Deuteronomy. This document mentioned that God would choose one place in Israel "as his habitation to put his name there" (Deut 12:5, passim).⁶² An important tenet of the theology of the books of Kings and Chronicles is that Jerusalem is the place God chose for his name to dwell (1 Kgs 9:3, passim; 2 Chr 7:12, passim). Theoretically, then, all the reforms anticipated in Deuteronomy should have been implemented with the inauguration of Solomon's temple. In practice, however, the fullest implementation of this reform came during the reign of Josiah (2 Kgs 23:1–27; 2 Chr 34:1–7; 35:1–19). The dedication of the temple marks, however, the beginning of this transition in the Israelite cult.

The inauguration of the Temple is understood as well as the confirmation of the covenant between God and the people. In his prayer of dedication, Solomon recognizes that the building of the temple evidences God's faithfulness to his covenant (1 Kgs 8:23–26). Though he refers explicitly to the Davidic covenant (1 Kgs 8:22–26), it is clear that he understands it in the context of the greater framework of the Mosaic covenant, which he mentions explicitly in 1

---

59 John W. Wright, "The Legacy of David in Chronicles: The Narrative Function of 1 Chronicles 23–27," *JBL* 110 (1991): 229–242.

60 de Vries, "Moses and David," 619, 639. Similarly, "if the Ancestral era marks Israel's birth as a people, the Sinaitic era marks the time in which Israel receives its national code of conduct, and the life of Joshua marks the time in which Israel receives and divides its land, the Davidic era marks the time in which the institutions associated with the Jerusalem Temple achieve standard definition" (Knoppers, *I Chronicles 10–29*, 798).

61 Mordechai Cogan, *1 Kings: A New Translation with Introduction and Commentary*, AB 10 (Doubleday, 2001), 293.

62 As I mentioned above (pp. 68–71), according to Deuteronomy, this election would implicate a reform for the cult: the laws of sacrifices (Deut 12), offerings and firstborn animals (14:22–29; 15:19–23; 26:1–15), jurisprudence (17:8–13), the festal calendar (16:1–17), priesthood (18:1–8), cities of asylum (19:1–13), and the special laws of Deut 16:21 and 31:11 would be modified. See Richard D. Nelson, *Deuteronomy: A Commentary*, OTL (Westminster John Knox, 2002), 148.

Kgs 8:56–58 (cf. vv. 9, 21, 51–53; 2 Chr 5:10; 6:14).[63] As a result, Solomon exhorts the people to be faithful to their covenantal obligations: "Devote yourselves completely to the Lord our God, walking in his statutes and keeping his commandments" (1 Kgs 8:61). The ceremony is culminated by God's indwelling of the temple, as a sign of his acceptance of the temple, the king, and his people (1 Kgs 8:10–13; 2 Chr 7:1–4), and a dream to the king (1 Kgs 9:1–14; 2 Chr 7:12–22). The king, then, functions as a covenant mediator between God and the people.

In summary, Solomon's first years of righteous rule over "all Israel" are characterized by his defeat of his enemies, the appointment of Zadok as faithful priest, the building of the temple, the implementation of David's reform of the cult, and the renewal of the covenant.

Asa

Like Solomon, Asa displays great confidence in and faithfulness to God in the first years of his rule. Toward the end, however, his confidence in God fails; yet, he is considered a righteous Davidic king (1 Kgs 15:11; 2 Chr 14:2). The expression "seeking the Lord" occurs nine times in the Chronicler's account of Asa's reign and sets the theme for the entire section (14:4, 7 [2x]; 15:2, 4, 12, 13, 17; 16:12).[64]

The first recorded action of his rule is the cleansing of the land from male temple prostitutes and idols (1 Kgs 15:12–13), foreign altars, high places, pillars, and sacred poles (2 Chr 14:3, 5; 15:8). By doing this, Asa fulfills the instructions of Deut 7:5 and 12:2.[65] Asa's reform is quite comprehensive. He is considered by the Chronicler as the first reformer of the cult. Abijah, his father, had been presented in a positive light also (1 Chr 13); but his reign was probably too short to make possible any significant reform.[66]

Only the Chronicler reports Azariah's sermon and the resulting renewal of the covenant (2 Chr 15:8–15). The king exhorted the people to make an oath to "seek the Lord ... with all their heart and with all their soul" (v. 12; cf.

---

63 See John Gray, *I & II Kings: A Commentary*, OTL (Westminster, 1963), 204.
64 Andrew E. Hill, *1 & 2 Chronicles*, NIVAC (Zondervan, 2003), 469.
65 Note how the Chronicler uses the same language as Deuteronomy (see ibid.). The Chronicler does not explain what are "the abominations" (הַשִּׁקּוּצִים) Asa purges from the land (2 Chron 15:8). This probably refers to the male cultic prostitutes referenced in 1 Kgs 15:12. It is important to note, though, that the same word is used of the pollutions of the sanctuary in Dan 9:27, William Johnstone, *2 Chronicles 10–36: Guilt and Atonement*, vol. 2, *1 and 2 Chronicles*, JSOTSup 254 (Sheffield Academic, 1997), 66.
66 Japhet, *I & II Chronicles*, 707.

14:4); thus, he functions as a covenant mediator.[67] The solemnity of this oath is remarkable because it included a penalty of death for those who broke the covenant (v. 13). In fact, Asa removed his own mother, Maacah, from being queen mother because "she had made an abominable image for Asherah" (2 Chr 15:16; cf. 1 Kgs 15:13). The penalty of death and the phrase "all their heart and soul" suggest that the covenant renewed is based on the tradition of the Sinai covenant (cf. Deut 6:5; 10:12; 13:6–10; 17:2–7).[68]

The renewal of the covenant included repair of the temple as well. Asa repaired the altar (2 Chr 15:8) and brought votive gifts into the house of the Lord (1 Kgs 15:15; 2 Chr 15:18).[69] In this respect, Asa follows David's example who is the premier exemplar of giving votive offerings and cultic implements (1 Chr 18:11; 22:3, 14; 29:1–5).[70]

Another important aspect of the theology of Chronicles is that the renewal of the covenant implies, as well, the reunification of "all" Israel.[71] Second Chronicles 15:9 reads: "He gathered all Judah and Benjamin, and those from Ephraim, Manasseh, and Simeon who were residing as aliens with them, for great numbers had deserted to him from Israel when they saw that the LORD his God was with him."

The renewal of the covenant has positive consequences for the nation. God rewards Asa's faithfulness by providing him "rest" from his enemies (2 Chr 14:1, 6, 7; 15:15, 19). The Chronicler's account includes Asa's victory over Zerah, the Cushite, as a result of God's direct intervention. Rest becomes a

---

67 Steven Shawn Tuell, *First and Second Chronicles*, IBC (John Knox, 2001), 167; Japhet, *I & II Chronicles*, 706–707.

68 Hill, *1 & 2 Chronicles*, 472; Tuell, *First and Second Chronicles*, 171–172. Note that this renewal took place in the third month, the same month as the establishment of the covenant at Sinai (Exod 19:1) and probably on the date of the Feast of Weeks or Pentateuch (2 Chr 15:10). See also, Thompson, *1, 2 Chronicles*, 271.

69 For a discussion regarding the identification of the altar Asa repaired, see Japhet, *I & II Chronicles*, 722–3.
Sara Japhet observed that Azariah's instruction to Asa in 2 Chr 15:7, "But you, take courage! Do not let your hands be weak, for your work shall be rewarded," recalls the language of Zech 8:9–13 (*I & II Chronicles*, 721). This passage refers to God's promise of peace as a result of the building of the temple. According to Steven S. Tuell, the use of this language evidences that "Asa is being encouraged to engage in temple-building and reform, an exhortation that he understands and follows" (*First and Second Chronicles*, 170). It is not clear, however, that this is what the Chronicler intended to convey. Azariah's prophecy is full of "citations and standard idioms" and may not be an allusion to Zech 8:9–13. Sara Japhet also notes, for example, that in the same passage (2 Chr 15:7) the phrase "Do not let your hands be weak" is a direct quotation of Zeph 3:16 and that the final clause "for your work shall be rewarded" is a citation of Jer 31:6 (*I & II Chronicles*, 721).

70 Dillard, *2 Chronicles*, 122.

71 Hill, *1 & 2 Chronicles*, 472.

thematic element of Asa's reign.[72] Asa is, in fact, the first king after Solomon to enjoy rest or peace as a gift from God (2 Chr 14:1; cf. 1 Chr 22:9).[73] Azariah's prophecy describes the period before David as "a time when there was no *shalom* in the land" (2 Chr 15:3–7).[74] This implies that God's promise of "rest" to the nation (Deut 12:8–10) was not fulfilled until the time of David and Solomon and, now, Asa.[75]

Joash

The Hebrew Bible characterizes the rule of Joash by stark contrasts. Joash was a king of lights and shadows. Richard D. Nelson nimbly captures the essence of his record:

> Joash was able to refurbish the temple, but in the end had to rob it. Rescued from death as a baby, he was struck down forty years later by his own servants. Heir to God's gracious promise to David, he received the testimony of the law and was a partner in the covenant between God and the people. Yet he failed to live up to the precepts of that covenant. He did right, but not completely right. His accomplishments were ordinary enough, but still significant.[76]

My interest here resides in those actions which caused him to be considered a righteous Davidic king (2 Kgs 12:2; cf. 14:3).

The ascension of Joash to the throne involves renewal of the covenant. This renewal involved three covenants that are referred to in the accounts of Kings and Chronicles.[77] The first is between Jehoiada and the captains of the Carites and of the guardians of the temple (2 Kgs 11:4; 2 Chr 23:1). Its purpose is to topple Athaliah from power and occurs before the enthronement of Joash.

The second covenant is between the Lord, the people, and the king (2 Kgs 11:17ab; 2 Chr 23:16). Its purpose is to renew Yahweh's relationship with Judah

---

72 Ibid., 469–70; Japhet, *I & II Chronicles*, 705. For the thematic use of rest in the Chronicler's account of Asa's reign, see especially Johnstone, *2 Chronicles 10–36*, 59–75.

73 Tuell, *First and Second Chronicles*, 166. Yet, in the actual description of Solomon's reign there is no single reference to rest (Japhet, *I & II Chronicles*, 705).

74 Tuell, *First and Second Chronicles*, 169.

75 Hill, *1 & 2 Chronicles*, 470; Japhet, *I & II Chronicles*, 705.

76 *First and Second Kings*, 214.

77 Both, 2 Kings and 2 Chronicles, use consistently the term בְּרִית for the three of them (2 Kgs 11:4, 17; 2 Chr 23:1, 3, 16). For a comparison between the covenants in the accounts of Kings and Chronicles, see Japhet, *I & II Chronicles*, 834–835.

so that they may be "the Lord's people"; thus, it makes necessary the eradication of Baal worship, restoration of Yahweh's temple, and the reorganization of the cult (2 Kgs 11:18; 2 Chr 23:17–19). This covenant is established during the enthronement ceremony.[78] The covenant here referred to is the Mosaic covenant as renewed at Moab (Deuteronomy) which established how Israel became "the people of the Lord" (Deut 27:9; cf. 4:20; 9:29; 14:2; 26:18). It required of Israel, regarding foreign forms of worship, to "break down their altars, smash their pillars, hew down their sacred poles, and burn their idols with fire. For you are a people holy to the LORD your God" (Deut 7:5–6; cf. 12:1–3).[79]

The third covenant is between the king and the people (2 Kgs 11:17c; 2 Chr 23:3). Its purpose is to reinstate Davidic kingship in Judah after the usurpation of Athaliah and is, also, a constitutive part of the enthronement ceremony of Joash (2 Kgs 11:19–20; 2 Chr 23:20–21). The covenant renewed here, then, refers to the Davidic covenant of 2 Sam 7:1–17 which promised David that "your throne shall be established forever" (v. 16).[80]

The second and third covenants are intimately related.[81] Since Davidic kingship was established under the authority of God's rule over Israel (2 Sam 7:1–17), the renovation of Judah's relationship with God makes the reinstallation of Davidic kingship necessary. Thus, "the relation between king and people [third covenant] is subordinate to the covenant between God and the people [second covenant]."[82]

The covenant plays a central role in the enthronement ceremony itself. Among other insignias vested on the new king, Jehoiada gives him a "covenant" or "testimony" (עֵדוּת; 2 Kgs 11:12; 2 Chr 23:11). Scholars do not agree regarding the identity of this covenant. Some believe it was a copy of the arrangement between Joash and the whole assembly by which he became their king (2 Chr 23:3; cf. 2 Kgs 11:17c), or a copy of the decree of his divine adoption by God.[83] More likely, the covenant here refers to a copy of the law (Deuteronomy) as envisioned in Deut 17:18. (Note that the term עֵדוּת typically refers to the Ten Commandments [e.g., Exod 31:18; 34:29].)[84] In any case, the reference to Jehoiada as crowning, anointing, and proclaiming Joash as king and giving

---

78   For the purposes and differences between the second and third covenants, see ibid.
79   See Dumbrell, *Covenant and Creation*, 160; Nelson, *First and Second Kings*, 210.
80   Dumbrell, *Covenant and Creation*, 160.
81   They are, in fact, bundled together in 2 Kgs 11:17.
82   Johnstone, *2 Chronicles 10–36*, 134.
83   E.g., Hill, *1 & 2 Chronicles*, 523. A similar covenant was also made for David's enthronement (2 Sam 5:3; 1 Chr 11:3). Regarding the "testimony" as a decree of the divine adoption of the king, see Gerhard von Rad, "The Royal Ritual in Judah," in *The Problem of the Hexateuch and Other Essays*, trans. E. W. Trueman Dicken (McGraw-Hill, 1966), 224–229.
84   Tuell, *First and Second Chronicles*, 191.

him the covenant underline his central role in the reform of Israel. Normally, it was the king who acted as covenant mediator between God and the people. As we have seen, Solomon and Asa exhorted the people to renew their allegiance to God. The same will be the case with Hezekiah and Josiah. Here, however, "Jehoiada seems to be a stand-in for the underage king as covenant mediator."[85]

The renewal of the covenant makes necessary the renovation of the temple. This renovation has special importance for both writers, which is clear from the amount of space that both accounts devote to its description (2 Kgs 12:1–16; 2 Chr 24:4–14).[86] A closer reading reveals that probably more than repair was meant. According to the Chronicler, "the children of Athaliah … had broken into the house of God, and had even used all the dedicated things of the house of the LORD for the Baals" (24:7). The defilement of all the sacred utensils most likely entailed discontinuation of the temple worship.[87]

If Joash's prohibition against making utensils for the cult from the money collected in the chest for repair of the temple (2 Kgs 11:13–14) was actually followed, the worship at the temple was resumed when the repair of the temple was finished (2 Chr 24:14). The end of v. 14 seems to confirm this view: It says that after the restoration was finished and new vessels provided, "They offered burnt offerings in the house of the LORD regularly all the days of Jehoiada."

It is clear that the cult was in fact reorganized—whether right after the enthronement of the king or after the repairs had been made. The Chronicler is very clear that Jehoiada reestablished the order that David had conceived originally for the inauguration of the temple: "Jehoiada assigned the care of the house of the LORD to the levitical priests whom David had organized to be in charge of the house of the LORD, to offer burnt offerings to the LORD, as it is written in the law of Moses, with rejoicing and with singing, according to the order of David" (2 Chr 23:18).

It is possible, as well, that Joash's rule also marked a major change in the way the money of the temple was handled. Accounts of the temple repairs show that the king exerted a growing power over the temple. For some reason the Levites were slow in following up the king's plans for the renovation of the temple (2 Kgs 12:7; 2 Chr 24:5). As a result, the king took control of the collection and handling of the money by delegating the task to the king's secretary (2 Kgs 12:10; 24:11).[88]

---

85 Nelson, *First and Second Kings*, 210.
86 For an attempt of explaining the process of repair, see Hill, *1 & 2 Chronicles*, 539–540.
87 Japhet, *I & II Chronicles*, 836.
88 House, *1, 2 Kings*, 303.

Finally, it is important to note that Jehoiada becomes a prototype of the post-exilic faithful priest who rules alongside a kingly figure.[89] For all practical purposes, Jehoiada was a king-priest during the first years of Joash (2 Kgs 12:2; 2 Chr 24:2).[90] Like other Davidic kings, he is remembered because he led Israel in covenant faithfulness and renovation of the temple (2 Chr 24:16).[91] He is buried "in the city of David among the kings" (2 Chr 24:16).[92] Sara Japhet notes that "this is the only case of the Chronicler reporting the death and burial of someone other than a king, and in fact, the terms used here are those regularly employed for kings."[93]

Hezekiah

After David and Solomon, no other king receives more attention in Chronicles than Hezekiah.[94] Second Kings, though shorter in its account of Hezekiah, is lavish in its praise of him: "He trusted in the LORD the God of Israel; so that there was no one like him among all the kings of Judah after him, or among those who were before him" (2 Kgs 18:5). The Chronicler's evaluation of his reign is almost entirely positive: "He did what was right in the sight of the LORD, just as his ancestor David had done" (2 Chr 29:2; 31:20–21; cf. 2 Kgs 18:3, 5).[95] "The Chronicler holds out hope for a united Israel under a Davidic king overseeing the true worship of God in the Jerusalem temple. For him Hezekiah and Josiah are the prototypes of such kingship."[96]

Covenant Renewal

According to 2 Chronicles, Hezekiah's first project after assuming power was repair of the temple and restoration of the cult. This was necessary because Ahaz had

---

89 Hill, *1 & 2 Chronicles*, 540.
90 Dillard, *2 Chronicles*, 192.
91 Hill, *1 & 2 Chronicles*, 540.
92 Ironically Joash was not buried among the kings (v. 25).
93 Japhet, *I & II Chronicles*, 847. See also Tuell, *First and Second Chronicles*, 195.
94 Thompson, *1, 2 Chronicles*, 342.
95 The Chronicler's only adverse report is that Hezekiah's heart was proud after God gave him a sign in relation to his sickness (2 Chr 32:25)—referring to the visit of the embassy from King Merodach-baladan of Babylon (2 Kgs 20:12–19)—but notes immediately that Hezekiah repented (2 Chr 32:26). For a comparison of the accounts of Hezekiah's rule in 2 Kings and 2 Chronicles, see Japhet, *I & II Chronicles*, 912–914. Interpreters consider that Chronicles closely parallels Hezekiah with Solomon and David, especially Solomon. For example, just as Solomon erected the temple and established proper worship (2 Chr 3–7), so Hezekiah repairs the temple and reinstitutes its cult; e.g., Dillard, *2 Chronicles*, 227–229; Hill, *1 & 2 Chronicles*; Thompson, *1, 2 Chronicles*, 340; Tuell, *First and Second Chronicles*, 211.
96 Hill, *1 & 2 Chronicles*, 579.

shut the doors of the temple, thus discontinuing the regular service (2 Chr 28:24). Chapters 29 to 31 are a lengthy and self-contained narrative devoted to this topic.[97]

Hezekiah opens the doors of the temple on the first month of the first year of his reign and exhorts the Levites to re-consecrate themselves and the temple (2 Chr 29:3–11). He clearly states that his purpose is to make a covenant with Yahweh and atone for the sins of Israel (v. 10). The context makes clear that he intends the renovation of the covenant mediated by Moses and later institutionalized by David, since it is Moses's cultic laws which are reinstated (cf. 30:16; chap. 31) and David's temple and organization of the cult which are renewed (e.g., 29:25).[98] Consequently, we must understand Hezekiah's restoration of the cult in terms of a covenant renewal between God and the nation. The king acts as a covenant mediator. He is also an intercessor. Like Moses, he cleanses the nation from idolatry so that God's "fierce anger may turn away from" the nation (2 Chr 29:10; Num 25:4).[99]

The process of restoration of the cult is remarkable. It required a re-consecration of the temple and its ministers, an expiation for the sin of the nation, a re-inauguration of the cult, and a re-consecration of the people to God because the cult had ceased and the covenant with Yahweh had been broken—Ahaz had shut up the doors of the temple and built altars to foreign gods in every city (2 Chr 28:24–25; cf. 29:6–8). This task is performed in three phases clearly delimited in the text: (1) re-consecration of the temple and its ministers (2 Chr 29:12–19), (2) re-inauguration of the cult (vv. 20–30), and (3) re-consecration of the people to God (vv. 31–36).[100]

Re-Consecration of the Priests and Temple

The process of re-consecrating the temple begins "on the first day of the first month" (2 Chr 29:17)— the same time of the year when Moses inaugurated the tabernacle (Exod 40:2, 17). It finishes sixteen days later (2 Chr 29:17) and comprehends three different actions: the consecration (קדשׁ) of the Levites,

---

97 Japhet, *I & II Chronicles*, 914.
98 Johnstone, *2 Chronicles 10–36*, 191–192. Contra Tuell, *First and Second Chronicles*, 213; Japhet, *I & II Chronicles*, 919, who see this call only as a renewed total commitment to the Lord.
99 Note the equivalent expressions:
Num 25:4: וַיִּשֹׁב חֲרוֹן אַף־יְהוָה מִיִּשְׂרָאֵל
"... in order that the fierce anger of the LORD may turn away from Israel."
2 Chr 29:10: וְיָשֹׁב מִמֶּנּוּ חֲרוֹן אַפּוֹ
"... so that his fierce anger may turn away from us."
See also, Hill, *1 & 2 Chronicles*, 580.
100 This account finishes with the assertion: "Thus the service of the house of the LORD was restored. And Hezekiah and all the people rejoiced because of what God had done for the people; for the thing had come about suddenly" (vv. 35–36).

the cleansing (טהר) of the temple, and its consecration (קדש; cf. 18–19). It is important to note that this corresponds to Moses's consecration of the sanctuary, which included the consecration of the priests (Exod 40:12–16; cf. 29:44; Lev 8–9; Num 7–8), but did not include the cleansing of the sanctuary.[101]

The text does not explain what the consecration of the Levites involves. (This should involve here the priests as well [see 2 Chr 29:16–19, 34; cf. 30:15].)[102] From 2 Chr 30:15 it is clear that the sanctification involved burnt offerings, but their nature and function are not explained.[103] These sacrifices are most likely part of a larger liturgical context that is connected to the consecration of the priests (קדש; Exod 29; 40; Lev 8), which should have included as well a sin offering (Lev 8:14–17) and a ram for consecration (vv. 22–29), in addition to the burnt offering (vv. 18–21).[104]

Hezekiah's re-inauguration of the temple is analogous to Moses's inauguration of the tabernacle with the difference that it included a ritual of purification.[105] This ritual of purification was not necessary for Moses's inauguration of the tabernacle because the tabernacle had not been previously defiled. In the case of Hezekiah, however, the temple had been polluted by Ahaz. This evil king not only "cut in pieces the utensils ... [and] shut up the doors of the house of the LORD" (2 Chr 28:24–25; cf. 29:6–8), but also "made his sons pass through fire" as a burnt offering to Molech (2 Chr 28:3; cf. 33:6; 2 Kgs 23:10). This last serious sin is especially significant. According to Lev 20:3,

---

101 However, Moses's consecration of the temple did include cleansing the altar of sacrifice prior to its consecration (Lev 8:15).

102 Japhet, *I & II Chronicles*, 920. Note, however, that in the Pentateuch the consecration of the Priests (Lev 8) and the purification of the Levites (Num 8; the Levites were not consecrated) are separate events.

103 Ibid., 949.

104 I proceed here on the basis that NT authors understand Leviticus to contain God's messages to Moses (Luke 2:22 [referring to Lev 12]; Matt 8:4 [par. Mark 1:44; Luke 5:14; referring to Lev 13–14]; Mark 7:10 [referring to Lev 20:9]) which are, therefore, prior to Hezekiah's reform. See Gane, *Leviticus, Numbers*, 27–28.

Sarah Japhet (*I & II Chronicles*, 922) mentions the possibility that these burnt offerings might be part of a process of atonement for a specific sin (Lev 4:3–12), or purification after defilement because of the death of a relative (Ezek 44:27). But those suggestions are less likely because their purpose is "atonement" (כפר; Lev 4: 26, 31, 35) and not "consecration" (קדש) as in our case.

105 I have noted (92, n.101), though, that Moses's inauguration of the Sanctuary did include the purification and consecration of *the altar* (Lev 8:15). For a discussion of the meaning of this text, see Gane, *Cult and Character*, 130–133, 140–142.

We should be careful not to confuse Hezekiah's purification (טהר/καθαρίζω or ἁγνίζω) of the temple with its consecration (קדש/ἁγνίζω). According to 2 Chr 29:18, 19 they are discrete processes; see Japhet, *I & II Chronicles*, 922.

the sacrifice of an offspring to Molech defiles God's sanctuary.[106] Thus, it was necessary to cleanse (טהר) the temple before it could be consecrated (קדש).

I want to suggest that Hezekiah's re-inauguration of the temple is analogous as well to the re-consecration of the altar on the Day of Atonement. Roy Gane's research has shown that serious moral faults—such as Ahaz's sacrifice of his sons to Molech—were cleansed from the sanctuary only on the Day of Atonement.[107] Thus, Hezekiah's ritual of purification (טהר) and consecration (קדש) of the temple from "all the unclean things" (טֻמְאָה; 2 Chr 29:15–16) is equivalent to the purification (טהר) and consecration (קדש) of the altar from the "uncleannesses [טֻמְאָה] of the people of Israel" performed every year on the Day of Atonement (Lev 16:19; Ezek 43:18–27; cf. Exod 39:36–37; Num 7:87–88).[108] Jacob Milgrom argues in his commentary on this passage that the reason for the annual re-consecration of the altar resides in the fact that it was the means of atonement for the people.[109] In the case of Hezekiah, it is the whole temple and not just the altar, which undergoes the same ritual of purification and re-consecration. The purpose is the same. As soon as the temple and its ministers are re-consecrated, Hezekiah commands that sacrifices be offered "to make atonement for all Israel" (2 Chr 29:20–24).

Hezekiah's re-inauguration of the temple has an intriguing similarity to the purification and atonement (כפר) sacrifices to be offered on the first and seventh days of the first month, according to the law of the temple in Ezek 45:18–20.[110] These sacrifices served a function related to the Day of Atonement in the ritual system of Ezekiel but did not supersede it. They were instead related to the celebration of the Passover (v. 21). Hezekiah's cleansing and re-consecration of the temple also has a preparatory function for the Passover that was celebrated one month later.

---

106 For a discussion of serious moral faults that pollute the sanctuary, see Roy E. Gane, *Cult and Character: Purification Offerings, Day of Atonement, and Theodicy* (Eisenbrauns, 2005), 144–151.

107 Gane, *Leviticus, Numbers*, 277–283, esp. 281. For an in-depth analysis, see Roy E. Gane, *Ritual Dynamic Structure*, Gorgias Dissertations 14, Religion 2 (Gorgias, 2004); Gane, *Cult and Character*.

108 Japhet, *I & II Chronicles*, 922; Tuell, *First and Second Chronicles*, 213–214. Jacob Milgrom suggests that the annual purification and consecration of the altar (which consisted in the discrete acts of daubing of blood on its horns and sprinkling of blood on it) is also equivalent to the daubing of blood on the right-ear lobes, right-hand thumbs, and right-foot big toes of the priests and the sprinkling of oil upon them on the day of their consecration (Lev 8:24–30; *Leviticus 1–16*, 1037). The difference is that priests were not re-consecrated every year.

109 Milgrom, *Leviticus 1–16*, 1038.

110 Japhet, *I & II Chronicles*, 922; Tuell, *First and Second Chronicles*, 214.

Re-Inauguration of the Service of the Temple

As in the inauguration of the tabernacle (Lev 8–9), Hezekiah's re-inauguration of the temple is followed by the inauguration of the system of sacrifices.

After the Mosaic tabernacle was inaugurated, Aaron and his sons offered sin and burnt offerings to atone for themselves and the people of Israel (Lev 9:7). In addition, they offered grain and well-being offerings (vv. 17–21). In total, these sacrifices included all the basic types of sacrifices except the reparation offering.[111] The inauguration of the sanctuary service was in some sense, then, a demonstration of the full capability of the sanctuary, but it is not clear that specific sins—whether those of the priests or the people—were atoned for.[112]

In the case of Hezekiah, however, the inauguration of the temple's worship included sin and burnt offerings with the purpose of atoning for specific sins. This is indicated by the fact that the king and the people laid their hands on the sacrificial animals (2 Chr 29:23) that were to be offered "for the kingdom and for the sanctuary and for Judah" (v. 21) in order "to make atonement for all Israel" (v. 24).[113] What we have here is a national act of confession, repentance, and atonement with the purpose of averting God's wrath upon Israel because of its apostasy during the rule of Ahaz (v. 10; cf. Lev 4:13–26).

The Chronicler is explicit when stating that the worship of the temple is renewed according to the reforms introduced by David.[114] The Levites are organized and stationed according to the dispositions of David to play the instruments he had designed for the service and sing the songs of David and Asaph the seer (vv. 25–30).

Re-Consecration of the Nation

The final phase of the restoration of the cult is the most remarkable. Now, once the temple has been re-consecrated and the cult re-inaugurated, Hezekiah invites the people to "come near, [and] bring sacrifices and thank offerings to the house of the Lord" (v. 31). The invitation itself is not extraordinary, but the terms in which the king refers to the people are. He

---

[111] Gane, *Leviticus, Numbers*, 180.

[112] Jacob Milgrom suggests that כפר carries here a general meaning of reconciliation between the people and God (*Leviticus 1–16*, 578; See also, Gane, *Leviticus, Numbers*, 180–182).

[113] The phrase "for the kingdom" may refer to the Davidic dynasty (Hill, *1 & 2 Chronicles*, 582).

[114] There are four references to David in 29:25–30. This is "the most condensed distribution of Davidic references outside his own story" (Japhet, *I & II Chronicles*, 928).

refers to the general audience as those who have "consecrated" themselves to the Lord, using a technical term for consecration to the priesthood (מִלְאתֶם יֶדְכֶם; e.g., Exod 32:29; 29:9; Lev 8:33).[115] Moreover, he considers them capacitated to "draw near" (נגשׁ) to present their offerings, a verb used of priestly activity (Exod 19:22).[116] This is the only event in which the Chronicler credits the people with "active participation in the contribution of sacrifices."[117] Does he mean that the congregation or nation has become a nation of priests (cf. Exod 19:5–6)?

Most likely, the Chronicler is using this expression (מִלְאתֶם יֶדְכֶם "consecrate," lit. "fill the hand") in a more general sense.[118] The same phrase is used by David when he instructed Solomon to build the temple: He invited the people to bring offerings for the service of the temple so that they could "consecrate" themselves (לְמַלֹּאות יָדוֹ) to the Lord (1 Chr 29:5).[119] Likewise, the people responded to Hezekiah's invitation by bringing abundant offerings so that "the service of the house of the Lord was established *again*" (2 Chr 29:35, NASB, emphasis original).

Celebration of Passover

After the covenant had been renewed and the cult restored, Hezekiah decided to celebrate the Passover (2 Chr 30). This event is very important because it makes evident additional aspects of Hezekiah's leadership.

First, the king promotes the reunification of the twelve tribes of Israel through the cult. Hezekiah sent invitations for the Passover to "all Israel, from Beer-sheba to Dan" (v. 5). The specific invitation to the "remnant" of Israel is "return to the Lord" (v. 6) and "do not ... be stiff-necked as your ancestors were, but yield yourselves to the LORD and come to his sanctuary" (v. 8). The invitation to come to the sanctuary *in Jerusalem* is important because it was the "prescribed" manner of keeping the Passover (cf. v. 5) according to the Chronicler's interpretation of Deut 16:1–8.[120] The temple at Jerusalem is the place God chose for the "dwelling of his name" (v. 6; cf. 2 Chr 30:8). Hezekiah, then, seeks to reunite Israel through proper worship.[121]

---

115 L. A. Snijders, "מָלֵא," *TDOT* 8:301–306. See also, Johnstone, *2 Chronicles 10–36*, 197–199.
116 Johnstone, *2 Chronicles 10–36*, 197.
117 Japhet, *I & II Chronicles*, 929.
118 According to 2 Chr 30:17 the "consecration" (קָדַשׁ) of lay people is not necessary to officiate at the altar, but to slay the Passover lamb.
119 Japhet, *I & II Chronicles*, 929–30; Snijders, "מָלֵא," 205.
120 See Japhet, *I & II Chronicles*, 940–941.
121 Hill, *1 & 2 Chronicles*, 585.

The response is mixed. The heralds are laughed at and mocked, but "a few from Asher, Manasseh, and Zebulun humbled themselves and came to Jerusalem" (v. 11; cf. v. 18). Like David, Hezekiah restores the unity of Israel under one cult.

Hezekiah is also, like Moses, an intercessor on behalf of the people. When the Passover was celebrated, "a multitude of people" participated in it without having first "cleansed themselves" (2 Chr 30:18). Leviticus 7:19–21 explicitly prohibits such participation. The king, then, intercedes on their behalf so that "the good LORD pardon all who set their hearts to seek God ... even though not in accordance with the sanctuary's rules of cleanness" (vv. 18–19). The Chronicler registers that God listened to Hezekiah and "healed the people" (v. 20). This reminds us of Solomon's prayer that God would "forgive their [the people's] sin and heal their land" if they "humble themselves, pray, seek my face, and turn from their wicked ways" (7:14).[122]

The Chronicler also describes the king as the main provider for the cult. Hezekiah provided for the cult 1,000 bulls and 7,000 sheep on the occasion of the festival of unleavened bread (v. 24). Later on, the Chronicler relates that the king became a consistent provider of the cult: "The contribution of the king from his own possessions was for the burnt offerings: the burnt offerings of morning and evening, and the burnt offerings for the sabbaths, the new moons, and the appointed festivals, as it is written in the law of the LORD" (2 Chr 31:3). Hezekiah anticipates, then, the role of the king in Ezek 40–48. According to the law for the new temple in Ezekiel the king (called prince) will be the main provider for the cult (Ezek 45:17; cf. 45:22; 46:4).[123]

The restoration of the cult triggers several responses from the people. First, the Chronicler emphasizes that the people rejoiced greatly (2 Chr 29:36; 30: 21, 23, 25, 26). In fact, there was so much joy that the nation decided to continue the festival of unleavened bread for seven more days (30:21, 23), just as Solomon had also extended the ceremonies accompanying the dedication of the temple (7:8–10).

The second response is that the people follow up on Hezekiah's reforms. They destroy pagan places of worship as well as the high places not only in Judah, but also in Ephraim and Manasseh (31:1). The high places here are probably not centers of idolatrous worship, but alternate centers of worship to YHWH.[124] At least this is the way Sennacherib understands Hezekiah's reforms

---

122 Ibid., 587; Japhet, *I & II Chronicles*, 952–953. Note, however, that in 1 Chr 7:14 what is healed is the "land," not the people.

123 Solomon (2 Chr 8:13) and the Persian Darius (Ezra 6:6–12) contribute as well for the liturgy of the temple, Tuell, *First and Second Chronicles*, 222–223.

124 The construction of the temple by Solomon did not immediately centralize the cult. Time and again, the historian informs us that the people continued to worship in the high

according to the Chronicler: "Was it not this same Hezekiah who took away his high places and his altars and commanded Judah and Jerusalem, saying, 'Before one altar you shall worship, and upon it you shall make your offerings'?" (2 Chr 32:12; cf. 2 Kgs 18:22). Thus, apparently, this destruction of high places intends the implementation of the centralization of the worship that had been anticipated in the Mosaic legislation (Deut 12:5, passim).

Finally, the Chronicler relates that the king organizes the work of the priests and Levites by appointing "everyone according to his service" (2 Chr 31:2; cf. 8:14–15; 23:18–19). The organization of the Levites and priests had been abolished when Ahaz closed the doors of the temple (28:24). After the king commanded the people to contribute for their support, the nation responded generously so that there was "plenty to spare" and store-chambers were necessary to be prepared to store the offerings of the nation (32:10–11).

Rest from Their Enemies

God responds favorably to Hezekiah's reforms by delivering Israel from Sennacherib (2 Kgs 18–20; 2 Chr 32; Isa 36–38). Second Kings relates that after Hezekiah cleansed the land from idolatry (18:4), he "rebelled against the king of Assyria" (v. 7). Sennacherib's attempt at reprisal creates a huge crisis for Hezekiah. But the Angel of the Lord saved him by killing 185,000 of Sennacherib's army (19:35). The chronicler summarizes this deliverance in meaningful terms: "[The Lord] gave them rest on every side" (2 Chr 32:22).[125] Hezekiah, then, enjoys the fulfillment of the promises made to David: "I will give you rest from all your enemies" (2 Sam 7:11).

Josiah

Josiah is the last of the righteous kings of the Davidic dynasty. Both Chronicles and Kings report that "he did what was right in the sight of the LORD, and walked in the ways of his ancestor David; *he did not turn aside to the right or to the left*" (2 Chr 34:2, emphasis mine; cf. 2 Kgs 22:2). Note that the last

---

places (1 Kgs 14:23; 15:14; 22:43; 2 Kgs 12:3; 14:4; 15:4, etc.; 2 Chr 15:17; 20:33).

These high places do not necessarily refer to pagan shrines. For example, Samuel used to offer sacrifices in them (1 Sam 9:12–27; cf. 10:5). Solomon offered sacrifices to the Lord at Gibeon, which is called a high place, and received a divine vision there (1 Kgs 3:3–4; cf. 2 Kgs 18:22; 23:9; 1 Chr 16:39; 21:29). See also, Auld, *Kings without Privilege*, 87. These high places are removed until the time of Hezekiah and Josiah (since Manasseh had rebuilt them; 2 Kgs 18:22; 23:5–9; 2 Chr 31:1; 32:12; 34:3) and signal the culmination of the reformation of the cult anticipated by Deuteronomy (see above note 40 in page 46).

125 See Johnstone, *2 Chronicles 10–36*, 219.

remark describes the ideal obedience to the covenant according to Deuteronomy (5:32; 17:11, 20; 28:14). Moreover, Josiah is the only king who "turned to the LORD with all his heart, with all his soul, and with all his might, according to all the law of Moses" (2 Kgs 23:25; cf. Deut 6:5).[126]

Cleansing of the Land

Josiah "began to seek" the Lord in the eighth year of his reign (2 Chr 34:3), but it was on the twelfth year that he began a work of reform by purging the land from idolatry (vv. 3–7; 2 Kgs 23:4–20).[127] He was by then twenty years old, which is the age of majority in the Hebrew cult and the age when Levites began their service for God (Num 1:3; 1 Chr 23:24). This was probably the first year he did not reign under the authority of a regent.[128] His work of reform begins in Judah and Jerusalem (2 Chr 34:3, 5), but he later extended it to the cities of Manasseh, Ephraim, Simeon, and Naphtali; that is, "throughout *all the land of Israel*" (v. 7; emphasis mine). The latter expression is related only to the reigns of David, Solomon, and Hezekiah, when Israel reached its largest expansion.[129] His reform intends, then, a unification of the northern and southern tribes into one cult.[130]

---

126 See Tuell, *First and Second Chronicles*, 234.

127 According to 2 Kings, Josiah's reform occurs six years later, in the 18th year of his reign, just after the repair of the temple and the renewal of the covenant (22:3). Chronicles registers two reforms; one before the finding of the book of the Law in the 12th year (2 Chr 34:3–7) and another after it in the 18th year of his reign (34:33), which coincides with the reform of 2 Kgs 23:4–20. There is a growing consensus among scholars that there were in fact early and late reforms in the reign of Josiah, previous and subsequent to the finding of the book. Dillard, *2 Chronicles*, 276–277; Thompson, *1, 2 Chronicles*, 373–375. The book was found in 622 BCE, the 18th year of Josiah's reign (2 Chr 34:8; 2 Kgs 22:3). According to the Chronicler, Josiah's earlier reforms began in the 12th year of his reign (2 Chr 34:3), around 628 BCE. The Assyrian empire was already disintegrating by this time. The death of Ashurbanipal in 627 BCE accelerated the process. In 625 BCE, Nineveh itself was under siege by Ciaxares and the Medes. It is not difficult to believe that Josiah would take advantage of this opportunity to advance his political and religious agenda. Dillard, *2 Chronicles*, 278; Hill, *1 & 2 Chronicles*, 618–619; Tuell, *First and Second Chronicles*, 235–236.

128 Dillard, *2 Chronicles*, 278. Also, Hill, *1 & 2 Chronicles*, 618; Johnstone, *2 Chronicles 10–36*, 233; Tuell, *First and Second Chronicles*, 235. See, however, the precaution of Japhet, *I & II Chronicles*, 1022.

129 Japhet, *I & II Chronicles*, 1024.

130 Note as well that the offerings for the repair of the temple come from Judah, Benjamin, and "the rest of Israel" (2 Chr 34:8). The NRSV translates this expression as the "remnant" of Israel, but this has theological nuances. Sarah Japhet (*I & II Chronicles*, 1027) argues that the best translation is "the rest of Israel" as in the case of the enthronement of David in 1 Chr 12:38, the only other place in biblical prose where this expression is found. The emphasis is, then, not in the survival of a remnant but on the universality of support for the renovation of the temple.

Josiah's reform parallels in form and content the reforms of Hezekiah.[131] His cleansing of the land and repair of the temple goes further, however, than previous reforms. Josiah not only destroyed idolatrous shrines, images, and altars; he broke them into dust, killed its pagan priests, and *defiled* the sites by "burning the bones of the priests on their altars" (v. 5).[132]

Repair of the Temple

Six years later, on the eighteenth year of his reign, Josiah initiates repair of the temple (34:14–28; 2 Kgs 22:3–7). The Chronicler reports that the temple had been previously cleansed in connection with the cleansing of the land begun six years earlier (2 Chr 34:8; see above); thus, the Chronicler understands the repair of the temple as one step in a comprehensive reform movement.[133] The king is, of course, the driving force behind the work of repair, especially in the Chronicler's account.[134] He has the initiative and appoints officials of his kingdom to hand in the money "to the workers who had the oversight of the house of the LORD" (2 Chr 34:10).[135] The organization of the Levites to oversee repairs of the temple reflects the reforms of David to the service of the Levites, including those in charge of music (vv. 12–13; cf. 1 Chr 25–26).[136]

The Book of the Law Is Found

During the repair of the temple, Hilkiah, the high priest, found "the book of the law of the Lord" (2 Chr 34:14–28; 2 Kgs 22:8–20). Though we are not sure of exactly what the book contained, it is clear that it exposed the gravity of Judah's apostasy and the dreadful curses that hung upon them.[137] The king consults the Lord through Huldah the prophetess who reveals that the calamity has been decreed and cannot be revoked, yet the king will "not see all

---

131 Tuell, *First and Second Chronicles*, 234.

132 Japhet, *I & II Chronicles*, 1021–1022.

133 In fact, toward the end of his reign, Manasseh had begun a cleansing of the temple (2 Chr 33:15–16).

134 See Japhet, *I & II Chronicles*, 1025–1026.

135 The Chronicler's account (34:8–13) is not necessarily different from 2 Kgs 22:3–7. It is possible to read in both cases that the king's officials received the money from Hilkiah, the high priest, and handed it to those who were overseeing the work in the temple.

136 Hill, *1 & 2 Chronicles*, 620.

137 The general consensus favors the idea that the book found was a copy of Deuteronomy or an early version of it. For a summary of the reasons see Dillard, *2 Chronicles*, 280. If the book was a copy of Deuteronomy, the terrifying curses of Deut 28:15–68 may have prompted the king's renewal of the covenant and extensive reform.

the disaster that ... [God] will bring on this place and its inhabitants" because he was "penitent" and "humbled" himself before the Lord (2 Chr 34:27–28).[138]

Renewal of the Covenant

Josiah decides, then, to renew the covenant with God which has been broken (2 Chr 28:29–33; 2 Kgs 23:1–3). He convenes the elders of Judah and Jerusalem and reads to them the book just found. Then the king makes a covenant "before the Lord," ostensibly with the assembly, to keep the "covenant of God" with "all his heart and all his soul" (2 Chr 34:31–32; 2 Kgs 23:3).

Both Kings and Chronicles emphasize the central role of the king in the making of this covenant. Not only did he convene the assembly and read the book, but "he made all who were present in Jerusalem and in Benjamin pledge themselves to it" (2 Chr 34:32). One wonders to what extent the nation was willing to enter into this covenant. Neither Chronicles nor Kings reports a joyous reaction to the making of the covenant. The Chronicler presents the king as taking not only the initiative but also assuming responsibility for the fidelity of the nation.

The following verse (v. 33) informs us that the king enforced the covenant upon the people. He literally "made them serve the Lord" (note the Hiphil stem of וַיַּעֲבֵד; v. 33). It is not surprising, then, that Judah's fidelity lasted only while the king lived (v. 33).

Reorganization of the Cult

The climax of Josiah's reform comes with the celebration of the Passover which both accounts consider unequaled since the time of the judges (2 Chr 35:18; 2 Kgs 23:22).[139] The focus is on the king as the organizer of the feast (2 Chr 35:1–10).

The celebration of the Passover after a long period of apostasy requires a major reorganization of the cult and its personnel. The preparations for the Passover are comprehensive and painstaking (2 Chr 35:1–10). The celebration of this Passover did not come "about suddenly" (2 Chr 29:36) and was not organized in a rush as in the case of Hezekiah. Instead, "Josiah works to establish a permanent institution, built on solid administrational and organi-

---

138 "Humbling" (כנע) is an important theological concept in the book of Chronicles. It is a prerequisite to forgiveness and deliverance by God (2 Chr 7:14; 12:6–7, 12; 28:19; 30:11; 33:12, 19; 34:27); see Thompson, *1, 2 Chronicles*, 378.

139 Note that Josiah's Passover doubles the size of Hezekiah's. Compare the number of sacrifices offered by Josiah (1 Chr 35:7–9) with those offered by Hezekiah (30:24).

zational foundations, with a clear division of roles and an undisputed legal basis."¹⁴⁰

The king organizes first the priests and Levites and appoints them to their offices according to the dispositions of David (2 Chr 35:4, 15). (Once again, the Chronicler emphasizes David and Solomon as founding figures of Israel's cult.)¹⁴¹ Next, the king exhorts the Levites to be prepared and sanctified so that they can help the priests by slaughtering the Passover lamb. This instruction is interesting. It makes standard practice what had been an emergency measure in the time of Hezekiah so that there would not be a shortage of Levites and priests to serve the worshipers (vv. 3–6).¹⁴² Apparently, the Levites continued to slaughter the sacrificial animals in post-exilic times as suggested in Ezra 6:20 (cf. Ezek 44:10–11).¹⁴³ It seems, then, that Josiah becomes a reformer of the cult on a small scale.

The king and their officials also make a generous donation of sacrifices for the feast (2 Chr 35:7–9). The provisions of sacrifices and cultic personnel are plentiful so the nation may celebrate without delay. The Chronicler's emphasis for the preparations, however, is that the temple, its offerings, and ministry be used correctly.

In the context of these preparations the king issues an enigmatic order to the Levites: "Put the holy ark in the house which Solomon the son of David king of Israel built" (2 Chr 35:3). Had the ark been taken out of the temple during the reign of Manasseh? We don't really know.¹⁴⁴ If this was the case, its reinstallation amounts to a re-inauguration or re-dedication of the temple. Though the Chronicler does not explicitly mention a service of re-inauguration of the temple, other elements associated with such liturgy appear. For example, the building or repair of the temple, the reorganization of the Lev-

---

140 Japhet, *I & II Chronicles*, 1045.
141 Tuell, *First and Second Chronicles*, 239.
142 Dillard, *2 Chronicles*, 280.
143 See, Hill, *1 & 2 Chronicles*, 626; Tuell, *First and Second Chronicles*, 239. For a differing opinion, see Thompson, *1, 2 Chronicles*, 382.
144 Sarah Japhet (*I & II Chronicles*, 1048) suggests that the text is corrupted in this passage (2 Chr 35:3). Her reconstructed text reads, "The holy ark was placed in the house which Solomon ... built ... you need no longer carry it." She suggests, then, that the ark had not been taken out of the temple and there was no need to reinstall it. If she is right, Josiah refers here to the installation of the ark in Solomon's temple as the reason for the reorganization or reassignment of the role of the Levites in the cult. The extant text implies, notwithstanding, that the ark had been taken out. Menaham Haran argues that Manasseh replaced the ark in the holy of holies with the "carved image of Asherah" (2 Kgs 21:3–8; 2 Chr 33:4–8, *Temples and Temple-Service in Ancient Israel: An Inquiry into the Character of Cult Phenomena and the Historical Setting of the Priestly School* [Clarendon, 1978], 277–284; also, Thompson, *1, 2 Chronicles*, 381–2). The evidence we have, however, is insufficient to reach hard conclusions regarding what happened to the ark previous to and during Josiah's reform.

ites, and the contributions of the king and the officials to the temple appear in those events organized by David and Solomon, and Hezekiah.

On the other hand, if the ark had not been taken out but Josiah required its reinstallation, then the command is highly symbolical. It would evidence the king's desire that the Passover be understood as a re-inauguration of the cult; that is, "a rerun ... of what was achieved under Solomon."[145] Second Chronicles 35:16 seems to support this view because it describes the Passover as the moment of the re-establishment of the temple's cult: "So all the service of the LORD was prepared [established; וַתִּכֹּן] that day, to keep the Passover and to offer burnt offerings on the altar of the LORD, according to the command of King Josiah."[146]

Summary

The study of the rule of those Davidic kings considered righteous—or of their loyal years—reveals a recurring pattern that culminates in the reigns of Hezekiah and Josiah. Seven main elements—which often do not appear in the same order—comprise this pattern: (1) renewal of the covenant, (2) cleansing of the land from spurious forms of worship, (3) building or repair of the temple, (4) emergence of a faithful high priest alongside the Davidic king, (5) reform of the cult, which implied the change of ritual laws and/or the reorganization of the priests; (6) a movement toward the reunification of Israel, and (7) "rest" from or defeat of enemies. (See Table 2.)

This pattern provides the basic elements of the ideal rule of the Davidic kings in the history of monarchic Israel according to the biblical record. The Hebrew Bible makes clear, however, that this ideal was not fully achieved—or at the best achieved only temporarily.

I would now like to analyze what the references to the Davidic covenant elsewhere in the Hebrew Bible tell us regarding how the biblical writers reacted to the failure of the Davidic kings in bringing the Davidic promises to fulfillment. I am especially interested in their interpretation of the future of the Davidic covenant.

---

145   Johnstone, *2 Chronicles 10–36*, 247.
146   Ibid., 252. Note again that Ezek 45 ties the cleansing of the sanctuary to the first month in preparation for Passover. See above section "Celebration of Passover" on page 65.

	Solomon	Asa	Joash	Hezekiah	Josiah
Renewal of the Covenant	1 Kgs 8:14–26, 56–58, 61; 2 Chr 5:7–10	2 Chr 15:10–14	2 Kgs 11:17ab; 2 Chr 23:16	2 Chr 29:10	2 Chr 34:29–33; 2 Kgs 23:1–3
Cleansing of the Land	1 Kgs 2 (from blood guilt)	1 Kgs 15:12–13; 2 Chr 14:3, 5; 15:8	2 Kgs 11:18; 2 Chr 23:17	2 Chr 31:1	2 Chr 34:3–7; 2 Kgs 23:4–20
Building or Repair of the Temple	1 Kgs 5–8; 2 Chr 2–7; (builds the temple)	2 Chr 15:8; cf. 1 Kgs 15:15; 2 Chr 15:18	2 Kgs 12:1–16; 2 Chr 24:4–14	2 Chr 29:3; cf. vv. 12–36	2 Chr 34:8–13; 2 Kgs 22:3–7
A Faithful High Priest	1 Chr 29:22 (cf. 1 Kgs 2:26–27)		2 Kgs 12:2; 2 Chr 24:2, 14, 16		2 Kgs 22:4–7; 2 Chr 34:9–14
Reform of the Cult	2 Chr 8:14–15		2 Chr 23:17–19	2 Chr 31:2	2 Chr 35:1–16
Reunification of Israel	1 Kgs 4:1; 2 Chr 1:2–3 (rules over "all Israel")	2 Chr 15:9		2 Chr 30:5–18	2 Chr 34:5–7
Rest from Enemies	1 Kgs 5:4; 8:56	2 Chr 14:1, 6, 7; 15:15, 19		2 Chr 32:22	

Table 2. Pattern of Rule of Righteous Davidic Kings in Monarchic Israel

The Davidic Covenant in the Rest of the Hebrew Bible

The Psalms

The Davidic covenant is referred to in the Psalms mainly as a request by the Davidic king, or in behalf of him, that God may fulfill his promises in his favor. Prominent among these are Pss 89 and 132.

Psalm 89

Psalm 89 claims the promises of the Davidic covenant (vv. 19–37) for the Davidic king who has fallen in disgrace: "Lord, where is your steadfast love of old, which by your faithfulness you swore to David?" (v. 49). The psalmist's appeal to God's "steadfast love" (vv. 1–8, 49–52) focuses on two promises of the Davidic covenant: God will defeat the enemies of the Davidic king (vv. 19–27; cf. 2 Sam 7:11) and one from David's progeny will sit on the throne forever (vv. 36–37; cf. 2 Sam 7:13). The basis for the psalmist's plea is that God's promise to David was perpetual and unconditional (vv. 28–37): "as long as the heavens endure" (v. 29), as the moon's "enduring witness in the skies" (v. 37).[147]

This psalm contains probably the most clear assertion of the eternal, unconditional nature of the Davidic covenant in the Hebrew Bible.

Psalm 132

Psalm 132 makes the same appeal to God—the throne for David's descendants (vv. 11–12) and the defeat of their enemies (v. 18)—requesting him to "remember" his "oath" to David. This psalm emphasizes, however, the conditional dimension of the Davidic covenant: "The LORD swore to David a sure oath from which he will not turn back: 'One of the sons of your body I will set on your throne. *If* your sons keep my covenant and my decrees that I shall teach them, *their sons also*, forevermore, shall sit on your throne' " (vv. 11–12; emphasis mine).

As I have mentioned above, this passage does not necessarily contradict the unconditional nature of the Davidic covenant, but emphasizes the necessity of fidelity for the Davidic king so that *his* children may sit *also* on the throne. It is not the Davidic progeny who are in danger of forfeiting the throne; but that of the individual Davidic king (cf. גַּם־בְּנֵיהֶם עֲדֵי־עַד יֵשְׁבוּ לְכִסֵּא־לָךְ "their sons also, forevermore, shall sit on your throne"). His progeny may be excluded from the promises of the Davidic covenant if he is unfaithful to God who established the covenant (see above section "Is the Davidic Covenant Unconditional?" on page 39).

---

147 Older commentators tended to see the crisis referred to in vv. 39–45 as pointing out to Jerusalem's fall in 586 BCE. More recent commentators consider that it probably refers to an earlier crisis (Pomykala, *The Davidic Dynasty Tradition*, 15, n. 6).

Other Psalms

Other psalms focus on specific aspects of the Davidic covenant without further reflection on its conditional or unconditional nature. God's promise to David is prominent in the Psalms: "I will give you rest from all your enemies" (2 Sam 7:11) understood in terms of universal dominion granted to the king.

Psalm 2 emphasizes the filial relationship between the Davidic king and the Lord (v. 7; 2 Sam 7:14) and the promise of his rule over the nations (vv. 8–9; 2 Sam 7:10–11a).[148] This is asserted in the context of the rebellion of the vassals against YHWH and his king (vv. 1–3).[149] The king's proclamation of his divine adoption is a claim on the Davidic promise that God will defeat his enemies. Psalm 18 stresses the triumph of the king over his enemies as an evidence of God's steadfast love to David (v. 50). Psalm 72 focuses on the justice and peace that the just rule of the Davidic king should bring about. It also stresses the promise of his dominion over the nations (vv. 8–11, 17).

Psalm 110 is packed with exegetical difficulties that have probably elicited more discussions and hypotheses than any other Psalm.[150] It is clear, however, that the psalm stresses the Davidic promise of God's defeat of the enemies on behalf of the king (vv. 1, 2, 5, 6). The most intriguing element of this psalm is v. 4 where the king is given priestly status: "You are a priest forever according to the order of Melchizedek." This passage is unique in the Hebrew Bible.[151] Priesthood was not part of the promises granted to the king in the Davidic covenant.[152] There is, however, as we will see, a tendency in the post-exilic prophets and Second Temple documents that express a hope for the restoration of Israel to closely associate the offices of the king and the high priest.

---

148 For an analysis of Ps 2 in the context of ANE royal rituals see Eckart Otto, "The Judean Legitimation of Royal Rulers in Its Ancient Near Eastern Contexts," in *Psalms and Liturgy*, ed. Dirk J. Human and Cas J. A. Vos, JSOTSup 410 (T&T Clark, 2004), 131–139.

149 Psalm 2:1–3 is similar in form to vassal accusations in the Amarna letters. Scott R. A. Starbuck, *Court Oracles in the Psalms: The So-Called Royal Psalms in Their Ancient Near Eastern Context*, SBLDS 172 (Society of Biblical Literature, 1999), 162.

150 Ibid., 142. This discussion is probably incited, at least in part, by the frequent use of Ps 110 in the NT.

151 D. J. Dumbrell has noted that by assigning the king a priestly role, the person on the throne now embodies "the values which the Sinai covenant required of the nation as a whole" (*Covenant and Creation*, 152).

152 There are some indications, however, that David may have been considered in some sense a king-priest or to have exercised some priestly functions (Eugene H. Merrill, "Royal Priesthood: An Old Testament Messianic Motif," *BSac* 150 [1993]: 50–61).

The Pre-exilic Prophets and the Davidic Covenant

Amos

Amos is probably the first prophet to refer to the Davidic covenant: "On that day I will raise up the booth of David that is fallen, and repair its breaches, and raise up its ruins, and rebuild it as in the days of old" (Amos 9:11).[153] The meaning depends on the referent of the phrase "the booth of David."

A number of scholars believe that the phrase refers to Jerusalem and, thus, the oracle concerns its restoration after its destruction in 586 BCE.[154] The language in this passage is similar to that of the restoration of Jerusalem in other places (e.g., Isa 58:12). In addition, it is argued that the term סֻכָּה "booth" is not used of a kingdom or dynasty, but is used of Jerusalem in Isa 1:8.[155]

Most recent scholars, however, see here a reference to the Davidic dynasty.[156] Vocabulary and expressions in Amos 9:11–12 parallel those of 2 Sam 7. For example, the expressions "*I will raise up* the fallen booth of David" (אָקִים; Amos 9:11a, emphasis mine) and "I will ... re*build* [the booth of David]" (וּבְנִיתִיהָ; Amos 9:11b, emphasis mine) remind us of the expressions "*I will raise up* your descendant after you" (וַהֲקִימֹתִי; emphasis mine) in 2 Sam 7:12b and "I will *build* you a house" (אֶבְנֶה־לְּךָ; emphasis mine) in 2 Sam 7:27.[157] In Amos, David's dynasty is called a "booth" or "hut" and not a "house" because of its pre-

---

153   Amos 1:1 establishes the reigns of "King Uzziah of Judah and ... King Jeroboam son of Joash of Israel"—that is, early 8th century—as the context for his ministry.

154   Consequently, they consider that Amos 9:11–15 is a postexilic insertion (Pomykala, *The Davidic Dynasty Tradition*, 61; Gakuru, *The Davidic Covenant*, 161).

155   Kenneth E. Pomykala argues that the similar phrase "the tent (אֹהֶל) of David" in Isa 16:5 refers not to the dynasty of David but to the place where the king sits; that is, Jerusalem (*The Davidic Dynasty Tradition*, 62). Yet, others consider that the image of a "booth in the field" is a military image referring to the king in campaign, e.g., Francis I. Andersen and David Noel Freedman, *Amos: A New Translation with Introduction and Commentary*, AB 24A (Doubleday, 1989), 913–915; Thomas J. Finley, *Joel, Amos, Obadiah*, Wycliffe Exegetical Commentary (Moody, 1990), 323. Moreover, William M. Schniedewind suggests that the enigmatic expression "You shall take up Sakkuth your king" in 5:26—from the same root for booth (סֻכָּה)—is a word play on the aspirations of the Davidic dynasty (*Promise to David*, 64).

156   They consider, accordingly, that the arguments for a late dating of this passage are weak and prefer to consider the oracle as part of Amos's preaching; e.g., Shalom M. Paul, *Amos: A Commentary on the Book of Amos*, Hermeneia (Fortress, 1991), 288–289; Douglas Stuart, *Hosea–Jonah*, WBC 31 (Word, 1987), 397. Francis I. Andersen and David Noel Freedman suggest a date "shortly after the beginning of the 6th century BCE," but consider that the restoration of the Davidic kingdom is meant (*Amos*, 893; also, James L. Mays, *Amos: A Commentary*, OTL [Westminster, 1969], 163–165). For a list of authors on each side of this argument, see Gerhard F. Hasel, *Understanding the Book of Amos: Basic Issues in Current Interpretations* (Baker, 1991), 116–120.

157   Gakuru, *the Davidic Covenant*, 160.

carious condition.[158] God promises, however, to "rebuild it as in the days of old," referring to the empires of David and Solomon. Note that the nations which are the object of God's judgment have in common that they were once subjects of the Davidic empire (Amos 1:2–2:3; cf. 2 Sam 8).[159]

If this is the case, then, the passage refers to the restoration of the Davidic kingdom after the breakup of 940 BCE.[160] This restoration implies the reunification of Israel (north) and Judah (south) under the rule of a Davidic king and the restoration of a place (the Davidic empire) in which the people of Israel will dwell in security and prosper, in this way fulfilling God's plan for Israel. This interpretation will be later attested among the Qumran documents: 4Q174 I, 1–13 (4QFlor) interprets Amos 9:11, in the context of 2 Sam 7:11–14, as predicting the coming of a deliverer. As we will see, the reunification of "all Israel" will be a main concern of the prophets and kings of this time.

Hosea

Hosea 3:4–5 predicts Israel's return to God and David. This message has an eschatological character:[161]

> For the Israelites shall remain *many days* without king or prince, without sacrifice or pillar, without ephod or teraphim. Afterward the Israelites shall return and seek the LORD their God, and *David their king*; they shall come in awe to the LORD and to his goodness *in the latter days*. (Hos 3:4–5; emphasis mine)

The context makes clear that this return includes a reunification of Judah with the kingdom of the North (cf. 1:11). This will happen, however, in the "latter days" (v. 5); that is, after the "many days" (v. 4) the Israelites are without

---

158 Billy K. Smith and Frank S. Page, *Amos, Obadiah, Jonah*, NAC 19B (Broadman & Holman, 1995), 165; Schniedewind, *Promise to David*, 63–65. The term "ruins" in the phrase "I will ... raise up its ruins" may refer to the ruins of the city or to "removal from authority" (Isa 22:19). If the latter, "the Lord promised to restore those who had repudiated the authority of the Davidic king" (Smith and Page, *Amos, Obadiah, Jonah*, 166).

159 Dumbrell, *Covenant and Creation*, 154.

160 Finley, *Joel, Amos, Obadiah*, 323–324; Paul, *Amos*, 290; Smith and Page, *Amos, Obadiah, Jonah*, 165; Gary V. Smith, *Hosea, Amos, Micah*, NIVAC (Zondervan, 2001), 412; Stuart, *Hosea–Jonah*, 398.

161 Hosea claims to have delivered his message "in the days of Kings Uzziah, Jotham, Ahaz, and Hezekiah of Judah, and in the days of King Jeroboam son of Joash of Israel" (1:1); that is, in the second half of the 8th century BCE.

king or prince and without priest.¹⁶² The perspective of this passage, then, reaches far into the future and has an "unmistakable ... note of finality, not in a cessation of time, but in the achievement of a state of affairs after which no new decisive events will occur."¹⁶³

This promise implies the currency of the Davidic covenant despite Israel's unfaithfulness and is eschatological in character. It contains the elements that are part of the age of restoration: "return and blessing after deprivation; restoration of Davidic rule; reunification of North and South, etc." (cf. Lev 26; Deut 4, 30; regarding Davidic rule, Jer 30:9; Ezek 34:23–24; 37:24–25).¹⁶⁴

Micah

Micah 5:1–5 is a passage riddled with difficulties.¹⁶⁵ Yet, it seems clear that vv. 2–5a predict the rise of a new David, alluding to the promises of the Davidic covenant.¹⁶⁶

> But you, O *Bethlehem of Ephrathah*, who are one of the little clans of Judah, from you shall come forth for me one who is to rule in Israel, *whose origin is from of old*, from ancient days. Therefore he shall give them up until the time when she who is in labor has brought forth; then the rest of his kindred shall return to the people of Israel. And he shall stand and

---

162 The cessation of sacrifices (Hos 3:4) implies that priesthood would cease together with the monarchy. Hosea does not make clear, however, if priesthood is restored with the Davidic dynasty as well.

163 Francis I. Andersen and David Noel Freedman, *Hosea: A New Translation with Introduction and Commentary*, AB 24 (Doubleday, 1980), 309. The reference to the king is considered by many scholars a later interpolation; e.g., Gale A. Yee, "The Book of Hosea," *NIB* 7:232. For a brief argument for its originality, see Andersen and Freedman, *Hosea*, 307; Stuart, *Hosea–Jonah*, 67–68.

164 Stuart, *Hosea–Jonah*, 68.

165 Micah claims to have delivered his message "in the days of Kings Jotham, Ahaz, and Hezekiah of Judah" (1:1); that is, in the second half of the 8th century BCE.
Francis I. Andersen and David Noel Freedman summarize appropriately the difficulties of this passage: For the interpretation of "the whole unit, much depends on establishing the connotation of some familiar words. Does *ṣā·ʿîr'* refer to the insignificance of Bethlehem or to the fact that David was youngest in the family (*qāṭān* in 1 Samuel 16; cf. Ps 151)? Does *yēṣē'* (verse 2bA) refer to birth or to a military expedition? And what is the meaning of the cognate *môṣā'ōt* in the next colon? What is the meaning of 'he will give them' in v. 2a? Who is the speaker, referred to by *lî*, 'to (or for) me,' in v. 1aB? Yahweh? And, in general, are the verb forms future or past tense? The answers to all these questions are interdependent, but where to begin?" (*Micah: A New Translation with Introduction and Commentary*, AB 24E [Doubleday, 2000], 470–477).

166 Ibid., 471; Kenneth L. Barker and Waylon Bailey, *Micah, Nahum, Habakkuk, Zephaniah*, NAC 20 (Broadman & Holman, 1998), 97–98; James Limburg, *Hosea–Micah*, IBC (John Knox, 1988), 188; Daniel J. Simundson, "Micah," *NIB* 7:570–571; Smith, *Hosea, Amos, Micah*, 524.

feed his flock in the strength of the LORD, in the majesty of the *name* of the LORD his God. And they shall live secure, for now *he shall be great* to the ends of the earth; and he shall be *the one of peace*. (Mic 5:2–5a; emphasis mine)

This passage promises a new ruler who will come from Bethlehem of Ephrathah, the city of Boaz, Jesse, and David of the tribe of Judah (Ruth 4:11; 1 Sam 16:1; 17:2). This probably refers to the fact that he comes from the Davidic line in fulfillment of God's promise to David: "Your house and your kingdom shall be made sure forever before me" (2 Sam 7:16).[167]

Other elements of the Davidic covenant are present in the context. The new David will "stand and feed his flock … in the majesty of the name of the Lord" (v. 4).[168] This expression implies a magnification of David's deliverance. David delivered the people by defeating Goliath "in the name of the Lord" (1 Sam 17:45); but the new David "in the *majesty* of the name of the Lord" (emphasis mine).[169] As a result "he shall be great to the ends of the earth" (Mic 5:4; cf. Isa 24:14). (Note that in the Psalms the Davidic king is often promised a dominion to the "ends of the earth" [e.g., Pss 2:8; 72:8].) This implies the fulfillment of God's promise to David: "I will make you a great name" and "cut off all your enemies from before you" (2 Sam 7:9). Finally, as a result of the defeat of his enemies (vv. 5b–6), the new David will be "the one of peace" (Mic 5:5a).[170]

---

167 Andersen and Freedman, *Micah*, 467. I do not agree with Kenneth E. Pomykala's claim: "What is clear, however, is that this new ruler will not emanate from the davidic line currently in power in Jerusalem. Consequently, some kind of genealogical break with the currently ruling royal line is envisioned, thus indicating a tradition here that is in opposition to the dynastic promise found in 2 Sam 7:11–16 and Psalm 89." His argument is that this new ruler is promised in contrast to the present king now under siege (Mic 5:1). Thus, the promised ruler's origin from Bethlehem Ephrathah is contrasted with the current Davidic line in Jerusalem. His argument is not convincing, however. Even if this passage intends a contrast between the current Davidic ruler from Jerusalem and a new ruler from Bethlehem, this does not necessarily mean the rejection of David's progeny; in fact, the mention of Bethlehem suggests the new ruler's identification with David's ancestry. Moreover, the prominence of Davidic traditions in Israel's monarchical thinking would require a clearer language for the rejection of the Davidic line than what we have in Mic 5:1–5. On the other hand, as we have seen above, the election of a new Davidic ruler from a different Davidic line than the one on the throne (which is what Pomykala seems to suggest) does not oppose the dynastic promises of 2 Sam 7 or Ps 89.

168 This phrase is intriguing because it is an intensification of the formula "in the name of the Lord" which indicates that the person is working under the authority of God (e.g., the priest and the prophet; Deut 18:5, 20; 1 Chr 21:19; 33:18).

169 Barker and Bailey, *Micah, Nahum, Habakkuk, Zephaniah*, 100.

170 Francis I. Andersen and David Noel Freedman consider that this is "a play on the name 'Solomon.'" They conclude that the "new king will combine the qualities and achievements of David and Solomon" (*Micah*, 476).

This is an allusion to God's promise to David, "I will give you rest from all your enemies" (2 Sam 7:11) which results in peace for the nation.

Isaiah

The book of Isaiah includes several references to the Davidic covenant that focus on the idea of an era of justice and righteousness brought about by a new righteous king.[171]

> *Isaiah 9:6–7.* For a child has been born for us, *a son* given to us; authority rests upon his shoulders; and *he is named* Wonderful Counselor, Mighty God, Everlasting Father, Prince of Peace. His authority shall grow continually, and there shall be *endless peace* for the *throne of David* and his kingdom. He will establish and uphold it with justice and with righteousness from this time onward and *forevermore*. The zeal of the LORD of hosts will do this. (Isa 9:6–7; emphasis mine)

There is a debate whether this passage refers to a future king or is a poem that celebrates the birth or an accession to the throne of a contemporary ruler.[172] Whatever the case may be, the poem evidences the currency of Davidic traditions in the theological thinking of Isaiah's time.

It is clear that God's promise to David that he would establish his throne forever (2 Sam 7:13) is either requested or asserted in this passage. The names/

---

171 Isa 11:1–10; 16:5; 32:1–8; 55:3. Isaiah 33:17 probably refers to God as king, not the Davidic king. The Davidic covenant is implied in other passages (e.g., Isa 37:35; 38:5); however, these will not be analyzed. (Though not explicitly Davidic, the idea of a righteous ruler is expressed also in Isa 32:1–8.) Isaiah claims to have delivered his messages "in the days of Uzziah, Jotham, Ahaz, and Hezekiah, kings of Judah" (1:1); that is, in the second half of the 8th century BCE.

172 The passage is mostly considered a poem celebrating an actual historical event; e.g., Joseph Blenkinsopp, *Isaiah 1–39: A New Translation with Introduction and Commentary*, AB 19 (Doubleday, 2000), 247–251; John D. W. Watts, *Isaiah 1–33*, WBC 24 (Word, 1985), 135–137. Others consider that the titles given to this child-king are too divine to be applied to an earthly ruler; therefore, the child "is clearly an eschatological figure, the Messiah," as referred to in the Targum (John N. Oswalt, *The Book of Isaiah: Chapters 1–39*, NICOT [Eerdmans, 1986], 245; Dumbrell, *Covenant and Creation*, 158). The Targum paraphrases this passage: "Messiah in whose days peace will be great for us" (quoted in Blenkinsopp, *Isaiah 1–39*, 250). Yet, the passage seems to refer to a present event. Note that both the Hebrew (MT) and Greek forms (LXX) of Isa 9:6 refer to the past, not to the future. The position of Christopher R. Seitz seems more convincing to me. This "child … born for us" is Emmanuel who was promised in Isa 7:14. In this sense the poem is both historical and prophetical in nature. The birth of Emmanuel referred to in 9:6 is the fulfillment sign God announced to Ahaz in 7:10–14. Yet, this historical event has eschatological overtones (*Isaiah 1–39*, IBC [John Knox, 1993], 84–87).

titles given to this child/king—"Marvelous Counselor," "God Warrior,"[173] "Eternal Father," and "Prince of Peace"—and the outcome of his government as "justice and ... righteousness from this time onwards and for evermore" imply the fulfillment of other elements of the Davidic covenant: "I will make for you a great name" (1 Sam 9:7) and "I will appoint a place for my people Israel and will plant them, so that they may live in their own place, and *be disturbed no more*; and evildoers shall afflict them no more" (v. 10; emphasis mine).

Both the names and the everlasting era of justice and righteousness suggest that the fulfillment in view has eschatological overtones.[174]

Isaiah 11:1–10. This passage focuses—again—on the idea of an era of justice and righteousness brought about by a promised righteous Davidic king:[175]

> A shoot shall come out from the stump of Jesse, and a branch shall grow out of his roots. The spirit of the LORD shall rest on him, the spirit of wisdom and understanding, the spirit of counsel and might, the spirit of knowledge and the fear of the LORD. His delight shall be in the fear of the LORD. He shall not judge by what his eyes see, or decide by what his ears hear; but with righteousness he shall judge the poor, and decide with equity for the meek of the earth; he shall strike the earth with the rod of his mouth, and with the breath of his lips he shall kill the wicked. Righteousness shall be the belt around his waist, and faithfulness the belt around his loins.
>
> The wolf shall live with the lamb, the leopard shall lie down with the kid, the calf and the lion and the fatling together, and a little child shall lead them. The cow and the bear shall graze, their young shall lie down together; and the lion shall eat straw like the ox. The nursing child shall play over the hole of the asp, and the weaned child shall put its hand on the adder's den. They will not hurt or destroy on all my holy mountain; for the earth will be full of the knowledge of the LORD as the waters cover the sea.

---

173 This is a better translation of the Hebrew אֵל גִּבּוֹר than NRSV's rendition "Mighty God." See Blenkinsopp, *Isaiah 1–39*, 250.

174 John N. Oswalt and Joseph Blenkinsopp argue that these names/titles do not reflect the actual practice of giving throne names to the Israelite king following the custom of the Egyptian ritual (*The Book of Isaiah*, 245–7; Blenkinsopp, *Isaiah 1–39*, 248–9). They disagree, however, in what this reflects. Blenkinsopp argues that the "language imitates the oratorical and declamatory style of the court and corresponds to aspiration rather than political and military reality" (*Isaiah 1–39*, 249). He does not give, however, further examples of this practice.

175 See, Gene M. Tucker, "The Book of Isaiah 1–39," *NIB* 6:140; Watts, *Isaiah 1–33*, 173.

On that day the root of Jesse shall stand as a signal to the peoples; the nations shall inquire of him, and his dwelling shall be glorious. (Isa 11:1–10)

This new era of righteousness is possible because of God's empowerment of the promised ruler with his spirit (vv. 2–3). The gift of the Spirit involves three pairs of abilities: (1) "wisdom and understanding"—probably, practical wisdom and fairness in judicial and political matters, (2) "counsel and might"—authority and judgment in the diplomatic and military realms, and (3) "knowledge and fear of the Lord"—the ideal king's piety.[176] Thus, the Davidic king will be able to rule righteously by judging the poor and destroying the wicked, as described in vv. 3–5.[177]

The context suggests, however, that the terms "poor" and the "wicked" refer beyond the internal life of Israel to its international circumstances. Verses 10–16 make clear that God intends to bring back the remnant of Israel from the Assyrian captivity (esp. v. 16), which implies the vindication of Israel in the international scene.[178] The passage implies, as well, the restoration of the Davidic empire. Verse 13 refers to the reunification of Ephraim and Judah; arguably, under the rule of the son of David (v. 10). Once restored, Israel will re-conquer the territory that once comprised the Davidic empire: Philistia, Edom, Moab, and Ammon (v. 14; cf. 2 Sam 8).

Finally, it is important not to miss the subtle parallel between vv. 3–5 and 6–9. In the latter, peace is understood as the absence of depredation in the relationships between the strong and the weak in the zoological realm: the wolf and the lamb, the leopard and the kid, the calf and the lion, etc., will live in harmony (vv. 6–9). Scholars disagree regarding the meaning of these verses. Some see here a figurative expression of a world without harm and danger.[179] Christopher R. Seitz has suggested that these animals stand for nations and that this passage describes international peace.[180] Finally, others see here the promise of the fundamental transformation of the natural order. Probably the latter is meant because in the prophetical writings the "political order and the order of creation as a whole can be and sometimes are connected and in-

---

176 See Tucker, "The Book of Isaiah 1–39," 6:141; Watts, *Isaiah 1–33*, 171–172. The promised king's righteousness probably stands in contrast to the spiritual bankruptcy of contemporary rulers (Oswalt, *Isaiah 1–39*, 279–280).

177 Note that the idea of the end of violence had already been introduced in Isa 9:7.

178 Cf. the book of Judges, in which deliverers "judged" in the sense of gaining justice for Israel on the international level (Roy E. Gane, *Heroes imperfectos de Dios*, trans. Félix Cortés A. [APIA, 1995], 32).

179 E.g., Oswalt, *Isaiah 1–39*, 283–284.

180 Seitz, *Isaiah 1–39*, 106–107.

terdependent."[181] This same idea appears in Hos 2:18; Ezek 34:23–31; and 37:26 where God makes a "covenant of peace" so that the "wild animals from the land" will not attack Israel anymore.[182]

Isaiah introduces in this passage a very important element: The righteous rule of the king results in the spread of the knowledge of the Lord so that the piety of the king will be replicated in the inhabitants of the land. Verse 9 affirms: "For the earth will be full of the knowledge of the LORD as the waters cover the sea." Thus, Isaiah includes in the fulfillment of the Davidic covenant the promise of the infusion of God's spirit on all creation (cf. vv. 2, 9). In Jeremiah and Ezekiel, this promise constitutes the essence of the "new covenant" (Jer 31:31–34; Ezek 36:25–28). As I will show below, both Jeremiah and Ezekiel relate the new covenant with the eschatological fulfillment of the Davidic covenant.

Isaiah 55:3. This is a difficult and intriguing passage that will require both a longer treatment and my conclusions to remain tentative. Isaiah 55:3 is the only reference to David in chs. 40–66.[183]

> Incline your ear, and come to me; listen, so that you may live. I will make with you *an everlasting covenant*, my steadfast, sure love for *David*. (Isa 55:3; emphasis mine)

---

181   Blenkinsopp, *Isaiah 1–39*, 263–265. Also, Watts, *Isaiah 1–33*, 175.

182   Though not in Davidic terms, the same expectation of righteousness is expressed in connection with the hope of fertility in the land in Ps 72 (esp. v. 16).

183   See Joseph Blenkinsopp, *Isaiah 40–55: A New Translation with Introduction and Commentary*, AB 19A (Doubleday, 2002), 370.

A majority of commentators consider that chs. 40–55 were written not by Isaiah ben Amoz (1:1) of Jerusalem—considered the author of most of chs. 1–39 and referred to as First Isaiah—in the 8th and 7th centuries BCE, but by another person—commonly referred to as Second Isaiah—in Babylon during the 540s BCE (Richard J. Clifford, "Second Isaiah," *ABD* 3:493; Tremper Longman III and Raymond B. Dillard, *An Introduction to the Old Testament*, 2d ed. [Zondervan, 2006], 303–306; Schniedewind, *Promise to David*, 114).

I have decided, however, to analyze this text in the context of the Davidic passages of Isaiah in the first section of the book because, as far as we know, this is the way in which early Jewish interpreters would have read it. I argued above (54, n. 4) that early Jewish interpreters viewed these writings as a "flat text"; that is, they viewed these writings as a unity and were either ignorant or oblivious of a redaction history. For example, Isaiah is cited by name about 20 times in the New Testament. These citations include references to both halves of Isaiah. John 12:38–41 is especially instructive in this regard. It cites Isa 6:10 and 53:1 in consecutive verses, identifying both as belonging to Isaiah. Acts 8:28 informs us also that the Ethiopian was reading in the book of Isaiah what we have now in 53:7–8. Sirach 48:24–25 (2nd century BCE) assigns the second half of the book to Isaiah the prophet in the time of Hezekiah (8th BCE). Finally, Qumran documents do not show awareness of any kind of break after chap. 39. See Longman III and Dillard, *An Introduction to the Old Testament*, 307.

This passage contains an invitation to the people of Israel to enter into a new covenant with God.[184] He offers them the promises made to David.[185] Like the Davidic, this covenant is both perpetual (2 Sam 23:5) and unconditional. The people are invited to *buy* something that is freely given, that is to say, it involves a transaction for something of value, but the price is free! (vv. 1–2).[186] Thus, unlike the Mosaic covenant, this offer is not contingent on their moral performance. All this leads us to an important question: What is the relationship between the Davidic covenant and this new covenant Isa 55:3 proposes? Should they be linked, or is Isaiah's new covenant intended to replace the Davidic promises?

Otto Eissfeldt has argued that Isa 55:3–4 reinterprets the Davidic covenant as a response to the calamity of 586 BCE. After suggesting a close relationship between Isa 55:3–4 and Ps 89, he argued that the former responded to the heartbreaking complaint of the latter ("You have renounced the covenant with your servant; you have defiled his crown in the dust" [Ps 89:39]) by transferring the promises of the Davidic covenant from David's descendants to the nation of Israel.[187] In other words, "Second Isaiah announced that God's plan had not been defeated by the ruin of the royal house of David but rather that the everlasting covenant was now to be expanded beyond the privileged elite to embrace the entire community of those obedient to God's word."[188] As a result, "the promise is no longer tied to David and assigned to the past, but is renewed as a present, active reality [in the community of faith]."[189] In a word, it is understood that "Second Isaiah [chs. 40–55] has transformed the Davidic convenantal [*sic*] tradition."[190] This view is commonly referred to as

---

184 Note that in this passage the imperatives are plural as well as both pronouns "you."

185 God's offer to the people of his "steadfast [הַנֶּאֱמָנִים], sure love [חַסְדֵי] for David" (Isa 55:3) recalls 2 Sam 7:15–16 where God offers David: "I will not take my steadfast love [חַסְדִּי] from him" and "your kingdom shall be made sure [נֶאְמַן] forever" (Schniedewind, *Promise to David*, 115).

186 Blenkinsopp, *Isaiah 40–55*, 369.

187 Otto Eissfeldt, "The Promises of Grace to David in Isaiah 55:1–5," in *Israel's Prophetic Heritage*, ed. Bernhard W. Anderson and Walter Harrelson (Harper, 1962), 196–207.

188 Paul D. Hanson, *Isaiah 40–66*, IBC (John Knox, 1995), 179. He does not mean that Isa 55:3 should be understood in terms of an inclusion; namely, that the covenant had been "expanded … to embrace the entire community" in addition to David's house. On the contrary, he means a transference of the Davidic promises from the Davidic house to the nation: "The vocation of being 'a witness to the people' assigned to David *would now pass* to the entire community of those faithful to God" (Hanson, *Isaiah 40–66*, 179, emphasis mine).

189 See Brevard S. Childs, *Isaiah*, OTL (Westminster John Knox, 2001), 435.

190 Ibid., 436. Note that this reinterpretation of the Davidic covenant would mean, in fact, a reinterpretation of Isa 1–39 as well. As we noted above, those chapters express the belief that the Davidic covenant is eternal and God intends to fulfill it in the future. Brevard S. Childs expresses this view in clear terms: "Second Isaiah [chs. 40–55] has incorporated the messianic

the democratization of the Davidic covenant and is widely accepted among commentators of Isaiah.[191]

The view that Isa 55:3-4 has reinterpreted the Davidic covenant is problematic, however.[192] First, we find no criticism of the royal house in this passage.[193] Second, the reference to the Davidic covenant in God's promise to the people in Isa 55:3 makes sense neither as a transference nor as an analogy. By definition, a covenant—much less an eternal one—is not transferable. The transference of the Davidic promises from David's children to the entire community implies that the Davidic covenant has been invalidated. On the other hand, the reference to the Davidic covenant as an analogy would show itself inconsequent. God's promise to the people—"I will make with you an everlasting covenant, [*just like*] my steadfast, sure love for David"—is difficult to understand if the author, the audience, or both were convinced that God's covenant with David was, after all, neither "everlasting" nor "steadfast."[194]

Finally, I believe that the view that Isa 55:3 transfers God's "steadfast, sure love for David" to the nation misses the point that that promise was intended for the people from the very beginning! God made clear in 2 Sam 7 that he intended to benefit the nation through his promise to David:

> Thus says the LORD of hosts: I took *you* from the pasture, from following the sheep to be prince over *my people Israel*; and I have been with *you* wherever *you* went, and have cut off all *your* enemies from before you; and I will make for *you* a great name, like the name of the great ones of the earth. And I will appoint a place for *my people Israel* and will plant *them*, so that *they* may live in *their* own place, and be disturbed no more; and evildoers shall afflict *them* no more, as formerly, from the time that I appointed judges over *my people Israel.* (vv. 8b–11a; emphasis mine)

Thus, if the original intention of the Davidic covenant was to benefit the people through the promises made to David and Isa 55:3 offers the nation God's

---

promise to David in First Isaiah [chs. 1–39] into a new version of God's future rule" (*Isaiah*, 437; cf., John N. Oswalt, *The Book of Isaiah: Chapters 40–66*, NICOT [Eerdmans, 1998], 439, n. 26).

191 See references in Pomykala, *The Davidic Dynasty Tradition*, 39, n. 118.

192 In fact, Eissfeldt's suggestion is probably irrelevant for this study because it assumes an exilic date for Isaiah which—as I mentioned above—early Jewish readers didn't contemplate as far as we know.

193 Christopher R. Seitz, "The Book of Isaiah 40–66," *NIB* 6:482.

194 Blenkinsopp, *Isaiah 40–55*, 370. Moreover, a reinterpretation of the Davidic covenant was unnecessary. Other writings did not reinterpret the Davidic covenant in their reaction to the calamity of 586 BCE, but held fast to it as a source of hope; e.g., Jer 23:5–8; 33:14–26; 30:8–9; Ezek 34:23–24; 37:24–28; Hag 2:20–23; Zech 3:8; 6:12 (Blenkinsopp, *Isaiah 40–55*, 370).

"steadfast, sure love for David," is it not more logical to see here a reference to the fulfillment of the Davidic covenant instead of its abrogation?

I agree, then, with those who see in this passage not the modification or abrogation of the Davidic covenant, but its confirmation in behalf of the nation. Isaiah 55:3 seems to provide the answer to the theological dilemma that would result from the nation's violation of the Mosaic covenant and their banishment from the land.[195] John N. Oswalt expresses this with clarity:

> How was the nation to continue in covenant with God [after they had broken the Mosaic covenant and gone into exile]? Through the life and work of the Davidic Messiah. God had made irrevocable promises to David. As he kept those promises, Israel could participate in the blessings. As David experienced God's *certain mercies* (utterly dependable acts of covenant love— *ḥesed*), so Israel could participate in them as well.[196]

I believe this reading makes better sense of the context of the passage; especially, the difficult issue of the change in number and tense in Isa 55:3–5.

God's generous promise to the nation in vv. 1–3 will be accomplished through an individual—note the singular number in vv. 4–5.[197] Verse 4 refers to the historical David—note the past tense in this passage—who was a "leader and commander of peoples."[198] Verse 5 refers to a future individual for whom David serves as a type. Just as David was "a leader and commander for the peoples," this future individual will "call nations ... and nations ... shall run" to him (v. 6). Who is he? Probably this individual is the servant of the Lord.[199] He accomplishes what was announced of the promised Davidic king in chs. 1–39. The basic function of the promised Davidic king was to bring justice to earth (Isa 9:7; 11:4–5, 10; 16:5) which is what the servant of the Lord accomplishes in Isa 40–55 (cf. 42:1–4; 49:1–13). The closest parallel to the language of vv. 4–5 is Isa 11:10: "On that day the root of Jesse shall stand as a

---

195 Regarding Isa 55:3–5 as a response to this theological dilemma, see also Schniedewind, *Promise to David*, 115–8.

196 Oswalt, *Isaiah 40–66*, 438.

197 Recent commentators consider that v. 5 refers to Israel, the nation. It is clear that vv. 1–3 refer to Israel because of the plural number in vv. 1–3. Verses 4 and 5, however, change to a singular number. I believe this change in number indicates a change in referent (Ibid., 439).

198 Note the past tense in v. 4. It is interesting that in this way David foreshadows the mission of the servant of the Lord who is to be a witness to the nations of the glory and power of God (Isa 43:10, 12; 44:8). See ibid., 439–40. Others disagree. For example, John D. Watts considers that vv. 4–5 refer to a person, specifically Darius (*Isaiah 1–33*, 246).

199 Isa 40–55 makes a clear connection between the servant of the Lord and God's covenant with the people; e.g., 42:6 (alluded to in Luke 2:32; Acts 26:23); 49:8. See Seitz, "Isaiah 40–66," 6:482.

signal to the peoples; the nations shall inquire of him, and his dwelling shall be glorious."[200]

Thus, Isa 55:3 announces that, as impossible as that may seem, God still intends to fulfill his promise to David:

> For as the rain and the snow come down from heaven, and do not return there until they have watered the earth, making it bring forth and sprout, giving seed to the sower and bread to the eater, so shall my word be that goes out from my mouth; it shall not return to me empty, but it shall accomplish that which I purpose, and succeed in the thing for which I sent it. (Isa 55:10–11)[201]

In summary, in Isa 55:3 God offers to renew his covenantal relationship with the nation after they broke the Mosaic covenant and were banished from the land. This renewal was in fact the fulfillment of God's "steadfast, sure love for David." God promises to raise an unidentified individual, similar to David, to be a "witness ..., a leader and commander" to glorify the nation. Thus, this passage is a theological precursor to the promise of a new covenant in Jer 31:31–34 and Ezek 36:25–28.[202]

---

200 Blenkinsopp, *Isaiah 40–55*, 370. Joseph Blenkinsopp, however, remains unsure about whether Isa 40–55 expect the restoration of the Davidic dynasty. Yet, he does not embrace O. Eissfeldt's view that the Davidic covenant has been democratized either.

201 William M. Schniedewind interprets this passage (Isa 55:10–11) in the context of v. 3 as promising the fulfillment of the Davidic covenant of 2 Sam 7. (Though he holds the view that Isa 55:3 democratizes the Davidic covenant, something which I believe is not warranted in the text, *Promise to David*, 115–6.)

Early Christians interpreted this passage as a promise of the fulfillment of the Davidic covenant in the future. Acts 13:34 quotes Isa 55:3 to identify Jesus as the heir of the promises made to David. C. K. Barrett paraphrases this passage in the following way: "I will fulfil for you (that is, for the Christian generation) the holy and sure (promises made to) David, by raising up, by not allowing to see corruption, (not David himself but) his greater descendant, who was himself holy," (*A Critical and Exegetical Commentary on the Acts of the Apostles*, ICC [T&T Clark, 1994], 1:647–648; see also, Joseph A. Fitzmyer, *The Acts of the Apostles: A New Translation with Introduction and Commentary*, AB 31 [Doubleday, 1998], 517).

202 Note that the promise of forgiveness is also prominent in this passage (vv. 6–7) as in Jeremiah and Ezekiel. Also, the promise of the spiritual reformation of the nation—essential to the promises of a new covenant in Jeremiah and Ezekiel as well—is made in the context of this passage: "All your children shall be taught by the Lord" (Isa 54:13). Isaiah stands close, also, to the thinking of Dan 9:25–27 where the covenant is confirmed for the many through the Messiah prince!

Exilic Interpretation of the Davidic Covenant

Jeremiah

Jeremiah's references to the future of the Davidic dynasty present a challenge to the interpreter. Some passages seem to betray an anti-monarchical attitude and assume the end of the Davidic dynasty (e.g., chs. 22, 40–41); yet others express the hope of its restoration (e.g., 23:5–8; 30:8–9). In view of these apparently contradictory statements, Kenneth E. Pomykala has concluded that, "on the whole ... the book of Jeremiah points to a variety of viewpoints concerning the fate of the Davidic royal house prior to and after the fall of the [*sic*] Jerusalem in 586 BCE."[203]

I believe, however, that these statements are not as contradictory as they first seem, but should be understood as focusing on the conditional and unconditional dimensions of the Davidic covenant.

Jeremiah 22: Judgment on the Davidic kings. Jeremiah 22:1–9 contains an exhortation to the "king of Judah, sitting on the throne of David" (and his officials) to "administer justice and righteousness."[204]

The Davidic covenant had the purpose of giving "rest" to the people and that "evildoers ... afflict them no more" (2 Sam 7:10–11). The king, however, had not only failed to administer justice to the oppressed but had himself done "violence to the alien, the orphan, and the widow, ... [and had] shed innocent blood" (Jer 22:3). God, therefore, exhorts the king to correct his ways. If the king repents, God promises: "Through the gates of this house shall enter kings who sit on the throne of David" (v. 4; cf. 17:25). (The house here refers more probably to the palace.) If he failed to reform his government, God's ultimatum was clear: "I swear by myself, says the LORD, that this house shall become a desolation" (22:5).

This passage focuses clearly on the conditional dimension of the Davidic covenant. The participation of the king in the promises of the Davidic covenant was contingent on his faithfulness to God and his administration of justice to the people. Yet, God's promise to David, "Your house and your kingdom shall be made sure forever before me," were not conditioned on the faithfulness of the individual king (see 2 Sam 7:14–16). It is not David's house (the dynasty) that God will make desolate, but the "house" of the king addressed

---

203 Pomykala, *The Davidic Dynasty Tradition*, 34.
204 Note that the "you" in vv. 4–5 is plural referring to the officials in addition to the king.

(palace and dynasty).[205] God will punish the king and his house. None of his children will sit anymore on the throne of David (Jer 22:4); yet, God will fulfill his promises through a different line. (This becomes clear in 23:1–8.[206])

Similarly, Jer 22:24–30 registers God's rejection of Coniah (=Jehoiachin), son of Jehoiakim, and his descendants to be rulers of Judah: "Thus says the LORD: Record this man as childless, a man who shall not succeed in his days; for none of his offspring shall succeed in sitting on the throne of David, and ruling again in Judah" (v. 30; cf. 36:30). This does not mean, however, the invalidation of the Davidic covenant but only the rejection of Coniah and his house (posterity) from the Davidic royal line. In fact, Jeremiah proceeds in 23:5–6 to predict the raising of a new Davidic king:

> The days are surely coming, says the LORD, when I will raise up for David a righteous Branch, and he shall reign as king and deal wisely, and shall execute justice and righteousness in the land. In his days Judah will be saved and Israel will live in safety. And this is the name by which he will be called: "The LORD is our righteousness."[207]

Evidently, the promised king will come from a different genealogical line, but still an offspring of David.[208] Coniah's (Jehoiachin) participation in the prom-

---

205 Contra Pomykala, *The Davidic Dynasty Tradition*, 21–22. See, William L. Holladay, *Jeremiah 1: A Commentary on the Book of the Prophet Jeremiah Chapters 1–25*, ed. Paul D. Hanson, Hermeneia (Fortress, 1986), 582. Some consider "house" to refer only to the palace; e.g., Terence E. Fretheim, *Jeremiah*, Smyth & Helwys Bible Commentary (Smyth & Helwys, 2002), 317. Others see here a reference to the destruction of the temple; e.g., Peter C. Craigie, Page H. Kelley, and Joel F. Drinkard, Jr., *Jeremiah 1–25*, WBC 26 (Word, 1991), 298. Others are unsure; e.g., Robert P. Carroll, *Jeremiah: A Commentary*, OTL (Westminster, 1986), 417–418.

206 This section (21:11–23:8) contains oracles addressed to several kings (Johoahaz, Jehoiakim, and Jehoiachin [Coniah]), Patrick D. Miller, "The Book of Jeremiah," *NIB* 6:739. Towards the end of the section, 23:1–4, Jeremiah refers "to the shepherds who destroy and scatter the sheep." This provides a collective summary of the indictments to the evil kings previously mentioned. Then the section closes with the promise that God "will raise up shepherds over them [Israel] who will shepherd them"; especially a "righteous Branch" for David who "shall execute justice and righteousness in the land" (vv. 5–8).

207 The name is probably a wordplay on Zedekiah ("Yahweh is righteousness"), the name of the last king of Judah. This name was given him by Nebuchadnezzar at the time of his appointment (2 Kgs 24:17). "The point would be, in effect, God is our righteous king, not Zedekiah" (Fretheim, *Jeremiah*, 327; Craigie, Kelley, and Drinkard, *Jeremiah 1–25*, 329; Holladay, *Jeremiah 1*, 629). Others see here a positive reference to him, though (Carroll, *Jeremiah*, 446–447).

208 Miller, *NIB* 6:744–5; Pomykala, *The Davidic Dynasty Tradition*, 31.
Jeremiah 40–41 is another passage that seems to assume the end of the Davidic dynasty. It narrates the assassination of Gedaliah son of Ahikam—governor of the land appointed by Nebuchadnezzar in 586 BCE (2 Kgs 25:22; Jer 40:5)—by Ishmael son of Nethaniah. Of the latter it is said explicitly that he was "of the royal family" (41:1; cf. 2 Kgs 25:25) and his actions are presented "in the worst possible terms" (Pomykala, *The Davidic Dynasty Tradition*, 33). The mo-

ises of the Davidic covenant is conditional. The Davidic covenant promises themselves, however, are not conditional.

Jeremiah 23: Hope for a new Davidic king. Other passages in Jeremiah confirm a hope for the restoration of the Davidic monarchy.

> The days are surely coming, says the LORD, when I will raise up for David a righteous Branch, and he shall reign as king and deal wisely, and shall execute justice and righteousness in the land. In his days Judah will be saved and Israel will live in safety. And this is the name by which he will be called: "The LORD is our righteousness" (Jer 23:5–6).
>
> On that day, says the LORD of hosts, I will break the yoke from off his neck, and I will burst his bonds, and strangers shall no more make a servant of him. But they shall serve the LORD their God and David their king, whom I will raise up for them (Jer 30:8–9).
>
> The days are surely coming, says the LORD, when I will fulfill the promise I made to the house of Israel and the house of Judah. In those days and at that time I will cause a righteous Branch to spring up for David; and he shall execute justice and righteousness in the land. In those days Judah will be saved and Jerusalem will live in safety. And this is the name by which it will be called: "The LORD is our righteousness." For thus says the LORD: David shall never lack a man to sit on the throne of the house of Israel, and the levitical priests shall never lack a man in my presence to offer burnt offerings, to make grain offerings, and to make sacrifices for all time. (Jer 33:14–18)

The latter passage is most interesting. It promises the restoration of the Davidic dynasty on the basis of the perpetual nature of God's promises to David.[209] What makes this passage fascinating is the fact that the fulfillment of

---

tivation of the murder seems clearly an attempt to reinstate Davidic leadership on the land; however, it ends in utter failure. (Presumably, Ishmael had sought to recover the royal princesses—who were entrusted to Gedaliah by Nebuzaradan [41:10]—as an assertion of his royal claim [cf. 2 Sam 16:21], Robert Althann, "Gedaliah [Person]," *ABD* 2:924.) Ishmael is persecuted by Johanan son of Kareah and the people are "glad" to see the latter and abandon Ishmael immediately. Ishmael, though, is able to escape with eight men and takes refuge with the Ammonites. Nothing else is heard of him.

This account assumes God's judgment and abandonment of the Davidic kings in 586 BCE announced in chs. 21–23; yet, it is not explicit regarding the revoking of the Davidic covenant promise.

209   Jeremiah 33:14–26 belongs to Jeremiah's "Book of Restoration" (chs. 30–33), also known as "(Little) Book of Comfort" or "Book of Consolation." It is possible that this book was once contained in a separate scroll (30:2). The first section of the book consists of chs.

the Davidic covenant is intimately related to the fulfillments of two other covenants: the perpetual covenant of priesthood with the Levites (cf. v. 19:22) and the "new covenant with the house of Israel and the house of Judah" (Jer 31:31–34; cf. 32:38–41).[210]

Jeremiah 33:14–26. Jeremiah 33:14–26 does not appear in the LXX version of Jeremiah.[211] The complex textual transmission history of Jeremiah makes it difficult to reach hard conclusions regarding the originality, integrity, and relationship of Jer 33:14–26 to its context (30:1–33:26).[212] The discovery of 4QJerc

---

30–31 which was later expanded in a second section (chs. 32–33). In its present form, it is a "book within a book." For an introduction to its form and the current state of research, see J. Andrew Dearman, *Jeremiah and Lamentations*, NIVAC (Zondervan, 2002), 267–271; Jack R. Lundbom, *Jeremiah 21–36: A New Translation with Introduction and Commentary*, AB 21B (Doubleday, 2004), 368–378.

210 Note the parallels between 33:19–22 and 31:35–37.

211 I am using the text of Joseph Ziegler, ed., *Ieremias, Baruch, Threni, Epistula Ieremiae*, Septuaginta: Vetus Testamentum Graecum 15 (Vandenhoeck & Ruprecht, 1957). See also, Sven Soderlund, *The Greek Text of Jeremiah: A Revised Hypothesis*, JSOTSup 47 (JSOT Press, 1985), 97–152. Jeremiah 33:14–26 "is the largest single block of MT material missing in the LXX," Johan Lust, "The Diverse Text Forms of Jeremiah and History Writing with Jer 33 as a Text Case," *JNSL* 20, no. 1 (1994): 37.

Many scholars have concluded, mainly because of their omission in the LXX, that vv. 14–26 are a later insertion, probably introduced in the text at the beginning of the 3rd century BCE (Lust, "The Diverse Text Forms of Jeremiah," 31–48; Geoffrey H. Parke-Taylor, *The Formation of the Book of Jeremiah: Doublets and Recurring Phrases*, SBLMS 51 [Society of Biblical Literature, 2000], 55–79. Cf. William McKane, *A Critical and Exegetical Commentary on Jeremiah: Commentary on Jeremiah XXVI–LII*, ICC [T&T Clark, 1996], 2:clxii–clxiv). They are also lacking in 4QJerb and 4QJerd (Schniedewind, *Promise to David*, 135). Additional arguments include (1) oddities in the Hebrew style, (2) repetition of material found earlier in the book (i.e., 23:5–6), and (3) insertion of ideas considered alien to Jeremiah (i.e., a covenant with the Davidic royal line and especially with the Levitical priesthood, Lust, "The Diverse Text Forms of Jeremiah," 31–48. Also, Lundbom, *Jeremiah 21–36*, 537–538; Parke-Taylor, *The Formation of the Book of Jeremiah*, 55–62).

Jack R. Lundbom disagrees, however. After evaluating the evidence, he concludes that the arguments are "less than conclusive." According to him, arguments brought by William L. Holladay regarding the careless Hebrew style of this passage "will not stand scrutiny, … [Holladay's examples] are unconvincing." Doublets are found throughout the book. They "are no more indicative of a late date here than elsewhere." Hopes regarding the restoration of the monarchy are present elsewhere (esp. 23:5–6, "which is widely taken to be Jeremianic"). The restoration of the priesthood is assumed in 31:14; "which can be dated originally to the reform years of Josiah," Lundbom, *Jeremiah 21–36*, 537–538. He points out that vv. 16–20 are extant in 4QJerc and that Theodotion included this passage in his Version. He suggests that the "best explanation for the LXX omission of vv 14–26 … is that the verses were lost by (vertical) haplography," Lundbom, *Jeremiah 21–36*, 538. Sadly, this possibility is not explored either by Johan Lust ("The Diverse Text Forms of Jeremiah," 31–48) or Geoffrey H. Parke-Taylor (*The Formation of the Book of Jeremiah*, 55–60).

212 The history of the transmission of the text of Jeremiah has been the object of scholarly research more than that of any other biblical book. The LXX differs from the MT in two major ways: (1) the LXX is substantially shorter—around one seventh of the MT is not repre-

makes clear, however, that Jer 33:14–26, as it appears in the MT, follows closely a textual tradition attested in Second Temple Judaism.[213] I will refer here to the heart of this passage:

> The word of the LORD came to Jeremiah: Thus says the LORD: If any of you could break my covenant with the day and my covenant with the night, so that day and night would not come at their appointed time, only then could *my covenant with my servant David* be broken, so that he would not have a son to reign on his throne, and *my covenant with my ministers the Levites*. Just as the host of heaven cannot be numbered and the sands of the sea cannot be measured, so I will increase the offspring of my servant David, and the Levites who minister to me. (Jer 33:19–22; emphasis mine)

God announces that he will restore Davidic rulership over Israel as well as the ministry of the Levitical priesthood. This is the first place in the Hebrew Bible where the restoration of Davidic kingship is related to the restoration of the priesthood. The promise is based on the eternal nature of both covenants.

Now, what is this covenant with "my ministers the Levites"? (cf. Neh 13:29; Mal 2:4, 8).[214] This is a covenant similar in nature to the Davidic. It refers to the grant of priesthood as a "perpetual ordinance" to Aaron and his sons (cf.

---

sented in the LXX—and (2) has a different arrangement of the material. At least four theories have been advanced to explain the differences: (1) the "abbreviation" theory, (2) the "editorial" theory (Jeremiah himself produced two different edition of his writings), (3) the "expansion" theory, and (4) the "mediating" theory (it is not correct to generalize one text as preceding the other; instead, each passage must be evaluated on its own merits, Soderlund, *The Greek Text of Jeremiah*, 11–3; Lust, "The Diverse Text Forms of Jeremiah," 34–5).

The Qumran discoveries, which produced some fragments from Jeremiah (esp. 4QJerb), reopened the question. The research of J. Gerald Janzen, who supported the "expansion" theory, has dominated the field in recent years (*Studies in the Text of Jeremiah*, HSM 6 [Harvard University Press, 1973]; see also, Lust, "The Diverse Text Forms of Jeremiah," 31–48). According to this view, the LXX version is the best witness to the original text of Jeremiah. Sven Soderlund, however, has challenged his findings and supported the "mediating" theory (*The Greek Text of Jeremiah*, 193–248).

213 4QJerc has been dated to the latter part of the 1st century BCE (James C. VanderKam and Peter W. Flint, *The Meaning of the Dead Sea Scrolls: Their Significance for Understanding the Bible, Judaism, Jesus, and Christianity* [HarperSanFrancisco, 2002], 134). For the *editio princeps* of 4QJerc, see Emanuel Tov, "4QJerc (4Q72)," in *Tradition of the Text: Studies Offered to Dominique Barthélemy in Celebration of His 70th Birthday*, ed. Gerard J. Norton and Stephen Pisano, OBO 109 (Vandenhoeck & Ruprecht, 1991), 249–276.

214 For a brief study of God's covenant with the Levites, see the excursus "Priests and Levites in Critical Perspective" in Richard A. Taylor and E. Ray Clendenen, *Haggai, Malachi*, NAC 21A (Broadman & Holman, 2004), 293–306. For a brief Historical-Critical analysis of the topic, see "Comment 3: Selectivity in the Descent of the Aaronide Priesthood" in Baruch A. Levine, *Numbers 21–36: A New Translation with Introduction and Commentary*, AB 4A (Doubleday, 2000), 297–300.

Sir 45:23–26).[215] As a result of their faithfulness in the midst of Israel's idolatry with the golden calf, God granted the priesthood to the Levites (Exod 32:26–29; Deut 10:8; 33:8–11), specifically to Aaron and his descendants (Exod 28–29). In Exod 29:9, 28–29 it is stated that "the priesthood shall be theirs [Aaron's and his sons'] by a perpetual ordinance."[216] Though a covenant is not explicitly mentioned, it seems to be implied (cf. Neh 13:29; Mal 2:1–9).[217] Soon after Aaron's death and on occasion of the apostasy with the Baal of Peor, God granted the priesthood to Phinehas (Aaron's grandson) as a "*covenant of peace[,] ... a covenant of perpetual priesthood*" because of his zeal for the Lord (Num 25:11–13; emphasis mine).

This covenant with Phinehas seems to be a further delimitation of God's "perpetual ordinance" of priesthood to the Levites indicating that "high priesthood will flow through his [i.e., Phinehas'] line of descendants."[218] Later on, however, the enthronement of Solomon would involve a change in the line of the high priesthood. Solomon replaced Abiathar with Zadok (1 Kgs 2:26–27, 35) in fulfillment of the curse upon Eli's house (1 Sam 2:29–35). He was the "faithful priest" who would walk before the Lord's anointed "forever" (v. 35).[219] Accordingly, Ezekiel prophesied that Zadokite priests, who are characterized by their faithfulness (44:15; 48:11), will minister in the future temple (Ezek 40:46; 43:19). On the other hand, non-Zadokite priests will be demoted (44:5–16).

Malachi 2:1–9 is the last reference to God's covenant of priesthood with Levi in the OT,[220] which Malachi identifies with God's covenant with Phinehas by referring to it as a "covenant of life and well-being [peace]" (cf. Num 25:12).[221] As I will show later, this covenant—and its relationship to the David-

---

215 The phrase הַלְוִיִּם הַכֹּהֲנִים, "the Levitical priests," refers to the priesthood of Aaron and his descendants. The expression appears in Deut 17:9, 18; 18:1; 24:8; 27:9; Josh 3:3; 8:33, as well as Ezek 43:19; 44:15 (Fretheim, *Jeremiah*, 478–479; Lundbom, *Jeremiah 21–36*, 541).

216 This was in fact a reversal of the curse Jacob placed upon them to divide and scatter them among Israel (Gen 49:5–7; cf. Josh 19:9).

217 Taylor and Clendenen, *Haggai, Malachi*, 298–300. Note that Mal 2:1–9 (esp. v. 5) identifies the covenant of Levi with the "covenant of peace" of Phinehas; see Levine, *Numbers 21–36*, 299.

218 Gane, *Leviticus, Numbers*, 719.

219 Dearman, *Jeremiah and Lamentations*, 304, n. 31. This did not imply the failure of God's covenant with Phinehas. Zadok was a descendant of Phinehas, too; see Ezra 7:1–7; cf. 1 Chr 24:1–5.

220 Although not in the Hebrew Bible which ends with 2 Chronicles.

221 Contra David L. Petersen, *Zechariah 9–14 and Malachi*, OTL (Westminster John Knox, 1995), 189–190. See, Levine, *Numbers 21–36*, 299. He notes several allusions to God's covenant with Phinehas in Mal 2. The most evident is the reference to the covenant with Levi as a covenant of peace (v. 5), a clear reference to Num 25:12.

Malachi's reference to Phinehas's covenant, however, comes as a warning to the priests that if they continue to fail in obeying God and honoring him, he will revoke his covenant with

ic covenant—will continue to have importance in Second Temple Judaism (e.g., Sir 45:23–25).

There are also allusions to the Noahic and Abrahamic covenants in this passage. God asserts that the Davidic and Levitical covenants are as firm and enduring as God's covenant with the day and night, and as sure as the fact that the "host of heaven cannot be numbered and the sands of the sea cannot be measured" (Jer 33:19–22). Psalm 89:36–37 compared the endurance of the Davidic covenant with the perpetuity of the sun and the moon; yet, this passage refers back to God's covenant with Noah after the flood: "As long as the earth endures, seedtime and harvest, cold and heat, summer and winter, *day and night, shall not cease*" (Gen 8:22; emphasis mine). The comparison with the "host of heaven" and the "sands of the sea" is an allusion to the Abrahamic covenant.[222] Thus, the passage (Jer 33:14–26) refers to the covenants with David and Phinehas and alludes to the covenants with Noah and Abraham. These four covenants have in common that they are unconditional and that they are a grant of God to an individual because of his exceptional loyalty.[223]

The covenants with David and Phinehas play a special function in Jeremiah's "Book of Restoration" (Jer 30–33). They explain *how* the restoration of the house of Israel and the promise of a new covenant is accomplished (cf. 31:31–34). The restoration includes the rebuilding of the palace (30:18; 33:4–6) and a new ruler (30:21). Jeremiah 33:14–26 explains that the ruler will be a Son of David (cf. 30:9). The restoration implies the reconstruction of the temple (33:11; cf. 30:19; 31:4, 6–7, 14). Jeremiah 33:14–26 explains that Levitical priests will minister there.[224]

I believe, however, that their most important function is theological. The covenants with David and Phinehas provide the theological basis upon which

---

them. God declares: "If you will not listen, if you will not lay it to heart to give glory to my name ... I will rebuke your offspring, and spread dung on your faces, the dung of your offerings, and I will put you out of my presence" (vv. 2–3). This warning amounts to the revocation of the covenant with them and their descendants by making them unfit to carry out the priestly service and carrying them out as the dung of their sacrifices is carried out. See Andrew E. Hill, *Malachi*, AB 25D (Doubleday, 1998), 200–203; Petersen, *Zechariah 9–14 and Malachi*, 189; David W. Baker, *Joel, Obadiah, Malachi*, NIVAC (Zondervan, 2006), 240–243. The purpose of the warning, however, was to make the covenant with Levi to stand (Mal 2:4). The decision about the future of the covenant, then, depends on the Levites.

222 "Look toward heaven and count the stars, if you are able to count them" and "I will surely ... make your offspring as the sand of the sea, which cannot be counted because of their number" (Gen 15:5; 32:12, respectively; cf. 22:17; 26:4); see Fretheim, *Jeremiah*, 479; Lundbom, *Jeremiah 21–36*, 544.

223 See my discussion above (page 72) regarding the unconditional nature of the Davidic covenant.

224 Carroll, *Jeremiah*, 638–639; Gerald L. Keown, Pamela J. Scalise, and Thomas G. Smothers, *Jeremiah 26–52*, WBC 27 (Word, 1995), 173.

the promise of a new covenant with Israel is offered. They explain the *why* of the new covenant. Note the inter-textual relationship between Jer 31:31–37 and 33:14–26 as shown in Table 3.

Note that the new covenant (31:31–34) is based on the fact that God maintains the created order: "Thus says the lord, who gives the sun for light by day and the fixed order of the moon and the stars for light by night, who stirs up the sea so that its waves roar" (v. 35). Accordingly, vv. 36–37 explain that the new covenant will be as permanent as the created order.

On the other hand, Jer 33:19–22 asserts that the covenants with David and Phinehas cannot be broken because the created order cannot be broken ("my covenant with the day and my covenant with the night," v. 20). The implication is clear: He who maintains the created order guarantees as well the covenants with David and Phinehas. Neither can be invalidated. Thus, it is God's faithfulness to his covenant with David and Phinehas (33:14–26) that makes possible—even necessary—the creation of a new covenant with the house of Israel (31:31–37) which comprises God's plan for the fulfillment of his promise to David.

Jer 31:31–37	*Jer 33:14–26*
31–34: The new covenant is offered.	14–18: The covenants with David and Phinehas are confirmed.
35–37: "Thus says the LORD, who gives *the sun for light by day and the fixed order of the moon and the stars for light by night*, who stirs up the sea so that its waves roar—the LORD of hosts is his name: If this fixed order were ever to cease from my presence, says the LORD, then also the offspring of Israel would cease to be a nation before me forever. Thus says the LORD: *If the heavens above can be measured, and the foundations of the earth below can be explored,* then I will reject all the offspring of Israel because of all they have done, says the LORD."	19–22: "The word of the LORD came to Jeremiah: Thus says the LORD: *If any of you could break my covenant with the day and my covenant with the night, so that day and night would not come at their appointed time,* only then could my covenant with my servant David be broken, so that he would not have a son to reign on his throne, and my covenant with my ministers the Levites. *Just as the host of heaven cannot be numbered and the sands of the sea cannot be measured,* so I will increase the offspring of my servant David, and the Levites who minister to me."

Table 3. The New Covenant and the Covenants with David and Phinehas in Jeremiah

Ezekiel

Ezekiel also shows interest in the promise of a Davidic figure in the future:

> My servant David shall be king over them; and they shall all have one shepherd. They shall follow my ordinances and be careful to observe my statutes. They shall live in the land that I gave to my servant Jacob, in which your ancestors lived; they and their children and their children's children shall live there forever; and my servant *David shall be their prince forever*. I will make a covenant of peace with them; it shall be *an everlasting covenant* with them; and I will bless them and multiply them, and will set my sanctuary among them forevermore. My dwelling place shall be with them; and I will be their God, and they shall be my people. Then the nations shall know that I the LORD sanctify Israel, when *my sanctuary* is among them forevermore. (37:24–28; emphasis mine)

This passage is an anthology of the restoration promises presented in chs. 34–36 and brings them to a fitting conclusion.[225] Nevertheless, more than a conclusion, this passage functions as a hinge on which Ezekiel's message of hope turns.

Several ideas of chs. 34–36 climax in these verses. God reunites Israel and Judah as one nation under "one shepherd," and transforms them so that they may be faithful to his statutes, restores them to the land he had promised their ancestors, provides them a ruler forever, renews the covenant with them forever, and promises to set his sanctuary in their midst.[226] Therefore, this passage closes the section (chs. 34–37) with the prospect of a "renewed Israel's living at peace within their own land" (37:26).[227] This is also, on the other hand, the precondition to the final onslaught of the forces of evil in chs. 38–39 and God's decisive triumph over them which finally establishes the conditions necessary for the temple-building plans of chs. 40–48.[228] Therefore, the promise of an eschatological David in Ezek 37:24–28 concludes the message of restoration for the nation of Israel and sets the stage for God's ultimate victory over his enemies and the building of his temple among his people.

What interests me is the reference to "My servant David" as a future ruler over Israel (Ezek 34:23–24; cf. Hos 3:5; Jer 30:9). The question that immediately comes to mind is this: Will this future "David" be from the line of David in

---

[225] Daniel I. Block, *The Book of Ezekiel: Chapters 25–48*, NICOT (Eerdmans, 1998), 408; Moshe Greenberg, *Ezekiel 21–37: A New Translation with Introduction and Commentary*, AB 22A (Doubleday, 1997), 758.

[226] See Iain M. Duguid, *Ezekiel*, NIVAC (Zondervan, 1999), 435–437.

[227] Ibid., 437.

[228] Likewise, the construction of the temple is possible only after God has given David (and Solomon) rest from his enemies (2 Sam 7; cf. Deut 12:10–11). Ibid.

fulfillment of the Davidic covenant or does "David" serve here only as a typological figure?

A few scholars have suggested a third possibility: This passage promises the resurrection of David to rule over Israel. They stress the apparently obvious meaning of the Hebrew expression וַהֲקִמֹתִי עֲלֵיהֶם "I will raise over them" (34:23; cf. LXX καὶ ἀναστήσω ἐπ᾽ αὐτοὺς "I will raise over them"). That this expression refers to the resurrection of David is unlikely, however, because the same expression is used "for the raising up of judges (Ju 2:16) 'deliverers' (Ju 3:9), prophets (Jer 29:15; cf. also Deut 18:18) and kings (1 Kgs 14:14)" throughout the OT without referring to a resurrection from death.[229]

Walther Eichrodt argues that the phrase "my servant David" (34:23; cf. 37:24) should be understood as "my servant of the family of David." He understands this passage as promising a line of rulers established forever in the context of the Davidic covenant.[230] (Similarly, Jer 23:4 promises: וַהֲקִמֹתִי עֲלֵיהֶם רֹעִים "I will raise up shepherds over them" which clearly refers to a Davidic dynasty of rulers [cf. v. 5].)

This agrees with Ezek 17:22–24 where the continuation of David's line on the throne is promised. This passage is an appendix to the allegory of the eagles (vv. 1–21) which refers to the fortune of the last two kings of Judah: Jehoiachin and Zedekiah.[231] The allegory explains how Zedekiah will not escape punishment because of his breaking of the covenant with the king of Babylon who "planted" him as king instead of Jehoiachin: "As I live, I will surely return upon his head my oath that he despised, and my covenant that he broke" (v. 19). Yet, God announces in vv. 22–24 that he himself will take a new "sprig" and will "plant" it "on the mountain height of Israel," referring to the restoration of kingship to David (vv. 22–23; cf. Isa 11:1; Jer 23:5; 33:15; Zech 3:8; 6:12).[232]

Further evidence is found in Ezek 37:25 where it is promised that "my servant David shall be their prince forever [לְעוֹלָם]." It is difficult to conceive that this means a king who will live forever; rather, probably a king whose

---

229 Walther Zimmerli, *Ezekiel 2: A Commentary on the Book of the Prophet Ezekiel Chapters 25–48*, ed. Paul D. Hanson and Leonard Jay Greenspoon, trans. James D. Martin, Hermeneia (Fortress, 1983), 219. Also, Walther Eichrodt, *Ezekiel: A Commentary*, OTL (Westminster, 1970), 476; Pomykala, *The Davidic Dynasty Tradition*, 27.

230 Eichrodt, *Ezekiel*, 476.

231 Daniel I. Block, *The Book of Ezekiel: Chapters 1–24*, NICOT (Eerdmans, 1997), 548–553; Pomykala, *The Davidic Dynasty Tradition*, 25–26; Walther Zimmerli, *Ezekiel 1: A Commentary on the Book of the Prophet Ezekiel Chapters 1–24*, ed. Frank Moore Cross, Klaus Baltzer, and Leonard Jay Greenspoon, trans. Ronald E. Clements, Hermeneia (Fortress, 1979), 359–361.

232 "There is a deliberate insistence on the inconspicuousness of the shoot chosen by Yahweh so as to display the miracle by Yahweh," Eichrodt, *Ezekiel*, 228. Note that the shoot is described in v. 22 as a "tender one." This is not, however, only a prediction of the restoration of the Davidic line but also a promise of its universal impact (v. 24, Zimmerli, *Ezekiel 1*, 367–368).

dynasty will rule forever.[233] Note that in the previous phrase (37:25) it is stated that "[the people] and their children and their children's children shall live there [in the land] forever [עַד־עוֹלָם]."

It seems logical to conclude, then, that just as the people will live forever in the land through their descendants, David, likewise, will "be their prince forever" through his descendants, even though this is not explicitly stated. This is, in fact, what God promised to David in 2 Sam 7. Here, however, more is said than merely that the line of David will be re-established, though this is implied. What is emphasized is that, more than being a mere descendant of David, the "future king ... will be the moral (and physical?) duplicate of the David idealized by late biblical writers."[234]

Other elements of the Davidic covenant can be discerned in the passage. The nation is restored to their "land" (Ezek 37:25; cf. 2 Sam 7:10) and God promises to set his "sanctuary" among them forever (Ezek 37:26–27; cf. 2 Sam 7:13).

Yet, more important is the relationship between the restoration of Davidic rule and the promised covenant in Ezek 36:22–28. The relationship is clear. There (Ezek 36), God promises to restore the house of Israel to their land (vv. 22–24), cleanse them (v. 25), give them a "new heart" (v. 26), that is a "new spirit" (i.e., God's spirit) within them so that they will "follow ... [his] statutes [חֹק] and be careful to observe ... [his] ordinances [מִשְׁפָּט]" (v. 27), and make a covenant with them ("you shall be my people, and I will be your God"; v. 28). The same elements are found in Ezek 37. Here God promises to restore Israel to the land (Joseph, who represents the northern tribes, and Judah; vv. 15–22, 25), cleanse them (v. 23), appoint "one shepherd" over them (v. 24ab), "make them follow ... [God's] ordinances [חֹק] and be careful to observe [God's] statutes [מִשְׁפָּט]" (v. 24c), make an "everlasting covenant with them" (v. 26ab; "I will be their God, and they shall be my people," v. 27), and "set ... [his] sanctuary among them forevermore" (v. 26d; cf. "dwelling-place," v. 27).

The parallels and relationship between chs. 36 and 37 are obvious; the differences, however, are significant. Ezekiel 36 speaks of the restoration of Israel to the land; chap. 37 explains that it involves the reunification of Joseph (northern tribes) and Judah. Ezekiel 36 promises a new covenant; chap. 37 indicates it will be an "eternal covenant." Ezekiel 36 pledges that God will put (נָתַן) his "spirit within you [pl.]"; chap. 37 expresses it as God setting (נָתַן) his "sanctuary among them." These differences suggest, however, that the pur-

---

233   Leslie C. Allen, *Ezekiel 20–48*, WBC 29 (Word, 1990), 194.
234   Greenberg, *Ezekiel 21–37*, 760.

pose of chap. 37 is to clarify the nature of the covenant promised in chap. 36 by providing further information.

The key difference between these passages is the insertion of the Davidic figure in chap. 37.[235] David is the unifying factor of the nation.[236] God's miraculous union of the "two sticks," Joseph and Judah (vv. 15–23), climaxes in the provision of "one king" over them (vv. 24–28). Chapter 37 sets in relief the great difference between the new covenant God promises and the Mosaic covenant that the nation had broken (36:16–21). The Mosaic covenant was conditional on the obedience of the people (Lev 26, Deut 28). In the new covenant God will provide the "obedience" ("I will make you follow my statutes" [36:27; 37:24]). As a result, the new covenant—like the Davidic—is "forever."

Ezekiel 37:25–28 mentions four things that God will provide that are "forever": (1) life in the land (v. 25ab), (2) a Davidic prince (v. 25c), (3) a covenant (v. 26), and (4) a sanctuary (vv. 26d–27).[237] It is important to note that these four elements can be found in 2 Sam 7. Thus, the new covenant of chap. 36 is elucidated in Davidic categories in chap. 37. Or, probably more accurately, the promised covenant of chap. 36 is interpreted as the fulfillment of the Davidic covenant in chap. 37. I believe Leslie C. Allen is right when he suggests that the Davidic dynasty functions as the guarantor of the covenant in this passage.[238]

A final note on the Davidic allusions in Ezekiel is important. Ezekiel 40–48 spells out the role of the "prince" in the program of restoration. There are no specific references in these chapters to the Davidic covenant, but readers in late Second Temple times more likely understood this "prince" as a Davidic figure since Ezek 37:25 refers to the promised Davidic ruler as "prince."[239] Cer-

---

235 Allen, *Ezekiel 20–48*, 194.
236 Zimmerli, *Ezekiel 2*, 276.
237 Ibid. עוֹלָם "forever" appears 8 times in 2 Sam 7 (vv. 13, 16 [bis], 24, 25, 26, 29 [bis], Block, *Ezekiel 25–48*, 418.
238 Allen, *Ezekiel 20–48*, 194. See also, Block, *Ezekiel 25–48*, 422–423. Walther Zimmerli concludes his analysis of this passage with a penetrating remark: "It is remarkable that in the case of the other prophet of the exile, with regard to the David promise, in spite of all the differences in the details in Is 55:3–5, one can make basically very similar observations" (*Ezekiel 2*, 279).
239 There are two positions. The first stresses the continuity between chs. 1–37 and 40–48. They consider that the Davidic king of the messianic oracles of chs. 1–37 is the same figure of chs. 40–48, though his authority has been limited to prevent the abuses of the Judean monarchy. A second view stresses the discontinuity between chs. 1–37 and 40–48. They consider that the authors of chs. 40–48 broke with the Davidic hope of the previous chapters. For the history of the question, see Jon D. Levenson, *Theology of the Program of Restoration of Ezekiel 40–48*, HSM 10 (Scholars Press for Harvard Semitic Museum, 1976), 55–74. Also, Pomykala, *The Davidic Dynasty Tradition*, 30–31.

tain privileges, obligations, and limitations are assigned to him.[240] He enjoys special access to some temple areas (44:3; 46:2, 8, 10) and an allotment of personal lands (45:7; 48:21–22). The only obligation described for him, however, is to provide offerings for sacrifice (45:16–17, 22; 46:4, 12–15). Mainly, then, he is seen as patron of the cult.[241]

The Post-Exilic Prophets and the Davidic Covenant

Haggai

Haggai 2:20–23 has no explicit reference to the Davidic covenant. Notwithstanding, it is possible that Zerubbabel is presented as foreshadowing the restoration of the Davidic line.[242]

> The word of the LORD came a second time to Haggai on the twenty-fourth day of the month: Speak to Zerubbabel, governor of Judah, saying, I am

---

240 E.g., it is explicitly stated that he cannot infringe on the land rights of others (45:8–9; 46:18).

241 Pomykala, *The Davidic Dynasty Tradition*, 30.

242 Kenneth E. Pomykala rightly points out that "there is no explicit reference to a dynastic promise, to David, or to the davidic dynasty tradition generally in these verses or elsewhere in the book of Haggai" (*The Davidic Dynasty Tradition*, 49). He is also right in pointing out that neither Haggai, nor Zechariah, Ezra, or Nehemiah explicitly mention Zerubbabel's Davidic descent (*The Davidic Dynasty Tradition*, 46). Only 1 Chr 3:16–19 refers to Zerubbabel as belonging to the line of David. Nevertheless, Pomykala considers that Zerubbabel was of non-Davidic lineage and was secondarily grafted by the Chronicler to David's line. He points out as evidence that 1 Chr 3:19 mentions that Zerubbabel was son of Pedaiah, and not of Shealtiel as the rest of the biblical record holds (*The Davidic Dynasty Tradition*, 46).

Yet, the idea that Zerubbabel was secondarily grafted into David's line is problematic. Why was he not inserted as son of Shealtiel, which was the easiest thing to do? Later tradition clearly understood Zerubbabel as belonging to the Davidic line (1 Esd 5:5; Matt 1:12–13; Luke 3:27). The NT evidence has its own problems, however. Luke considers that Zerubbabel comes through the line of Nathan (brother of Solomon; 3:27–31) and not through the line of Jeoiachin (i.e., Jeconiah or Coniah; Jer 17:24–30) and Solomon. Matthew, on the other hand, considers that Zerubbabel comes through the line of Jeoiachin and Solomon (1:7–13). Eugene H. Merrill has tried to reconcile these differences, conjecturing that Zerubbabel is a descendant of Jehoiachin through one of his daughters who married Neri, a descendant of David through the line of Nathan (*An Exegetical Commentary: Haggai, Zechariah, Malachi* [Moody, 1994], 325). In any case, Zerubbabel's Davidic descent remains problematic (for the different solutions that have been given to this problem, see Gary N. Knoppers, *1 Chronicles 1–9: A New Translation with Introduction and Commentary*, AB 12 [Doubleday, 2003], 328.)

I believe, however, that Kenneth E. Pomykala has overstated his case. He fails when he discounts the Davidic implications of Haggai's reference to Zerubbabel as a "signet ring" (2:23), which is an allusion to Jer 22:24–30 (*The Davidic Dynasty Tradition*, 49). While it is true that the image of the "signet ring" can be applied to non-Davidics, the intention of the image in Hag 2:23 is a reversal of the prophecy against Jeoiachin (i.e., Jeconiah or Coniah; Jer 17:24–30). Thus, a restoration of the Davidic line seems to be in mind.

about to shake the heavens and the earth, and to overthrow the throne of kingdoms; I am about to destroy the strength of the kingdoms of the nations, and overthrow the chariots and their riders; and the horses and their riders shall fall, every one by the sword of a comrade. On that day, says the LORD of hosts, I will take you, O Zerubbabel my servant, son of Shealtiel, says the LORD, and make you like a signet ring; for I have chosen you, says the LORD of hosts.

Two things call our attention: the allusion to Jeremiah's prophecy against Jehoiachin and the eschatological framework of the oracle.

Jeremiah had prophesied against Jehoiachin (i.e., Jeconiah or Coniah), king of Judah, that none of the children who had gone with him into exile would rule in the future. God rejected him and his descendants as a "signet ring" that has been cast off (Jer 22:24–30). With his rejection and that of Zedekiah, the rule of the house of David came to an end. Yet, Haggai announces that God will take Zerubbabel, grandson of Jehoiachin (1 Chr 3:16–19), as a "signet ring" in this way reversing the prophecy of Jeremiah.[243] If Zerubbabel is a grandson of Jehoiachin, as 2 Chr 3:19 and later tradition understood him to be (Matt 1:12–13; Luke 3:27; 1 Esd 5:5), this oracle implies the restoration of the Davidic line.[244] The interesting fact, and yet puzzling, is that Zerubbabel himself is not the fulfillment of the restoration of the Davidic line to the throne. The oracle has a future reference. It will be fulfilled "on that day" (v. 23), when God shakes "the heavens and the earth" and overthrows kingdoms and armies (vv. 21–23). For now, Zerubbabel is the governor of Judah (2:21), "a

---

243 Pieter A. Verhoef, *The Books of Haggai and Malachi*, NICOT (Eerdmans, 1987), 147. Mark J. Boda claims that Jeremiah's prophecy against Jehoiachin (17:24–30) applied only to his children who went with him into exile (v. 28). Interestingly, Zerubbabel means "seed of Babel" (*Haggai, Zechariah*, NIVAC [Zondervan, 2004], 164.)

244 Note that Zerubbabel is called "my servant" (Hag 2:23), a term used throughout the Hebrew Bible to denote those whom the Lord has appointed to a particular task, but especially for David (Taylor and Clendenen, *Haggai, Malachi*, 196, n. 22). Twice David is identified by God as "my servant" in 2 Sam 7 (vv. 5, 8). David recognizes this role no less than ten times (2 Sam 7:19, 20, 21, 25, 26, 27 [bis], 28, 29 [bis] (Block, *Ezekiel 25–48*, 418).

The reference to Zerubbabel in 1 Esd 5:5 is intriguing. This passage closes the "Story of the Three Youth" (1 Esd 3:1–5:6) which has no parallel in the canonical books. This book was probably composed between 165 BCE and the middle of the 1st century CE (Josephus used it for his account of the post-exilic period, William R. Goodman, "First Book of Esdras," *ABD* 2:610). First Esdras 5:5 juxtaposes the line of Aaron through Phinehas and the line of David. Interestingly, it considers Joakim, son of Zerubbabel, a priest together with Jeshua (NRSV). Scholars believe, however, that an emendation of the text is necessary and that Joakim should be understood as son of Jeshua (so NEB, R. J. Coggins, "Commentary on 1 Esdras," *The First and Second Books of Esdras*, CBC [Cambridge University Press, 1979], 36–37). For a critical edition of the text, see Robert Hanhart, *Esdrae liber I*, Septuaginta: Vetus Testamentum Graecum 8/1 (Vandenhoeck & Ruprecht, 1974), 87.

small political player in the bureaucracy of the Persian empire."[245] Zerubbabel is here, instead, an eschatological symbol in a similar fashion to the reference to David in Hos 3:5; Jer 30:9; Ezek 34:23–24; 37:24–25.[246]

Zechariah

Zechariah 6:9–15. Probable allusions to the Davidic promises can be found in Zechariah 6:9–15.

> The word of the LORD came to me: Collect silver and gold from the exiles — from Heldai, Tobijah, and Jedaiah — who have arrived from Babylon; and go the same day to the house of Josiah son of Zephaniah. Take the silver and gold and make a crown, and set it on the head of the high priest Joshua son of Jehozadak; say to him: Thus says the LORD of hosts: Here is a man whose name is Branch: for he shall branch out in his place, and he shall build the temple of the LORD. It is he that shall build the temple of the LORD; he shall bear royal honor, and shall sit upon his throne and rule. There shall be a priest by his throne, with peaceful understanding between the two of them. And the crown shall be in the care of Heldai, Tobijah, Jedaiah, and Josiah son of Zephaniah, as a memorial in the temple of the LORD. Those who are far off shall come and help to build the temple of the LORD; and you shall know that the LORD of hosts has sent me to you. This will happen if you diligently obey the voice of the LORD your God. (Zech 6:9–15)

This is a very difficult passage, the meaning of which depends on the answer we give to a number of questions for which we have little information.[247] The questions that concern me here, however, are the following: Who is the "Branch"? Is the "Branch" a Davidic figure? When did the prophet expect the Messiah to bring about the new age?

---

245 Boda, *Haggai, Zechariah*, 164.
246 Ibid., 166–167; Carol L. Meyers and Eric M. Meyers, *Haggai, Zechariah 1–8: A New Translation with Introduction and Commentary*, AB 25B (Doubleday, 1987), 83–84; Taylor and Clendenen, *Haggai, Malachi*, 195–200; Verhoef, *The Books of Haggai and Malachi*, 148–149. Against those who see here a reference to the restoration of David's rule in Zerubbabel: e.g., W. Eugene March, "Haggai," *NIB* 7:730–731. In fact, not long after this prophecy, Zerubbabel falls into obscurity (Taylor and Clendenen, *Haggai, Malachi*, 199; Verhoef, *The Books of Haggai and Malachi*, 149).
247 For example: Who were the men who came from Babylon? Were there four or more of them? Why did they go into Josiah's house? Were there two crowns or one? Who is "Branch"? Why is Zerubbabel not mentioned? How many thrones will there be? See Ralph L. Smith, *Micah–Malachi*, WBC 32 (Word, 1984), 217–218.

Regarding the first question, the NRSV translation (quoted above) privileges the view that Joshua, the high priest, is identified here as the Branch. This would seem likely because a crown is placed on Joshua's head and the oracle predicts that "[Branch] shall bear royal honor, and shall sit upon his throne and rule" (v. 13). I believe, however, that this is not the correct reading of the passage. The function assigned to Branch in this passage is that he will build the temple. Zechariah 4:6b–10a, on the other hand, makes clear that it is Zerubbabel—not Joshua—who will build the temple. Moreover, the expression "Behold a man" is not used for direct address, but normally refers to a third party (1 Sam 9:6, 17; 2 Sam 18:26).[248] It is possible, then, that Branch denotes here not Joshua but a third person who is probably not present.[249]

Zechariah 3:6–10 is a parallel oracle that throws light on our text. This passage contains the following revelation—which is given to Joshua the high priest after he has been crowned with a "clean turban" in a vision (v. 5):[250] "If you will walk in my ways and keep my requirements, then you shall rule my house and have charge of my courts, and I will give you the right of access.... I am going to bring my servant the Branch, ... and I will remove the guilt of this land in a single day." Note that four things are promised to Joshua: future rule, right of access, a third person whom God will bring (probably Zerubbabel who will build the temple; cf. 4:6–10), and atonement for Israel.

The parallels are evident. Both passages contain a symbolic act of crowning (3:5; 6:11).[251] Zechariah 6 contains promises that had been given to Joshua in Zech 3, though in reverse order: God will bring Branch (vv. 12–13b; cf. v. 15) and rule is promised to Joshua (v. 13). Note that in both cases these promises are contingent on the faithfulness of Joshua and fellow priests to

---

248 Boda, *Haggai, Zechariah*, 339.

249 Ben C. Ollenburger, "Zechariah," *NIB* 7:787. Mark J. Boda suggests that Branch belongs to those whom God will bring from "far off" to build the temple (*Haggai, Zechariah*, 342–3). Others think that he was there and addressed but his name is not mentioned, e.g., Smith, *Micah–Malachi*, 218.

If Branch is not Joshua but a third party that God will bring, it probably does not refer to Zerubbabel either. "According to the dates in Ezra 3:8 and Zech 1:7, Joshua and Zerubbabel would have come to Judah two years earlier" (Ollenburger, "Zechariah," 787). By the time the oracle was given, according to the extant literary structure of Zechariah, the temple "was already well on the way to completion" (Smith, *Micah–Malachi*, 219). If this is the case, Zerubbabel is not Branch but acts as a type of an eschatological figure who will build an eschatological temple (cf. Zech 4:8–10; 6:12–13). Note that, in Haggai, Zerubbabel plays a similar function. He is the sign of a future fulfillment (see above section "Haggai").

250 For the royal connotations of the turban, see Meyers and Meyers, *Haggai, Zechariah 1–8*, 369–370.

251 That the crowning of Joshua in 6:9–15 is symbolic is clear from the instruction given that the crowns be kept in the temple "as a memorial" (v. 14).

God (3:7): "This will happen if you diligently obey the voice of the LORD your God" (6:15c).[252]

In Zech 3:6–10 it is clear, however, that Joshua is not Branch but a third person God will bring, though the promise is given to Joshua as it was in Zech 6.[253] I believe, then, based on the parallel with Zech 3:6–10, that in Zech 6 Joshua is not Branch but a third person God will bring.

Is the Branch a Davidic figure? The majority of scholars believe he is.[254] The oracle announces that Branch will build God's temple. This work was assigned in the Davidic covenant to the scion of David (2 Sam 7:13). Accordingly, in Zech 4:6–10 the building of the temple is assigned to Zerubbabel who belongs, most likely, to the line of David.[255] Zechariah 6:12 probably alludes to Jer 33:15: "In those days and at that time I will cause a righteous Branch to spring up [צֶמַח] for David; and he shall execute justice and righteousness in the land" (cf. 23:5).[256]

---

252 For the fact that the individuals referred to in Zech 6:10, 14 are priests, see Boda, *Haggai, Zechariah*, 336.

253 In his analysis of this text, James C. VanderKam concludes: "Joshua is invested with his splendid garments as a sign that a new age is dawning. That new age is characterized by two facts: a Davidic heir is coming, but more importantly in this context the temple cult will once more serve its function of removing guilt and atoning for sin. Zechariah 3 reminds one of Exod 40:12–13.... Harmony and security are not associated with the physical laying of the temple foundation but with resumption of the cult. Investiture of the high priest means the divine remembrance of his people and his regular communication with them" ("Joshua the High Priest," in *From Revelation to Canon: Studies in the Hebrew Bible and Second Temple Literature*, Supplements to the Journal for the Study of Judaism 62 [Brill, 2000], 175–176).

254 E.g., Elizabeth Achtemeier, *Nahum–Malachi*, IBC (John Knox, 1986), 131; Merrill, *Haggai, Zechariah, Malachi*, 197–198; Meyers and Meyers, *Haggai, Zechariah 1–8*, 369; Boda, *Haggai, Zechariah*, 338.

Kenneth E. Pomykala rejects the idea that "Branch" here is a Davidic figure. He notes that "there is nowhere an appeal to the Davidic dynastic promise." In addition, he argues that Zerubbabel was probably not a descendant of David and that צֶמַח is probably not an allusion to Jer 23:5 and 33:15 but a pun on Zerubbabel's name. Zerubbabel means "Seed of Babylon" and צֶמַח may be a pun referring to the "growth" the Lord will bring (cf. Isa 4:2). He observes, also, that in Jer 23:5 and 33:15 the צֶמַח springs up "for David," but that explanation is absent in Zechariah (Pomykala, *The Davidic Dynasty Tradition*, 53–60). On the other hand, I have argued above that his argument for the secondary development of Zerubbabel's Davidic ancestry in 1 Chr 3:19 is unconvincing. Later tradition understood Zerubbabel as a scion of David (Matt 1:12–13; Luke 3:27; 1 Esd 5:5).

Pomykala concedes, however, that allusions to such traditions are possible. He concludes that if "Branch" were to be understood as a Davidic figure, the passage would imply a transformation of the Davidic promise. His function is to "build the temple" and he would rule alongside a priestly figure (*The Davidic Dynasty Tradition*, 60). I do not agree that this is a transformation of the Davidic traditions, because the building of the temple was something expected from the son of David according to 2 Sam 7:13. It is, instead, a change of emphasis on his role in view of the events of 586 BCE.

255 Regarding the Davidic ancestry of Zerubbabel, see page 100, n. 242.

256 Cf. "Here is a man whose name is Branch: for he shall branch out [צֶמַח] in his place, and he shall build the temple of the Lord" (Zech 6:12).

It is intriguing, however, that Branch is expected to rule alongside a priestly figure (Zech 6:12–13). Zechariah 6 refers to the coronation of two individuals: Joshua the priest and Branch (vv. 11, 14).²⁵⁷ They will both sit on their thrones and there will be a "peaceful understanding between them" (v. 13). This is in fact a development in the interpretation of the Davidic covenant which did not foresee a diarchic rule (2 Sam 7:16). The idea of diarchic rule had been suggested already by Jeremiah (see above section "Jeremiah" on page 88). In fact, just as Branch in Zech 6:9–15 is probably an allusion to Jer 33:15, the prediction of the diarchic rule of a Davidic and a Levitical (Zadokic) figure is probably an allusion to Jer 33:17–18: "For thus says the LORD: David shall never lack a man to sit on the throne of the house of Israel, and the levitical priests shall never lack a man in my presence to offer burnt offerings, to make grain offerings, and to make sacrifices for all time."²⁵⁸ Thus, Zech 6 probably points to the restoration of the Levitical and Davidic lines that Jer 33:17–18 had predicted.

When did Zechariah expect the messiah to bring about the new age?²⁵⁹ The crowning of Joshua in 6:9–15 is an "acted out" oracle that conveys a message to the people.²⁶⁰ (Similarly, Joshua and his colleagues in Zech 3 "are an omen of things to come" [v. 8].) They were an acted out parable of what God intended to do in the future. The question is: What is the meaning of this

---

257 עֲטָרוֹת is plural ("crowns"; cf. the LXX στεφάνους "crowns"); therefore, two different persons are meant. This coincides with the idea of "two anointed ones" in 4:14, e.g., Julia M. O'Brien, *Nahum, Habakkuk, Zephaniah, Haggai, Zechariah, Malachi*, Abingdon Old Testament Commentaries (Abingdon, 2004), 205; Smith, *Micah–Malachi*, 218; Merrill, *Haggai, Zechariah, Malachi*, 195; Meyers and Meyers, *Zechariah 1–8*, 349–354; Boda, *Haggai, Zechariah*, 335.

Others observe, however, that in Job 31:36 עֲטָרוֹת refers to one crown and that the singular verb תִּהְיֶה in v. 14 implicates that only one crown is meant (Pomykala, *The Davidic Dynasty Tradition*, 58. Also, Achtemeier, *Nahum–Malachi*, 132).

258 Boda, *Haggai, Zechariah*, 335. "It is significant that Josiah [Zech 6:10] is associated with Zephaniah, the name of the deputy priest to Seraiah (2 Kgs 25:18), and that Joshua is associated with Jehozadak, who was Seraiah's son (1 Chr 5:39–40 [6:13–14]). Both Zephaniah and Seraiah were executed by Nebuchadnezzar (2 Kgs 25:18–21). Here their descendants collaborate with Zechariah in Joshua's coronation. Afterwards, Zechariah delivers an oracle to Joshua (v. 12)" (Ollenburger, "Zechariah," 787). If this is so, the case for the restoration of the Levitical and Davidic lines is stronger. For some caveats regarding the priestly identity of these figures, see Merrill, *Haggai, Zechariah, Malachi*, 194–195. For a more comprehensive analysis of the identity of these individuals, see Meyers and Meyers, *Zechariah 1–8*, 340–345.

259 Ralph L. Smith identifies the central issue in similar terms: "The real issue is: Did Zechariah identify Zerubbabel as the messianic king and expect the new age to begin in his lifetime? Or did he say that the time is coming when the branch or shoot of David (the Messiah) will come and be both king and priest?" (*Micah–Malachi*, 218).

260 Similar sign-acts can be found in Isa 20:2–4; Jer 27:2–7; Ezek 12:1–12. See, Ibid., 216–7. "Sign-acts usually comprise three segments: exhortation, execution, and explanation. This passage contains an exhortation (vv. 10–14) and explanation (v. 15) but omits the middle segment" (Boda, *Haggai, Zechariah*, 335).

sign-act? Should it be interpreted in the sense that Joshua's and Zerubbabel's leadership and the temple they are constructing prefigure the diarchic rule of a kingly and priestly figure and the construction of a more glorious temple in the future?[261] Or, did Zechariah understand the rise of Joshua and Zerubbabel as leaders in Judah to be a fulfillment of the Davidic promises (confirmed by Jeremiah, Isaiah, and Ezekiel) and the beginning of a new age for Israel?[262] I am not sure.[263] I tentatively suggest that both views are not mutually exclusive.[264] The consecration of Joshua as high priest marks the renewal of the Levitical priesthood and evidences that the fulfillment of Jeremiah's and Ezekiel's prophecies had been set in motion (Jer 33:19–22; Ezek 44:15; 48:11).[265] Yet, it is not clear whether Zechariah himself believed that Joshua, Zerubbabel, and the temple they were building exhausted the prophecies that had been made for the restoration of Israel.[266] Most likely, later readers believed that they did not exhaust them and, therefore, a future fulfillment was still due.[267]

Zechariah 12:2–13:1. An explicit reference to the "house of David" is found in Zech 12:2–13:1. This passage describes a battle for Jerusalem in which God

---

261 E.g., Achtemeier, *Nahum–Malachi*, 131; Smith, *Micah–Malachi*, 219; Merrill, *Haggai, Zechariah, Malachi*, 200; Meyers and Meyers, *Zechariah 1–8*, 356–7.

262 O'Brien, *Nahum, Habakkuk, Zephaniah, Haggai, Zechariah, Malachi*, 206; Boda, *Haggai, Zechariah*, 336–343.

263 For example, it is not entirely clear whether two crowns (Joshua's and Branch's) are stored in the temple as "a memorial" or only Branch's crown (Zech 6:14). If both are, a future reference beyond Joshua and Zerubbabel is meant. The Hebrew construction is awkward. The noun translated as "crown" is plural in the MT (וְהָעֲטָרֹת "and the crowns") but the verb is singular (תִּהְיֶה "it will be"). The LXX translates both in the singular, δὲ στέφανος ἔσται, "and the crown will be" (Joseph Ziegler, ed., *Duodecim prophetae*, Septuaginta: Vetus Testamentum Graecum 12 [Vandenhoeck & Ruprecht, 1943], 303).

264 Meyers and Meyers, *Zechariah 1–8*, 374.

265 Elizabeth Achtemeier makes the same point regarding sign-acts oracles, which she calls prophetic symbolic actions: "That which is spoken or symbolized [in these prophetic symbolic actions] is at the same time set in motion, and it works its effects in Israel's history until it is fully fulfilled" (*Nahum–Malachi*, 130).

266 The present literary structure of Zechariah suggests that Zechariah himself considered Joshua and Zerubbabel and their temple symbols of the future. Ben C. Ollenburger claims that "according to the dates in Ezra 3:8 and Zech 1:7, Joshua and Zerubbabel would have come to Judah two years earlier" ("Zechariah," 787). By the time the oracle was given, according to the extant literary structure of Zechariah, the temple "was already well on the way to completion" (Smith, *Micah–Malachi*, 219). If this is the case, the idea is given that another more glorious temple and rule is meant by these sign-oracles.

267 It is interesting that neither Joshua nor Zerubbabel is mentioned in Ezra's report of the Temple's completion, but only the "elders of the Jews" (Ezra 6:14–15). Ollenburger, "Zechariah," 788. The silence regarding Zerubbabel in later Jewish writings is very telling in this respect as well. Qumran literature witnesses to the fact that at least that sector of Israel continued to expect the messiah from Levi and David, and the construction of a legitimate temple. See section "Dead Sea Scrolls" below on page 123.

obtains the victory over the enemies (12:2–9). As a result of this victory, the inhabitants of Jerusalem are exalted, but especially the house of David (v. 8). After this, God "pours out a spirit of compassion and supplication on the house of David and the inhabitants of Jerusalem, so that, when they look on the one whom they have pierced, they shall mourn for him, as one weeps over a firstborn" (v. 10). Though all Jerusalem experiences this conversion, four families are especially mentioned: the families of David, Nathan, Levi, and Shimei (12:10–14). Finally, the passage closes with God's purification of "the house of David and the inhabitants of Jerusalem" from their "sin and impurity" by opening a fountain for them (13:1; cf. vv. 2–6).[268]

It is clear from this passage that the house of David has a leading role in future Jerusalem. Zechariah 12:8 says that David's house will be exalted above the rest of the inhabitants of Jerusalem. The house of David is also singularized as recipient of God's "spirit of compassion and supplication" (12:10) and cleansing (13:1). As a result, many interpreters see behind this passage the assumption of a promise of rule given to David's dynasty forever (2 Sam 7).[269] The mention of the houses of David, Nathan, Levi, and Shimei is understood as a reference to royal and priestly lines which undergo a process of conversion and purification as it is made evident in their mourning (cf. 13:2–6).[270]

Kenneth E. Pomykala disagrees. He argues that the phrase "[house of David] must be understood within the social structures of post-exilic Judah."[271] Whereas this phrase denoted in pre-exilic Judah the rule, king, court, or dynasty of the Davidic family, he considers that its meaning changed in post-exilic Judah.[272] "House of David" denotes now one of several social units or clans.[273] The houses of Nathan, Levi, and Shimei mentioned in vv. 12–14 would

---

268 Note the similarity with Ezek 36:25.
269 E.g., Achtemeier, *Nahum–Malachi*, 160–162; Merrill, *Haggai, Zechariah, Malachi*, 323–326; Carol L. Meyers and Eric M. Meyers, *Zechariah 9–14: A New Translation with Introduction and Commentary*, AB 25C (Doubleday, 1993), 329–330, 357–9; O'Brien, *Nahum, Habakkuk, Zephaniah, Haggai, Zechariah, Malachi*, 262; Smith, *Micah–Malachi*, 277.
270 Achtemeier, *Nahum–Malachi*, 162; Boda, *Haggai, Zechariah*, 488–489; Merrill, *Haggai, Zechariah, Malachi*, 325–6; Meyers and Meyers, *Zechariah 9–14*, 359–360; O'Brien, *Nahum, Habakkuk, Zephaniah, Haggai, Zechariah, Malachi*, 265; Petersen, *Zechariah 9–14 and Malachi*, 122–123; Smith, *Micah–Malachi*, 277. Others see here royal, prophetic, priestly, and wisdom lines.
271 Pomykala, *The Davidic Dynasty Tradition*, 118–119. He follows the research of Joel Weinberg, *The Citizen-Temple Community*, trans. Daniel L. Smith-Christopher, JSOTSup 151 (JSOT Press, 1992).
272 Pomykala, *The Davidic Dynasty Tradition*, 117–118, nn. 204–207. Rule: 1 Sam 20:16; 2 Sam 3:1, 6; 1 Kgs 12:19, 20, 26; 14:8. King or court: Isa 7:2, 13; Jer 7:2. Dynasty: 1 Kgs 13:2; 1 Chr 17:24; 2 Chr 21:7; 2 Sam 7:11b. He also notes that in a couple of cases it denotes a building: 1 Sam 19:11; Isa 22:22.
273 Ibid., 118–120.

be other examples of such social units. In addition, he notes that no reference is made to the terminology and imagery associated with the Davidic dynasty tradition and that royal ideology is absent in this passage.[274] He concludes: "There is no evidence that messianic or royalist hopes were fixed upon the house of David. No individual figure is in view—whether royal or messianic."[275] Therefore, though it is clear that the "house of David ... will retain its prominence in the ideal future when all of Jerusalem is glorified" (12:8), this does not imply a "divine, royal, or messianic status" because it is not focused on an individual, but on "a clan consisting of hundreds or thousands of members."[276]

Pomykala's view depends on the new understanding of the term "house of David" as a clan and not as a line of rulers. Many scholars remain unconvinced, however, of the existence of such clans and prefer to see in the mention of the four houses in 12:12–14 a reference to the total leadership of Jerusalem.[277] If "house of David" continues to refer to the royal line, as it did in pre-exilic Judah; then, Zech 12:2–13:1 confirms a leadership role for it and presupposes the promises given to David in 2 Sam 7.[278]

Summary

The Davidic covenant is a recurring theme in the Hebrew Bible beyond the books of Kings and Chronicles. Reference to the Davidic covenant in the Psalms most often accompanies the request that God may give the king victory over his enemies or expresses the hope that he will exercise universal dominion (Pss 2, 18, 89, 110, 132). This petition is made on the basis that the Davidic covenant is eternal and in some cases its conditional/unconditional dimensions are also mentioned (Pss 89, 110).

Among the prophets, the Davidic covenant was a common concern too. Their oracles focused mostly on the need of the contemporary king to rule righteously and the people's need to return to God. The prophets warned that their unfaithfulness was pushing the fulfillment of God's promises into the future and drawing near the execution of God's judgment.[279] As apostasy increased, however, the hope expressed in these oracles acquired eschatological overtones. The nation would be disciplined for her unfaithfulness but

---

274 Ibid., 123.
275 Ibid., 124.
276 Ibid., 120. Also, Petersen, *Zechariah 9–14 and Malachi*, 116–118.
277 For example, Carol L. Meyers and Eric M. Meyers consider these four families mentioned here an expansion of 12:10 (*Zechariah 9–14*, 333–5, 346).
278 This leadership role, however, is shared now with priestly lines as in Zech 6:9–15.
279 See Limburg, *Hosea–Micah*, 188.

after the punishment God would raise a new righteous Davidic ruler. Not surprisingly, his main attribute would be righteousness and fear of the Lord (Isa 9:7; 11:2; Jer 33:15–16)

I noted above that seven main elements comprised the pattern of the rule of righteous Davidic kings.[280] These elements appear in the oracles of the prophets concerning the Davidic ruler God will raise in the future. In Isaiah, the exilic, and post-exilic prophets, however, these elements are elevated to an eschatological dimension.

Thus, righteous kings attempted to reunite Israel by means of the cult; the eschatological king, however, will "gather the dispersed of Judah [and Ephraim] from the four corners of the earth" (Isa 11:10–13; cf. Amos 9:11–12; Hos 3:5; Ezek 37:16–22; Mic 5:3). Righteous kings promoted the renewal of the nation's covenant with God; the eschatological king will mediate a new "covenant of peace ... an everlasting covenant" between God and the nation (Ezek 37:26–27; Isa 55:3). Righteous kings cleansed the land from idolatry; the eschatological king "will save them from all the apostasies into which they have fallen, and will cleanse them" and forgive them (Ezek 37:23; cf. Isa 55:7). Righteous kings reformed the cult by modifying the laws of the sacrifices and reorganizing the priesthood; the eschatological fulfillment implicates the writing of the law in the heart of the nation so that "the earth will be full of the knowledge of the LORD" (Isa 11:9; Ezek 37:24; cf. Hos 3:5; Zech 12:10; also related are Jer 31:31–34; Ezek 36:26–27). God defended the righteous king from his enemies and provided rest for the land; the eschatological king "shall strike the earth with the rod of his mouth" and even the natural order will be transformed so that no one will "hurt or destroy on all my holy mountain" (Isa 11:3–9; cf. Isa 9:5–7; Mic 5:4–5). Righteous kings repaired the temple; the eschatological king "shall build the temple of the LORD" (Zech 6:13; cf. Ezek 37:26, 28). Finally, alongside the righteous king often appeared the figure of a faithful priest; alongside the eschatological king "there shall be a priest by his throne, with peaceful understanding between the two of them" (Zech 6:13; cf. Jer 33:16–26; Hos 3:4–5).

In summary, according to the prophets, the failure of the Davidic dynasty in making possible the fulfillment of the Davidic promises caused their fulfillment to be projected into the future. God will remain faithful to his promise to David even though their fulfillment may require an act from him. David,

---

280 (1) renewal of the covenant, (2) cleansing of the land from spurious forms of worship, (3) building or repair of the temple, (4) emergence of a faithful high priest alongside the Davidic king, (5) reform of the cult, which implicated the change of the ritual laws and/or the reorganization of the priests; (6) a movement toward the reunification of Israel, and (7) "rest" from or defeat of enemies (see page 72).

the prototypical righteous king, served as the model that later righteous kings would emulate. In the prophets, David and his rule are a type as well of the person and rule of the coming redeemer.

I will now turn to an analysis of the fate of the Davidic covenant in the writings of Early Judaism.

THE DAVIDIC COVENANT IN EARLY JUDAISM

Early Judaism is characterized by the fragmentation of its beliefs and points of view.[281] Its views regarding a royal messiah are also pluralistic.[282] In this chapter I will study those documents that refer explicitly to the Davidic covenant or a Davidic Messiah.[283]

Wisdom of Ben Sira

The Wisdom of Ben Sira (Sirach) refers explicitly to the Davidic covenant in several places (e.g., 45:25; 47:11, 22; 49:4–5), mostly in the Hymn in Praise of

---

281 See Nickelsburg and Kraft, "The Modern Study of Early Judaism," 1–30, esp. 20–21.

282 See for example, Jacob Neusner, William Scott Green, and Ernest S. Frerichs, eds., *Judaisms and Their Messiahs at the Turn of the Christian Era* (Cambridge University Press, 1987).

283 I will not deal here with passages about a royal messiah that are not explicitly Davidic. For example, the ideal king described in the section "Statutes of the King" of the *Temple Scroll* (11QTemple LVI, 12–LIX, 21) which is not a Davidic figure (see Pomykala, *The Davidic Dynasty Tradition*, 232–7; Martin Hengel, James H. Charlesworth, and D. Mendels, "The Polemical Character of 'On Kingship' in the Temple Scroll: An Attempt at Dating 11QTemple," *JJS* 37 [1986]: 28–38; cf. Jacob Milgrom, "New Temple Festivals in the Temple Scroll," in *The Temple in Antiquity: Ancient Readers and Modern Perspectives*, ed. Truman G. Madsen, RSMS 9 [Religious Studies Center Brigham Young University, 1984], 132) or the six references in Qumran texts to the Messiah of Israel (CD XII, 23–XII,1; XIV, 18; XIX, 10–11; XIX, 20–XX,1; 1QS IX, 9b–11; 1QSa [1Q28a] II, 11b–22). Lincoln D. Hurst has challenged the view that Qumran expected two Messiahs ("Did Qumran Expect Two Messiahs?" *BBR* 9 [1999]: 157–180).

The future king of the tribe of Judah in the *Testaments of the Twelve Patriarchs* will not be treated as well. The references are *T. Reu.* 6:7; *T. Sim.* 7:1–2; *T. Levi* 8:14 (cf. *T. Levi* 18); and *T. Jud.* 24. This royal figure from Judah is sometimes assumed to be Davidic; for example, Cleon L. Rogers, Jr., "The Promises to David in Early Judaism," *BSac* 150 (1993): 290–293. His Davidic nature, however, is not explicit in the text. Moreover, the history of its composition is uncertain. The text in its present state incorporates Christian interpolations and is dated to the latter half of the 2nd century CE. M. de Jonge, "The Future of Israel in the Testaments of the Twelve Patriarchs," *JSJ* 17 (1986): 210–211. Finally, recent research agrees that "Christian elements in the *Testaments* cannot be removed by textual criticism ... [and] in the end the *Testaments* can be used much more confidently in the study of second-century Christianity than of pre-Christian Judaism" (John J. Collins, "The Testamentary Literature in Recent Scholarship," in *Early Judaism and Its Modern Interpreters*, ed. Robert A. Kraft and George W. E. Nickelsburg, SBLBMI 2 [Fortress; Scholars Press, 1986], 276).

Other references to royal non-Davidic messianic figures that will not be analyzed include *Sib. Or.* 3.652–656, *Ant.* 17.271–274; 17.278–281; *J. W.* 2.434; 4.507–508; 7.29.

the Fathers (44:1–50:24).[284]

The most important text of Sirach regarding the Davidic covenant is 45:25. This passage presents the interpreter with several challenges, the first of which is the establishment of its text. For the purposes of this study I will follow the critical edition of the LXX by Joseph Ziegler; which is, in fact, very close to the reconstruction of the Hebrew text by F. V. Reiterer:[285]

Καὶ διαθήκην τῷ δαυιδ
υἱῷ Ιεσσαι ἐκ φυλῆς Ιουδα
κληρονομία βασιλέως υἱοῦ ἐξ υἱοῦ μόνου
κληρονομία Ααρων καὶ τῷ σπέρματι αὐτοῦ.

Just as a covenant was established with David
son of Jesse of the tribe of Judah,

---

284 A majority of commentators consider that Sirach was written between 198–175 BCE during the high-priesthood of Onias III (196–175 BCE), or more precisely between 185 and 180 (James L. Crenshaw, "Sirach," *NIB* 5:610–611; Milward Douglas Nelson, *The Syriac Version of the Wisdom of Ben Sira Compared to the Greek and Hebrew Materials*, SBLDS 107 [Scholars, 1988], 1–2; Skehan and Di Lella, *The Wisdom of Ben Sira*, 9–10). The tone of Sirach's reference to Simon, the high priest, suggests that he had died (ca. 190 BCE; cf. Sir 50). On the other hand, there is no mention of the events that transpired during the rule of Antiochus IV Epiphanes (175–164 BCE).

Regarding the Greek translation, its prologue mentions that it was prepared after the thirty-eighth year of the reign of king "Euergetes" (132 BCE). It was published, however, after 117 BCE (Skehan and Di Lella, *The Wisdom of Ben Sira*, 8–9; Crenshaw, "Sirach," 610).

285 Joseph Ziegler, ed., *Sapientia Iesu Filii Sirach,* Septuaginta: Vetus Testamentum Graecum 12/2 (Vandenhoeck & Ruprecht, 1965), 340. Joseph Ziegler's edition of the LXX has been highly praised and is considered the best critical text available of Sirach (Skehan and Di Lella, *The Wisdom of Ben Sira*, 62). Though it is clear that Sirach was written originally in Hebrew, the Hebrew text of this book began to disappear after the rabbis denied it a place in the Hebrew canon. For centuries it was only known through quotations in the Talmudic and rabbinic literature. Because of several discoveries at the end of the 19th and throughout the 20th centuries, about 68 percent of the book is now extant in Hebrew. These discoveries include fragments found in the Cairo Synagogue Geniza, the Adler Geniza collection, Qumran caves 2 and 11, and in the ruins of Massada. Two things, among many others, make it difficult to work with the Hebrew text: no extant witness gives us the whole Hebrew text (the most ancient and reliable witnesses are the Massada fragments that contain only 39:27–44:17) and no reliable critical edition of these texts exists (Skehan and Di Lella, *The Wisdom of Ben Sira*, 60–61).

For a reconstruction of the Hebrew text, see Friedrich Vinzenz Reiterer, *"Urtext" und Übersetzungen: Sprachstudie über Sir 44,16–45,26 als Beitrag zur Siraforschung*, Arbeiten zu Text und Sprache im Alten Testament 12 (EOS, 1980), 30–31, 225–229. Cf. Israel Lévi, ed., *The Hebrew Text of the Book of Ecclesiasticus*, 3d ed. Semitic Studies Series 3 (Brill, 1969), 62. A list of other Hebrew editions is found in Nelson, *Syriac*, 2–5. A list of Syriac editions is found in Nelson, *Syriac*, 19–26.

This is the Hebrew text as reconstructed by F. V. Reiterer:/ וגם ברתו עם דוד / נחלת אהרן לזרעו / נחלת מלך לבנו לבדו / בן ישי למטה יהודה; And his covenant with David / son of Jesse of the tribe of Judah / an inheritance of a king is to his son alone / an inheritance of Aaron is to his seed. See also, Pomykala, *The Davidic Dynasty Tradition*, 132–139.

that the king's heritage passes only from son to son,
so the heritage of Aaron is for his descendants alone. (NRSV)

Sirach's mention of the Davidic covenant occurs in the context of his description of Phinehas' courageous actions of faithfulness to the Lord and of God's covenant with him for an eternal high priesthood (45:23–26; cf. Num 25:10–13; Ps 106:28–31). Sirach uses it as an example of the legitimate method of succession for the high-priesthood on the basis of the similarity between the Davidic covenant and God's covenant with Phinehas.[286] Just as the Davidic covenant extends from son to son only, also the high-priestly covenant applies through a direct line of descendants of Aaron only, not to all Aaronic priests.[287]

There were probably good reasons for this. Sirach was written during the time Onias III was high priest (190–175 BCE). Onias III became high priest at the peak of the influence of this office but was also the last legitimate priest through hereditary succession (cf. 2 Macc 4:7).[288] He engaged in a fierce controversy with Simon, of the priestly order of Bilga, who had also the office of captain of the temple (προστάτης τοῦ ἱεροῦ; 2 Macc 3:1–4). Simon was brother of Lysimachus and Menelaus and possibly the second in rank after the high priest.[289] Since Menelaus became high priest later through bribery, it is not difficult to conceive that there existed during his time a dispute regarding what constituted a legitimate succession for the high-priesthood.[290] The Davidic covenant here, then, serves to explain God's covenant with Phinehas "as if to settle the dispute over priestly lineage once and for all."[291]

---

286 Pomykala, *The Davidic Dynasty Tradition*, 140. Also, Burton L. Mack, *Wisdom and the Hebrew Epic: Ben Sira's Hymn in Praise of the Fathers*, CSJH (University of Chicago Press, 1985), 39.

287 Pomykala, *The Davidic Dynasty Tradition*, 141. Against others who understand this passage as a contrast between the Davidic Covenant and Phinehas's covenant in the sense that the Davidic applied only to one son (i.e., Solomon) but Phinehas's covenant applied to all his descendants; e.g., Skehan and Di Lella, *The Wisdom of Ben Sira*, 514.

288 Uriel Rappaport, "Onias (Person)," *ABD* 5:23–24; James C. VanderKam, *From Joshua to Caiaphas: High Priests after the Exile* (Fortress and Van Gorcum, 2004), 188.

289 VanderKam, *From Joshua to Caiaphas*, 191.

290 Pomykala, *The Davidic Dynasty Tradition*, 141; Rappaport, "Onias (Person)," 23–24; VanderKam, *From Joshua to Caiaphas*, 188–197. Cf. Skehan and Di Lella, *The Wisdom of Ben Sira*, 513.

There had been, in fact, a struggle for the control of the priesthood between the Oniads and the Tobiads a little before; that is, very early in the 2nd century BCE. "The Oniads were related to Aaron on the paternal side, but the Tobiads laid claim to Aaronite ancestry through the maternal side. The latter group sought to wrest the priesthood from the Oniads in the early 2nd century BCE" (Crenshaw, "Sirach," 843).

291 Crenshaw, "Sirach," 843.

Sirach's interest in the Davidic covenant goes beyond the proper method of succession for the office of the high priest. Burton L. Mack's analysis suggests that Sirach considered the high priest the climax and fulfillment of all the offices and covenants of Israel's history.[292] The first seven figures of the Hymn in Praise of the Fathers have in common the theme of the covenant and may be considered a literary unit (Noah, Abraham, Isaac, Israel, Moses, Aaron, Phinehas; Sir 44–45).[293] Sirach is also interested in the offices of the fathers (Noah, Abraham, Isaac, and Jacob), the priests (Aaron, Phinehas, Samuel, Simon), the prophets (e.g., Elijah, Jeremiah) and the kings (e.g., David, Solomon, Hezekiah). Many of these figures have, in fact, multiple offices (e.g., Moses, Phinehas, Samuel, Simon).[294] According to Burton L. Mack, all these figures climax in the multiple-office figure of the high priest Simon in Sir 50. This becomes clear, for example, in Sirach's description of the function of the high priest in 50:1–4.

While describing kings, Sirach considered that their primary function was to build and defend the civil and religious institutions (David, 47:1–11; Solomon, 47:12–22; and Hezekiah, 48:17–25).[295] This is the function, however, for which Sirach praises Simon, the high priest, in 50:1–4. Pomykala notes also that Sirach assigns a royal symbol to the high priest.[296] Sirach adds upon the turban and flowered plate of the Pentateuch's description of Aaron's headdress (45:12), a crown of gold (עֲטֶרֶת פָּז).[297] This crown of gold, of course, has royal connotations (cf. 2 Sam 12:30; Jer 13:18; Ezek 21:31; Ps 21:4). Note that a crown of gold (עֲטֶרֶת פָּז) is used to describe the headdress of the Davidic king in Ps 21:4.

The high priest's inheritance of the roles and functions of the Davidic king in Sirach is significant. It is a powerful witness that the Davidic covenant had not fallen into oblivion.[298] Yet, Sirach does not express hope for a future ruler from the house of David in fulfillment of an eternal Davidic covenant. He does not comment on the eternal nature of the Davidic covenant.

---

292 Mack, *Wisdom and the Hebrew Epic*, 36, 41, 54–55. See also, Thomas R. Lee, *Studies in the Form of Sirach 44–50*, SBLDS 75 (Scholars, 1986).

293 Mack, *Wisdom and the Hebrew Epic*, 39. The mention of the Davidic covenant (45:25) and the prayer of blessing upon Phinehas (45:26) close this unit. The Davidic covenant, however, is not a central concern of the author, but is brought in to explain the appropriate form of succession for the high-priesthood. Note that the Davidic covenant is the only element out of chronological sequence and does not become the occasion for David's description and praise (cf. 47:2–11) (Mack, *Wisdom and the Hebrew Epic*, 39).

294 Mack, *Wisdom and the Hebrew Epic*, 26–36.

295 Ibid., 29.

296 Pomykala, *The Davidic Dynasty Tradition*, 143.

297 Exod 28:36–38; 29:6; 39:30; Lev 8:9.

298 Pomykala, *The Davidic Dynasty Tradition*, 144.

A further mention of the Davidic covenant is found in 47:11:[299]

κύριος ἀφεῖλεν τὰς ἁμαρτίας αὐτοῦ
καὶ ἀνύψωσεν εἰς αἰῶνα τὸ κέρας αὐτοῦ
καὶ ἔδωκεν αὐτῷ διαθήκην βασιλέων
καὶ θρόνον δόξης ἐν τῷ Ισραηλ.

The Lord took away his sins,
and exalted his power [horn] forever;
he gave him a covenant of kingship
and a glorious throne in Israel. (NRSV)

The covenant with David is mentioned in positive terms. The passage mentions that God exalted "David's horn" forever. Horn is used here in the metaphorical sense of power and prestige (note the parallelism between κέρας and δόξα in 49:5; cf. 47:5, 7).[300] The idea is confirmed in the second part of the verse where it is said that David is given "a glorious throne [θρόνον δόξης] in Israel." (Note, again, the parallel between κέρας and δόξα.) Thus, it is his fame or glory that has been exalted forever. His rule will be commemorated in Israel through the ages. But nothing is said of an eternal dynasty.[301]

The promise of an eternal dynasty to David is referred to, however, in the following section which is devoted to Solomon (vv. 12–22). Verse 22 reads:

ὁ δὲ κύριος οὐ μὴ καταλίπῃ τὸ ἔλεος αὐτοῦ
καὶ οὐ μὴ διαφθείρῃ ἀπὸ τῶν λόγων αὐτοῦ
οὐδὲ μὴ ἐξαλείψῃ ἐκλεκτοῦ αὐτοῦ ἔκγονα
καὶ σπέρμα τοῦ ἀγαπήσαντος αὐτὸν οὐ μὴ ἐξάρῃ·
καὶ τῷ Ιακωβ ἔδωκεν κατάλειμμα
καὶ τῷ Δαυιδ ἐξ αὐτοῦ ῥίζαν.[302]

But the Lord will never give up his mercy,
or cause any of his works [words] to perish;
he will never blot out the descendants of his chosen one,
or destroy the family line of him who loved him.

---

299   For the text of the LXX, Ziegler, ed., *Sapientia Iesu Filii Sirach*, 347.

300   The image of horn appears often in Davidic texts, Pss 89:18, 25; 132:17; Luke 1:69; see Skehan and Di Lella, *The Wisdom of Ben Sira*, 524.

301   Ivor H. Jones, *The Apocrypha*, Epworth Commentaries (Epworth, 2003), 124; Pomykala, *The Davidic Dynasty Tradition*, 145. Contra Skehan and Di Lella, *The Wisdom of Ben Sira*, 526.

302   Ziegler, ed., *Sapientia Iesu Filii Sirach*, 349.

So he gave a remnant to Jacob,
and to David a root from his own family. (NRSV)

After praising Solomon for his building of the temple and wisdom (vv. 12–18b), Sirach describes Solomon's sins, but notes that he reigned in security (vv. 18c–21).[303] He explains the reason: "The Lord will never give up his mercy, or cause any of his works [words; τῶν λόγων αὐτοῦ] to perish." The "words" that do not "perish" are those of 2 Sam 7:14–16.[304] The implication is clear: Solomon lived in security because of God's covenant with David. Just as at the beginning of the section Sirach points out how David's victories provided Solomon an "ample space" to live (47:12), he explains at the end of the same section that the Davidic covenant secured a descendant for Solomon upon the throne (47:22e–23). This passage, then, emphasizes God's faithfulness to the Davidic covenant despite Solomon's unfaithfulness. It is because God "[will never] destroy the family line of him who loved him" that Rehoboam succeeds Solomon upon the throne, despite the fact that he was "broad in folly and lacking in sense" (v. 23).[305] Sirach uses οὐ μή with the aorist subjunctive to indicate that God "*will never* give up his mercy … [or] blot out the descendants of his chosen one … or destroy the family line of him who loved him" (emphasis mine). This "is the most definite form of negation regarding the future."[306] Thus, Sirach betrays in this passage an understanding of the Davidic covenant as unconditional—possibly eternal—as the reason for the existence of a Davidic line of kings in Israel's history.[307] There is no indication, however, that Sirach expects a son of David to rise in the future based on the promises made to David.[308]

This unconditional—possibly eternal—understanding of the Davidic covenant seems to be contradicted in a later passage, Sir 49:4–5, which refers to the end of the Davidic line.

---

303 Skehan and Di Lella, *The Wisdom of Ben Sira*, 527–528.

304 Ibid., 528. Note the parallels: τὸ δὲ ἔλεός μου οὐκ ἀποστήσω ἀπ' αὐτοῦ (2 Sam 7:15a); But my mercy I will not take from him (translation mine). And then, ὁ δὲ κύριος οὐ μὴ καταλίπῃ τὸ ἔλεος αὐτοῦ (Sir 47:22a); But the Lord will never abandon his mercy (translation mine).

305 The original says "the people's (λαοῦ) folly and lacking in sense" (λαοῦ ἀφροσύνην καὶ ἐλασσούμενον συνέσει). This was a play on Rehoboam's name. The line begins in Hebrew with רחב (broad) and finishes with עם (people), forming in this way the name רחבעם (Rehoboam). Lévi, ed., *The Book of Ecclesiasticus*, 66; Skehan and Di Lella, *The Wisdom of Ben Sira*, 530.

306 BDF §365. Cf. Daniel B. Wallace, *Greek Grammar Beyond the Basics: An Exegetical Syntax of the New Testament* (Zondervan, 1996), 468.

307 Skehan and Di Lella, *The Wisdom of Ben Sira*, 528.

308 Pomykala, *The Davidic Dynasty Tradition*, 146. The rule of Rehoboam, the fool of the nation, is understood by Sirach as both the evidence of God's mercy (47:22) as well as the cause for the eventual exile and divine punishment (47:25; Jones, *The Apocrypha*, 124).

Πάρεξ Δαυιδ καὶ Εζεκιου καὶ Ιωσιου
πάντες πλημμέλειαν ἐπλημμέλησαν·
κατέλιπον γὰρ τὸν νόμον τοῦ ὑψίστου,
οἱ βασιλεῖς Ιουδα ἐξέλιπον·
ἔδωκαν γὰρ τὸ κέρας αὐτῶν ἑτέροις
καὶ τὴν δόξαν αὐτῶν ἔθνει ἀλλοτρίῳ.[309]

Except for David and Hezekiah and Josiah,
all of them were great sinners,
for they abandoned the law of the Most High;
the kings of Judah came to an end.
They gave their power to others,
and their glory to a foreign nation. (NRSV)

Sirach asserts that because of their unfaithfulness "the kings of Judah came to an end." Mack notes that, in the Hymn in Praise of the Fathers (chs. 44–50), Sirach mentions 7 kings with a collective reference at the end (49:4–5) suggesting that this phase of Israelite history has come to an end.[310] Again, Sirach does not suggest any hope for a future Davidic ruler as a result of the Davidic covenant. The book does not explain the apparent contradiction of the end of the dynasty and the assertion made before that "[God] will never blot out the descendants of his chosen one, or destroy the family line of him who loved him" (47:22). The LXX suggests a possible explanation in its assertion that it was "they," the Davidic kings, who gave their own powers to others.[311] In other words, the failure of the Davidic covenant did not evidence the unfaithfulness of God to his promises, but the rejection by David's line of God's promise to David.[312] In the LXX's view, the Davidic covenant has not been forfeited but repudiated.

Sirach, then, considers the Davidic covenant as having come to an end with the end of the Davidic line in the exile. The Davidic covenant is not claimed as a source of hope for a messianic figure in the future as in the prophets. Sirach does not conceive explicitly a diarchic rule for Israel either.

---

[309] Ziegler, ed., *Sapientia Iesu Filii Sirach*, 354–355.

[310] Mack, *Wisdom and the Hebrew Epic*, 62.

[311] In the Hebrew text, however, it is God [he] who gave away their powers (Lévi, ed., *The Book of Ecclesiasticus*, 69; Pomykala, *The Davidic Dynasty Tradition*, 147).

[312] Sir 49:11–12 mentions Zerubbabel, but there is no clear indication that Sirach considered him a renewal of the Davidic line. There is as well a reference to Hag 2:23 but no clear messianic implications (Pomykala, *The Davidic Dynasty Tradition*, 148).

Instead, Sirach is interested in the present. For him, the high priest is in reality a high-priest-king, though he is never called so.[313]

First Maccabees

First Maccabees 2:57 refers to the Davidic covenant:

Δαυιδ ἐν τῷ ἐλέει αὐτοῦ ἐκληρονόμησεν θρόνον βασιλείας εἰς αἰῶνας.[314]

David, because he was merciful, inherited the throne of the kingdom forever. (NRSV)

This is an explicit reference to God's promise to David that he would "establish his throne forever" (2 Sam 7:13, 16). Now the question is, How does 1 Maccabees understand this promise? Is there an expectation for the restoration of Israel's throne to the line of David?

---

313 Mack, *Wisdom and the Hebrew Epic,* 35. It is probable that the political realities of the time prevented him from doing it. See also, Crenshaw, "Sirach," 843; Skehan and Di Lella, *The Wisdom of Ben Sira,* 514; Jones, *The Apocrypha,* 123.
   The Hebrew version of Sirach contains a further mention of the Davidic covenant in a Psalm found between vv. 12 and 13 of chap. 51 of the LXX. Lines 8 and 9 of this Psalm interest me (text from Lévi, *The Book of Ecclesiasticus,* 74): / הודו למזמיח קרן לבית דוד כי לעלם חסדו‎ הודו לבוחר בבני צדוק לכהן כי לעלם חסדו‎ ; Give thanks to him who makes a horn to sprout for the house of David, for his mercy endures forever; / Give thanks to him who has chosen the sons of Zadok to be priests, for his mercy endures forever; (NRSV).
   The authenticity of this Psalm has been seriously questioned because of its absence in the LXX and Syriac versions; moreover, the Psalm does not fit the context. (For a survey of scholarly opinions and bibliography, see Alexander A. Di Lella, *The Hebrew Text of Sirach: A Text-Critical and Historical Study,* Studies in Classical Literature 1 [Moulton, 1966], 101–105.)
   The mention of David in line 8 comes from Ps 132:17 (cf. Ezek 29:21). It is difficult to know, however, what the author meant without having a clear historical context for this Psalm. Alexander A. Di Lella concedes that this Psalm in Sirach was not written by Ben Sira but suggests that it dates from "the time when the Zadokites were still high priests (as is clear from 51:12 ix), i.e., before 152 BCE." Skehan and Di Lella, *The Wisdom of Ben Sira,* 569–570. If this were the case (though see the critique of Di Lella's suggestion in Pomykala, *The Davidic Dynasty Tradition,* 149–150), it is not clear whether the writer considered that God had made "a horn to sprout for the house of David" or he expected a future fulfillment of this promise.
   Whatever the case, it is worth noting that this Psalm envisions the horn for David and the Sons of Zadok as parallel figures in the line of the message of the Jeremiah, Ezekiel, and other OT prophets.

314 Greek text from Werner Kappler, *Maccabaeorum libri I–IV,* Septuaginta: Vetus Testamentum Graecum 9/1 (Vandenhoeck & Ruprecht, 1936), 61. "Not even fragments have survived of the Hebrew original of First Maccabees," Jonathan A. Goldstein, *I Maccabees: A New Translation with Introduction and Commentary,* AB 41 (Doubleday, 1976), 176. This book was written towards the end of the 2nd century BCE (Thomas Fischer, "First and Second Maccabees," *ABD* 4:441).

There is no clear evidence of such expectation in 1 Maccabees, as Pomykala argues.³¹⁵ He notes correctly that the expression εἰς αἰῶνας (עולמים in the putative original Hebrew) can mean either "long time" or "unlimited time" and concludes that the context of 1 Macc 2:57 privileges the understanding of εἰς αἰῶνας in its limited sense of "long time."³¹⁶

Maccabees expresses little concern for the future. George W. E. Nickelsburg succinctly summarizes what is widely believed to be the purpose of 1 Maccabees' author:

> He has recorded the history of the founding, the succession, and the establishment of the Hasmonean house, and he has documented its legitimacy by royal decree, popular acclaim, and the attestation of the God who has worked the divine purposes through the Hasmonean family and its early heroes. He has told the story of "the family of those men through whom deliverance was given to Israel" (5:62). Thereby he has proclaimed the gospel according to the Hasmoneans.³¹⁷

The author is not interested in what God will do in the future; instead, he describes the Hasmoneans as the fulfillment of God's purpose for Israel in the present.

Second, the immediate literary context of 1 Macc 2:57 does not suggest an eschatological dimension for the Davidic covenant. The reference to David is part of a long list of heroes that Mattathias presents to his sons on his

---

315 Some have found in 1 Macc 14:41 evidence that there was hope for the miraculous restoration of the throne to the Davidic line. This passage relates how perpetual high-priesthood and leadership were granted to Simon "forever" but with the proviso "until a trustworthy prophet should arise" (cf. vss 41–49). Some have argued that the reason for this proviso was the expectation of the restoration of throne to the Davidic line in the future; e.g., Joseph Klausner, *The Messianic Idea in Israel: From Its Beginning to the Completion of the Mishnah*, trans. W. F. Stinespring (Macmillan, 1955), 260. See also, John J. Collins, "Messianism in the Maccabean Period," in *Judaisms and Their Messiahs at the Turn of the Christian Era*, ed. Jacob Neusner, William Scott Green, and Ernest S. Frerichs (Cambridge University Press, 1987), 104. This proviso does not necessarily imply hope for restoration of the Davidic line to the throne, but only hope in a messianic figure (Goldstein, *I Maccabees*, 508). In fact, the proviso could refer not to the Hasmonean claim to leadership, but to their high-priesthood which was not from the line of Zadok.

316 BDAG, 32; Pomykala, *The Davidic Dynasty Tradition*, 154–155, cf. 95; Preuss, "עוֹלָם," *TDOT* 10:531. The same would be true for the textual variants εἰς [τὸν] αἰῶνα or αἰωνίου noted by Kappler, *Maccabaeorum libri I–IV*, 61. First Maccabees 14:41 uses, for example, the phrase in the limited sense: Simon is appointed "leader and high priest forever [εἰς τὸν αἰῶνα]"; but a time limit is added, "until a trustworthy prophet should arise." Thus, the NAB translates: "Simon shall be their permanent leader and high priest until a true prophet arises."

317 George W. E. Nickelsburg, *Jewish Literature between the Bible and the Mishnah: A Historical and Literary Introduction*, 2d ed. (Fortress, 2005), 106.

deathbed as examples of piety and action so as to spur them to perform similar deeds and reap corresponding rewards (1 Macc 2:49–68). Throughout the rest of the book the author of 1 Maccabees echoes the language of the biblical stories of these heroes (as they appear in Judges, 1–2 Samuel, and 1–2 Kings) to suggest that the achievements of the Hasmoneans equaled those of the heroes mentioned by Mattathias.[318]

Harold W. Attridge concludes that by comparing the Hasmoneans' actions and rewards with those of Abraham, Joseph, Phinehas, Joshua, Caleb, David, Elijah, and the companions of Daniel, the author provides "an implicit defense of the legitimacy of the irregular, charismatic leadership exercized [sic] by the Hasmoneans."[319] Moreover, Jonathan A. Goldstein suggests that 1 Macc 5:62 asserts "for the Hasmoneans the prerogatives reserved for David's line in earlier Jewish tradition." There, the Hasmoneans are referred to as "the family of those men through whom deliverance was given to Israel" (ἐκ τοῦ σπέρματος τῶν ἀνδρῶν ἐκείνων οἷς ἐδόθη σωτηρία Ισραηλ διὰ χειρὸς αὐτῶν). He suggests that "the strange syntax [of this phrase] can have come only from 2 Sam 3:18, '... the Lord hath spoken of David saying, "Deliverance of [hōshīaʻ] My people of Israel is through the agency of David My servant."'"[320] In conclusion, David and the promises made to him are not a source of hope for the future in 1 Maccabees, but a model the Hasmoneans have emulated.[321]

Psalms of Solomon 17

The most extensive description of an expected Davidic king and his kingdom in Early Judaism is found in *Pss. Sol.* 17.[322] Verse 4 reads:

---

318 Jonathan A. Goldstein, "How the Authors of 1 and 2 Maccabees Treated the 'Messianic' Promises," in *Judaisms and Their Messiahs at the Turn of the Christian Era*, ed. Jacob Neusner, William Scott Green, and Ernest S. Frerichs (Cambridge University Press, 1987), 79–81.

319 Harold W. Attridge, "Historiography," in *Jewish Writings of the Second Temple Period: Apocrypha, Pseudepigrapha, Qumran Sectarian Writings, Philo, Josephus*, ed. Michael E. Stone, CRINT (Van Gorcum; Fortress, 1984), 2:172. Also, Pomykala, *The Davidic Dynasty Tradition*, 156–158.

320 Goldstein, " 'Messianic' Promises," 80. The Greek reads: κύριος ἐλάλησεν περὶ Δαυιδ λέγων Ἐν χειρὶ τοῦ δούλου μου Δαυιδ σώσω τὸν Ισραηλ ἐκ χειρὸς ἀλλοφύλων καὶ ἐκ χειρὸς πάντων τῶν ἐχθρῶν αὐτῶν (2 Sam 3:18).

321 David plays also a prototypical role in 1 Macc 4:30; 14:4–15, 41–49. Cf. Pomykala, *The Davidic Dynasty Tradition*, 156–158.

322 George W. E. Nickelsburgh suggests a date for this psalm between 37 and 30 BCE. *Jewish Literature between the Bible and the Mishnah: A Historical and Literary Introduction*, 243. Others suggest an earlier date (61–57 BCE). Gene L. Davenport, "The 'Anointed of the Lord' in Psalms of Solomon 17," in *Ideal Figures in Ancient Judaism: Profiles and Paradigms*, ed. John J. Collins and George W. E. Nickelsburg, SBLSCS 12 (Scholars, 1980), 71; Pomykala, *The Davidic Dynasty Tradition*, 159, n. 148.

Σύ, κύριε, ᾑρετίσω τὸν Δαυιδ βασιλέα ἐπὶ Ισραηλ,
καὶ σὺ ὤμοσας αὐτῷ περὶ τοῦ σπέρματος αὐτοῦ εἰς τὸν αἰῶνα
τοῦ μὴ ἐκλείπειν ἀπέναντί σου βασίλειον αὐτοῦ.

Lord, you chose David to be king over Israel,
and swore to him about his descendants forever,
that his kingdom should not fail before you.[323]

This recollection of God's promise to David is made in the general context of the psalm as a communal lament or complaint.[324] The author evokes God's promise to David in the context of his conviction that God rules with justice and mercy over the affairs of humankind and especially of Israel (vv. 1–4). This is why God has expulsed and punished by means of alien hands those who usurped the throne of David (vv. 5–10).[325] In the process, however, the land and people have been devastated (vv. 11–15), the righteous scattered (16–18a), and the remnant of Israel is in an utterly sinful condition (18b–20).[326] It is in this context that the author makes a plea for the restoration of Israel (vv. 26–42).

First, he appeals to God's promises to David requesting a legitimate king (v. 21):

Ἰδέ, κύριε, καὶ ἀνάστησον αὐτοῖς τὸν βασιλέα αὐτῶν
υἱὸν Δαυιδ εἰς τὸν καιρόν, ὃν εἵλου σύ, ὁ θεός,
τοῦ βασιλεῦσαι ἐπὶ Ισραηλ παῖδά σου·

---

323   Translation by Wright, "Psalms of Solomon," 665–669. The Greek text is taken from Rahlfs, ed., 2:486–488. A majority of scholars agree that the Psalms of Solomon were written in Hebrew. There are, however, no Hebrew manuscripts extant; only late Greek and Syriac ones (10th–16th century CE). R. B. Wright, "Psalms of Solomon: A New Translation and Introduction," *OTP* 2:640.

324   Davenport, "The 'Anointed of the Lord,'" 71. These verses explicitly reflect the language of the Davidic promise as expressed in 2 Sam 7:11–16; Ps 89:3–4, 19–37; and Jer 33:17. There is also a similarity in theme between *Pss. Sol.* 17 and Ps 89.
A majority of scholars concur that the historical background of this text was the rise of the Hasmonean dynasty, Pompey's capture of Jerusalem (63 BCE), the banishment of Aristobolus II, the puppet regime of Hyrcanus II, and the resulting lamentable situation of Israel (M. de Jonge, "The Psalms of Solomon," in *Outside the Old Testament*, ed. M. de Jonge, Cambridge Commentaries on Writings of the Jewish and Christian World 200 BC to AD 200 4 [Cambridge University Press, 1985], 160–161; Nickelsburg, *Jewish Literature between the Bible and the Mishnah: A Historical and Literary Introduction*, 242; Pomykala, *The Davidic Dynasty Tradition*, 159, 161; Wright, "Psalms of Solomon," 640–641).

325   The usurpers are described as "those to whom you did not (make the) promise. ... With pomp they set up a monarchy because of their arrogance" (vv. 5–6).

326   This sinful state of rulers and inhabitants has affected nature as well. There is no more rain and the springs have stopped (vv. 19–20). Davenport, "The 'Anointed of the Lord,'" 71.

> See, Lord, and raise up for them their king,
> the son of David, to rule over your servant Israel
> in the time known to you, O God.

This king is expected to be the means by which God will purge Israel from Jewish sinners and gentile enemies (22–25).[327]

Second, a vision of restored Israel is articulated in the remainder of the plea (26–42). The restoration amounts to the inauguration of a new age for Israel and includes the ingathering of the Jews to their land and the wise, righteous, and universal rule of the Davidic king.[328]

It is clear that the author considered God's promises made to David as eternal in nature; thus, a source of hope for Israel in his time.[329] He uses those promises as "a frontal assault on the legitimacy of the Hasmonean rule."[330] Some scholars believe that this psalm is evidence that there had been a continuing belief in the restoration of the Davidic rule in early Judaism which was disappointed when the Hasmoneans claimed royal status.[331] Kenneth E. Pomykala differs, arguing that it was the opposition to the Hasmonean rule that led the author of the psalm and his community to interpret the Davidic promises as eternal and, thus, promising the restoration of Davidic kingship for Israel.[332] The current state of scholarship on early Jewish messianism tends to support Pomykala's position. It should be noted that *Pss. Sol.* 17 provides evidence only for the beliefs of a sector of Judaism.[333] A study of the few references to the Messiah in the Pseudepigrapha reveals that the idea that first-century Jews "held a recognizable and definable, if not common, messianic belief" is wrong.[334]

---

327 Arguably, a reference to Hyrcanus II, his associates, and Roman enemies. Pomykala, *The Davidic Dynasty Tradition*, 163.

328 Davenport, "The 'Anointed of the Lord,' " 78–79.

329 Ibid., 72.

330 Pomykala, *The Davidic Dynasty Tradition*, 166.

331 E.g., Karl Georg Kuhn, "The Two Messiahs of Aaron and Israel," in *The Scrolls and the New Testament*, ed. Krister Stendahl (Harper, 1957; reprint, with a new Introduction by James H. Charlesworth, Crossroad, 1992), 60–63.

332 Pomykala, *The Davidic Dynasty Tradition*, 166–167.

333 Three groups of people are the focus of these psalms: the gentiles, the sinners, and the devout. The psalms, of course, present the point of view of the devout. Some have identified the devout with the Pharisaic or Essene communities. The fact is, however, that we do not know enough to make the attribution certain or probable (Wright, "Psalms of Solomon," 642).

334 Charlesworth, "From Jewish Messianology," 225. "First-century Palestinian Jews held many different, often mutually exclusive, ideas and beliefs regarding the Messiah" (Charlesworth, "From Jewish Messianology," 225). Kenneth E. Pomykala considers *Pss. Sol.* 17 "the first evidence for the expression of hope for a davidic Messiah in early Jewish literature" (*The Davidic Dynasty Tradition*, 169). For the opposite case, see Davenport, "The 'Anointed of the Lord,' " 67–68.

The description of the hoped-for Davidic king in *Pss. Sol.* 17 is interesting. First, the priest and the temple are notoriously absent; instead, holiness for Israel is achieved under the rule of the expected Davidic king (esp. vv. 26–30).[335] The king is described in terms that exalt his *justice, power, mercy, and wisdom*. He is appointed by God (vv. 21–25) and taught by him (v. 32). Accordingly, he is a righteous king (vv. 32, 40, passim), free from sin (v. 36), who does not tolerate sin among his people (v. 27). He is powerful as well to cleanse Jerusalem from sin "(and make it) holy" (v. 30).[336] He will destroy the unrighteous rulers, expel gentiles from Jerusalem, and condemn the sinners (vv. 22–25, 36 passim).[337] As a result he rules over a holy people (vv. 26, 32, 41, 43). He is also compassionate (v. 34b). Finally, he is wise. He trusts tenaciously in God and has been endowed with the Holy Spirit (v. 37). He destroys his enemies, not with the power of arms, but "with the word of his mouth" which are as pure "as the words of the holy ones" (vv. 24, 43; cf. 33, 35). In summary, he "rules with all the ancient virtues heightened to superlatives"; almost a supernatural being.[338] In his description of the Davidic king, the author of *Pss. Sol.* 17 has been influenced by Ps 2:9, Jer 23:5, and Isa 11:2 which speak of a righteous king who is endowed with power and a spirit of wisdom.[339]

The righteousness and faithfulness of the Davidic king to God is also important for a second reason: it becomes "the means by which God is faithful to the larger covenant with Israel as a whole."[340] In v. 15 the Israelites are referred to as "children of the covenant." They had broken their covenant with God by their sinful behavior (v. 5). Verse 20 says: "From their leader to the commonest of the people, (they were) in every kind of sin: The king was a criminal and the judge disobedient; (and) the people sinners." According to the author, it was the usurpation of the throne by those to whom it was not promised (arguably Hasmoneans) that led the nation to its present state of sinfulness. In response, God, "faithful in all his judgments" (v. 9), has "reward-

---

335 This echoes Zech 3:8–9 where the guilt of the land is removed by Branch; a kingly figure. See the section above on "Zechariah" on page 102.

336 Nickelsburg, *Jewish Literature between the Bible and the Mishnah: A Historical and Literary Introduction*, 243. Gene L. Davenport suggests that according to v. 32 the Davidic king will purify the whole world from sin. He considers that "they" refers to the nations of v. 31 ("The 'Anointed of the Lord,'" 76).

337 Davenport, "The 'Anointed of the Lord,'" 74–75.

338 Wright, "Psalms of Solomon," 643. "Although the messianic king will be a human being, the author attributes to him semidivine characteristics that are typical of the older (esp. Isaianic) oracles. As God's vicar and agent on earth the king shares in, or embodies, divine qualities" (Nickelsburg, *Jewish Literature between the Bible and the Mishnah: A Historical and Literary Introduction*, 242).

339 Davenport, "The 'Anointed of the Lord,'" 72; Pomykala, *The Davidic Dynasty Tradition*, 168–169.

340 Davenport, "The 'Anointed of the Lord,'" 76–77.

ed them ... according to their sins" (v. 8). The banishment of the rulers and the destruction and scattering of the nation are considered, then, God's punishment for their covenantal unfaithfulness. The restoration of the nation follows an opposite course of action. A righteous king will cleanse the nation from sin. Because of his unwavering trust in and faithfulness to God (vv. 32–34, 36), God will fulfill in him the covenantal promises made to David so he will rule "with an iron rod" (*Pss. Sol.* 23–24; Ps 2:9; cf. 2 Sam 7:9–10) and restore the land for and to the people of Israel (*Pss. Sol.* 17:28; Ezek 45:8; 47:13, 21; cf. 2 Sam 7:10). This means then that the Davidic ruler is himself "the very means by which God's own holiness and strength are mediated to [Israel and] all the nations."[341] In summary, the king becomes the mediator of God's covenantal blessings for his people.

Dead Sea Scrolls

Five documents of the Dead Sea Scrolls contain references to the Davidic dynastic tradition.

Words of the Luminaries (4Q504)

The first reference is found in *Words of the Luminaries* (4Q504 1–2 IV, 5–8 or 4QDibHam^a 1–2 IV, 5–8) .

5 את ישראל מכול העמים ותבחר בשבט
6 יאודה ובריתכה הקימותה לדויד להיות
7 כרעי נגיד על עמכה וישב על כסא ישראל לפניך
8 כול הימים וכול הגוים ראו את כבודכה

5 Israel more than all the peoples. And you chose the tribe of
6 Judah, and established your covenant with David so that he would be
7 like a shepherd, a prince over your people, and would sit in front of you on the throne of Israel
8 for ever. And all the countries have seen your glory.[342]

---

341 Ibid., 85.
342 Text and translation from Florentino García Martínez and Eibert J. C. Tigchelaar, eds., *The Dead Sea Scrolls Study Edition* (Brill, 1997–1998), 2:1014–1015. For the original publication and plaques, Maurice Baillet, *Qumran grotte 4: III (4Q482–4Q520)*, Discoveries in the Judaean Desert 7 (Clarendon, 1982), 143–144, pl. xlix–liii. These texts have been dated on the basis of paleography between the middle of the 2nd century BCE and the middle of the 1st century CE.

This translation suggests the presence of hope for the restoration of Davidic rule over Israel. A number of scholars consider this passage to be evidence of the expectation of a Davidic messiah in the Qumran sect.[343]

There are, however, two variables that make three interpretations of the text possible. First, the text could refer to David alone or to David as a corporate person which includes his descendants.[344] Second, וישב could be a continuation of the purpose clause introduced by להיות or it could introduce an independent clause. This passage allows, then, three different meanings which are all grammatically possible:[345]

> 1. And you chose the tribe of Judah, and established your covenant with David so that *he* would be like a shepherd, a prince over your people; and *he sat* in front of you on the throne of Israel *all the days* [i.e., of his life] [emphasis mine].
> 2. And you chose the tribe of Judah, and established your covenant with David so that *he* [i.e., David and his descendants] would be like a shepherd, a prince over your people; and *he* [i.e., David and his descendants] *sat* in front of you on the throne of Israel *all the days* [i.e., of their dynasty] [emphasis mine].
> 3. And you chose the tribe of Judah, and established your covenant with David so that *he* [i.e., David and his descendants] would be like a shepherd, a prince over your people, *and would sit* in front of you on the throne of Israel all the days [i.e., forever] [emphasis mine].

Readings one and two look to the past. The first focuses on King David and his 40 years of rule. The second focuses on the Davidic dynasty which came to an end in 586 BCE. The third reading looks to the future. It focuses on God's promise of an eternal dynasty to David. It is the literary context that decides what was meant by the author. Sadly, only a small portion of that context is extant.[346]

For an introduction to this document, see Daniel K. Falk, *Daily, Sabbath, and Festival Prayers in the Dead Sea Scrolls*, STDJ 27 (Brill, 1998), 59–94.

343 E.g., Collins, "Messianism," 105.

344 A similar or analogous idea would be the new David of Hos 3:5; Jer 30:9; Ezek 34:23–24; 37:24–25.

345 See Pomykala, *The Davidic Dynasty Tradition*, 176.

346 Our text comprises lines 6–8 of a fragment that contains 21 lines. Lines 1 and 15–21 are not readable, though. Thus the only context we have is 4 lines that precede our text and 6 that follow it (García Martínez and Tigchelaar, eds., *The Dead Sea Scrolls Study Edition*, 2:1014–1015).

It has been pointed out that 4Q504 belongs to a genre of prayer common in biblical and early Jewish sources known as Taḥanunim.³⁴⁷ These prayers have a basic pattern that combines three elements: (1) supplication for God's help, (2) remembrance of God's saving actions in the past, (3) repentance and prayer for forgiveness.³⁴⁸ Kenneth E. Pomykala notes the similarity between 4Q504 and Neh 9:6–37. After reviewing God's abundant blessings for Israel throughout its history (vv. 6–24), Neh 9:25 summarizes God's mercies in the following phrase: "So they ate, and were filled and became fat, and delighted themselves in your great goodness." Afterwards, it recounts how Israel rebelled and God punished them (vv. 26–30). Likewise, col. IV of 4Q504 is part of the remembrance of God's merciful acts in favor of Israel. The reference to David and his throne for "all the days" (col. IV, lines 5–6) is part of this section which, intriguingly, finishes in line 14 with the following assertion: "and they a[t]e, were replete, and became fat [...]."³⁴⁹ Afterwards, col. V refers to God's punishment of the people because of their rebellion. Kenneth E. Pomykala concludes from this that our passage is "a historical reminiscence referring to the time of David" and the most probable interpretation is number 1 above in which the Davidic covenant refers only to David's rule without implications for his descendants.³⁵⁰

Pomykala's conclusion, though possible, is not necessarily correct, however. Beyond the fact that there are lacunae in the text, Daniel K. Falk has more recently downplayed the relationship between 4Q504 and the Taḥanunim. He adds that "the common themes and most of the terminological similarities between *Word of the Luminaries* and the Taḥanunim are also shared by the penitential supplications for fast days and the Day of Atonement."³⁵¹

The major problem of Pomykala's argument, however, is the assumption that a reference to the Davidic covenant in the section of remembrances im-

---

347 D. Flusser, "Psalms, Hymns and Prayers," in *Jewish Writings of the Second Temple Period: Apocrypha, Pseudepigrapha, Qumran Sectarian Writings, Philo, Josephus*, ed. Michael E. Stone. *CRINT* (Van Gorcum; Fortress, 1984), 567; M. R. Lehmann, "A Re-interpretation of 4 Q Dibrê Ham-me'oroth," *RevQ* 17, no. 5 (1964): 106–110; Bilhah Nitzan, *Qumran Prayer and Religious Poetry*, trans. Jonathan Chipman, STDJ 12 (Brill, 1994), 89–99; Pomykala, *The Davidic Dynasty Tradition*, 176, n. 21. Contra Falk, *Daily, Sabbath, and Festival Prayers*, 73–75. The term *taḥanunim* (supplication) comes from Dan 9:3, 17. Among examples of such prayers in the Hebrew Bible are Neh 9; Pss 44, 74, 89; Isa 63; Dan 9. For further examples in Second Temple literature, see Flusser, "Psalms, Hymns and Prayers," 570–573.

348 Flusser, "Psalms, Hymns and Prayers," 570–571.

349 García Martínez and Tigchelaar, eds., *The Dead Sea Scrolls Study Edition*, 2:1015.

350 Pomykala, *The Davidic Dynasty Tradition*, 179. He adds that immediately after the reference to David in lines 6–7, lines 8–12 probably refer to the reign of Solomon, (Ibid).

351 Falk, *Daily, Sabbath, and Festival Prayers*, 75. He notes, also, thematic and terminological parallels with the Amidah or Eighteen Benedictions (Shemoneh Esreh), that is an ancient Jewish daily prayer.

plies that this covenant was understood as applying to David only; that is, only a historical reminiscence of his rule. Bilhah Nitzan studies the remembrances of 4Q504 and finds that they invoke events that are among the fundamentals of Jewish faith; for example, "the creation, the covenant with the patriarchs, the exodus from Egypt, the giving of the Torah, the relations of election and covenant between God and His people over the course of the generations, all given in apparently chronological order."[352] She concludes that this act of remembrance had the purpose of creating "a link between the worshippers and the generations of their ancestors, and ... [to] arouse perpetual hope."[353] The references to the Sinaitic covenant and the covenant with the patriarchs as part of God's mercy to the nation in the past do not imply that they were matters of the past, or applied only to the past. For example, in the following column (4Q504 1–2 V, 5–14) the Sinaitic covenant is invoked for the restoration of Israel. Thus, a reference in this passage to an eternal covenant with David remains possible, in spite of its inclusion in the remembrances section of this prayer.

Commentary on Genesis A (4Q252)

A second reference is found in *Commentary on Genesis A* (4Q252 or 4QCommGen A) col. V, lines 1–7. This passage is a commentary on Gen 49:10:

1 [...לו]א יסור שליט משבט יהודה בהיות לישראל ממשל
2 [לוא י]כרת יושב כסא לדויד כי המחקק היא ברית המלכות
3 [ואל]פי ישראל המה הדגלים ... עד בוא משיח הצדק צמח
4 דויד כי לו ולזרעו נתנה ברית מלכות עמו עד דורות עולם אשר
5 שמר י[...] [התורה עם אנשי היחד כי
6 [...]. היא כנסת אנשי
7 [...]. נתן

1 *Gen 49:10* The scepter shall [no]t depart from the tribe of Judah. While Israel has the dominion,
2 there [will not] be cut off someone who sits on the throne of David. For «the staff» is the covenant of royalty,
3 [and the thou]sands of Israel are «the standards». *Blank* Until the messiah of righteousness comes, the branch
4 of David. For to him and to his descendants has been given the cove-

---
352 Nitzan, *Qumran Prayer and Religious Poetry*, 98.
353 Ibid., 92.

nant of the kingship of his people for everlasting generations, which
5 he observed [...] the Law with the men of the Community, for
6 [...] it is the assembly of the men of [...]
7 [...] He gives³⁵⁴

This passage expresses a clear hope that "while Israel has dominion" (line 1) a Davidic king will reign perpetually (line 2).³⁵⁵ The basis for this belief is the "covenant of the kingship" that has been granted to David "for everlasting generations" (line 4), a clear reference to 2 Sam 7:11–16; 23:5 and Ps 89:4–5; 20–38. The clause "while [or when] Israel has dominion" is probably included to explain why a Davidic king was not ruling over Israel at the time.³⁵⁶

We should note that the only characteristic given of the future Davidic king is that he will be a "righteous messiah." This document interprets, then, the Davidic covenant similarly to Jer 23:5–6 and 33:15–17 that promise "I will raise up a righteous Branch."

Florilegium (4Q174)

A third reference is found in *Florilegium* (4Q174 or 4QFlor).³⁵⁷ This document offers a commentary on several passages with the purpose of illuminating the circumstances in the last days.³⁵⁸ Lines 1–13 in col. I are a commentary on

---

354 Text and translation from García Martínez and Tigchelaar, eds., *The Dead Sea Scrolls Study Edition*, 1:504–505. See also George J. Brooke, "4Q252 as Early Jewish Commentary," *RevQ* 17 (1996): 185–208, pl. xii–xiii. For a discussion regarding what kind of work 4Q252 is, see Brooke, "4Q252 as Early Jewish Commentary," 385–402; Pomykala, *The Davidic Dynasty Tradition*, 180–83.

355 Pomykala, *The Davidic Dynasty Tradition*, 184–185. עד in line 3 would be better translated as "when" and not "until." Evidently, the coming of "the messiah of righteousness ... , the branch," does not mark the end limit of the Davidic line on the throne; instead, his coming secures the throne for the Davidic line (ibid., 186–187).

356 H. Stegemann identified the script of this document as Herodian yielding a date between 30 BCE and 70 CE. "Weitere Stücke von 4QPsalm 37, 4QPatriarchal Blessings, und Hinweis auf eine unedierte Handschrift aus Höhle 4Q mit Exzerpten aus dem Deuteronomium," [More Fragments from 4QPsalm 37, 4QPatriarchal Blessings, and Reference to an Unpublished Manuscript from Cave 4Q with Excerpts from Deuterononmy,] *RevQ* 6 (1967–1969): 193–227; as cited by Pomykala, *The Davidic Dynasty Tradition*, 180–81. Pomykala suggests that the Davidic covenant is used polemically to challenge the legitimacy of a reigning king; probably against Herodian or Roman kings (*The Davidic Dynasty Tradition*, 188–91).

357 This document has been dated on the basis of paleography to the end of the 1st century BCE and the 1st century CE (Jonathan G. Campbell, *The Exegetical Texts*, Companion to the Qumran Scrolls, no. 4 [London: T&T Clark, 2004], 35; Pomykala, *The Davidic Dynasty Tradition*, 192). For an introduction, see Campbell, *The Exegetical Texts*, 33–44.

358 The phrase אחרית הימים (the last days) occurs repeatedly in the text (col. I, lines 2, 12, 15, 19).

2 Sam 7:10–14. Lines 10–13 express in clear terms a hope for the restoration of Davidic rule in the last days:

10 [וה]גיד לכה יהוה כיא בית יבנה לכה והקימותי את זרעכה
אחריכה והכינותי את כסא ממלכתו
11 [לעו]לם אני אהיה לוא לאב והוא יהיה לי לבן הואה צמח דויד
העומד עם דורש התורה אשר
12 [ ] יקים [בצי]ו[ן בא]חרית הימים כאשר כתוב והקימותי את סוכת
דויד הנופלת היאה סוכת
13 דויד הנופל[ת א]שר יעמוד להושיע את ישראל *vacat*
14 מדרש מאשרי[ן ה]א[יש אשר לוא הלך בעצת רשעים פשר
הדב]ר המה [סרי מדרך] הרשעים]
15 אשר כתוב בספר ישעיה הנביא לאחרית [ה]י[מים ויהי כחזקת
[ ] היד ויסרני מלכת בדרך]
16 העם הזה והמה אשר כתוב עליהמה בספר יחזקאל הנביא
אשר לו[א יטמאו עוד בכול]
17 [ג]ו[ל]ו[]ליהמה המה בני צדוק וא[נ]שי עצת[מ]ה רוד[פי צ]דק
מאחריהמה לעצת היחד
18 [למה רגש]ו גויים ולאומים יהג[ו ריק ית]יצבו [מלכי ארץ ור]
וזנים נוסדו ביחד על יהוה ועל
19 [משיחו פ]שר הדבר[] אשר ירגשו מלכי הגו[י]ים וה[גו ריק על]
בחירי ישראל באחרית הימים

10 [And] YHWH [de]clares to you that *2 Sam 7:12–14* «he will build you a house. I will raise up your seed after you and establish the throne of his kingdom
11 [forev]er. I will be a father to him and he will be a son to me.» This (refers to the) «branch of David», who will arise with the Interpreter of the law who
12 [will rise up] in Zi[on in] the [l]ast days, as it is written: Amos 9:11 «I will raise up the hut of David which has fallen», This (refers to) «the hut of
13 David which has fall[en», w]ho will arise to save Israel. *Blank*
14 Midrash of Ps 1:1 « Blessed [the] man who does not walk in the counsel of the wicked ». The interpretation of this wor[d: they are] those who turn aside from the path of [the wicked,]

15 as it is written in the book of Isaiah, the prophet, for [the] last days: Isa 8:11 « And it happened that with a strong [hand he turned me aside from walking on the path of]
16 this people». And (this refers to) those about whom it is written in the book of Ezekiel, the prophet, that Ez 44:10 « [they should] no[t defile themselves any more with all]
17 their [i]d[o]ls ». This (refers to) the sons of Zadok and (to) the m[e]n of [the]ir council, those who see[k jus]tice eagerly, who have come after them to the council of the community.
18 Ps 2:1 [« Why ar]e the nations [in turmoil] and hatch the peoples [idle plots? The kings of the earth t]ake up [their posts and the ru]lers conspire together against YHWH and against
19 [his anointed one ». Inter]pretation of the saying: [the kings of the na]tions [are in turmoil] and ha[tch idle plots against] the elect ones of Israel in the last days.³⁵⁹

It is important to note that the hope for the restoration of the throne to the Davidic line is one of several aspects of the events of the "last days." The others are the building of the sanctuary of the Lord (I, 1–6), the provision of rest from the sons of Belial (I, 7–9), and the restoration of a righteous priesthood from the line of Zadok (I, 14–19; quoting Ezek 44:10 in line 16).

The building of the sanctuary of the Lord and the provision of rest from enemies are elements clearly included in the Davidic covenant of 2 Sam 7.³⁶⁰ The expectation of a righteous priesthood through the line of Zadok shows, however, that this document has followed the interpretation of the post-exilic prophets who expected the rule of the scion of David alongside a priestly figure. This is clear. The mention of the line of Zadok (lines 16–17) quotes Ezek 44:10, something that helps to explain the figure of the "Interpreter of the law" in lines 11–12 as being a priest. The identification of the seed of David as Branch of David (צמח דויד) is an allusion to Jer 23:5; 33:15.³⁶¹ Finally, it is the quotation of Amos 9:11 in line 12 which establishes the promise of the restoration of the throne to David's line in the future.

---

359 Text and translation from García Martínez and Tigchelaar, eds., *The Dead Sea Scrolls Study Edition*, 1:352–353. See also, John M. Allegro and with the collaboration of Arnold A. Anderson, *Qumrân Cave 4: I (4Q158–4Q186)*, Discoveries in the Judaean Desert 5 (Clarendon, 1968), 53–57, pl. xix–xx.

360 For the building of the temple, see Michael Owen Wise, "4QFlorilegium and the Temple of Adam," *RevQ* 15 (1991): 103–132.

361 Schniedewind, "King and Priest," 75–76; Pomykala, *The Davidic Dynasty Tradition*, 195.

Commentary on Isaiah (4Q161)

A fourth reference is found in 4Q161 (or 4QpIsa^a) which contains a commentary on Isa 10:21–11:5. The manuscript consist of 10 fragments arranged in 3 columns.[362] The commentary of Isa 11:1–5 is found in frags. 8–10, col. III, 11–25.[363] After citing Isa 11:1–5 (lines 11–17); lines 18–25 interpret the text in the following way:

18 [פשר הדבר על צמח] דויד העומד באח[רית הימים אשר]
19 [ברוח שפתיו ימית או]יבו ואל יסומכנו ב[רוח ג]בורה [...]
20 [... כ]סא כבוד נזר ק[ודש] ובגדי ריקמו[ת]
21 [...]ן בידו ובכול הגו[אי]ם ימשול ומגוג
22 [... כו]ל העמים תשפוט חרבו ואשר אמר לוא
23 [למראה עיניו ישפוט]ולוא למשמע אוזניו יוכיח פשרו אשר
24 [...]וכאשר יורוהו כן ישפוט ועל פיהם
25 [...]עמו יצא אחד מכוהני השם ובידו בגדי

18 [The interpretation of the word concerns the shoot] of David which will sprout in the fi[nal days, since]

19 [with the breath of his lips he will execute] his [ene]my and God will support him with [the spirit of c]ourage [...]

20 [... thro]ne of glory, h[oly] crown and multi-colour[ed] vestments

21 [...] in his hand. He will rule over all the peo[ple]s and Magog

22 [...] his sword will judge [al]l the peoples. And as for what he says: «He will not

23 [judge by appearances] or give verdicts on hearsay», its interpretation: which

24 [...] and according to what they teach him, he will judge, and upon their authority

25 [...] with him will go out one of the priests of renown, holding in his hand clothes (of)

---

362 Regarding the problem of ordering the fragments, see Maurya P. Horgan, *Pesharim: Qumran Interpretations of Biblical Books*, CBQMS 8 (Catholic Biblical Association of America, 1979), 70–73. This text has been dated between 30 BCE and 20 CE on the basis of paleography (Pomykala, *The Davidic Dynasty Tradition*, 198).

363 Text and translation are from García Martínez and Tigchelaar, eds., *The Dead Sea Scrolls Study Edition*, 1:316–317. For the *editio princeps*, Allegro and Anderson, 11–15, pl. iv-v.

Three elements of this interpretation are relevant for us. First, the "shoot ... from the stump of Jesse" of Isa 11:1 is identified by 4Q161 as a Davidic figure that will take office in the "last days" (line 18). According to most reconstructions of the text, 4Q161 refers to this Davidic figure not as נצר (shoot) but as צמח (Branch) of David which is a common messianic designation in other Qumran manuscripts (e.g., 4Q285 5, 3 [*Sefer Hamilḥama*]; 4Q174 1–2, 21 I, 11 [4QFlor]).[364]

Second, the context makes clear that the scion of David is a military figure that will take part in a battle against the Kittim in the final days and utterly defeat them (cols. I–II). The fragmentary nature of the text hinders us from knowing with certainty what the relationship between the Prince of the Congregation (נשיא עדה), who was mentioned earlier (2–6 II, 15), and the scion of David is. It is possible that they were originally identified as one.[365] 4Q161 comments little on the spiritual attributes of David's scion mentioned in Isa 11:1–5. It only says that God will support him with "the spirit of courage," something very appropriate for a warrior. This small amount of interest in his spiritual attributes is also noted in the interpretation of the "rod of his mouth" and the "breath of his lips" which refer in Isa 11 to the wisdom of David's scion (see above section "Isaiah" on page 80). 4Q161 considers this rod, instead, a "sword [with which he] will judge all the peoples" (line 22).

Finally, though a royal figure, David's scion will share the rule with another figure.[366] Line 24 says that he will judge "according to what they teach him ... and upon their authority [על פיהם]." Thus, he will rule under the supervision of "instructors." The explicit identity of who these "instructors" are is lost. Most probably, this document interprets the Davidic covenant along the lines set by Jer 33:15 and Zech 3:8; 6:12 where the "Branch of David" rules alongside a priest. The phrase על פיהם is often used in connection with the Sons of Zadok, the priests (1QS V, 2 *passim* [*Rule of the Community*]; 1Q28a I, 2 [*Rule of the Congregation*]). In fact, line 25 may refer to this figure: "with him will go out one of the priests of renown."

Sefer Hamilḥama (4Q285)

Finally, 4Q285 (*Sefer Hamilḥama*) has a further reference to a Davidic messiah. This document comprises 10 fragments which probably represent the

---

364 Horgan, 85. Note that this is how the scion of David is referred to in Jer 23:5; 33:15; and Zech 3:8; 6:12.
365 Pomykala, *The Davidic Dynasty Tradition*, 201.
366 Line 20 talks about a "throne of glory, [a] holy crown and multi-coloured vestments."

remains of six successive columns.³⁶⁷ Fragment 7 reads:

1 [... כאשר כתוב בספר]ישעיהו הנביא ונוקפ[ו]
2 [סבכי הי]ר בברזל ולבנון באדיר יפול ויצא חוטר מגזע ישי
3 [ונצר משרשין יפרה ...] צמח דויד ינשפטו את
4 [...] והמיתו נשיא העדה צמ[ח]
5 [דויד ... בנגעי]ם ובמחוללות וצוה כוהן
6 [השם ... ח]לל[י]ן כתיים [ל]

1 [As it is written in the book of]Isaiah the prophet: 'Cut down shall be
2 [the thickets of the forest with an axe, and Lebanon by a majestic one shall f]all. And there shall come forth a shoot from the stump of Jesse,
3 [and out of his roots a sapling will grow'. ...] the Branch of David, and they will enter into judgment with
4 [...] and the Prince of the Congregation, the Bran[ch of David,] shall put him to death
5 [... by stroke(?)]s and wounds(?). And a priest [of renown(?)] will command
6 [... the s]lai[n] of the Kittim[...] [...]³⁶⁸

In the first half of the 1990s there was a highly publicized debate over whether the Davidic messiah pierces someone or is himself killed in the war with the Kittim (lines 4–5).³⁶⁹ The debate focused on the vocalization of והמיתו in line 4. The two suggested readings, וְהֱמִיתוֹ ("and he will kill him") and וְהֵמִיתוּ ("and they will kill"), are grammatically possible. The context, however, strongly suggests—at least in my view—the former reading in which it is Branch who kills another person. This document suggests a triumphant Messiah and, as we saw above, 4Q252 mentions that Israel's victory in the eschatological battle marks the beginning of the restoration of dominion to Israel and the time when the Davidic kingship will not be cut off.³⁷⁰

The fragment contains an isolated commentary on Isa 10:34 and 11:1. The context is a battle between Israel and the Kittim.³⁷¹ Lebanon and the forest,

---

367 Stephen J. Pfann and others, *Qumran Cave 4: XXVI Criptic Texts and Miscellanea*, Discoveries in the Judaean Desert 36 (Clarendon, 2000), 228–229.

368 Ibid., 238–239. Cf. frg. 5 in García Martínez and Tigchelaar, eds., *The Dead Sea Scrolls Study Edition*, 2:642–643. This manuscript has been dated towards the end of the 1st century BCE (Pfann and others, *Qumran Cave 4*, 232).

369 For references see Pomykala, *The Davidic Dynasty Tradition*, 203, n. 132.

370 For further discussion, see Martin G. Abegg, Jr., "Messianic Hope and 4Q285: A Reassesment," *JBL* 113 (1994): 81–91; Pomykala, *The Davidic Dynasty Tradition*, 207–209.

371 For details, see Abegg, Jr., "Messianic Hope and 4Q285," 82.

which are cut down, symbolize enemy nations (the Kittim) and the kings who are slain (lines 2, 6).[372] The reference to the Davidic figure in lines 2–4 is important for several reasons. First, this document explicitly identifies the figure promised in Isa 11:1 with the Branch of David, a title taken from Jer 23:5; 33:15; Zech 3:8; 6:12. This suggests the influence of the post-exilic prophets Jeremiah (and Zechariah?) in Qumran's expectation of a messianic figure. Second, line 4 also indicates that the figure designated by the title Branch of David is for the first time definitely identified with the נשיא העדה (Prince of the Congregation).[373] Finally, the נשיא העדה rules alongside a priestly figure. It is, in fact, the priest who orders the execution of the Kittim (line 5). The נשיא העדה follows the commands and is supervised in his judgments by the priestly figure. This view is also attested in 4Q161 8–10, III, 24 "and according to what they teach him, he will judge" (see above section "Commentary on Isaiah [4Q161]" on page 130).

Apocryphon of Daniel or "Son of God" Document (4Q246)

This is a fragmentary text that has produced widely divergent interpretations.[374] It consists of two columns, the first of which has suffered a vertical tear resulting in the loss of about a third to half of each line.[375]

Col. I

1 [... ע]לוהי שרת נפל קדם כרסיא
2 [... מ]לכא לעלמא אתה רגז ושנוך

---

372 In fact, 4Q161 identifies the cedars of Lebanon as the Kittim in its interpretation of Isa 10:34.

373 This is important because the activities of the נשיא העדה elsewhere in the document can be attributed to the Branch of David.

374 For a detailed summary of the different positions, see Collins, *The Scepter and the Star*, 155–167; Joseph A. Fitzmyer, "4Q246: The 'Son of God' Document from Qumran," *Bib* 74 (1993): 153–174. For a brief introduction, see Craig A. Evans, "Son of God Text (4Q246)," *DNTB* 1134–1137.

375 The text was first published in full by Émile Puech ("Fragment d'une Apocalypse en Araméen [4Q246=pseudo DanJ] et le 'Royaume de Dieu,' " *RB* 99 [1992]: 104–109; idem, "4QApocryphe de Daniel ar [Pl. XI]," in *Qumran Cave 4 XVII: Parabiblical Texts, Part 3*, ed. James C. VanderKam, DJD 22 [Clarendon, 1996], 165–184). See also the reconstruction by Frank Moore Cross ("Notes on the Doctrine of the Two Messiahs at Qumran and the Extracanonical *Daniel Apocalypse* [4Q246]," in *Current Research and Technological Developments on the Dead Sea Scrolls: Conference on the Texts from the Judean Desert, Jerusalem, 30 April 1995*, ed. Donald W. Parry and Stephen D. Ricks, STDJ 20 [Brill, 1996], 1–13; Frank Moore Cross, "The Structure of the Apocalypse of 'Son of God' [4Q246]," in *Emanuel: Studies in Hebrew Bible Septuagint and Dead Sea Scrolls in Honor of Emanuel Tov*, ed. Shalom M. Paul and others, VTSup 94 [Brill, 2003], 154–158).

3] ... [.א חזוך וכלא אתה עד עלמא
4] ... בר]בין עקה תתא על ארעא
5] ... ונחשירון רב במדינתא
6] ...]מלך אתור [ום]צריך
7] ... רב להוה על ארעא
8] ... יע]בדון וכלא ישמשון
9] ... בר]בא יתקרא ובשמה יתכנה

Col. II

1 ברה די אל יתאמר ובר עליון יקרונה כזיקיא
2 די חזיתא כן מלכותהן תהוה שני[ן] ימלכון על
3 ארעא וכלא ידשון עם לעם ידוש ומדינה למדני[נ]ה
4 *vacat* עד יקום עם אל וכלא יניח מן חרב
5 מלכותה מלכות עלם וכל ארחתה בקשוט ידי[ן]
6 ארעא בקשט וכלא יעבד שלם חרב מן ארעא יסף
7 וכל מדינתה לה יסגדון אל רבא באילה
8 הוא יעבד לה קרב עממין ינתן בידה וכלהן
9 ירמה קדמוהי שלטנה שלטן עלם וכל תהומי

Col. I

1 [...] settled [up] on him and he fell before the throne
2 [... k]ing forever. You are angry, and have changed you
3 [...] ... your vision, and everything that shall come forever.
4 [... mi]ghty ones, oppression will come upon the earth
5 [...] and great slaughter in the provinces
6 [...] king of Assyria [and E]gypt
7 [...] and he will be great over the earth
8 [...] they [will d]o, and all will serve
9 [... gr]eat will he be called and he will be designated by his name.

Col. II

1 He will be called son of God, and they will call him son of the Most High. Like the sparks
2 that you saw, so will their kingdom be; they will rule several year[s] over
3 the earth and crush everything; a people will crush another people, and a province another provi[n]ce.
4 *Blank* Until the people of God arises and makes everyone rest from the sword. *Blank*

5 His kingdom will be an eternal kingdom, and all his paths in truth. He will jud[ge]
6 the earth in truth and all will make peace. The sword will cease from the earth,
7 and all the provinces will pay him homage. The great God is his strength,
8 he will wage war for him; he will place the peoples in his hand and
9 cast them all away before him. His rule will be an eternal rule, and all the abysses[376]

The principal question that divides scholars in their interpretation of this text is whether the personage designated "son of God" is a positive or negative figure.[377] A slight majority of scholars favor a positive view of this figure and consider him a Davidic eschatological redeemer who will overthrow God's enemies and establish the eternal kingdom of God.[378] The basis of this interpretation is the title "son of God" which is considered a Davidic title (2 Sam 7:14; Pss 2:7–8; 89:26–27).[379] Furthermore, the notion in lines 8–9 that God "will place the peoples in his hand" reminds us as well of Ps 2:8 where God promises his "messiah," "I will make the nations your heritage, and the ends of the earth your possession." Similarly, lines 4–6 refer to his kingdom as being eternal and establishing "rest" or "peace" upon the earth. These were also part of the Davidic promises in 2 Sam 7:11, 13, 16.[380]

---

376 I am quoting here García Martínez and Tigchelaar, eds., *The Dead Sea Scrolls Study Edition*, 1:492–495. They follow Puech ("4QApocryphe," 165–184).

377 E.g., J. T. Milik suggested that it refers to the Seleucid king Alexander Balas (son of Antiochus Epiphanes) who proclaimed himself "son of God." In this reading, the text predicts that his reign will be destroyed ("Les modèles Araméens du livre d'Esther dans la grotte 4 de Qumran," *RevQ* 15 [1992]: 383). David Flusser understood the first part to refer to the antichrist who takes for himself the title "son of God" ("The Hubris of the Antichrist in a Fragment from Qumran," *Imm* 10 [1980]: 31–37). See also, Karl A. Kuhn, "The 'One Like a Son of Man' Becomes the 'Son of God'," *CBQ* 69 (2007): 23, n. 8.

378 Collins, *The Scepter and the Star*, 154–172; Cross, "Notes on the Doctrine of the Two Messiahs," 1–13; Fitzmyer, "4Q246," 153–157; Kuhn, "The 'One Like a Son of Man' Becomes the 'Son of God'," 22–42; Johannes Zimmermann, "Observations on 4Q246—The 'Son of God'," in *Qumran-Messianism: Studies on the Messianic Expectations in the Dead Sea Scrolls*, ed. James H. Charlesworth, Hermann Lichtenberger, and Gerbern S. Oegema (Mohr Siebeck, 1998), 175–190.

379 John J. Collins cites two passages to support the view that the Davidic messiah was regarded as son of God at Qumran (1QSa [1Q28a]; 4Q369) in *The Scepter and the Star*, 164–165. Cf. John J. Collins, "The *Son of God* Text from Qumran," in *From Jesus to John: Essays on Jesus and New Testament Christology in Honour of Marinus de Jonge*, ed. Martinus C. De Boer, JSNT-Sup 84 (JSOT Press, 1993), 80. See esp. Craig A. Evans, "Are the 'Son' Texts at Qumran Messianic? Reflections on 4Q369 and Related Scrolls," in *Qumran-Messianism: Studies on the Messianic Expectations in the Dead Sea Scrolls*, ed. James H. Charlesworth, Hermann Lichtenberger, and Gerbern S. Oegema (Mohr Siebeck, 1998), 135–153.

380 See Jon Laansma, *"I Will Give You Rest": The Rest Motif in the New Testament with Special Reference to Mt 11 and Heb 3–4*, WUNT II/98 (Mohr Siebeck, 1997), 112.

Summary

Those Qumran sectarian writings that refer to the Davidic covenant interpret its fulfillment in eschatological terms. In the last days, the Branch of David will arise and take office. They identify the Branch of David with the Prince of the Congregation. His main function is military. He will lead the war against the enemy (the Kittim). At the time of the victory, Davidic rule is restored never to be cut off. His role, however, is subordinated to the authority of the priests. His main role, then, is to lead in the war against the eschatological enemies.[381] Note as well that 4Q174 I, 6–13 contains the intriguing remark that the Branch of David will build a "temple of man."

4 Ezra

Fourth Ezra refers to the Davidic dynasty in the interpretation of its fifth vision.[382] This vision (*4 Ezra* 11:1–12:3) describes an eagle with 3 heads and 12 wings that reigns over the earth. Its rule is oppressive. Next, a lion rises from the forest and pronounces the judgment of The Most High against the eagle. As a result, the eagle loses its heads and wings and its body is burned. The eagle is interpreted as referring to Rome, "the fourth kingdom which appeared in a vision to your brother Daniel" (12:11; cf. Dan 7:7). Finally the figure of the lion is interpreted in 12:31–34:

> And as for the lion that you saw rousing up out of the forest and roaring and speaking to the eagle and reproving him for his unrighteousness, and as for all his words that you have heard, this is the Messiah whom the Most High has kept until the end of days, who will arise from the posterity of David, and will come and speak to them; he will denounce them for their ungodliness and for their wickedness, and will cast up before them their contemptuous dealings. For first he will set them living before his judgment seat, and when he has reproved them, then he will destroy them. But he will deliver in mercy the remnant of my people, those who

---

381   See Pomykala, *The Davidic Dynasty Tradition*, 212–214.
382   This work has been dated to ca. 100 CE (cf. *4 Ezra* 3:1) (Bruce M. Metzger, "The Fourth Book of Ezra: A New Translation and Introduction," *OTP* 1:520). Michael E. Stone provides a further analysis of the external and internal evidence and provides a date between 81 and 96 CE on the basis of the imagery of the fifth vision (chs. 11–12), (*Fourth Ezra: A Commentary on the Book of Fourth Ezra*, ed. Frank Moore Cross, Hermeneia [Fortress, 1990], 9–10). It is believed that *4 Ezra* was originally written in Hebrew and later translated into Greek. No manuscript is extant either in Hebrew or Greek. Here I will use Bruce M. Metzger's translation from a Latin version. Cf. Stone, *Fourth Ezra*, 2–9.

have been saved throughout my borders, and he will make them joyful until the end comes, the day of judgment, of which I spoke to you at the beginning.

The interpretation of the image of the lion interests us here. First, the image probably derived from Gen 49:9–10 and applied to the Davidic figure. Second, it is called the "posterity [seed] of David" and specifically named the Messiah. Finally, he was "kept until the end of days."[383] The author clearly expects, then, a Davidic figure to arise in the end of time. Some aspects of *4 Ezra*'s expectation of a Davidic Messiah are peculiar, though. Its main function is to pronounce judgment against the eagle and probably to execute it as well (11:36–12:3). This is not strange. Isaiah 11:1–5 considers judgment and its execution the main function of the "shoot of David." What is notable is the absence of monarchic and militaristic terminology in the description of his functions. He is never spoken of in terms of kingship.[384] The Davidic Messiah will not rule over Israel, but he "will make them [i.e., Israel's remnant] joyful." Even if we consider this to refer to his rule over Israel, this rule would not be forever, but only "until the end." It is interesting that *4 Ezra* 7:28–29 says that the Messiah will live 400 years and then he will die. Thus, the arrival of the Davidic messiah and his kingdom are not seen as the inauguration of a new ideal age for Israel but only a stage on the way to those events.[385] The Davidic covenant is no longer the focus of the author's hope but only a part—and not the central one—of God's design for the future.

Josephus

There are several references to the Davidic dynasty in *The Jewish Antiquities*.[386] None of them states or implies a hope for its restoration. The first reference is located in its account of the story of Ruth: "Of Obed was born Jesse, and of him David, who became king and bequeathed his dominion to his posterity

---

383 Michael E. Stone believes that on the basis of this and similar assertions regarding the Messiah in the rest of the book, the scion of the David is considered to be a preexistent figure (*Fourth Ezra*, 212).

384 Pomykala, *The Davidic Dynasty Tradition*, 218; Stone, *Fourth Ezra*, 209, 212–3.

385 Stone, *Fourth Ezra*, 213.

386 Josephus himself dated this work to the 13th year of Domitian and 56th of his own life; that is, to 93–94 CE (*Ant.* 20.267; Harold W. Attridge, "Josephus and His Works," in *Jewish Writings of the Second Temple Period: Apocrypha, Pseudepigrapha, Qumran Sectarian Writings, Philo, Josephus*, ed. Michael E. Stone, vol. 2. CRINT [Van Gorcum; Fortress, 1984], 210–211).

As far as I know, there is no work devoted to the interpretation of Davidic traditions in Josephus. I will follow here mostly the work of Pomykala (*The Davidic Dynasty Tradition*, 222–229).

for one and twenty generations" (*Ant.* 5.336 [Thackeray, LCL]). This reference to the Davidic dynasty does not allude to the promise of an eternal throne; instead, it refers to it as enduring for a long time but not eternally.

This is clearer in the narrative of the end of the kingdom of Judah: "Thus, then, did the kings of David's line end their lives; there were twenty-one of them including the last king, and they reigned altogether for five hundred and fourteen years, six months and ten days" (*Ant.* 10.143 [Thackeray, LCL]). Again, Josephus refers here to the end of the Davidic dynasty without any reference to a hope for its restoration.

For Josephus, the monarchy was one of the different phases in the government of Israel. These phases included the rule of the judges and the leadership of the Hasmonean high priests:

> For the high priests were at the head of affairs until the descendants of the Asamonaean family came to rule as kings. Before the captivity and deportation they were ruled by kings, beginning first with Saul and David, for five hundred and thirty-two years, six months and ten days; and before these kings the rulers who governed them were the men called judges and monarchs, and under this form of government they lived for more than five hundred years after the death of Moses and the commander Joshua. (*Ant.* 11.112 [Thackeray, LCL])

Thus, Josephus considered the Davidic monarchy a stage in the history of the Jewish people, a stage that was glorious but had finished.

Josephus's account of the Davidic promise itself does not refer to its unconditional and/or perpetual nature. He interprets God's promise to David as clearly conditional. We first find an allusion in Josephus's account of David's anointing by Samuel:

> He also exhorted him to be righteous and obedient to His commandments, for so would the kingship long continue to be his, and his house would become splendid and renowned; he would subdue the Philistines and, victorious and triumphant over all nations with whom he might wage war, he would in his lifetime attain glorious fame and bequeath it to his posterity. (*Ant.* 6.165 [Thackeray, LCL])

Josephus refers here to several elements that would later become part of God's promises to David—for example, victory over enemies, a great name, and posterity—but they are clearly conditional and apparently not eternal. The account of the promise itself is, likewise, conditional and not eternal:

> He [God] said, after David's death at an advanced age and at the end of a long life, the temple should be brought into being by his son and successor to the kingdom, whose name would be Solomon, and whom He promised to watch over and care for as a father for his son, and to preserve the kingdom for his children's children and transmit it to them, but He would punish him, if he sinned, with sickness and barrenness of the soil. (*Ant.* 7.93–95 [Thackeray, LCL])

A comparison of Josephus's account of David's exhortation to Solomon with the biblical text (1 Chr 2:1) shows clearly that Josephus avoids the Chronicler's reference to an eternal dynasty:

> See, a son shall be born to you; he shall be a man of peace. I will give him peace from all his enemies on every side; for his name shall be Solomon, and I will give peace and quiet to Israel in his days. He shall build a house for my name. He shall be a son to me, and I will be a father to him, and I will establish his royal throne in Israel *forever*. (1 Chr 22:10, emphasis mine)
>
> He had also foretold that his youngest son Solomon would build Him a temple, and should be called by this name, and promised to watch over him like a father, and bring prosperity to the country of the Hebrews *in his reign*, with, among other things, the greatest of all blessings, namely peace and freedom from war and civil dissension. (*Ant.* 7.337 [Thackeray, LCL], emphasis mine)

The conditional nature of the dynastic promise to David is repeated, as well, in Josephus's account of David's last words to Solomon (*Ant.* 7.384–385; par. 1 Kgs 2:1–4).

Finally, the noneternal nature of the promise becomes clear in the account of God's confirmation of the Davidic promise to Solomon in a dream (1 Kgs 9:4–9):

> As for the king himself, God said that if he abided by his father's counsels, He would first raise him to a height and greatness of happiness beyond measure, and that those of his own line should forever rule the country and the tribe of Judah. If, however, he should be faithless to his task and

forget it and turn to the worship of foreign gods, *He would cut him off root and branch and would not suffer any of their line to survive.* (*Ant.* 8.126–127 [Thackeray, LCL], emphasis mine)

The condition is clear: If Solomon is not faithful, God will "cut off" (ἐκκόπτω) his line of descendants.

In summary, the several references to the Davidic covenant in *The Jewish Antiquities* make it clear that Josephus considered the Davidic dynasty a glorious period in the history of Israel that had come to an end because of its unfaithfulness.

This agrees with Josephus's general theological interpretation of Jewish history. Josephus replaces covenantal language with benefactor/alliance terminology. God intervenes in history to reward the righteous and punish the wicked.[387] Thus, there is no such thing as an unconditional eternal promise of a Davidic dynasty. In fact, "there is not a trace of Davidic messianism in the *Antiquities*."[388]

Summary

There is a diverse reaction to the failure of the Davidic dynasty in early Judaism. The Davidic promises are not ignored but the political realities of the time color their interpretation.

For Sirach, the Davidic covenant was God's unconditional promise to David of an eternal dynasty which made the rule of Solomon, Rehoboam, and other kings possible despite their sin and folly (47:12–22). Yet, the Davidic dynasty came to an end. It is not that they forfeited the promise because of their great sins, but, in fact, repudiated it (49:4–5). Sirach presents, instead, the office of the high priest as the heir and climax of the Davidic office. This becomes clear in the eulogy of Simon the high priest in Sir 50 (esp. vv. 1–4). In fact, the contemporary relevance of the Davidic covenant for Sirach is that it helps to explain the appropriate method of succession for the office of the high priest (45:25).

First Maccabees 2:57 refers to the Davidic dynasty. David and the promises made to him are part of the glorious past that the Hasmonean rulers have emulated (1 Macc 2:49–68, esp. 57). First Maccabees does not express a hope for the future.

On the other hand, *Psalms of Solomon* 17 is probably a direct assault on the legitimacy of the Hasmonean monarchy. The author blames the sorry condi-

---

387 Attridge, "Josephus," 218–219.
388 Pomykala, *The Davidic Dynasty Tradition*, 228.

tion of the nation on the usurpation of the throne by those it didn't belong to (vv. 5–10), arguably the Hasmoneans. The author claims that the Davidic promises are eternal and expresses hope for the restoration of the Davidic dynasty. The author expects that the hoped-for Davidic king—almost a divine figure—will mediate the renewal of the covenant, gather the Jews from the land of their exile, cleanse the nation from sin, and bring righteousness and holiness to the nation. Expectations regarding the priests and temple are notoriously absent, however.

The Qumran covenanters expect the fulfillment of the Davidic covenant in the last days. The Branch of David is an eschatological figure who will lead the forces of the Sons of Light to victory against their eschatological enemies (the Kittim). This figure, however, has a subordinate role to the priests who oversee his activities.

In 4 Ezra, the Davidic king is an eschatological figure whose main (only?) function is to pronounce judgment against the eagle (Rome) and probably execute it as well. His function is of limited time, however. He rules until "the end." Thus, he fulfills a function preliminary to the end of time.

Finally, for Josephus the Davidic dynasty is a stage in the history of the Israelite nation that ended because of its sinfulness. His references to the Davidic promise consistently avoid language regarding its perpetual or unconditional nature. He does not entertain any hope for Israel based on the Davidic covenant.

The Early Judaism period attests to the diversification of the messianic hope in general and the Davidic hope in particular. Some have renounced a Davidic hope (Josephus). For others, the Davidic covenant is part of a glorious past that continues to live in the heroics of present rulers (1 Macc 2:57), or consider that its functions have been taken over by the present priesthood (Sirach). Finally, a third group still clings to the Davidic covenant as a source of eschatological hope that promises a holy and righteous ruler who restores Israel (*Pss. Sol.* 17), or a military figure who leads in the war against eschatological enemies (Qumran), or a figure who pronounces judgment but whose function is only temporary (4 Ezra). This state of affairs reflects the fragmentary nature of early Judaism.

Conclusion

The purpose of this chapter was to provide a conceptual map of the expectations regarding the rule of the ideal Davidic king in the Early Judaism period. The range of these expectations is determined by the different interpretations of the Davidic covenant upon which the Davidic dynasty was established. Therefore, I examined two groups of writings—the Hebrew Bible and Early Jewish writings—in four stages: (1) the institution of the Davidic covenant, (2) the history of righteous kings and the Davidic covenant in monarchic Israel, (3) the Davidic covenant in the psalms and the prophets, and (4), the Davidic covenant in early Jewish writings. These are the results.

The Davidic covenant consists of God's promise to establish the "house" of David—dynasty, throne, rule—forever and letting David's son build a "house" for God —temple (2 Sam 7; 1 Chr 17). The purpose of the Davidic covenant is to engraft the Davidic monarchy into the existing covenant relationship between God and the nation established at Sinai. This, however, implicates a deep transformation of the theological foundations of Israel in two ways.

First, God's relationship to the nation is now mediated through the Davidic king. By means of his divine adoption the Davidic king becomes Israel's proxy. Accordingly, God's promises to the nation—land and rest from enemies—are assigned to him so that he becomes the channel through which the covenantal blessings will flow. The Davidic mediation makes possible, as well, the eternal validity of God's promises to Israel that were only conditional in the past (Mosaic covenant). This is so because the Davidic promises are eternal and unconditional. Though God reserves the right to punish individual kings for their sins, this does not invalidate God's promises to David. Thus, the Davidic covenant renews the Mosaic covenant "under better promises."

Second, the building of the temple implies changes in the cult. God's choosing of this temple as a dwelling place for his "name" makes necessary the centralization of the cult that had been anticipated in Deuteronomy. This includes, for example, changes to the law of sacrifices and modifications to the cultic function of the priests and Levites.

In summary, the most important function the Davidic covenant assigns to the Davidic king is to be the mediator of the covenantal blessings. His rule should apply this ideal.

The analysis of the rule of righteous Davidic kings in biblical history showed a pattern of their actions that reached its most complete expression in the reigns of Hezekiah and Josiah. Seven main elements—not always in the same order—comprise this pattern. After ascending the throne, the king would (1) renew the covenant between God and the nation, (2) cleanse the land from spurious forms of worship, (3) build or repair the temple, (4) modify the cult by ordinances that secured a better service for the worshipers and reorganize or reestablish the cultic function of the priests and Levites, (5) promote the reunification of Israel, and (6) achieve "rest" by defeating enemies, and, in several cases, the rise to power of the Davidic king coincides with (7) the emergence of a faithful priest.

Notwithstanding, the catastrophic failure of the Davidic dynasty made a reinterpretation of the Davidic covenant necessary. The prophets projected the fulfillment of the Davidic covenant to the future. The seven elements that comprised the actions of righteous Davidic kings in Jewish history appear as well in their description of the rule of the future scion of David, but now they are elevated to eschatological proportions. The renewal of the covenant becomes a new covenant, the cleansing of the land becomes a cleansing of the spiritual life of the nation, an eschatological temple is built, the law is implanted in the heart of the nation, Israel is brought from the "four corners of the earth," and the rest includes the transformation of the natural order so that war and violence will not arise again. There is also the expectation that a faithful priest will arise alongside the Davidic king. According to Zechariah the eschatological king and priests will co-rule in harmony.

Reaction to the failure of the Davidic dynasty is diverse in early Judaism. Some renounce or reject any contemporary or future significance for the Davidic covenant (Josephus). Others limit its significance to the past. Either they consider David's rule one of many historical examples that current rulers should emulate (1 Maccabees), or suggest that its purposes are being fulfilled by contemporary non-Davidic rulers (Sirach). A third group continues to support the validity of the Davidic covenant for their time. They differ in their interpretations, though. The Davidic covenant may be the source of an eschatological hope that promises a holy and righteous ruler who restores the nation (*Pss. Sol.* 17), a military figure who leads in the war against eschatological enemies (Qumran), or a figure who pronounces judgment but whose function is only temporal (4 Ezra).

What are the implications of this study? This chapter has shown that expectations for the rule of the ideal Davidic king in the Hebrew Bible include seven elements/actions. These seek to fulfill the purposes of the Davidic covenant in the reign of these kings. These elements appear as well in those writings that continue to hold the validity of the Davidic promises (esp. *Psalm of Solomon* 17 and Qumran's sectarian writings).

I want to suggest that these elements provide the necessary subtext to understand Jesus's rule in heaven in the Letter to the Hebrews. Thus, Jesus is the "son" enthroned at the right hand of God (1:3, 5–6). He has defeated "death," the enemy (2:14–16), built the "house of God" (3:1–6; 8:1–5), and provided "rest" to his people (4:1–10). His ascension to the throne also implies a change in the cult. The new ministry for the temple implies the emergence of a new faithful priest from the order of Melchizedek (chs. 5–7) and a change to the law of sacrifices (9:9–10). The new king cleanses his people (9:11–14), mediates a new covenant (9:15–23), and reforms the cult by establishing one sacrifice that is effective "once for all" (9:24–10:18) and multiple spiritual sacrifices (13:10–16), all of which conclude in a joyous celebration at Mount Zion (12:22–29).

I turn now to analysis of these elements of the Davidic hope in the Letter to the Hebrews.

CHAPTER 3

Ascension and Inauguration of the Rule of the "Son" in the Letter to the Hebrews

This chapter has a simple structure. I will analyze, in order, the six passages in which the ascension of Jesus is explicitly referred to in the Letter to the Hebrews. These passages are Heb 1:6; 4:14–16; 6:19–20; 9:11–14; 9:24; 10:19–25.[1] This analysis will include two steps.

The first step concerns the imagery of the passage and its logic. In other words, we want to understand "how" the ascension is described in each passage and what that implies. Study of the imagery implies two questions: (1) "where" has Jesus entered? and (2) "what for"? Thus, for example, the study of the imagery of Heb 6:19–20 implies analysis of the image "entrance within the veil," and whether this identifies Jesus's ascension as part of a heavenly Day of Atonement.

The second step analyzes the rhetorical function of the ascension in the argument of the section of Hebrews to which that passage belongs. In other words, we want to know "why" the author of Hebrews decided to refer explicitly to the ascension in that particular place.

At the end of this chapter, I will also analyze Heb 12:18–29, which refers to the "ascension" of believers to Mount Zion. My decision to include this passage may seem strange at first because it does not refer explicitly to Jesus's ascension (only assumes it). I will argue, however, that this passage articulates the varying descriptions of Jesus's ascension as a single, multifaceted, yet harmonious event and its place in the general argument of Hebrews. This passage is key to understanding the Davidic traditions as essential to the ex-

---

1 Multiple passages in which Jesus's ascension is assumed but not directly referred to will not be studied (e.g., 8:1, etc.). In the end, the argument of the Letter as a whole assumes Jesus's ascension.

position of the ascension in Hebrews. It also explains the relationship of the Davidic traditions to the argument of the Letter as a whole.

"... When He Brings the Firstborn into the World" (Heb 1:6): Ascension and the Enthronement of the Son

ὅταν δὲ πάλιν εἰσαγάγῃ τὸν πρωτότοκον εἰς τὴν οἰκουμένην, λέγει· καὶ προσκυνησάτωσαν αὐτῷ πάντες ἄγγελοι θεοῦ.

And again, *when he brings the firstborn into the world*, he says, "Let all God's angels worship him" [emphasis mine].

The event referred to in this passage has been and continues to be a matter of debate among the interpreters of Hebrews. Three events have been suggested as being referred to in this passage: the Parousia, the incarnation, and the exaltation of Jesus in heaven. It is necessary, then, before I embark on an analysis of the ascension in this passage, to explain why I consider this passage to be, in the first place, a reference to the ascension in Hebrews.

Does This Passage Refer to the Ascension of Jesus?

The Case for the Incarnation

In his Homily on Heb 1:6–8, John Chrysostom (b. ca. 349, d. 407 CE)[2] understood this passage as referring to the incarnation:

> Our Lord Jesus Christ calls His coming in the flesh an exodus [or going out]: as when He saith, "The sower went out to sow." (Matt. xiii. 3.) And again, "I went out from the Father, and am come," (John xvi. 28.) And in many places one may see this. But Paul calls it an [eisodus or] coming in, saying, "And when again He bringeth in the First-Begotten into the world," meaning by this Bringing in, His taking on Him flesh. (*On the Epistle to the Hebrews* 3.1 [*NPNF*1 14:375])[3]

This interpretation has remained popular among current scholars of He-

---

2 P. W. Harkins, "St. John Chrysostom," *NCE* 7:945.

3 Similarly Theodoret of Cyr (b. ca. 393; d. before 466 c.e.) a few years later wrote: "Both phrases, 'brings the firstborn' and 'let them worship,' suggest the incarnation" (*Interpretation of Hebrews* 1 [PG 82:685], translation from Erik M. Heen and Philip D. W. Krey, eds., *Hebrews* ACCS 10 [InterVarsity, 2005], 22). On Theodoret of Cyr, see P. Canivet, "Theodoret of Cyr," *NCE* 13:878.

brews.⁴ They argue, correctly, that οἰκουμένη—where Jesus is brought into—normally denotes "the earth as inhabited area, exclusive of the heavens above and nether regions" (BDAG, 699) and, therefore, they conclude that this passage cannot refer to Jesus's ascension to heaven but only to his coming to earth. Harold W. Attridge suggests, then, that Heb 1:6 is part of a "three-stage" Christology, implied in the exordium, that includes Jesus's pre-existence, incarnation, and exaltation.⁵ In addition, Otto Michel and Ceslas Spicq note that the phrase "introduce into the world" (הֵבִיא לְעוֹלָם) is a Hebrew idiom for giving birth.⁶ Finally, there are, as well, possible parallel traditions to this view in early Judaism. According to *Life of Adam and Eve* 13–16, when God created Adam in his own image, Michael ordered the angels to worship him

---

4 Harold W. Attridge, *The Epistle to the Hebrews*, ed. Helmut Koester, Hermeneia (Fortress, 1989), 56; Charles A. Gieschen, *Angelomorphic Christology: Antecedents and Early Evidence*, AGJU 42 (Brill, 1998), 299; Robert P. Gordon, *Hebrews*, Readings: A New Biblical Commentary (Sheffield Academic, 2000), 43; Thomas D. Lea, *Hebrews & James*, Holman New Testament Commentary (Holman Reference, 1999), 10; Jim Girdwood and Peter Verkruyse, *Hebrews*, College Press NIV Commentary (College Press, 1997), 49; Philip Edgcumbe Hughes, *A Commentary on the Epistle to the Hebrews* (Eerdmans, 1977), 60; Ceslas Spicq, *L'épître aux Hébreux*, EBib (Gabalda, 1952), 2:17; Hugh Montefiore, *A Commentary on the Epistle to the Hebrews*, HNTC (Harper & Row, 1964), 46.

5 Attridge, *The Epistle to the Hebrews*, 56. Also, F. C. Synge, *Hebrews and the Scriptures* (SPCK, 1959), 2–4; John P. Meier, "Structure and Theology in Heb 1,1–14," *Bib* 66 (1985): 168–189; John P. Meier, "Symmetry and Theology in the Old Testament Citations of Heb 1,5–14," *Bib* 66 (1985): 504–533.

Harold W. Attridge suggests that the author of Hebrews has reinterpreted in 1:5–14 an original catena that expressed the early church's belief in Christ as exalted Lord (*The Epistle to the Hebrews*, 50). If this is the case, however, it seems strange to me that no scriptural support is given in the catena for Jesus's purification of sin (i.e., his death on the cross), which is a very important element for the argument of Hebrews—and early Christians—and was just mentioned in 1:3. Others argue, instead, that the opposite is true: The original catena demonstrated Christ's eternal existence, divine nature, incarnation, baptism, resurrection, and ascension, but was applied to the ascension of Jesus by the author of Hebrews (Montefiore, *the Epistle to the Hebrews*, 43–44).

For the argument that the catena refers only to the exaltation of Christ, see Kenneth L. Schenck, "A Celebration of the Enthroned Son: The Catena of Hebrews 1," *JBL* 120 (2001): 469–485; idem, "Philo and the Epistle to the Hebrews: Ronald Williamson's Study after Thirty Years," in *Studia Philonica Annual: Studies in Hellenistic Judaism* 14, BJS 335 ([Brown University], 2002), 40–55. I will argue below that the catena focuses only on the enthronement of Christ and is preparatory to the interpretation of Ps 8 in chap. 2. (See section "The Catena Describes the Enthronement Ceremony of the Son" on page 153.)

6 Otto Michel, *Der Brief and die Hebräer*, KEK 13 (Vandenhoeck & Ruprecht, 1966), 113, n. 1; Spicq, *L'épître aux Hébreux*, 2:17. James Moffatt, *A Critical and Exegetical Commentary on the Epistle to the Hebrews*, ICC (T&T Clark, 1924), 10, provides some examples of the use of εἰσάγω for birth in Greek literature (e.g., *Diatr.* 4.1.104). Hugh Montefiore suggested that here Hebrews alludes to the angels' worship in Luke 2:13. Harold W. Attridge is correct when he argues that "there is no need to posit any allusion to Luke 2:13, where, in any case, the angels do not worship the Son" (*The Epistle to the Hebrews*, 56, n. 67).

but Satan refused.[7]

Several scholars find it difficult to believe, however, that Hebrews refers here to God's command to worship the Son at the incarnation. They usually note that, according to Hebrews, Jesus's incarnation entailed his humiliation of being made "lower than the angels" (2:7, 9).[8] If he is made lower than the angels, how is it that God orders angels to worship him at this point?

The Case for the Parousia

Gregory of Nyssa (335/340–394 CE), on the other hand, understood this passage as referring to the second coming of Jesus.[9] His exegesis was based on the use of πάλιν (again) which he understood to modify the verb εἰσαγάγῃ (he brings); therefore, the introduction of the "firstborn into the world" was, in fact, a reintroduction, a second coming to the world:

> The addition of "again" shows, by the force of this word, that this event happens not for the first time: for we use this word of the repetition of things which have once happened. He signifies, therefore, by the phrase, the dread appearing of the Judge at the end of the ages, when He is seen no more in the form of a servant, but seated in glory upon the throne of His kingdom, and worshipped by all the angels that are around Him. (*Against Eunomius* 4.3 [*NPNF2* 5:157])[10]

More recently, this position has been advocated mostly—but not exclusively—by German authors on the same basis.[11] The strength of this position is

---

7 This work was written between 100 BCE and 200 CE, most probably towards the end of the 1st century CE (M. D. Johnson, "Life of Adam and Eve: A New Translation and Introduction," *OTP* 2:252).

This is probably a rabbinic tradition also referred to in *Sanh.* 59b and *2 En.* 31:2 (F. F. Bruce, *The Epistle to the Hebrews*, rev. ed., NICNT [Eerdmans, 1990], 57, n. 77).

8 Albert Vanhoye, *Situation du Christ: Hébreux 1–2*, LD 58 (Cerf, 1969), 154–155. Also, William L. Lane, *Hebrews 1–8*, WBC 47a (Word, 1991), 27; Kenneth L. Schenck, "Celebration," 478; Craig R. Koester, *Hebrews: A New Translation with Introduction and Commentary*, AB 36 (Doubleday, 2001), 152.

9 Regarding St. Gregory of Nyssa, see R. F. Harvanek and K. B. Steinhauser, "St. Gregory of Nyssa," *NCE* 6:517.

10 For the Greek text, see PG 45.634–635.

11 Ernst Käsemann, *The Wandering People of God: An Investigation of the Letter to the Hebrews*, trans. Roy A. Harrisville and Irving L. Sandberg (Augsburg, 1984), 101; Herbert Braun, *An die Hebräer*, HNT 14 (Mohr Siebeck, 1984), 36–37; William R. G. Loader, *Sohn und Hoherpriester: Eine traditionsgeschichtliche Untersuchung zur Christologie des Hebräerbriefes*, WMANT 53 (Neukirchener, 1981), 24–25; Eduard Riggenbach, *Der Brief an die Hebräer* (Deichertsche, 1922); reprint, Brockhaus, 1987), 19–20; Brooke Foss Westcott, *The Epistle to the Hebrews: The Greek Text with Notes and Essays* (Mcmillan, 1892; repr., Eerdmans, 1984), 22–23; Jean Héring, *The*

that St. Gregory of Nyssa's reading of πάλιν is common elsewhere in Hebrews; that is, πάλιν often has a temporal function and modifies the verb (e.g., 4:7; 5:12; 6:1, 6).[12] Scholars also note—together with those who see here a reference to the incarnation—that the firstborn is introduced not to heaven, but to the "world" (οἰκουμένη); therefore, they argue, it cannot refer to the former.[13]

Against this position, it is noted that in the sentence immediately before (v. 5) πάλιν does not modify the verb (temporal function) but introduces a quotation from Scripture (connective function; cf. 1:5; 2:13a, 13b; 4:5; 10:30). Since Heb 1:6 also quotes Scripture, it is not difficult to believe that here too πάλιν introduces a citation and, therefore, does not refer to a second introduction of the firstborn into the world.[14]

Brooke F. Westcott provides a third argument for a future understanding of the introduction of the Son to the world. He contends that the construction of ὅταν with the aorist subjunctive (εἰσαγάγῃ) "must look forward to an event (or events) in the future regarded as fulfilled at a time (or times) as yet undetermined."[15] Westcott is right in that this is normally the case.[16] Thus,

---

Epistle to the Hebrews, trans. A. W. Heathcote and P. J. Allcock (Epworth, 1970), 9; Michel, *die Hebräer*, 113; Friedrich Schröger, *Der Verfasser des Hebräerbriefes als Schriftausleger*, Biblische Untersuchungen 4 (Pustet, 1968), 50–51; Franz Delitzsch, *Commentary on the Epistle to the Hebrews*, trans. Thomas L. Kingsbury (Eerdmans, 1952), 1:67.

12 Note that Erich Gräßer argues instead that πάλιν does have a temporal function and refers to Jesus's second entrance or re-entrance into the heavenly place of rulership, but this refers to his ascension or enthronement (*An die Hebräer*, Evangelisch-Katholischer Kommentar zum Neuen Testament 17 [Benziger Neukirchener, 1990–1997], 1:78).

13 See previous section, pages 146–147.

14 The connective function of πάλιν seems to be suggested by the fact that both passages (Heb 1:5–6) form part of a catena of passages from Scripture (vv. 5–14). This was also the way it was interpreted in the Old Latin and Syriac versions (Lane, *Hebrews 1–8*, 26. Cf. Westcott, *The Epistle to the Hebrews*, 21–22). On the other hand, Herbert Braun has cited examples from Philo [*Drunkenness* 207, 208, 210] and others where πάλιν is used more than once performing different functions, including temporal and connective ones in the same passage (*An die Hebräer*, 36). This makes possible, then, that this passage refers to the second coming. I am convinced, however, by Kenneth Schenck's suggestion that πάλιν is used twice to link two passages from Scripture (2 Sam 7:14 [Heb 1:5b] and Deut 32:43 [Heb 1:6]) to Ps 2:7 (Heb 1:5a) so as to bear in its interpretation (*Understanding the Book of Hebrews: The Story Behind the Sermon* [Westminster John Knox, 2003], 49; also Girdwood and Verkruyse, *Hebrews*, 49).

It is debated exactly what passage—and in what form—is cited in Heb 1:6. The passages suggested are: Deut 32:43b, Deut 32:43d, Ps 97:7 (LXX 96:7); Odes Sol. 2:43b; 4QDeut. I tend to agree with Paul Ellingworth that the text cited is Deut 32:43b, though "in a form not now directly attested, but to which 4QDeuteronomy gives indirect support" (*The Epistle to the Hebrews: A Commentary on the Greek Text*, NIGTC [Eerdmans, 1993], 119).

15 Westcott, *The Epistle to the Hebrews*, 22. He offers as examples Matt 5:11; 10:19; Mark 4:15; Luke 6:22; Jas 1:2.

16 See Daniel B. Wallace, *Greek Grammar Beyond the Basics: An Exegetical Syntax of the New Testament* (Zondervan, 1996), 479. Though Nigel Turner adds that the aorist subjunctive usually refers to "a definite action taking place in the future but concluded before the action of the main verb" (*A Grammar of New Testament Greek*, 3.112, quoted by Ellingworth, *The Epis-*

even if πάλιν referred not to a second coming to the world, the syntactical structure of the sentence would denote that this coming is still future. The problem with Westcott's case is that in this case ὅταν ... εἰσαγάγῃ refers to a quotation; therefore, whose future is it—that of the author of Hebrews, or of the author of the OT quotation?[17] For example, Ceslas Spicq notes that the same syntactical structure is found in 1 Cor 15:27 (ὅταν ... εἴπῃ), also referring to an OT quotation. There, this syntactical structure denotes not the future, but the past.[18] Also, it must be noted that, if πάλιν is not connected with εἰσαγάγῃ, the main verb of the sentence (λέγει) would imply that the temporal aspect of εἰσαγάγῃ refers to the present too, however general this may be.[19]

Finally, damaging to this position is the fact that this section shows little interest in the Parousia. Actually, there is no reference to it, but only possible inferences from 1:13 and 2:8.[20]

The Case for the Exaltation

A slight majority of contemporary scholars hold that Heb 1:6 refers to Jesus's exaltation after his resurrection.[21] They argue that the immediate context of Heb 1:6 is Jesus's session at the right hand of God. In Heb 1:1–4, the exaltation of the Son as heir (v. 2b) is connected with his enthronement and superiority over the angels (vv. 3d–4). Since vv. 5–14 describe the adoption of the Son (v. 5) and his enthronement (vv. 8, 9, 13), it is natural to understand God's command to the angels to worship the Son (v. 6) as part of his enthronement ceremony. Moreover, the title "firstborn" itself (v. 6) is probably a Davidic ti-

---

tle to the Hebrews, 117). For the argument that ὅταν plus the aorist subjunctive does not express by itself the future and the analysis of some examples, see Vanhoye, *Situation du Christ*, 152–3.

17 Ellingworth, *The Epistle to the Hebrews*, 119.

18 Spicq, *L'épître aux Hébreux*, 2:17. Also, Moffatt, *Epistle to the Hebrews*, 10–11.

19 The present form of the verb (λέγει) suggests the permanent validity of the word of God (as in vv. 7, 3:7; 5:6; 8:8). Ellingworth, *The Epistle to the Hebrews*, 117. Also, Lane, *Hebrews 1–8*, 26.

20 Koester, *Hebrews*, 192. Regarding allusions to the Parousia, see Ellingworth, *The Epistle to the Hebrews*, 117; Bruce, *The Epistle to the Hebrews*, 56–58.

21 Samuel Bénétreau, *L'épître aux Hébreux*, CEB 10 (Édifac, 1989), 1:80–83; Bruce, *The Epistle to the Hebrews*, 56–58; David A. deSilva, *Perseverance in Gratitude: A Socio-Rhetorical Commentary on the Epistle "to the Hebrews"* (Eerdmans, 2000), 97; Ellingworth, *The Epistle to the Hebrews*, 117; Gräßer, *An die Hebräer*, 1:78; George H. Guthrie, *Hebrews*, NIVAC (Zondervan, 1998), 69; Luke Timothy Johnson, *Hebrews: A Commentary*, NTL (Westminster John Knox, 2006), 79; Martin Karrer, *Der Brief an die Hebräer: Kapitel 1,1–5,10*, Ökumenischer Taschenbuchkommentar zum Neuen Testament 20/1 (Gütersloher Verlag, 2002), 135; Koester, *Hebrews*, 192, 199–202; Lane, *Hebrews 1–8*, 26–28; Victor C. Pfitzner, *Hebrews*, ANTC (Abingdon, 1997), 54; Schenck, *Understanding*, 41; Gerd Schunack, *Der Habräerbrief*, Zürcher Bibelkommentare 14 (Theologischer Verlag, 2002), 27; Vanhoye, *Situation du Christ*, 154–157; Hans-Friedrich Weiß, *Der Brief an die Hebräer*, KEK 13 (Vandenhoeck & Ruprecht, 1991), 162.

which evokes the promise regarding the Davidic kings: "I will make him the firstborn, the highest of the kings of the earth" (Ps 89:27).[22]

The view that Jesus was worshipped by the angels when he was exalted in Heaven is well attested in early Christian literature. The "begetting" of the Son—referred to in Heb 1:5 (quoting Ps 2:7 and 2 Sam 7:14; par. 1 Chr 17:13)—is applied to the resurrection of Jesus in Rom 1:3–4.[23] Likewise, according to Phil 2:9–10, God gave Jesus "the name that is above every name" after his death on the cross "so that at the name of Jesus every knee should bend, in heaven and on earth and under the earth" (cf. Eph 1:20–22; 4:8–10; 1 Pet 3:22).[24] Finally, the apocalyptic document *Martyrdom and Ascension of Isaiah* (ca. 2nd century CE),[25] in a section of Christian origin, is more explicit:

> And I saw when he ascended into the sixth heaven, that they worshiped him and praised him; but in all the heavens the praise grew louder. And I saw how he [Jesus] ascended into the seventh heaven, and all the righteous and all the angels praised him. And then I saw that he [Jesus] sat

---

22 See Schenck, *Understanding*, 49. "Hier wird der davidische König als πρωτότοκος (υἱός) bezeichnet, und zwar als derjenige, dem die Weltherrschaft verheißen ist" (Here the Davidic king is called πρωτότοκος (υἱός), to be precise the person to whom the rule of the world is promised) (Weiß, *Der Brief an die Hebräer*, 163). Martin Karrer's insight in this context is important: "Durch die Auswahl des Zitats kombiniert der Hebr damit einen weiteren, nicht minder bedeutsamen Akzent: Die Engel, die vor dem Sohn niederfallen, stehen im Moselied über den Völkern. Sie stecken daher den universalen Horizont ab, in dem sich die Leserinnen und Lesser des Hebr aus den Völkern vorfind, und bekunden indireckt die Unterwerfung der Völker unter den Sohn" (Through the selection of the citation, Hebrews combines with it a wider, not less significant, accent: the angels, who prostrate themselves before the Son, stand above the nations in the Song of Moses. They define the universal horizon in which the readers of Hebrews find themselves coming out of the nations, and express indirectly the subjugation of the nations under the Son) (*Der Brief an die Hebräer*, 135).

It is also possible, though less likely, that an allusion is made to Deut 6:10; 11:29 which refer to Israel's entrance into Canaan: ὅταν εἰσαγάγῃ σε ... εἰς τὴν γῆν. Hebrews would replace, in this case, σε with πρωτότοκον. (Note that according to Exod 4:22, Israel is the firstborn of God.) In this sense, Jesus, as the firstborn of God, is introduced into the promised land, just as Israel was introduced into Canaan (Paul C. B. Andriessen, "La Teneur Judéo-Chrétienne de HE I 6 et II 14B–III 2," *NovT* 18 [1976]: 395–400). In Exod 16:35, the οἰκουμένη refers to the promised land into which God introduces Israel. Note that Heb 4:1–11 reinterprets the promised land as the future world (Koester, *Hebrews*, 193).

23 Probably also Acts 13:33, though there are some doubts regarding whether the begetting of the Son is connected with the resurrection or the incarnation in this passage. See below page 176, n. 132.

24 A similar view seems to be behind 1 Tim 3:16: "He [Jesus] was ... seen by angels." See also Vanhoye, *Situation du Christ*, 140–142; Weiß, *Der Brief an die Hebräer*, 162.

25 This is a composite work of which chs. 6–11 are of Christian origin and known as "the Vision of Isaiah." This section probably originated in the 2nd century CE. The first section (chs. 1–5), known as the "Martyrdom of Isaiah," includes a good deal of Jewish material and originated earlier, around 1st century CE (M. A. Knibb, "Martyrdom and Ascension of Isaiah: A New Translation and Introduction," *OTP* 2:149–150).

down at the right hand of that Great Glory, whose glory I told you I could not behold. (11:22–33; cf. 10:7–16 [Knibb, *OTP* 2:176])

This view receives two important critiques, however. First—as mentioned above—this understanding has the inconvenience that it requires the term οἰκουμένη not to carry its normal meaning in Heb 1:6.[26] Οἰκουμένη would not denote here the world, but heaven. Proponents of this view argue, however, that this is exactly what Heb 2:5—the only other place where the term οἰκουμένη is used in the epistle—tries to explain. It is noted there that the world (οἰκουμένη) which he is talking about—i.e., the one that has been subjected to the Son—is the "coming world" (τὴν οἰκουμένην τὴν μέλλουσαν), not the present one.[27] Besides, whenever Hebrews refers to the present world, it uses a different term, κόσμος (4:3; 9:26; 10:5; 11:7, 38).[28] Οἰκουμένη denotes, then, in Heb 1:6 the sphere over which the Son reigns; that is, the world to come.[29] This use of οἰκουμένη is similar, in fact, to the use of the term in the imperial rhetoric of the time. In those cases οἰκουμένη denoted not the inhabited world itself but the Roman Empire, the sphere over which the emperor ruled (e.g., Luke 2:1).[30] Thus, the introduction of the "firstborn into the world" (1:6) denotes his introduction into his dominion—represented by the heavenly court—as ruler; which is what fulfills his appointment by God as "heir of all things" (1:2).

---

26 E.g., Attridge, *The Epistle to the Hebrews*, 56.

27 Harold W. Attridge counters that οἰκουμένη in Heb 2:5 has an eschatological qualifier to distinguish it from 1:6 (*The Epistle to the Hebrews*, 56). Likewise, William R. G. Loader has argued that if the author of Hebrews wanted to refer to "the coming world," he would have added an explaining adjective as in 2:5 (*Sohn und Hoherpriester*, 24). Attridge's and Loader's critique could be answered, however, with the claim in 2:5 that the "coming world" is the one "about which we are speaking." There is no other mention of the world in this section, except 1:6 (deSilva, *Perseverance in Gratitude*, 97).

28 Albert Vanhoye argues that the OT also uses the term οἰκουνένη to denote the world to come as Hebrews does; for example, Isa 62:4 and Pss 96:9–11 [95:9–11 LXX]; 93:1 [92:1 LXX]. This οἰκουμένη is the authentic world that is established by the just work of God (Vanhoye, *Situation du Christ*, 154–157; idem, "L' οἰκουμένη dans *l'épître aux Hébreux*," *Bib* 45 [1964]: 248–253). I do not agree, however, with his suggestion that οἰκουμένη is a technical term in the OT for the eschatological kingdom of God. Harold W. Attridge correctly critiques this view, noting that in those passages οἰκουμένη simply contrasts with ἔρημος, referrring to the creation of the world, but is not a technical term for God's eschatological kingdom (*The Epistle to the Hebrews*, 56, n. 66). Nevertheless, this does not prevent the author of Hebrews from using this term to denote the eschatological realm of God's rule (deSilva, *Perseverance in Gratitude*, 97).

29 Exod 16:35 refers to the promised land as γῆ οἰκουμένη. Note that in Heb 4:1–11 the promised land refers to the future world (Koester, *Hebrews*, 193).

30 BDAG, 699; O. Flender, "οἰκουμένη," *NIDNTT* 1:518–519; Otto Michel, "ἡ οἰκουμένη," *TDNT* 5:157–159; George Johnston, "Οἰκουμένη and κόσμος in the New Testament," *NTS* 10 (1963–1964): 352–354; Vanhoye, "L'οἰκουμένη," 248–253.

Hebrews' use of οἰκουμένη, then, is ironic. It implies that the true kingdom—the unshakable one (12:28)—and the true world—the homeland of believers (11:13–15; 13:14)—are not on this earth but in heaven.[31] This is a strategy the author will use later in the epistle when he refers to the true rest for the people of God not as the one given by Joshua (4:8), and the true tabernacle as the one in heaven (8:1–2, 5). Note that in both cases, the terms κατάπαυσις and τὰ ἅγια designate *without any qualifications* an eschatological reality. It is the context that makes clear their eschatological or heavenly sense.

Hebrews 1:6 refers, then, to God's introduction of Jesus to the heavenly court. The author refers here to the ascension as an act of God in which God has brought Jesus into the heavenly realm.

It is necessary, now, to answer the following two questions. First, in terms of the imagery of the passage, how is the ascension described? Or, what is the event of which the ascension is a part? Second, in terms of the argument of Hebrews, why is the ascension referred to here?

I will address these two issues in order in the following two sections.

The Enthronement of the Firstborn over the World to Come

The Catena Describes the Enthronement Ceremony of the Son

Hebrews 1:6 is the third link in a catena of seven OT quotations (vv. 5–14).[32]

---

31 Schenck, "Celebration," 478; idem, *Understanding*, 49. Also, Gräßer, *An die Hebräer*, 1:79.

32 Similar series of OT passages can be found in Rom 3:10–18; 1 Cor 6:16–18. Outside the NT, Tatian's *Testimonia* is a similar collection (3rd century CE) which was, in fact, an enlargement of a previous document (Montefiore, *The Epistle to the Hebrews*, 43–44). Other Jewish sects also produced similar chains of OT passages; for example, 4QTestimonia (4Q175) (without commentary) and 4QFlorilegium (4Q174) (with commentary).

It has been suggested that the author of Hebrews borrowed the passages for this catena from an existing collection of Christian proof-text passages: "The author has not got the Scriptures in front of him at all. What he has in front of him is a catena of passages, a Testimony Book which may be used to persuade Jews that their Scriptures tell of Jesus the Christ. It is not he who has assembled the passages; that work has been done by predecessors, Hebrews expounds them as they stand in the Testimony Book, not as they stand in the Bible" (Synge, *Hebrews and the Scriptures* 54, cf. 3–6).

While F. C. Synge believes this is the case of all the OT quotations in Hebrews, others apply this notion only to 1:5–14, e.g., David M. Hay, *Glory at the Right Hand: Psalm 110 in Early Christianity*, SBLMS 18 (Abingdon, 1973), 38–39; Käsemann, *The Wandering People of God*, 168–72; Montefiore, *The Epistle to the Hebrews*, 43–44; Gerd Theißen, *Untersuchungen zum Hebräerbrief*, SNT 2 (Gütersloher Verlag, 1969), 34–37. (For a brief introduction to the discussion, see Schröger, *Der Verfasser*, 43–45.) Others consider that the author may have used material from a traditional catena but has reinterpreted it to reproduce his own argument, e.g., Attridge, *The Epistle to the Hebrews*, 50.

The arguments for this view include the lack of relationship between this catena and the rest of the argument and the obvious similarity between the OT lists of Heb 1:5–14 and

The nature of the catena itself and its relationship to the rest of the argument of Hebrews has been a matter of debate, however.[33]

Some argue that the sole purpose of the catena is to provide the scriptural grounds for the affirmation made in 2:1–4 that Christ is an agent of revelation superior to the angels (cf. 1:1–2). The corollary is that the readers should pay greater attention to what God has said through the Son than to what God said through the angels in the inauguration of the Mosaic covenant (2:1–4; cf. 1:1–4; 12:25–29). The superiority of the Son to the angels is part, then, of the author's contrast between the old and new covenant developed throughout the document.[34] In this sense, the catena is *an argument* whose purpose is to prove that Jesus is superior to the angels. But, why would this be necessary?[35]

Some have suggested that the author is combating here some kind of worship of angels (e.g., Col 2:18).[36] This is unlikely, however, because there is no explicit reference to this practice in Hebrews.[37] Furthermore, the angels seem to be not that important for the author or audience because they are mentioned again only in the concluding section of the argument (12:22; 13:2).[38] The similar view that the author was combating some kind of angel Christology—which would assimilate Jesus to the angels or other heavenly figures who carried salvific and/or intermediating roles according to beliefs in different first-century Jewish circles—lacks any explicit polemic elsewhere in Hebrews as well. Thus, this thesis is rendered unlikely too.[39] Finally, David

---

1 Clem. 36 which has been considered as evidence that both passages borrowed from a common source. Gareth Lee Cockerill has demonstrated, however, that 1 Clem. 36 depends, in fact, on Heb 1:5–14 and not on a preexisting source to both ("Heb 1:1–4, *1 Clem.* 36:1–6 and the High Priest Title," *JBL* 97 [1978]: 437–440; see also Koester, *Hebrews*, 198, n. 50).

33 For a list of the different suggestions and introductory bibliography, see Loren T. Stuckenbruck, *Angel Veneration and Christology: A Study in Early Judaism and in the Christology of the Apocalypse of John*, WUNT II/70 (Mohr Siebeck, 1995), 124–125.

34 Kiwoong Son, *Zion Symbolism in Hebrews: Hebrews 12:18–24 as a Hermeneutical Key to the Epistle*, Paternoster Biblical Monographs (Paternoster, 2005), 105–124. Also, deSilva, *Perseverance in Gratitude*, 83–84, 94–95; George Guthrie, *Hebrews*, 74; Lane, *Hebrews 1–8*, 32–33; Michel, *die Hebräer*, 125–126; Spicq, *L'épître aux Hébreux*, 2:52.

35 The author does not endeavor, for example, to prove Jesus's superiority over the prophets—mentioned in Heb 1:1.

36 Robert Jewett, *Letter to Pilgrims: A Commentary on the Epistle to the Hebrews* (Pilgrim, 1981), 5–13; Stuckenbruck, *Angel Veneration and Christology*, 119–139; Hans Windisch, *Der Hebräerbrief*, 2d ed. Handbuch zum Neuen Testament 14 (Mohr Siebeck, 1931), 17. For a more nuanced evaluation of the problem and comprehensive bibliography, see Stuckenbruck, *Angel Veneration and Christology*, 124–26.

37 In fact, the thesis that angel worship is addressed elsewhere (e.g., Col 2:18) is also problematic (Attridge, *The Epistle to the Hebrews*, 51; see also, deSilva, *Perseverance in Gratitude*, 95; George Guthrie, *Hebrews*, 72).

38 See Koester, *Hebrews*, 83–86.

39 Proponents include, Lala Kalyan Kumar Dey, *The Intermediary World and Patterns of Perfection in Philo and Hebrews*, SBLDS 25 (Scholars Press for Society of Biblical Literature,

A. deSilva has correctly observed that for the author of Hebrews to begin a polemic here would be bad rhetoric. He would "run the risk of alienating the hearers by 'correcting' them too quickly (before trust has been fully established within the speech)."[40]

Others consider that the catena *describes* the scene of the enthronement of the Son at the right hand of God.[41] The seven quotations of the catena are grammatically arranged in three sentences.[42] It is argued that each sentence introduces a stage of the enthronement ceremony: (1) the declaration that the king has been adopted by God as Son (v. 5), (2) the presentation of the Son to his people, the bestowal of royal symbols, and his proclamation as king (vv. 6–12), and (3) the enthronement proper, which is the actual conferral of power (v. 13).[43] In this reading, the angels have the literary function of a

---

1975), 154; Ronald H. Nash, "The Notion of Mediator in Alexandrian Judaism and the Epistle to the Hebrews," *WTJ* 40 (1977): 89–115. See also discussion in Donald A. Hagner, *Hebrews*, NIBC 14 (Hendrickson, 1990), 30; Attridge, *The Epistle to the Hebrews*, 51–52. In relation to beliefs attested in the Dead Sea Scrolls, see Yigael Yadin, "The Dead Sea Scrolls and the Epistle to the Hebrews," in *Aspects of the Dead Sea Scrolls* 4 (Magnes, 1965), 39–49; Hughes, *Hebrews*, 52–53. On the other hand, Charles A. Gieschen proposes that Hebrews embraces an angelomorphic Christology (*Angelomorphic Christology*, 294–314).

40 deSilva, *Perseverance in Gratitude*, 95. See also, Ellingworth, *The Epistle to the Hebrews*, 109–10.

41 Ellingworth, *The Epistle to the Hebrews*, 108–10; Gräßer, *An die Hebräer*, 71–72; Joachim Jeremias, *Die Briefe an Timotheus und Titus*, NTD 9 (Vandenhoeck & Ruprecht, 1975), 28; Käsemann, *The Wandering People of God*, 99–101; Koester, *Hebrews*, 201; Franz Laub, *Bekenntnis und Auslegung: Die paränetische Funktion der Christologie im Hebräerbrief*, Biblische Untersuchungen 15 (Pustet, 1980), 56; Susanne Lehne, *The New Covenant in Hebrews*, JSNTSup 44 (JSOT Press, 1990), 28; Michel, *die Hebräer*, 116–117; C. F. B. Moule, *The Birth of the New Testament*, 3d rev. and rewritten ed., HNTC (Harper & Row, 1982), 33–34; Schenck, *Understanding*, 40–55; F. J. Schierse, *The Epistle to the Hebrews*, trans. Benen Fahy, New Testament for Spiritual Reading (Herder & Herder, 1969), 5–7.

42 Each of the sentences is provided with an introductory phrase:

Heb 1:5: Τίνι γὰρ εἶπέν ποτε τῶν ἀγγέλων ... (For to which of the angels did He ever say ...)

Heb 1:6: ὅταν δὲ πάλιν εἰσαγάγῃ τὸν πρωτότοκον εἰς τὴν οἰκουμένην, λέγει ... (And again, when he brings the firstborn into the world, he says ...)

Heb 1:13: πρὸς τίνα δὲ τῶν ἀγγέλων εἴρηκέν ποτε ... (But to which of the angels has he ever said ...)

Note, as well, the similarity of the introduction to sentences 1 and 3 (Ellingworth, *The Epistle to the Hebrews*, 108).

The sources of the seven quotations are the following: Heb 1:5 quotes Ps 2:7 and 2 Sam 7:14 (par. 1 Chr 17:13). Hebrews 1:6–12 quotes (a form not directly attested to) Deut 32:43b LXX, Pss 104:4 (103:4 LXX), 45:6–7 (44:6–7 LXX), and 102:25–27 (101:26–28 LXX). (We cannot be certain of the source of the quotation of Heb 1:6. Beyond Deut 32:43b LXX, other possibilities are Ps 96:7 LXX, *Odes Sol.* 2:43b, and 4QDeut 32:43. *Odes Sol.* 2:43b is the closest text, but MS evidence suggests that this reading is not older than the 5th century CE and that it is the result of Christian editing. For an analysis of the different solutions to the problem, see Schröger, *Der Verfasser*, 53.) Hebrews 1:13 quotes Ps 110:1 (109:1 LXX).

43 Ellingworth, *The Epistle to the Hebrews*, 108–10; Gräßer, *An die Hebräer*, 1:71; Laub, *Bekenntnis und Auslegung*, 56; Michel, *die Hebräer*, 116–117; Schierse, *The Epistle to the Hebrews*,

"scenic background" to Jesus's enthronement. This seems to be confirmed by the fact that Heb 2:5 summarizes the catena as the "subjection of the coming world" to Jesus.[44]

The three-stage substructure of the catena corresponds to the coronation liturgies evidenced in ancient Near Eastern texts—especially from Egypt—and the Hebrew Bible.[45] Joachim Jeremias also argues that the same three-stage substructure of exaltation, presentation, and enthronement is found in 1 Tim 3:16, Phil 2:9–11, Matt 28:18–20, and Rev 5:5–14.[46]

This view has received the critique that it is not possible to reconstruct with any degree of certainty the overall process of the enthronement liturgies of Israel or other ancient Near East nations (e.g., Egypt), and that even if this were possible it is not clear that such ancient ceremonies were current in the Judaism of the period.[47]

It is true that extant sources regarding ancient Near Eastern enthronement ceremonies are fragmentary in nature and do not allow a complete reconstruction of the ritual.[48] For example, the OT contains two considerable descriptions of royal coronations: 1 Kgs 1:33–53 and 2 Kgs 11:4–21 (par. 2 Chr 23:8–21); yet, both of them describe coronations in extraordinary circumstances.[49] The critique is only correct, however, in the sense that we cannot be certain that Heb 1:5–14 reproduces exactly the enthronement ritual practiced in monarchic Israel, early Judaism, or the ancient Near East. We can safely say, however, that the three stages of the coronation ritual identified in Heb 1:5–14 formed part of ancient Near Eastern coronation rituals, although they probably did not exhaust them. There is, indeed, enough evidence for this.

6–7. See also, Jeremias, *Timotheus und Titus*, 27–29.

44 Schierse, *The Epistle to the Hebrews*, 6. Also, Edgar V. McKnight and Christopher Church, *Hebrews–James*, Smyth & Helwys Bible Commentary (Smyth & Helwys, 2004), 43–45.

45 Gerald Cook, "The Israelite King as Son of God," *ZAW* 73 (1961): 202–225; Aubrey Johnson, *Sacral Kingship in Ancient Israel*, 2d ed. (University of Wales Press, 1967), 28, n. 4; Othmar Keel, *The Symbolism of the Biblical World: Ancient Near Eastern Iconography and the Book of Psalms*, trans. Timothy J. Hallett (Seabury, 1978), 247–268; Eduard Norden, *Die Geburt des Kindes: Geschichte einer religiösen Idee* (1924; reprint, Teubner, 1969); Gerhard von Rad, "The Royal Ritual in Judah," *The Problem of the Hexateuch and Other Essays*, trans. E. W. Trueman Dicken (McGraw-Hill, 1966), 222–231; Eric Voegelin, *Israel and Revelation, Order and History* (Louisiana State University Press, 1956), 1:303–310.

46 Jeremias, *Timotheus und Titus*, 28.

47 For example, Lala K. K. Dey asserts that "the evidence given does not support the view that the schema of such an ancient ceremony was current in the Judaism of the period" (*The Intermediary World*, 147). See also Mathias Rissi, *Die Theologie des Hebräerbriefs: Ihre Verankerung in der Situation des Verfassers und seiner Leser*, WUNT I/41 (Mohr Siebeck, 1987), 49.

48 Keel, *The Symbolism of the Biblical World*, 256. For references regarding the several reconstructions of these rituals in Egypt, see Keel, *The Symbolism of the Biblical World*, 257, n. 28.

49 Von Rad, "The Royal Ritual in Judah," 222.

First, similar to Egypt and other nations of the ancient Near East, the Davidic king was considered God's son.[50] Second Samuel 7:14 registers God's promise to David regarding the heir of his throne: "I will be a father to him, and he shall be a son to me" (par. 1 Chr 17:13). Later kings claimed this promise on their behalf. For example, Ps 2:7 says: "I will tell of the decree of the LORD: He said to me, 'You are my son; today I have begotten you.'" Likewise, LXX Ps 109:3 (110:3) reads: "The authority to rule is with you in the day of your power [and] in the splendors of [your] saints: *I begot you* from the womb before the morning" (translation and emphasis mine, see also, Ps 89:20–30).[51] Gerhard von Rad has suggested that the decree of the divine adoption of the king was part of the Hebrew royal ritual referred to in 2 Kgs 11:12. He argues that the "testimony" (וְאֶת־הָעֵדוּת /τὸ μαρτύριον) given to Joash as he was proclaimed king was in fact a copy of the decree of his divine adoption (cf. Ps 2:7).[52] This is

---

50 For Egypt, see the references to the royal rituals for Hatshepsut and Tutmosis III in Keel, *The Symbolism of the Biblical World*, 247–256; Rad, "The Royal Ritual in Judah," 226–227. For other ancient Near East nations, see Henri Frankfort, *Kingship and the Gods: A Study of Ancient Near Eastern Religion as the Integration of Society and Nature* (University of Chicago Press, 1948); René Labat, *Le caractère religieux de la royauté assyro-babylonienne* (Librairie d'Amerique et d'Orient, 1939); Jarl Fossum, "Son of God," ABD 6:128–129. Regarding Hebrew royal theology, see Gerald Cook, "The Israelite King as Son of God."

It should be noted, however, that although there are real similarities between the Jewish and Egyptian royal theologies, there are also fundamental divergences. For example, Gerald Cook notes: "The Egyptian tradition of the physical begetting of Pharaoh by a god is absent; the Hebrew materials remain consistent in their treatment of the king's divine sonship in terms of adoption" ("The Israelite King as Son of God," 214).

51 μετὰ σοῦ ἡ ἀρχὴ ἐν ἡμέρᾳ τῆς δυνάμεώς σου ἐν ταῖς λαμπρότησιν τῶν ἁγίων· ἐκ γαστρὸς πρὸ ἑωσφόρου ἐξεγέννησά σε. The Greek text is from the critical edition by Alfred Rahlfs, *Psalmi cum Odis*, Septuaginta: Societatis Scientiarum Gottingensis 10 (Vandenhoeck & Ruprecht, 1931). In his analysis of this passage, Gerald Cook argues that this is the original intent of the Hebrew text as well, which he translates: "In holy array from the womb of the dawn go forth; as the dew I have begotten you." This reading is supported by the LXX, Syriac, and several MSS, and does not require a change to the consonantal text of the MT (Cook, "The Israelite King as Son of God," 222).

Contemporary scholars often consider that Pss 2 and 110 were composed for the enthronement of Israelite kings. For example, Leslie C. Allen, *Psalms 101–50: Revised*, WBC 21 (Thomas Nelson, 2002), 111; Peter C. Craigie, *Psalms 1–50*, WBC 19 (Word, 1983), 67; Mitchell Dahood, *Psalm 1–50: Introduction, Translation, and Notes*, AB 16 (Doubleday, 1965), 7; James L. Mays, *Psalms*, IBC (John Knox, 1994), 45–46, 351–353; J. Clinton McCann, Jr., "The Book of Psalms: Introduction, Commentary, and Reflections," NIB 4:689, 1129; Artur Weiser, *The Psalms: A Commentary*, OTL (Westminster, 1962), 109, 693. Other Psalms believed to have the same *Sitz im Leben* are 72 and 101 (possibly also 20 and 21). Keel, *The Symbolism of the Biblical World*, 256.

52 Von Rad, "The Royal Ritual in Judah," 224–229. The coronation rite of Pharaoh included a document that contained the ancient titles, the sovereign rights, and the duties conferred on Pharaoh by the god, von Rad, "The Royal Ritual in Judah," 225; Roland de Vaux, *Les institutions de L'Ancien Testament*, 2d rev. ed. (Cerf, 1961), 1:159–160. See also Norden, *Die Geburt des Kindes*; Johnson, *Sacral Kingship*, 27–28.

Similarly, it is possible that a new name was given to the Israelite king at his enthronement. The only two clear examples of this in the OT (2 Kgs 23:34; 24:17) may involve a sign of vassal-

improbable, however. More likely, the "testimony" refers here to a copy of the law (Deut 17:18).⁵³ Notwithstanding, what remains certain is that the divine adoption of the king was an important element of Hebrew royal ideology.

The concept of the divine adoption of the ruler was also common in the Greco-Roman world. Greece took over kingship ideology from the east. The turning point was when Alexander the Great was called the "Son of Ammon" by an oracle in the desert of Lybia in 331 BCE⁵⁴ This was understood by the Greeks as Alexander being son of Zeus whom Alexander addressed thereafter as "my father" (Plutarch, *Alex.* 27–28; cf. Arrian, *Anab.* 7.8.3).⁵⁵ Later on, Ptolemaic rulers adopted such titles as "son of God," "son of Helios," "son of Zeus."⁵⁶ Similarly, in imperial Rome, the title *Divi filius*, given to Augustus and his successors, was translated θεοῦ υἱός—son of God.⁵⁷

Second, the introduction of the king to the assembly as part of the coronation solemnities is also attested. In the case of Joash, Jehoiada brought him into the assembly to make him king (2 Kgs 11:12).⁵⁸ At this time the symbols of royal office are vested on him: "Then he brought out the king's son, put the crown on him, and gave him the covenant; they proclaimed him king, and anointed him; they clapped their hands and shouted, 'Long live the king!' " (2 Kgs 11:12). Likewise, the scene of Jesus's introduction to the assembly in Heb 1:6–12 includes the vesting of royal symbols on him. The following are men-

---

age and not a native enthronement custom of Israel; however, the existence of two names for David (Elhanan, 2 Sam 21:19), Solomon (2 Sam 12:24–25), and other kings may point to this. See Vaux, *Les institutions de L'Ancien Testament*, 1:165–167; Nicolas Wyatt, " 'Jedidiah' and Cognate Forms as a Title of Royal Legitimation," *Bib* 66 (1985): 112–125. Perhaps this custom is behind the expression "I will make you a great name" (2 Sam 7:9; 1 Chr 17:8). Notice that Hebrews emphasizes the conferral of a "name ... more excellent than theirs [i.e., the angels]" (Heb 1:4).

53 See above section "Joash" on page 57

54 Peter Wülfing von Martitz, "υἱός," *TDNT* 8:336. Several illustrious persons were venerated as sons of God before Alexander the Great, Fossum, "Son of God," 6:133.

55 Fossum, "Son of God," 6:133; Petr Pokorný, *Der Gottessohn: Literarische Übersicht und Fragestellung*, ThSt 109 (Theologischer Verlag, 1917), 15.

56 Martitz, "υἱός," 8:336.

57 Adolf Deissmann, *Light from the Ancient East: The New Testament Illustrated by Recently Discovered Texts of the Graeco-Roman World*, trans. Lionel R. M. Strachan, new and completely rev. ed. (Hodder & Stoughton, 1927), 346. See also, Fossum, "Son of God," 6:133; Martin Hengel, *The Son of God: The Origin of Christology and the History of Jewish-Hellenistic Religion*, trans. John Bowden (SCM, 1976), 25–30. The use of υἱός θεοῦ by the emperors marks the only instance in which it is used as a title (Hengel, *The Son of God*, 28–31).

58 In the case of Solomon, this introduction was carried out by having him ride on the king's own mule (1 Kgs 1:33, 38). Later he is introduced to the court itself (vv. 46–48). Cf. Esth 6:7–11; Zech 9:9; Judg 5:10; 10:4; 12:14.

tioned: the throne (v. 8b), the scepter (v. 8c), and the anointing (v. 9). All this is followed by the acclamation of his eternal rule (vv. 10–12).[59]

Third, the enthronement proper of the king as the culmination of the ritual is self-explanatory (Heb 1:13). This marked the moment of his assumption of power and authority and the beginning of his rule (e.g., 1 Kgs 1:35, 46–47; 2 Kgs 11:19).

Finally, it is necessary to note that the author of Hebrews does not adopt his views regarding the kingship and enthronement of Christ in heaven di-

---

59 Regarding the anointing, see 1 Kgs 1:32–40; 2 Kgs 11:12; also, Judg 9:8; 1 Sam 9:16; 16:1, 12; 1 Kgs 19:15, 16. The anointment symbolized the conferring of grace by the Spirit of God (1 Sam 10:10; 16:13) so that the king became the Lord's anointed (e.g., 1 Sam 24:6; 26:9). In the case of Solomon, the anointing in Gihon probably implied a baptism or royal washing (1 Kgs 1:32–40). This royal washing was part of the coronation rites of Pharaoh (Fossum, "Son of God," 6:133; Keel, *The Symbolism of the Biblical World*, 258–259).

Regarding the acclamation, it was signaled in the Hebrew royal ritual by the trumpet sounding and expressed in the shout: "Long live the king" (1 Kgs 1:25, 34, 39; 2 Kgs 11:12; also, 1 Sam 10:24; 2 Sam 16:16). This shout, however, is not a wish, but an acquiescence which showed that the people accepted the king (Vaux, *Les institutions de L'Ancien Testament*, 1:163–164; Baruch Halpern, *The Constitution of the Monarchy in Israel*, HSM 25 [Scholars, 1981], 134. In the case of Solomon, the obeisance by the officials to the king is also described [1 Kgs 1:47].) The quotation of Ps 101:26–28 LXX (102:25–27) in Heb 1:10–12 fits in this context. Its purpose is manifold. First, it compares the eternal nature of Jesus with the transient nature of the angels (cf. Heb 1:7). Second, it contrasts the "son" as the creator of all things and the angels as part of God's creation (note, "he makes [ὁ ποιῶν] his angels winds ..." [Heb 1:7]). Third, it complements the notion of the divinity of the Son (v. 8) with the notion that he is creator (v. 10). Most important, however, it emphasizes the eternal nature of the rule of the son whose "years will never end" (v. 12d); therefore, it has a function equivalent to the shout "Long live the king" (see above).

The reference to Jesus as the creator of the cosmos in the context of his enthronement is appropriate. In Egypt and Mesopotamia, the enthronement of the king was considered a recreation of the world, the conquering of chaos. The king also maintained order in creation (Frankfort, *Kingship and the Gods*, 148–61, 307–12). Israelite kingship theology had similar views. Those Psalms that celebrate the kingship of Yahweh, usually referred to as "enthronement Psalms" (Pss 96–99, often linked to 47, 93 and 95; for discussion, see Marvin E. Tate, *Psalms 51–100*, WBC 20 [Word, 1990], 504–505), commonly refer to God as creator (Pss 96:5b; 98:1b; 93:1c; 96:10b; 99:4b; 99:4c). See Allen Eugene Combs, "The Creation Motif in the 'Enthronement Psalms' " (Ph.D. diss., Columbia University, 1963; University Microfilms International, 1988), 148–166. In fact, God is declared king over the earth by virtue of his victory over the forces of Chaos (i.e., creation, 93:3–4; 74:12–17; 89:10–12). God also sustains the order of creation by his righteous rule (Pss 96:10–13; 97:2, 8; 98:9; 99:4); see Keith W. Whitelam, "King and Kingship," *ABD* 4:43. Hebrews transfers these attributes to Jesus. This transference was prefigured in the theology of the Davidic rule perceived in the Psalms. For example, Ps 89:9–14 asserts that God is king over the universe because he has dominated "the raging sea" and crushed its monsters, a reference to creation (cf. Ps 74:12–17). See Tate, *Psalms 51–100*, 421. Verse 25, however, asserts that the Davidic king will share in God's victory over chaos: "I will set his hand on the sea and his right hand on the rivers." On the other hand, the king participates in the sustenance of creation by ruling justly. Thus, the Psalmist requests of God, "Give the king your justice" so that he may be "like rain that falls on the mown grass, like showers that water the earth" and "May there be abundance of grain in the land; may it wave on the tops of the mountains; may its fruit be like Lebanon; and may people blossom in the cities like the grass of the field" (Ps 72:1, 6, 16). See Michael D. Guinan, "Davidic Covenant," *ABD* 2:70.

rectly from the Jewish or Greco-Roman first-century-CE context, but through a mediated process.⁶⁰ These enthronement traditions had undergone a process of reinterpretation in at least three stages. First, foreign liturgies of enthronement were adapted to Israelite views of God and kingship. Second, these views were idealized in pre-Christian Messianic expectations. Finally, Christians found the concretization of these expectations in the coming and exaltation of Jesus.⁶¹

It seems to me persuasive in general, then, that the catena describes the enthronement of the Son "at the right hand of the majesty on high" (Heb 1:3).⁶²

The Enthronement of the Son Culminates His Victory over Death

Hebrews 2:9 asserts that Jesus was crowned "with glory and honor *because of the suffering of death*" (emphasis mine; cf. Phil 2:6–11).⁶³ We find a similar assertion in 12:2: "looking to Jesus the pioneer and perfecter of our faith, who *for the sake of the joy* [ἀντὶ τῆς χαρᾶς] that was set before him *endured the cross*, disregarding its shame, and has taken his seat at the right hand of the throne of God" (emphasis mine).⁶⁴ It seems to be important for the hortatory argu-

---

60 See Dey's critique above (p. 228, n. 47). For the suggestion, for example, that Egyptian traditions of the divine sonship of the king were mediated to the Lukan Christology, see J. Kügler, *Pharao und Christus? Religionsgeschichtliche Untersuchung zur Frage einer Verbindung zwischen altägyptischer Königstheologie und neutestamentlicher Christologie im Lukasevangelium*, BBB 113 (Philo, 1997). See also, Cook, "The Israelite King as Son of God," 202–225; Keel, *The Symbolism of the Biblical World*, 247, n. 8. For a study of the effect of the Egyptian and broader ancient Near Eastern traditions of the king as representing God on earth on Roman politics during the Republic and early empire, see J. Rufus Fears, *Princeps a diis electus: The Divine Election of the Emperor as a Political Concept at Rome*, Papers and Monographs of the American Academy in Rome 26 (American Academy in Rome, 1977), 85–188.

61 See Ellingworth, *The Epistle to the Hebrews*, 108–109.

62 This reading of the catena, however, raises two questions that I need to answer. First, if "Son" is a royal title that Jesus received at his enthronement (1:5), why are there passages that refer to him as Son already on earth (e.g., 5:7–8); that is, before his enthronement? Second, why is the description of the enthronement of the Son important for the argument of the letter? I will deal with both questions below.

63 Luke Timothy Johnson observes that the phrase διὰ τὸ πάθημα τοῦ θανάτου ("because of the suffering of death") could explain either *how* the Son was lowered beneath the angels or *why* he was enthroned (*Hebrews*, 92). A great majority of scholars prefer the latter: Jesus was enthroned *because* of his suffering death, e.g., Attridge, *The Epistle to the Hebrews*, 73, n. 35; deSilva, *Perseverance in Gratitude*, 110–112; Ellingworth, *The Epistle to the Hebrews*, 155; Gräßer, *An die Hebräer*, 1:121; George Guthrie, *Hebrews*, 100; Koester, *Hebrews*, 217; Karrer, *Der Brief an die Hebräer*, 172; Pfitzner, *Hebrews*, 62. The position of the phrase διὰ τὸ πάθημα τοῦ θανάτου right next to δόξῃ καὶ τιμῇ ἐστεφανωμένον—but separated by the subject and the verb from τὸν βραχύ τι παρ' ἀγγέλους ἠλαττωμένον—suggests that death explains why Jesus was enthroned and not how he was lowered below the angels.

64 The logic is that Jesus endured the cross in order to obtain "the joy that was set before him." Philippians 2:6–11 has the same logic: "… he humbled himself and became obedient to

ment of Hebrews that just as Jesus's enthronement was achieved through suffering, the readers need to be patient under their trials so that they may also "receive what was promised" (Heb 10:35–36; cf. 2:17; 12:1–3, 10–11; 13:13–14). I am only interested at this moment, however, with the description of Jesus's death as a victory over the devil and its relationship with Jesus's enthronement in the argument of Hebrews.

> Since, therefore, the children share flesh and blood, he himself likewise shared the same things, so that through death he might destroy [καταργέω] the one who has the power of death, that is, the devil, and free those who all their lives were held in slavery by the fear of death. For it is clear that he did not come to help angels, but the descendants of Abraham. (Heb 2:14–16)

Commentators have suggested points of contact between Hebrews' description of Jesus's victory over the devil, the one "who has the power of death," and several different traditions.[65]

Legends about Hercules (=Heracles) are one of these traditions.[66] Cynic and Stoic philosophers considered Hercules' sufferings a way to glorification. For example: "Never does glorious valour pass / to the Stygian shades. / Live, all, with courage, / and the cruel fates will then not haul you / over Lethe River. / No: when the final hour is imposed / at the end of your days, / glory

---

the point of death—even death on a cross. Therefore [διό] God also highly exalted him and gave him the name that is above every name …"

65 Harold W. Attridge offers a brief but helpful introduction to the different traditions that have been suggested to stand behind this text (*The Epistle to the Hebrews*, 79–82). His perspective, however, is wider than the one I have adopted here. He explores the models that have been used to explain a Christology that includes the incarnation, death, and exaltation. This is the result of his view that the Christology of Heb 1 reproduces all these elements, while I believe that Hebrews focuses instead on Christ's exaltation or enthronement.

66 See David E. Aune, "Heracles and Christ: Heracles Imagery in the Christology of Early Christianity," in *Greeks, Romans, and Christians: Essays in Honor of Abraham Malherbe*, ed. D. L. Balch, Everett Ferguson, and W. A. Meeks (Fortress, 1990), 13–19. Also Attridge, *The Epistle to the Hebrews*, 80, nn. 20–21; Lane, *Hebrews 1–8*, 61. For the bold proposition that the life of Christ was shaped by the author of an "Urevangelium" (a putative source for the Synoptic gospels) "in enger Abhängigkeit" (in narrow dependence) to a cynic-stoic type of biography of Hercules, see Friedrich Pfister, "Herakles und Christus," *AR* 34 (1937): 59–60. For a critique, Herbert Jennings Rose, "Herakles and the Gospels," *HTR* 31 (1938): 113–142; Aune, "Heracles and Christ," 11–12.

Fathers of the church recognized as early as the middle of the 2nd century CE the parallels between gods and heroes of Greek mythology and Jesus, which they dismissed as imitations; e.g., Justin, *1 Apol.* 21.1; *Dial.* 69.3; Origen, *Cels.* 3.22, 42. See also Aune, "Heracles and Christ," 3–4. Hercules was the single most popular hero in the ancient Greco-Roman world and was considered by the Stoics an embodiment of the ideal king, see Aune, "Heracles and Christ," 6, 9.

will open a path to heaven (Seneca *Herc. Ot.* 1982–1988 [Fitch, LCL]; see also, 1434–1440, 1557–1559, 1940–1988). These philosophers also considered his tragic end a victory that liberates others from the fear of death. For example: "He crossed the waters of Tartarus, / pacified the underworld, and returned. / Now no fear remains: nothing lies beyond the underworld" (Seneca *Herc. Fur.* 889–892 [Fitch, LCL]).⁶⁷ David E. Aune concludes in his analysis, however, that these are phenomenological parallels that should not be explained by literary dependence or as a Christian conceptualization of Jesus in terms of the Hercules myth, but "are rather to be attributed to the more general tendency of traditions about great personalities to conform to the morphology of Greco-Roman heroes through the folkloristic process of the communal re-creation of tradition."⁶⁸

Others find in Hebrews' description of Jesus's victory over the devil allusions to the idea of the Messiah's victory over demonic forces prevalent in Jewish apocalyptic tradition and early Christianity.⁶⁹ Gustaf Aulén has identified Jesus's victory over the devil as constitutive of the early Christian view of the atonement, which he calls "the classic idea of atonement" and traces throughout the NT (Rom 8:38–39; 1 Cor 15:24; Gal 1:4; Eph 4:8–10; Phil 2:10; Col 2:15; 1 Pet 3:18–22).⁷⁰ In many cases, NT writers explained the gospel as Jesus's victory over death; for example, 2 Tim 1:10: "the appearing of our Savior Christ Jesus, who abolished [καταργέω] death and brought life and immortality to light through the gospel" (see also, Rom 8:38–39; 1 Cor 15:26, 55; Rev 21:4; cf. *Odes Sol.* 15.9; 29.4; Barn. 5.6; 14.5).

---

67   See Attridge, *The Epistle to the Hebrews*, 80, nn. 20–21; Aune, "Heracles and Christ," 7.
    David E. Aune notes other parallels to traditions about Hercules in Hebrews ("Heracles and Christ," 13–19). For example, like the Son who "sustains all things by his powerful word" (Heb 1:3), Hercules is "the Logos permeating everything, giving nature its force and cohesion" (Cornutus, *Thelogiae Graecae compendium*, 31). Hercules undergoes a process of education that includes suffering like Jesus (Heb 5:8–9). See Dio Chrysostom *Or.* 4 (*4 Regn.*) 29–32; Epictetus 3.22.56–57. The term ἀρχεγός is applied to Hercules (e.g., Dio Chrysostom *Or.* 33 [*1 Tars.*] 47) as well as Jesus (2:10; 12:2). He was also a provider of help in the struggles of life (e.g., Pindar, *Nem.* 7.94–97), like Jesus (Heb 4:14–16).

68   Aune, "Heracles and Christ," 19.

69   *As. Mos.* 10.1; *T. Levi* 18.1–2; *T. Jud.* 25.3; *T. Dan* 5.10; *Sib. Or.* 3.63–74; *1 En.* 10.13; *4 Ezra* 13.1; 1QM I, 11, 13, 15; Matt 12:25–30; Luke 10:18; John 12:31; 14:30; 16:11; 1 John 3:8; Rev 12:7–10, see Adela Yarbro Collins, *The Combat Myth in the Book of Revelation*, HDR 9 (Scholars, 1976), 57–206; Attridge, *The Epistle to the Hebrews*, 92, nn. 153–155; Johnson, *Hebrews*, 100.

70   *Christus Victor: An Historical Study of the Three Main Types of the Idea of Atonement*, trans. A. G. Hebert (Macmillan, 1958), 61–80. Also, Ellingworth, *The Epistle to the Hebrews*, 172–173.

    John McRay suggests unconvincingly that "Hebrews was written to a Jewish audience which was so well acquainted with the main tenets of apocalyptic Judaism that the author could set the classical view of atonement [i.e., Aulen's] against that background and argue it as the Jewish Christian understanding of Jesus's high priestly work" (emphasis his, "Atonement and Apocalyptic in the Book of Hebrews," *ResQ* 23 [1980]: 9).

Still others consider that Jesus's victory is conceptualized in light of OT motifs.[71] An intriguing suggestion is that this passage contains an exodus typology.[72] In this sense Jesus is compared with Moses who liberates the Israelites from the "house of slavery" (Exod 13:3; 20:2; Deut 5:6; passim). Thus, Moses was not ashamed of calling the slaves his brethren (Exod 2:11; 4:18; Heb 11:24–26), declared the name of God to others (Exod 3:13–14; cf. Heb 2:12), trusted God (Exod 14:13–14; cf. Heb 2:13), and delivered the people by destroying Pharaoh's army (Exod 14:21–31; cf. Heb 2:14b–15).[73] Finally, Heb 3:7–4:13 refers explicitly to Israel's journey through the wilderness.[74]

William L. Lane has suggested that the OT motif of God as the Divine Warrior provides a closer background to this text.[75] The OT describes God on several occasions as a champion who engages in individual combat on behalf of his people:

The LORD goes forth like a soldier, like a warrior he stirs up his fury; he cries out, he shouts aloud, he shows himself mighty against his foes. (Isa 42:13; cf. 49:24–26; 59:15b–20)[76]

In fact, Jesus described himself as a champion who overpowers Satan and "divides his plunder" to explain his exorcisms (Luke 11:21–22; cf. Matt 12:29; Mark 3:27). Probably the most similar passage in this tradition is Isa 49:24–26:

---

71 In addition to what is considered below, George Wesley Buchanan has suggested the liberation from debt during the Sabbatical year as the OT background to Heb 2:14–16 (*To the Hebrews: Translation, Comment and Conclusions*, AB 36 [Doubleday, 1972], 34–35). However, there is no reference to liberation from "the fear of death" in connection with the Sabbatical year.

72 Andriessen, "La Teneur Judéo-Chrétienne," 304–13; Koester, *Hebrews*, 240.

73 According to Paul C. B. Andriessen, this typology is part of an extended comparison between Jesus and Moses which becomes explicit in Heb 3:1–6, but had already been introduced in Heb 1:6 where Israel's entrance into Canaan provides the OT background to Jesus's ascension to heaven ("La Teneur Judéo-Chrétienne," 293–304, 312–313).

74 Koester, *Hebrews*, 240.

75 Lane, *Hebrews 1–8*, 62–66; Charles Sherlock, *The God Who Fights: The War Tradition in Holy Scripture*, Rutherford Studies in Contemporary Theology 6 (Rutherford, 1993), 356–360. For a description of this motif, see Neil Forsyth, *The Old Enemy: Satan and the Combath Myth* (Princeton University Press, 1987); Tremper Longman III and Daniel G. Reid, *God Is a Warrior*, Studies in Old Testament Biblical Theology (Zondervan, 1995); Patrick D. Miller, Jr., *The Divine Warrior in Early Israel*, HSM 5 (Harvard University Press, 1973); Sherlock, *The God Who Fights*.

76 See Thomas R. Yoder Neufeld, *"Put on the Armour of God": The Divine Warrior from Isaiah to Ephesians*, JSNTSup 140 (Sheffield Academic, 1997). This idea also appears in apocalyptic writings of the Second Temple period; for example: "And thereafter the Lord himself will arise upon you, the light of righteousness with healing and compassion in his wings. He will liberate every captive of the sons of men from Beliar, and every spirit of error will be trampled down" (*T. Zeb.* 9.8 [*OTP* 1:807]; cf. *T. Levi* 18.10–12; *T. Mos.*10.1–10; 11Q13 [11QMelch] II, 13).

Can the prey be taken from the mighty, or the captives of a tyrant be rescued? But thus says the LORD: Even the captives of the mighty shall be taken, and the prey of the tyrant be rescued; for I will contend with those who contend with you, and I will save your children. I will make your oppressors eat their own flesh, and they shall be drunk with their own blood as with wine. Then all flesh shall know that I am the LORD your Savior, and your Redeemer, the Mighty One of Jacob.

William L. Lane argues that the fact that the description of Jesus as champion (2:14–16) is developed in cultic terms (2:17–18) is not a problem.[77] Hebrews 2:17–18 introduces Jesus as the merciful high priest whose death and ascension are interpreted in terms of a sacrifice for sins and entrance into the heavenly sanctuary (Heb 5–10:18). Lane notes that these two apparently very different imageries are integrated in the *T. Lev.* 18:10–12 where an eschatological priest, like a champion of Israel, will bind Beliar and "grant to his children the authority to trample on wicked spirits" (*OTP* 1:795).[78]

We have to acknowledge, however, that the diversity of possibilities suggests that none of them is entirely satisfactory. Hebrews bears resemblance in this or that aspect to all of them but does not seem to clearly privilege any of them. I want to suggest that the reason for this is that Hebrews draws upon a motif that is basic to all of these models. All of them are, in fact, reinterpretations of the "divine warfare" motif that was widespread in the ANE and the Greco-Roman world of the 1st century CE[79]

In ANE mythology, a war between deities typically followed a narrative pattern, usually called by contemporary scholars the Divine Warrior motif or Combat Myth. In brief terms, this motif consists of a war between deities in which the eventual victor is enthroned as king above the gods. Then a temple or palace is built in his honor where he celebrates his victory with those loyal to him. The main elements of the pattern are, then, (1) warfare, (2) vic-

---

77 Cf. Phineas, the priest, in Num 25 and 31, using a spear and going into battle.

78 See also the comparison that Hans Windisch makes between *T. Levi* 18:2–12 and the catena of Heb 1:5–14 (*Der Hebräerbrief*, 15).

The *T. 12 Patr.* was probably written around 150 BCE. Howard Clark Kee, Introduction to "Testaments of the Twelve Patriarchs," *OTP* 1:777–778. The *T. 12 Patr.*, however, is Christian in its present form and probably received this form sometime in the second half of the 2nd century CE. M. de Jonge, "Testaments of the Twelve Patriarchs," *ABD* 5:183. M. de Jonge also concludes that "it is very difficult, if not impossible, to establish the exact contents of this 'original' (pre-Christian) Jewish document, let alone to detect different stages in the redaction of that document" ("Testaments," 183).

79 Joseph Fontenrose, *Python: A Study of Delphic Myth and Its Origins* (University of California Press, 1959), 321–364.

tory, (3) kingship/enthronement, (4) building of the palace/temple, and (5) celebration.[80]

The Divine Warrior motif was widespread in the ANE and the Mediterranean world.[81] In Ugarit, this narrative structure was used in two cycles to explain Baal's supremacy over the gods because of his victories over the gods Yamm (sea/chaos) and Mot (death).[82] Likewise, the Babylonian Epic of Creation or *Enuma Elish* uses this narrative structure to explain Marduk's rise to cosmic supremacy. Marduk attains this supremacy because of his victory over Tiamat, the god of sea. In the Greek world, the Divine Warrior motif is present in several succession narratives; for example, the battles between Ouranos and Kronos, Zeus and Kronos, Zeus and the Titans, and Zeus and the Giants (the Gigantomachy).[83] Regarding the consistency of this widespread narrative pattern in the ancient world, David E. Aune commented: "While the names of the combatants, as well as their roles, change from culture to culture, many of the constituent folklore motifs of the Combat Myth or legend either remain constant or are subject to a limited range of variation."[84]

It is important to note that nations used the imagery and conceptual framework of this motif to interpret their political and religious situations. Usually a claim of the superiority of a god was explained in terms of his victory over other gods and creation.[85] This, of course, had important political implications. For example, king Eumenes II (2nd century BCE) built the

---

80 For a table comparing divine warfare myths from different cultures, see Forsyth, *The Old Enemy*, 446–452. Also, David E. Aune, *Revelation 6–16*, WBC 52B (Word, 1998), 667–668; Frank Moore Cross, *Cannanite Myth and Hebrew Epic: Essays in the History of the Religion of Israel* (Harvard University Press, 1973), 162–163; Timothy G. Gombis, "Ephesians 2 as a Narrative of Divine Warfare," *JSNT* 26 (2004): 405–407; Longman III and Reid, *God Is a Warrior*, 83–88. Cf. Harold Wayne Ballard, Jr., *The Divine Warrior Motif in the Psalms*, BIBAL Dissertation Series 6 (BIBAL, 1999), 27–29. For similar narrative structures in Egypt and India, see Fontenrose, *Python*, 177–216.

81 For study of this motif throughout the ancient world, see Fontenrose, *Python*; Forsyth, *The Old Enemy*, 44–66.

82 Fontenrose, *Python*, 129–138.

83 Aune, *Revelation 6–16*, 667. For a full study, see Fontenrose, *Python*.

84 Aune, *Revelation 6–16*, 667. For further study of the Combat Myth, see Adela Yarbro Collins, *Combat Myth*; Richard J. Clifford, "The Roots of Apocalypticism in Near Eastern Myth," in *The Origins of Apocalypticism in Judaism and Christianity*, ed. John J. Collins, *The Encyclopedia of Apocalypticism*, ed. Bernard McGinn, John J. Collins, and Stephen J. Stein (Continuum, 1998), 1:3–38; John Day, *God's Conflict with the Dragon and the Sea: Echoes of a Canaanite Myth in the Old Testament*, University of Cambridge Oriental Publications 35 (Cambridge University Press, 1985); Fontenrose, *Python*; Forsyth, *The Old Enemy*; Paul D. Hanson, *The Dawn of Apocalyptic: The Historical and Sociological Roots of Jewish Apocalyptic Eschatology*, rev. ed. (Fortress, 1979), 292–333; Longman III and Reid, *God Is a Warrior*.

85 Gombis, "Ephesians 2 as a Narrative," 405.

Great Altar of Pergamon in which the outer frieze included the Combat Myth describing the battle between the gods and the Giants. The purpose of this frieze was to celebrate the victory of the Attalid kings over the Gauls. The interpretation of the frieze, however, did not remain static. The frieze was later interpreted in terms of the victories of the Romans.[86]

The Combat Myth is also present in early Jewish literature and the New Testament, carrying both religious and political implications. In the Hebrew Bible it is especially common in references to God as creator and king in Israelite poetry.[87] The prophets, however, used this narrative structure to describe God's victory over Israel's historical enemies.[88] One of the most commonly cited examples is the so-called "Song of the Sea" in Exod 15. In a majority of cases, the prophets used this motif to interpret Israel's current political situation and to express their hope in God's future defeat over their enemies.

The Divine Warrior motif is also present in Jewish apocalyptic literature. In this literature the motif is not used as metaphorical language; instead, God battles against a cosmic adversary—Satan and his angelic forces—to whom suffering and evil are attributed. For example, in *1 En.* 6–11 God defeats Semihazeh and Azazel, leaders of rebel angelic forces (the watchers), and confines them under the earth until the Day of Judgment.[89] Apocalyptic literature uses this motif to explain the origin of evil in the world and to express the hope that the final judgment of God's cosmic enemy will bring about a period of righteousness and peace.[90]

In the New Testament, the motif is prominent in Revelation, especially in the narrative of the "great red dragon" in chap. 12.[91] Further examples, however, can be found in Jesus's rebuke of the sea in the Gospels (e.g., Mark 4:35–41)

---

86   Adela Yarbro Collins, "Pergamon in Early Christian Literature," *Pergamon, Citadel of the Gods: Archaeological Record, Literary Description, and Religious Development*, ed. Helmut Koester, HTS 46 (Trinity, 1998), 180–183.

87   E.g., Pss 74:12–17; 89:10–15; Job 26. For further examples, Aune, *Revelation 6–16*, 667–668; Forsyth, *The Old Enemy*, 90–146; Hanson, *The Dawn of Apocalyptic*, 300–324; Longman III and Reid, *God Is a Warrior*, 85–87. For deeper study of this motif, Ballard , Jr., *The Divine Warrior Motif in the Psalms*; Rebecca S. Watson, *Chaos Uncreated: A Reassessment of the Theme of "Chaos" in the Hebrew Bible*, BZAW 341 (Walter de Gruyter, 2005).

88   Isa 14:10–15; 51:9–11; Jer 51:34; Ezek 28:1–9; 29:3–5; 32:2–8. See Day, *God's Conflict with the Dragon*, 88–140.

89   Cf. God's defeat of *Mastema* (an alias of Satan) and his angelic forces who are confined under the earth until the day of judgment in *Jub.* 5:6–11. On the Combat Myth in early Judaism, see Clifford, "Roots of Apocalypticism," 3–38; Hanson, *The Dawn of Apocalyptic*; K. William Whitney, *Two Strange Beasts: Leviathan and Behemoth in Second Temple and Early Rabbinic Judaism*, HSM 63 (Eisenbrauns, 2006). Also, Aune, *Revelation 6–16*, 668–669; Forsyth, *The Old Enemy*, 147–212.

90   Aune, *Revelation 6–16*, 669.

91   See Adela Yarbro Collins, *Combat Myth*; idem, "Pergamon," 163–184.

and Jesus's victory over the powers in Pauline literature (e.g., Rom 8:38–39; 1 Cor 15:24; Eph 1:20–2:22; 4:8–10; Phil 2:10; Col 2:15; 1 Pet 3:18–22).[92] In fact, Marie Huie-Jolly has suggested that "a version of the divine warrior myth based on early Christian exegesis of Scripture was foundational for death-and-resurrection speech patterns. It undergirds the form of early Christian speech that juxtaposes images of threats to the life of Jesus with speech exalting him as son."[93] As I have noted, Gustaf Aulén argues that the image of the Divine Warrior is essential to what he calls the classic idea of the atonement.[94]

Neil Forsyth's comment summarizes well, in my view, the significance of the Combat Myth for the ANE: "The combat paradigm, in fact, seems to have generated the central myth that supported and justified the kingship in many different societies of the ancient world."[95]

This motif was central to the theology of YHWH's and Davidic kingship in the Old Testament and the kingship of Jesus in the New Testament.[96] It is not strange, then, that it is also essential to Hebrews' understanding of Jesus's death and enthronement as the royal Son. It is clear that Hebrews shares with other New Testament documents the idea that Jesus's victory over death is constitutive of his kingship over the cosmos.[97]

It is possible, as well, that the Combat Myth provides a narrative substructure to chs. 1–4. I described the main elements of the pattern of the Combat Myth as consisting of (1) warfare, (2) victory, (3) kingship/enthronement, (4) building of the palace/temple, and (5) celebration. Note that Heb 2:14–16 refers to Jesus's warfare with the devil. Hebrews 1:5–14 refers to Jesus's enthronement "at the right hand of the majesty on high" as a result of this victory (cf. 2:9). Hebrews 3:3 refers to Jesus as the builder of the house of God,

---

92 For the Gospels, see Mary R. Huie-Jolly, "Threats Answered by Enthronement: Death/Resurrection and the Divine Warrior Myth in John 5.17–29 and Daniel 7," in *Early Christian Interpretation of the Scriptures of Israel: Investigations and Proposals*, ed. Craig A. Evans and James A. Sanders, JSNTSup 148; Studies in Scripture in Early Judaism and Christianity 5 (Sheffield Academic, 1997), 191–217; Longman III and Reid, *God Is a Warrior*, 91–135; Foster R. McCurley, *Ancient Myths and Biblical Faith: Scriptural Transformations* (Fortress, 1983), 58–71; Sherlock, *The God Who Fights*, 243–380. For Pauline literature, see Peter W. Macky, *St. Paul's Cosmic War Myth: A Military Version of the Gospel*, The Westminster College Library of Biblical Symbolism 2 (Lang, 1998). Also, Forsyth, *The Old Enemy*, 258–284; Gombis, "Ephesians 2 as a Narrative," 403–418; Longman III and Reid, *God Is a Warrior*, 136–79.

93 "Threats Answered by Enthronement," 200, 208–211. She finds this pattern in John 5 (211–217). See also McCurley, 58–71; Sherlock, *The God Who Fights*, 243–380.

94 Aulén, *Christus Victor: An Historical Study of the Three Main Types of the Idea of Atonement*, trans. A. G. Hebert (Macmillan, 1958), 79.

95 Forsyth, *The Old Enemy*, 45.

96 Guinan, "Davidic Covenant," 69–70. Note that Ps 89:9–14 presents God's victory over the sea as the basis for his kingship. In v. 26, the Davidic king shares in this victory of God. Also Whitelam, "King and Kingship," 43–45.

97 For victory over Death in Apocalyptic literature, see Johnson, *Hebrews*, 100.

which suggests the possibility that this refers to the construction of an eschatological temple by Jesus.[98] Finally, Jesus invites his faithful ones to enter into "the rest" (3:7–4:11), which suggests the possibility that we should understand this "rest" as an eschatological celebration of God's victory (cf. 12:22–24).[99]

Let me summarize the findings thus far. Hebrews 1:6 describes God's introduction of Jesus to the heavenly court as part of an enthronement ceremony described in the catena of 1:5–14. Jesus's enthronement in heaven follows his victory over the devil "who has the power of death" (2:14–16; cf. 2:9). Thus, the Combat Myth is essential to the understanding of the ascension of Jesus referred to in Heb 1:6, and both justifies and supports his kingship over the cosmos.

If Hebrews is not combating here the worship of angels or an angelomorphic Christology, as I have argued above, why is the description of the enthronement of Jesus above the angels important for the argument of Hebrews? In other words, what is the rhetorical function of the ascension and enthronement of Jesus in Heb 1:5–14 for the argument of Heb 1–2?

Enthronement as the Basis for Exhortation: The Son's Exaltation Prefigures and Makes Possible the Glorification of the Sons

Why does the author of Hebrews open his "word of exhortation" with a description of the Son's enthronement in heaven? What did he try to accomplish by this?[100] In order to understand what the role of the ascension and enthronement of the Son in the Letter is, it is first necessary to understand the meaning of the title "Son" in the Letter. Both are inextricably connected.[101]

---

98 I will argue below that Heb 8:2, 5; 9:23 refer to the inauguration of the heavenly sanctuary.

99 The invitation to enter into "the rest" could be understood as an invitation to enjoy the results of God's victory and kingship. God's description of the "rest" as "my rest," however, also makes possible an allusion to the heavenly sanctuary (cf. Isa 66:1). Note that this section ends with an invitation to "approach the throne of Grace [the heavenly holy of holies?] with boldness" (4:16).

The rest in 3:7–4:11 is described by God as "my rest." An allusion is also possible to the rest as participation in God's victory and kingship as the celebration of God's heavenly sanctuary. I will not explore this possibility here, as it will take me beyond the purpose of this section.

100 A similar question is, why does he refer so often to Jesus's royal worthiness throughout the letter (1:3, 5–14; 2:5–9; 5:5; 7:28; 8:1–2; 10:12–13; 12:1–3; 13:20)?

101 The analysis of this question will permit me to address a question I left pending above: If "Son" is a royal title that Jesus received at his exaltation, why are there passages that refer to him as Son already on earth (e.g., 5:7–8)?

I have argued above that "Son" is a royal Davidic title in Heb 1:5–14. According to Hebrews, Jesus received this title when he was enthroned at the right hand of God (Heb 1:4). Hebrews likewise applied to Jesus the promises made to the Son of David in 2 Sam 7:14 and Ps 2:7 (Heb 1:5) and used in the catena (1:5–14) psalms originally related to the Davidic dynasty to describe

Jesus as "Son" in Hebrews

The Christology of the Letter to the Hebrews is one of the most developed in the NT.[102] Hebrews speaks of Jesus in unusually varied ways to emphasize two aspects of his function in God's plan: He is both the one who brings salvation to humanity from God and the first human being in whom God's original purpose for humanity is finally realized.[103] My interest here lies in Hebrews' designation of Jesus as "Son" and what aspect of Jesus's mission it emphasizes in the argument of the Letter.[104]

---

his enthronement. Though Ps 102:25–27 is not a royal Davidic psalm, some think that this psalm received a messianic interpretation in the translation of the LXX. (See above section "The Catena Describes the Enthronement Ceremony of the Son" on page 153.)

102 L. W. Hurtado, "Christology," *DLNT* 173. "The conception of Christ in this composition [Hebrews] is indeed one of the richest in the New Testament Canon" (Johnson, *Hebrews*, 48).

103 Hebrews' use of the name "Jesus" underscores the author's interest in the humanity of Jesus (2:9–11, passim; cf. 2:11, 17; 4:15; 5:7–10). On the other hand, Hebrews also emphasizes the divinity of Jesus. He is addressed as "Lord" (1:10; 2:3; 7:14; 13:20), "God" (Heb 1:8), and "Son of God" (Heb 4:14, passim; see next footnote). Hebrews does not seem to be interested in reconciling both assertions; see J. W. Drane, "Son of God," *DLNT* 1112–1113; Johnson, *Hebrews*, 50–56, esp. 55. Instead, the symbiosis of both emphases is intimately related to the two-aspect mission of Jesus.

As the one who "brings salvation to humanity from God," Jesus is the "apostle" (3:1), the "Christ" (3:6, passim), the "cause of salvation" (5:9), the "sanctifier" (2:11), "the great shepherd of the sheep" (13:20), the "minister" (8:2), the "builder of God's house" (3:3), the "guarantor" (7:22). As the "human being who reaches first what all seek," Jesus is "heir" (1:2), "the firstborn" (1:6), "the pioneer" (or "captain" [ἀρχηγός], 2:10; 12:2), the "perfecter" (12:2), the "forerunner" (6:20). Finally, the designation of Jesus as "mediator" (8:6; 12:24) embraces both functions in a single title. See, Johnson, *Hebrews*, 48–49.

104 Jesus is referred to in Hebrews either as "Son" (Heb 1:2; 1:5 [x2]; 1:8; 3:6; 5:5; 5:8; 7:28) or "Son of God" (Heb 4:14; 6:6; 7:3; 10:29).

The concept "Son of God" was widely used in ancient culture. In early Judaism, the term was applied to Israel itself (Exod 4:22; Jer 31:9; Hos 11:1; Wis 9:7; 18:13; *Jub.* 1:24–25; *Pss. Sol.* 17:27), angels and other heavenly beings (MT Job 1:6–12; 2:1–6 [cf. Deut 32:8]; 38:7; Pss 29:1; 89:6; Dan 3:25), the Davidic king (2 Sam 7:14; 1 Chr 17:13; 22:10; 28:6; Pss 2:7; 89:26–27; 4Q174 I, 10–12; 4Q246 II, 1–3), the messiah (*4 Ezra* 7:28; 13:32, 37, 52; 14:9 [though these may be later Christian interpolations]; 4Q174 I, 10–13), and later to individual rabbis (*b. Taan.* 24b). See Drane, "Son of God," 1112; Fossum, "Son of God," 128–32.

In the Greco-Roman world, men of extraordinary gifts and acts, heroes, and rulers could be considered or referred to as "son[s] of God." For example, Pompey and Apollonius of Tyana, the heroes Dionysus and Heracles, and the Ptolemaic rulers and the Caesars, could all be considered "Son of God." See Fossum, "Son of God," 132–133; Martitz, "υἱός," 336–340. For a study of the divine election of the chief magistrate in the Roman republic, or later in the empire, and its political implications, see Fears, *Princeps a diis electus*, 85–188.

See also, Oscar Cullmann, *The Christology of the New Testament*, trans. Shirley C. Guthrie and Charles A. M. Hall, rev. ed. (Westminster, 1963), 270–274; James D. G. Dunn, *Christology in the Making: A New Testament Inquiry into the Origins of the Doctrine of the Incarnation* (Westminster, 1980), 14–22; Hahn, *Christologische Hoheitstitel*, 280–333; Hengel, *The Son of God*, 21–56.

Donald A. Hagner opines that "[Son] is clearly the central christological designation of Hebrews."[105] It is clear from the beginning of the Letter that the title "son" plays a fundamental role in its argument. In the introduction to his work (Heb 1:1–4), the author of Hebrews divides salvation history into two ages: (1) the "long ago" in which God revealed himself "in many and various ways by the prophets" and (2) "these last days" in which he "has spoken to us by a Son" (Heb 1:1–2). Thus, the present age, in which the readers of Hebrews find themselves, is characterized by the revelation in a "Son." In the rest of the Letter, this title is prominent in both the expositional and hortatory sections of the work. In the first, it is used to express Jesus's superiority over the angels (Heb 1:4, cf. vv. 5–14), Moses (3:1–6), and Aaron (5:4–6; 7:28).[106] As I will show below, Jesus's sonship is not only the basis of his superiority over Aaron, but also essential for his appointment as high priest of the heavenly sanctuary (5:5, 8; 7:3, 28; cf. 4:14; see section " 'A Hope that Enters the Inner Shrine behind the Curtain' (Heb 6:19–20): Ascension and the Appointment of a Faithful Priest" on page 202). In the hortatory sections, the importance of this title is evidenced in the fact that rejection of the "Son" is considered the ultimate sin and the readers are warned sternly against "spurning the Son of God" (10:29; cf. 6:6).

Now, what is the meaning of the Christological title "Son" or "Son of God" in Hebrews? More specifically, does this title emphasize Jesus's divine nature as co-eternal and co-creator with God (ontology) or his role as the eschatological "son of David" whose rule brings salvation to Israel (function)?

---

105 Hagner, "The Son of God," 249.

106 Regarding the title Son as expressing superiority over the angels, I understand that the "name" referred to in Heb 1:4 that Jesus inherited at his ascension and expresses his superiority over the angels is "Son" (McKnight and Church, *Hebrews–James*, 36; Koester, *Hebrews*, 181; Dmitri Royster, *The Epistle to the Hebrews: A Commentary* [St. Vladimir's Seminary Press, 2003], 21; Kenneth L. Schenck, "Keeping His Appointment: Creation and Enthronement in Hebrews," *JSNT* 66 [1997]: 93). Others consider that the name referred to in Heb 1:4 is "Lord" (cf. Phil 2:9–11), or the three names "Son, God, and Lord" (Johnson, *Hebrews*, 73; Rissi, *Die Theologie des Hebräerbriefs*, 52). Or, a broad range of meanings including "status," "rank," "reputation," etc. (George Guthrie, *Hebrews*, 50). These positions are not mutually exclusive, however. The early church believed that as the "Son of David" who has been enthroned "at the right hand" of God, Jesus is "Lord" (Acts 2:31–36; see Ps 110:1; Matt 22:41–45; par. Mark 12:35–37; Luke 20:41–44).

It is clear, however, that Son is the primary title in the catena (Heb 1:2, 5, 8). Note that it is the Son (1:8) who is addressed as "God" (vv. 8–9) and "Lord" (vv. 10–11) (Ellingworth, *The Epistle to the Hebrews*, 110).

Regarding the relationship between the titles Son and high priest in Hebrews, Marie E. Isaacs concludes: "Thus we can see that for the author of Hebrews, Jesus's primary status is not that of Melchizedekian high priest but son of God.... In many ways Jesus's work may be compared with that of his biblical predecessors, namely Moses and the high priest, but in each case it is his sonship which is used to highlight the contrast between his status and theirs" (*Sacred Space*, 178).

Though expressed in different terms, the following question is essentially the same: Did Jesus became the "Son" when he was enthroned "at the right hand" of God (Son denoting a royal function), or was he always the "Son" (Son denoting filial identity)?

"Son" as a royal title. In his article "Son by Appointment," G. B. Caird has made the case that Hebrews' Christology is basically functional and not ontological. In other words, he considers that Hebrews does not go further than describing a human being—Jesus—who *became* the Son by virtue of an appointment from God. In this sense, Son is a title that refers to the function Jesus assumed at his exaltation and not to the essence of his personal nature as co-eternal and co-pre-existent with God. Thus, he suggests that Jesus's perfection, preeminence, and even eternity—as far as the argument of Hebrews goes—are attributes that the human Jesus *attained* at his exaltation.[107]

Caird's argument is built upon the *appointment language* that is present in the Letter. He argues that Heb 1:1–4 refers to the human Jesus whom God "appointed [ἔθηκεν] heir of all things" (cf. 3:2). He points out that Heb 1:5 explains that this appointment refers to the *royal status* of "Son" and that Heb 5:5 adds that this appointment includes the further office of priest in perpetuity (cf. 6:20; 7:28).[108] The royal nature of Jesus's sonship is emphasized throughout the letter. Jesus, as promised to the Son of David, was appointed "heir of all things" (1:2; cf. Ps 2:8), sat "at the right hand of God (1:3, 13; 8:1; 10:12–13; 12:2; cf. Ps 110:1),[109] royal insignias are vested on him (throne and scepter in 1:8, anointment in 1:9, and crowning in 2:9), and designated shepherd

---

107 He makes clear, however, that we should not confuse Hebrews' functional Christology with a low Christology. He concludes that Jesus holds "the highest place that heaven affords ... by right." In his view, however, this does not include or require the idea of Jesus's preexistence as an ontological concept. Jesus preexisted only in the "eternal purpose of God" ("Son by Appointment," in *The New Testament Age*, ed. William C. Weinrich [Mercer University Press, 1984], 1:81).

108 Ibid., 75.

109 Psalm 110 was understood as messianic in the NT (Matt 22:42–45 [par. Mark 12:35–37; Luke 20:41–44]; Matt 26:64 [par. Mark 14:62; Luke 22:69]; Mark 16:19; Acts 2:34–35; Rom 8:34; 1 Cor 15:25; Eph 1:20; Col 3:1).
 Ancient Jewish interpretation of the Psalm is varied, however. Some scholars have detected allusions to Ps 110 in the description of the enthronement of the Son of Man in *1 Enoch* (45:1, 3; 51:3; 52:1–7; 55:4; 61:8; this section has been dated to 105–64 BCE). *Testament of Job* 33:3 (1st century BCE or CE) applied Ps 110 to Job, who is described as king of a heavenly kingdom. 11QMelchizedek (second half of 1st cent. BCE or first half of 1st cent. CE) does not refer clearly to Ps 110. It describes Melchizedek, however, as a heavenly eschatological warrior and savior. It is difficult to think that any Jew acquainted with both passages would fail to make the connection. It is probable that 1 Macc 14:41 alludes to Ps 110:4 and applies it to Hasmonean rulers.
 A messianic interpretation of Ps 110 appears frequently in rabbinic writings after ca. 250 CE. See Hay, *Glory at the Right Hand*, 19–33.

of God's people (13:20; cf. Ps 78:71; Ezek 34:23; 37:24; Matt 2:6; 26:31 [par. Mark 14:27]; John 10:11–16).[110]

In fact, according to Caird, the promises of the Davidic covenant are explicitly applied to him (Heb 1:5–6; quoting Ps 2:7 and 2 Sam 7:14, par. 1 Chr 17:13). In this sense, then, Jesus was not inherently superior to the angels but *became* superior to the angels when he *inherited* a "more excellent [name] than theirs," that is, the royal name of "Son." All the glory and dignity ascribed to the Son is not his because of some "preincarnate status" but because he "qualified for it by his earthly career."[111]

We might ask Caird: How is it, then, that Hebrews asserts that the Son "founded the earth, and the heavens" "in the beginning" (1:10; cf. v. 2) if he became Son only later at the exaltation? First, he argues that in the redaction of Hebrews the attribution of creation to Jesus presupposes his exaltation or enthronement. The attribution of creation to Jesus in v. 10 presupposes the anointment of v. 9, which refers to the exaltation. Likewise, the ascription of creation in v. 2 presupposes his appointment as "heir of all things" (v. 3). Second, he explains that it is possible for Hebrews to ascribe the creation to Jesus at the exaltation because "he is the man in whom the divine Wisdom has been appointed to dwell."[112] He does not develop this idea, but it seems clear that he understands that Hebrews discloses a wisdom Christology in the sense that, by virtue of his exaltation, Jesus embodies or incarnates Wisdom and thus can be rightfully ascribed the work of creation.[113]

A majority of commentators believe that Hebrews' knowledge and use of early Jewish wisdom speculation is evident in its allusion to Wis 7:26 in Heb 1:3. Note the similarity between both passages:

He [the Son] is the reflection [ἀπαύγασμα] of God's glory and the exact imprint [χαρακτὴρ] of God's very being [ὑποστάσεως], and he sustains all things by his powerful word. (Heb 1:3)

For she [wisdom] is a reflection [ἀπαύγασμα] of eternal light, a spotless mirror of the working of God, and an image [εἰκὼν] of his goodness [ἀγαθότητος]. (Wis 7:26)

---

110 For a discussion of the royal connotations in the description of Jesus as the great shepherd of the sheep, see Hagner, "The Son of God," 263–265.

111 Caird, "Son by Appointment," 76. Jesus was "crowned with glory and honor because of the suffering of death" (2:9). Likewise, he was perfected, which means that he obtained access to God (7:19) through suffering and the learning of obedience (2:10; 5:8–9).

112 Ibid.

113 For a discussion of wisdom Christology, see Dunn, *Christology in the Making*, 163–212; Ben Witherington, *Jesus the Sage: The Pilgrimage of Wisdom* (Fortress, 1994).

Both Wisdom and Jesus are described as the reflection [ἀπαύγασμα] of God's glory or light. (It is striking that the Greek term ἀπαύγασμα does not appear elsewhere in the LXX or the NT.) There are further similarities between both texts. The expression "the exact imprint of God's very being" in Heb 1:3 resembles the expression "an image of his goodness" in Wis 7:26. More remarkable still, in Wis 9:1–4, pseudo-Solomon requests from God the wisdom "that sits by your throne" and by whom God has made "all things" and "formed humankind" (cf. Prov 8:27–31).[114] This clearly parallels the Son, who "sat down at the right hand of the majesty on high" (Heb 1:3) and "through whom he [God] also created the worlds" (v. 2).

There are differences as well, however. In Wis 7:26, Wisdom is a personification of an attribute of God, not a separate entity. It is a capacity God grants to the king. Note that this passage (Wis 7–9) draws on the story of 1 Kgs 3:1–15 where Solomon requests God "an understanding mind." In Heb 1:3, on the other hand, the Son is a historical person, Jesus (Heb 2:9).

Wisdom was a conceptual parallel to the word of God (λόγος) in Hellenist Jewish speculation.[115] In the writings of Philo (ca. 20 BCE – 50 CE)—where this concept reached its climax[116]—the Logos of God is clearly personalized but is not conceived as a separate entity from God, namely, the Logos does not acquire a real personal existence.[117] That is why Philo may use the Logos of God to describe angels as a personification of God's guidance (e.g., *Conf. Ling.* 28, *Migr. Abr.* 173–175); the Law as God's reason and purpose within the

---

114 See, Lincoln D. Hurst, "The Christology of Hebrews 1 and 2," in *The Glory of Christ in the New Testament: Studies in Christology*, ed. Lincoln D. Hurst and N. T. Wright (Clarendon, 1987), 161–162.

115 In Wis 9:1–4, for example, wisdom is equivalent to the word of God: "O God of my ancestors and Lord of mercy, who have made all things by your *word*, and by your *wisdom* have formed humankind to have dominion over the creatures you have made, ... give me the wisdom that sits by your throne, and do not reject me from among your servants [emphasis mine]."

116 Philo's concept of the word of God is complex because he went further than other Jewish literature in combining Stoic and Platonic language with wisdom language. For a good introduction to Philo's concept of the Word of God, see Ronald Williamson, *Jews in the Hellenistic World: Philo*, Cambridge Commentaries on Writings of the Jewish and Christian World 200 BC to AD 200 (Cambridge University Press, 1989), 103–143; Isaacs, *Sacred Space*, 195–198. Lincoln D. Hurst has rejected the influence of Philonic or Platonic thought in Hebrews (*The Epistle to the Hebrews*, 7–42). There remains, however, a tendency among Hebrews' scholars to acknowledge that Hebrews uses terminology from the linguistic and conceptual world of Middle Platonism, though used differently and independently from Philo (Andrew T. Lincoln, *Hebrews: A Guide* [T&T Clark, 2006], 47; Johnson, *Hebrews*, 15–21. Cf. James W. Thompson, *The Beginnings of Christian Philosophy: The Epistle to the Hebrews*, CBQMS 13 [Catholic Biblical Association of America, 1982], 156–159).

117 The word is referred to in Philo as the First-Begotten Son (*Confusion* 146, *Dreams* 1:215), the High Priest of the Cosmos (*Flight* 108), a suppliant on behalf of the mortal race as well as an ambassador from God (*Heir* 205), the Man of God (*Confusion* 41), etc.

creation (e.g., *Migr. Abr.* 130, where the righteous person *performs* the word); the man of God (the incorporeal Adam), who represents the reason God has given humanity in resemblance to his own (*Conf. Ling.* 41, 62–63); and perhaps even Moses as an embodiment of God's wisdom for his people (*Rer. Div. Her.* 205–207).[118]

Thus, like wisdom, in Philo and Hellenistic Jewish speculation, the word of God is "a metaphor for divine action and reason,"[119] or "the mind of God expressed in the created order ... the face which God shows to the world."[120]

From the use of language identified with Wisdom speculation to describe Jesus in Heb 1:2–3, Caird and others infer that Jesus—like Solomon—is described as the bearer of Wisdom. Therefore, since Wisdom—who "created the worlds [and] is the reflection of God's glory and the exact imprint of God's very being"—"dwells" in the Son, it is inferred that it can be said of the Son appropriately that he created the worlds and is the reflection of God's glory, but this does not mean that the Son personally pre-existed.[121] They conclude, then, that these passages do not require the personal pre-existence of Christ. Instead, Jesus only pre-existed in the eternal purpose of God.[122]

Lincoln D. Hurst has picked up the argument of Caird and extended it in two ways. First, he emphasizes that all the assertions in Heb 1:3–14 are appropriate of an "idealized royal figure," if we understand their original intent. The quotations of the catena are mostly royal Psalms and should be understood in their original context as addressed to a human king.[123] He argues that even LXX Ps 101:25–27 (quoted in Heb 1:10–12), though not originally a royal Psalm, is a messianic interpretation of the Hebrew original. The LXX implies in vv. 24b–29 that two persons are speaking. It is suggested that God "was ad-

---

118 Schenck, "Keeping His Appointment," 110.

119 Ibid., 109. He uses as an example *Alleg. Interp.* 3.96: "The shadow of God is his word, by which he was making the world, having used it as an instrument. But this shadow and, as it were, representation, *is an archetype of other things*, for just as God is the model of the image, which he has now called "shadow," so the image becomes a model of other things" (Colson, LCL; emphasis mine; cf. *Heir* 230–231).

120 Isaacs, *Sacred Space*, 197. Similarly, Dunn, *Christology in the Making*, 228.

121 See, Hurst, "Christology," 156.

122 Caird, "Son by Appointment," 77.

123 Thus, Ps 110:1—quoted in Heb 1:3c and 1:13—was originally addressed to a Davidic king on the day of his enthronement (Hurst, "Christology," 156). Likewise, the quotations of 2 Sam 7:14 and Ps 2:7 in Heb 1:5 refer again to the enthronement of a Davidic king (Hurst, "Christology," 157). The "firstborn" of Heb 1:6 is a royal title in Ps 89:28, which may also encompass the reference to Israel as God's "firstborn" (Exod 4:22). He argues that the reference to Jesus as the "son of man" in Heb 2:6–10 makes him the representative of humanity; thus, we have here the image of a king who embodies the nation. In this sense, Heb 1:6 might have the two passages in mind (Hurst, "Christology," 157–159). Finally, Ps 45:6–7 (quoted in Heb 1:8–9) was originally addressed to the king apparently on the occasion of a royal wedding (it is described in the title as a love song, see v. 1).

dressing an appeal by the Messiah to shorten the appointed days."[124] Second, he builds on Caird's argument that these assertions about the Son as "idealized royal figure" in chap. 1 are necessary for the argument of chap. 2.[125] The purpose of chap. 2 is to point out that Jesus, as representative of humanity, proleptically fulfills God's original purpose for the creation of humankind. This original purpose was expressed in Ps 8 where it is said of human beings: "You have crowned them with glory and honor subjecting all things under their feet" (Heb 2:7–8, quoting Ps 8:5–6).[126] The purpose of the catena is to prove, then, that this purpose was proleptically fulfilled in the human being Jesus who was crowned with "glory and honor" when he was enthroned "at the right hand of the majesty on high." In virtue of this fact, Jesus has become the "pioneer of ... salvation," who leads other "sons (υἱοί) to glory" (2:10). Thus, he concludes, Jesus's sonship is functional, not ontological.

The value of this position resides in the fact that it calls our attention to the appointment language of the Letter. There is language in Hebrews that refers explicitly to the fact that Jesus was *appointed to* or *inherited* new functions so that he *became* something he was not before.[127] This language of "be-

---

124 The LXX translates עִנָּה ("he has broken"; MT 102:24) by ἀπεκρίθη (LXX 101:24). See Hurst, "Christology," 160–162. He depends here on the work of B. W. Bacon, "Hebrews 1:10–12 and the Septuagint Rendering of Ps. 102:23," *ZNW* 3 (1902): 280–285; and C. F. D. Moule, *The Birth of the New Testament* (1962), 78–79. See also, S. Kistemaker, *The Psalm Citations in the Epistle to the Hebrews* (van Soest, 1961), 79–80.

125 Hurst, "Christology," 151–164.

126 The expression "son of Man" is to be understood as a generic term for humanity and not as a Christological title, ibid., 153.

127 Passages that refer to Jesus as being appointed to an office or becoming something include:

"... whom he appointed [ἔθηκεν] heir of all things" (1:2).

"... having become [γενόμενος] as much superior to angels as the name he has inherited [κεκληρονόμεκεν] is more excellent than theirs" (1:4).

"You are my Son; today I have begotten [γεγέννηκά] you" (1:5; 5:5).

"Sit [κάθου] at my right hand ..." (1:13; cf. 10:12; 12:2).

"... now crowned [ἐστεφανωμένον] with glory and honor because of the suffering of death" (2:9).

"... should make the pioneer of their salvation perfect [τελειῶσαι] through sufferings" (2:10).

"... was faithful to the one who appointed [ποιήσαντι] him" (3:2).

"So also Christ did not glorify himself in becoming [γενηθῆναι] a high priest" (5:5).

"... and having been made perfect [τελειωθείς], he became [ἐγένετο] the source of eternal salvation" (5:9).

"... having been designated [προσαγορευθείς] by God a high priest according to the order of Melchizedek" (5:10).

"... having become [γενόμενος] a high priest forever according to the order of Melchizedek" (6:20).

"... one who has become [γέγονεν] a priest ... through the power of an indestructible life" (7:16).

coming" concerns the offices of king and priest. In both cases, what qualifies Jesus for these offices is not attributes of divine pre-existence but his suffering and death on earth.[128] A second strength is that its reading of the Psalms in the catena is straightforward in terms of their original intention: They are addressed to a Davidic king.

Moreover, the idea that Jesus became the Son at the ascension is not foreign to other NT documents. Paul in Rom 1:3b–4 makes the same point:

> The gospel concerning his Son, who was descended from David according to the flesh and was declared [ὁρισθέντος] to be Son of God with [ἐν] power according to the spirit of holiness by resurrection from the dead.

According to this passage Jesus became "Son of God with power" in virtue of two things: his Davidic descent and his resurrection. These qualifications related to his earthly life—and not preexistence or eternity—entitled him to become the Son of God. Thus, "Son of God with power" here refers to a function Jesus assumes after his resurrection; that is, at the exaltation.[129] James D. G. Dunn concludes in his analysis of this passage that "it remains significant that ... Paul saw in the resurrection of Jesus a 'becoming' of Jesus in status and role, not simply a ratification of a status and role already enjoyed on earth or from the beginning of time."[130] It is significant that this passage is commonly believed to be a pre-Pauline confession formula; that is, Paul is not introducing here a new concept but emphasizing what he and his readers held in common.[131] It would be quite strange that Paul would begin his epistle—that has the purpose of introducing him to new readers with the hope that they would support his ministry (cf. 1:13; 15:24)—with a point of contention regarding Christ.[132]

"This one became [γέγονεν is implied] a priest with an oath" (7:21).

"Jesus has also become [γέγονεν] the guarantee of a better covenant" (7:22).

"... but the word of the oath ... appoints [καθίστησιν] a Son who has been made perfect forever" (7:28).

"Jesus has now obtained [τέτυχεν] a more excellent ministry" (8:6).

128 His appointment as king (mainly chs. 1–2) presupposes his suffering of death: "but we do see Jesus ... now crowned with glory and honor because of [διὰ τὸ ...] the suffering of death" (2:9; cf. 1:3; 2:10, 14–16). Likewise, he has been appointed as high priest (mainly chs. 3–7) after he was perfected, that is, after having "learned obedience through what he suffered" (5:8–9; cf. 2:18; 3:6; 4:15; 7:26–28).

129 It is possible that a similar view is behind 1 Thess 1:9–10.

130 James D. G. Dunn, *Romans 1–8*, WBC 38A (Word, 1988), 14.

131 For the confessional nature of Rom 1:3b–4, see ibid., 5; J. N. D. Kelly, *Early Christian Creeds*, 3d ed. (David McKay, 1972), 17.

132 A similar assertion could be found in Acts 13:32–34: "And we bring you the good news that what God promised to our ancestors he has fulfilled for us, their children, by *raising Jesus*;

A similar functional understanding of Jesus's sonship can be found throughout the New Testament. For example, Acts 9:20–22 reports that Paul's preaching from the beginning consisted in demonstrating that Jesus was the "Son of God," which is explained as demonstrating that Jesus was the Messiah (cf. Acts 17:3–4; 18:5; 24:24).¹³³

"Son" as a filial title. There are tensions, however, in Hebrews' use of sonship language for Jesus. Some passages refer to Jesus as Son *before* the exaltation.¹³⁴ For example,

> In the days of his flesh, Jesus offered up prayers and supplications, with loud cries and tears, to the one who was able to save him from death, and he was heard because of his reverent submission. *Although he was a Son*, he learned obedience through what he suffered. (Heb 5:7–8, emphasis mine)

---

as also it is written in the second psalm, 'You are my Son; today I have begotten you.' As to his raising him from the dead, no more to return to corruption, he has spoken in this way, 'I will give you [ὑμῖν] the holy promises made to David' " (emphasis mine; cf. Acts 2:22–36).

It is not clear, however, if the phrase "raising Jesus" in v. 33 refers to Jesus's resurrection (which is clearly referred to in v. 34; see Dunn, *Christology in the Making*, 36) or to the fact that God brought Jesus onto the stage of history (e.g., Luke 1:69; Acts 3:22, 26; see Barrett, *Acts of the Apostles*, 1:645–646). In any case, it is clear that "by raising Jesus" God has fulfilled the Davidic promises. "Son of God" is here a royal title, a function that Jesus assumed by virtue of events that happened in relation to his life on earth. C. K. Barrett concludes: "Jesus is both Son of David (cf. Rom. 1.3) and Son of God; these are complementary, not contradictory propositions" (*Acts of the Apostles*, 1:646). Finally, note that 1 Cor 15:24–28 also connects Davidic traditions, the resurrection, and Jesus's sonship.

See also, John H. Hayes, "The Resurrection as Enthronement and the Earliest Church Christology," *Int* 22 (1968): 333–345.

133 For a discussion of the title "Son of God" in the New Testament, see Cullmann, 270–305; Hahn, *Christologische Hoheitstitel*, 280–333; Hengel, *The Son of God*; Martin Hengel, *Studies in Early Christology* (T&T Clark, 1995), 372–379; I. Howard Marshall, *The Origins of New Testament Christology*, Issues in Contemporary Theology (InterVarsity, 1976); Dunn, *Christology in the Making*, 12–64; Fossum, "Son of God," 128–137. It is usually understood that Christian understanding of Jesus as the Son of God experienced development throughout time (evidenced in the different uses of the title in the NT) from a functional understanding (Son of God = the messiah Son of David) to an ontological one (Son of God = pre-existent divine sonship) that was already formulated at the end of the 1st century but became dominant centuries later. See Dunn, *Christology in the Making*, 60–64; Drane, "Son of God."

134 Commentators have suggested several moments in which Jesus became Son (see Attridge, *The Epistle to the Hebrews*, 54, nn. 47–49): (1) The creation or another primeval event (Eugène Ménégoz, *La théologie de L'Epitre aux Hébreux* [Fischbacher, 1894], 82; Montefiore, *The Epistle to the Hebrews*, 44–45; Michel, *die Hebräer*, 110. For further references among the church fathers, see Spicq, *L'épître aux Hébreux*, 2:16), (2) the incarnation (Riggenbach, *an die Hebräer*, 18–19; Windisch, *Der Hebräerbrief*, 14–15; Spicq, *L'épître aux Hébreux*, 2:16; and most church fathers [see Heen and Krey, eds., 20–25 passim]), (3) and the baptism (Hermann Strathmann, *Der Brief an die Hebräer*, 9th ed., NTD 9 [Vandenhoeck & Ruprecht, 1968], 79).

There are also passages that do not refer to Jesus as Son to denote his royal status but to denote his filial relationship to God. For example,

> For the one who sanctifies and those who are sanctified *all have one Father*. For this reason Jesus is not ashamed to call them brothers and sisters, saying, "I will proclaim your name to my brothers and sisters, in the midst of the congregation I will praise you." And again, "I will put my trust in him." And again, "Here am I and the children whom God has given me." (Heb 2:11–13, emphasis mine; cf. 3:6)

How should we deal, then, with these apparently contradictory understandings of Jesus's sonship?

Some scholars believe that Hebrews incorporates two different sonship traditions without any attempt at reconciliation; therefore, we should not try to reconcile them either.[135] They note that both early Jewish and Christian writings independently combined traditions about exaltation and pre-existence that seem contradictory. For example, the identification of pseudo-Enoch as the Son of Man in the Similitudes of Enoch (105–64 BCE) is apparently contradictory. In *1 En.* 48:2 the Son of Man, the Chosen One, is named in the presence of God *before* the creation of the cosmos. At the end of the section, however, in 71:14–17, pseudo-Enoch is exalted and apparently identified as the Son of Man.[136] Similarly, Luke saw no difficulty in including assertions that seem to set the decisive moment of Jesus's divine sonship at three different moments: conception or birth (Luke 1:32, 35; cf. 2:49), baptism (Luke 3:22; cf. 3:23–28), and resurrection (Acts 13:33).[137] Paul, likewise, may refer to Jesus becoming the Son of God at the exaltation in Rom 1:3 and to Jesus's pre-existence in 1 Cor 8:6. Apparently, these contradictions didn't bother early Jewish or Christian writers. For example, Thomas H. Tobin shows how Philo uses different and sometimes contradictory exegetical traditions regarding the creation of Man without any attempt to reconcile them.[138] The fact, however, that the author of Hebrews refers in Heb 5:7–8 to Jesus as Son on earth right after referring to his exaltation and royal adoption as Son (Heb

---

135 E.g., Dunn, *Christology in the Making*, 53; Loader, *Sohn und Hoherpriester*, 140. Harold W. Attridge seems to favor this option as well, *The Epistle to the Hebrews*, 54–55.

136 See Attridge, *The Epistle to the Hebrews*, 55, n. 58. This identification is problematic, though, because different Ethiopic terms are used for "Son of Man" in these passages, see note in *OTP* 1:50.

137 Dunn, *Christology in the Making*, 50–51. It is not clear, however, whether Acts 13:33 refers to the incarnation or to the exaltation; see page 176, n. 132.

138 Thomas H. Tobin, *The Creation of Man: Philo and the History of Interpretation*, CBQMS 14 (Catholic Biblical Association of America, 1983), 162–172.

5:5–6) suggests that for him there is no contradiction between these views but they somehow complement each other.[139]

Others have suggested that Hebrews applies the title Son to Jesus before the exaltation in proleptic fashion. In other words, Hebrews calls Jesus Son while on earth in anticipation of his exaltation when he will truly become the Son.[140] Hebrews 5:8, however, does not seem to allow for this view. This passage reads, "Although he was a Son, he learned obedience through what he suffered" (5:8). This argument requires that Jesus was in some sense a son while he was on earth, not that he was going to be. "The point of 5.8 is that even though Christ was a son, and thus might be thought exempt from suffering, he still suffered and, even further, learned obedience from his suffering."[141]

Therefore, if this passage says that Jesus was already a Son on earth (5:8), right after referring to the fact that he became the Son at the ascension (5:5), then there is a progression in the meaning of the term "son" from 5:5 to 5:8. The first use of the term "son" has *royal* connotations. It harks back to the enthronement of Jesus following his ascension to heaven as described in chap. 1. In v. 8, however, the term son has *filial* connotations. It focuses on the process of learning in the context of the relationship between a father and his son, which is common to humanity. Jesus, as son of God, submits to his father's discipline (5:7) and fulfills his will (10:5–10). In this sense he has learned obedience (5:8). This is why God has appointed him "heir of all things" (Heb 1:2).

This progression in the meaning of the term "son" suggests a solution to our dilemma. The author of Hebrews uses the term "son" in two different ways. Obviously he does not see a contradiction in asserting that Jesus became the "Son" at the exaltation (Heb 1; 5:5) and asserting that he was already Son while on earth (5:8; cf. 2:11–13; 3:6). The first refers to his assumption of a *royal office*; the latter to his *filial identity*. While Jesus *became* the Son at the ascension in terms of royal power, he *was already* Son in terms of his identity.[142] Luke T. Johnson suggests that these two concepts are complementary: "The Son's capacity to inherit 'all things' from God is, in turn, connected to his role in fashioning 'all things' in the universe. He is to inherit

---

139 The participle λαλήσας in Heb 5:5 refers back to Heb 1:5–6 to the moment of Jesus's enthronement. This is the moment in which, for the author of Hebrews, Jesus is appointed high priest according to the order of Melchizedek (5:1–10).
140 E.g., Käsemann, *The Wandering People of God*, 99; Thompson, *Beginnings*, 131.
141 Schenck, "Keeping His Appointment," 97.
142 Here I am following the argument of Schenck, "Keeping His Appointment," 91–117.

what he himself participated in bringing into being."¹⁴³ The Son, in his filial identity, participates with the Father in the creation of the universe (Heb 1:2); but in his royal identity, he assumes the rulership of the universe (cf. Ps 2:8). Thus, "the protological function of the Son points to his eschatological victory."¹⁴⁴

Paul probably held a similar view. I have already mentioned Paul's assertion that Jesus "was declared to be Son of God with power according to the spirit of holiness by resurrection from the dead" (Rom 1:4). It is commonly accepted that the qualification "with power" should be taken with the noun (υἱοῦ θεοῦ) in the sense that the role Jesus assumed after the resurrection was "Son of God with power."¹⁴⁵ This suggests that in Paul's view Jesus did not become Son of God at the resurrection but that he acquired royal or executive power at the resurrection. James D. G. Dunn clearly expresses this view:

> "In power" was presumably important to Paul. It indicated that Jesus' divine sonship (v. 3) had been "upgraded" or "enhanced" by the resurrection, so that he shared more fully in the very power of God, not simply in status (at God's right hand ...), but in "executive authority," able to act on and through people in the way Paul implies elsewhere (e.g., [Rom] 8:10; 1 Cor 15:45; Gal 2:20; Col 2:6–7).¹⁴⁶

Finally, this progression in the meaning of the term "Son" is not an isolated phenomenon in the Book of Hebrews. For example, the author of Hebrews moves back and forth between the temporal and spatial meanings of the adjective πρῶτος in Heb 9:1–10. In fact, as I will show below, the author will develop a parable to illustrate the inauguration of the new age from these two uses of the adjective πρῶτος. I will suggest below that there is also a rhetorical intention in the progression of the meaning of the term "Son" in the overall argument of the letter.

The Son and the Sons in the Argument of Hebrews

I suggest that this ambiguity in the use of the term son in Hebrews plays a decisive role in the hortatory argument of the Letter. On the one hand, Hebrews' reference to the royal worthiness of the Son and his enthronement in heaven is the basis for the call to show allegiance to the new king. The

---

143 Johnson, *Hebrews*, 67.
144 Ibid.
145 See references in Dunn, *Romans 1–8*, 14.
146 Ibid.

author suggests that this allegiance should be shown by their "holding fast to the confession" (Heb 2:17–3:1; 4:14–16; 10:19–23; 13:12–15). He also issues a stern warning of judgment against those who decide to "spurn" the Son of God (Heb 6:4–8; 10:26–31; 12:25, 29). On the other hand, Hebrews' reference to the Son's sufferings and his total identification with human beings are the basis for the call to believers to endure and go forward to the reception of the promises (e.g., Heb 4:11, 16; 10:22, 35–39; 12:1–3).

The second aspect, however, constitutes the core of the argument of chs. 1 and 2. The exhortation to the believers to endure suffering and press forward to the inheritance of the promises is based on the Letter's interpretation of Ps 8:4–6 quoted in Heb 2:6–8. Interestingly enough, the force of the exhortation resides in the ambivalence in the use of the term Son.

The purpose of the author's long description of Jesus's enthronement in heaven in the catena (1:5–14) becomes clear with the interpretation of Ps 8:4–6 in Heb 2:5–9.[147] In Heb 2:5, the author picks up the topic left at 1:14 and advances the argument of the catena towards its culmination.[148] The author wants to show that the enthronement of Jesus in heaven and his rule over the world to come is of decisive importance for human beings.

---

147 The insight that the interpretation of Ps 8 in Heb 2 controls the argument of the preceding chapter (esp. the catena of 1:5–14) was introduced by G. B. Caird, "The Exegetical Method of the Epistle to the Hebrews," *CJT* 5 (1959): 44–51. Others have built on this insight; e.g., Hurst, "Christology," 151–164; Craig R. Koester, "Hebrews, Rhetoric, and the Future of Humanity," *CBQ* 64 (2002): 110–112.

148 The conjunction γάρ is better translated here by "now" in the sense of denoting the resumption of the argument left at 1:14. E.g., NRSV; Attridge, *The Epistle to the Hebrews*, 69–70; Ellingworth, *The Epistle to the Hebrews*, 144–5; Koester, *Hebrews*, 213; Lane, *Hebrews 1–8*, 44. Contra, NASB; Johnson, *Hebrews*, 89. There are several reasons for this. The phrase οὐ γὰρ ἀγγέλοις ... (2:5) is equivalent to the rhetorical questions Τίνι ... τῶν ἀγγέλων ("to which of the angels ... ?," 1:5) and πρὸς τίνα ... τῶν ἀγγέλων ("to which of the angels ... ?," 1:13). Hebrews 2:5, then, resumes the comparison between Christ and the angels of 1:5–14 with the exception that it introduces a new element in the contrast: human beings. Note that this comparison is of a different nature to the comparison between angels and Christ in 2:1–4. In 1:5–14 and 2:5–9 the angels play a negative role vis-à-vis Christ. In 2:1–4, however, the angels play a more positive role as the lesser component in an *a fortiori* comparison. Moreover, the negative assertion that "God did not subject the coming world, about which we are speaking, to angels" repeats in different terms the assertion of 1:13, "Sit at my right hand until I make your enemies a footstool for your feet." The explanatory phrase "about which we are speaking" suggests that this negative statement functions as a summary of what has been shown in 1:5–14. Hebrews 2:5 also marks a change in genre from exhortation (2:1–4) to exposition (2:5–18). There is, as well, a change in the subject and references of the passage. As in 1:5–14, "God" and the "Son" are the main referents, and God is the subject in 1:5–14 and 2:5–9. In 2:1–4, "we" is the subject and the "believers" are the main referents. See Ellingworth, *The Epistle to the Hebrews*, 144–145; George H. Guthrie, *The Structure of Hebrews: A Text-Linguistic Analysis*, NovTSup 73 (Brill, 1994), 63–64. Finally, it is worth noting that Ps 8 is tied with Ps 110—the last OT quotation of the catena (1:13)—in several Christological passages in the NT (1 Cor 15:26–27; Eph 1:20–22), see Michel, *die Hebräer*, 138.

> Now God did not subject the coming world, about which we are speaking, to angels. But someone has testified somewhere, "What are human beings [ἄνθρωπος] that you are mindful of them, or mortals [υἱὸς ἀνθρώπου], that you care for them? You have made them for a little while lower than the angels; you have crowned them with glory and honor, subjecting all things under their feet." Now in subjecting all things to them, God left nothing outside their control. As it is, we do not yet see everything in subjection to them, but we do see Jesus, who for a little while was made lower than the angels, now crowned with glory and honor because of the suffering of death, so that by the grace of God he might taste death for everyone. (Heb 2:5–9)

This quotation of Ps 8:4–6 can be read at two levels. On the first level, this psalm refers to God's broad intentions regarding human beings.[149] His purpose is to crown them with "honor and glory" and subject "all things under their feet." God has subjected the world to come to them! This reading is anticipated by the author's affirmation, twice mentioned, that human beings are destined for salvation (1:13; 2:3). The author makes an objection, however: "As it is, we do not yet see everything in subjection to them" (v. 8). This is painfully clear for the audience of the Letter. They have experienced persecution in the past (10:32–34) and continue to suffer verbal harassment (13:13). Some of them are still in prison (13:3) and the rest are experiencing a crisis of faith (5:11; 6:12; cf. 2:1).

The author responds to this disparity between promise and fulfillment by suggesting an interpretation of the Psalm at a second level. This Psalm refers to the death and exaltation of Jesus Christ. The author explains that he "was made lower than the angels" in order that "he might taste death for everyone." This was only for "a little while" but now he has been "crowned with glory and honor."[150] Thus the psalm refers to the majesty of the Son of God, whom God appointed "heir of all things" (1:2) and promised "I [will] make your enemies a footstool for your feet" (1:13). The author assumes the audience's knowledge and acceptance of what he described in the catena (1:5–14); namely, that Jesus has ascended to heaven and has been enthroned "at the right hand of the

---

149 Most commentators take αὐτῷ—repeated three times in most manuscripts (except 𝔓46 B d v vgmss boms)—to refer to humankind, not Christ. See, Ellingworth, *The Epistle to the Hebrews*, 150–152. Contra, Braun, *An die Hebräer*; Windisch, *Der Hebräerbrief*.

150 This implies a reinterpretation of Ps 8. In Ps 8 the phrases "lower than the angels" and "crowned with glory and honor" are parallel and, therefore, could be understood as being synonymous. Hebrews, however, interprets them as being contradictory. See James Swetnam, *Jesus and Isaac: A Study of the Epistle to the Hebrews in the Light of the Aqedah*, AnBib 94 (Biblical Institute Press, 1981), 139; Lane, *Hebrews 1–8*, 48.

majesty on high."¹⁵¹ Thus, "when applied to the exalted Christ, the psalm describes his present glory; when applied to the beleaguered people of God, the psalm promises future glory (1:14; 2:10)."¹⁵²

The reality of Jesus's enthronement is of fundamental importance to believers. It proves that God's purpose for human beings—as expressed in Ps 8—is for real. Jesus is the *royal* Son of God in whom God accomplished his purposes for human beings when he enthroned him Lord of the "coming world" (2:5; cf. 1:5–14). But this is not the end of the story. Jesus is the Son of God in a filial sense too. "For a little while" Jesus was made "lower than the angels … so that by the grace of God he might taste death *for everyone*" (2:9, emphasis mine). In other words, he identified fully with human beings in order to bring "many sons [υἱοί] to glory" (2:10, NASB). God has fulfilled his purpose for humanity in Christ in such a way that it anticipates and brings about fulfillment for the rest of humankind.¹⁵³ Hebrews 2:10–18 concentrates, then, on how the Son makes the fulfillment of God's purpose possible for "many sons." The author builds his argument on the filial sense of the term Son. Instead of emphasizing Jesus's royal worthiness, it focuses on his total identification with human beings.¹⁵⁴

There are seven instances of familial terminology in this passage: "many sons" (πολλοὺς υἱούς; v. 2:10), "brothers and sisters" (ἀδελφούς; v. 11), "my brothers and sisters" (τοῖς ἀδελφοῖς μου; v. 12), "the children" (τὰ παιδία; v. 13), "the children" (τὰ παιδία; v. 14); "his brothers and sisters" (τοῖς ἀδελφοῖς), and "of the people" (τοῦ λαοῦ; v. 17).¹⁵⁵ The passage emphasizes, then, that Jesus belongs to the human family.

The passage also implies, however, that Jesus is Son in a unique way. As Son, he is the brother of human beings because he has identified with them.¹⁵⁶ In fact, the language of identification is even more pervasive: "that … he might taste death for everyone" (2:9), "the pioneer of their salvation" (v. 10), "the one

---

151 The author does not try to prove in the catena by means of Scripture Jesus's ascension and enthronement over the cosmos. The catena describes, rather than argues for, Jesus's heavenly glorification. Most likely, this belief was already part of their confession (cf. 3:1; 4:14; 10:23; 13:15).

152 Koester, "Hebrews, Rhetoric, and the Future of Humanity," 111.

153 See, e.g., Swetnam, *Jesus and Isaac*, 137–141; Lane, *Hebrews 1–8*, 48.

154 For an analysis of the function of Jesus's identification with humankind in the argument of Hebrews, see Scott D. Mackie, "Confession of the Son of God in Hebrews," *NTS* 53 (2007): 114–129; *Eschatology and Exhortation in the Epistle to the Hebrews*, WUNT II/223 (Mohr Siebeck, 2007), 213–229.

155 See Mackie, "Confession of the Son of God," 119.

156 That Jesus "was made lower than the angels" implies that he preexisted. Regarding the debate about the mode of Jesus's preexistence in Hebrews, see Isaacs, *Sacred Space*, 198–204.

For an analysis of the role solidarity plays throughout Hebrews, see G. W. Grogan, "The Old Testament Concept of Solidarity in Hebrews," *TynBul* 49 (1998): 159–173.

who sanctifies and those who are sanctified all have one Father" (v. 11), "he himself likewise shared the same things [flesh and blood]; so that ... he might destroy ... the devil" (v. 14), "He gives help to the descendants of Abraham" (v. 16, NASB), "he had to become like his brothers and sisters in every respect, so that he might be a merciful and faithful high priest" (v. 17), and "Because he himself was tested by what he suffered, he is able to help those who are being tested" (v. 18).[157]

Jesus's full identification with humanity has a saving purpose. Jesus partakes of "flesh and blood" (2:14) and suffers death "so that he might be a merciful and faithful high priest in the service of God" and be "able to help" them, that is, to lead them to glory. That is why the "sons" are given to him (2:13). Jesus's death and filial obedience have made their "adoption" possible (2:9, 14). Thus, the believers' sonship is *mediated* through the sufferings of the Son. The "sons" achieve "glory" only through him. Jesus's sonship, instead, is genuine and unmediated. He "is the reflection of God's glory and the exact imprint of God's very being" (1:3).[158]

Craig R. Koester suggests, then, that Hebrews' two-level interpretation of Ps 8:4–6 in 2:5–9 should be considered the proposition (*propositio*), that is, the section "which identifies the principal issue to be addressed in the speech."[159] The author interprets Ps 8 to say two things. First, this Psalm expresses God's glorious purpose for human beings. Second, this glorious purpose has been accomplished in Jesus *on account of* (διά) his suffering of death "for everyone" (v. 9).

This interpretation sets the course for the rest of the document. It gives origin to three series of arguments. The first series (chs. 1–7) focuses on the crowning of Jesus "with glory and honor" in the sense that he has been enthroned as Son (king; esp. 1:5–14) and appointed as priest (esp. 5:1–10). In both cases, his sufferings (i.e., death) qualify him for his office (2:9, 17–18; 5:7–10). The second series (chs. 8–10) focuses on Jesus's death as a sacrifice "for everyone" that makes possible a new covenant in which his purpose for human beings can be attained. Finally, the third series (chs. 11–13) focuses on what readers should do. It acknowledges the dilemma regarding their situation. The readers "do not yet see" all things subjected to them as God intended. He shows them, on the one hand, that they need faith and that faith concerns those things that are unseen (10:38–11:40). On the other hand, he exhorts them "to see" Jesus (12:1–3; cf. 2:9) who has been "crowned with honor and

---

157 Mackie, "Confession of the Son of God," 119.
158 See Schenck, "Keeping His Appointment," 98–99.
159 Koester, "Hebrews, Rhetoric, and the Future of Humanity," 110.

glory because of the suffering of death" (2:9) and endure the necessary trials (12:5–11) as they journey towards the consummation of their hope (12:12–13; cf. vv. 22–29).[160]

Summary

I have argued that Heb 1:6 refers to the ascension of Jesus into heaven as an act of God in which he introduces the Son to the heavenly court as their ruler. In the ANE, the motif of divine warfare or Combat Myth was commonly used to support and justify kingship claims. Similarly, Hebrews describes Jesus's warfare with and victory over the devil (Heb 2:14–16) as part of a narrative substructure that justifies and supports Jesus's kingship over the world and, therefore, a strong reason for encouragement.

I have also argued that Heb 1:6 is part of a catena of OT passages that describes the enthronement of Jesus at the right hand of God. This description of the enthronement of Jesus fulfills an important function in the argument of chs. 1–2. It provides the basis to interpret Ps 8 (in Heb 2:6–10) on two levels. On the first level, Hebrews understands that Ps 8 refers to God's glorious purpose for humanity—that they should rule over creation—and recognizes that this purpose has not been fulfilled yet. On the second level, Hebrews asserts that God has fulfilled this purpose in the person of Jesus who has received "honor and glory" and has been given dominion over all things. This is not the end of the story, however. The enthronement of the Son "because of the suffering of death" makes it possible that Jesus may lead "many sons" to glory. Thus, the readers of Hebrews should see in the enthronement of Jesus a prefiguration and foretaste of their own enthronement over all things (cf. 12:28). This powerful fact is the basis of the exhortation of Hebrews. The "today" of the enthronement of the Son is not the time to "drift away" and "disobey" but to "pay greater attention" to the Son (2:1–4). This hortatory argument will be developed in new ways in the following sections of Hebrews.

" ... A Great High Priest Who Has Passed through the Heavens" (Heb 4:14–16): Ascension and Entrance into God's Rest

> Since, then, we have a great high priest *who has passed through the heavens*, Jesus, the Son of God, let us hold fast to our confession. For we do not have a high priest who is unable to sympathize with our weaknesses, but we have one who in every respect has been tested as we are, yet without

---

160 Ibid., 112.

sin. Let us therefore approach the throne of grace with boldness, so that we may receive mercy and find grace to help in time of need. (Heb 4:14–16, emphasis mine)

This is the second passage in the letter that refers to Jesus's ascension to heaven. It is significant for several reasons. First, it is a simple and straightforward affirmation of the ascension.[161] Second, it connects Jesus's ascension to important themes of the letter; for example, the important Christological titles "Son of God" and "high priest," and the exhortations "hold fast to the confession" and "approach" God "with boldness."[162] Finally, it is commonly recognized that this passage is one of the pivotal points in the argument of the Letter.[163]

I will deal, first, with the image of a high priest ascending to heaven. Second, I will explore the role the ascension plays in the immediate argument.

High Priesthood and Ascension "through the Heavens"

In terms of imagery, there are two components in the description of the ascension in this passage. First, Jesus is described as a high priest. Second, the ascension is described as a passage "through the heavens."

The image of a high priest ascending "through the heavens" into the presence of God was not strange in early Jewish and Christian apocalyptic literature. Martha Himmelfarb has argued that *1 Enoch* and later early Jewish and Christian apocalypses that involved ascent to heaven conceived heaven as a temple; thus, the ascension implied in many cases the investiture of the visionary as a heavenly priest.[164] For example, the *Testament of Levi* refers to two

---

161 Similarly Heb 9:24. The remaining ascension passages use more elaborate royal (1:6) or cultic imagery (6:19–20 [7:19]; 9:12 [26, 28]; 10:19–22).

162 Regarding the call to "hold fast to the confession," see Heb 3:6; 10:23; cf. 2:1; 6:18; 10:35; 12:3; 13:15.

163 Scholars have normally recognized clear formal and semantic parallels between 4:14–16 and 10:19–25. This parallelism is so prominent that Wolfgang Nauck suggests a tripartite structure on this basis ("Zum Aufbau des Hebräerbriefes," in *Judentum, Urchristentum, Kirche*, ed. Walther Eltester, BZNW 26 [Töpelmann, 1964], 199–208). For brief evaluations of this view, see George Guthrie, *The Structure of Hebrews*, 17–19; Cynthia Long Westfall, *A Discourse Analysis of the Letter to the Hebrews: The Relationship between Form and Meaning*, Library of New Testament Studies 297 (T&T Clark, 2005), 12–14. Though Nauck's thesis has not gained much support, most scholars believe that 4:14–16 and 10:19–25 are in fact clear peaks in the structure of the work (George Guthrie, *The Structure of Hebrews*, 17–19; Long Westfall, *A Discourse Analysis*, 137).

164 *Ascent to Heaven in Jewish and Christian Apocalypses* (Oxford University Press, 1993), 29–46. Himmelfarb analyzes early Jewish and Christian apocalypses (the Book of the Watchers [*1 En.* 1–36], the *Testament of Levi, 2 Enoch,* the Similitudes of Enoch [*1 En.* 37–71], the *Apoca-*

visions in which Levi is consecrated to serve as priest. In the first, he ascends to heaven (chs. 2–5) where God himself charges him with the work of priesthood (5:2). The second vision (chap. 8) describes two angels who come and consecrate him as priest.

In other documents the priestly function is only implicit. For example, in the case of the Book of the Watchers, Enoch himself is not called priest, but "scribe of righteousness" (*1 En.* 12.4; 15.1). However, he fulfills such priestly functions as intercession and has access to the heavenly temple (*1 En.*14.9–15.2). (Note, however, that in *Jub.* 4.25 Enoch is considered a priest.) Also, very often the ascension of a visionary implied his transformation into an angel, who were often understood to fulfill priestly roles in the heavenly sanctuary. This was indicated in a variety of ways; for example, participation in the heavenly liturgy or the investiture of the visionary with an special "robe" (e.g., *1 En.* 62:15–16; *2 En.* 22.8–10 [*OTP* 1:138]; *3 En.* 4; *Apoc. Zeph.* 8:3–4 [*OTP* 1:514]; *Ascen. Isa.* 6–9, esp. 9:1–2; *Apoc. Ab.* 13:14).[165]

James C. Vanderkam warns, however, that Martha Himmelfarb may have overemphasized the point. Some of the roles that she has taken as priestly, such as mediator, are also eminently prophetic.[166] In any case, it seems that in general her point is well taken. Since God's dwelling in heaven was consid-

---

lypse of Zephaniah, the *Apocalypse of Abraham*, the *Ascension of Isaiah*, and *3 Baruch*) spanning 400–500 years (from 3rd century BCE to 2nd century CE). She suggests that this view is the result of the influence the Book of the Watchers exerts on later apocalypses. This book describes the "house" of God as a three-chambered structure (a wall, and first and second houses), following the pattern of the First and Second Temples (*1 En.* 14.9, 10–14, 15–17; "Apocalyptic Ascent and the Heavenly Temple," in *Society of Biblical Literature: 1987 Seminar Papers*, ed. Kent Harold Richards, *SBLSP* 26 (Scholars Press, 1987), 210–217; idem, *Ascent to Heaven*, 14–16).

Regarding heavenly ascent in early Judaism and early Christianity, see J. M. Scott, "Heavenly Ascent in Jewish and Pagan Traditions," *DNTB* 447–452; Zwiep, *The Ascension of the Messiah*, 36–79; Collins, "A Throne in the Heavens," 43–58; Tabor, "Ascent," 3:91–94; idem, *Things Unutterable*, 57–112; Dean-Otting, *Heavenly Journeys*; Segal, "Heavenly Ascent," 1352–1376; Lohfink, *Die Himmelfahrt Jesu*, 51–73.

The conception of heaven as a temple is in itself not extraordinary. The OT already refers to God's dwelling as a temple in heaven. Commonly agreed references in the OT include Gen 28:11–22; Exod 25:8–9, 40; 2 Sam 22:7=Ps 18:6; Pss 29:9; 150:1; Isa 6:1–8; Zech 2:17; 3:1–10. Elias Brasil de Souza suggests that there are a total of 43 references in the Hebrew Bible ("The Heavenly Sanctuary/Temple Motif in the Hebrew Bible: Function and Relationship to the Earthly Counterparts" [Ph.D. diss., Andrews University, 2005]; see also Beale, *The Temple and the Church's Mission*, 31–44; R. J. McKelvey, *The New Temple: The Church in the New Testament*, OTM [Oxford University Press, 1969], 25–41).

165 Himmelfarb, "Apocalyptic Ascent," 212–215; idem, *Ascent to Heaven*, 29–70. It is interesting that in *3 En.* 4, Enoch is transformed into the angel Metatron, God's second in command. A similar transformation is the one of Enoch into the Son of Man in *1 En.* 71. See Himmelfarb, *Ascent to Heaven*, 44–45.

166 James C. VanderKam, review of *Ascent to Heaven in Jewish and Christian Apocalypses*, by Martha Himmelfarb, *JBL* 114 (1995): 325.

ered a temple, the ascension of the visionary into God's presence implied the assumption of priestly privileges and roles too.

The apocalypses also developed the idea of a plurality of heavens—mostly 7.[167] The highest heaven, where God's throne was, represented by implication the holy of holies of the heavenly sanctuary. (In fact, the seventh heaven is explicitly identified as the holy of holies of the heavenly sanctuary in *T. Lev.* 3.4.) A similar fusion of royal and priestly imagery is found in Hebrews' expression "throne of mercy" (4:16) which refers to God's throne in heaven from which mercy was given (Heb 8:1; 12:2; cf. Jer 17:12–14) and was represented by the ἱλαστήριον in Heb 9:5 (the lid of the ark, from the Hebrew כַּפֹּרֶת, mistakenly translated "mercy seat" in several English translations, e.g., NASB, NRSV, etc.), the place of atonement in the holy of holies, God's throne on earth (Exod 25:22; 2 Kgs 19:15; Pss 80:1; 99:1; Isa 6:1).[168]

Jesus's ascent to heaven is simply described as a passage "through the heavens." There is no place in Hebrews for the detailed and fantastic descriptions of heavenly tours that appear in early Jewish and Christian apocalypses.[169] Its interest lies, instead, in the result of the process (i.e., that Jesus has been exalted), rather than in the process itself (cf. 7:26).[170] The simple image, however, of Jesus as a high priest ascending "through the heavens" (4:14; cf. 7:26) presages the more developed image of Jesus as a high priest entering the heavenly sanctuary, which is so important later in the argument (6:19–20;

---

167   Documents referring to 1 heaven include: *1 En.* 14. Documents referring to 3 heavens include: earlier recension of the Greek version of *T. Levi* 2–3; 2 Cor 12:2–4; and probably *1 En.* 71.1–5. Documents referring to 7 heavens include: later recension of the Greek version of *T. Levi* 2–3; *L.A.E.* 35.2; *Apoc. Ab.* 10.8; 19.4; *2 En.* 3–22; *Mart. Ascen. Isa.* 6–11; and probably *3 Bar.* 11–17. See also, the description of the heavenly temple in the *Shirot 'Olat Hashabbat* (ShirShabb; Songs of the Sabbath Sacrifice) as composed of seven sanctuaries (Carol Newsom, *Songs of the Sabbath Sacrifice: A Critical Edition*, HSS 27 [Scholars Press, 1985], 48–58) and the description of multiple heavens in the non-canonical Christian writings *Apoc. Pet.* and *Apoc. Paul*. See Adela Yarbro Collins, "The Seven Heavens in Jewish and Christian Apocalypses," in *Death, Ecstasy, and Other Worldly Journeys*, ed. John J. Collins and Michael Fishbane (State University of New York Press, 1995), 57–92.

Carol Newsom considers that the use of multiple sanctuaries/heavens in the "Songs of the Sabbath Sacrifice" is "an attempt to communicate something of the elusive transcendence of heavenly reality" (49). Note, in this connection, that the 7 heavens are referred to in the singular in *T. Levi* 5.1; cf. 2.5–3.4. See Himmelfarb, *Ascent to Heaven*, 32–33.

168   This passage probably refers to God's throne and not to Christ's (1:3; 8, 13; 10:12) because elsewhere in the Letter the readers are invited to approach God (7:25; 11:6).

For the intersection of priestly, royal, and other imagery regarding Christ's exaltation and the throne of God, see Timo Eskola, *Messiah and the Throne: Jewish Merkabah Mysticism and Early Christian Exaltation Discourse*, WUNT II/142 (Mohr Siebeck, 2001), 338–374.

169   See Himmelfarb, *Ascent to Heaven*.

170   Attridge, *The Epistle to the Hebrews*, 139. The ascension is not mystical, either. Jesus's ascension implies the early Christian doctrine of Jesus's death, resurrection, and exaltation at the "right hand" of God (Heb 13:20; cf. 2:14–16; 12:2). See Johnson, *Hebrews*, 139.

8:1–2; 9:11–12; 10:19–20).¹⁷¹ Both representations merge in 9:24: "For Christ did not enter a *sanctuary* made by human hands, a mere copy of the true one, but he entered into *heaven itself*, now to appear in the presence of God on our behalf" (emphasis mine).

The assertion that Christ "has passed through the heavens" presents a problem to the interpreter as well. This passage implies a three-part universe: earth, the heavens, and above the heavens.¹⁷² Other passages, instead, imply only a two-part universe. For example, "For Christ did not enter a sanctuary made by human hands, a mere copy of the true one, but he entered into heaven itself, now to appear in the presence of God on our behalf" (Heb 9:24). We have in this case only earth and heaven.¹⁷³

César Augusto Franco Martínez has argued that there is no contradiction between the cosmological presuppositions of 4:14 and 9:24. He suggests that the apparent differences between both views may be explained by understanding the Semitic substructure of 4:14 and that this passage should read: "Teniendo, pues, un gran sumo sacerdote que entró en los cielos (o en el cielo) mantengámonos adheridos a la confesión."¹⁷⁴

First, the plural οὐρανοί could be understood as an assimilation to the Hebrew word שָׁמַיִם, which is plural in form but not in meaning.¹⁷⁵ In this sense, the plural οὐρανοί in 4:14 is equivalent to the singular οὐρανός in 9:24.¹⁷⁶ This

---

171 I am not convinced, however, that the "heavens" may stand for several rooms of the heavenly sanctuary as in the multiple heavenly temples of the Jewish apocalypses. I will argue below that the view of Jesus passing through the heavens as the high priest passed through the outer room into the inner room of the heavenly sanctuary (e.g., Koester, *Hebrews*, 282) is problematic. See the section " 'The Greater and Perfect Tent' Denotes the Sanctuary of the New Covenant" below on page 233. For Hebrews' view of the universe, see Ellingworth, "Jesus and the Universe," 337–350.

172 Paul Ellingworth suggests that also Heb 2:9 and 7:26 imply a three-part view of the universe (e.g., Eph 4:10), "Jesus and the Universe," 340–341. It is not clear that something beyond status is meant in 2:9 and 7:26 (e.g., see César Augusto Franco Martínez, *Jesucristo, su persona y su obra, en la Carta a los Hebreos: Lengua y cristología en Heb 2, 9–10; 5, 1–10; 4, 14 y 9, 27–28*, Studia Semitica Novi Testamenti 1 [Ciudad Nueva, 1992], 285; Otfried Hofius, *Der Vorhang vor dem Thron Gottes: Eine exegetisch-religionsgeschichtliche Untersuchung zu Hebräer 6,19 und 10,19 f.*, WUNT I/14 [Mohr Siebeck, 1972], 68–69).

173 This is the case in other passages that use imagery from the heavenly sanctuary (6:19; 8:1–2; 9:11–14; 10:19–21). Hebrews emphasizes Jesus's entrance into τὰ ἅγια and does not to refer to an outer room or division in the heavenly sanctuary. See Ellingworth, "Jesus and the Universe," 342–348. This is a complicated issue, however, and deserves a fuller treatment. See my analysis of the imagery of each passage below.

174 (Since we have a great high priest that entered in the heavens [or in heaven] let us hold fast to our confession.) Franco Martínez, *Jesucristo, su persona y su obra*, 308.

175 Bruce, *The Epistle to the Hebrews*, 115; Hughes, *Hebrews*, 170, n. 2. Note that in many cases שָׁמַיִם is translated with the singular in the LXX; e.g., Gen 1:1; 2:1; passim.

176 Hebrews uses the plural form in 1:10; 4:14; 7:26; 8:1; 9:23; 12:23, 25. The singular is used in 9:24; 11:12; 12:26.

shifting between plural and singular forms of οὐρανός in a single document is not strange in the NT.[177] For example, note that 1 Thess 1:10 refers to Jesus's coming "from heaven" (ἐκ τῶν οὐρανῶν) using the plural, but 1 Thess 4:16 refers to the same event with "from heaven" (ἀπ' οὐρανοῦ) in the singular.[178] In fact, this equivalency helps us to understand the shift from the plural to the singular of οὐρανός in contiguous verses in Heb 9:23–24 and 12:25–26. Franco Martínez is right, then, that we should not read too much into the plural "heavens" of 4:14.

His second point, however, is unconvincing. He argues that the term διέρχομαι in 4:14 does not carry here the sense "go through" but "to enter."[179] He notes that in the LXX διέρχομαι may translate the verbs עבר or בוא and that both verbs may refer either to "go through" or just "go, arrive at, enter." None of the examples he presents from the LXX, however, show clearly that διέρχομαι should be understood as "entering" instead of "going through."[180] His examples from the NT are similarly not convincing.[181] The problem remains, then: The author of Hebrews juxtaposes two different views of the universe in his Letter.

Paul Ellingworth, after analyzing eight passages that combine cosmological presuppositions with a description of the work of Christ, concludes that the author of Hebrews "works with two types of spatial language."[182] One is vertical and is concerned with the *exaltation* of Jesus Christ (Heb 2:9; 4:14; 7:26). This language presupposes an intermediate sphere populated with angels which he does not describe in detail over which Jesus exerts authority. The second is horizontal, typological in nature, and concerned with Jesus's sacrifice (6:19–20; 8:1–2; 9:1–14; 9:24; 10:19–21). This language presupposes a

---

177 BDAG, 738.
178 Note, as well, the shift from the plural in Col 1:5, 16, 20 to the singular in 1:23; 4:1; likewise, from the plural in 1 Pet 1:4 to the singular in 1:12 and 3:22.
179 Sometimes διέρχομαι plus the accusative may refer to movement within an area; e.g., Acts 13:6; 18:23, Ellingworth, "Jesus and the Universe," 341. This does not fit the argument of Hebrews, however, where the expression διεληλυθότα τοὺς οὐρανούς explains why Jesus is a "great high priest." The greatness of this priest resides in that he transcended the earthly and even the heavenly realms (cf. 7:26). The suggestion of César A. Franco Martínez is different, however. He suggests, instead, that the sense of διέρχομαι here is one of entering to stay, not a movement through an area and beyond.
180 For example: Deut 29:11 and 2 Chr 15:12, "enter [διέρχομαι] into a covenant"; Nah 2:1 and Joel 4:17, the wicked will never again "invade" (διέρχομαι) you; etc., see Franco Martínez, *Jesucristo, su persona y su obra*, 294–303. See also, J. Lust, E. Eynikel, and K. Hauspie, comps., *A Greek-English Lexicon of the Septuagint* (Deutsche Bibelgesellschaft, 1992–1996), 1:114; T. Muraoka, *A Greek-English Lexicon of the Septuagint: Twelve Prophets* (Peeters, 1993), 53.
181 Luke 2:15; John 4:15; Rom 5:12, Franco Martínez, *Jesucristo, su persona y su obra*, 303–307.
182 Ellingworth, "Jesus and the Universe," 349. The passages he analyzes are Heb 2:9; 4:14; 6:19–20; 7:26; 8:1–2; 9:1–14; 9:24; 10:19–21.

simple contrast between heaven and earth—without any reference to an intermediate sphere—and its purpose is to present the first covenant institutions as prefiguring Jesus's achievements in the heavenly sanctuary.[183] He suggests that both types of language complement each other. They are used in close proximity (e.g., 7:26; 8:1–2) and both describe the full access to the immediate presence of God that Jesus enjoys as high priest, first for himself and then for believers.[184]

Jesus Leads Believers into the Rest

Now, what is the function of the ascension in the argument of this passage? The answer to this question on a first level is simple. The participial phrase "who has passed through the heavens" modifies the expression "a great high priest." It has the purpose of explaining the idea that Jesus is "a great high priest."[185] In this sense, Jesus is "a great high priest" because he "has passed through the heavens"; that is, he has gone through and beyond the heavens (4:14).[186] Similarly, the implicit reference to the ascension in Heb 7:26 has the same purpose of explaining what a great high priest believers have (it also

---

183 Attempts to equate both types of spatial language by, for example, arguing that the veil represents the middle sphere populated by angels or that there are two rooms in the heavenly sanctuary are problematic. See ibid., 344–349.

184 Ibid., 350. I have not addressed here the important debate regarding Hebrews' worldview. The suggestion that Hebrews holds a Platonic/Philonic understanding of the universe that is based on a metaphysical dualism probably reached its clearest expression in Thompson, *Beginnings*. This view continues to be held, at least to some extent, by some recent commentaries, e.g., Johnson, *Hebrews*, 15–30. A second suggestion is that Hebrews holds an apocalyptic worldview that posits a dualism between two ages. This has probably reached its clearest expression in Hurst, *The Epistle to the Hebrews*.

For the most recent evaluation of the cosmology of Hebrews, of which I am aware, see Adams, "The Cosmology of Hebrews." After interacting with the work of James W. Thompson throughout his essay, he concludes: "Rather than displaying a radical cosmological dualism that negates creation and the material world, the cosmological ethos of the epistle to the Hebrews, as I read it, is decidedly *pro*-creational. The cosmology of Hebrews is, therefore, less theologically problematic than might be assumed." (Adams, "The Cosmology of Hebrews," 139, emphasis original). See also, Ronald Williamson, *Philo and the Epistle to the Hebrews*, ALGHJ 4 (Brill, 1970).

185 Attridge, *The Epistle to the Hebrews*, 139; Ellingworth, "Jesus and the Universe," 341. The expression ἀρχιερέα μέγαν (great high priest) appears redundant at first sight. The argument of the Letter will make clear, however, that Jesus is superior to all the high priests in the history of Israel. Jesus's high priesthood belongs in an altogether different category. This expression is similar to τὸν ποιμένα τῶν προβάτων τὸν μέγαν (the great shepherd of the sheep, Heb 13:20) which also emphasizes that Jesus is superior to any king in the history of Israel. See Hagner, "The Son of God," 263–265.

186 Ἔχοντες οὖν ἀρχιερέα μέγαν διεληλυθότα τοὺς οὐρανούς, Ἰησοῦν τὸν υἱὸν τοῦ θεοῦ, κρατῶμεν τῆς ὁμολογίας ("Since, then, we have a great high priest *who has passed through the heavens*, Jesus, the Son of God, let us hold fast to our confession") (4:14, emphasis mine).

has a parallel structure):[187] "For it was fitting that we should have such a high priest, holy, blameless, undefiled, separated from sinners, and *exalted above the heavens*" (emphasis mine).[188]

This leads us to a second question, however: Why has the author chosen the ascension together with Jesus's sinlessness to characterize Jesus as "a great high priest"? In order to answer this question we need to explore the relationship between this passage and its co-text.

Hebrews 4:14–16 in the Argument of the Letter

Hebrews 4:14–16 introduces the exposition of Hebrews 5–10. Most commentators agree that this passage has impressive literary connections to Heb 10:19–23. In fact, George H. Guthrie considers this connection "the most striking use of *inclusio* in the book of Hebrews."[189] (Notice the connections in Table 4.)

This relationship is important for the overall structure of the letter. These passages frame the major central section of the exposition of Hebrews (5:1–10:18).[190] The first phrase of 4:14–16—"Since, then, we have a great high priest who has passed through the heavens"—seems to enclose the two overall arguments of the central section of Hebrews (5:1–10:18).[191] The author explains

---

187 Note that in both passages, the ascension is only one of the qualifications that makes Jesus a great high priest. These passages also mention a second qualification, Jesus is sinless or, in other words, a faithful high priest.

188 Τοιοῦτος γὰρ ἡμῖν καὶ ἔπρεπεν ἀρχιερεύς, ὅσιος ἄκακος ἀμίαντος, κεχωρισμένος ἀπὸ τῶν ἁμαρτωλῶν καὶ ὑψηλότερος τῶν οὐρανῶν γενόμενος (emphasis mine).

189 George Guthrie, *The Structure of Hebrews*, 79–82. Also Nauck, 203–206; Long Westfall, *A Discourse Analysis*, 137. Cf. deSilva, *Perseverance in Gratitude*, 179; Ellingworth, *The Epistle to the Hebrews*, 265. All of them recognize the importance of the connection between these passages. Both George H. Guthrie and Wolfgang Nauck develop their understanding of the structure of Hebrews on the basis of this connection and Cynthia Long Westfall considers the two passages "clear peaks in the discourse" (*A Discourse Analysis*, 137, 299–301). However, the inclusion of 4:11–13 by Long Westfall and 10:24–31 by Nauck appears to me unwarranted.

It is puzzling that Albert Vanhoye failed to consider the connection between these passages but recognized a less clear *inclusio* formed by 3:1 and 4:14 (see page 194, n. 193). In any case, the connection between 4:14–16 and 10:19–23 does not fit the chiastic structure he suggests for Hebrews. This significantly weakens his overall approach to the structure of Hebrews, even though his analysis of Hebrews' techniques of composition remains valuable. For an evaluation of Albert Vanhoye's views, see George Guthrie, *The Structure of Hebrews*, 33–35; Long Westfall, *A Discourse Analysis*, 7–11.

190 Here I am following the argument of George Guthrie, *The Structure of Hebrews*, 79–82, 102–104, 144. Albert Vanhoye differs regarding the extension of this central section. He identifies 5:11–10:39 as the central section of the argument of Hebrews. He discerns, however, a similar progression in the argument that begins with the appointment of Jesus as high priest and continues to the exposition of his sacrifice. *La structure littéraire de l'Épitre aux Hébreux*, 2nd ed. (Desclée De Brouwer, 1976), 40a–40b.

191 George Guthrie, *The Structure of Hebrews*, 103. Note, however, that the train of thought is interrupted by the hortatory section that goes from 5:11–6:20.

in the first half (Heb 5:1–7:28) the appointment of the Son as high priest ("we have a great high priest"). In the second half (Heb 8:1–10:18), he discusses Jesus's superior offering in heaven as constituting the inauguration of a new covenant ("who has passed through the heavens"). Note that Heb 7:11–12 makes explicit the logic of the progression of the argument of this central section by pointing out that the change of priesthood (5:1–7:28) makes necessary a change in the law (8:1–10:18).

4:14–16	10:19–23
Since, then, we have a great high priest who has passed through the heavens, Jesus, the Son of God, let us hold fast to our confession. For we do not have a high priest who is unable to sympathize with our weaknesses, but we have one who in every respect has been tested as we are, yet without sin. *Let us therefore approach the throne of grace with boldness,* so that we may receive mercy and find grace to help in time of need [emphasis mine].	Therefore, my friends, *since we have confidence* to enter the sanctuary by the blood *of Jesus,* by the new and living way that he opened for us *through the curtain* (that is, through his flesh), and *since we have a great priest* over *the house of God, let us approach with* a true heart in full assurance of faith, with our hearts sprinkled clean from an evil conscience and our bodies washed with pure water. *Let us hold fast to the confession* of our hope without wavering, for he who has promised is faithful [emphasis mine].
Ἔχοντες οὖν ... (since we have)	Ἔχοντες οὖν ... (since we have)
ἀρχιερέα μέγαν (a great high priest)	ἱερέα μέγαν (a great priest)
διεληλυθότα τοὺς οὐρανούς (who has passed through the heavens)	διὰ τοῦ καταπετάσματος (through the curtain)
Ἰησοῦν (Jesus)	Ἰησοῦ (Jesus)
τὸν υἱὸν τοῦ θεοῦ, (the Son of God)	τὸν οἶκον τοῦ θεοῦ (the house of God)
κρατῶμεν τῆς ὁμολογίας (let us hold fast to the confession)	κατέχωμεν τὴν ὁμολογίαν (let us hold fast to the confession)
προσερχώμεθα ... μετά (let us approach with ...)	προσερχώμεθα μετά (let us approach with)
παρρησίας (boldness)	παρρησίαν (confidence)

Table 4. Literary Relationship between Hebrews 4:14–16 and 10:19–23[192]

---

192 Adapted from George H. Guthrie, *The Structure of Hebrews: A Text-Linguistic Analysis*, NovTSup 73 (Brill, 1994), 80.

In this sense, then, the reference to the ascension in Heb 4:14 functions as a harbinger of Hebrews' discussion of Jesus's sacrifice and entrance into heaven in 8:1–10:18.

Hebrews 4:14–16 concludes the exhortation of Hebrews 3–4. This passage, however, also has a clear relationship with its preceding argument. Albert Vanhoye has correctly noted that 4:14 closes an *inclusio* opened at 3:1.[193] The author crafts this *inclusio* around four verbal elements common to both passages: Ἰησοῦς (Jesus), ἀρχιερεύς (high priest), ἐπουράνιος/οὐρανός (heavenly/heaven), and ὁμολογία (confession). (See Table 5.)

Heb 3:1	Heb 4:14
Therefore, brothers and sisters, holy partners in a *heavenly* calling, consider that *Jesus*, the apostle and *high priest* of our *confession*. (emphasis mine)	Since, then, we have a great *high priest* who has passed through the *heavens*, *Jesus*, the Son of God, let us hold fast to our *confession*. (emphasis mine)

Table 5. Literary Relationship between Hebrews 3:1 and 4:14

I believe, however, that the correspondence between 3:1 and 4:14 goes beyond these four elements if we broaden the comparison to include thematic elements and a comparison between the wider passages 3:1–6 and 4:14–16. The latter describes Jesus as the "Son of God," a concept that plays a very important function in the argument of the first where Jesus's faithfulness is superior to that of Moses because Jesus is a Son while Moses was a servant (3:5–6). Also, 4:15 presents Jesus as "one who in every respect has been tested as we are, yet without sin"; again, a concept that resides at the core of the argument of Heb 3:1–6 which presents Jesus as the one who "was faithful [πιστός] to the one who appointed him" (v. 2). Finally, and more important, 3:1–6 opens a

---

193 *La structure littéraire*, 54, 104; idem, *Structure and Message*, 26; George Guthrie, *The Structure of Hebrews*, 78. Albert Vanhoye, however, mistakenly separates 4:14 from 4:15–16 (*Structure and Message*, 26). Likewise, Lane, *Hebrews 1–8*, 110–11. It seems better to me to consider vv. 14–16 a unit that both concludes the preceding argument and introduces a new stage in it. The parallels between 4:14–16 and 10:19–23 suggest that the author considered the former to have an inherent unity. Furthermore, the progression of three hortatory subjunctives introduced by οὖν (4:11, 14, 16) with a close semantic relationship between them ("all three are behavioural [sic] processes that are physiological, involving the body" [Long Westfall, *A Discourse Analysis*, 135]) makes it unlikely that there is a break between vv. 14 and 15. Similar progressions of hortatory subjunctives are found in 10:19–25, which is clearly a unit (*A Discourse Analysis*, 133–137).

hortatory argument of the Letter that it is not interrupted until it concludes in 4:14–16.[194]

Thus, these two passages also frame Hebrews' exhortation contained in 3:7–4:13. In this sense, 4:14–16 functions more as a hinge or pivot on which the overall argument of Hebrews turns.[195] It functions both as an introduction to the following exposition and a conclusion to the foregoing exhortation. This raises a question. If Heb 4:14–16 concludes the hortatory argument of the unit (3:1–4:16), what is the function of the ascension and Jesus's priesthood in it?

The Exalted High Priest Helps the People to Enter the Rest

In this section (Heb 3–4) the author uses the language and events of Ps 95 and Num 14 to call the attention of the readers to the danger of disregarding the word of God.[196] The author describes the readers as in the same situation that the wilderness generation of Num 14 was: the moment of the fulfillment of the promise or, in other words, the moment to enter "the rest."[197] According to the argument of Hebrews, the repetition of the promise by David in Ps 95 (94 LXX) shows that the promise had not been fulfilled in the time of Joshua (Heb 4:8). The Psalm's exhortation "Today, if you hear his voice, do not harden your hearts" (94:7–8 LXX, as quoted in Heb 3:7–8; cf. 3:15; 4:7) implies that the reason for the failure of the wilderness generation was disobedience (ἀπείθεια) resulting from lack of faith (ἀπιστία; Heb 3:18–19).[198] The author, then, exhorts the readers to obey the voice of God by entering "the rest."[199]

---

194 Contra Lane, *Hebrews 1–8*; Vanhoye, *La structure littéraire*. They argue that Hebrews begins a new expository section in 4:15. For the unity of Heb 4:14–16, see above page 194, n. 193.

195 Attridge, *The Epistle to the Hebrews*, 138; deSilva, *Perseverance in Gratitude*, 179; George Guthrie, *The Structure of Hebrews*, 78, 102–104.

196 The author introduces this section with the warning: "Today, if you hear his voice, do not harden your hearts" (3:7–8). This is a warning he repeats two other times in the section (cf. 3:15; 4:7).

197 See John Dunnill, *Covenant and Sacrifice in the Letter to the Hebrews*, SNTSMS 75 (Cambridge University Press, 1992), 141–143.

Psalm 95 refers to Meribah and Masah (Exod 17:7; Num 20:13). Hebrews reads Ps 95 in relation to Num 14 (Heb 3:17), where the "rest" implied is the land of Canaan (Deut 3:20; 12:9, 10; 25:19; Josh 1:13, 15; 21:44; 22:4). Rabbi Aqiba made also the same connection (*b. San.* 110b; *t. San.* 13:10 *j. San* 9.29c). See Otfried Hofius, *Katapausis: Die Vorstellung vom endzeitlichen Ruheort im Hebräerbrief*, WUNT I/11 (Mohr Siebeck, 1970), 41–47; Attridge, *The Epistle to the Hebrews*, 125, n. 33.

198 The Psalmist's exhortation refers to God's incrimination in Num 14:22 "[They] have tested me these ten times and *have not obeyed my voice*" (emphasis mine).

199 Scholars continue to debate the meaning of "rest" in Heb 3–4. The debated issues include whether rest is a place or a state, a present reality or a promise about the future, the heavenly temple or a Christian Sabbath. For an evaluation of the several views, see Jon Laansma, *"I Will Give You Rest": The Rest Motif in the New Testament with Special Reference to Mt 11 and*

The author closes the unit with three exhortations—all of them expressed with an hortatory subjunctive and introduced by οὖν: "Let us therefore make every effort to enter that rest" (4:11), "Let us hold fast to our confession" (4:14), and "Let us therefore approach the throne of grace with boldness" (4:16).[200] These three exhortations are supported by two explicit arguments: one negative and one positive. The readers may reject the voice of God and face the "word of God" as their Judge (4:12–13) or believe the voice of God and accept Jesus as their "helper along the way" (4:14–16).[201]

First, the author exhorts them to obey the "voice of God" and enter the "rest" (4:11). If they choose to disobey, however, they will have the "Word of God" as judge and executioner who will exclude them from receiving the promise (Heb 4:12–13).[202] These verses "are crafted to arouse fear."[203] The "Word of God" is a formidable Judge with the power to penetrate "the thoughts and intentions of the heart" like a "two-edged" sword, that is, to expose hidden things, and overpower his subjects.[204] Readers might as well have remembered that those Israelites in the desert who challenged God's oath died by the sword (μάχαιρα) of the Amalekites and the Canaanites (Num 14:43–45).[205] Thus, readers may avoid the judgment of the Word of God by obeying the voice of God, which is the same as accepting the exhortation, "Let us therefore make every effort to enter that rest."

The second and third exhortations—"Let us hold fast to our confession" and "Let us therefore approach the throne of grace with boldness" (4:14, 16)—do not seem to fit the context at first sight. The implicit argument of Heb 3–4 is that Jesus is a greater ἀρχηγός than Joshua was because he is leading believers into the true rest.[206] Thus, when he says, "For if Joshua ['Ἰησοῦς] had given

---

Heb 3–4, WUNT II/98 (Mohr Siebeck, 1997), 276–332. In addition, different views regarding the religio-historical origin of the concept of "rest" have produced different solutions, for example: entry into the gnostic pleroma, liberation from foreign oppression (Buchanan, *To the Hebrews*, 9, 63–65, 71), entry into the eschatological temple (Hofius, *Katapausis*, 53–54), entry into the heavenly spiritual world (Thompson, *Beginnings*, 99).

200 See Long Westfall, *A Discourse Analysis*, 133–137. The first exhortation summarizes the preceding argument (3:7–4:11). The last two perform a double duty. They provide the transition to the next section but also culminate the argument of the hortatory unit (3:7–4:11).

201 deSilva, *Perseverance in Gratitude*, 184.

202 Ibid. The word of God is here a personification of God or the Son of God; probably the first, Johnson, *Hebrews*, 132.

203 deSilva, *Perseverance in Gratitude*, 184.

204 The part. τετραχηλισμένα comes from τραχηλίζω which may have the connotation of pinning down "an opponent in wrestling by seizing the neck (Plutarch, *Anthony* 33)," Johnson, *Hebrews*, 135–136.

205 Lane, *Hebrews 1–8*, 102.

206 Num 13:1–16 explicitly identifies Joshua and the other spies sent ahead of the people into the land of Canaan as ἀρχηγοί.

them rest, God would not speak later about another day" (4:8), he implies that "today" Jesus ['Ιησοῦς] is leading believers into the rest.[207] The identity of the names of both leaders suggests a typological comparison.[208] This, however, is not developed; instead, this implicit comparison between Joshua (4:8) and Jesus in 4:1–11 seems to be excluded in 4:14–16. Jesus is not referred to as a leader (ἀρχηγός) into the rest, but as a high priest before the throne of God in the heavenly sanctuary!

It is considered, then, that this passage creates "an abrupt shift in tone and imagery."[209] We should note, however, that while the imagery changes abruptly, the content of the exhortation remains stable. Let me explain this.

The exhortation "let us hold fast to our confession" (4:14) culminates the call to obedience and faith in 3:7–4:11. The author emphasized here that the danger that the believers are facing—in the context of God's exhortation to enter the rest—is "disobedience" (ἀπείθεια) because of unbelief (ἀπιστία; 4:11; cf. 3:18–19, passim). This was the "sin" of the wilderness generation that prevented them from entering God's rest (3:17). "Disobedience" in this section translates the verb ἀπειθέω or the noun ἀπείθεια, which carry in the NT the "connotation of disbelief in the Christian gospel."[210] Thus, the author explains that it is the rejection of the "good news" that may prevent readers of today from entering the rest, as it did for the wilderness generation:

> Therefore, while the promise of entering his rest is still open, let us take care that none of you should seem to have failed to reach it. For indeed *the good news came to us just as to them*; but the message they heard did

---

207 Scholars dispute if Ἰησοῦς in 4:8 refers to Joshua, Jesus, or both. Some see here a reference to Joshua who led Israel into the land (Josh 21:44; 22:4). Ellingworth, *The Epistle to the Hebrews*, 252–253; Koester, *Hebrews*, 271–272, 278; Riggenbach, *an die Hebräer*. Others see a reference to Jesus here, in the sense that Jesus did not give rest to the Israelites in the time of Joshua. For example, Paul and the author of Hebrews associate Jesus with the time of Moses (1 Cor 10:4; Heb 11:26 KJV); Anthony Tyrrell Hanson, *Jesus Christ in the Old Testament* (SPCK, 1965), 61. I agree with those who see here suggested a typological relationship between Joshua and Jesus. Attridge, *The Epistle to the Hebrews*, 130; Héring, *The Epistle to the Hebrews*; Johnson, *Hebrews*, 128; Loader, *Sohn und Hoherpriester*, 122; Windisch, *Der Hebräerbrief*, 97. This typology was explicitly developed in later Christian writings (Barn. 12:8 and Justin, *Dial.* 75).

208 For an analysis of the role of Joshua in Hebrews, see Dunnill, *Covenant and Sacrifice*, 170–172. He notes that the promise "I will never leave you or forsake you"—registered in Deut 31:8, 6 and quoted in Heb 13:5—was originally made to Joshua (Josh 1:5; cf. Gen 28:15). He suggests that Joshua might be considered in this epistle to occupy the role of covenant mediator also fulfilled by Moses, Abel, Abraham, and Jesus.

209 Koester, *Hebrews*, 291.

210 BDAG, 99. The noun ἀπείθεια appears in Heb 4:6, 11. In Rom 11:30, 32, this term denotes the rejection of the gospel by Israel. The verb ἀπειθέω appears in Heb 3:18 (cf. 11:31). Likewise, it is related in the NT to the rejection of the gospel; see Acts 14:2, 9; Rom 15:31; 1 Pet 2:8; 3:1; 4:17.

not benefit them, because they were not united by faith with those who listened. For *we who have believed* enter that rest. (Heb 4:1–3, emphasis mine; cf. v. 6)

In this passage, the author identifies the announcement by Caleb and Joshua regarding the goodness of the land and God's command to the wilderness generation to enter Canaan as the "good news" that they disobeyed because of their unbelief (Num 13:30; 14:7–9).[211] Based on this negative example, the author of Hebrews exhorts readers to not commit the same mistake but to do the opposite. They should, instead, demonstrate their faith by holding fast to their "confession" (4:14).[212]

This exhortation is central to the purpose of Heb 3–4. At the beginning of the exhortation (3:1) the author noted that the believers are "holy partners [with Jesus] in a heavenly calling" (3:1).[213] At the beginning of this section the author repeats the notion introduced in Heb 2:5–18 that believers are destined to "glory" just as Jesus was.[214] The author, however, carries the ar-

---

211 Ellingworth, *The Epistle to the Hebrews*, 241; Lane, *Hebrews 1–8*, 98. God's order to enter Canaan was the realization of his promise—made through Moses to the Israelites in Egypt—that he would liberate them and give them the land of the Canaanites, etc. (Exod 3:16–17). The Israelites, however, vacillated between belief (4:2) and unbelief (6:1–10), when they first received this message of "good news" in Egypt. At the border of Canaan, however, they finally rejected the "good news" and named a new captain (ἀρχηγός) to lead them back to Egypt (Num 14:4). Only Joshua and Caleb remained as faithful ἀρχηγοί (Num 14:1–10). See also Koester, *Hebrews*, 269.

212 Note that Hebrews refers to "the confession" using the definite article which indicates that it had a content "that could be identified and grasped." Koester, *Hebrews*, 126. This confession may not have included all the teaching known to the listeners (cf. 6:1–2) but most likely it stated the core beliefs of the community. James D. G. Dunn, *Unity and Diversity in the New Testament: An Inquiry into the Character of Earliest Christianity* (Westminster, 1977), 58–59; Laub, *Bekenntnis und Auslegung*, 12. In this sense, to hold fast to the confession was equivalent to being faithful to the gospel, the good news (Heb 4:2, 6). In 4:14, the confession is referred to in relation to Jesus as high priest and Son of God. We cannot know if the confession referred to these two titles, but very probably it referred at least to Jesus as Son of God. The confession of Jesus as Son of God was common in the NT (Acts 9:20; Rom 1:4; 1 Cor 1:9; 2 Cor 1:19; 1 Thess 1:9–10; 1 John 4:15; 5:5). For a study of common elements in NT creeds, see Dunn, *Unity and Diversity*, 33–59; Kelly, *Early Christian Creeds*, 1–29.

213 The people of God are the object of God's call for salvation in the OT (Isa 41:9; 42:6) as well as in the NT (Rom 11:29; 1 Cor 1:26; Eph 1:18; Phil 3:14; 2 Pet 1:10).

214 The adjective "heavenly" refers here both to the origin of the call and its destination. Harold W. Attridge, " 'Let Us Strive to Enter That Rest': The Logic of Heb 4:1–11," *HTR* 73 (1980); Braun, *An die Hebräer*; Ellingworth, *The Epistle to the Hebrews*, 198; Grässer, *An die Hebräer*; Spicq, *L'épître aux Hébreux*. For "heavenly" as implying only origin, see the Peshitta, Spicq, *L'épître aux Hébreux*, 2:77. For "heavenly" as implying only destination, see Montefiore, *The Epistle to the Hebrews*; Windisch, *Der Hebräerbrief*. According to Heb 1–2, God is speaking to the believers in Jesus (1:1–4) and has confirmed the message delivered through his messengers (2:4). Therefore, it seems clear on the one hand that the call originates from God in heaven. On the other hand, it refers, as well, to the destination of the call. The author has made clear that

gument a step further. He makes clear that the believers are partners of Jesus *only if* they "hold firm [κατάσχωμεν] the confidence and pride that belong to hope" (3:6). This is confirmed in 3:14: "For we have become partners of Christ, *if only* [ἐάνπερ] we hold [κατάσχωμεν] our first confidence firm to the end" (emphasis mine).[215] What the author is trying to do in chs. 3–4 is to emphasize that if the believers want to realize God's purpose for them and achieve "glory"—which was explained in Heb 1–2, esp. 2:5–10—they need to "hold fast" (κρατῶμεν) to their confession (4:14).[216] Thus, the flow of the argument in the macrostructure of Heb 1–4 follows this pattern. Hebrews 1–2 consists of an exposition (with the exception of 2:1–4) where the author presents the enthronement of Jesus in heaven (1:5–14) and the fact that believers are called to share Jesus's glory (2:5–18). Hebrews 3–4 consists of an exhortation where the author calls his readers to "consider that Jesus, the apostle and high priest of our confession, was faithful to the one who appointed him" (3:1–6) and, therefore, they need to be faithful as well if they want to share his glory (3:7–4:11).

Therefore, the expression, "Since, then, we have a great high priest who has passed through the heavens, Jesus, the Son of God" is a summary of the

---

human beings are destined to "glory" which is considered their "salvation" (2:10; cf. 1:14). Later on, Hebrews will refer to this call as an invitation to enter the heavenly sanctuary (8:5; 9:23; cf. 10:19) and the heavenly city (11:16; 12:22). See Koester, *Hebrews*, 242.

For a study of the different senses in which heavenly language is used in Hebrews (cosmological, axiological, eschatological), see Aelred Cody, *Heavenly Sanctuary and Liturgy in the Epistle to the Hebrews: The Achievement of Salvation in the Epistle's Perspective* (Grail, 1960), 77–85.

215   The believers are partners (μέτοχοι) of Jesus's heavenly call, in the first place, only because Jesus "shared" (μετέσχεν) the human nature (flesh and blood, 2:14) and sufferings (πάθημα, 2:9–10; cf. 10:32) with human beings and became like them "in every respect" (2:17). See Ellingworth, *The Epistle to the Hebrews*, 198. The author explains that Jesus identified himself with humans in order that through his death he might lead them to "glory" (2:5–18). On the difficulties involved in the translation of 3:14, see Ellingworth, *The Epistle to the Hebrews*, 225–228.

I understand that "become partners of Christ" (3:14) means here to be partakers in the heavenly destiny of Christ (3:1)—which is associated in this section with entering God's "rest"—and not only in a more general sense of fellowship with Christ (cf. Heb 1:9); see e.g., Attridge, *The Epistle to the Hebrews*, 117–118; Bruce, *The Epistle to the Hebrews*, 149–52; Gräßer, *An die Hebräer*; Lane, *Hebrews 1–8*, 87–88; Moffatt, *Epistle to the Hebrews*; Spicq, *L'épître aux Hébreux*, 2:76–77; August Strobel, *Der Brief an die Hebräer*, NTD 9 (Vandenhoeck & Ruprecht, 1975), 113–114. Contra Braun, *An die Hebräer*; Ellingworth, *The Epistle to the Hebrews*, 226–227; Hughes, *Hebrews*, 149–150; Westcott, *The Epistle to the Hebrews*, 84–85. It is difficult, however, to distinguish between both, because fellowship with Christ suggests partaking in the benefit of his achievements; see Hughes, *Hebrews*, 150; Westcott, *The Epistle to the Hebrews*, 85.

216   The verbs κατέχω (3:6, 14) and κρατέω (4:14) may express the idea of "holding fast" to something. BDAG 532–533, 564–565. They are used as synonyms in Hebrews as shown, e.g., in the expressions κρατῶμεν τῆς ὁμολογίας (4:14) and κατέχωμεν τὴν ὁμολογίαν (10:23). Attridge, *The Epistle to the Hebrews*, 139 n. 35.

main points of the exposition of chs. 1–2.[217] Jesus is the Son of God (1:1–4) who "passed through the heavens" when he was enthroned "at the right hand of the majesty on high " (1:3; cf. 1:5–14, 2:5–9) but became our high priest when he shared our human nature in order to lead us to "glory" (2:10–18). The call, "let us hold fast to our confession," summarizes the exhortation in 3:7–4:11 to faithfulness by "holding fast" to our "hope" (3:6; 3:14) in order that they may share in Jesus's glorious destiny.[218] Thus, Heb 4:14 contains in a nutshell the argument of the Letter to the Hebrews so far.

The author closes the section with a call to "approach the throne of grace with boldness" (4:16). This exhortation is based on the fact that believers have in Jesus a high priest speaking on their behalf before the throne of God.[219] Jesus is a merciful high priest because he has been tempted "in every respect" as the believers are, "yet without sin" (4:15). The author invites readers to accept Jesus as a "helper along the way."[220]

Jesus is an ideal helper because he can understand the temptations and sufferings that the believers are experiencing. On his way to heavenly glory, Jesus passed through a day of testing (πειρασθείς, 2:17) just as the believers are passing through now (2:17–18; 4:15; cf. 10:32–34).[221] Hebrews emphasizes that Jesus chose to identify with human beings in their sufferings and temptations with the purpose of being "able to help" those who were being tempted (2:9–18, esp. 18; 5:8–9; cf. 10:5–10).[222]

---

217 See Johnson, *Hebrews*, 139.

218 Note that the enthronement of a new emperor in imperial Rome called for expressions of allegiance throughout the empire. These expressions of allegiance were repeated every year on the anniversary of the ascension of the emperor. See page 309, n. 10.

219 We find similar concepts throughout the NT. Ephesians 3:12 mentions that in Jesus we have "access to God in boldness [παρρησία]" (cf. Rom 5:2; Eph 2:18). Acts 3:20 relates the "times of refreshing [ἀνάψυξις]" with the parousia of the Messiah "appointed for you." See Laansma, *"I Will Give You Rest,"* 347.

The "throne of grace" could refer here to where Jesus is seated "at the right hand of God" (1:3, 8, 13; 10:12). More likely, this phrase refers here to the throne of God (8:1; 12:2): First, because in my view this passage emphasizes Jesus's mediation instead of his majesty and, second, because elsewhere in the Letter the invitation to "approach" is issued with respect to God (7:25; 11:6; cf. 10:1, 22; Koester, *Hebrews*, 284. Contra Johnson, *Hebrews*, 141).

220 deSilva, *Perseverance in Gratitude*, 184. Cf. Laansma, *"I Will Give You Rest,"* 334.

221 Regarding the "testing" of Jesus, see Dunnill, *Covenant and Sacrifice*, 188–226. Note that Heb 3:9 (quoting Ps 95:9 [94 LXX]) describes the day in the wilderness when the invitation to enter the rest came as a day of testing. The original sense refers to the testing of God by the Israelites in the desert. Here Hebrews may intend a double entendre because it clearly sees the believers as going through a day of testing (4:15; cf. 2:18; 10:32–34). Abraham, one of the examples of faith, also passed through a day of testing (11:17).

222 Note that Hebrews emphasizes Jesus's death as a suffering (πάθημα) on our behalf, 2:9; cf. 2:10, 18; 5:8–9; 9:26; 13:12. Also, that Jesus chose to suffer on our behalf (10:5–10; cf. 2:13a).

The description of Jesus as "one who in every respect has been tested as we are, *yet without sin*" is important (4:15, emphasis mine). While his sufferings enable him to be merciful toward human beings, his faithfulness (sinlessness) qualifies him to be an effective mediator before God. "Jesus ... is perfectly suited as broker between humans, for whom he has complete sympathy (and hence greater willingness and eagerness to help), and God, with whom he remains in an unblemished relationship at all times."[223]

Note as well that Jesus's faithfulness is an important concept in this hortatory section and the Letter in general (2:18; 4:15; 7:26; 9:14).[224] The author introduced this hortatory section by presenting Jesus as an example of faithfulness to the believers: "Therefore, brothers and sisters ... consider [κατανοήσατε] that Jesus, the apostle and high priest of our confession, was faithful [πιστός] to the one who appointed him" (Heb 3:1–2).[225] The author refers again to this in 7:26 and 10:5–10. Finally, toward the end of the document he refers to Jesus as "the pioneer [ἀρχηγός] and perfecter of our faith" (12:2). He is the "pioneer" in the sense that, being the only faithful person to have reached the goal of faith (cf. 11:39–40), he runs ahead of believers, and guarantees that the prize is for real (cf. 2:5–10).[226] In this sense he is the basis for our faith. On the other hand, he is the "perfecter of our faith" because he models the correct form to run. He reached the goal despite the "hostility against himself from sinners" (12:2–3). Thus, he is "the one who has displayed trust or faith in its complete and perfect form."[227]

Regarding mercy and priesthood, see William Horbury, "Aaronic Priesthood in Hebrews," *JSNT* 19 (1983): 59–66; Harold S. Songer, "A Superior Priesthood: Hebrews 4:14–7:28," *RevExp* 82 (1985): 346.

223   deSilva, *Perseverance in Gratitude*, 182.

224   The sinlessness of Christ is affirmed throughout the NT as well; cf. John 7:18; 8:46; 2 Cor 5:21, 1 Pet 1:19; 2:22; 3:18; 1 John 3:5–7.

225   Something that reminds us of the assertion in 2:9: "but we see Jesus." Similarly, Heb 12:1–3 presents Jesus as an example to believers and invites them to "consider" (ἀναλογίσασθε) him. See Johnson, *Hebrews*.

226   See deSilva, *Perseverance in Gratitude*, 431–432; Koester, *Hebrews*, 523. For a study of ἀρχηγός, see J. Julius Scott Jr., "*Archegos* in the Salvation History of the Epistle to the Hebrews," *JETS* 29 (1986): 47–54; George Johnston, "Christ as Archegos," *NTS* 27 (1981): 381–384.

227   deSilva, *Perseverance in Gratitude*, 432. It is appropriate, then, that he has been placed at the very end of the list of examples (Heb 11). Regarding the meaning of the extremely rare term τελειωτής, see N. Clayton Croy, "A Note on Hebrews 12:2," *JBL* 114 (1995): 117–119. After studying the only other place where this term appears (Dionysius of Halicarnasssus, *On Dinarchus*), N. Clayton Croy concludes: "A τελειωτής is one who perfects, refines, or brings to full flower that which is (in this case) the original work of others" (118). He notes that "perfecters" were compared with "inventors" (εὑρετής). Jesus seems to be both, however, because he is the "pioneer" (ἀρχηγός, a near synonym of εὑρετής) and "perfecter" (τελειωτής) of faith.

See also Richard B. Hays, "Apocalyptic Hermeneutics: Habakkuk Proclaims 'The Righteous One,'" in *The Conversation of the Imagination: Paul as Interpreter of Israel's Scripture* (Eerdmans, 2005), 119–142.

This attractive picture of Jesus as a merciful high priest able to help those who are being tested is completely opposite, then, to the stern description of the "Word of God" as Judge of those who decide to disobey (4:12–13). This reference to the polarity of alternatives the readers have is an important rhetorical strategy in the author's playbook. He frequently appeals to emotions of fear and confidence and discusses the dreadful results of apostasy and the favorable outcome of holding on to the confession.[228]

Summary

The ascension in Heb 4:14 has the purpose of explaining why Jesus is "a great high priest." It appears in a section that fulfills a double purpose. Hebrews 4:14–16 introduces the new expository section 5:1–10:18. It also concludes the hortatory argument that began in 3:1. Accordingly, this reference to Jesus's ascension fulfills a double purpose as well. It anticipates, on the one hand, the discussion of Jesus's sacrifice and entrance into the heavenly sanctuary on our behalf in 8:1–10:18. On the other hand it recapitulates—together with references to Jesus's sonship and high priesthood—the exposition of Jesus's becoming "lower than the angels" on our behalf and subsequent enthronement at the right hand of God. This is especially appropriate for the argument of Hebrews. The description of Jesus's passage "through the heavens" and his "tested" faithfulness make him an exceptional "helper" for those who are exhorted to enter into God's rest.

"A Hope That Enters the Inner Shrine behind the Curtain" (Heb 6:19–20): Ascension and the Appointment of a Faithful Priest

Ascension as Entering behind the Curtain

> We have this hope, a sure and steadfast anchor of the soul, a hope that enters the inner shrine behind the curtain, where Jesus, a forerunner on our behalf, has entered, having become a high priest forever according to the order of Melchizedek. (Heb 6:19–20)

This passage is the first to use cultic imagery in denoting Jesus's ascension to heaven.[229] The expression ἐσώτερον τοῦ καταπετάσματος ("behind the cur-

---

228 E.g., Heb 6:4–12; 10:19–31; 12:18–24; deSilva, *Perseverance in Gratitude*, 184, n. 11. See also, Koester, *Hebrews*, 330–331.

229 The idea of ascension as an entrance into a heavenly sanctuary is insinuated in 4:14–16 by the fact that Jesus is described as a high priest and in fact anticipates the use of cultic im-

tain"), which designates the place where Jesus has entered "on our behalf," identified in the LXX the holy of holies of the Israelite sanctuary (Exod 26:33; Lev 16:2, 12, 15).[230] In this way, the author creates an analogy between Jesus's

agery in 6:19–20; 9:11–14, 24; 10:19–21. Jesus's ascension in 4:14, however, is not explicitly cultic but described as a passage "through the heavens." Accordingly, Jesus's high priesthood is not understood in terms of expiation, but of mediation (cf. 4:15–16; 2:17–18).

On the other hand, the term καταπέτασμα itself in 6:19–20 may be exclusively cultic in nature. It has been found to date only in cultic contexts (Daniel M. Gurtner, "Καταπέτασμα: Lexicographical and Etymological Considerations on the Biblical 'Veil'," *AUSS* 42 [2004]: 107–108).

Regarding 6:19–20, ascension to heaven is clearly assumed in the context. The reference to the high priest Jesus as our πρόδρομος ("forerunner") into the holy of holies clearly assumes 4:14 where it is said that "we have a great high priest who has passed through the heavens." The term πρόδρομος has a similar function to ἀρχηγός ("pioneer") in 2:10 and ἀπόστολος ("one who is sent") in 3:1. Thus, Jesus is our "forerunner" into the heavenly holy of holies just as he is the "pioneer" who leads "many children to glory" (2:10).

Ἀρχηγός and ἀπόστολος are terms connected in the account of Israel's failure in the wilderness to enter God's rest (Num 13, cf. Heb 3–4). Numbers 13:2 says: "Send out [ἀπόστειλον] for yourself men so that they may spy out the land of Canaan, which I am going to give to the sons of Israel; you shall send a man from each of their fathers' tribes, every one a leader [ἀρχηγόν] among them" (cf. LXX Judg 5:15 and Neh 2:9) (Koester, *Hebrews*, 243). Ἀπόστολος refers in 3:1 to a "messenger" or "envoy" (BDAG, 122) and does not denote an ecclesiastical title (e.g., Acts 15:2, 6). (There is no intention here to counteract any tendencies toward ecclesiastical hierarchy as suggested by Theißen, 107. In fact, Hebrews has a positive view of church leaders [cf. 13:7, 17].) Though the application of the title "apostle" to Jesus is intriguing—this is the only place in the NT where it is applied to Jesus but appears later in Justin *1 Apol.* 12.9; 63.5 (Attridge, *The Epistle to the Hebrews*, 107, n. 34; Ellingworth, *The Epistle to the Hebrews*, 199; Lane, *Hebrews 1–8*, 75)—it is likely, however, that this title continues the idea expressed in 2:10 of Jesus as the ἀρχηγός of the believers (Ellingworth, *The Epistle to the Hebrews*, 200; Koester, *Hebrews*, 243) and, thus, equivalent to πρόδρομος in 6:20. For different interpretations of the title "apostle," see Ellingworth, *The Epistle to the Hebrews*, 199–200; Lane, *Hebrews 1–8*, 75–76; Michel, *die Hebräer*, 171–175.

230 George E. Rice correctly pointed out that in the LXX the term καταπέτασμα may refer to the screen of the court (e.g., Exod 38:18 [37:16 LXX]), the screen at the entrance of the outer room of the sanctuary (e.g., Exod 36:37 [37:5 LXX]; 26:37 [= LXX]), or the inner veil that separated the outer room from the inner room, the holy of holies (e.g., Exod 26:31, 33, 34, 35; Rice, 65–71). The phrase ἐσώτερον τοῦ καταπετάσματος, however, appears 4 times in the LXX and consistently denotes the holy of holies (Exod 26:33; Lev 16:2, 12, 15; cf. Num 18:7; Gane, "Re-Opening Katapetasma," 5–8). See also Young, "Where Jesus Has Gone," 165–170. This phrase translates the Hebrew מִבֵּית לַפָּרֹכֶת (which also appears in Num 18:7) so that καταπέτασμα translates the Hebrew פָּרֹכֶת. Note, that in the OT the term פָּרֹכֶת occurs 25 times and refers only to the inner veil of the sanctuary (Roy E. Gane and Jacob Milgrom, "פָּרֹכֶת," *TDOT* 12:95–97).

Richard M. Davidson—though he does not oppose this view—has observed that "the case is strong but not watertight" ("Christ's Entry," 175, n. 4). He points out some differences in wording and syntax (Heb 6:19 adds the article to the phrase and εἰς is part of the compound verb in the LXX but stands alone in Heb 6:19 [though note the part. εἰσερχομένην in Heb 6:19]), but, more importantly, the case of Num 18:7. There, ἔνδοθεν τοῦ καταπετάσματος translates the Hebrew מִבֵּית לַפָּרֹכֶת. Numbers 18:7 reads: "But you [Aaron the high priest] and your sons with you shall diligently perform your priestly duties in all that concerns the altar and the area behind the curtain [מִבֵּית לַפָּרֹכֶת / ἔνδοθεν τοῦ καταπετάσματος]. I give your priesthood as a gift; any outsider who approaches shall be put to death." Richard M. Davidson points out that "the area behind the curtain" in Num 18:7 may refer to the sanctuary as a whole and not to the holy

ascension and the entrance of the high priest into the holy of holies of the Israelite sanctuary. In the Israelite cult, this entrance regularly happened only on the Day of Atonement (Lev 16:1–3). There is one exception, however. The inner room of the sanctuary was also entered during the inauguration of the sanctuary by Moses (Exod 26:33–34; cf. 40:1–9; Lev 8:10–12; Num 7:1), or by the priests in the inauguration of the first temple (2 Chr 5:7). This exception is important because the book of Hebrews refers to the inauguration of the heavenly sanctuary in 9:23.[231]

A majority of commentators believe that Heb 6:19–20 foreshadows Hebrews' cultic argument in chs. 9–10 in the sense that it interprets Jesus's ascension in terms of the entrance of the high priest into the holy of holies on the Day of Atonement to make expiation for the sins of the people.[232]

The relationship between the meaning of the ascension in 6:19–20 and that of chs. 9–10 is by no means straightforward, however. There are three issues that complicate this relationship. The first has to do with terminology. Hebrews 6:19–20 describes Jesus's ascension as an entrance εἰς τὸ ἐσώτερον τοῦ καταπετάσματος (6:19), which—as mentioned above—denotes in the LXX the holy of holies. Hebrews 9–10, however, describe Jesus's ascension as an entrance εἰς τὰ ἅγια (9:12; cf. 9:24; 10:19), which denotes in the LXX the sanc-

---

of holies exclusively because it is indicated there that Aaron *and his sons* will perform their duties in that area. (According to Lev 16:1–3 [cf. v. 32], only the high priest could enter the holy of holies.)

Roy Gane answers this objection by suggesting that in Num 18:7, "the altar and the area behind the curtain" refer to the altar of sacrifices and the holy of holies as the two extremes of the sanctuary. They constitute, then, a merism that by enumerating the extremes refer to a single entity, i.e., "the entire area of priestly officiation" ("ReOpening *Katapetasma*," 6, n. 5; cf. Gane, *Leviticus, Numbers*, 652–653. He suggests as further examples "near and far" in Jer 25:26; cf. Jer 48:24. In this way, the verse does not say that Aaron *and his sons* will perform their duties in the holy of holies ("the area behind the curtain"), but that Aaron and his sons will perform their duties in the sanctuary as a whole, assuming further delimitations of their responsibilities.

Timothy R. Ashley offers a complementary observation. He suggests that the question in Num 18:7 is not the "entrance" of Aaron or his sons into the holy of holies but "guarding what was behind it against encroachment" (*The Book of Numbers*, NICOT [Eerdmans, 1993], 343). Jacob Milgrom agrees, noting that the literal translation of תִּשְׁמְרוּ אֶת־כְּהֻנַּתְכֶם (Num 18:7) is "guard your priesthood." This expression explicates and forms an inclusion with וְאַתָּה וּבָנֶיךָ אִתְּךָ תִּשְׂאוּ אֶת־עֲוֹן כְּהֻנַּתְכֶם "you and your sons alone shall bear responsibility for offenses connected with the priesthood" in 18:1. Thus, Num 18:7 may refer to the performance of cultic duties in relation to the guarding of "the sancta against encroaching nonpriests and disqualified priests" (*Numbers: The Traditional Hebrew Text with the New JPS Translation*, JPS Torah Commentary [Jewish Publication Society, 1990], 148).

231 Davidson, "Christ's Entry," 177. (This is also implied in 2 Chr 35:3. See above section "Josiah" on page 67.)

232 Regarding this, see the debate between Richard M. Davidson and Norman H. Young in *AUSS* 39 (2001) and 40 (2002).

tuary as a whole or the outer court but *not the holy of holies*.²³³ This raises the following question: Is this discrepancy a minor lapse on the part of the author, or indicative of a nuance in his argument?²³⁴ The second has to do with the purpose of Jesus's entrance "within the veil." The immediate context of 6:19–20 does not describe the purpose of Jesus's ascension as one of expiation.²³⁵ The author may have that in mind, but he does not develop this aspect of Jesus's ascension in our passage. Finally, the third has to do with the nature of the general argument in both sections. We need to recognize that the idea of an eschatological or transcendent Day of Atonement dominates neither the argument of 6:19–20 nor the one of chs. 8–10. In the first case, the author is concerned—in the immediate context—with the danger that the readers may commit apostasy (5:11–6:12) and—in the mediate context—with the appointment or inauguration of Jesus as high priest (5:1–10; 7:1–28). In the case of chs. 8–10, although the Day of Atonement plays a more prominent role, it is the inauguration of a new covenant that rules the shape of the argument.²³⁶ Thus, an elucidation of the complex relationship between the

---

233 BDAG, 11; Alwyn P. Salom, "*Ta Hagia* in the Epistle to the Hebrews," *Issues in the Book of Hebrews*, ed. Frank B. Holbrook, DARCOM 4 (Biblical Research Institute, General Conference of Seventh-day Adventists, 1989), 219–227; Henry S. Gehman, " Ἅγιος in the Septuagint, and Its Relation to the Hebrew Original," *VT* 4 (1954): 337–348. See also, Carl P. Cosaert, "The Use of ἅγιος for the Sanctuary in the Old Testament Pseudepigrapha, Philo, and Josephus," *AUSS* 42 (2004): 91–103. See below section "Τὰ ἅγια denotes the Sanctuary of the new covenant" on page 229.

234 This discrepancy is the more evident when Heb 9:3 uses ἅγια ἁγίων and not ἅγια (cf. 9:2) to refer to the holy of holies. See Ellingworth, *The Epistle to the Hebrews*, 447.

235 The author has explained, thus far, the purpose of Jesus's priesthood as one of providing "help" for those who are being tempted (2:18; 4:15–16). It is true that the author has also referred to Jesus's priesthood as being able to provide "atonement for the sins of the people" (1:3; 2:17; cf. 5:1). This aspect, however, has not been developed in the argument thus far.

236 I think that this cannot be overemphasized. For example, William R. G. Loader recognizes that "Einerseits muß klar gesehen werden, daß diese Typologie eine wichtige Rolle in den Gedanken des Vf in 9,1–10,18 spielt; andererseits darf ihre Besonderheit nicht so weit hervorgehoben werden, daß sie als eigentliches Thema oder vorherrschender Gedanke dieses Abschnittes bezeichnet Wird" (On the one hand, it must be clearly seen that this typology [Day of Atonement] plays an important role in the ideas of the author in 9:1–10:18; on the other hand, their peculiarity should not be overly emphasized to the extent that it be considered the actual subject or the dominant thought of this section), (Loader, *Sohn und Hoherpriester*, 172). Nevertheless, this recognition does not seem to have adequately impacted his own work. Note Harold W. Attridge's critique: "In his discussion of the high priestly act of Christ, Loader, while noting the rich texture of Hebrews, concentrates primarily on the Yom Kippur typology. While this is certainly an important element of the author's complex argument in chap. 9, it is not clear that it is the dominant one. Rather, what seems ultimately to control the development of his theme is the notion that Christ's death is primarily a *covenant* sacrifice, a theme to which Loader gives insufficient attention" (Review of *Sohn und Hoherpriester: Eine traditionsgeschichtliche Untersuchung zur Christologie des Hebräerbriefes*, by William R. G. Loader, *JBL* 103 [1984]: 304 [emphasis his]). James P. Scullion, in his study of Yom Kippur in Hebrews, reaches a similar conclusion to that of William R. G. Loader: "It should be noted that the key to this central sec-

references to the ascension in 6:19–20 and chs. 9–10 requires an analysis of the argument of chs. 8–10, which I will attempt only later. I believe, then, that we should interpret Heb 6:19–20 on its own terms and resist the temptation of interpreting Heb 6:19–20 in terms of the argument to be developed in chs. 8–10.

In summary, Jesus's ascension is described in 6:19–20, in terms of its imagery, as the entrance of the high priest into the holy of holies, something Moses did only at the initial setting up of the structure and that the Aaronic high priest could do only on the Day of Atonement. Now, what is the function of the ascension in the argument of Heb 6:13–20?

The Ascension Shows the Unchangeable Character of God's Promises

The Role of the Ascension in Hebrews 6:19–20

Hebrews 6:20 closes a hortatory digression that began at 5:11. Hebrews 5:1–10 had explained that Jesus was appointed high priest by God on behalf of men after having suffered on earth. This was accomplished through God's oath to him, "You are a priest forever, according to the order of Mechizedek" (5:6). Hebrews 5:11 interrupts the argument by introducing an exhortation to the readers that closes in 6:20, where the author indicates his return to the original topic by repeating the topic sentence of the interrupted argument "having become a high priest forever according to the order of Melchizedek" (6:20).[237]

The hortatory argument of 5:11–6:20 is composed of 4 units.[238] In the first unit (5:11–6:3), the author confronts the readers' "dullness" to understand "the basic elements of the oracles of God" and lack of spiritual "maturity" and exhorts them to "go on towards perfection [maturity]." In the second unit (6:4–8), the author issues a blistering warning against "falling away" from the "Son of God," of which they are in danger if they continue to neglect the "word of

---

tion is not Yom Kippur itself, but the connection that the author makes between the cult and the *new covenant*" ("A Traditio-Historical Study of the Day of Atonement" [Ph.D. diss., Catholic University of America, 1990; UMI, 1991], 252, emphasis mine).

237 Note the similarity with the last statement of 5:10: "having been designated by God a high priest according to the order of Melchizedek" (5:10); "having become a high priest forever according to the order of Melchizedek" (6:20).

238 Here I am following George Guthrie, *The Structure of Hebrews*, 69–71. Similarly, Vanhoye, *Structure and Message*, 87–88. Contra Long Westfall, *A Discourse Analysis*, 141–68. She suggests the following sections: 4:11–6:3 (unit subdivision: 4:11–16; 5:1–10; 5:11–14; 6:1–3) and 6:1–7:3 (unit subdivision: 6:1–3; 6:7–8; 6:9–12; 6:13–7:3). Her inclusion of 5:11–14 as part of exposition material with 5:1–10 and the inclusion of 7:1–3 in the exhortation of 6:13–20 are unconvincing to me.

God" (6:5; cf. 5:12).[239] The third unit (6:9–12) mitigates the previous warning with an expression of confidence in the audience's outcome and an invitation to show "diligence" so that "through faith and patience" they might "inherit the promises." In the final unit (6:13–20), the author drives the discourse back toward the main topic he had left behind: the appointment of Jesus as high priest (5:1–10).[240] He deftly accomplishes this by showing how the appointment of Jesus as high priest is in fact God's confirmation of his promises to them, providing an effective conclusion to the previous unit (6:9–12). The clear inference is that the readers would commit a gross error if they abandon their confidence now that the promises have been confirmed in the appointment of the Son as high priest of the heavenly sanctuary.

Hebrews 6:13–20 complements the positive exhortation of 6:9–12 by providing critical information regarding two of its points.[241] The first point has to do with the author's call "to realize the full assurance of [their] hope to the very end" (6:11). The second point has to do with the exhortation to be "imitators of those who through faith and patience inherit the promises" (v. 12). He complements these points in 6:13–20 in reverse order. The author of Hebrews provides Abraham as an example of faith and patience in vv. 13–15 and explains the ascension of Jesus as the assurance of their hope in vv. 16–20.[242]

Abraham was a celebrated example of faith and patience in Second Temple Judaism and early Christianity, particularly because of his offering of Isaac.[243] The author of Hebrews refers to this event and presents Abraham as an example "of those who through faith and patience inherit the promises" (6:15; cf. v. 12). He refers to the fact that, on the occasion of Abraham's offering of Isaac, God promised him an abundant offspring.[244] He quotes in 6:14 the first part of the promise registered in Gen 22:17. His point, however, is that God confirmed his promise to Abraham with an "oath"—something that is mentioned only in the original context of the passage he quotes:

---

239 The expression "word of God" (θεοῦ ῥῆμα) is a common designation for the Hebrew scriptures (Num 24:16; Deut 33:9–10; Pss 12:6 [11:7 LXX]; 18:30 [17:31 LXX]; 107:11 [106:11 LXX]; Acts 7:38; Rom 3:2; 1 Pet 4:11; 1 Clem. 19.1; 53.1; 62:3; Pol. *Phil.* 7.1) or the utterances of God recorded in Scripture (Philo *Posterity* 28; *Unchangeable* 50). See Koester, *Hebrews*, 301.

240 See George Guthrie, *The Structure of Hebrews*, 110–111.

241 Pierre Grelot, *Une lecture de l'épître aux Hébreux* (Cerf, 2003), 51. See also, Ellingworth, *The Epistle to the Hebrews*, 334.

242 Regarding the structure of this last unit, see Vanhoye, *La structure littéraire*, 120–123.

243 E.g., Jub. 17:17–18; Rom 4; Gal 3:6–18; Heb 11:8–19; Jas 2:18–24. See Swetnam, *Jesus and Isaac*, 23–85.

244 The author of Hebrews refers to himself in 11:32 with a masculine, singular participle. This suggests that the author was male.

By myself I have sworn, says the LORD: "Because you have done this, and have not withheld your son, your only son, I will indeed bless you, and I will make your offspring as numerous as the stars of heaven and as the sand that is on the seashore." (Gen 22:16–17; emphasis mine)[245]

The author of Hebrews makes the point, then, that after Abraham "patiently endured," he "received [ἐπέτυχεν] what was promised" (Heb 6:15, NIV).

This statement seems to conflict with Heb 11:13, 39 where Abraham is included among all those who "did not receive [ἐκομίσαντο] what was promised." Some suggest that 6:15 means that what Abraham obtained according to Hebrews was a *confirmation* of the promise.[246] This is improbable, however, because the whole point of the passage is to emphasize that God's "oath" is reliable (cf. 6:17–18), something that could not be proven unless it was shown that God had fulfilled his promise.[247] It would be of little comfort for the readers to know that Abraham, after "having patiently endured," received only a confirmation of the promise. Instead, the author wishes to emphasize that God fulfilled his promise to Abraham through Isaac and the readers themselves are part of the evidence (cf. 2:16).[248] This argument would appropriately fit the author's description of the readers as being at the threshold of the fulfillment of the promises. The promises have already been confirmed and have begun to be fulfilled in Jesus (2:9).[249] They have already "tasted" the "heavenly gift, ... the goodness of the word of God and the powers of the age to come" (6:4–5). Thus, they are not in the position to "shrink back" but to "have faith" and be "saved" (10:35–39).

In Heb 6:16–20, the author develops the first point made in the previous unit: "And we want each one of you to show the same diligence so as to realize

---

245 Hebrews quotes only a part of v. 17, but it clearly implies v. 16 where the oath is mentioned.

246 E.g., NRSV; NASB; Lane, *Hebrews 1–8*, 151; Swetnam, *Jesus and Isaac*, 184–5.

247 Note that 3:7–4:11 registers a previous oath by God. The force of the exhortation there relies on the fact that God fulfilled that oath (3:16–19).

248 E.g., NIV; NJB; Koester, *Hebrews*, 326; Ellingworth, *The Epistle to the Hebrews*, 338–339; Michel, *die Hebräer*, 251; Spicq, *L'épître aux Hébreux*, 2:160.

Most likely, the term ἐπαγγελία in 6:15 has a different referent than in 11:13, 39; that is, God fulfilled his promise to Abraham but not in the sense that believers are able to enjoy now (11:39–40). See, Ellingworth, *The Epistle to the Hebrews*, 338–339. Additionally, Harold W. Attridge suggests that the verbs κομίζω (Heb 11:39; cf. 10:36; 11:19) and ἐπιτυγχάνω (Heb 6:15; cf. 11:33) may carry slight distinctions in nuance, *The Epistle to the Hebrews*, 180, n. 21. In this sense, κομίζω refers to those promises that Christians can receive now (10:36) but OT individuals did not receive (11:19, 39), while ἐπιτυγχάνω refers to those promises that OT persons, such as Abraham (6:15) and other heroes of faith (11:33), did receive.

249 For Hebrews' description of the readers as being at the threshold of the fulfillment of the promise, see Dunnill, *Covenant and Sacrifice*, 134–148.

the full assurance of hope to the very end" (6:11, emphasis mine). His argument is that the oath of God is the basis for the believer's "full assurance of hope": "when God desired to show even more clearly to the heirs of the promise the unchangeable character of his purpose, *he guaranteed it by an oath*" (6:17, emphasis mine). Here the author refers not to the oath that God swore to Abraham but to the oath referred to in 5:6: "You are a priest forever, according to the order of Melchizedek" (quoting Ps 110:4 [109:4 LXX]).[250] This is clearly shown by the fact that 6:20 refers back to that oath. Then, just as God confirmed his promise to Abraham with an oath (vv. 13–14), God has confirmed (ἐμεσίτευσεν) the promises to his children with an oath. This oath is the believers' "full assurance of hope to the very end" (6:11) and has the purpose of "strongly" encouraging them "to seize the hope set before us [them]" (v. 18).[251]

What is, then, the function of Jesus's ascension to heaven in 6:19–20?

Jesus Is the Hope That Enters "within the Veil"

In this passage the author describes the believers' hope as a "sure and steadfast anchor of the soul … that enters the inner shrine behind the curtain" (6:19).[252] Hope is described as entering the holy of holies in the sense that it is anchored on God's throne itself in the heavenly sanctuary by means of the

---

250 Attridge, *The Epistle to the Hebrews*, 181–182; deSilva, *Perseverance in Gratitude*, 250; Ellingworth, *The Epistle to the Hebrews*, 342; George Guthrie, *The Structure of Hebrews*, 110–111. Contra Koester, *Hebrews*, 328; Johnson, *Hebrews*, 170; Lane, *Hebrews 1–8*, 152.

Here, the author is introducing a new element in this unit, of which the promise to Abraham is a paradigm and possibly a precursor as well. This verse (6:17) compares believers today with Abraham as "heirs" of a "promise" that has been mediated through an oath (cf. 6:12). The author creates an analogy here between the oath made to Abraham and the oath made to Jesus at his appointment as high priest (Heb 5:5–6; cf. 7:20–22)—which is, in fact, a promise for believers today (6:18–20). Thus, the assertion "when God desired to show even more clearly to the heirs of the promise the unchangeable character [τὸ ἀμετάθετον] of his purpose, he guaranteed it by an oath [ἐμεσίτευσεν ὅρκῳ]" (Heb 6:17) alludes to Ps 110:4 (109:4 LXX; quoted in Heb 5:6): "The LORD has sworn [ὤμοσεν] and will not change his mind [μεταμεληθήσεται], 'You are a priest forever according to the order of Melchizedek.'"

251 The text refers to the encouragement provided by "two unchangeable things, in which it is impossible that God would prove false." What are these two things? These have been understood mostly as referring to the promise (or the word of God by which he promises) and the oath (Attridge, *The Epistle to the Hebrews*, 181–182; Ellingworth, *The Epistle to the Hebrews*, 342; Johnson, *Hebrews*, 171; Koester, *Hebrews*, 328; Lane, *Hebrews 1–8*, 152; Michel, *die Hebräer*, 253; Schröger, *Der Verfasser*, 128–129). Or, God's issuing the oath and God's witnessing the oath (David R. Worley, "Fleeing to Two Immutable Things—God's Oath-Taking and Oath-Witnessing: The Use of Litigant Oath in Hebrews 6:19–20," *ResQ* 36 [1994]: 223–236).

252 On the legal, nautical, and cultic elements of the imagery, see Johnson, *Hebrews*, 172–173.

oath.²⁵³ That is to say, since God has guaranteed the promise with an oath, the honor of his throne has been grounded on the fulfillment of that promise.²⁵⁴ The author adds immediately that this is exactly the place where Jesus has entered on our behalf (6:20). Thus, Jesus is identified as the believers' hope.²⁵⁵

Furthermore, just like the believers' hope was anchored in God's throne because of the oath, Jesus was able to enter the heavenly holy of holies because of the oath by means of which he was appointed "high priest forever according to the order of Melchizedek" (6:20; cf. 5:5–6). The author describes, then, Jesus's ascension to heaven as the anchoring of the believers' hope of salvation in the throne of God by means of an oath.

Jesus Embodies God's Oath Which Confirms God's Promises to the Believers

In a deeper and more important level of the discourse, the author identifies Jesus with God's oath.

The author has said that God guaranteed (ἐμεσίτευσεν) his promise with an oath (6:17).²⁵⁶ The oath is an act of God by which he corroborates the veracity of his intentions regarding the heirs of the promise. Jesus's appointment as high priest fulfills the same function. Hebrews 5:1–10 makes clear that Jesus's appointment as high priest on our behalf was an act of God (esp. v. 5). God called Jesus (5:4; cf. v. 10), appointed him (5:5), and perfected him (v. 9) so as to make him high priest "on behalf" of humanity (ὑπὲρ ἀνθρώπων; 5:1). Thus, we should understand the reference in Heb 6:20 to Jesus's appointment as high priest and his entrance into the heavenly holy of holies as an act of God.²⁵⁷

This act of God, in the context of 6:13–20, has the purpose of corroborating the promise made to the believers. Jesus has entered as a "forerunner

---

253 The ark of the covenant is considered in the OT as the footstool of God's throne (1 Sam 4:4; 1 Chr 28:2; Pss 99:5; 132:7). See, Choon-Leong Seow, "Ark of the Covenant," *ABD* 1:388–389.

254 Regarding the importance of the honor of God's throne and its maintenance by judgment and expiation, see Gane, *Cult and Character*, 334–354.

255 Johnson, *Hebrews*, 172.

256 Because God cannot swear by any other than himself, he is at the same time the one who promises and the guarantor of his promises.

257 When Hebrews refers to the sufferings of Jesus, it makes clear that they were the result of God's plan. (It was God's purpose that he would suffer on our behalf [2:10–18; 4:14–16; 5:1–10; 8–10 passim].) Thus, Jesus "*was made* lower than the angels" (2:9), *God made* "the pioneer of their salvation *perfect* through sufferings" (2:10), "he ... *was tested*" (2:18; cf. 4:15), he *was* "*made* perfect" through sufferings (5:8–9). Finally, his appointment as high priest after the suffering of death presupposes his resurrection, which was also an act of God (cf. 13:20).

[πρόδρομος] *on our behalf* (πρόδρομος ὑπὲρ ἡμῶν, 6:20).²⁵⁸ In this sense, the ascension evidences for believers the certainty of God's purpose of salvation for them. This should be understood in relation to Hebrews' interpretation of Ps 8 in chap. 2. The author says there that God's original purpose of crowning human beings "with glory and honor, subjecting all things under their feet" (2:6–8) was fulfilled when Jesus was enthroned "at the right hand of the majesty on high" (1:3; cf. 2:9). Notwithstanding, Jesus's enthronement did not exhaust God's purpose for humanity. God led Jesus to glory through the suffering of "death *for* everyone" (ὑπὲρ παντὸς, emphasis mine) so that he might bring "many children to glory" (2:10). Therefore, Jesus's ascension *confirms* God's original purpose of "glory and honor" for human beings not only in the sense that it brings that purpose into realization in the person of Jesus but, more importantly, in the sense that it makes possible its fulfillment for them.²⁵⁹ Thus, Jesus is appointed as high priest by means of an oath (6:17–18, referring to 5:5–6) but his appointment and ascension, in turn, functions figuratively as an oath that confirms God's promise of salvation to the believers.

The author expresses this notion later in the epistle by assigning Jesus the title μεσίτης τῆς καινῆς διαθήκης (mediator of the new covenant, cf. 8:6; 9:15; 12:24). The noun μεσίτης derives from μέσος ("middle") and denotes the one who walks or stands in the middle. In Hellenistic usage, μεσίτης "became one of the most varied technical terms in the vocabulary of Hellen. law."²⁶⁰ It could denote (1) an arbiter, (2) a negotiator or business broker, (3) a witness in the legal sense of the word, or (4) one who stands as a surety and thus guarantees the execution of an agreement.²⁶¹

The English term "mediator," however, is probably too narrow a translation for μεσίτης in Hebrews. Since it is normally understood as "one that mediates between parties at variance," it focuses only on the first two or three uses of the Greek term.²⁶² Hebrews, however, emphasizes its fourth meaning. Jesus is not conceived as μεσίτης in the sense that he settles a dispute between God and humans, or a peacemaker that reconciles parties in disaffection, or a witness that certifies the existence of a contract or its satisfac-

---

258 The πρόδρομος was the one who came first in a military campaign or a race. See references in Koester, *Hebrews*, 330, 335.

259 Note that the author of Hebrews has focused, thus far, on the function of Jesus's priesthood as one of "helping" believers (2:17–18; 4:15–16).

260 A. Oepke, "μεσίτης," *TDNT* 4:599. Cf. O. Becker, "μεσίτης," *NIDNTT* 1:372–373; Ceslas Spicq, *TLNT* 2:465–468.

261 Spicq, *TLNT* 2:465–467. For additional nuances, see Oepke, "μεσίτης," 4:599–601.

262 See Mish, ed., s.v. "mediator."

tion.²⁶³ The term μεσίτης describes in Hebrews only the role of Jesus regarding the new covenant (8:6; 9:15; 12:24).²⁶⁴ The author describes his death as the sacrifice that confirms the covenant (9:15–22) and his blood as the blood of the covenant (10:29; 13:20). This role is better described, then, as the surety or pledge that guarantees the execution of the covenant.²⁶⁵ Thus, μεσίτης is equivalent in Hebrews to ἔγγυος (guarantor).²⁶⁶ The author states this explicitly in Heb 7:22, "Jesus has also become the guarantee [ἔγγυος] of a better covenant."

Jesus guarantees the covenant in two ways. His death makes the institution of the new covenant possible because it satisfies the claims of the first (Mosaic) covenant which had been broken (9:15–22).²⁶⁷ In this sense, Jesus is the guarantor that "prend[s] sur soi toutes les obligations juridiques dans un contrat de garantie."²⁶⁸ In a second sense, Jesus's ascension to and exaltation in heaven guarantees that God's promises to human beings will be fulfilled (2:5–18; 6:19–20).²⁶⁹

In summary, the ascension of Jesus to the presence of God in this passage is the realization of his appointment as high priest "forever" on behalf of human beings according to the order of Melchizedek. By this fact, God wanted to "show even more clearly to the heirs of the promise [i.e., the believers] the

---

263   The covenant, however, has the effect of reconciling God and humankind: God will forgive the sins of humans (Heb 8:12; 10:17). Thus, it is true that Jesus plays the role of a mediator or negotiator when he intercedes on behalf of humans before God (7:25; cf. 4:15–16; 2:17–18); nevertheless, this role is not described in Hebrews with the term μεσίτης.

264   David Peterson, *Hebrews and Perfection: An Examination of the Concept of Perfection in the 'Epistle to the Hebrews'*, SNTSMS 47 (Cambridge University Press, 1982), 193, n. 12.

265   Note that "in Hebrews, as elsewhere in the Bible, the covenant, whether old or new, is not a mutual agreement, contract, or negotiation, for which an arbitrator may be needed; it is a unilateral gift from God." Ellingworth, *The Epistle to the Hebrews*, 410.

266   Becker, 1:374–375; Oepke, "μεσίτης," 4:620; Spicq, *TLNT* 2:468. See, Ellingworth, *The Epistle to the Hebrews*, 410; George Guthrie, *Hebrews*, 312; Moffatt, *Epistle to the Hebrews*, 100. Contra, Attridge, *The Epistle to the Hebrews*, 208, n. 32.

267   See Hahn, "A Broken Covenant," 416–436; idem, "Covenant, Cult, and the Curse of Death," 65–88. See below section "Heb 9:15–23 Describes Jesus's Sacrifice and Ascension as the Inauguration of a New Covenant" on page 242.

268   (... takes upon himself all the legal obligations in a contract of guarantee.) Spicq, *L'épître aux Hébreux*, 2:196. In this connection, Sir 29:15–17 is significant: "Do not forget the kindness of your guarantor [ἐγγύου], for he has given his life for you. A sinner wastes the property of his guarantor, and the ungrateful person abandons his rescuer."

Moses may also have prefigured the role of Jesus as mediator of the covenant in this sense. Note Gudmundur Olafsson's interpretation of Exod 32:32: "Either you, God, *nāśā'* the wrongs of the people [i.e., forgive them] or let me *nāśā'* them and suffer the consequences [i.e., die]" ("The Use of NS' in the Pentateuch and Its Contribution to the Concept of Forgiveness" [Ph.D. diss., Andrews University, 1992], 261).

269   See Spicq, *L'épître aux Hébreux*, 2:196.

unchangeable character of his purpose" (6:17). This is the result of a play of ideas on a deeper level of this passage. Jesus was appointed high priest by an oath from God (6:17 referring to 5:5–6; cf. 7:20–22). This oath, however, though originally given to Jesus as an assurance of the permanence of his ministry (5:5–6; cf. 7:20–22), is interpreted in the passage as given to the believers (6:17). Therefore, just like the oath confirmed the promises given to Abraham (6:13–16), Jesus's ascension to heaven confirms God's purpose of salvation for human beings. In this sense, Jesus's ascension has become the surety of the fulfillment of the promises (cf. 7:22). From the point of view of the believers, then, Jesus is "the hope that enters the inner shrine behind the curtain" (6:19). This makes the fulfillment of the desire expressed in 6:11 possible that the readers may "realize the full assurance of hope to the very end" (6:11).

When Did Jesus Become a High Priest?

I am suggesting here, then, that Jesus's entrance into the presence of God is an integral part of his appointment as high priest and that this appointment, in turn, is the believers' assurance of their hope. This raises a problem, however: Did Jesus become a high priest when he was enthroned in heaven? Was this the moment in which God pronounced the oath, "The LORD has sworn and will not change his mind, 'You are a priest forever according to the order of Melchizedek' " (Ps 110:4, quoted in Heb 5:5–6)?[270]

This question is difficult to answer. The syntactical construction of the phrase ὅπου ... εἰσῆλθεν Ἰησοῦς ... ἀρχιερεὺς γενόμενος ("where Jesus ... has entered, having become a high priest" [Heb 6:20]) allows for two interpretations: (1) Jesus became high priest before his ascension or (2) at his ascension.[271] The problem, as we will see, is that the wider context of the epistle

---

270 Note that Jesus's high priesthood is based on the Christian belief that Jesus is the Son of David. If Jesus was not the Son of David, the Davidic Messiah, the author of Hebrews would not have scriptural basis for Jesus's high priesthood of the heavenly sanctuary because he would not have been able to apply Ps 110:4 to Jesus (Heb 5:5–10; 7:28). A similar phenomenon, but in the opposite direction, is found in *T. Levi* 4:2. There, royal language (sonship) is applied to the high priest: "The Most High has given heed to your prayer that you be delivered from wrongdoing, that you should become a son to him, as minister and priest in his presence" (cf. 18:3; *T. Jud.* 21:1–5).

271 The author uses an aorist participle (γενόμενος) to refer to Jesus's appointment as high priest and an aorist verb (εἰσῆλθεν) to refer to the ascension. The time denoted by the participle is relative and is determined by its relationship with the main verb. An aorist participle when related to an aorist verb may denote an action antecedent to the action of the main verb or an action coordinated with that of the main verb. See BDF, §339; Wallace, *Greek Grammar Beyond the Basics*, 624–625. Also, Peterson, *Hebrews and Perfection*, 192.

does not help us much. Hebrews associates Jesus's priesthood with his sufferings on earth, as well as with his exaltation in heaven.

The difficulty in defining the point in time in which Jesus became high priest is related to the difficult question of when Jesus became the Son of God (see above section "Jesus as 'Son' in Hebrews" on page 169). The sonship of Jesus and his high priesthood are intimately connected.

> So also Christ did not glorify himself in becoming a high priest, but was appointed by the one who said to him, "You are my Son, today I have begotten you"; as he says also in another place, "You are a priest forever, according to the order of Melchizedek." (Heb 5:5–6)

The argument of the author is that the one who adopted Jesus as his royal Son (Heb 1:5, quoting Ps 2:7) is the same one who appointed him as high priest. The author's connection of Jesus's sonship and high priesthood seems not incidental but deliberate. If he wanted just to connect the concept of kingship to the concept of priesthood, it was only necessary for him to say that if Ps 110:1 (quoted in Heb 1:3, 13) applied to Jesus, then v. 4 should apply to him as well.[272] The quotation of Ps 2:7 in this context, however, is a deliberate attempt to connect the notions of sonship and priesthood. This is confirmed by the fact that sonship plays an important role in the "perfecting" of Jesus as high priest in 5:8–10:

> Although he was a *Son*, he learned obedience through what he suffered; and *having been made perfect*, he became the source of eternal salvation for all who obey him, *having been designated by God a high priest* according to the order of Melchizedek. (emphasis mine)

In fact, in 7:28 the author connects the appointment of Jesus as high priest with his perfecting as Son:

> For the law *appoints as high priests* those who are subject to weakness, but the word of the oath, which came later than the law, *appoints a Son* who *has been made perfect* forever. (emphasis mine; cf. 4:14; 7:3)

Thus, both aspects of Hebrews' Christology are intimately related.[273] It is pos-

---

272 Koester, *Hebrews*, 298–299.

273 It is possible that by this association the author wants to substantiate the transcendent nature of Jesus's high priesthood. Jesus's death was an event of human history which

sible, then, that Hebrews is ambiguous regarding the moment when Jesus became a high priest, just as in the case of his sonship.

Jesus's earthly life and death are essential to his priestly ministry.[274] According to Hebrews, Jesus's high priesthood has two purposes: to provide "help" for those who are tempted (2:14–18; 4:14–16; 7:25) and expiate the sins of those who confess him (1:3; 2:17; 9:11–14, 24–26; 10:5–10, 12; 13:12). The author of Hebrews argues that Jesus is qualified for fulfilling these purposes by two actions he accomplished while on earth. First, Jesus "shared" with human beings their "sufferings" so that he might become a "merciful" high priest who is "able" to help (2:17–18; 4:15). Second, Jesus offered himself as a sacrifice for

---

outsiders considered shameful (12:2). Hebrews, however, interprets it as the sacrificial act of the eternal/royal Son of God culminated in the heavenly holy of holies which provided Jesus's priesthood a transcendental nature. More likely, Jesus's priesthood reinterprets and revitalizes the concept of Jesus's sonship. The Son is an effective mediator because he has suffered for us and is now enthroned in heaven. Attridge, *The Epistle to the Hebrews*, 147; Moffatt, *Epistle to the Hebrews*, 64; Riggenbach, *an die Hebräer*, 128; Schröger, *Der Verfasser*, 119; Laub, *Bekenntnis und Auslegung*, 122, 135.

This passage (Heb 5:9–10) relates the "designation" (προσαγορευθεὶς) of Jesus as high priest with the fact that he was "perfected" (τελειωθεὶς) through "sufferings." This suggests the idea that Hebrews may be using the verb τελειόω in the technical sense found in the LXX of consecration to the priesthood. (The technical sense of the phrase τελειοῦν τὰς χεῖρας is commonly reviewed in Hebrews' literature, e.g., Gerhard Delling, "τελειόω," *TDNT* 8:80–81; Loader, *Sohn und Hoherpriester*, 40, 47–48; Peterson, *Hebrews and Perfection*, 26–30. For an analysis of the language of perfection in Philo and its relation to Hebrews, see Charles Carlston, "The Vocabulary of Perfection in Philo and Hebrews," in *Unity and Diversity in New Testament Theology*, ed. Robert A. Guelich [Eerdmans, 1978], 133–160.) This view has found two main critiques. Hebrews does not use the complete phrase τελειοῦν τὰς χεῖρας; instead, it uses the absolute τελειόω. (There is one case in the LXX [Lev 21:10], however, where the absolute τελειόω translates the phrase וּמִלֵּא אֶת־יָדוֹ, "and his hands filled," i.e., consecrated.) Furthermore, the cultic sense of τελειόω as consecration in the LXX depends on the presence of a ritual context. In Hebrews, however, τελειόω—and its cognates τέλειος (5:14; 9:11), τελειότης (6:1), τελειωτής (12:2), and τελείωσις (7:11)—appears in a diversity of contexts in which the cultic sense of consecration is not warranted (John M. Scholer, *Proleptic Priests: Priesthood in the Epistle to the Hebrews*, JSNTSup 49 [JSOT Press, 1991], 190). This objection is not catastrophic either because the author is not obligated to use a term with absolute consistency (Moises Silva, "Perfection and Eschatology in Hebrews," *WTJ* 39 [1976]: 62.) It is usually considered, then, that τελειόω carries its general or formal sense of "to complete," "to fill," "to make perfect" in relation to his ministry as Son/high priest in Hebrews. Thus, the perfection of Jesus refers to his effectiveness in achieving the goal of his mission in the sense of bringing "many sons to glory" (Peterson, *Hebrews and Perfection*, 187), or his "intimacy with God" which qualifies him as a high priest able to help a persecuted community (Kevin McCruden, "Christ's Perfection in Hebrews: Divine Beneficence as an Exegetical Key to Hebrews 2:10," *BR* 47 [2002]: 40–62), or his access to the direct presence of God (Scholer, *Proleptic Priests*, 200). For a brief evaluation of the different understandings of the vocabulary of perfection in Hebrews, see Scholer, *Proleptic Priests*, 185–200.

274 A majority of Catholic commentators assert that Christ was consecrated as high priest at the moment of his incarnation, e.g., Cody, *Heavenly Sanctuary and Liturgy*, 97, 102. See also Peterson, *Hebrews and Perfection*, 193.

the sins of the people (7:27; 9:14, 26; 10:10).²⁷⁵ Furthermore, both actions are qualified by his life on earth. His life of faithfulness qualifies him to be both a competent helper to those who are being "tested" (4:15) and a sacrificial victim "offered ... without blemish to God, [to] purify our conscience" (9:14; cf. 7:26; 3:1–6). Thus, in this sense, Jesus's priestly ministry includes his life on earth.²⁷⁶

Hebrews, however, emphasizes the heavenly aspect of Jesus's ministry and sacrifice. Jesus is able to "help" those who are tempted because he has ascended to heaven and is in the presence of God (4:14–16). Hebrews also emphasizes the heavenly dimension of Jesus's sacrifice (9:11–14, 23–26; 10:12–14). For example, Heb 8:4 says: "Now *if he were on earth*, he would not be a priest at all, since there are priests who offer gifts according to the law" (emphasis mine). Finally, Heb 7:16 presupposes Jesus's resurrection to his becoming high priest: "one who has become a priest, not through a legal requirement concerning physical descent, but *through the power of an indestructible life*" (emphasis mine).²⁷⁷ This agrees with the fact that Jesus became a high priest with an oath which, arguably, was uttered at the moment of his enthronement as Son.²⁷⁸

We need to recognize, then, that Hebrews considers Jesus's sacrifice and appointment as high priest as heavenly in nature (Heb 8:4). This does not exclude events which occurred on earth. Jesus's identification with human beings in adopting their human nature (2:14) and his sufferings and death on earth (5:7–10; 12:2–3) are an integral part of his heavenly appointment and ministry as high priest. One cannot exist without the others.

---

275 When the author speaks about Jesus's sacrificial death, he is certainly thinking about the cross (12:2–3).

276 The author may have considered Jesus's "prayers and supplications" as part of his sacrificial offering: "In the days of his flesh, Jesus offered [προσφέρω] up prayers and supplications, with loud cries and tears, to the one who was able to save him" (5:7; cf. the believers' praise as a sacrifice to God in 13:15). E.g., Ellingworth, *The Epistle to the Hebrews*, 289; Johnson, *Hebrews*, 145–146; Koester, *Hebrews*, 298. Contra Attridge, *The Epistle to the Hebrews*, 149; Delitzsch, *Epistle to the Hebrews*.

277 Contra Ceslas Spicq and others who see the incarnation as the moment in which Jesus acquired "the power of an indestructible life." Montefiore, *The Epistle to the Hebrews*, 125–126; Spicq, *L'épître aux Hébreux*, 193. See the discussion in Michel, *die Hebräer*, 272–273. The problem is that Jesus's life did experience destruction. Hebrews emphasizes that Jesus identified with men even regarding death (2:9, 14–18; 4:15; 5:7–8; Peterson, *Hebrews and Perfection*, 110–111).

278 The fact that the author relates Jesus becoming a high priest with his adoption as the Royal Son (5:5–6) suggests that this was the moment when God designated him high priest "forever according to the order of Melchizedek." Likewise, the fact that the author uses Ps 110:4 to substantiate the appointment of Jesus as high priest and 110:1 for his enthronement at the right hand of God.

The question, then, regarding the moment in time when Jesus became the eternal high priest of the heavenly sanctuary has a complex answer. This "moment" includes several "points in time": incarnation, sufferings and death, resurrection, and exaltation in heaven. Each of these "points in time" is an essential component of a larger entity (i.e., Jesus's inauguration as priest) which cannot be ignored without destruction of the whole. Thus, "attempts to be overly precise about when Christ became High Priest ignore this complexity."[279] It is better to conclude, then, with David Peterson: "If the enthronement marks also the proclamation of his eternal high–priesthood at the Father's right hand, this new representation of Christ cannot be divorced from his previous work as high priest but must be viewed as its consummation."[280]

Summary

The purpose of Heb 6:13–20 is to explain how believers may "realize the full assurance of hope to the very end" (6:11) and become "imitators of those who through faith and patience inherit the promises" (6:12). The author explains both elements in reverse order. Verses 13–16 present Abraham as one who through patient endurance inherited the promises and vv. 17–20 present Jesus as the full assurance of the hope of the believers. He argues, then, that God's oath to Jesus by which he becomes our high priest (6:17 referring to 5:5–6) is one of the "two immutable things" on which their certainty of salvation is established (cf. 6:9).

In this passage Jesus's entrance into heaven is considered the attainment of salvation (6:9) or inheritance of the promises (v. 12). In this sense Jesus is the "forerunner" who confirms that God's purpose for humanity (i.e., to bring them to "honor and glory") is for real. Jesus's entrance into heaven is considered also the consummation of the appointment of Jesus as high priest "on our behalf" so he becomes a powerful helper "in time of need" (4:16). This "help" is related to the help Jesus provides those who are "tested" by sufferings (2:18; 4:15).

---

279 Attridge, *The Epistle to the Hebrews*, 147. Note that rituals—e.g., the ritual of the consecration of a high priest—are *systems* of actions and sounds whose meaning, by necessity, is derived from the whole. For an application, e.g., of Frits Staal's "Ritual Syntax" to the Israelite Day of Atonement, see Gane, *Ritual Dynamic Structure*. For an analysis of the ritual of the consecration of the high priest, see Frank H. Gorman, Jr., *The Ideology of Ritual*, JSOTSup 91 (Sheffield: JSOT Press, 1990), 103–139; Gerald A. Klingbeil, *A Comparative Study of the Ritual of Ordination as Found in Leviticus 8 and Emar 369* (Mellen, 1998).

280 Peterson, *Hebrews and Perfection*, 193.

"When Christ Came as a High priest of the Good Things That Have Come" (9:11–14, 24; 10:19–25): Ascension and the Inauguration of the New Covenant

The Ascension Inaugurates the New Covenant (Hebrews 9:11–14)

> But when Christ came as a high priest of the good things that have come, then through the greater and perfect tent (not made with hands, that is, not of this creation), he entered once for all into the Holy Place [τὰ ἅγια], not with the blood of goats and calves, but with his own blood, thus obtaining eternal redemption. For if the blood of goats and bulls, with the sprinkling of the ashes of a heifer, sanctifies those who have been defiled so that their flesh is purified, how much more will the blood of Christ, who through the eternal Spirit offered himself without blemish to God, purify our conscience from dead works to worship the living God! (Heb 9:11–14)

Jesus's ascension to heaven plays a central role in Heb 9:11–14. Jesus is described here as a high priest entering τὰ ἅγια with "his own blood" to obtain "eternal redemption." This redemption is explained as the purification of the conscience that permits believers "to worship the living God."

This description is very similar to that of the Day of Atonement ritual in which the high priest entered the holy of holies to cleanse the sanctuary from sins committed throughout the year (Heb 9:7; cf. Lev 16; cf. 23:26–32; Num 29:7–11).[281] Most commentators see here an analogy between the Day of Atonement ritual and Jesus's death.[282] In many cases this analogy is understood in terms of a typological relationship to the effect that the description of Jesus's death and ascension in Hebrews is understood as an eschatological Day of Atonement of sorts. The following passage (Heb 9:15–23), however, interprets Jesus's death in vv. 11–14 not as an eschatological Day of Atonement that provides cleansing of the conscience but as the eschatological fulfillment of the inauguration of the new covenant that provides forgiveness.[283]

---

281 For an analysis of the Day of Atonement ritual and its purpose, see Gane, *Ritual Dynamic Structure*.

282 See references on page 9, n. 32. For a different position, see Davidson, "Christ's Entry," 175–190; idem, "Inauguration," 69–88.

283 Note that the author introduces vv. 15–23 with διὰ τοῦτο making vv. 11–14 the basis for his identification of Jesus's death as the sacrifice for the inauguration of the new covenant.

Jesus's death and ascension are described here as making possible "the good things that have come." This expression has eschatological significance (cf. Heb 1:1–2). Note that in Isa 52:7 ἀγαθά is used absolutely to refer to eschatological gifts (likewise, Rom 10:7). This passage

This agrees with the main burden of the whole section (8:1–10:18) that describes Jesus as inaugurating a new covenant; therefore, making the first covenant obsolete (8:13). Therefore, any analogy between the Day of Atonement and Jesus's sacrifice and ascension should be understood in the context of the inauguration of the new covenant, which is the dominant concern of the central section of the Letter to the Hebrews.[284]

I will proceed here in two stages. The first analyzes Heb 9:11–14 and its description of Jesus's death and ascension and the OT imagery it uses to this end. The second considers the role of the ascension in Heb 9:11–14 and the wider argument.

Hebrews 9:11–14 Describes Jesus's Entrance into the (Heavenly) Sanctuary of the New Covenant

The author's use of imagery from the Israelite cult to describe Jesus's death and ascension in 9:11–14 is complex for several reasons. First, in terms of the imagery, we are not very clear regarding the "whither" of Jesus's ascension. For example, what are the referents for the expressions τῆς μείζονος καὶ τελειοτέρας σκηνῆς ("the greater and perfect tent") and τὰ ἅγια? Did Jesus pass through the first in order to enter the latter, or do they denote the same entity in heaven? Second, the identification of the purpose of Jesus's ascension—in terms of the imagery—is as well complicated. Should Jesus's entrance into τὰ ἅγια be understood as an eschatological Day of Atonement, the inauguration of a new covenant, or both?

On the one hand we have the relationship between Jesus's entrance into the τὰ ἅγια and the high priest's entrance into the "second tent" (holy of holies) once a year described in Heb 9:7; but, on the other hand, we have the relationship between Jesus's sacrifice in Heb 9:11–14 and the sacrifice for the inauguration of a new covenant in Heb 9:15–23. The same question could be posed in different terms: Does the comparison of Jesus's death with the sacrifices of "goats and calves" (9:12) allude to the sacrifices of the Day of Atonement (9:7), the sacrifices for the inauguration of the covenant (9:19), or the sacrifices of the Israelite cult in general? Finally, if there is an allusion to the

---

(Isa 52:7) was interpreted messianically in the rabbinic tradition. See Str-B 3:282–283; Ellingworth, *The Epistle to the Hebrews*, 450.

The adjective ἀγαθός (good) is regularly applied in the LXX to the promised land (e.g., Exod 3:8; 20:12, Num 14:7; Deut 1:25; 8:7).

284 Forgetting that the inauguration of the new covenant is the dominant concern of 8:1–10:18 has led to a distorted understanding of the argument of the central section of Hebrews (Attridge, review of *Sohn und Hoherpriester*, 304; See also Loader, *Sohn und Hoherpriester*, 172; Scullion, "the Day of Atonement," 252).

Day of Atonement ritual in this passage, what is its relationship to the imagery of the inauguration of the covenant that controls the wider argument?

I will proceed to explain first the relationship between our passage (9:11–14) and the preceding argument (9:1–10). Second, I will explain the use of cultic imagery to explain Jesus's ascension in Heb 9:11–14. (For example, what are the referents of the "greater and more perfect tent" and τὰ ἅγια? etc.) This will prepare the way to answer the question of the function of Jesus's ascension in Heb 9:11–14 in the next section.

The Day of Atonement in Heb 9:1–10 illustrates the transition between covenants. There is a consensus that vv. 11–14 form a comparison with vv. 1–10.[285] These two paragraphs contrast the "earthly sanctuary" (vv. 2–5) with the "greater and more perfect tent" (9:11), the continuous entrance of the priests into the first tent (v. 6) with Jesus's "once for all" entrance into τὰ ἅγια (v. 11–12), the (animal) blood of the sacrifices (v. 7) with Jesus's "own blood" (v. 12), the gifts and sacrifices offered in the first tent (v. 9) with Jesus's offering of "himself" (v. 14), the "regulations for the body" (v. 9–10) and Jesus's offering "through the eternal spirit" (v. 14), and the impossibility that offerings and sacrifices may "perfect the conscience of the worshiper" (v. 9) with Jesus's purification of our "conscience" through the offering of himself (v. 14).[286] Thus, the relationship between these two passages has been described as a "rigorous antithetical parallelism."[287]

Some further argue that this antithetical relationship is confirmed by a μέν ... δέ construction that connects vv. 1–10 and vv. 11–14. In this sense the emphatic μὲν οὖν of 9:1 opens an antithesis that is closed with the δέ of v. 11.[288] Given this antithesis, it is concluded that the Day of Atonement—which has a prominent place in the argument of 9:1–10—provides the imagery neces-

---

285 E.g., Attridge, *The Epistle to the Hebrews*, 245; deSilva, *Perseverance in Gratitude*, 303; Ellingworth, *The Epistle to the Hebrews*, 445; Koester, *Hebrews*, 412; Lane, *Hebrews 9–13*, 233–234; Spicq, *L'épître aux Hébreux*, 2:246; Vanhoye, *La structure littéraire*, 149–151; Long Westfall, *A Discourse Analysis*, 196–205.

286 Vanhoye, *La structure littéraire*, 150–151. Cf. Buchanan, *To the Hebrews*, 150; Ellingworth, *The Epistle to the Hebrews*, 445. Cynthia Long Westfall suggests a comparison in three steps—from the general to the particular—that includes the priests, the high priest, and Jesus (*A Discourse Analysis*, 201). This is not convincing to me. Instead, it seems that the high priest in this text is not an intermediate step, but a type or figure that points forward to Christ.

287 Ellingworth, *The Epistle to the Hebrews*, 445.

288 Koester, *Hebrews*, 412; Lane, *Hebrews 9–13*, 229, n. a; Long Westfall, *A Discourse Analysis*, 197. It has been protested, however, that the δέ of v. 11 is too far from the μὲν of v. 1 to be directly related. Ellingworth, *The Epistle to the Hebrews*, 420. Thus, others consider that the μὲν οὖν of 9:1 is a resumption of the covenant theme from 8:7. Attridge, *The Epistle to the Hebrews*, 231; Ellingworth, *The Epistle to the Hebrews*, 420; Spicq, *L'épître aux Hébreux*, 2:247.

Regarding the use of μὲν οὖν, see BDF §450; L&N 2:812; BDAG, 630.

sary to understand Jesus's entrance into heaven.[289] Norman H. Young, for example, suggests that the description of the entrance of the high priest in the holy of holies is used by the author of Hebrews to explain Jesus's entrance into heaven:

> The terms in Heb. 9. 11–12 and in 9. 25 [which describe Jesus's sacrifice and ascension] follow an identical pattern to those in 9.7 [which describe the Day of Atonement], as the table below demonstrates:[290]

Heb. 9.7	Heb. 9.11–12	Heb. 9.25
ὁ ἀρχιερεύς	[ὁ] ἀρχιερεὺς	ὁ ἀρχιερεὺς
[εἴσεισι]	εἰσῆλθεν	εἰσέρχεται
εἰς τὴν δευτέραν	εἰς τὰ ἅγια	εἰς τὰ ἅγια
ἅπαξ τοῦ ἐνιαυτοῦ	ἐφάπαξ	κατ' ἐνιαυτὸν
οὐ χωρὶς αἵματος	οὐδὲ δι' αἵματος ... διὰ δὲ τοῦ ἰδίου αἵματος	ἐν αἵματι ἀλλοτρίῳ

While it is clear that these two passages contrast Jesus's achievements with the ineffective rituals of the first covenant, I believe that the Day of Atonement ritual described in vv. 6–7 does not have the purpose of explaining Jesus's sacrifice and ascension to heaven but has a more general purpose: it is a "parable" (παραβολή) that illustrates the *transition* from the first (Mosaic) covenant and its imperfect institutions (earthly sanctuary and ministry) that are ineffective to the new covenant and its heavenly institutions (heavenly sanctuary and ministry) that bring perfection.[291] Let us take first, then, a look into the argument of Heb 9:1–10 before considering its relationship to 9:11–14.

Hebrews 9:1–10 is a description of the first (Mosaic) covenant. It describes two of its aspects: its "regulations for worship" (δικαιώματα λατρείας) and its "earthly sanctuary" (τό τε ἅγιον κοσμικόν; 9:1). These are discussed in an inverted order: first the sanctuary (vv. 2–5) and then the regulations of worship (vv. 6–10). The author creates in its description of the earthly sanctuary a contrast between two tents that are separated by the veil. The first tent, or holy place, is described in simple terms (v. 2) while the second tent is described in glowing terms (vv. 3–5). Regarding the second, the author repeats three times that its furniture was built of gold and culminates its description with the "glorious cherubim" (Χερουβὶν δόξης) that overshadowed the "atonement cover"

---

289 See references on page 9, n. 32.
290 Young, "Gospel," 199.
291 I will be following here the argument I advanced in Félix H. Cortez, "From the Holy to the Most Holy Place: The Period of Heb 9:6–10 and the Day of Atonement as a Metaphor of Transition," *JBL* 125 (2006): 527–547.

(ἱλαστήριον).²⁹² Franz Laub correctly notes that there is a theological intention behind this antithetical description.²⁹³ The antithesis between the first and second rooms of the sanctuary lays the ground for the building of the more important antithesis between the ministries in the first and second rooms of the sanctuary introduced in vv. 6–7 and interpreted in vv. 8–10. Thus, the description of the earthly sanctuary in Heb 9:2–5 is geared towards the exposition of Heb 9:6–10 which crowns the argument of this section.

Hebrews 9:6–10 is a carefully constructed "period."²⁹⁴ Periods were important rhetorical devices used to introduce or conclude sections of the argument "by summarizing the points that preceded [or followed] the sentence itself."²⁹⁵ Quintilian, the most influential rhetorician of the 1st century CE, emphasized the importance of the period in the art of persuasion:²⁹⁶ "The Period is well suited to the Prooemia of important Causes, where the subject calls for anxiety, recommendation of the client, or pity; it also suits Commonplaces and every kind of Amplification. A severe type is required for prosecution, a more diffuse type for praise. The Period is also very important in the Epilogue"

---

292 Note that the furniture of the first tent was also made of gold but the author chose not to mention this fact (cf. Exod 25:23–40; 37:10–24).

Regarding the inclusion of the altar of incense in the second tent, see Harold S. Camacho, "The Altar of Incense in Hebrews 9:3–4," *AUSS* 24 (1986): 5–12. He notes that, like Heb 9:3–4, the altar of incense is described as "belonging" to the holy of holies in 1 Kgs 6:19–22 (cf. Exod 30:6; 40:5). The altar of incense belongs to the holy of holies in the sense that its function is directed to it.

293 Laub, " 'Ein für allemal hineingegangen in das Allerheiligste'," 69.

294 Several scholars have identified this sentence as a "period." E.g., Young, "Gospel," 200; Lane, *Hebrews 9–13*, 216; Gräßer, *An die Hebräer*, 216. According to Quintilian, other rhetoricians referred to the same structure by different names (*Inst*. 9.4.124).

The period is "a sentence that compresses several ideas into a complete thought and has a circular structure [hence its name: περί ὁδός]. This structure may be achieved by, though not limited to, four figures of speech: antithesis, paromoiosis, isocolon, and hyperbaton" (Cortez, "From the Holy to the Most Holy Place," 529–534; See also, Manuel Alexandre Jr., "The Art of Periodic Composition in Philo of Alexandria," in *Studia Philonica Annual: Studies in Hellenistic Judaism*, ed. David T. Runia, BJS [Scholars Press, 1991], 3:135–150; R. Dean Anderson Jr., *Glossary of Greek Rhetorical Terms Connected to Methods of Argumentation, Figures and Tropes from Anaximenes to Quintilian*, CBET 24 [Peeters, 2000], 94–101; Doreen C. Innes, "Period and Colon: Theory and Example in Demetrius and Longinus," in *Peripatetic Rhetoric after Aristotle*, ed. William W. Fortenbaugh and David C. Mirhady, Rutgers University Studies in Classical Humanities 4 [Transaction, 1994], 36–53; Heinrich Lausberg, *Handbook of Literary Rhetoric: A Foundation for Literary Study*, ed. David E. Orton and R. Dean Anderson, trans. Matthew Bliss, Annemiek Jansen, and David E. Orton [Brill, 1998], 414; Galen O. Rowe, "Style," in *Handbook of Classical Rhetoric in the Hellenistic Period: 330 B.C.–A.D. 400*, ed. Stanley E. Porter [Brill Academic, 2001], 121–157).

295 Koester, "Hebrews, Rhetoric, and the Future of Humanity," 105.

296 Quintilian's "*Institutio Oratoria* is the longest and most complete technical treatise on rhetoric to survive from Antiquity," however, it was Cicero (1st century BCE) who became "Rome's greatest orator and most influential writer on rhetorical technique" (Ruth Majercik, "Rhetoric and Rhetorical Criticism," *ABD* 5:711).

(*Inst.* 9.4.128 [Russell, LCL]). I want to suggest that the period of Heb 9:6–10 introduces the argument to follow in chs. 9–10.

The period is divided in two sections that are antithetical in nature. Each part is clearly introduced by a genitive absolute:

Vv. 6–7: Τούτων δὲ οὕτως κατεσκευασμένων …
Vv. 8–10: τοῦτο δηλοῦντος τοῦ πνεύματος τοῦ ἁγίου [297]

The first genitive absolute looks back forming an *inclusio* with v. 2 (note the use of the verb κατασκευάζω), but the second looks forward (9:11–10:18).

The first section (vv. 6–7) describes a transition from the ministry in the first room to the ministry in the second room of the Mosaic sanctuary as it occurred in the Day of Atonement. This section itself contains several antithetical structures that are very important for the argument (vv. 6–7). The antithetical structure is very clear and signaled by a tight syntactic μέν … δέ construction that describes and compares the ministries in the first and second rooms of the sanctuary. Three antithetical elements are set out in clear terms: (1) multiple priests (οἱ ἱερεῖς) versus one high priest (ὁ ἀρχιερεύς), (2) continuous entering (διὰ παντὸς εἰσίασιν) versus one entrance (ἅπαξ τοῦ ἐνιαυτοῦ [εἰσίασιν]), and (3) unrestricted access versus the requirement of blood (οὐ χωρὶς αἵματος).[298]

The author considered this annual transition in the OT cultus—i.e., the Day of Atonement—a parable (παραβολή, v. 9) the secret of which the Holy Spirit interprets for the believer.[299] The Day of Atonement—as a parable—*illustrates*

---

297 Vv. 6–7: Such preparations having been made …
Vv. 8–10: By this the Holy Spirit indicates …

298 The construction of the sentence implies that the high priest cannot enter the inner room without the blood of the sacrifice. The case for the outer room was different because the priests could enter the outer room without bringing any sacrifice. The author's understanding seems to be derived from Lev 16:1–3 where the blood of the bull and ram are described as prerequisites so that Aaron may not die as he enters the inner room. On the other hand, there was a requirement that the priests should wash their feet and hands any time they entered the first room of the tabernacle or approached the altar of burnt offering (Exod 30:17–21). The author, however, does not mention this fact.

299 Cf. Gräßer, *An die Hebräer*, 2:133. I agree with him that the interpretation implies some secret γνῶσις. However, I disagree with his general bent toward Gnosticism; cf. Hurst, *The Epistle to the Hebrews*, 67–75. In my view, the Holy Spirit's actions should be understood in the context of Jesus's explanation of the meaning of the parables to his disciples (e.g., Matt 13:10–17).

My reading implies a use of the term παραβολή in the sense of "a narrative or saying … designed *to illustrate* a truth especially through comparison or simile" (BDAG, 759, emphases are mine). Thus, the "narrative" or "saying" the Spirit interprets is the two-phased ministry of the two-room Israelite tabernacle.

A majority of commentators and translators have understood it, rather, in the sense of a *symbol*; namely, "something that serves as a model or example pointing beyond itself for later realization." E.g., NASB; NRSV; Attridge, *The Epistle to the Hebrews*, 241; Ellingworth, *The Epistle to the Hebrews*, 440; Koester, *Hebrews*, 398; Lane, *Hebrews 9–13*, 224. The main reasons have

the transition from the first tent into the second tent. This transition between "tents" and their ministries involves a transition from the ministry of several priests to the ministry of one, from several sacrifices to one sacrifice, and from unrestricted access to the outer tent to access only "through blood" into the inner tent. Finally, the author interprets this transition between tents as a transition from the cleansing of the body to the cleansing of the conscience in the second section of the sentence (vv. 8–10).[300]

The author of Hebrews uses the Day of Atonement to illustrate the transition from the first (earthly) tent and the first (Mosaic) covenant into the second (heavenly) tent and the new covenant in 9:11–10:18.[301] This transition includes a transition from the ministry of many Levitical priests to one heav-

---

been their identification of the "first tent" (an object, not a saying or narrative) as the referent of the parable as well as its prefigurative function. Friedrich Hauck, "παραβολή," *TDNT* 5:752. Nevertheless, Hebrews' use of παραβολή as illustration does not preclude its prefigurative function. I believe the term παραβολή is used again in Heb 11:19 in a similar manner to Heb 9:9. There, as James Swetnam argues, παραβολή refers not only to Isaac's "resurrection" from the sacrifice but also to the wider narrative which includes Abraham's offering of Isaac. Abraham's offering of Isaac prefigures an offering; his reception of Isaac, a resurrection. The narrative illustrates and foreshadows, then, Jesus's sacrifice as well as his resurrection (Swetnam, *Jesus and Isaac*, 119–123).

300 Notice the intentional analogy between the temporal standing (acc. of στάσις; v. 8) of the "first tent" and the description of the present age as "standing/present" (ptc. pf. of ἐνίστημι, v. 9). Also, notice the antithesis between flesh (σάρξ) versus conscience (συνείδησις) in vv. 9–10. The antithesis is signaled now not by a μέν ... δέ construction (on the one hand ... on the other hand) but by the adverb μόνον (only). The NRSV recognizes the antithetical function of both constructions (vv. 6–7; 9–10) and translates them in the same way: "but only."

301 There are two main variables in the exegesis of Heb 9:8. First, does the expression πρώτης σκηνῆς have a "spatial" or "temporal" sense; that is, does it refer to the outer room (spatial) or the whole sanctuary (temporal)? Second, does the expression ἐχούσης στάσιν have a physical or legal meaning; namely, is the tent destroyed or does it just lose its legal significance? These two variables make four interpretations possible. (1) The outer room is destroyed, e.g., Buchanan, *To the Hebrews*, 144–145. (2) The first sanctuary is destroyed, e.g., Gerhard Delling, "στάσις," *TDNT* 7:570. (3) The outer room loses cultic standing, e.g., Attridge, *The Epistle to the Hebrews*, 240; Gräßer, *An die Hebräer*, 2:132–134; Donald A. Hagner, *Encountering the Book of Hebrews: An Exposition*, Encountering Biblical Studies (Baker Academic, 2002), 120; Koester, *Hebrews*, 397–398; Lane, *Hebrews 9–13*, 223–224; Weiß, *Der Brief an die Hebräer*, 457–459. (See esp. Hofius, *Der Vorhang*, 60–65; Otfried Hofius, "Das 'erste' und das 'zweite' Zelt: Ein Beitrag zur Auslegung von Hebr 9,1–10," *Neutestamentliche Studien*, WUNT I/132 [Mohr Siebeck, 2000], 203–209). (4) The first sanctuary loses cultic standing, e.g., Bruce, *The Epistle to the Hebrews*, 208; Ellingworth, *The Epistle to the Hebrews*, 437–438; Simon J. Kistemaker, "Exposition of the Epistle to the Hebrews," *Exposition of Thessalonians, the Pastorals, and Hebrews*, New Testament Commentary (Baker, 1995), 243; Ray C. Stedman, *Hebrews*, IVP New Testament Commentary Series (InterVarsity, 1992), 95.

As indicated in the sample of supporters mentioned above, the majority of scholars choose the third option (3) and interpret Heb 9:8 in the following way: The Holy Spirit is signifying that the way into the inner room of the sanctuary (τὰ ἅγια) has not yet been disclosed as long as the outer room (τῆς πρώτης σκηνῆς) still has cultic standing (ἐχούσης στάσιν). A very important tenet of this interpretation is that the term (τὰ) ἅγια in Heb 8–10 denotes the inner room of the sanctuary, the holy of holies. I will argue below, however, that there is no support

enly high priest (7:23–25), from many animal sacrifices to the "once for all" sacrifice of Jesus (9:25–28; 10:11–13), from lack of access to access into the presence of God in the heavenly sanctuary (9:11–14, 24; 10:19–21), and from the cleansing of the "flesh" to the cleansing of the conscience (9:14; 10:2, 22).[302] In other words, it is suggested that the parable contains *in nuce* the argument for the central section of Hebrews. The period of Heb 9:6–10 introduces, then, the Day of Atonement not as a typology for Jesus's sacrifice, but as an illustration (παραβολή) of the transition between covenants.[303]

This interpretation suggests that ὁδός is the antecedent of ἥτις in vv. 8–9: "By this the Holy Spirit indicates that the way into the sanctuary has not yet been disclosed, as long as the first tent is still standing. This [i.e., the way into the sanctuary] is an illustration of the present time …"[304] The "way into the sanctuary" refers to the cultic system that requires a sequence of ministries; first in the outer tent (daily), then in the inner tent (annually). In fact, the carrying on of a ministry in the first tent impedes access into the second (Lev 16:17). Therefore, the "way into the sanctuary" was more an evidence of restriction than of access (Heb 9:6–7). Nevertheless, the author of Hebrews plays with the concept of the "way into the sanctuary" brilliantly by transforming the annual transition between tents and their cultic systems in the Day of Atonement (vv. 6–8) into an illustration of the transition between ages and their respective cultic systems (vv. 9–10).

The use of the transition in the ministry of the tents in the Day of Atonement as a parable removes a hurdle in the current interpretations of the "first tent" (τῆς πρώτης σκηνῆς) and its alleged relationship to "present time" (τὸν καιρὸν τὸν ἐνεστηκότα) of v. 9. Neither the "mosaic tabernacle" nor the "outer

---

for this translation, neither in the LXX, nor in the Pseudepigrapha, Philo, or Josephus. See, Cosaert, "The Use of ἅγιος," 91–103.

302 See Cortez, "From the Holy to the Most Holy Place," 543–546.

303 For a study of the relationship between the old and new covenants see Skip MacCarty, *In Granite or Ingrained?: What the Old and New Covenants Reveal about the Gospel, the Law, and the Sabbath* (Andrews University Press, 2007).

304 Admittedly, the antecedent (ὁδός) is somewhat removed from the relative pronoun (ἥτις); however, this is not strange in Hebrews (cf. 9:2; 8:5).

A majority of interpreters consider that the phrase τῆς πρώτης σκηνῆς—which is closer to the relative pronoun—is the antecedent, e.g., Attridge, *The Epistle to the Hebrews*, 241; Ellingworth, *The Epistle to the Hebrews*, 439; Gräßer, *An die Hebräer*, 2:135; Koester, *Hebrews*, 398; Lane, *Hebrews 9–13*, 224. This position, as I will argue below, has the problem of the awkward relationship between the symbol ("first tent") and the referent ("present time"). Others argue that the antecedent is the whole situation of vv. 6–8, e.g., Bruce, *The Epistle to the Hebrews*, 209; Loader, *Sohn und Hoherpriester*, 164; Michel, *die Hebräer*, 307; Montefiore, *The Epistle to the Hebrews*. Though this interpretation is tempting for my argument, it has the problem of the awkward explanation of the relative pronoun whose gender is defined not by the antecedent, but by παραβολή, an element of its own clause. In my view, it is unnecessary.

room" (understood as the referents of "first tent" [v. 8] in a majority of interpretations; see above page 224, n. 301) is an appropriate symbol of the "present time." Both refer to non-fulfillment and imperfection; however, the main thrust of Hebrews is that Jesus *has inaugurated* the time of fulfillment and perfection. He is the "high priest of the good things that *have come*" (9:11; emphasis mine). Harold W. Attridge has argued, following J. H. Davies, that Hebrews uses "the inverse image" (first tent/imperfection) to symbolize the "present time" of perfection.[305] However, this is unconvincing because the author of Hebrews had a better option. If the main point of Hebrews is that Jesus "is seated at the right hand of the throne of the majesty in the heavens" (8:1; cf. 1:3); that he has "entered the inner shrine behind the curtain" (6:19; cf. 4:14–16; 10:19–22); why didn't he use the "second tent" (the inner room), a symbol of God's throne room and presence, to symbolize the "present age"? It seems a poor choice in one of the better argued documents of the New Testament. Craig R. Koester, on the other hand, rightly points out that the author holds a view of an overlap of ages similar to that of Paul.[306] His identification, however, of the "present time" as the time where the first covenant regulations are still in force, and the "time of correction" as the time when those regulations are set aside is awkward. It would say that the author uses the phrase "present time" to refer to what he considers is only one of the two aspects of the "present time." In any case, the "first tent" continues to be an ill-adapted symbol for the "present time" where the two ages overlap.

The Day of Atonement, however, as a time of transition between the ministries of the first (outer) and second (inner) rooms is a fitting illustration of the "present time," which is also a time of transition. In the OT cultus, the ministries in the outer and inner rooms were juxtaposed in the Day of Atonement. The regular rituals, performed every day in the morning and evening in the outer room, were *also* performed on the Day of Atonement; however, between the morning and evening ritual, the special ritual of purification of the sanctuary was "inserted" which included the "once a year" ministry in the inner room.[307] The ritual in the inner room, however, implied not only co-existence but also a supersession of the outer room cultus (Heb 9:8; cf. Lev 16:17). The Day of Atonement illustrates appropriately, then, what is happening in the "present time": Jesus has come and made the old covenant cultus "obsolete" so that it "will soon disappear" (8:13). This transition, however, has not

---

305 *The Epistle to the Hebrews*, 241–242; Davies, *Hebrews*, 86.
306 *Hebrews*, 398.
307 See, Gane, *Ritual Dynamic Structure*, 297–305.

totally transpired. The new covenant has been inaugurated, but the old has not yet vanished (8:13).[308] (See Table 6 on this respect.)

I suggest then the following reading of Heb 9:6–10:

> When such preparations have been made, the priests go continually into the first tent to carry out their ministry; but only the high priest goes into the second, and he but once a year, and not without taking the blood that he offers for himself and for the sins committed unintentionally by the people. This is what the Holy Spirit reveals: the way into the [*heavenly* or *second*] sanctuary has not yet been disclosed as long as the *first* [earthly] sanctuary continues to have [cultic] standing. *The way of the sanctuary* [first, ministry in the outer tent; then, access to the second tent] *is a parable* for the present time, according to which gifts and sacrifices are offered that cannot perfect the conscience of the worshiper, but deal only with food and drink and various baptisms, regulations for the body imposed until the time comes to set things right.[309]

This understanding of the Day of Atonement as a parable of the transition to the new covenant provides a fitting culmination to the immediately preceding argument. Hebrews 8:7–13 argued that the promise of a new covenant in Jer 31:31–34 (quoted in Heb 8:8–12) implied the obsolescence and soon disappearance of the first covenant (esp. v. 13).[310]

Daily Ritual	*Yearly Ritual*
Ministry in the outer room	Ministry in the inner room
Ministry of many Levitical priests	Only the high priest ministers
Many daily sacrifices	One yearly sacrifice
No access to the immediate presence of God	Access through sacrifice to the immediate presence of God
Old (Mosaic) Covenant	*New Covenant*
Ministry in the *earthly* tabernacle	Ministry in the *heavenly* tabernacle

---

308 See Koester, *Hebrews*, 398.

309 Franz Laub has a similar position in which Jesus's movement through the tent should be understood—following a history-of-religions matrix—as a transition into the coming age and which is also the higher sphere of the philosophical speculation. In this sense, in Hebrews both the apocalyptic worldview that distinguishes between ages and the philosophical (Plato/Philo) contrast between lower and higher spheres intersect (" 'Ein für allemal hineingegangen in das Allerheiligste,'" 65–85).

310 George H. Guthrie suggests that 8:7 and 13 create an inclusion around the word "first" (πρῶτος) (*The Structure of Hebrews*, 85–86).

Ministry of *many* Levitical (High) Priests	Ministry of *one*, eternal high priest
Many sacrifices	*One* sacrifice ("once for all")
No access to the presence of God	Access to the presence of God through the blood of Jesus
Cleansing of the *flesh*	Cleansing of the *conscience*

Table 6. Transition from the Daily to the Yearly Ritual in the Israelite Cult (the Day of Atonement) and the Transition between the Old and New Covenants in Hebrews

Hebrews 9:1–10 rounds off the argument by suggesting that the ritual of the sanctuary itself (esp. the Day of Atonement) illustrated this transition. Note that the concluding argument of this section (vv. 9–10) is in essence equivalent to 8:13, as shown in Table 7.[311]

Hebrews 9:9–10	*Hebrews 8:13*
"This is a symbol of the present time, during which gifts and sacrifices are offered that cannot perfect the conscience of the worshiper, but deal only with food and drink and various baptisms, regulations for the body …"	"… what is obsolete and growing old …"
"… imposed until the time comes to set things right."	"… will soon disappear."

Table 7. Literary Relationship between Hebrews 9:9–10 and 8:13

Thus, Heb 9:1–10 has the purpose of pointing out that the first covenant itself—through the Day of Atonement ritual—illustrates its own inefficacy and the need of a better covenant with better institutions. In this sense, it fulfills the same function that the story of Abraham's encounter with Melchizedek (7:1–10) and God's promise of rest in Ps 95 (3:7–4:11) played in previous sections of the argument. The story of Levi paying the tithes to and being blessed by Melchizedek—through Abraham—served as evidence of the inferiority—therefore, inefficacy—of the Levitical priesthood and the need of a greater priesthood established under a better law (7:11–28). Similarly, God's

---

311 Thus, I agree with those who consider that the μὲν οὖν of 9:1 is a resumption of the covenant theme from 8:7 (Attridge, *The Epistle to the Hebrews*, 231; Ellingworth, *The Epistle to the Hebrews*, 420; Spicq, *L'épître aux Hébreux*, 2:247). I consider that the μὲν οὖν here functions as a marker of result and could be translated in the sense of "accordingly" (L&N 2:783–4; cf. BDF §450; L&N 2:794–795, 812; BDAG, 630). On the other hand, the μὲν οὖν of 9:1 is not directly related to the δέ of v. 11 (Ellingworth, *The Epistle to the Hebrews*, 420).

promise of rest through David in Ps 95 had the purpose of showing that the rest given by Joshua was inferior and there remained a need for a superior rest for the people of God.

This view of the Day of Atonement as a "parable" of the transition to the new covenant fits perfectly with the argument of 9:11–18 because there—as we will see—Jesus is not described as entering the heavenly holy of holies, but entering the heavenly sanctuary. Therefore, this passage refers not to an eschatological Day of Atonement but to the inauguration of the new covenant ministry and its heavenly sanctuary.

Τὰ ἅγια denotes the sanctuary of the new covenant. The term Hebrews uses for the place Jesus entered at his ascension (τὰ ἅγια) does not refer to the inner room of the sanctuary specifically, but to the sanctuary in general (8:2; 9:2, 8, 12, 24, 25; 10:19; 13:11).[312]

In his study of the term τὰ ἅγια in the LXX when it appears in connection to the sanctuary, Alwyn P. Salom found that with one exception τὰ ἅγια does not refer to the inner room (holy of holies) but to the sanctuary in general and—in a few cases—to the outer room.[313] Carl P. Cosaert studied the use of the term in the OT Pseudepigrapha, Philo, and Josephus and reached the same conclusion: "Despite the variety of uses of ἅγιος, one pattern, however, does appear to be consistent throughout: *the plural form by itself is never used to describe the Holy of Holies alone.* Whenever the plural form by itself is used, it exclusively describes the whole sanctuary in general. Moreover, whenever specific reference is made to the Most Holy Place, the plural form by itself is never used" (emphasis his).[314] Hebrews itself refers to the inner room in 9:3 with a different term: ἅγια ἁγίων. Thus, to say that Jesus entered the holy of holies at his ascension would entail a new meaning for the term τὰ ἅγια and

---

312 BDAG, 11.

313 Alwyn P. Salom concluded that ἅγιος appeared 170 times in the LXX in connection to the tabernacle or temple. Of the 66 times it appears *in singular*, 45 times refer to the sanctuary, 13 to the outer compartment, and 8 to the inner compartment. Of the 104 times it appears *in plural*, 97 refer to the sanctuary, 6 to the outer compartment, and 1 to the inner compartment ("*Ta Hagia* in the Epistle to the Hebrews," 221). This study is of limited utility, however, because it fails to include the references to the LXX on which the findings are based. For example, we don't know where ἅγια denotes the inner room, the holy of holies. Though somewhat dated, Henry S. Gehman's article is more useful. He agrees with Salom in the fact that τὰ ἅγια translates the Hebrew term מִקְדָּשׁ in the LXX when it refers to 'sanctuary' in the general sense. When מִקְדָּשׁ refers to the tabernacle, it may be translated by τὸ ἅγιον; still the plural occurs more frequently ("Ἅγιος in the Septuagint," 340–341). The only place in the LXX where Gehman identifies that τὰ ἅγια refers to the inner room is Ezek 41:21 ("Ἅγιος in the Septuagint," 345). (Probably, Salom had the same verse in mind.)

314 Cosaert, "The Use of ἅγιος," 102–103.

"identifying what is called τὰ ἅγια in v. 12 as the heavenly counterpart of what was called Ἅγια ἁγίων in v. 3."[315]

Erich Gräßer and others hold, however, that Hebrews follows Lev 16 (vv. 2, 3, 16, passim) where τὸ ἅγιον refers to the inner room.[316] Erich Gräßer notes:

> Der Hebr folgt dieser Terminologie [i.e., Lev 16], ersetzt den Singular aber durch den Plural (9,8.12.24f; 10,19; 13:11[38]), der in der LXX nur vereinzelt für das Allerheiligste steht (Ez 41,21).
> [38] Den Beweis findet Hofius*, Vorhang 57 Anm. 60 m.R. in 13,11, wo Lev 16,27 zitiert wird, der dortige Singular τὸ ἅγιον aber als Plural erscheint. Vgl. A.P. Salom, *TA HAGIA* in the Epistle to the Hebrews, *AUSS* 5 (1967) 59–70.[317]

A second argument refers to the literary context in which τὰ ἅγια is used. As noted above, Norman H. Young shows in a table how Hebrews' description of Jesus's entrance into the heavenly sanctuary (τὰ ἅγια, Heb 9:11–12, 25) follows "an identical pattern" to the description of the entrance of the high priest into the inner room on the Day of Atonement in Heb 9:7. Because of this alleged connection between Jesus's entrance into heaven and the high priest's entrance into the most holy place on the Day of Atonement, it is concluded that τὰ ἅγια in Hebrews refers to the inner room of the heavenly sanctuary and not the sanctuary as a whole.[318]

What has tipped the balance in most cases in favor of understanding τὰ ἅγια as referring specifically to the holy of holies is the typological correspondence most scholars believe is developed in Hebrews between Jesus's entrance into heaven and the high priest's entrance into the inner room on the

---

315 Ellingworth, *The Epistle to the Hebrews*, 447.

316 Attridge, *The Epistle to the Hebrews*, 218; Gräßer, *An die Hebräer*, 81; Hofius, *Der Vorhang*, 56–57. Others hold that τὰ ἅγια refers to the inner room not because of Lev 16, but for other reasons. Chief among them, the typological correspondence between Jesus's entrance into heaven and the high priest's entrance into the inner room on the Day of Atonement. Michel, *die Hebräer*, 311–2; Loader, *Sohn und Hoherpriester*, 363; Rissi, *Die Theologie des Hebräerbriefs*, 37–41; Laub, *Bekenntnis und Auslegung*, 203–207; Scholer, *Proleptic Priests*, 160; Wilson, *Hebrews*, 150; Bénétreau, *L'épître*; Young, "Gospel"; Hughes, *Hebrews*, 281, n. 54.

317 Gräßer, 2:81–82. Translation: "Hebrews follows this terminology [i.e., Lev 16], but he replaces the singular with the plural (9:8, 12, 24f; 10:19; 13:11), which stands for the most holy place in the LXX only occasionally (Ezek 41:21). [Translation of note 38:] Hofius finds the evidence correctly in 13:11 where Lev 16:27 is cited (*Vorhang*, 57 n. 60). There [Lev 16:27] it is the singular τὸ ἅγιον but here [Heb 13:11] appears the plural. Cf. A. P. Salom, *TA HAGIA* in the Epistle to the Hebrews, *AUSS* 5 (1967) 59–70.

318 Young, "Gospel," 199. I will deal with 9:25 below.

Day of Atonement.³¹⁹

This position is not convincing, however. It must be borne in mind that Lev 16 LXX uses *the singular* (τὸ ἅγιον) to refer to the inner room of the sanctuary, while Hebrews uses *the plural* (τὰ ἅγια).³²⁰ In using the plural—which elsewhere refers to the sanctuary in general—and not the singular (which in Lev 16 refers to the inner room), Hebrews sides with the rest of the LXX and not with Lev 16. Erich Gräßer overstates his case when he says that τὰ ἅγια (plural) "occasionally" (vereinzelt) refers to the inner room. There is only one verse in the LXX where τὰ ἅγια refers to the inner room: Ezek 41:21. This verse, however, is riddled with text-critical problems. Referring to vv. 15b–26, Brandon L. Fredenburg notes: "These verses are among the most difficult to translate in the entire book because of the rare terms used and the high probability of copyists' errors due to their rarity."³²¹ In my opinion, it is not wise to establish the meaning of a term on the evidence of one passage that belongs to a section with a high probability of copyists' errors, against the majority of biblical texts.

Moreover, the "proof" Otfried Hofius presents that Hebrews changes the singular τὸ ἅγιον of Lev 16 for the plural τὰ ἅγια is not compelling.³²² He argues that Heb 13:11 alludes to Lev 16:27 but substitutes the singular τὸ ἅγιον with the plural τὰ ἅγια.³²³ We cannot be sure, however, that Heb 13:11 is referring to Lev 16:27. Day of Atonement sacrifices were not the only ones whose blood was taken into the tent by the high priest, the priests could not eat from them, and their carcasses were burned "outside the camp." The carcasses of purification

---

319 For references, see page 9, no. 32.

320 It is not clear why Lev 16 uses the singular. The fact is that the singular is not used to refer to the inner room outside of Lev 16. Cosaert, "The Use of ἅγιος," 98, n. 35. Cf. John William Wevers, *Notes on the Greek Text of Leviticus*, SBLSCS 44 (Scholars Press, 1997), 240–241.

321 Brandon L. Fredenburg, *Ezekiel*, College Press NIV Commentary (College Press, 2002), 368–369.
Walther Zimmerli's conclusion about the textual status of this section, especially vv. 21b–22, is more severe: "Rather one must suppose that vv 21b–22 ... have been added by the hand which took over vv 15b–26 from another" (Zimmerli, *Ezekiel 2*, 386). Steven Shaun Tuell reaches a different conclusion: "The terminological evidence cited by Zimmerly for the secondary character of 41:15b–26 in particular is strong, but not finally compelling; such shifts may be for stylistic effect, to break up the monotony of the interminable rounds of measurement and description" (Steven Shawn Tuell, *The Law of the Temple in Ezekiel 40–48*, HSM 49 [Scholars Press, 1992], 31, n. 34).

322 See above, page 230, n. 317.

323 "For the bodies of those animals whose blood is *brought into the sanctuary* [εἰσφέρεται ... εἰς τὰ ἅγια] by the high priest as a sacrifice for sin are burned outside the camp" (Heb 13:11, emphasis mine).
"The bull of the sin offering and the goat of the sin offering, whose blood was *brought* in to make atonement *in the holy place* [εἰσηνέχθη ... ἐν τῷ ἁγίῳ], shall be taken outside the camp; their skin and their flesh and their dung shall be consumed in fire" (Lev 16:27, emphasis mine).

offerings as well as the consecration offerings were burned outside the camp (Exod 29:14; Lev 4:12, 21; 8:17; 9:11).[324] More specifically, however, the blood of the purification offering for the high priest (Lev. 4:5–7) and the blood of the sin offering for the community (Lev. 4:16–21; 6:30) were brought into the sanctuary,[325] and the priests could not eat from them (Lev 6:30; cf. Heb 13:10).[326] Therefore, Hebrews 13:10–13 could allude either to the purification offerings of the Day of Atonement (Lev 16:27) or the purification offerings on behalf of the community or the high priest (Lev 6:30; cf. Lev 4:1–21). The terminology is on the side of the latter because, in the LXX idiom, the term τὰ ἅγια equivalent to the τὴν σκηνὴν τοῦ μαρτυρίου of Lev 6:30 (6:23 LXX) and not to the τῷ ἁγίῳ of Lev 16:27.

Some scholars adopt a middle position. Craig R. Koester and others believe that τὰ ἅγια denotes the whole sanctuary.[327] For example, he argues that in the expression τῶν ἁγίων λειτουργὸς καὶ τῆς σκηνῆς τῆς ἀληθινῆς, ἣν ἔπηξεν ὁ κύριος, οὐκ ἄνθρωπος (and who serves in the sanctuary, the true tabernacle set up by the Lord, not by man; Heb 8:2 NIV) καὶ has an explanatory function making τῶν ἁγίων and τῆς σκηνῆς τῆς ἀληθινῆς synonyms: "The two nouns are followed by the singular 'which' (*hēn*), suggesting that only one tent is intended."[328] They argue, as well, that the main contrast in Hebrews is not between two parts of the heavenly sanctuary (an outer and inner room), but between the earthly and heavenly sanctuary. In their opinion, however, this does not invalidate the typological role of the Day of Atonement for Jesus's ascension. The entrance of the high priest into the most holy place foreshadows Jesus's transition from earth to heaven (cf. Heb 9:6–10).[329]

A problem with this view is that we cannot infer from it that Hebrews considers heaven to be the inner room and earth the outer room of Hebrews'

---

324 Johnsson, "Day of Atonement," 115.
325 "The rabbis add the he-goat of the community (Num 15:22–26), which, in their view, is brought for the sin of idolatry (*m. Hor.* 1:4; *Siphre* Shelaḥ 112; *Sipra*, ḥobah 6:10). Some commentators feel that this rule applies only to the previously mentioned purification offerings (4:1–21; Ibn Ezra, Ramban), but its generalized formulation argues for greater comprehensiveness" (Milgrom, *Leviticus 1–16*, 407–408. Also, Gane, *Leviticus, Numbers*, 144).
326 Gane, *Leviticus, Numbers*, 144.
327 Koester, *Hebrews*, 376; Bruce, *The Epistle to the Hebrews*, 180, n. 3; Ellingworth, *The Epistle to the Hebrews*, 400; Lane, *Hebrews 1–8*, 199, n. e, 205; Harald Hegermann, *Der Brief an die Hebräer*, THKNT 16 (Evangelische, 1988), 163; Weiß, *Der Brief an die Hebräer*; Peterson, *Hebrews and Perfection*, 130–31.
328 Koester, *Hebrews*, 376. As I will argue below, the same relationship between ἅγια and σκηνή is found in 9:11–12. See below section "'The Greater and Perfect Tent' Denotes the Sanctuary of the New Covenant" on page 233.
329 Ibid.

true (heavenly/cosmic) sanctuary.³³⁰ If this were the case, Jesus was sacrificed in the outer room of this cosmic sanctuary; yet, Hebrews does not show any interest in relating the work of Jesus on earth with the outer room of the heavenly sanctuary and its ministry. Hebrews does not show interest in a division in the heavenly sanctuary.³³¹ In fact, Hebrews considers that Jesus suffered "outside of the camp" (Heb 13:10–13). Moreover, the view presented above that Hebrews uses Day of Atonement imagery to illustrate a transition from the first covenant and the earthly sanctuary to the new covenant and the heavenly sanctuary is less problematic in this sense.³³²

"The greater and perfect tent" denotes the sanctuary of the new covenant. The plethora of different interpretations of διὰ τῆς μείζονος καὶ τελειοτέρας σκηνῆς ("through the greater and more perfect tabernacle," NASB) attests to the difficulty of its interpretation. The referent of this expression depends in great measure on whether the preposition διά has a locative or instrumental meaning.

The preposition διά, when used with verbs of motion, usually has the locative sense of "extension through an area or object."³³³ The prepositional phrase "through [διά] the greater and more perfect tabernacle" modifies the verb of motion εἰσῆλθεν (entered). On this basis, some conclude that "the greater and more perfect tabernacle" denotes a location through which Jesus entered into the "Holy Place."³³⁴ In terms of the cultic imagery of the Mosaic sanctuary, "the greater and more perfect tabernacle" would refer to the outer room and the "Holy Place" to the inner room of the heavenly sanctuary. This is possible because the term "tabernacle" (σκηνή) in Hebrews may denote both the whole sanctuary (8:5; 9:21; 13:10) or one of its compartments (9:2, 3, 6). Since Heb 9:1–10 describes two "tents" or rooms of the earthly sanctuary, it is not difficult to conclude that the heavenly sanctuary has also two rooms.³³⁵

---

330 Philo believed that the heavenly sanctuary was a symbol of the soul or the universe (Philo, *Dreams* 1.215). He preferred the latter, however. Heaven symbolizes in his view the most sacred part of this sanctuary (*Spec. Laws* 1.66; cf. *Moses* 2.101–108; *QE* 2.91). For Josephus, also, the most sacred section of the sanctuary symbolized heaven (*Ant.* 3:123, 179–181; *J.W.* 5.211–214). Lincoln D. Hurst, however, argues that those who hold this view of the heavenly sanctuary as a symbol of the universe fall short of proof. Hurst, *The Epistle to the Hebrews*, 24–33.

331 Ellingworth, *The Epistle to the Hebrews*, 446–447; Hughes, *Hebrews*, 289; Koester, *Hebrews*, 409.

332 Cortez, "From the Holy to the Most Holy Place," 527–547.

333 BDAG, 223–224.

334 E.g., Attridge, *The Epistle to the Hebrews*, 246; Bénétreau, *L'épître*; Ellingworth, *The Epistle to the Hebrews*, 450; Gräßer; Johnson, *Hebrews*, 235–236; Lane, *Hebrews 9–13*, 236–237; Michel, *die Hebräer*, 310–312; Thompson, *Beginnings*, 106.

335 Lane, *Hebrews 9–13*, 236; Paul C. B. Andriessen, "Das größere und vollkommenere Zelt (Hebr 9, 11)," *BZ* 15 (1971): 76–92; Gräßer; Spicq, *L'épître aux Hébreux*; Héring, *The Epistle to the*

The cultic imagery of 6:19 and Heb 10:20 seems to support this view because they refer to Jesus's entrance as going through the celestial equivalent of the curtain that divided the outer from the inner room in the Mosaic tabernacle; thus implying the existence of a heavenly anteroom to the place of God's presence. This understanding might fit, as well, 4:14 where Jesus's ascension is described as passing "through the heavens" into the presence of God and 7:26 where it is said that Jesus has been "exalted *above* the heavens" (emphasis mine).[336]

There are several problems with this view, however. First, it seems awkward that Hebrews would refer to the anteroom as "the greater and more perfect tabernacle" while the object of its concern—the place of God's presence—is referred to simply as the "Holy Place."[337] Second, Paul Ellingworth has shown that Heb 4:14–16 and 9:11–14 employ two different types of spatial language in Hebrews and that it is problematic to equate them.[338] We cannot simply consider both types of language equivalent as if their only difference was their respective vertical and horizontal orientations. For example, 4:14–16 asserts that Jesus "has passed *through* the heavens" (emphasis mine)—implying that Jesus is now somewhere *beyond* "the heavens"—while 8:1 asserts that Jesus sits "at the right hand of the throne of the Majesty *in* the heavens" (emphasis mine; cf. 12:23, 25).[339] Thus, while we may concur that both 4:14–16 and 9:11–14 are equivalents in terms of their meaning, they are not in terms of their imagery; therefore, we cannot explain the imagery of one in terms of the other.[340] Third, Hebrews does not seem to be interested in any distinction between two sections in the heavenly sanctuary.[341] Instead, it compares two

---

Hebrews; Helmut Koester, "Outside the Camp: Hebrews 13:9–14," *HTR* 55 (1962): 309–310. Cf. Attridge, *The Epistle to the Hebrews*, 223, 246–247.

336 Riggenbach, *an die Hebräer*, 255; Moffatt, *Epistle to the Hebrews*, 120; Laub, *Bekenntnis und Auslegung*, 186.

337 Koester, *Hebrews*, 409.

338 Ellingworth, "Jesus and the Universe," 337–350. The first belongs to vertical language and is perhaps largely traditional (4:14–16; 2:9; 7:26). It is mainly used to convey the reality of Christ's exaltation over creation and the angels and presupposes an intermediary sphere populated by angels. In other words, it presupposes a three-tiered universe: earth, heavens (angels), above the heavens.

The second belongs to horizontal language and is used to express the significance of Jesus's sacrifice as providing direct access to God (6:19–20; 9:11–14; 10:19–20). This type of language *does not* presuppose an intermediate sphere but a simple contrast between heaven and earth. In other words, it presupposes a two-tiered universe—an outer and an inner region in reference to the throne of God. (Note that Heb 8:1–2 and 9:24 convey this two-tiered universe in vertical fashion.)

339 Similarly, 9:24 asserts that Jesus "entered into heaven itself."

340 Though their imageries are contradictory (Jesus is above/in "the heavens"), both images coincide in that Jesus is in the presence of God interceding in our favor.

341 Ellingworth, *The Epistle to the Hebrews*, 446–447; Hughes, *Hebrews*, 289; Koester, *Hebrews*, 409. Also, Cody, *Heavenly Sanctuary and Liturgy*, 150–59; Hofius, *Der Vorhang*, 65–66;

covenants and their sanctuaries (8:1–6; cf. 9:1). If "the greater and more perfect tabernacle" denotes the outer room of the heavenly sanctuary, this "greater and more perfect tabernacle" is irrelevant both in 9:11–14 and elsewhere in Hebrews. At the most, its existence is implied in 6:19–20 and 10:19–21 but its significance never explained. Finally, this interpretation makes necessary that τὰ ἅγια denotes the heavenly holy of holies which is incorrect—as shown above.[342]

Others consider that διά has an instrumental meaning. Albert Vanhoye and others have noted that the preposition modifies both the verb εἰσῆλθεν (entered) *and* the participial phrase "obtaining eternal redemption." Therefore, they suggest, it is incorrect to determine the function of the preposition on the basis of the verb only.[343] In this sense, Jesus entered into the "Holy Place" *by means of* "the greater and more perfect tabernacle." The phrase "through [διά] the greater and more perfect tabernacle" is one of three prepositional phrases that explain *how* Jesus "entered [εἰσῆλθεν] ... the Holy Place [τὰ ἅγια] ... *obtaining* eternal redemption" (v. 12, emphasis mine). All three use the preposition διά: (1) "through [διά] the greater and more perfect tabernacle," (2) "not through [διά] the blood of goats and calves," (3) "but through [διά] His own blood." Since it is clear that διά in the prepositional phrases 2 and 3 has an instrumental meaning, it is likely that διά also has an instrumental sense in the phrase "through the greater and more perfect tabernacle."[344]

Many of those who adopt this view interpret "the greater and more perfect tent" metaphorically as referring to the body of Christ.[345] This view can

---

Laub, *Bekenntnis und Auslegung*, 186; Loader, *Sohn und Hoherpriester*, 166–167.

342 See previous section on page 229.

343 Lindars, *Theology of Hebrews*, 94; James Swetnam, " 'The Greater and More Perfect Tent': A Contribution to the Discussion of Heb 9:11," *Bib* 47 (1966): 91–106; Albert Vanhoye, "Par la tente plus grande et plus parfaite (He 9:11)," *Bib* 46 (1965): 1–28; Young, "Gospel," 204; Norman H. Young, "Τοῦτ'ἔστιν τῆς σαρκὸς αὐτοῦ (Heb. X. 20): Apposition, Dependent or Explicative?," *NTS* 20 (1974): 100–104. Cf. Nello Casalini, *Dal simbolo alla realta': L'expiazione dall'Antica alla Nuova Allenaza secondo Ebr 9,1–14: Una proposta esegetica*, Studium Biblicum Franciscanum Analecta 26 (Franciscan, 1989), 152.

344 Hebrews can use the same preposition in different senses in the same context; e.g., πρός in 1:7–8, ὑπέρ in 5:1, εἰς in 7:25, and probably διά in 10:20. Attridge, *The Epistle to the Hebrews*, 245, n. 18; Ellingworth, *The Epistle to the Hebrews*, 451; Hofius, *Der Vorhang*, 67, n. 110; Moffatt, *Epistle to the Hebrews*, 121. For a study of how διά changes its meaning from spatial to instrumental in 10:20, see Young, "Heb. X. 20," 100–104.

Craig R. Koester claims that nowhere else in Hebrews does the preposition διά, plus the genitive have a spatial sense. *Hebrews*, 408. Yet, the phrases διὰ ξηρᾶς γῆς in 11:29 and διὰ τοῦ καταπετάσματος in 10:20 have the spatial sense of extension through an area and an object respectively. See also, Attridge, *The Epistle to the Hebrews*, 245, nn. 12, 14.

345 Chrysostom *PG* 63.119; Ps.-Oecumenius *PG* 119.336; Theophylact; Calvin. They base their interpretation on the basis that God's Word "became flesh" and "tented" among us (John 1:14) and that Jesus identified his body as a "temple" (John 2:21). William L. Lane suggests that "if διά is understood in an instrumental sense ..., it becomes necessary to give to σκηνῆς a sym-

take many forms. It has been suggested that the tent denotes Christ's humanity, his resurrected body, his eucharistic body, or the church as the body of Christ.[346] In support of this view, it is noted that this paragraph has a chiastic structure in which "tabernacle" parallels "his own blood."[347] Similarly, they argue, 10:19–20 introduces Jesus's flesh metaphorically as the "veil" of the heavenly temple.[348]

There are several drawbacks, however, to a metaphorical understanding of the "tabernacle." First, the fact that the lines containing "tabernacle" and "his own blood" are parallel in form does not necessarily mean that they are parallel in content.[349] Second, if the body of Christ is meant, how do we understand the description of the "tabernacle" as not belonging to this creation?[350] Finally, and more important, the justification for the symbolic interpretation of the "tabernacle" rests on Christian symbolism extrinsic to Hebrews. Nowhere else in Hebrews does the tabernacle denote the church or Christ's body.[351]

An instrumental understanding of διά, however, does not require a metaphorical understanding of the expression, "the greater and more perfect tabernacle." As mentioned above, διά modifies not only the verb εἰσῆλθεν but also the participial phrase αἰωνίαν λύτρωσιν εὑράμενος (obtaining eternal redemption). In other words, it explains how Jesus entered *with the result that*

---

bolic value" (*Hebrews 9–13*, 236). Craig R. Koester evidently disagrees because he understands διά as instrumental but understands the σκηνή to refer to the heavenly sanctuary (*Hebrews*, 408–409).

346 Christ's humanity: Cody, *Heavenly Sanctuary and Liturgy*, 161–165; Schierse, *The Epistle to the Hebrews*, 56. Jesus's resurrected body: Albert Vanhoye, *Old Testament Priests and the New Priest: According to the New Testament*, trans. J. Bernard Orchard, Studies in Scripture (St. Bede's, 1986), 193–196. Jesus's eucharistic body: Swetnam, "'The Greater and More Perfect Tent,'" 91–106. The church as Jesus's body: Westcott, *The Epistle to the Hebrews*; Bruce, *The Epistle to the Hebrews*.

347 This is the suggested chiastic structure:
A But Christ, having arrived as high priest of the good things that have occurred,
    B through (διά) the greater and perfect tent
        C not (οὐ) fabricated by hands—that is, not of this creation—
        C1 and not (οὐδὲ) through (διά) blood of goats and calves,
    B1 but through (διά) his own blood, thus obtaining eternal redemption.
A1 He entered once for all into the sanctuary and secured an eternal redemption

Vanhoye, "Par la tente," 2. Also, Hofius, *Der Vorhang*, 66; Koester, *Hebrews*, 407; Vanhoye, *La structure littéraire*, 149–151.

348 On 10:19–20, see below the section "The Ascension Is Described as Providing Full Access to the Presence of God" on page 277.

349 Koester, *Hebrews*, 409.

350 See also Hughes, *Hebrews*, 285–286.

351 See ibid., 283–290. Also, Attridge, *The Epistle to the Hebrews*, 246. The assertion in Heb 3:6 that "we [the believers] are his house" does not necessarily imply that the church is a heavenly sanctuary.

he "obtained eternal redemption." The phrase διὰ τῆς μείζονος καὶ τελειοτέρας σκηνῆς οὐ χειροποιήτου refers to one of the prevailing circumstances which makes possible Jesus's entrance *to provide* "eternal redemption."³⁵² A more literal translation of Heb 9:11–14 would be this:

> But when Christ came as a high priest of the good things that have come, *in virtue of* the greater and perfect tent (not made with hands, that is, not of this creation), and not *in virtue of* the blood of goats and calves, but *in virtue of* his own blood, [he] entered once for all into the sanctuary obtaining eternal redemption. (emphasis mine)

This third option makes better sense in my view. The "greater and more perfect tabernacle" denotes the heavenly sanctuary as a whole.³⁵³ In this sense, it is equivalent to τὰ ἅγια in v. 12.³⁵⁴ Τὰ ἅγια—where Jesus entered—is the "greater and more perfect tabernacle" because it is superior to the Mosaic (first covenant) sanctuary. This understanding fits the overall comparison between the first and new covenants in the larger context (8:1–10:18). Jesus's entrance into the "greater and more perfect tabernacle" inaugurates the greater realities of the new covenant that make possible what the first covenant cult was not able to accomplish: provide forgiveness and access to God.

This description of the heavenly sanctuary as "the more perfect tabernacle" is particularly appropriate. In Hebrews the process of perfection involves suffering and entrance into God's glory (2:10; 5:9; 7:11, 19, 28). This

---

352 I understand, then, διά in the specific sense that it marks "the circumstance whereby someth. is accomplished or effected" (BDAG, 224. Cf. Rom 2:27; 4:11; 8:25; 14:20; 2 Cor 2:4; 2 Pet 1:3).

353 Johnson, *Hebrews*, 235–236; Koester, *Hebrews*, 409; Montefiore, *The Epistle to the Hebrews*, 153; deSilva, *Perseverance in Gratitude*, 304. Paul Ellingworth argues that the τὰ ἅγια and ἡ σκηνή refer to the same heavenly reality. *The Epistle to the Hebrews*, 447–448. He strongly argues, also, that the διά has a locative sense. He does not explain, however, the awkward expression that results from identifying τὰ ἅγια and ἡ σκηνή (He entered the heavenly sanctuary *through* the heavenly sanctuary).

If I understand David A. deSilva correctly, "the greater and more perfect tabernacle" refers to the sanctuary as a whole, of which the "Holy Place" is a part (*Perseverance in Gratitude*, 304–305). This interpretation is unsatisfactory because it understands τὰ ἅγια as referring to the inner room of the sanctuary, a meaning that is not attested in the LXX or other early Jewish literature.

354 Note that the expression τῶν ἁγίων λειτουργὸς καὶ τῆς σκηνῆς τῆς ἀληθινῆς ("a minister in the sanctuary and true tent") in 8:2 is a hendiadys; that is, it refers to one entity and not two. This is suggested by the comment ἣν ἔπηξεν ὁ κύριος, οὐκ ἄνθρωπος ("that the Lord, and not any mortal, has set up") in which the singular relative pronoun ἣν suggests that the τὰ ἅγια and ἡ σκηνή constitute a single entity that has been built by God. See Koester, *Hebrews*, 375–376. Contra Attridge, *The Epistle to the Hebrews*, 217–8.

sanctuary is "more perfect" in the sense that it provides access to the presence of God.[355]

The sacrifice of "goats and calves" does not refer particularly to the sacrifices of the Day of Atonement. Hebrews 9:12 contrasts Jesus's sacrifice to those "of goats and calves." The expression "goats and calves" (τράγων καὶ μόσχων), however, does not refer specifically to the animals sacrificed on the Day of Atonement (Lev 16). Richard M. Davidson notes correctly that, according to the LXX, τράγοι (he-goats) were not offered on the Day of Atonement.[356] The LXX refers, instead, to χίμαροι (young male goats, Lev 16:5, 7–10).[357] In fact, τράγοι and χίμαροι translate different Hebrew nouns: עַתּוּד and שָׂעִיר respectively.[358] The sacrifices of τράγοι appear in cultic contexts in the Pentateuch *only* in Num 7 as part of the sacrifices for the inauguration of the tabernacle.[359] Richard M. Davidson suggests, then, that the phrase "with the blood of goats and calves" (δι' αἵματος τράγων καὶ μόσχων) is an allusion to the complex of events related to the inauguration of the covenant and not to the Day of Atonement. This seems to be confirmed by the fact that Heb 9:19 refers to the sacrifice of τράγοι and μόσχοι as part of the ritual for the inauguration of the Mosaic covenant.[360]

Hebrews also refers to the sacrifices of τράγοι and ταύροι in Heb 9:13 and 10:4. In the latter verse, the sacrifices of these animals are referred to in the context of the ineffectiveness of the annual ritual of the Day of Atonement (10:3).[361] What is the relationship between the sacrifices of these two pairs of animals?

---

355   deSilva, *Perseverance in Gratitude*, 304; Johnson, *Hebrews*, 235–236; Koester, *Hebrews*, 409.

356   Davidson, "Christ's Entry," 182–185.

357   Ibid., 183. Also, Westcott, *The Epistle to the Hebrews*, 258; Spicq, *L'épître aux Hébreux*, 2:257. James Moffatt mistakenly says that the term μόσχων substitutes χιμάρων (*Epistle to the Hebrews*, 121). See also, Lust, Eynikel, and Hauspie, comps., *Greek-English Lexicon*, 2:479, 516.

358   See, Davidson, "Christ's Entry," 183–184. The Greek noun τράγοι translates the Hebrew noun [עַתּוּד] (Num 7:17, 23, 29, and so on).

359   Ellingworth, *The Epistle to the Hebrews*, 452. In non-cultic contexts it appears also in the list of Jacob's animals and in the divine promise of abundance (Gen 30:35; 31:10, 12; Deut 32:15); see, Davidson, "Christ's Entry," 183, n. 24. In non-cultic contexts it translates either [עַתּוּד] (Gen 31:10, 12; Deut. 32:14) or [תַּיִשׁ] (Gen 30:35; 32:15).

360   The reading "καὶ τῶν τράγων" is probably original (see page 23, n. 79). For a short discussion of the text, see Metzger, *Textual Commentary*, 599.

361   Similarly, the Greek versions of Aquila (early 2d c. CE) and Symmachus (late 2d–early 3d c. CE) use the term τράγος instead of χίμαρος for the he-goat of Lev 16. Field, ed., 2:194. See especially the discussion in Young, "Day of Dedication," 65. Also, Westcott, *The Epistle to the Hebrews*, 258; Moffatt, *Epistle to the Hebrews*, 121; Spicq, *L'épître aux Hébreux*, 257. Regarding the versions of Aquila and Symmachus, see Stanley E. Porter, "Septuagint/Greek Old Testament," *DNTB* 1102.

Paul Ellingworth argues that the references to these two pairs of animals ("blood of goats [τράγων] and calves [μόσχων]" in 9:12, 19 and "blood of goats [τράγων] and bulls [ταύρων]" in 9:13; 10:4) are synonyms and, thus, both refer to the sacrifices of the Day of Atonement: The phrase "goats and calves" (v. 12) becomes "goats and bulls" (ταύρων replaces μόσχων) in v. 13 because "the young bullock of Lev 16:3 could be called either μόσχος or ταῦρος."[362] This view faces the problem, however, that Heb 9:19 identifies one pair of these sacrificial animals as belonging to the ceremony of the inauguration of the covenant; therefore, if these references are synonyms, they cannot refer to the sacrifices of the Day of Atonement.

It seems to me, then, that we have two options.

First, if these two references to sacrificial animals are not synonyms, then Hebrews' references to sacrificial animals is more sophisticated: The sacrifices of τράγοι and μόσχοι refer to the sacrifices for the inauguration of the Mosaic covenant (9:12, 19) and the sacrifices of τράγοι and ταῦροι refer in general to all the sacrifices of the Israelite cult (9:13–14; 10:1–4). Similar general expressions referring to animal sacrifices can be found in Ps 50:13 (Ps 49:13 LXX; "Do I eat the flesh of bulls [ταύρων], or drink the blood of goats [τράγων]?") and Isa 1:11 ("I do not delight in the blood of bulls [ταύρων], or of lambs [ἀρνῶν], or of goats [τράγων]").[363] The sacrifice of τράγοι and ταῦροι in Heb 9:14 is mentioned together with the "ashes of a heifer."[364] Note that these ashes were not used on the Day of Atonement in particular,[365] but their juxtaposition to the sacrifices of τράγοι and ταῦροι may have had the intention of representing all the means of purification under the first covenant to which Jesus's blood is contrasted as superior:[366] "By grouping 'the blood of goats and bulls' and 'the sprinkled ashes of a heifer,' the writer implies that *all the sacrifices of the old covenant were able to provide merely an external and symbolic removal of defilement*"

---

362 Ellingworth, *The Epistle to the Hebrews*, 452.
363 Cf. Pss 51:19 (50:21 LXX); 69:31 (68:32 LXX).
364 The ashes of a red heifer were used to cleanse those who had incurred ritual contamination through contact with a corpse (Num 19; cf. Philo, *Spec. Laws* 1.262–72; Josephus, *Ant.* 4.78–81).
365 Attridge, *The Epistle to the Hebrews*, 249; Koester, *Hebrews*, 410. Although Heb 10:4 refers to "the blood of bulls and goats" in the context of the Day of Atonement (10:3), the Day of Atonement itself represents in this section all the sacrificial systems of the Israelite cult (cf. 10:1). See below section "Jesus's ascension and the Day of Atonement" on page 266.
366 Note that the ashes of the red cow functioned as blood and when mixed with water became a "purification offering" (Num 19:9). This is because the ashes already contained blood. This is further emphasized by the fact that the ashes were made by burning a red cow with cedar wood and crimson yarn, all of which emphasized the color red (Num 19:6). See Gane, *Leviticus, Numbers*, 660; Jacob Milgrom, "The Paradox of the Red Cow (Num. XIX)," *VT* 31 (1981): 63.

(emphasis mine).³⁶⁷ In this sense, Hebrews' comparison of Jesus's death to the sacrifice of "goats and calves" (9:11–12) has the purpose of identifying Jesus's death as the inauguration of a new covenant (cf. 9:19). Hebrews' comparison of Jesus's death with the sacrifice of "goats and bulls" (9:13–14), then, would have the purpose of emphasizing the superiority of Jesus's death over all the sacrificial systems of the Israelite cult (cf. 10:1–4).

Second, if the references to the sacrifices of these two pairs of animals are synonyms, both kinds of references denote all the animal sacrifices of the Israelite cult. In this case, then, the specific terms for neither pair of animals have the purpose of identifying a specific ritual, but refer in general to the animal sacrifices of the Israelite cult. Further specification of the ritual in question is made only through the context that surrounds each reference to the sacrificial animals (e.g., Heb 9:19).

Whether we accept option one or two, it seems clear that the references to the sacrificial animals in 9:12–14 do not have the intention of comparing Jesus's death to the ritual of the Day of Atonement.

Hebrews 9:11–14 Understands the Ascension as the Inauguration of the Ministry of the New Covenant

This passage is considered by Albert Vanhoye (9:11–14)—especially the word Χριστός—the fulcrum or "keystone for the entire structure" of Hebrews.³⁶⁸ Whether we agree with his judgment or not, we can agree that this passage strikes the theological core of the exposition of Hebrews.³⁶⁹ According to this passage, Jesus accomplishes through his death and ascension to heaven what the first covenant institutions were not able to. The first covenant did not provide access to the presence of God because its institutions (priesthood, ritual, sanctuary) were not able to perfect the conscience of the worshiper (τὸν λατρεύοντα; Heb 9:8–10). Now, however, Jesus is able to cleanse the conscience of believers and habilitate them "to serve [λατρεύειν] the living God" (v. 14 NASB) because he has offered himself as a sacrifice on their behalf and has entered the heavenly sanctuary as a high priest on their behalf.³⁷⁰ Thus, Jesus's death and ascension inaugurate an age of forgiveness and direct ac-

---

367 Lane, *Hebrews 9–13*, 239. Thus, Jesus's sacrifice seems to be compared in this passage (9:14) not to the sacrifices of the Day of Atonement in particular, but to all the sacrifices of the first covenant in general.

368 Vanhoye, *Structure and Message*, 36, 40a–40b.

369 Ellingworth, *The Epistle to the Hebrews*, 445; Koester, *Hebrews*, 411. For further discussion, see Long Westfall, *A Discourse Analysis*, 202.

370 In this sense, Heb 9:1–14 repeats and develops the idea introduced in 8:1–6 that "Jesus has now obtained a more excellent ministry, and to that degree he is the mediator of a better

cess to God or—in cultic categories—Jesus's sacrifice and entrance into the heavenly sanctuary inaugurates the new covenant which promised such forgiveness and access to God (Heb 8:8–12; 9:8–10).

This is what the author wants to say with the assertion that Jesus has arrived as the "high priest of the good things that have come" (9:11).[371] The expression "good things" (ἀγαθός), which describes the benefits brought about by Jesus (also 10:1; cf. 13:21), anticipates the expression "eternal redemption" (αἰώνιος λύτρωσις) in 9:12.[372] In the LXX, ἀγαθός, is often applied to the promised land (Exod 3:8; Num 14:7; Deut 1:25; 8:1) and sometimes it was used as a noun to denote the eschatological gifts (Rom 10:15, quoting Isa 52:7).[373] It is probable that here it carries a comparative sense ("better things") emphasizing, therefore, that what Jesus offers is better than what the first covenant was able to offer.[374] In this sense, Jesus has arrived as the "high priest of the *better things that have come*," that is, the new covenant and its institutions.

Jesus's ascension to the heavenly sanctuary, then, inaugurates the new covenant. It is important to note in this connection that the heavenly sanctuary was central in the OT to God's *covenantal* relationship with Israel. Elias Brasil de Souza concluded in his study of the heavenly sanctuary/temple motif in the OT that

> the impression emerges of a heavenly sanctuary/temple fully active in the covenantal experience of ancient Israel. These covenantal activities may be thus classified in three categories. First, the heavenly sanctuary/tem-

---

covenant, which has been enacted through better promises." See especially Long Westfall, *A Discourse Analysis*, 203–205.

371 This is based on the reading γενομένων supported by mss 𝔓⁴⁶ B D* 1739 it^d syr^(p), h, (pal) geo, among others. The variant reading μελλόντων is supported by mss ℵ A D² I^vid 075 0150 33 81 it^ar, b, comp, t vg cop^sa, bo, fay arm, etc. Though both readings are well supported, the first "appears to have superior attestation on the score of age and diversity of text type." Metzger, *Textual Commentary*, 598. It is probable that μελλόντων is the result of assimilation to the expression τῶν μελλόντων ἀγαθῶν in 10:1. Thus, there is a growing tendency among interpreters to accept γενομένων as the superior reading. NA²⁷; UBS⁵; Attridge, *The Epistle to the Hebrews*; Braun, *An die Hebräer*; Bruce, *The Epistle to the Hebrews*; Buchanan, *To the Hebrews*; Cody, *Heavenly Sanctuary and Liturgy*, 138–141; Ellingworth, *The Epistle to the Hebrews*, 449; Héring, *The Epistle to the Hebrews*; Hughes, *Hebrews*; Koester, *Hebrews*, 407–408; Kistemaker, "Exposition of the Epistle to the Hebrews"; Lane, *Hebrews 9–13*; Weiß, *Der Brief an die Hebräer*; Westcott, *The Epistle to the Hebrews*. Contra, Michel, *die Hebräer*, Moffatt, *Epistle to the Hebrews*; Montefiore, *The Epistle to the Hebrews*; Spicq, *L'épître aux Hébreux*.

372 In 10:1, ἀγαθά recapitulates σωτηρίας (9:28).

373 Ellingworth, *The Epistle to the Hebrews*, 450.

374 Ἀγαθός has no regular comparative. The term κρείττων (stronger, mightier, more powerful) is one of its substitutes which, in fact, constantly emphasizes in Hebrews the superiority of the new covenant (e.g., 7:19, 22; 8:6; 9:23; 10:34; 11:16, 35, 40; 12:24, Ellingworth, *The Epistle to the Hebrews*, 450).

ple functioned as a surety for the covenant, as implied in Gen 28:1–11 and Exod 24:9–11. Second, the heavenly sanctuary functioned as a place where YHWH granted atonement and forgiveness to his people in the context of covenant transgression [e.g., Exod 32–34]. Third, the heavenly sanctuary/temple relates with the covenant inasmuch as it is depicted as the place wherein YHWH undertakes a covenant lawsuit against his people because of their breaking of the covenant [e.g., Mic 1:2–3].[375]

Note, also, that the first covenant was consummated with a covenant meal where the 70 elders of Israel ascended to a certain distance from the top of the mountain and had a heavenly sanctuary/temple vision and with Moses's ascension to the presence of God at the top of Sinai. Similarly, Jesus has ascended into the very presence of God to consummate the new covenant on behalf of Christian believers.

This idea that Jesus's sacrifice and ascension implies the inauguration of the new covenant and its superior blessings for believers is developed in 9:15–23, which compares Jesus's death with the sacrifice for the inauguration of the new covenant.

Hebrews 9:15–23 describes Jesus's sacrifice and ascension as the inauguration of a new covenant. The interpretation of Jesus's death as the sacrifice for the inauguration of the new covenant in 9:15–23 is the subject of debate. Most commentators see a semantic shift in the use of the word διαθήκη from the sense "covenant" to the sense "will/testament" in vv. 16–17 and back to the sense "covenant" in vv. 18–22.[376] This view, however, faces several crippling difficulties.[377]

First, nowhere else in Hebrews does διαθήκη have the sense of testament.[378] Thus, we should be cautious in identifying a shift in the use of this term. Second, certain peculiar expressions of 9:16–17 do not fit the understanding of διαθήκη as testament. For example, a literal translation of the clause διαθήκη

---

375 de Souza, "The Heavenly Sanctuary/Temple Motif," 490.

376 It is argued that the mention of the "promised eternal inheritance" (τὴν ἐπαγγελίαν ... τῆς αἰωνίου κληρονομίας) "provides the logical basis for a semantic shift that otherwise seems arbitrary" (Johnson, *Hebrews*, 241). Others who understand a semantic shift in vv. 16–17 include Attridge, *The Epistle to the Hebrews*, 253–256; Buchanan, *To the Hebrews*, 151; Ellingworth, *The Epistle to the Hebrews*, 462–463; Koester, *Hebrews*, 418, 424–426; Thomas G. Long, *Hebrews*, IBC [John Knox, 1997], 99; Pfitzner, *Hebrews*, 131.

377 See esp. John J. Hughes, "Hebrews IX 15ff. and Galatians III 15 ff.: A Study in Covenant Practice and Procedure," *NovT* 21 (1979): 27–96. I will follow here the argument of Hahn, "A Broken Covenant," 416–436; idem, "Covenant, Cult, and the Curse of Death," 65–88.

378 Johannes Behm, "διαθήκη," *TDNT* 2:132; Lane, *Hebrews 9–13*, 230.

γὰρ ἐπὶ νεκροῖς βεβαία (v. 17a) is "for a διαθήκη is confirmed *upon dead [bodies]*" (emphasis mine).[379] The problem is that the plural νεκροῖς is awkward if the death of a testator is in view.[380] Third, wills or testaments in Greek, Egyptian, and Roman laws were ratified or validated (βέβαιος) not upon "dead bodies" but when they were written down, witnessed, and deposited with a notary.[381] Therefore, it is difficult to understand in what sense Hebrews argues that a διαθήκη is confirmed upon dead bodies. Fourth, inheritance did not have to follow the death of the testator. In "Hellenistic testamentary practice, a testament disposition could take effect either at the testator's death, as *donatio*, or immediately, as parental distribution *inter vivos*."[382] Thus, Hebrews' argument that a διαθήκη "is not [μήποτε; lit. "never"] in force as long as the one who made it is alive" (v. 17) or that where there is a διαθήκη, "there *must of necessity* [ἀνάγκη] be the death of the one who made it" (v. 16 NASB; emphasis mine) would be just plainly false if understood as referring to testamentary practice.[383] Finally, a shift in the meaning of διαθήκη would obscure the argument because the concept of testament does not fit in the argument of the inauguration of a new covenant in Heb 8–10. Scott W. Hahn expresses this problem with clarity:

> A "testament" simply is not a "covenant," and it is hard to see how the analogy between the two has any validity. In a "testament," one party dies and leaves an inheritance for another. In a "covenant," a relationship is established between two living parties, often through a mediator. Testaments do not require mediators, and covenants do not require the death of one of the parties. Moreover, it is hard to understand either the "new" or the "old" covenants—as portrayed in Hebrews—as a "testament." If the

---

379 Hahn, "Covenant, Cult, and the Curse of Death," 73.

380 Similarly, v. 16 is awkward: Ὅπου γὰρ διαθήκη, θάνατον ἀνάγκη φέρεσθαι τοῦ διαθεμένου· (lit. "where there is a διαθήκη, it is necessary the death of the testator to be borne"). The only thing that the author had to say is that "where there is a covenant, it is necessary for the testator to die."

381 John J. Hughes, "Hebrews IX 15," 60–61. He quotes the studies of Raphael Taubenschlag, *The Law of Greco-Roman Egypt in the Light of the Papyri: 332 B.C.–640 A.D*, 2d ed. (Panstwowe Wydawnictwo Naukowe, 1955), 207–209; H. J. Wolff, "Hellenistic Private Law," in *The Jewish People in the First Century: Historical Geography, Political History, Social, Cultural, and Religious Life and Institutions* 1, CRINT (Van Gorcum, 1974), 1:543.

382 John J. Hughes, "Hebrews IX 15," 61–62. He refers to examples in Taubenschlag, *The Law of Greco-Roman Egypt*, 23; Wolff, "Hellenistic Private Law," 1:543.

383 Regarding Craig R. Koester's reference to a papyrus death-notice as evidence that "legally people had to present evidence that the testator had died for a will to take effect" (Koester, *Hebrews*, 418, 425), Scott W. Hahn argues that "the papyrus cited does not actually mention a will or inheritance as being at issue in the notice of death" (Hahn, "Covenant, Cult, and the Curse of Death," 74, n. 32; see also, John J. Hughes, "Hebrews IX 15," 62–63).

old covenant is understood as a "testament," God would be the "testator"; yet it is absurd to think of God dying and leaving an inheritance to Israel. In the new covenant, Christ indeed dies, but he is a mediator (9:15; 12:24), not a "testator." Moreover, he does not die in order to *leave* an inheritance to the Church, but rather to *enter* the inheritance himself (Heb 2:10–3:6).

Clearly, then, the mode of the inheritance of salvation in Hebrews is based on a Jewish covenantal and not a Greco-Roman testamentary model. Therefore, it is hard to see how the analogy the author draws in Heb 9:15–18 has any cogency.[384]

In view of these problems, a few authors have decided to maintain the usual meaning of "covenant" for διαθήκη in vv. 16–17.[385] This understanding is built on four facts regarding ANE covenant practice.[386] Covenant making invariably implied (1) the swearing of an oath,[387] (2) this oath was a conditional self-malediction or curse,[388] (3) the self-malediction referred to the death of the covenant maker,[389] and (4) this curse of death was often ritually enacted, often through the sacrifice of animals.[390]

If we apply the covenantal background to vv. 16–17 it would produce the following reading. The assertion "Where a covenant is involved, the death of the one who made it must be introduced [lit. "borne"]" (v. 16) would refer to the death of the covenant maker as symbolically represented by the sacrificial animals. The assertion, "for a covenant is confirmed upon dead bodies" (v. 17a) would describe covenant-making practice. The assertion "since it [a covenant] is never in force while the covenant-maker lives" would be understood symbolically, in the sense "while the covenant-maker is still rit-

---

384 Hahn, "Covenant, Cult, and the Curse of Death," 70–71. For a more detailed analysis of the incongruity of a testamentary interpretation of διαθήκη in the context of Heb 7–10, see Hahn, "A Broken Covenant," 421–426.

385 E.g., John J. Hughes, "Hebrews IX 15," 27–96; Lane, *Hebrews 9–13*, 226–252; George Milligan, *The Theology of the Epistle to the Hebrews* (T&T Clark, 1899), 166–70; Darrell J. Pursiful, *The Cultic Motif in the Spirituality of the Book of Hebrews* (Mellen Biblical, 1993), 77–79; Westcott, *The Epistle to the Hebrews*, 298–302.

386 Hahn, "A Broken Covenant," 427–430; idem, "Covenant, Cult, and the Curse of Death," 75–80.

387 E.g., in Ezek 17:13–19 "oath" and "covenant" are in some cases interchangeable. For extra-biblical examples, see Hahn, "Covenant, Cult, and the Curse of Death," 75–76.

388 Thus, the invocation of deities in covenant making (ibid., 76–77).

389 Thus, the covenant curses of Lev 26 and Deut 28, and other biblical passages that refer explicitly to the transgression of a covenant (Deut 4:25–26; 17:2–7; Josh 7:10–15; 23:16; Jer 22:8–12; 34:18–21) and refer to its punishment as death or leading to death (Deut 31:16–17; Isa 33:8–12; Jer 11:10–16; Hos 7:13 [cf. 6:7]). Ibid., 77.

390 Jer 34:18–20 (cf. Gen 15:9–21). For extra-biblical examples, ibid., 78–79.

ually alive, not yet having undergone the death represented by the sacrificial animals."[391]

This interpretation is not satisfactory either. First, covenants were not always ratified by the sacrifice of animals. Therefore, the author could not say that it was "necessary" to establish the ritual or symbolic death of the covenant maker to establish the covenant (v. 16).[392] Second, this view understands the reference to the death of the testator in symbolic terms. It seems clear, however, that the author of Hebrews is speaking of the *actual* death of the covenant maker.[393]

I have been convinced, however, by Scott W. Hahn's argument that Heb 9:15–22 becomes clearly intelligible if we understand that the author is not referring here to covenant making in general but *specifically* to the first or Sinai Covenant which is understood as a *covenant* that has been *breached* and, thus, requires the penalty of death for the transgressors.[394]

Hebrews 9:15 clearly explains that Jesus's death had the purpose of redeeming believers "from the transgressions [παραβάσεων] under the *first covenant*." Verses 16–17 explain why Jesus's death was necessary. Since this covenant was ratified with a ritual enactment of the curse of death (9:18–22; cf. Exod 24:1–11), the covenant-maker who transgressed the covenant must endure death. Thus, v. 16 should read: "*Since* there is a [breached] covenant, the death of the covenant-maker *must* [ἀνάγκη] be *borne* [φέρεσθαι]."[395] (Note that this translation does not do violence to the syntax or lexical meaning of the terms.)

Admittedly, at first sight, the second clause of the verse is circumlocutory, that is, it uses more words than necessary to express the simple idea that the covenant maker should die. He could have just said διαθέμενον ἀναγκη ἀποθανεῖν ("the covenant-maker must die"). A closer look reveals, however, that there is probably a deeper intention in the circumlocution of the second clause. The construction θάνατον ἀνάγκη φέρεσθαι τοῦ διαθεμένου ("the death

---

391 Ibid., 80.

392 "Covenants or contracts, of whatever sort, simply do not require the death of one of the parties" (Attridge, *The Epistle to the Hebrews*, 256).

393 Ibid.

394 The first covenant has been breached in the sense that the people of Israel did not meet their end of the agreement with God as established at Sinai (Exod 20–24) and renewed at Moab (Deut 29–30); therefore, their transgression has brought upon them the penalty of sin established in that covenant.

395 Ὅπου is taken here as indicating cause or reason "with special reference to a set of relevant circumstances." L&N 89.35; also, BDAG, 717. This adverb is clearly causal in 1 Cor 3:3–4. A causal sense is also probably appropriate in Heb 6:20; 10:18.

On the other hand, φέρεσθαι carries its normal sense "to bear, to endure." L&N 90.64; BDAG, 1052, meaning 9.

of the covenant-maker must be endured") asserts not that the covenant-maker must die but that his death must be borne. This opens the possibility for a representative of the covenant-maker to bear/endure the death of the transgressors in their stead. This is what happened in the case of Jesus's death. Jesus did not break the covenant (cf. 3:1–6; 4:15; 7:26–27) but he died as a representative of the covenant transgressors (i.e., as their high priest) so as to redeem them from the penalty of death (9:15). In fact, the author's use of φέρω is probably influenced by the use of ἀναφέρω in Isa 53 which is clearly alluded in Heb 9:28.[396] A similar use of φέρω, but in the opposite direction, is found in Heb 13:13. There the author invites believers to respond to Jesus's sacrifice on their behalf (13:12) by "bearing (φέροντες) his reproach" (13:13 NASB); that is, by enduring an abuse that belongs to another, in this case to Jesus.

Hebrews 9:17a elaborates on this concept: διαθήκη γὰρ ἐπὶ νεκροῖς βεβαία ("For a [breached] covenant is confirmed upon dead [bodies]").[397] This passage asserts, then, that the only way to enforce a covenant after it has been breached is to enforce its punishment. Thus, the execution of the penalty of death upon Jesus attests to the validity of the first covenant (cf. 2:1–2). The following clause (17b) confirms this idea: ἐπεὶ μήποτε ἰσχύει ὅτε ζῇ ὁ διαθέμενος ("for it [i.e., the breached covenant] is never in force while the one who made it lives" NASB). This expresses the principle that a covenant created under the penalty of death is not in force (when breached) unless that penalty is enforced.[398] Thus, Scott W. Hahn shows that the flow of thought of 9:16–22 can be paraphrased in this way:

---

396 Hahn, "Covenant, Cult, and the Curse of Death," 83. Note that according to Lev 10:17 the priest must eat the meat of the sin offering so that he may "bear" (נָשָׂא) the guilt (עָוֹן) of the people. "To bear the guilt" means that a person is culpable and "deserve[s] and may suffer any consequences" (Gane, *Leviticus, Numbers*, 196). Thus, the culpability remains on the priest—who is immune to its consequences—until the Day of the Atonement where he transfers the culpability to Azazel's goat (ibid.). According to Exod 34:7, God forgives in the same way by "bearing" (נָשָׂא) the "guilt" (עָוֹן) of the sinner. Thus, the priest who eats the meat of the sin offering participates with God (of whom he is a representative) in the expiation of the sin of the offerer by "bearing his guilt." Likewise, the Servant of the Lord has "borne" (נָשָׂא) our infirmities (Isa 53:4). See ibid., 195–197; esp. idem, *Cult and Character*, 91–105; Olafsson, "The Use of NS' in the Pentateuch."

This throws light on the argument of Hebrews. Jesus, as the mediator and guarantee of the covenant (Heb 7:22; see section "Jesus Embodies God's Oath which Confirms God's Promises to Believers" on page 210), has "borne" our culpability and thus endured the punishment for our transgression of the covenant, that is, he literally bore our death (φέρω; Heb 9:16; cf. 9:28).

397 Νεκροῖς is used as a substantive here. It refers to dead persons or corpses. See BDAG, 667–668. It is plural because it refers to the people as covenant makers who, after breaking the covenant, should endure death.

398 Hahn, "Covenant, Cult, and the Curse of Death," 84.

A broken [breached] covenant requires the death of the covenant-maker (Heb 9:16–17); hence, the first covenant liturgically portrayed the death of the covenant-maker by bloody sacrifice (9:18–21). Nearly everything about the first covenant was covered in blood, representing the necessity of death for the forgiveness of transgressions of the covenant (Heb 9:22, cf. 9:15).[399]

Thus, Jesus's sacrifice functions at two levels. It redeems from the penalties incurred under the first covenant—i.e., it has an *expiatory* function—and mediates a new covenant with better promises—i.e., it has a *bonding* function.[400]

Hebrews' comparison of Jesus's death with the sacrifice for the ratification of the Mosaic covenant implies that the latter (Exod 24) had also both

---

399 Ibid., 85. This may have important consequences for the argument of Hebrews which we can only adumbrate here. The first covenant was breached at the golden calf apostasy (Exod 32:1–14). God wanted to enforce the covenant at that time by destroying the people (v. 10), but Moses interceded for them, invoking the oath God had sworn to Abraham that he would bless his offspring (Gen 22:16–18; quoted in Heb 6:13–15). Thus, God could not enforce the covenant and at the same keep his oath to Abraham. In response God instituted the Levitical priesthood (Exod 32:25–34) and promised that a time would come to punish the people for their sin (v. 34). This implies that the covenant was not enforced then; but was held in abeyance until the time for its enforcement.

Meanwhile, according to the author of Hebrews, the law was instituted on the basis of the Levitical priesthood (Heb 7:11). Hebrews is referring here to its cultic aspect that prefigured Jesus's death and ministry on our behalf (cf. Susan Haber, "From Priestly Torah to Christ Cultus: The Re-Vision of Covenant and Cult in Hebrews," *JSNT* 28 [2005], 105–124; Lehne, *The New Covenant in Hebrews*, 119). This law was only "a shadow of the good things to come and not the true form of these realities" (10:1). This law, however, was "weak and useless" (7:18) because it could not perfect the conscience of the people (9:9), instead it was more like a pedagogical apparatus ("a shadow of the things to come") that only reminded the people of their covenant violation (Heb 10:3). On the other hand, it pointed forward to the "heavenly realities" (which include the heavenly sanctuary *and* Jesus's ministry in it according to the argument of Hebrews) that would be able to provide "perfection."

Thus, Hebrews seems to understand that the penalties have not been enforced upon the people because of God's oath to Abraham. That is why he identifies the readers as the "descendants of Abraham" (2:16) and refers to that oath as part of the basis for their confidence of salvation (6:13–15; in this context it is tempting to consider that God's oath to Abraham is one of the two things "in which it is impossible that God would prove false" [v. 15]. The other is God's oath to Jesus in Ps 110:4). Note, however, that that oath was the result of Abraham's offering of Isaac. Hebrews considers the offering of Isaac and his deliverance from death a "parable" (11:19). It is not difficult to infer that it is a parable of the death and resurrection of Jesus. If this is correct, we may conclude that Jesus's sacrifice is the place where two things happen at the same time. First, it is the place where the first covenant is finally enforced (9:16–17). God discharges the penalties of the transgression of the first covenant upon Jesus. Second, it is also the place where God fulfills his oath to Abraham to bless his descendants by making possible, through the sacrifice of Jesus, the believer's entrance into the inheritance (9:15). See Hahn, "Covenant, Cult, and the Curse of Death," 85–88.

400 Both views are introduced together in 9:15; cf. 10:29; 12:24; 13:20.

bonding and expiatory functions. It is possible, however, that Hebrews is not providing a Christological revision of the event at Sinai—as it is commonly understood among Hebrews scholars—but that that sacrifice already included both aspects.[401] The covenant sacrifice of Exod 24 had primarily a bonding function. In other words, the sacrifice of "young calves" (μοσχάρια) in Exod 24 established a bond of blood between God and Israel and a curse of death for the transgressor. Commenting on the sacrifice of young calves in Exod 24, William H. C. Propp comments:

> Because the blood comes from a common source, it symbolizes the horizontal, literal kinship of all Israelites and also their vertical, fictive kinship with their Heavenly Father. Herodotus 3.8 describes a similar Semitic ritual whereby parties to an oath mingle their blood on sacred pillars, presumably symbolizing their fictive kinship. In a Greek parallel, Aeschylus *Seven Against Thebes* 43–47 describes heroes taking an oath by touching bull's blood collected in a shield (cf. also Xenophon *Anabasis* 2.2.9).
>
> Covenantal bloodletting has another function: it represents the sanguinary fate that awaits the traitor to the pact. In 24:8, sprinkling the people is as much as to say, "if you do not keep the Covenant, your blood is forfeit like this blood" (Saadiah *apud* ibn Ezra). It follows that the blood sprinkled against the altar in v 6 constitutes Yahweh's own bleeding wound. He, too, must keep his promises.[402]

He continues, however, arguing that the covenant sacrifice of Exod 24 may have included a redemptive dimension as well.[403] It is worthwhile to quote him at length again:

---

401 On Heb 9:18–22 as a Christological revision of the OT event, see, e.g., D'Angelo, *Moses*, 243–249; Haber, "From Priestly Torah to Christ Cultus," 108–112. For a list on the ways in which Hebrews deviates from the account of Exod 24, see Moffatt, *Epistle to the Hebrews*, 129–130.

Thus, if the covenant sacrifice of Exod 24 did not include a redemptive aspect in addition to its covenantal bonding, Hebrews sees in the use of blood a prefiguration of the expiatory function of Jesus's sacrifice in addition to its bonding function because in the cult of the first covenant the shedding of blood had mainly an expiatory function—as Hebrews points out (Heb 9:22).

402 William H. C. Propp, *Exodus 19–40*, AB 2A (Doubleday, 2006), 308. See also, Douglas K. Stuart, *Exodus*, NAC 2 (Broadman & Holman, 2006), 552. For the covenant sacrifice as a substitution ritual that represents the sanguinary fate of the one who transgresses the covenant, see the examples from the neo-Assyrian period in Gerhard Hasel, "The Meaning of the Animal Rite in Genesis 15," *JSOT* 19 (1981): 65–67.

403 Moshe Weinfeld notes that the cutting of the animals that often accompanied the making of a covenant (Gen 15, Exod 24, Ps 50) was not only a symbolic act denoting the fate that will befall the one who transgresses the covenant, it is also considered sacrificial and, thus,

Apropos of circumcision and the paschal rite, I have had occasion to describe the Arab rite of *fidya/fedu* 'redemption,' wherein, during rites of passage, blood is applied to persons or things—originally to repel demons. In Exodus 24, "Covenant blood" has a similar purifying, protective function. According to Zech 9:11, for example, "covenant blood" liberates captives from "the pit" (i.e., exile).

Exodus 24 may in fact be read as the mirror image of the *Pesaḥ*. The blood ritual in Exodus 12 initiates Israel's freedom; the blood ritual of Exodus 24 terminates it. Released from involuntary servitude to Pharaoh, Israel voluntarily enters Yahweh's servitude. (Compare 21:6, where a man becomes a permanent slave by standing "before the Deity" and having blood drawn from his ear.) Later Judaism would apply the phrase of 24:8, *dam bərît* 'Covenant blood,' to the surgical operations whereby each Jewish boy separately enters into the Covenant, symbolically dramatizing the conceit that all later generations stood with their ancestors at Sinai (see already Deut 5:2–4; 29:13–14). The people will finally leave Sinai after making the second *Pesaḥ*.

In 19:6, Yahweh promised to make Israel "a priests' kingdom and a holy nation." The prerogative of holy priesthood is to approach God without suffering harm. The blood of Exodus 24 functions like the blood applied to the priest in 29:20, 21: it is a symbolic wound that confers protection from the divine presence. From Sinai onward, all Israel is Yahweh's "priests' kingdom and holy nation." In confirmation that the rite of passages has been efficacious, Exodus 24 describes Israel's representative elders beholding God unscathed.[404]

Thus, for William H. C. Propp, the sacrifice of Exod 24 has three functions: It is a sacrifice that consummates (1) the covenantal bond between YHWH and Israel, (2) the redemption of Israel from servitude from Egypt, and (3) consecrates the nation to priesthood.

Note that *Targum Onqelos* interprets also the sacrifice of Exod 24 as providing atonement. It translates Exod 24:8 in this way: "Moses took the blood

---

subordinate to the laws of the cult (M. Weinfeld, "בְּרִית," *TDOT* 2:262–3; Hasel, "The Animal Rite of Gen 15.")

It is noteworthy that the "blood of the covenant"—which ratified the first covenant (דַּם הַבְּרִית; Exod 24:8)—is mentioned in Zech 9:11 as the basis of God's redemption of Israel (בְּדַם בְּרִיתֵךְ שִׁלַּחְתִּי אֲסִירַיִךְ; lit. "because the blood of your covenant [i.e., of my covenant with you], I will set your prisoners free") and not as the basis of Israel's punishment. See Meyers and Meyers, *Zechariah 9–14*, 139–40. Cf. Ezek 16:59–63.

404 Propp, *Exodus 19–40*, 309. He actually makes a reference to Heb 9:19–22 in this context.

and sprinkled (it) on the altar *as an atonement for the people*. He said, 'This is the blood of the covenant which the Lord has made with you concerning all these things" (emphasis mine).[405] This is very significant because—as I mentioned above—Jesus's death as a covenant sacrifice both mediates a new covenant and redeems from transgressions under the first covenant.

Hebrews includes, however, two other dimensions that we need to explore. Jesus's new covenant sacrifice implies as well the consecration of the heavenly sanctuary and of the believers as priests.

The inauguration of the new covenant includes the consecration of the heavenly sanctuary. It is important to note in this connection that Hebrews' description of the inauguration of the first covenant deviates from the account of Exod 24:1–11 in several respects.

> Hence not even the first covenant was inaugurated without blood. For when every commandment had been told to all the people by Moses in accordance with the law, he took the blood of calves and goats, with water and scarlet wool and hyssop, and sprinkled both the scroll itself and all the people, saying, "This is the blood of the covenant that God has ordained for you." And in the same way he sprinkled with the blood both the tent and all the vessels used in worship. (Heb 9:18–21)

Exodus 24 refers to the sacrifices of μοσχάρια ("young bulls") but Hebrews to the sacrifices of μόσχων ("calves") and τράγων ("goats").[406] Hebrews inserts "with water and scarlet wool and hyssop." Exodus 24 does not refer to the sprinkling of "the scroll." Hebrews changes ἰδοὺ τὸ αἷμα ... ("Behold, the blood ...") to τοῦτο τὸ αἷμα ... ("This is the blood ...").[407] Hebrews follows a later Jewish view (e.g., Josephus *Ant* 3.8.6) that Moses used blood to sprinkle the tent and the vessels used for worship, but Exod 40:9–10 and Lev 8:10–11 refer to the use of oil.[408] The most striking deviation is, however, that Hebrews merges the

---

405 Israel Drazin, *Targum Onkelos to Exodus: An English Translation of the Text with Analysis and Commentary* (Ktav, Center for Judaic Studies University of Denver and Society for Targumic Studies, 1990), 238.

406 For the reading "καὶ τῶν τράγων," see page 23, n. 79.

407 Luke T. Johnson mentions five other ways in which the explicit quotation of Exod 24:8 differs from the LXX. He suggests that the author of Hebrews is consciously or unconsciously accommodating Moses's words to those of Jesus (Johnson, *Hebrews*, 241).

408 Moffatt, *Epistle to the Hebrews*, 129–130. For further analysis, see D'Angelo, *Moses*, 243–249; Haber, "From Priestly Torah to Christ Cultus," 108–12.

ratification ceremony of the first covenant with the ceremony for the consecration of the tent found in Num 7:1.[409]

These deviations, however, are important for the argument of Hebrews. They make possible the description of the sacrifice of Christ as a complex event that included—in addition to its bonding and expiatory functions (see previous section on page 242)—the consecration of the heavenly sanctuary (9:23) and the inauguration of the believers' priestly access to the presence of God (10:19–23).[410]

Thus, the author of Hebrews extrapolates from his description of the inauguration of the first covenant and the tent with blood that there was a need of better sacrifices for the "heavenly things":

> Thus it was necessary for the sketches of the heavenly things to be purified with these [τούτοις] rites, but the heavenly things themselves need better sacrifices than these. (Heb 9:23)

The problem of this passage is that it describes the heavenly things as in need of cleansing. Why would they need to be cleansed?[411]

A majority of commentators understand v. 23, in one way or another, not as a reference to the cleansing of heaven itself. For example, Crysostom and

---

409 "Even if the author of Hebrews is not trying to suggest that the consecration of the tent took place as part of the covenant ceremony, he certainly intends it to be understood as an extension of that ceremony" (D'Angelo, *Moses*, 244).

410 The building of a sanctuary was an integral part of the covenant between God and Israel. It was ordered in the context of the establishment of the covenant (Exod 25) and had the purpose of providing a residence for God in the midst of its people (Exod 25:8) and as a means of communication (v. 22). This was accomplished with the inauguration of the sanctuary (Lev 9:23–24; Num 7:89).

Mary Rose D'Angelo has suggested that the inclusion of the consecration of the sanctuary in the inauguration of the covenant ceremony may agree with the description of Moses's vision at Mount Sinai (Exod 25:40, quoted in Heb 8:6, *Moses*, 231–236). According to Hebrews, the vision was given when Moses "was about to erect [ἐπιτελεῖν] the tent" (Heb 8:5). This explanation of the circumstances of the vision connects the inauguration of the covenant and the building of the tent. (I remain unconvinced by D'Angelo's argument that "Hebrews does not mean to cite Ex. 25.40 in 8.5 but rather refers to another oracle, or a repetition of this oracle on another occasion" (*Moses*, 234). She argues, however, that the vision referred not only to the building of the tent, but also to its consecration. She argues that the verb ἐπιτελεῖν may mean "to complete, finish, or accomplish" (a building in this case; e.g., 1 Esd 4:55); or, "discharge a religious duty, celebrate" (*Moses*, 233). Cf. LSJ, 665. In fact, Heb 9:6 uses ἐπιτελοῦντες to refer to the rites performed by the priests in the tent. From this she argues that what Moses saw in the vision included instructions for building as well as performance of the rituals. In this sense, what Moses saw in the vision was not only the "sketch and shadow" of the heavenly sanctuary but also those rituals which included the consecration of the tent.

411 Ceslas Spicq considers the idea that heavenly things need cleansing as nonsense. *L'épître aux Hébreux*, 267.

many others identified the "heavenly things" with the church.[412] But this idea is little warranted by the context. Similarly, Harold W. Attridge considers that the "heavenly things" represents the conscience.[413] This is appealing because the cleansing of the conscience is clearly referred to in Heb 9:9, 14 and in the ultimate sense the cleansing of the "heavenly things" implies the cleansing of sins committed by humans. The spatial language of v. 24, however, suggests that Hebrews is referring to heaven itself.[414] Others allow that this passage refers to the cleansing of the heavenly sanctuary. They argue that because sin affects all creation, the purification provided by Christ's sacrifice extends to all creation—including heaven.[415]

In trying to understand this passage, we need to notice first that Hebrews refers to the inauguration of the Mosaic tabernacle as a *purification* ritual. Note its description of the inauguration of the first sanctuary: "It was necessary for *the sketches of the heavenly things* [i.e., "the tent and all the vessels used in worship" (v. 21)] *to be purified* [καθαρίζεσθαι] with these rites" (v. 23, emphasis mine). Thus, the first question we need to answer is, in what sense was the inauguration of the first sanctuary a cleansing?

The inauguration of the Mosaic sanctuary was a complex event (Lev 8; cf. Exod 29, 40; Num 7).[416] The ritual consisted of three stages:[417] (1) anointing the sanctuary and the high priest (Lev 8:6–13), (2) the offering of sacrifices, and (3) anointing of the priests.[418] This complex event alternated rites of purifica-

---

412   See Bruce, *The Epistle to the Hebrews*; Montefiore, *The Epistle to the Hebrews*; Vanhoye, *Old Testament Priests*, 205.

413   Attridge, *The Epistle to the Hebrews*.

414   For a critique of this view see, Johnsson, "Defilement/Purification," 94–95.

415   Koester, *Hebrews*, 421. Also, Bénétreau, *L'épître*; Dunnill, *Covenant and Sacrifice*, 232; Johnson, *Hebrews*, 243; Lane, *Hebrews 9–13*.

It is not necessary, however, to infer that this refers to Satan's expulsion from heaven (Luke 10:18; John 12:31; Rev 12:7–9) and other evil spirits inhabiting heaven (Eph 6:12; Col 1:20). Héring, *The Epistle to the Hebrews*; Michel, *die Hebräer*. Or, that this cleansing is a kind of immunization of heaven to prevent the entrance of sin. Riggenbach, *an die Hebräer*; Spicq, *L'épître aux Hébreux*.

416   Exod 29 is a prescriptive text and Lev 8 is a description of how the ritual was carried out (Gane, *Leviticus, Numbers*, 162; Gorman, *The Ideology of Ritual*, 103–105). For a study of Lev 8, see Klingbeil, *The Ritual of Ordination*, 117–323.

417   The ritual lasted seven days. All the sacrifices were repeated on each of these days (Exod 29:35–37). See Milgrom, *Leviticus 1–16*, 541. For the structure of the ritual see Gane, *Leviticus, Numbers*, 163–164; Klingbeil, *The Ritual of Ordination*, 111–114; Milgrom, *Leviticus 1–16*, 542–544. Cf. Gorman, *The Ideology of Ritual*, 113–115.

418   The first stage included the (1) washing of Aaron and his sons with water (v. 6), (2) dressing of Aaron in his high priestly regalia (vv. 7–9), (3) anointing of the sanctuary and its utensils (v. 10), (4) anointing of the altar and its utensils (v. 11), (5) anointing of Aaron's head (v. 12), and (6) the dressing of Aaron's sons in their priestly vestments (v. 13).

The second stage included (1) a purification offering (LXX μόσχος, young bull) on behalf of the priests by which the altar is purified and consecrated (vv. 14–17), (2) a burnt offering (LXX

tion with rites of consecration and blended them in the sprinkling of oil and blood on the priests and their vestments (Lev 8:30).[419]

This alternation is most clearly seen in the purification and consecration of the altar. Exodus 29:36–37 instructed explicitly: "Also you shall offer a sin offering for the altar, when you make atonement for it, and shall anoint it, to consecrate it."[420] This was carried out—according to Lev 8:15—by Moses when he daubed the blood on the horns of the altar and then poured the rest on the base of the altar, thus purifying and consecrating it.[421]

What were the tabernacle and priests purified from? This is a difficult question and a variety of solutions have been suggested.[422] Most likely, no specific sins were in view. Roy E. Gane argues to this effect: "Since the altar was in the process of becoming qualified for its function, it was not ready for expiation of specific sins or ritual impurities of the priests or anyone else."[423] More likely, purification here is inherent to the consecration process itself and implies preparation to enter a higher state of holiness but does not imply puri-

---

χριός, ram) on behalf of the priests (vv. 18–21), and (3) an ordination sacrifice (LXX χριός, ram) on behalf of the priests by which they are consecrated by the application of blood on the lobe of the right ear, the thumb of the right hand, and the big toe of the right foot of Aaron and his sons. Parts of the sacrifice with some cakes, oil, and wafers were placed in the hands of Aaron and his sons and then elevated (vv. 22–29).

The third stage consisted of a second anointing with blood from the altar mixed with oil and includes Aaron and his vestments and Aaron's sons and their vestments (v. 30).

419 The purification aspect of the ritual included washing of Aaron and his sons (Lev 8:6), a purification sacrifice for the altar (vv. 14–17), and a burnt offering sacrifice (vv. 18–21). In fact, however, the whole ceremony was considered "to make atonement" for them (Lev 8:34). The consecration aspect of the ritual included dressing the high priest (8:7–9), anointing the tent and its utensils, the altar and its utensils, and Aaron's head (vv. 10–12), the dressing of the priests (v. 13), the sacrifice of the ram of consecration (vv. 22–29), and the sprinkling of the priests and their vestments with oil and blood (v. 30).

420 This poses a problem. Leviticus 8:10–12 refers to the anointing of the altar *before* its purification (8:15). A closer look shows, however, that Lev 8:15 interprets the manipulation of the blood of the purification sacrifice as accomplishing the (1) purification and (2) consecration in the appropriate order, though it is not clear what its relationship to the anointing with oil mentioned in v. 11 is. (Cf. Lev 16:18–19 where the re-consecration of the altar on the Day of Atonement by the application of blood and sprinkling had the same purpose.) For different solutions to the problem see Klingbeil, *The Ritual of Ordination*, 264–270; Milgrom, *Leviticus 1–16*, 522–523.

421 Similarly, Moses daubed blood on the lobe of the right ear, the thumb of the right hand, and the big toe of the right foot of the priests (v. 22–23), arguably to purify them (see Klingbeil, *The Ritual of Ordination*, 290–295; Milgrom, *Leviticus 1–16*, 528–529), and sprinkled them with oil and blood to consecrate them (Lev 8:30). The parallelism between the blood ritual for the altar and the priests is made more evident in Ezek 43:20 where the blood is applied to the altar "on its four horns, and on the four corners of the ledge, and on the border round about; thus you shall cleanse it and make atonement for it," corresponding to the right lobes, thumbs, and big toes of the priests. Milgrom, *Leviticus 1–16*, 529. Cf. Zimmerli, *Ezekiel 2*, 433.

422 See Milgrom, *Leviticus 1–16*, 521–522.

423 Gane, *Leviticus, Numbers*, 164.

fication from previous specific acts of contamination.[424] "The theological implication is that outside Yahweh practically everything is under the influence of impurity. Everything or every person who comes into contact with Yahweh must go through a cleansing ritual."[425] Cleansing is part of the habilitation of the tent and its ministers for the service or worship of God.

Interestingly, the idea of cleansing was also closely associated with the inauguration of the future sanctuary in Ezekiel. The book refers to the inauguration of the altar following closely the instructions of Exod 29:36–37 (cf. Lev 8:15): "Seven days shall they make atonement for the altar and cleanse it, and so consecrate it" (Ezek 43:26, cf. vv. 19–27). This passage contains links to Ezek 45:18–20, which refers to the cleansing of the sanctuary. It is not clear, however, if this purification presupposes specific acts of contamination. The passage says the following:[426]

> "Thus says the Lord GOD: In the first month, on the first day of the month, you shall take a young bull without blemish, and purify the sanctuary. The priest shall take some of the blood of the sin offering and put it on the doorposts of the temple, the four corners of the ledge of the altar, and the posts of the gate of the inner court. You shall do the same on the seventh day of the month for anyone who has sinned through error or ignorance; so you shall make atonement for the temple."

The event referred to in this passage is the subject of debate. Some see here Ezekiel's answer to the annual Day of Atonement of Lev 16.[427] Daniel I. Block argues, however, that Ezekiel refers here to "a one-time event, analogous to, if not associated with, the inaugural decontamination of the altar described in 43:18–27."[428] If this is the case, this passage described the inauguration of the future temple as an act of purification.[429]

---

424 See also, Milgrom, *Leviticus 1–16*, 541.

425 Angel Manuel Rodriguez, *Substitution in the Hebrew Cultus* (Andrews University Seminary Doctoral Dissertations Series 3; Andrews University Press, 1979), 110, quoted in Klingbeil, *The Ritual of Ordination*, 263.

426 Block, *Ezekiel 25–48*, 662–664.

427 Allen, *Ezekiel 20–48*, 266; Zimmerli, *Ezekiel 2*, 482. Note that the LXX places the second cleansing (Ezek 45:20) not seven days after the first day of the first month, but in the seventh month on the first day of the month, thus, closer to the date of the Day of Atonement—though not precisely on it. It is improbable, however, that this reading reflects the original intention. Zimmerli, *Ezekiel 2*, 482–483.

428 Block, *Ezekiel 25–48*, 664.

429 I have mentioned (see above section "Ezekiel" on page 95) that Ezek 45 has an intriguing similarity to Hezekiah's re-inauguration of the temple (2 Chr 29). See Japhet, *I & II Chronicles*, 922; Tuell, *1 & 2 Chronicles*, 214. Hezekiah's cleansing and re-consecration of the temple was carried out in the first month of the first year of his reign (v. 3) and was prepara-

In early Judaism, the cleansing of the temple was integral to its inauguration especially because it presupposed previous transgressions.[430] The dedication of the temple after the return from exile—which was also preparatory for the Passover according to Ezra 6:14–22[431]—included a purification of the people as the sin offerings of 12 male goats for the 12 tribes of Israel indicate (6:17).[432] Likewise, the dedication of the temple in 1 Macc 4:36–59, after the atrocities of Antiochus IV, also relates both the cleansing and consecration of the temple: Ἰδοὺ συνετρίβησαν οἱ ἐχθροὶ ἡμῶν, ἀναβῶμεν καθαρίσαι τὰ ἅγια καὶ ἐγκαινίσαι. ("See, our enemies are crushed; let us go up to *cleanse the sanctuary and dedicate* it," emphasis mine). This celebration was the origin of Hanukkah or festival of dedication (ἐγκαίνια; cf. John 10:22).[433] Finally, the

tory for the Passover that was celebrated one month later (2 Chr 30). The Passover was celebrated in the second month, instead of the first, because the priests (and the house) had not been consecrated on time for the Passover (2 Chr 30:3). (Similarly, the Passover was kept after the reparation of the temple in the time of Josiah [2 Chr 34–35]. Similarly, the celebration of the inauguration of the first temple by Solomon probably also included the celebration of the Feast of Booths [2 Chr 7:8–10], Japhet, *I & II Chronicles*, 611–613.)

In the case of Ezekiel this seems to be the case. The cleansing of the temple is ordered to be carried out on the first day of the first month (cf. Exod 40:2) and is, arguably, preparatory for the celebration of the Passover (Ezek 45:21–24).

430   Regarding the inauguration of temples in the late Roman republic and the early empire, this was accomplished through an act of *dedicatio* and *consecratio*. The first term indicated the "surrender of an object into divine ownership, the latter its transformation into a *res sacra* ('thing consecrated')," *The Oxford Dictionary of the Classical World* (Oxford University Press, 2005), s.v. "*dedicatio*." (These two terms were used synonymously, however, since the late Republic. See also Christa Frateantonio, "*Consecratio*," BNP 3:698–699; idem, "*Dedicatio*," BNP 4:167.) The ceremony consisted mainly of the pronunciation of a formula in which the dedicant transferred ownership to the divinity. For a fuller description of a *dedicatio*, see PW, s.v. "*dedicatio*."

The performance of purifications, however, was closely related with new beginnings. A ceremony of purification was called *lustrātiō*. The most important was the *lustrātiō* of the Roman people as the conclusion of a census performed every five years (from where it comes the word "lustrum") and was related with new beginnings. "The ceremony excluded evil ... but it also denoted a new beginning, esp. for the Roman people at the census or for an army when a new commander arrived or when two armies were joined together" (*The Oxford Dictionary of the Classical World*, s.v. "lustration").

431   The temple was finished "on the third day of the month of Adar" (Ezra 6:15) which was the 12th month. The Passover was celebrated on the 14th day of the first month (v. 19). Thus, it is not difficult to conceive that the inauguration of the temple was carried out on the first day of the first month. See Joseph Blenkinsopp, *Ezra–Nehemiah: A Commentary*, OTL (Westminster, 1988), 128–131.

432   Arguably, these sacrifices atoned for the transgressions that led the people into exile. See Ralph W. Klein, "The Books of Ezra & Nehemiah," *NIB* 3:712; Mark A. Throntveit, *Ezra–Nehemiah*, IBC (John Knox, 1992), 35.

433   VanderKam, "Dedication," 2:123–125. Jesus would later identify himself in the context of this festival as "the one whom the Father has sanctified [ἡγίασεν; cf. Num 7:1] and sent into the world."

James C. VanderKam has suggested that we should understand the narrative of John 10:22–39 in the context of this feast. He suggests that Jesus's assertion "The Father and I are one" (v.

Temple Scroll (11Q19 or 11QT^a) also juxtaposes purification and consecration aspects in the inauguration ritual (11Q19 XV, 16–18; cf. Exod 29:10; Lev 8:14).[434]

Thus, Hebrews' reference to the inauguration of the first sanctuary as a purification ritual is not awkward.[435] The flow of the argument suggests that the author is describing here an antitypical day of inauguration and not an antitypical Day of Atonement.[436] Hebrews introduces 9:23 with the coordinating conjunction οὖν ("therefore") to signal the drawing of inferences from the preceding context. Furthermore, the demonstrative pronoun τούτοις refers back to the inauguration sacrifices described in 9:15–22. In other words, "Moses's inauguration of the covenant has become the antitype of the cleansing of the heavenly sanctuary, which must be cleansed with better sacrifices than these, that is, through the entry of Christ into the holy of holies in his own self-offering with his own blood."[437]

---

30) was pregnant with meaning because the Jews would remember on Hanukkah the blasphemies of Antiochus IV who proclaimed himself "god manifest" and, as a result, they would try to stone Jesus: 'Jesus's unbelieving audience ... sees in the divine Son only another blasphemer who, like the Seleucid king, claimed to be god. Perhaps it is also no coincidence that just two verses before the notice about Hanukkah [vv. 20, 22] one reads: 'Many of them said: "He has a demon, and he is mad ..."' (10:20: the word is μαίνεται). Is this charge meant to remind one of Antiochus whom some considered a madman (μαινόμενος)?" ("John 10 and the Feast of the Dedication," *Of Scribes and Scrolls: Studies on the Hebrew Bible, Intertestamental Judaism, and Christian Origins*, ed. Harold W. Attridge, John J. Collins, and Thomas H. Tobin, College Theology Society Resources in Religion 5 [University Press of America, 1990], 213).

434 The ritual for the consecration of the priests and dedication of the altar is described in 11Q19 XV, 3–XVI, 4. For differences in the consecration ritual presented in the Temple Scroll from Exod 29 and Lev 8, see Milgrom, *Leviticus 1–16*, 561–566; Yigael Yadin, ed., *The Temple Scroll*, English ed. (The Israel Exploration Society, the Institute of Archaeology of the Hebrew University of Jerusalem, the Shrine of the Book, 1983), 3:91–96.

435 This answers the objection that this passage speaks of "purification" not "inauguration," Johnsson, "Defilement/Purification," 96. There is no contradiction. The simple fact that the author of Hebrews refers to the inauguration of the first tent as the *purification* of "the sketches of the heavenly things" shows that he refers to the inauguration of the heavenly sanctuary as a purification as well. Note that purity is a prerequisite to holiness. Because impurity excludes holiness there cannot be consecration of an object that has not been purified first. See especially Georg Gäbel, *Die Kulttheologie des Hebräerbriefes: Ein exegetisch-religionsgeschichtliche Studie*, WUNT II/212 (Mohr Siebeck, 2006), 420–424.

436 Those who hold this view include Ellingworth, *The Epistle to the Hebrews*, 477: "The 'purification' of the sanctuary, whether the earthly or the heavenly one, does not necessarily imply any previous 'impurity': it is a consecratory and inaugural rite." Also, Spicq, *L'épître aux Hébreux*, 2:267. Philip E. Hughes: "There is much to attract in this proposal, which has both simplicity and strength" (*Hebrews*, 380). Also, Gäbel, *Die Kulttheologie des Hebräerbriefes*, 420–424; Wolfgang Kraus, *Der Tod Jesu als Heiligtumsweihe: Eine Untersuchung zum Umfeld der Sühnevorstellung in Römer 3,25–26a*, WMANT 66 (Neukirchener Verlag, 1991), 387–388. For other proponents, see Spicq, *L'épître aux Hébreux*, 2:267.

437 D'Angelo, *Moses*, 247. It is interesting, in this context, that though the Pentateuch does not refer to Moses's entrance into the sanctuary on the occasion of its inauguration (though it is presupposed, cf. Exod 40), Philo does draw the picture of Moses's entrance into the sanctuary in the context of the inauguration (*Moses* 2.153).

I want to suggest that we need to understand Jesus's cleansing of the heavenly sanctuary (9:23) in the context of the double function of Jesus's sacrifice regarding the inauguration of the new covenant. Jesus's sacrifice both inaugurates a new covenant (bonding function) and redeems from "the transgressions under the first covenant" (expiation function, 9:15). Thus, regarding the heavenly sanctuary, Jesus's sacrifice both inaugurates the heavenly sanctuary and cleanses it from transgressions.[438] The inauguration of the heavenly sanctuary is constitutive of the inauguration of the new covenant (cf. 9:1, 11) and its cleansing of the heavenly sanctuary essential to the redemption from transgressions promised by the new covenant (9:22; cf. 8:8–12).[439]

Hebrews, however, emphasizes in 9:23 not the inauguration aspect of Jesus's sacrifice and ascension, but the cleansing aspect. That is why the author decided to refer to Jesus's sacrifice as accomplishing the *cleansing* (καθαρίζω) of "the heavenly things."[440] This refers back to the redemption from the transgression committed under the first covenant (9:15). This is confirmed in 10:18 where ἄφεσις is used absolutely—in a statement that epitomizes the argument thus far—to refer to the forgiveness of sin promised in the new covenant of Jer 31:31–34. (Note that the καθαρίζω of the heavenly sanctuary [v. 23] parallels the ἄφεσις of v. 22.)[441] Thus, the important thing about the inauguration of the new covenant for the author of Hebrews is that it provides forgiveness of sin (ἄφεσις), while the first covenant could not. He will explain in 9:24–10:18 that Jesus's ministry in the heavenly sanctuary accomplishes this in two phases. First, Jesus will "appear in the presence of God" in order to "remove sin by the sacrifice of himself" (εἰς ἀθέτησιν [τῆς] ἁμαρτίας, 9:25–26). Second, he will "appear a second time ... to save those who are eagerly waiting for him" (9:27–28).[442]

---

438 In this sense Craig R. Koester is correct when he concludes that "since sin affects all creation, Christ's work extends to all creation," including the heavenly sanctuary (*Hebrews*, 421).

439 For a study of how the expiation of transgression implies the cleansing of the heavenly sanctuary in the sense that there has been a tainting of God's justice and holiness, see Gane, *Cult and Character*, chs. 14–16. This work expands on the original insight of Jacob Milgrom that theodicy is foundational to the Israelite expiatory system.

440 Verse 23's assertion that "the heavenly things themselves need better sacrifices [plural] than these" does not affect Hebrews' argument of the uniqueness ("once for all") sacrifice of Jesus. Luke T. Johnson is correct in arguing that "this may be a case where grammatical choice is governed by the logic of the image rather than by the logic of the argument" (*Hebrews*, 243).

441 Attridge, *The Epistle to the Hebrews*, 261.

442 The multiple functions of the sacrifice of Jesus should not disconcert us. In fact, we should expect this because "in Hebrews Christ's sacrifice is the offering *par excellence* against which all other offerings are measured" (emphasis original). Haber, "From Priestly Torah to Christ Cultus," 117. Similarly, "le sacrifice du Christ résumant d'ailleurs en lui toutes les espèces

Summary

I have argued in this section that Heb 9:11–14 describes Jesus's ascension to heaven as an entrance into the heavenly sanctuary. Against the majority position, I suggest that Hebrews does not describe this entrance as an eschatological or transcendental Day of Atonement, but as the inauguration of Jesus's ministry in heaven and—therefore—of the new covenant. I have argued that Heb 9:11–14 does not refer to Jesus's entrance specifically into the heavenly holy of holies but into the heavenly sanctuary in general.[443] (Τὰ ἅγια denotes the sanctuary in general and not the holy of holies in particular. The expression "the greater and perfect tent" refers also to the heavenly sanctuary.) This agrees with the flow of the argument in the section. First, the contrast developed between 9:1–10 and 9:11–4 is a contrast between covenants—including a contrast of their sanctuaries and ministries—and not of specific rituals; therefore, Jesus's transition implies a transition from the earthly sanctuary of the first covenant to the heavenly sanctuary of the new covenant. Second, the function of the Day of Atonement in 9:1–10 is to illustrate the transition between covenants and not specifically Jesus's entrance into the heavenly sanctuary. Third, neither the blood of "goats and calves" nor the blood of "goats and bulls" refers specifically to the sacrifices of the Day of Atonement.

I have argued that this is further confirmed by the fact that the immediately following section (9:15–23) interprets Jesus's death and ascension as the inauguration of the new covenant, which, in the argument of Hebrews, implies the inauguration of the heavenly sanctuary.

The Ascension Inaugurates the Fulfillment of the New Covenant Promises (Hebrews 9:24–28)

Hebrews 9:24 contains the second explicit reference to Jesus's ascension in this section:

---

de sacrifices en usage dans le culte israëlite" ("… moreover, the sacrifice of Christ summarizes all the kinds of sacrifices in use in the Israelite cult"), (Spicq, *L'epître aux Hébreux*, 2:266).

443 Heb 6:19–20 and 10:19–23 refer specifically to Jesus's entrance "within the veil," an expression that denotes the holy of holies (see page 203, n. 230). This image is used in 6:19 in the context of the inauguration of Jesus's priesthood to refer to the total access he enjoys to the presence of God. The image of entering "through the curtain" in 10:20 (referring to the holy of holies again) refers again to the total access believers enjoy by virtue of Jesus's sacrifice. I will suggest below that the imagery of 10:19–22 describes the privileges of the believers as the inauguration of a priestly function of access. See section "The Ascension as the Basis for Exhortation (10:19–25)" on page 281.

οὐ γὰρ εἰς χειροποίητα εἰσῆλθεν ἅγια Χριστός, ἀντίτυπα τῶν ἀληθινῶν, ἀλλ' εἰς αὐτὸν τὸν οὐρανόν, νῦν ἐμφανισθῆναι τῷ προσώπῳ τοῦ θεοῦ ὑπὲρ ἡμῶν

For Christ did not enter a sanctuary made by human hands, a mere copy of the true one, but he entered into heaven itself, now to appear in the presence of God on our behalf.

The purpose of this verse and the following (Heb 9:24–28) is to explain what happened when Jesus entered into the heavenly sanctuary after the ascension.[444] Verse 23 said that if "the sketches of the heavenly things (i.e., the heavenly sanctuary and its utensils, v. 21)"[445] were purified with the sacrifices of the inauguration of the first covenant (cf. 9:15–22), "the heavenly things themselves need better sacrifices than these." The γάρ that introduces v. 24 marks the development of the contrast between the heavenly things and their earthly counterparts which the author introduced in v. 23.[446] Thus, in brief terms, this passage explains the ministry of Jesus in the heavenly sanctuary in order to bring about the "purification" of the heavenly things.

---

444 Jesus's ascension is described here as entering *heaven itself*; that is, not "a sanctuary [ἅγια] made by hands, a mere copy of the true one" (9:24). The description of the earthly sanctuary as "a mere copy of the true one" implies the existence of a heavenly sanctuary (cf. Heb 8:5; quoting Exod 25:40). Regarding the reality of a heavenly sanctuary in the worldview of the Hebrew Bible and the ANE, see de Souza, "The Heavenly Sanctuary/Temple Motif"; also Beale, *The Temple and the Church's Mission*, 31–44. Commonly agreed references to a heavenly sanctuary in the OT include Gen 28:11–22; Exod 25:8–9, 40; 2 Sam 22:7=Ps 18:6; Pss 29:9; 150:1; Isa 6:1–8; Zech 2:17; 3:1–10. Elias Brasil de Souza suggests a total of 43 references in the Hebrew Bible. For the idea of a heavenly sanctuary in the ANE, see de Souza, "The Heavenly Sanctuary/ Temple Motif," 26–82. Regarding the idea of a heavenly sanctuary in Jewish and Greek literature, see McKelvey, *The New Temple*, 25–41. He refers, e.g., to *1 En.* 14:16–18, 20; 26:1–2; 90:28–36; 91:13; 71:5–7; *T. Levi* 3:4–6; 5:1–2; *2 Bar.* 4:2–6; *4 Ezra* 10:44, 48–50; Philo *Moses* 2.74–76; 1.158; *QE* 2.52–82; Plato *Resp.* 9.592 a, b. (some passages refer to the heavenly Jerusalem implying the presence of a temple there). Regarding the idea of a heavenly sanctuary in the NT, see Beale, *The Temple and the Church's Mission*; McKelvey, *The New Temple*, 140–178. References in the NT include John 1:51; 14:2–3; 4:26; 2 Cor 5:1–5; Rev 4–20. (Again, some passages refer to the heavenly Jerusalem implying the presence of a temple there.) For typological language and the relationship between the earthly and heavenly sanctuary in the argument of Hebrews, see Richard M. Davidson, *Typology in Scripture: A Study of Hermeneutical Τυπος Structures*, AUSDDS 2 (Andrews University Press, 1981), 336–367. For the argument that τὰ ἅγια refers to the tabernacle as a whole and not to the holy of holies in particular, see above section "Τὰ ἅγια denotes the Sanctuary of the new covenant" on page 229.

445 The heavenly things refers only, in my view, to "the tent and all the vessels used in worship" (v. 21) because these were the only ones explicitly identified in Hebrews as being modeled after a heavenly pattern (Heb 8:5).

446 Ellingworth, *The Epistle to the Hebrews*, 480.

Since this passage describes Jesus's ministry as the act of "appearing in the presence of God on our behalf," I will explore first the meaning of this phrase and then the role of this image in the argument of Heb 9:24–28.

Ascension as an Act of Appearance before God on Our Behalf

Hebrews explains that Jesus entered the heavenly sanctuary ἐμφανισθῆναι τῷ προσώπῳ τοῦ θεοῦ ὑπὲρ ἡμῶν (lit., "in order to appear before the face of God in our behalf"). This expression is equivalent to the Hebrew יֵרָאֶה אֶל־(אֶת־)פְּנֵי יְהוָה (lit. "to be seen before the face of God") which was "a technical term for a cultic encounter with the deity."[447] It referred to people coming to the sanctuary in order to worship the Lord (Ps 42:2 [LXX 41:3]; cf. Deut 31:11; Isa 1:12).[448] This act implied a pilgrimage up to Jerusalem and bringing an offering. The Israelites were, in fact, required to make this pilgrimage to "appear before the Lord" three times a year, and it was clearly indicated that they should bring an offering in order to worship the Lord (Exod 23:15; 17; 34:23; Deut 16:16).[449]

Here the author of Hebrews describes Jesus as accomplishing the ideal act of worship in the Israelite cult. Jesus has made the ultimate pilgrimage and has arrived before the very presence of God. He has arrived at the heavenly sanctuary, "the true one," in order to "appear" (ἐμφανισθῆναι) before God not empty-handed but with a "better sacrifice" (v. 23)—his own blood. Note that in the argument of Hebrews Jesus is a forerunner into the presence of God (6:19–20; cf. 12:1–3; 2:10) who realizes the ideal of believers who journey "seeking a homeland," desiring "a better country," looking "forward to the city ... whose architect and builder is God" (Heb 11:10, 13–16).[450]

Now the fact that Jesus has appeared "on our behalf" implies a second purpose as well. Mark S. Smith has shown that the purpose of pilgrimage in ancient Israel was to "see God" (e.g., Ps 42:2 [LXX 41:3]).[451] This meant to ex-

---

447 H. Simian-Yofre, "פָּנִים," *TDOT* 11:604–605. The expression אֶל־פְּנֵי יְהוָה (lit. "before the face of God") was translated in the LXX either with τῷ προσώπῳ τοῦ θεοῦ (lit. "in the face of God"; e.g., Ps 41:3) or ἐνώπιον τοῦ θεοῦ ("before God"; e.g., Exod 23:15, 17; 34:23; Deut 31:11) or ἐναντίον τοῦ θεοῦ ("before God"; e.g., Deut 16:16). See Johnson, *Hebrews*, 243.

On the other hand, Hebrews does not seem to use ἐμφανισθῆναι in a different sense to the LXX's ὀφθήσομαι. Note that Hebrews' ἐμφανισθῆναι τῷ προσώπῳ τοῦ θεοῦ is equivalent to the LXX's ὀφθήσομαι τῷ προσώπῳ τοῦ θεοῦ in Ps 41:3 (MT 42:3). See Koester, *Hebrews*, 422; Ellingworth, *The Epistle to the Hebrews*, 480. See also BDAG, 325–326, and TDNT, 9:7.

448 Similar expressions in the NT are found in Matt 18:10; Rev 22:4.

449 Simian-Yofre, "פָּנִים," 604–605..

450 For the motif of pilgrimage in Hebrews, see Käsemann, *The Wandering People of God*; William G. Johnsson, "Pilgrimage Motif in the Book of Hebrews," *JBL* 97 (1978): 239–251.

451 Mark S. Smith, " 'Seeing God in the Psalms': The Background of the Beatific Vision in the Hebrew Bible," *CBQ* 50 (1988): 171–183; Mark S. Smith, *The Pilgrimage Pattern in Exodus*, JSOTSup 239 (Sheffield Academic, 1997), 100–109.

perience God's favor (Pss 17:15 [16:15]; 42:3 [41:3]).[452] Similarly, the Hebrew expression to "seek the face of God" meant to ask God for help (2 Sam 21:1; 2 Chr 7:14; Pss 27:8 [26:8 LXX]; 105:4 [104:4] Hos 5:15).[453] This sense is appropriate here because Hebrews emphasizes that Jesus's sacrifice and ascension to the presence of God qualify him to provide help to the believers (2:18; 4:15–16; 7:25).[454] This verse, then, is equivalent to Heb 7:25 where it is said that Jesus has been appointed as a high priest in order that he might "intercede" in behalf of believers.[455] The question is, What is Jesus interceding for in our behalf?

The Ascension Has the Purpose of Removing Sin and Executing Judgment

The context of the passage (vv. 24–28) suggests the purpose for Jesus's appearance before God. Verse 26 explains that "[Jesus] has appeared [πεφανέρωται] once for all at the end of the age *to remove sin by the sacrifice of himself*" (emphasis mine).

It is necessary, however, to ask two questions regarding this passage and its relationship to v. 24. First, is it possible to identify Jesus's "appearance" (πεφανέρωται) in v. 26 as the same event referred to as Jesus's "appearance" (ἐμφανισθῆναι) "in the presence of God" in v. 24? Second, how should we understand the expression "to remove sin" (εἰς ἀθέτησιν [τῆς] ἁμαρτίας)?

Hebrews 9:26 probably has a wider focus than v. 24. There, the author referred specifically to Jesus's entrance into the heavenly sanctuary. In this passage, however, no specific mention is made of Jesus's entrance into heaven, only the general statement that "he [Jesus] has appeared [πεφανέρωται] once for all at the end of the age to remove sin by the sacrifice of himself."[456] Now, in what sense has Jesus "appeared [πεφανέρωται] once for all at the end of the age" according to v. 26?

The use of the verbal form πεφανέρωται (manifest, reveal) creates a verbal connection to Heb 9:8 where it was said that "the way into the sanctuary has

---

452 Simian-Yofre, "פָּנִים," 605; Koester, *Hebrews*, 422.

453 It is used in a general sense of seeking out a person with authority (e.g., 1 Kgs 10:24, par. 2 Chr 9:23; Prov 29:26); see Simian-Yofre, "פָּנִים," 598–599.

454 Johnson, *Hebrews*, 243–244; Koester, *Hebrews*, 422.

455 Johnson, *Hebrews*, 243–244.

456 The expression συντελείᾳ τῶν αἰώνων—with some variations—is common in Jewish apocalypses; e.g., Dan 9:27; 11:35; 12:13; *T. Dan* 11:3; *T. Levi* 10:2; *T. Benj.* 11:3; 1QM I, 5 (cf. Matt 13:39, 40, 49; 24:3; 28:20). See Attridge, *The Epistle to the Hebrews*, 264; Ellingworth, *The Epistle to the Hebrews*, 484–485; Johnson, *Hebrews*, 244; Koester, *Hebrews*, 422.

That Christ's incarnation, death, and resurrection have inaugurated the time of the end is a common concept in the NT (e.g., Heb 1:2; cf. Acts 2:17; Gal 4:14). See Bruce, *The Epistle to the Hebrews*.

not yet been disclosed [πεφανερῶσθαι] as long as the first tent is still standing." This connection, however, is more than incidental.[457] The manifestation of Jesus Christ at the end of the age (1:2; 9:11, 26) has put an end to the sacrificial system of the first tent (10:18) and opened the way into the heavenly sanctuary (10:20). Thus, the "manifestation" of Christ has brought about another "manifestation": that of the way of the sanctuary into the presence of God (9:8; cf. 10:19–23).[458] I have not answered yet, however, in what sense Christ has been manifested.

Hebrews changes in this verse (9:26), from the imagery of the Day of Atonement introduced in v. 25, to the use of traditional language for the salvation brought about by Jesus.[459] Other NT authors refer to God's bringing of Jesus onto the stage of human history to save us from sin as the "appearance" (φανέρωσις) of Jesus (1 Tim 3:16; 1 Pet 1:20; 1 John 3:5; cf. Rom 3:21; 16:26; 1 John 1:2; 1 Pet 5:4). (All of these passages use diverse forms of the verb φανερόω.) Likewise, his sacrifice is qualified as "once for all" (ἅπαξ/ἐφάπαξ; 1 Pet 3:18; Rom 6:10; cf. Heb 7:27; 9:12, 26, 28; 10:10). Logically, then, the "manifestation" of Jesus "once for all" in 9:26 is usually understood as referring to the incarnation and the death of Jesus on the cross.[460] Moreover, the passage itself makes clear that Jesus's sacrifice on the cross is an essential element of this "manifestation."[461]

However, I think it is a mistake to make a hard distinction here between Jesus's appearance before God in heaven (v. 24) and the manifestation of Jesus on earth to offer his life as a sacrifice (v. 26).[462] We need to remember that,

---

457 The verb φανερόω is not used elsewhere in Hebrews. Cognate terms do appear, though: φαίνω (Heb 11:3); φαντάζω (12:21).

458 Attridge, *The Epistle to the Hebrews*, 265.

459 Regarding the function of imagery of the Day of Atonement in this passage, see the following two sections.

460 Ellingworth, *The Epistle to the Hebrews*, 485; Gräßer; Koester, *Hebrews*, 422. Contra, Weiß, *Der Brief an die Hebräer*, 490–492.

461 James Swetnam suggests that Jesus's sacrifice is the means of his own revelation. "Sacrifice and Revelation in the Epistle to the Hebrews: Observations and Surmises on Hebrews 9,26," *CBQ* 30 (1968): 227–34. He argues that Jesus's sacrifice may have a revelatory function in the NT. He presents as examples Rom 3:21–26—the sacrifice of Jesus reveals the righteousness of God—and Rev 4:1—the sacrifice of Christ provides an open door into heaven as a revelation of heavenly things. Likewise, he argues that Jesus's sacrifice in Heb 10:20 has a revelatory function: the ripping of the flesh of Christ permits the entrance into or the vision (revelation) of the holy of holies (10:20).

I remain unconvinced, however, that this is true of Heb 9:26. The text could be read in two ways: "He has been manifested through the sacrifice of himself at the end of the age ... to remove sin"; or, "he has been manifested ... at the end of the age to remove sin by the sacrifice of himself." I think that the latter makes more sense. The manifestation of Jesus results in his sacrifice for the removal of sins and not the other way around.

462 See Ellingworth, *The Epistle to the Hebrews*, 485.

according to Hebrews, Jesus's sacrifice is an event of the heavenly cult and belongs to the heavenly sanctuary (9:11–12; 23–26). Thus, the "manifestation" of Jesus in 9:26 includes Jesus's death, resurrection, and exaltation. In this sense, Hans-Friedrich Weiß is correct:

> Gewiß ist das Geschehen jener „Offenbarung" untrennbar mit dem einmaligen Eintritt des Hohenpriesters Christus in das himmlische Heiligtum (V.24), also mit seiner „Selbstdarbringung" (V.25) bzw. mit seinem „Leiden" (V.26a) verbunden, also mit seinem Opfer; sofern es sich jedoch bei alledem um ein „himmlisches", alles Irdische überschreitendes Geschehen handelt, eröffnet sich von jenem „Einst-einmal" her zugleich eine alle Gegenwart (und Zukunft!) umgreifende Perspektive.[463]

In summary, we should identify the entrance of Christ into the heavenly sanctuary in v. 24 with his manifestation at the end of the age in v. 26 because the first (v. 24) presupposes his sacrifice; and the second (v. 26), the heavenly nature of that sacrifice.

Now Jesus's sacrifice—and, therefore, his heavenly ministry—has as its purpose "to remove [ἀθέτησιν] sin." This means more than the forgiveness of sin (cf. 9:22; 10:18). The unusual term ἀθέτησις means literally "removal" of something and is used also in the legal sense of the "annulment" of something (cf. Heb 7:18).[464] Here, it refers to sin and denotes either figuratively the "removal" of sin or, in a juridical sense, the "annulment" of sin. Both uses are, of course, intimately related and a distinction between them in this passage is probably artificial.[465]

---

463 (Certainly, the occasion of that "revelation" is inseparable from the unique entrance of the high priest Christ in the heavenly sanctuary [v. 24] and, therefore, from the "offering of himself" [v. 25], that is to say, it is bound with his "suffering" [v. 26a], and, also, with his sacrifice; provided, however, that it deals with a "heavenly" happening which exceeds all of the earthly, opening itself from the "once-at-a-time" to an all present [and future!] encompassing perspective.) Weiß, *Der Brief an die Hebräer*, 490. Similarly: "But the Christ who has been made manifest is not just a Christ who has died. He is above all a Christ who is risen and who is alive" (James Swetnam, "Sacrifice and Revelation," 231, cf. 232).

464 BDAG, 24; Spicq, TLNT 1:39–40. Cf. LSJ, 31; L&N 13.36; 76.24; TDNT, 8:158–159. Beyond Hebrews, it does not appear again in the NT and only in 1 Sam 24:12 in the LXX. The verb ἀθετέω is more common and has the sense of rejecting something as invalid (nullify), or rejecting by not recognizing something (reject), or simply to make of no account (be insolent or offensive). BDAG, 24. In the LXX ἀθετέω "is frequently used for breaking faith with God and man, and for profanely disregarding and abusing something holy (e.g., God's sacrifice, 1 Sam [1Ki.] 2:17; God's law, Ezek. 22:26)" (J. I. Packer, "Abolish, Nullify, Reject," *NIDNTT* 1:74. Ἀθετέω is used in the latter sense, e.g., in Heb 10:28).

465 For example, Harold W. Attridge blends both meanings in his interpretation of this passage. *The Epistle to the Hebrews*, 264–265.

An overemphasis on the legal sense could be misleading, however. Some consider, for example, that just as the

> institution of the Aaronic priesthood has been abolished [ἀθέτησις] (Heb 7:18) ... Christ has been manifested to destroy the reign of sin by his own sacrifice (9:26). In both cases, *athetēsis* is chosen to express a judicial and official annulment; the hereditary priesthood is radically abolished; sin can never regain its power, since it has been conquered by the blood of Christ.[466]

Against this, Paul Ellingworth notes that the context does not suggest a legal connotation and, more important, that a close parallel to the legal use of ἀθέτησις in 7:18 would implicitly identify the first covenant with sin.[467] This would obviously be incorrect because Hebrews considers the first covenant ineffective, but not sinful (e.g., Heb 9:9–10; 10:1–2).

It seems better to see here more the idea of the "removal" of sin or the breaking of its power in a sense that goes *beyond* legal connotations. This passage goes beyond the "annulment" of a sentence against the believer because of sin to the breaking of the power of sin over the believer. As Craig R. Koester argues, the removal of sin—or the breaking of its claim over humankind—implies a change in the human condition.[468] This is possible because the sacrifice of Christ has inaugurated the new covenant which promises the writing of God's laws on human hearts (9:20; 10:16). As David A. deSilva notes, " 'Sin will cease' not only because sins are forgiven and forgotten but also because human beings are effectively equipped to bring forth the fruits of righteousness, living lives pleasing to God (see Heb. 11:6; 12:18; 13:16, 21)."[469] He is referring here to the idea, common in apocalyptic traditions, that the Messiah would bring about an era of righteousness (T. Lev. 18:9; Pss. Sol. 17:36, 41).[470] This passage is equivalent, then, to 1 John 3:5: "You know that he was revealed [ἐφανερώθη] to take away [ἄρῃ] sins, and in him there is no sin." According to the following verses (cf. vv. 6–10), this results in the breaking of the power of sin over believers and their lives of obedience to God.

---

466 Spicq, TLNT, 1:39. Also, Christian Maurer, "ἀθετέω," TDNT, 8:159; Bruce, *The Epistle to the Hebrews*, 231; Koester, *Hebrews*, 422.
467 Ellingworth, *The Epistle to the Hebrews*, 482–483.
468 Koester, *Hebrews*, 429.
469 deSilva, *Perseverance in Gratitude*, 314.
470 See Michel, *die Hebräer*. Also, Attridge, *The Epistle to the Hebrews*, 264–265. The same idea is expressed in Heb 10:22 as the cleansing of the heart from an "evil conscience" (cf. 13:18).

In summary, Jesus's appearance before God—that is, the inauguration of his ministry in the heavenly sanctuary on our behalf (cf. 7:25)—has the purpose of "removing sin."[471] This amounts to the inauguration of the new covenant promise:

> This is the covenant that I will make with the house of Israel after those days, says the Lord: I will put my laws in their minds, and write them on their hearts, and I will be their God, and they shall be my people. And they shall not teach one another or say to each other, "Know the Lord," for they shall all know me, from the least of them to the greatest. For I will be merciful toward their iniquities, and I will remember their sins no more. (Heb 8:10–12; cf. 10:16–17)

To reduce the purpose of Jesus's sacrifice to the cancellation of the penalty of sin is to misunderstand both the nature of Jesus's sacrifice and the nature of the new covenant. The new covenant promises both the forgiveness of sins ("I will remember their sins no more") and the power to be obedient ("I will put my laws in their minds, and write them on their hearts"). Likewise, Jesus's sacrifice both redeems from the transgressions under the first covenant *and* mediates a new covenant (Heb 9:15) which promises the power to the people to be righteous.[472]

---

471 Cf. Dan 9:24. The same idea is probably repeated in negative terms in Heb 10:4: "For it is impossible for the blood of bulls and goats to take away [ἀφαιρεῖν] sins." The author seems to refer there to the inability of the first covenant sacrifices to "take away sins" themselves, not only their guilt. If the sacrifices were able to produce faithfulness in addition to clearing the guilt for transgressions committed, there would truly be no "consciousness of sin" (10:2; cf. v. 22) in the believer nor a remembrance of sins "year after year."

472 I have mentioned that though the author of Hebrews considers the *sacrifice* as being "once for all," he envisions the *ministry* of Jesus's in the heavenly sanctuary as consisting in two phases. I would like to make only some introductory remarks regarding the second phase because it stands beyond the scope of this study. The author of Hebrews says that "just as it is appointed for mortals to die once to bear the sins of many, and after that the judgment, so Christ, having been offered once to bear [ἀνενεγκεῖν] the sins of many, will appear a second time, not to deal with sin, but to save those who are eagerly waiting for him" (9:27–28).

In other words, the experience of human beings consisting in "death" and "judgment" represents two phases in the ministry of Jesus. The first phase, "death," refers to the sacrifice of Jesus "to bear [ἀνενεγκεῖν] the sins of many." The author explained the first phase ("death") in Heb 9:25–26 where he argued that Jesus's sacrifice had the purpose of "removing sin." This fulfills the promise of the new covenant ("I will put my laws …"). It is important to remember also that the *first* "appearance" of Jesus Christ (9:26) is an event that included both a sacrifice on earth and Jesus's appearance before God in heaven.

The second phase is represented by "judgment." Hebrews 9:28 argues that the "second" appearance has the purpose of "saving" those who are "eagerly waiting" (ἀπεκδεχομένοις) for him. Almost all commentators see here a reference to the second coming. I think this is correct, but,

This helps us to understand better the comparison Hebrews makes between Jesus's ascension and the Day of Atonement in Heb 9:25–26.

Jesus's ascension and the Day of Atonement. Hebrews 9:24–26a directly and explicitly compares the Day of Atonement ritual with Jesus's ascension to heaven. The text says:

> For Christ did not enter a sanctuary made by human hands, a mere copy of the true one, but he entered into heaven itself, now to appear in the presence of God on our behalf. Nor was it to offer himself again and again, as the high priest enters the Holy Place *year after year* [κατ'ἐνιατὸν] with

---

just as the first appearance involved acts on earth (sacrifice) and in heaven (appearance before God), the second appearance should include an act in heaven as well as on earth.

This explains better the sense of Heb 9:28. The literal translation of the last phrase of 9:28 has a problem that often goes without mention: ἐκ δευτέρου χωρὶς ἁμαρτίας ὀφθήσεται τοῖς αὐτὸν ἀπεκδεχομένοις εἰς σωτηρίαν ("[Jesus] shall appear a second time for salvation without *reference to* sin, to those who eagerly await Him" [NASB]). The problem is that at his second coming Jesus will "appear" to *all* not only to "those who eagerly wait for him." Thus, the dative τοῖς αὐτὸν ἀπεκδεχομένοις *should probably* be translated as a dative of advantage. The translation would be this way: "so Christ also, having been offered once to bear the sins of many, shall appear a second time [ἐξ δευτέρου ... ὀφθήσεται], without *reference to* sin, in favor of those who are eagerly waiting for him [τοῖς αὐτὸν ἀπεκδεχομένοις] for salvation [εἰς σωτηρίαν]." In this sense, Jesus's appearance is in fact a "second time" before God, now "without relation to sin," in order to save those who believe in him. This, I believe, better explains the sense of the verse. These two phases in the ministry of Jesus are probably also meant in Heb 10:12–13 with a different (royal) imagery: "But when Christ had offered for all time a single sacrifice for sins, 'he sat down at the right hand of God,' and since then has been waiting 'until his enemies would be made a footstool for his feet.'" Note that there is first a sacrifice and exaltation in heaven (in the past from the perspective of the author) and, second, a subjugation of the enemies under his feet (in the future from the perspective of the author). The first refers to Jesus's sacrifice and intercession in heaven; the second, to the "salvation" of his people. (Note also the two "shakings" in Heb 12:26–29.)

Finally, this passage has an intriguing thematic resemblance to Dan 9:24–27 that would be worthwhile to explore. The theological argument of Heb 9–10 is that Jesus's sacrifice has inaugurated a new covenant (9:15) and a new heavenly sanctuary (9:23). Thus, it has redeemed from transgression (9:15), removed the sacrifices (10:18), and removed sin (9:26). Notice as well, that Jesus's removal of sin is preliminary to the judgment (9:27–28).

On the other hand, Dan 9:24 says that 70 weeks are decreed in order to "finish the transgression, to put an end to sin [removal of sin? Heb 9:26], and to atone for iniquity [redeem from transgressions? Heb 9:15], to bring in everlasting righteousness, to seal both vision and prophet, and to anoint a most holy place [inauguration of the heavenly sanctuary? Heb 9:23]." Daniel 9:27 adds: "He shall make a strong covenant with many for one week [inaugurate the new covenant which is in fact a confirmation of the old? Heb 9:15–21], and for half of the week he shall make sacrifice and offering cease [cf. Heb 10:18]; and in their place shall be an abomination that desolates, until the decreed end is poured out upon the desolator."

Finally, note that there is a possible allusion to Dan 7:14, 18 (LXX) in Heb 12:28 where it is said that believers "are receiving a kingdom" (Lane, *Hebrews 9–13*, 484–485).

blood that is not his own; for then he would have had to suffer again and again since the foundation of the world. (emphasis mine)

How does this comparison of Jesus's death and ascension with the Day of Atonement ritual fit in the wider interpretation of Jesus's death and ascension as the inauguration of a new covenant (and its heavenly sanctuary)?

I have argued above that the Day of Atonement in Heb 9:6–10 functions as a parable that illustrates the transition from the first covenant to the new covenant.[473] I will argue that here the Day of Atonement has a different function. It serves as the epitome of the Israelite cult, against which Jesus's sacrifice and ascension are compared and shown superior.

It is important to note, first, that in the argument of Hebrews the comparisons between Jesus's sacrifice and the inauguration of the new covenant—on the one hand—and Jesus's sacrifice and the Day of Atonement—on the other hand—are of a different nature. The first builds upon the *similarities* between both events to establish their *identity* while the second emphasizes the *differences* between them to establish their different *worth*. Let me explain.

It is clear that the purpose of Hebrews' comparison of Jesus's death and ascension to Moses's sacrifice for the inauguration of the first covenant (9:15–23) was to *identify* Jesus as the "mediator of the new covenant" (8:6; 9:15; 12:24) and his sacrifice as the "blood of the covenant" (10:29; 13:20; cf. 7:22). The comparison between Jesus's death and ascension with the Day of Atonement is of a different nature. Let's review the explicit references to the Day of Atonement ritual in this section.

> He [Jesus] does not have to offer himself again and again, as the high priest goes into the sanctuary year after year [κατ'ἐνιατὸν] with the blood that is not his own. (9:25 NJB)

> It can never, by the same sacrifices that are continually offered year after year [κατ'ἐνιατὸν], make perfect those who approach. (10:1)

> But in these sacrifices there is a reminder of sin year after year [κατ'ἐνιατὸν]. For it is impossible for the blood of bulls and goats to take away sins. (10:2–3)

These explicit references to the Day of Atonement emphasize three aspects of

---

473 See section "The Day of Atonement in Hebrews 9:1–10 illustrates the transition between covenants" on page 220.

the Day of Atonement ritual: (1) its yearly repetition,[474] (2) the fleshly nature of the sacrificial offering, and (3) its inability to provide forgiveness or perfection.[475] (In fact, the Day of Atonement is considered an annual "reminder" of sins [10:2].) These negative characteristics of the Day of Atonement are the same characteristics the author has critiqued from the first covenant. In the first place, the first covenant was not able to bring perfection (7:11, 19; 9:9). In the second place, the sacrifices of the first covenant consisted of the blood of animals (9:12, 13, 19); thus, the regulations of the first covenant are characterized as "regulations for the body" (δικαιώματα σαρκός, 9:10). Finally, as a result of their ineffectiveness, it was necessary that its sacrifices be repeated "day after day [καθ'ἡμέραν]" (7:27).[476] (Note that the sacrifices of the first covenant are always referred to in the plural; See Table 8.)[477]

The Day of Atonement, then, epitomizes the weaknesses of the first covenant. Hebrews, on the other hand, underlines the opposite characteristics in Jesus's sacrifice and ascension.

First, the uniqueness of Jesus's sacrifice is clearly emphasized: Christ did not enter heaven "to offer himself again and again" (πολλάκις, 9:25) nor "to suffer again and again" (πολλάκις, v. 26), but he was "offered once to bear the sins of many" (ἅπαξ, v. 28). The terms ἅπαξ or ἐφάπαξ (once for all) are used to characterize Jesus's sacrifice 6 times in Hebrews (7:27; 9:12; 9:26, 27, 28; 10:10; cf. 10:14). The contrast reaches its climax in 10:11–13 where the first covenant priests *stand* (ἕστηκεν) "day after day ... offering again and again the same sacrifices," while Jesus is *seated* (ἐκάθισεν) waiting the fulfillment of the Father's promise after having "offered for all time one sacrifice."

---

474   The common expression κατ'ἐνιατὸν does not mean "throughout the year" but "every year"; thus, it refers to the Day of Atonement. It appears 27 times in the LXX and 3 times in the NT (all of them in Hebrews). It is used to refer to the yearly celebration of the feast of dedication or Hanukkah (1 Macc 4:59; 2 Macc 10:8; cf. 1 Macc 7:49; 13:52), the Day of Atonement (3 Macc 1:11), and the Feast of Tabernacles (Zech 14:16). See BDAG, 336–337 (cf. 512 under "marker of temporal aspect: distributively").

475   Cf. Haber, "From Priestly Torah to Christ Cultus," 117–121.

476   Sacrifices for the high priest (and his house) and for the people were offered on a regular basis "every year" on the Day of Atonement (Lev 16:5–6). Similar sacrifices, though much simpler, could be offered on other occasions as needed (Lev 4:1–21). In my view, Heb 7:27 is not referring to the Day of Atonement rituals in particular (otherwise, he should have said "year after year") but to the need of repeating sacrifices because of the sinfulness of the high priests and people. In this sense, the phrase "day after day" is equivalent to the phrase "again and again" in 10:11.

477   Heb 9:9, 12, 13, 19, 23, 25, 26–28; 10:1, 4, 6, 9–10, 11–12. When sacrificial animals are mentioned, they appear in pairs (9:12, 13, 19, 10:4). Note that if the reading "καὶ τῶν τράγων" in 9:19 is not original, this would be an exception. (For a short discussion of the text, see Metzger, *Textual Commentary*, 599.)

First Covenant Sacrifices	Day of Atonement Ritual
They are repeated "day after day" (Heb 7:26; cf. 10:11)	It is repeated "year after year" (Heb 9:25; 10:1, 3)
They consist of the blood of animals (Heb 9:12, 13, 19)	The high priest offers the blood that is not his own (Heb 9:25; 10:4)
They cannot provide perfection (Heb 7:11, 19; 9:9)	It cannot provide perfection (Heb 10:1, 2)

Table 8. The First Covenant and the Day of Atonement in the Argument of the Letter to the Hebrews

Second, the author contrasts the sacrifices of "bulls and goats" (10:4; cf. 9:12, 19) to the offering of Jesus's body and "will" to obey (10:5–10). In other words, Jesus's sacrifice includes two dimensions, the flesh and the conscience. (These two dimensions of Jesus's sacrifice are condensed in the assertion that Jesus "offered himself" [7:27; 9:14, 25, 26].)[478] The dimension of the conscience is important for the argument of Hebrews. The word συνείδησις appears for the first time in Heb 9:9 as part of the antithesis between the first and second covenants. It refers to the individual's *internal* awareness of sin and always appears in opposition to flesh (σάρξ).[479] After Heb 9:9, it shows up again in 9:14; 10:2, 22. This antithesis strikes the core of the argument of Heb 8–10. The inefficacy of the old covenant and its cultus resided in its external nature. It consisted only of "regulations for the body" (δικαιώματα σαρκός, 9:10) that purified only the flesh (9:13); thus, its sacrifices could not cleanse the conscience (10:2). In fact, these sacrifices reminded of sins (v. 3). There was a need, then, for a better sacrifice (9:23) because "it is impossible for the blood of bulls and goats to take away sins" (10:4).

---

478 Jesus's offering of "himself" implies the sacrifice of a person as the result of a *conscious* decision over against the sacrifice of an animal that does not have the power of choice.

479 Gary S. Selby, "The Meaning and Function of Συνείδησις in Hebrews 9 and 10," *ResQ* 28 (1985–1986): 145–154. The exception is 13:18 where no opposition to flesh is present. Selby contrasts Paul's understanding of the conscience as a "positive moral guide" with Hebrews' understanding of it as "the individual's personal cognizance of sin" (147); however, Philip Bosman's study of the linguistic and conceptual development of the term in Philo and Paul shows that the concept of conscience as the awareness of sin was present from the earliest stages (*Conscience in Philo and Paul: A Conceptual History of the Synoida Word Group*, WUNT I/166 [Mohr Siebeck, 2003], 276–283). Philip Bosman's work brings to the fore another element in the discussion of conscience which is important for Hebrews: παρρησία ("boldness, confidence"). The cleansing of the conscience provides παρρησία to the individual which is essential in his approach to God (Heb 3:6; 4:16; 10:19; 10:35).

Third, the sacrifice of Jesus perfected him (2:10; 5:9; 7:28) and brings perfection to the believers (7:19; 10:14; 12:2) because it is able to purify their consciences (9:14; 10:22; cf. 13:18). The underlying reasoning is that the blood of animals, since it belongs to the realm of the flesh, purifies only the body. Jesus's sacrifice is superior in this respect because it belongs to both realms: flesh and conscience. Hebrews 10:5–10 explains that Jesus's sacrifice included his body—"a body you have prepared for me"—as well as his will—"See, God, I have come to do your will."[480] Hebrews concludes that it is the volitional nature of Jesus's sacrifice that cleanses our conscience: "By this will [that is, Jesus's determination to obey] we have been sanctified through the offering of the body of Jesus Christ once for all."[481]

There is a transition here from the external efficiency of the old covenant to the internal cleansing power of Jesus's blood. This transition is essential in the new covenant passages of the OT. They expressly indicate that the difference between the first covenant and that which God will institute is that God will transform the inner selves of the people, enabling them to obey. It is the inward thrust of God's action that is new in the new covenant (cf. Jer 31:31–34; Ezek 36:24–28).[482] (See Table 9.)

The Day of Atonement, then, works as a foil that provides the appropriate contrast to gauge the greatness of Jesus's sacrifice and ascension.

To some extent, the Day of Atonement plays the same role that the angels and the Levitical priesthood played in earlier moments of the argument. The author did not introduce the angels to explain the nature of Jesus's exaltation in heaven but as a background that brings into focus by contrast the significance of his enthronement. The angels, though considered powerful beings in the world of 1st century CE,[483] are introduced as servants, created, and transient (1:5–14). On the other hand, Jesus is the enthroned Son, creator of all things, and eternal (1:1–14). It is, instead, the "son of Man" of Ps 8 (Heb 2:5–10) who explains the nature of Jesus's exalted status.[484]

---

480 See, Attridge, "The Uses of Antithesis," 9.
481 I take issue here with the NRSV translation: "And it is by God's will ...," which makes univocal what is ambivalent in the text. The phrase ἐν ᾧ θελήματι explains the phrase τοῦ ποιῆσαι ὁ θεὸς τὸ θέλημά σου (v. 7). In other words, Jesus's will is to do God's will. Therefore, there are two wills involved in the passage, not only one as NRSV would make us believe. Cf. Lane, *Hebrews 9–13*, 265.
482 See Zimmerli, *Ezekiel 2*, 248.
483 See, Stuckenbruck *Angel Veneration and Christology*.
484 It should be remembered that the Son of man of Ps 8 is not a type of Jesus. Instead, Ps 8 is understood in Hebrews as the expression of God's purpose for humanity which is finally fulfilled in Jesus. See above section "Enthronement as the Basis for Exhortation: The Son's Exaltation Prefigures and Makes Possible the Glorification of the Sons" on page 168.

First Covenant Sacrifices	Day of Atonement Ritual (epitome of the first covenant)	Jesus's Sacrifice
They are repeated "day after day" (Heb 7:26; cf. 10:11)	It is repeated "year after year" (Heb 9:25; 10:1, 3)	Jesus died "once for all" (Heb 7:27; 9:12; 9:26, 27, 28; 10:10, 14)
They consist of the blood of animals (Heb 9:12, 13, 19)	The high priest offers the blood that is not his own (Heb 9:25; 10:4)	Jesus offered his body and will (Heb 10:5–10; cf. 7:27; 9:14, 25, 26)
They cannot provide perfection (Heb 7:11, 19; 9:9)	It cannot provide perfection (Heb 10:1, 2)	Jesus's sacrifice brings perfection (Heb 7:19; 10:14; 12:2; cf. 2:10; 5:9; 7:28) Jesus's sacrifice purifies the conscience (Heb 9:14; 10:22; cf. 13:18)

Table 9. Jesus's Sacrifice and the Sacrifices of the Day of Atonement and First Covenant in the Argument of the Letter to the Hebrews

Similarly, the Levitical priesthood does not explain the heavenly priesthood of Jesus. The author of Hebrews emphasizes that the Levitical priests appointed through the law of descent are mortal (therefore, the multiplicity of priests), and sinful (7:11–28). Jesus, on the other hand, was appointed through the oath of God, lives forever, and is sinless (7:11–28). It is, instead, the priesthood of Melchizedek that explains the nature of Jesus's priesthood. Melchizedek is a priest who "remains forever." His name suggests righteousness. And, he was not appointed through the law of descent; in fact, he does not have a genealogy.

There are, then, at least two types of comparisons in Hebrews.[485] One builds upon *similarities* in order to identify the nature and purpose of Jesus's work. The

---

485 The comparison between Jesus and Moses in Heb 3:1–6 is complex and needs further study. One the one hand, the faithfulness of Moses prefigures the faithfulness of Jesus. On the other hand, Moses contrasts with the Son; for example, Jesus is Son while Moses is servant and Jesus is builder of the house while Moses is part of the house. For a study of the relationship between Jesus and Moses in the argument of Hebrews, see D'Angelo, *Moses*.

other emphasizes *differences* in order to stress the superiority of Jesus's achievements. The first identifies Old Testament persons and institutions as *patterns* for the work of Jesus. The second identifies Old Testament persons and institutions as foils that bring into focus the greater reality of the new covenant. (See Table 10).

The relationship, then, between Jesus's death and the sacrifice for the inauguration of the new covenant on the one hand and between Jesus's death and the ritual of the Day of Atonement on the other hand is complex but harmonious. The first comparison (with the inauguration of the Mosaic covenant) has the purpose of explaining the nature and purpose of Jesus's death. The second comparison (with the Day of Atonement ritual) has the purpose of bringing out the superiority of Jesus's achievements.

The Day of Atonement and the inauguration of the first covenant in the argument of Hebrews. There is a more subtle reason why the author of Hebrews adds the Day of Atonement to the comparison of Jesus's death and ascension with the inauguration of the first covenant: the close relationship that exists between the Day of Atonement and the inauguration of the sanctuary in the Israelite cult.[486]

Pattern	Jesus	Foil
	The Son is ruler	Angels are servants
	(Heb 1:3, 13, passim)	(Heb 1:7, 14)
	The Son is creator	Angels are created beings
	(Heb 1:3, 10)	(1:7; cf. 1:2–3)
	The Son is eternal	Angels are transient
	(Heb 1:8, 11–12)	(1:7)

---

486 John Dunnill argues that a number of covenantal narratives in Jewish tradition associate the inauguration of the covenant with the Day of Atonement and identified the latter as " 'the day' in which the covenant of salvation is complete" (*Covenant and Sacrifice*, 139). He mentions—for example—that according to *Pirqe Rabbi Eliezer* 29, Abraham was circumcised on the Day of Atonement at Mount Moriah and, by this means, inaugurated the covenant; cf. *Pirke de Rabbi Eliezer: (The Chapters of Rabbi Eliezer the Great) According to the Text of the Manuscript of the Manuscript Belonging to Abraham Epstein of Vienna*, trans. and annotated Gerald Friedlander (New York: Blom, 1971), 203–204. Likewise, also on the Day of Atonement, Abraham offered Isaac (Pirqe R. El. 31) and Moses descended from Mount Sinai to give Israel the law (Pirqe R. El. 46). The traditions to which he refers, however, are late. *Pirqe Rabbi Eliezer* achieved its present form probably around the 9th century CE (Miguel Pérez Fernández, trans., *Los capítulos de Rabbí Eliezer*, Biblioteca Midrásica 1 [Institución S. Jerónimo para la Investigación Biblica, 1984], 20–21). I will argue, instead, that the intimate relationship between the inauguration of the covenant and the Day of Atonement is clear from the ritual itself.

Melchizedek is a priest without genealogy (Heb 7:3)	The Son is appointed priest through an oath (Heb 7:20–22; cf. vv. 13–14)	Levitical priests are appointed through the law of descent (Heb 7:16)
Melchizedek remains a priest forever (Heb 7:3; cf. v. 8)	The Son has an eternal priesthood (Heb 7:16, 23–25)	Levitical priests are many because they are mortal (Heb 7:23)
Melchizedek's name means "king of righteousness" (Heb 7:2)	The Son is a sinless priest (Heb 7:26–28)	Levitical priests are sinful (7:27–28)
Covenant sacrifices are inherently "once for all" (Thus, the transgression of the covenant requires the death of the transgressor, Heb 9:16)	Jesus's sacrifice is "once for all" (Heb 7:27; 9:12; 9:26, 27, 28; 10:10, 14)	Day of Atonement is repeated "year after year" (Heb 9:25; 10:1, 3)
Moses offered "the blood of calves and goats" (Heb 9:19)[487]	Jesus offered his body and will (Heb 10:5–10; cf. 7:27; 9:14, 25, 26)	The high priest offers the blood that is not his own (Heb 9:25; 10:4)
Moses's inauguration of the covenant purified the people and the sanctuary (Heb 9:18–23)	Jesus's sacrifice brings perfection (Heb 7:19; 10:14; 12:2; cf. 2:10; 5:9; 7:28)	It cannot provide perfection (Heb 10:1, 2)
	Jesus's sacrifice purifies the conscience (Heb 9:14; 10:22; cf. 13:18)	It reminds of sins (Heb 10:3)

Table 10. Patterns and Foils That Explain the New Covenant Realities

---

487 Moses's offering of "the blood of calves and goats" could fit just as well on the side of the foils because it consists of the blood of animals—like the Day of Atonement sacrifices. OT patterns—or types—are limited in nature and therefore cannot express with precision all the aspects of the greater reality of the NT. (For a list of limitations of the sanctuary and the Israelite cult system as a pattern of the NT realities, see Roy E. Gane, Altar Call [Diadem, 1999], chs. 8–9.) There is, however, an explicit intention to describe the events of the inauguration of the first covenant as a pattern for Jesus's actions. This intention is clearly indicated by the use of the adverb ὅθεν (hence) in 9:18 and the coordinating conjunction οὖν in 9:23. More importantly, from the description of the ceremony of inauguration of the first covenant, the author extrapolates that "it was necessary" (ἀνάγκη) that Jesus's actions accomplished similar things.

The Day of Atonement had the purpose of restoring the sanctuary to its original status of purity by cleansing it of the ritual and moral evils that had accumulated during the year.[488] In this sense, the Day of Atonement was a re-inauguration or re-consecration of the sanctuary.

> The ritual [of the Day of Atonement] clearly reflects the structure of a community rite of passage. More specifically, it reflects community passage to a renewed and reordered state of existence. Thus, it must be seen primarily as a ritual of *restoration*—it serves to restore the community to its prescribed and founded state. Thus, restoration will include in this context the idea of *re-founding*—a return to the founded order of creation [emphasis mine].[489]

This is explicitly shown in the fact that the ritual required that after the priest had cleansed the sanctuary with the blood of the bull (Lev 16:11–14) and the goat (vv. 15–17), he was to go to the altar in order to cleanse it and *consecrate it*.

> Then he shall go out to the altar that is before the Lord and make atonement on its behalf, and shall take some of the blood of the bull and of the blood of the goat, and put it on each of the horns of the altar. He shall sprinkle some of the blood on it with his finger seven times, and cleanse it [וְטִהֲרוֹ/καὶ καθαριεῖ αὐτὸ] and hallow it [וְקִדְּשׁוֹ/καὶ ἁγιάσει αὐτὸ] from the uncleannesses of the people of Israel. (Lev 16:18–19)

This act of cleansing and consecration of the altar was, in fact, an act of *re-consecration*. The altar had been cleansed and consecrated at the inauguration of the sanctuary, as Lev 8:15 shows:

> Moses took the blood and with his finger put some on each of the horns of the altar, purifying the altar [וַיְחַטֵּא/καὶ ἐκαθάρισεν]; then he poured out the blood at the base of the altar. Thus he consecrated it [וַיְקַדְּשֵׁהוּ/καὶ ἡγίασεν], to make atonement for it (cf. Exod 29:36–37).[490]

---

488 For a study of the accumulation of ritual and moral evils in the sanctuary throughout the year and how they were cleansed through the Day of Atonement in order to prevent God from leaving the sanctuary, see Gane, *Ritual Dynamic Structure*; *Cult and Character*, referring to aspects of Jacob Milgrom, "Israel's Sanctuary: The Priestly 'Picture of Dorian Gray,'" *RB* 83 (1976): 390–399.
489 Gorman, *The Ideology of Ritual*, 61.
490 Milgrom, *Leviticus 1–16*, 1036–1038, 1040.

Thus, the Day of Atonement brings the tabernacle back to its original state of purity and, in this sense, re-founds it or re-inaugurates it.

This relationship between the Day of Atonement and the inauguration of the sanctuary is important for the argument of Hebrews. I mentioned above that Hebrews refers to the sacrifice of the inauguration of the first covenant and its sanctuary (9:15–23) as a blood sacrifice that *cleanses* the people and the sanctuary (see esp. vv. 22–23).[491] In this way, the ceremony for the inauguration of the covenant becomes the "first of the yearly cleansings," that is, the first of the Days of Atonement.[492]

This helps us understand the logic of the argument of Hebrews. The first covenant and its sanctuary were inaugurated with the blood of "calves and goats" (v. 19). But these sacrifices are not effective because they "cannot perfect the conscience of the worshipper" (vv. 9–10). In other words, they cannot "remove sin" (v. 26) in the sense that they cannot enable a life pleasing to God in the believer.[493] Thus, the iterative nature of the animal sacrifices—their repetition "year after year" (9:25–26)—attests to their inefficacy in general and to the inefficacy of the inauguration sacrifices in particular.

This argument reaches its climax in 10:1–4. The assertion that the animal sacrifices are ineffective—that is, they "can never ... make perfect those who approach"—is that they are repeated "year after year" (10:1). The author argues that if they had been able to "perfect those who approach" they would "have ceased to be offered" because, "having once been cleansed, [they] would no longer have had consciousness of sin" (10:2 NASB). Instead, the Day of Atonement reminds them every year of their sins and their sinfulness (v. 3). The argument requires that here the cleansing of the conscience be understood as more than the "removal" of guilt to include the "removal" of sin itself as evidenced in a life pleasing to God (cf. Heb 11:6). Thus, v. 4 says: "For it is impossible for the blood of bulls and goats to *take away* [ἀφαιρεῖν] sins" (emphasis mine).[494] The "yearly" repetition of the Day of Atonement becomes, then, the *proof* that the sacrifices for the inauguration of the covenant—representing animal sacrifices in general—were ineffective. Note that, in the same way,

---

[491] See above section "The inauguration of the new covenant includes the consecration of the heavenly sanctuary" on page 250.

[492] D'Angelo, *Moses*, 247.

[493] See above section "The Ascension Has the Purpose of Removing Sin and Executing Judgment" on page 261 for the argument that to "remove sin" in v. 26 refers to a change in the human condition that enables people to live lives pleasing to God.

[494] This was the problem of the first covenant people. They forfeited the blessings because of the sin of disobedience that resulted from their unbelief (3:17–19; cf. chs. 3–4). The first covenant sacrifices—represented here by the inauguration sacrifices and the Day of Atonement—were not able to solve this problem.

the Day of Atonement in 9:8 was a parable that "shows" (δηλοῦντος) that "the way into the sanctuary has not yet been disclosed."[495] That is, according to 9:8, the Day of Atonement was the evidence that there was not access to the presence of God under the first covenant; according to 10:1–4, the repetition year after year of the Day of Atonement is the evidence that animal sacrifices, in general, and the sacrifice for the inauguration of the first covenant, in particular, were ineffective.

Jesus's sacrifice for the inauguration of the covenant, on the other hand, is effective because it is "once for all" (7:27; 9:12, 26, 27, 28; 10:2, 10). In other words, in contrast to the sacrifices of the inauguration of the covenant, "by a single offering he [Jesus] has perfected *for all time* those who are sanctified" (10:14, emphasis mine; cf. 10:12). This helps to explain the apparently harsh transition from the comparison of Jesus's death and ascension with the inauguration of the covenant in 9:23–24 to the comparison with the Day of Atonement in 9:25–10:4. Jesus's sacrifice for the inauguration of the new covenant (and its heavenly sanctuary) is "once for all"; not like the sacrifice for the inauguration of the first covenant (and its sanctuary) that had to be repeated "year after year" on the Day of Atonement.

The rhetorical strategy of the argument is brilliant. The Day of Atonement was the greatest of the festivals of the Israelite cult in the 1st century CE.[496] The author, however, chose to epitomize in this greatest festival the weaknesses of the Israelite cult in order to compare it with Jesus's sacrifice and ministry in the heavenly sanctuary (9:25–10:4). Also, he had previously used this greatest festival as an illustration of the passing away of the first covenant (9:6–10). Thus, the author transformed the climax of the Israelite cult into the evidence of its ineffectiveness (9:25–10:4) and an illustration of its own demise (9:6–10).[497]

---

495 See above section "The Day of Atonement in Hebrews 9:1–10 illustrates the transition between covenants" on page 220.

496 "It is certain that during the time of the Second Temple the Day of Atonement was already considered the greatest of the festivals" (*EncJud* 5:1378).

497 Note that the different roles the Day of Atonement plays in the argument of Hebrews are evidenced in one detail of its description which is often overlooked. When the Day of Atonement is used as an illustration of the transition from the first to the new covenant, the author describes the event as happening "once a year" (ἅπαξ τοῦ ἐνιαυτοῦ, 9:7). That is to say, just as that transition is unique in salvation history, the Day of Atonement is unique among the rituals of Israel. On the other hand, when the Day of Atonement epitomizes the deficiencies of the first covenant, the author describes the event as happening "year after year" (κατ' ἐνιαυτόν, 9:25; 10:1, 3). That is to say, the iterative nature of the Day of Atonement is emphasized to express the inefficacy of the animal sacrifices of the first covenant.

Hebrews' comparison of Jesus's death to the sacrifices of the Day of Atonement is particularly significant when studied in the context of the use of "amplification" (αὔξεσις) in Greek rhetoric. (For an introduction to αὔξεσις, see Anderson Jr., *Glossary of Greek Rhetorical Terms*,

Summary. The purpose of Jesus's ascension, according to 9:24, is that Jesus may appear in the presence of God on our behalf. According to this passage, Jesus has ascended in order to "remove sin" by the sacrifice of himself. This not only refers to the forgiveness of sin but implies a change in the human condition so as to bring about righteousness in the lives of the people. This refers to the fulfillment of God's new covenant promise: "I will put my laws in their minds, and write them on their hearts ... for they shall all know me" (Heb 8:10–11; 10:16). Thus, Jesus's ascension inaugurates the fulfillment of God's new covenant promises.

Ascension as the Basis for Exhortation (Hebrews 10:19–25)

Jesus's Ascension Is Described as Providing Full Access to the Presence of God

Ἔχοντες οὖν, ἀδελφοί, παρρησίαν εἰς τὴν εἴσοδον τῶν ἁγίων ἐν τῷ αἵματι Ἰησοῦ, ἣν ἐνεκαίνισεν ἡμῖν ὁδὸν πρόσφατον καὶ ζῶσαν διὰ τοῦ καταπετάσματος, τοῦτ' ἔστιν τῆς σαρκὸς αὐτοῦ,

Therefore, my friends, since we have confidence to enter the sanctuary by the blood of Jesus, by the new and living way that he opened for us through the curtain (that is, through his flesh) ...

This text describes Jesus's ascension to heaven as a passage "through the curtain" (διὰ τοῦ καταπετάσματος) of the heavenly sanctuary which "inaugurates" (ἐνεκαίνισεν) for the believers "a new and living way" into the (heavenly) sanctuary (εἰς τὴν εἴσοδον τῶν ἁγίων), that is, into the presence of God (cf. 4:16; 6:19–20; 7:19, 25).[498]

26–29.) Αὔξεσις was a method used to promote (or denigrate) any given matter that had already been demonstrated (Aristotle, *Rhet.* 1.9.40). Anaximenes (3rd century BCE), for example, suggested that one of the ways to accomplish this was "to set in comparison with the thing you are saying the smallest of the things that fall into the same class, for thus your case will appear magnified, just as men of medium height appear taller when standing by the side of men shorter than themselves" (Anaximenes of Lampsacus, *Rhet. Alex.* 3 [Rackham, LCL]). Hebrews, instead, compares Jesus's death to the greatest of Israelite sacrifices. Similarly, Aristotle suggested that comparisons with ordinary people should be attempted only if comparison with superior personages was not possible (Aristotle, *Rhet.* 1.9.39): "And you must compare him with illustrious personages, for it affords ground for amplification and is noble, if he can be proved better than men of worth" (Aristotle, *Rhet.* 1.9.38 [Freese, LCL]).

498 For a discussion regarding the use of καταπέτασμα in Hebrews, see page 203, n. 230. Καταπέτασμα is used in the LXX only in relation to the Israelite sanctuary. It is also used only in cultic contexts elsewhere (Gurtner, "Καταπέτασμα"). In the LXX, it could refer either to the veil that divided the forecourt from the temple proper or the outer from the inner room of the sanctuary. BDAG, 524.

The author's use of similar language to that of 6:19 (cf. 9:3) suggests that the veil referred to here is that which separated the inner from the outer room of the Israelite sanctuary. The image is simple. The holy of holies—where the ark of the covenant stands (cf. Heb 9:3–5)—represents God's throne room.[499] The imagery denotes that Jesus has entered heaven into the very presence of God with his own blood. Here, like in 6:19–20, the author emphasizes that Jesus has full access to the presence of God, something that was illustrated but not achieved by the Levitical priests on the Day of Atonement (cf. 9:8).[500] That is, "through Jesus's death and mediation all barriers between God and humanity have been broken down and we now have full access to the Father."[501]

This simple cultic image, however, is paradoxically complicated by the explanatory phrase τοῦτ' ἔστιν τῆς σαρκὸς αὐτοῦ—"that is, through his flesh"—in at least two ways.[502] First, it is not clear what the antecedent of this explanatory phrase is; that is, does this phrase qualifies the "way" or the "veil"?[503] Second, if it qualifies "veil," which immediately precedes the phrase, it needs to be explained whether the implied preposition διά should be understood as

---

The wider argument of the document makes clear that the author is referring here to Jesus's entrance into heaven (9:24; cf. 1:3; 4:14–16; 8:1–5; 9:11–12, 24; 12:22–25).

499   For the ark of the covenant as embodying God's presence, see Num 10:35–36: "Whenever the ark set out, Moses would say, 'Arise, O LORD, let your enemies be scattered, and your foes flee before you.' And whenever it came to rest, he would say, 'Return, O LORD of the ten thousand thousands of Israel' " (cf. vv. 33–34; likewise, 1 Sam 4:2–9).
For the Ark of the Covenant as God's footstool, see 1 Chr 28:2: "Then King David rose to his feet and said: 'Hear me, my brothers and my people. I had planned to build a house of rest for the ark of the covenant of the LORD, for the footstool of our God ...' " (likewise, 1 Sam 4:4; Pss 99:5; 132:7). Also, Seow, "Ark of the Covenant," 1:386–393.

500   Two elements of Jesus's entrance into the sanctuary in Heb 10:19–21 follow the description of the Day of Atonement ritual in Heb 9:7: (1) Jesus is described as a high priest (ἱερέα μέγαν, 10:21; cf. Lev 21:10; Num 35:25; 2 Kgs 12:11; 22:8; Neh 3:1; Hag 1:12; 2:4; Zech 3:8; Jdt 4:6, 15:8; Sir 50:8; passim) and (2) he enters with his "blood" into the sanctuary (10:19; cf. 9:25; Lev 16:3). Hebrews 9:6–10, however, illustrates the transition from the first to the second covenant.
Note, however, that in the argument of Hebrews, Jesus's entrance follows, instead, the model of the inauguration of the (Mosaic) first sanctuary which consisted in a sprinkling of the tent and its vessels with blood (cf. 9:18–23).

501   Ekkhardt Mueller, *Come Boldly to the Throne: Sanctuary Themes in Hebrews* (Pacific Press, 2003), 90.

502   This phrase is not a "later gloss" as suggested by C. C. J. Holsten, *Exegetische Untersuchungen zu Hb 10,20* (Bern: 1875), 15, quoted in Young, "Heb. X. 20," 100. See also, Héring, *The Epistle to the Hebrews*; Buchanan, *To the Hebrews*, 168. Hans-Martin Schenke considers the phrase awkward, but does not seem to challenge its originality; instead, he points out that this phrase complements ἐν τῷ αἵματι Ἰησοῦ—"by the blood of Jesus"— of v. 19, whose originality is not challenged ("Erwägungen zum Rätsel des Hebräerbriefes," *Neues Testament und christliche Existenz*, ed. Hans Dieter Betz and Luise Schottroff [Mohr Siebeck, 1973], 427). Finally, there is no MSS evidence to support the challenge to its originality.

503   If it qualifies the term "way," the passage would read in the following way: "by the new and living way that he opened for us through the curtain (that is, *a way consisting in his flesh*)" (emphasis mine).

locative ("a new and living way which He inaugurated for us *through* the veil, that is, *through* His flesh"!) or instrumental ("a new and living way which He inaugurated for us through the veil, that is *by means of* His flesh").[504] The answer we give to these questions will define the role that Jesus's "flesh" played in his ascension according to Hebrews.

It is possible to understand τῆς σαρκὸς αὐτοῦ as a genitive of dependence that refers back to ὁδόν (=τοῦτ᾽ ἔστιν [ὁδὸς] τῆς σαρκὸς αὐτοῦ).[505] This would yield the following translation: "He inaugurated for us a new and living way through the veil, that is, *a way consisting in his flesh*" (emphasis mine).[506] Jesus's "flesh" would be here an instance of metonymy that denotes Jesus's earthly existence through which he passed in order to access the presence of God (cf. Heb 2:14; 5:7; 2 Cor 5:16). This implies, of course, Jesus's suffering and sacrifice and parallels the concept of the previous verse that "[believers] have confidence to enter the sanctuary by the blood of Jesus" (Heb 10:19). Just as Jesus entered into the presence of God through the way of his life in the flesh (i.e., suffering), believers access God through Jesus's blood (cf. 9:12–14).

The major objection against this view has been the word-order. The expression τοῦτ᾽ ἔστιν τῆς σαρκὸς αὐτοῦ follows immediately after καταπέτασμα; thus, it seems logical that they are connected.[507] This is not, however, a strong argument. Paul C. B. Andriessen has claimed that the author uses τοῦτ᾽ ἔστιν throughout the work to refer back to substantives that do not immediately precede it (Heb 2:14; 7:5; 9:11; 11:16; 13:15).[508] Though closer analysis shows that

---

504 There is also the related matter of whether καταπέτασμα is understood in the passage as a hindrance or a means of access (Young, "Heb. X. 20," 100, n. 4; Ellingworth, *The Epistle to the Hebrews*, 519).

505 Those who relate τῆς σαρκὸς αὐτοῦ to ὁδόν include Westcott, *The Epistle to the Hebrews*, 319–321; Alexander Nairne, *The Epistle of Priesthood* (Edinburgh: T&T Clark, 1913), 161, 381–382; Alexander Nairne, *The Epistle to the Hebrews*, The Cambridge Bible for Schools and Colleges (Cambridge University Press, 1921), 78; Spicq, *L'épître aux Hébreux*, 2:316; Montefiore, *The Epistle to the Hebrews*, 173; Héring, *The Epistle to the Hebrews*, 91; Hofius, *Der Vorhang*, 81–82; George W. MacRae, "Heavenly Temple and Eschatology in the Letter to the Hebrews," *Semeia* 12 (1978): 188.

Similarly, Otfried Hofius suggests that τοῦτ᾽ ἔστιν is explicative of the preceding sentence as a whole ("Inkarnation und Opfertod Jesu nach Hebr 10,19 f.," in *Der Ruf Jesu und die Antwort der Gemeinde*, ed. E. Lohse [1970], 132–141, quoted in Young, "Heb. X. 20," 101). For an answer to this article of Otfried Hofius, see Joachim Jeremias, "Hebräer 10:20: τοῦτ᾽ ἔστιν τῆς σαρκὸς αὐτοῦ," *ZNW* 62 (1971): 131.

506 See Westcott, *The Epistle to the Hebrews*, 320.

507 E.g., Bruce, *The Epistle to the Hebrews*; Koester, *Hebrews*, 443.

508 Paul C. B. Andriessen and A. Lenglet, "Quelques passages difficiles de *l'Épître aux Hébreux* (5,7.11; 10,20; 12,2)," *Bib* 51 (1970): 214–215; Andriessen, "Das größere und vollkommenere Zelt," 80–81. He points out with a question mark, however, his uncertainty regarding 9:11. Brooke Foss Westcott had mentioned before the case of 7:5 (*The Epistle to the Hebrews*, 320).

not all of these passages support his argument, it is clear that at least 7:5 and 13:15 do.[509] This is not, then, a convincing objection.

Norman H. Young has shown, however, that the author of Hebrews *consistently* uses τοῦτ' ἔστιν elsewhere to introduce *appositional phrases*.[510] This strongly suggests that τῆς σαρκὸς αὐτοῦ should be connected to καταπετάσματος and not to ὁδόν. Τοῦτ' ἔστιν cannot introduce τῆς σαρκὸς αὐτοῦ as an appositional statement to ὁδὸν πρόσφατον καὶ ζῶσαν because the former is genitive and the latter accusative.[511] Additionally, the word order, though not decisive (see above), privileges a connection to καταπετάσματος over ὁδόν.

This realization leads us to the second question. Since τοῦτ' ἔστιν introduces an appositional statement to διὰ τοῦ καταπετάσματος, the preposition διὰ governs τῆς σαρκὸς αὐτοῦ (= διὰ τοῦ καταπετάσματος, τοῦτ' ἔστιν [διὰ] τῆς σαρκὸς αὐτοῦ). This poses a problem. Διὰ τοῦ καταπετάσματος should be understood as locative, not instrumentally. It has been often argued that the "veil" represents a barrier that Jesus overcomes to enter into the presence of God (cf. 6:19; 9:2), not an instrument.[512] On the other hand, Jesus's "flesh" is not an obstacle into the presence of God, but the instrument that makes possible that entrance.[513] This is very clear—as Joachim Jeremias has shown—in the parallelism between vv. 19–20.[514] Jesus's "flesh" in v. 20 parallels his "blood" as a means of access:

v. 19:
Ἔχοντες οὖν, ἀδελφοί, παρρησίαν
a) εἰς τὴν εἴσοδον
b) τῶν ἁγίων
c) ἐν τῷ αἵματι Ἰησοῦ

v. 20
ἣν ἐνεκαίνισεν ἡμῖν
a) ὁδὸν πρόσφατον καὶ ζῶσαν
b) διὰ τοῦ καταπετάσματος,
c) τοῦτ' ἔστιν τῆς σαρκὸς αὐτοῦ

---

509 Young, "Heb. X. 20," 101.
510 Ibid., 103.
511 Ibid.
512 E.g., Spicq, *L'épître aux Hébreux*, 2:316; Héring, *The Epistle to the Hebrews*, 91; Hofius, *Der Vorhang*, 83–84.
513 Contra Braun, *An die Hebräer*; Gräßer, *An die Hebräer*. The flesh is not the curtain that blocks access to the holy of holies in the sense that it confines the person to the realm of fear, death, and impurity (2:14–15; 5:7–8; 9:10–13). This view has some affinities with gnostic sources (*Hyp. Arch.* 94.9–10; *Gos. Phil.* 84.23–85.10). In Hebrews, however, "flesh" and "body" play a positive role in redemption. Koester, *Hebrews*, 444. Regarding the relationship between Gnosticism and Hebrews, see Hurst, *The Epistle to the Hebrews*.
The "flesh," instead, which refers to Jesus's earthly existence and suffering, is what makes possible Jesus's (and the believer's) entrance into the presence of God. See Spicq, *L'épître aux Hébreux*; Peterson, *Hebrews and Perfection*, 154; Attridge, *The Epistle to the Hebrews*; Bruce, *The Epistle to the Hebrews*, 252; Lane, *Hebrews 9–13*; Weiß, *Der Brief an die Hebräer*; Koester, *Hebrews*, 443–444.
514 Jeremias, "Hebräer 10 20: τοῦτ' ἔστιν τῆς σαρκὸς αὐτοῦ"; Young, "Heb. X. 20," 102–103.

It seems to me, however, that this problem is artificial. The locative sense of διά identifies the "veil" as the point of access to the presence of God; a meaning that is, in fact, because of the image, analogous to the instrumental. The veil as a point of access (locative) is in an analogous sense a *means* of access as well (instrumental).[515] Admittedly, there is a progression in the meaning of the preposition, but this is something that we should expect from the use of metaphorical images.[516] Thus, we should understand this expression in the following way: "by the new and living way that he opened for us through the curtain, that is, [by means] of his flesh."[517]

The Ascension Is the Basis for the Exhortation to Approach God

What is the function of Jesus's ascension in the argument of this passage?

Verses 19–25 form a single periodical sentence.[518] I have mentioned above (pp. 222–223) that periods were important rhetorical devices used by Greco-Roman writers to introduce or conclude sections of the argument "by summarizing the points that preceded [or followed] the sentence itself."[519] This periodic sentence is structured in two sections and has a double function.[520] The first section is introduced by the participle: Ἔχοντες and involves vv. 19–21. It explains what believers have: (1) boldness to enter the sanctuary and (2) a great high priest. This summarizes the argument of the central section of Hebrews (5:1–10:18) but in reverse order. The assertion "since we have a great priest over the house of God" summarizes the argument of the appointment of Jesus as high priest developed in 5:1–7:28. Verses 19–20 ("we have confidence to enter the sanctuary by the blood of Jesus ...") summarize the argument that Jesus's death is a sacrifice that cleanses the conscience of the believer and provides him with access to the presence of God that was presented in 8:1–10:18.[521] This summary of the argument has the purpose of serving as the basis for a call to action.

---

515 See Laub, *Bekenntnis und Auslegung*, 181; Peterson, *Hebrews and Perfection*, 154; Attridge, *The Epistle to the Hebrews*, 287.

516 See Young, "Heb. X. 20," 104.

517 Peterson, *Hebrews and Perfection*, 154; Koester, *Hebrews*, 444. Also Attridge, *The Epistle to the Hebrews*; Lane, *Hebrews 9–13*; Ellingworth, *The Epistle to the Hebrews*.

518 Koester, "Hebrews, Rhetoric, and the Future of Humanity," 116; Lane, *Hebrews 9–13*, 281. For the study of periods, see Anderson Jr., *Glossary of Greek Rhetorical Terms*, 94–101; Cortez, "From the Holy to the Most Holy Place"; Lausberg, *Handbook of Literary Rhetoric*, §431–442.

519 Koester, "Hebrews, Rhetoric, and the Future of Humanity," 105.

520 See the analysis in Ellingworth, *The Epistle to the Hebrews*, 516; Vanhoye, *La structure littéraire*, 175–177.

521 Cf. Koester, "Hebrews, Rhetoric, and the Future of Humanity," 116.

The second section (vv. 22–25) exhorts the believers to act on the basis of what they already have (vv. 19–21). This is expressed with three hortatory subjunctives: "Let us draw near [προσερχώμεθα] with a sincere heart in full assurance of faith" (NASB), "Let us hold fast [κατέχωμεν] the confession of our hope without wavering," and "Let us consider [κατανοῶμεν] how to provoke one another to love and good deeds." It is interesting to note that these three exhortations are, in fact, developed in the final section of Hebrews (Heb 11–13). We cannot explore this relationship further here, though.[522] What I want to emphasize now is that this sentence is an important transition in the macro-structure of the argument of Hebrews.

What is the function of the ascension, then, in this important transitional passage of Hebrews? The author is very clear: By virtue of his ascension, Jesus "inaugurated for us a new and living way through the curtain" (10:20, translation mine). Thus, "[believers] have confidence to enter the sanctuary by the blood of Jesus" (10:19). In this sense, Jesus has "opened the way to the heavenly sanctuary [into the presence of God] by himself going first and thus making it possible for others to follow after him."[523] This agrees with the conception introduced before in Hebrews that Jesus is the pioneer (ἀρχηγός, 2:10; cf. 12:2) and forerunner (πρόδρομος, 6:19–20) of the believers.[524]

What is this "new and living way" that has been inaugurated?[525] I want to suggest that it is the new covenant that has been inaugurated with Jesus's sacrifice and ascension into the heavenly sanctuary as the author has argued in Heb 8–10. Let me explain.

---

522 See George Guthrie, *The Structure of Hebrews*.

523 Nils A. Dahl, "A New and Living Way: The Approach to God According to Hebrews 10:19–25," *Int* 5 (1951): 403. An often noted and striking parallel to this idea is Lucius Annaeus Florus's comment on the legendary devotion of Decius Mus. I quote here from Attridge, *The Epistle to the Hebrews*, 285, n. 26: "While the other consul [*scil.*, Decius Mus], as though acting upon a warning from heaven, with a veiled head devoted himself to the infernal gods in front of the army, in order that, by hurling himself where the enemy's weapons were thickest, he *might open up a new path to victory along the track of his own blood*" (*Epitome* 1.14.3, emphasis mine).

524 Attridge, *The Epistle to the Hebrews*, 285.

525 Craig R. Koester notes, "The spatial quality of the 'way' suggests associations from the practice of making new roads" (*Hebrews*, 443). In the Roman Empire, dedicatory inscriptions celebrating new highways honored the emperor who had both royal and priestly functions (Naphtali Lewis and Meyer Reinhold, eds., *Roman Civilization: Selected Readings*, 3d ed. [Columbia University Press, 1990], 2:72–75; Spicq, *Theological Lexicon of the New Testament*, 397, n. 7). N. A. Dahl suggests that Heb 10:19–23 refers instead to the inauguration of the heavenly sanctuary ("A New and Living Way," 404). As far as I was able to understand, also Ellingworth, *The Epistle to the Hebrews*, 518–519. He mentions 2 Macc 14:36 in which πρόσφατος "recently" refers to the recently rededicated temple (also, Jdt 4:3–14). They are correct as long as it is recognized that the inauguration of the heavenly sanctuary is inherent to the inauguration of the new covenant and, thus, inextricable from it.

The term ἐνεκαίνισεν (10:20) has cultic connotations. In the LXX, ἐγκαινίζω translated either the piel of חָדַשׁ or חָנַךְ. The former Hebrew term—"to make anew, restore"[526]— usually carried the connotation of a new beginning (cf. Pss 51:12; 104:30; Lam 5:21; Job 10:17; cf. Sir 36:5); hence, it was used for the installation of royalty (1 Sam 11:14), the renovation of the altar (2 Chr 15:8), or the restoration of the temple (2 Chr 24:4, 12).[527] The latter—"dedicate" (חָנַךְ)[528]— carried the sense of "begin to put into use," and was used for the dedication of a private house (Deut 20:5), but especially the inauguration of the Mosaic tabernacle and Solomon's temple (Num 7:10–11 [ἐγκαινισμός]; 1 Kgs 8:63; 2 Chr 7:5; 1 Macc 4:36, 54, 57; cf. ἐγκαίνια in John 10:22).[529]

In Heb 10:20 what Jesus inaugurated was a "new and living way." I believe this expression refers to the new covenant. First, the author uses this term for the inauguration of the covenant in 9:18—the only other place in the NT where ἐγκαινίζω appears.[530] Second, "like the covenant he inaugurated, the way that Christ opened is 'new,' providing unprecedented access to God."[531] Third, like the inauguration of the covenant, Jesus's "inauguration" of the way includes a sacrifice.[532] And fourth, the expression "new [πρόσφατον] and living [ζῶσαν]" contrasts the description of the old covenant (8:13), "obsolete [παλαιούμενον] and growing old [γηράσκον]."[533]

Finally, the inauguration of the "way" parallels the inauguration of the first covenant in another respect. According to the argument of Hebrews, the inauguration of the first covenant was ratified through a covenant sacrifice that cleansed the people and sanctuary through the sprinkling of blood (and its vessels; 9:15–23). Similarly, the inauguration of the "way" in Heb 10:19–20 implies the cleansing of believers through the sacrifice of Jesus. Verse 22 says that in order to approach God, believers need to have their "hearts sprinkled clean from an evil conscience and … bodies washed with pure water" (v. 22).[534] This refers to the "blood of Jesus" that gives us the "confidence to enter the

---

526 *HALOT* 1:294.
527 In 2 Chr 24:4, 12, ἐπισκευάσαι (inf. aor. of ἐπισκευάζομαι) translates לְחַדֵּשׁ.
528 *HALOT* 1:334.
529 Spicq, *Theological Lexicon of the New Testament*, 1:396–397.
530 The cognate ἐγκαίνια appears in John 10:22.
531 Koester, *Hebrews*, 443.
532 Attridge, *The Epistle to the Hebrews*, 285; Dahl, "A New and Living Way," 403.
533 Dahl, "A New and Living Way," 404.
534 Regarding the cleansing of conscience in our particular passage, the author "would not only say that we need no longer have a bad conscience because of our past sins. He would probably say as well that we have been made free from an evil attitude of mind, a consciousness full of evil inclination" (ibid., 408). Note that the cleansing of the conscience manifests itself in a life full of faith (10:22), which in Hebrews involves "faithfulness" (3:18–19, Koester, *Hebrews*, 444).

sanctuary" (v. 19). Thus, the inauguration of the "new and living way" is equivalent to the inauguration of the new covenant because it includes the purification of the believers through the blood of Jesus and implies the inauguration of the heavenly sanctuary.[535] On the other hand, Jesus's death and ascension accomplish what the sacrifice for the first covenant was not able to: "access into the presence of God." Thus, the Spirit indicated that in the first covenant "the way into the sanctuary has not yet been disclosed" (9:8), but now the author asserts that "by the blood of Jesus" a "new and living way" has been *inaugurated* "through the curtain" into the very presence of God (10:19–20).

N. A. Dahl considers correctly that "the juxtaposition of sprinkling and ritual washing more closely parallels another Old Testament ceremony, the initiation of priests."[536] This is an interesting observation for several reasons. The inauguration of the sanctuary, which in Hebrews is subsumed under the inauguration of the covenant, included the initiation of the priests (Exod 40; Lev 8–9). Similarly, the inauguration of the new covenant in Hebrews implies priestly roles for believers. They are enabled to access the sanctuary through the veil (10:19–23). In fact, they are the "house" of the great high priest (10:21; cf. 3:6) who serve at a new altar (13:10) where they offer spiritual sacrifices of thanksgiving and praise (12:28; 13:15–16).[537]

Summary

I have argued that the main concern of the author in Heb 8–10 is the inauguration of the new covenant prophesied by Jeremiah through the sacrifice of Jesus.

Hebrews 9:11–14 describes Jesus's ascension as his entrance into the heavenly sanctuary. Jesus's ascension marks a transition from the earthly sanctuary to the heavenly sanctuary and therefore from the first to the new covenant which they represent. This transition had been illustrated—according to the argument of Heb 9:6–10—by "the way of the sanctuary," that is, the transition in the ministry of the Israelite sanctuary from the outer (first tent) to the inner room (second tent) as it happened on the Day of Atonement. This annual transition in the Israelite cult between the ministries of the two

---

535 I do not see here an identification of the "new and living way" with the heavenly sanctuary. Instead, the inauguration of the new covenant implies the inauguration of the heavenly sanctuary.

536 Dahl, "A New and Living Way," 406–407.

537 Note the cultic nuance of the terms προσέρχομαι and εἰσέρχομαι in Hebrews. Regarding this, see Scholer, *Proleptic Priests*, 91–149.

rooms (or tents in the argument of Hebrews) illustrated the transition between two sanctuaries and their covenants. Thus, Jesus's sacrifice and ascension inaugurate the new covenant and the fulfillment of its promise of providing forgiveness (i.e., the cleansing of conscience, 9:14).

Hebrews 9:15–23 confirms this idea by comparing Jesus's death and ascension to the ritual for the inauguration of the first covenant, which included the consecration of its tent. Hebrews 9:24–10:18 will flesh out this idea by explaining that Jesus's sacrifice has been able to accomplish what no sacrifice (including Day of Atonement sacrifices) of the first covenant was able to: the forgiveness of sin and the empowerment of the believer to be faithful to the covenant requirements. Thus, Jesus's sacrifice will "remove sin," which includes forgiveness and the empowerment of the believer.

Finally, Heb 10:19–25 exhorts the readers to "approach God" as a result of the benefits that result from Jesus's inauguration of the new covenant. The new covenant is described here as a "new and living way" into the presence of God. This is so because it cleanses believers from their evil consciences so that they have a "full assurance of faith" in order to approach God.

"You Have Come to Mount Zion" (12:18–29): The Ascension of the Believers to the Heavenly Jerusalem

The book of Hebrews finishes with one last description of an ascension, only in this case it is not Jesus who ascends, but the believers who come into the presence of God—through the "way" Jesus has opened.

> You have not come to something that can be touched, a blazing fire, and darkness, and gloom, and a tempest, and the sound of a trumpet, and a voice whose words made the hearers beg that not another word be spoken to them. (For they could not endure the order that was given, "If even an animal touches the mountain, it shall be stoned to death." Indeed, so terrifying was the sight that Moses said, "I tremble with fear.")
>
> But you have come to Mount Zion and to the city of the living God, the heavenly Jerusalem, and to innumerable angels in festal gathering, and to the assembly of the firstborn who are enrolled in heaven, and to God the judge of all, and to the spirits of the righteous made perfect, and to Jesus, the mediator of a new covenant, and to the sprinkled blood that speaks a better word than the blood of Abel.
>
> See that you do not refuse the one who is speaking; for if they did not escape when they refused the one who warned them on earth, how much

less will we escape if we reject the one who warns from heaven! At that time his voice shook the earth; but now he has promised, "Yet once more I will shake not only the earth but also the heaven." This phrase, "Yet once more," indicates the removal of what is shaken—that is, created things—so that what cannot be shaken may remain.

This is an intriguing passage. It describes the readers as already experiencing what the author has exhorted them to endure and struggle for throughout the Letter. He had encouraged them to "approach" (προσερχώμεθα) God with confidence (4:14; 10:22; cf. 7:25, 10:1; 11:6); now, he asserts that they "have come [προσεληλύθατε] ... to God the judge of all" (10:22–23).[538] He had encouraged them to enter into the "rest" (4:1–11) and described the patriarchs as "strangers and foreigners on the earth" (11:13) who were looking for a "city that has foundations, whose architect and builder is God" (11:9, 16) and for a "homeland" (11:14, 16); now, the author describes them as having reached the end of their journey. They "have come to Mount Zion and to the city of the living God, the heavenly Jerusalem" (12:22).[539] They have come not as visitors but as citizens, members of the heavenly city's assembly (ἐκκλησία).[540] Similarly, the author had exhorted the readers to "go on towards perfection" (6:1); now, he

---

538 For a study of use of προσέρχομαι in Hebrews, see ibid., 91–149.

539 George Wesley Buchanan has argued that the author does not refer in this passage to a heavenly reality: " 'Heavenly Jerusalem' was not used to mislead the reader into thinking Mount Zion was in heaven, although Jews and Christians believed there was a Jerusalem in heaven as well, but to affirm its divine origin, just as in 6:5 the heavenly gift was something believers on earth had tested, meaning it was a teaching considered divine or heavenly" (*To the Hebrews*, 222).

His argument is unconvincing. The idea of a heavenly gift in Heb 6:5 does not exclude the notion that believers are destined for heaven. There is a clear sense in Hebrews that Jesus has ascended into heaven (e.g., 9:24; 4:14; passim) and that believers will follow him there (e.g., 6:19–20, 2:10). In fact, the notion of a heavenly city had already appeared in Heb 11:10, 14, 16. Finally, it is difficult to believe that "heavenly Jerusalem" refers to an earthly restoration of Jerusalem (G. W. Buchanan offers as examples of the restoration of Jerusalem, Zech 14:9–11 and Ezek 40–48 [*To the Hebrews*, 222–223]), since in the immediate context Hebrews refers to the "removal" of the "created things" (12:26–27). For further critique of this position, see Attridge, *The Epistle to the Hebrews*, 374; Ellingworth, *The Epistle to the Hebrews*, 678.

540 The members of the "assembly of the firstborn" are not actually specified. Some critics consider it as parallel to the immediately preceding expression; therefore, they identify its members as angels (Käsemann, *The Wandering People of God*, 50; Spicq, *L'épître aux Hébreux*, 2:407; Montefiore, *The Epistle to the Hebrews*, 231). The idea of being "enrolled in heaven," however, suggests that it refers to faithful human beings (Exod 32:32; Ps 69:28 [68:29 LXX]; Isa 4:3; Dan 12:1; Luke 10:20; Rev 13:8; 17:8; 1QM XII, 1–4; cf. Phil 3:20). The " 'firstborn' are those who share the inheritance (12:16) of the Firstborn par excellence (1:6)" (Attridge, *The Epistle to the Hebrews*, 375; also deSilva, *Perseverance in Gratitude*, 466–467; Ellingworth, *The Epistle to the Hebrews*, 679–80; Johnson, *Hebrews*, 332; Koester, *Hebrews*, 545; Lane, *Hebrews 9–13*, 468–9). Note, as well, that God's people are called his firstborn in Exod 4:22–23 (cf. Sir 36:17 [36:11 LXX]; 2 Esd 6:58 [55]).

describes them as joining the "spirits of the righteous made perfect" in the heavenly assembly (12:23; cf. 7:11, 19; 9:9; 10:1, 14; 11:40).[541]

Two questions arise from this passage. First, in what sense have the readers arrived at the heavenly Jerusalem? Second, what is the role of this description of the readers' "ascension" in the argument of Hebrews?

The Believers Have Ascended to the Heavenly Jerusalem in the World of the Scriptures

In what sense have the readers already arrived at Mount Zion (12:22–24)?

The context suggests that, in addition to the present dimension of the passage, there is a future thrust in this description of the believers' "ascension" to the heavenly Jerusalem. The believers' participation in the *heavenly* "festal gathering" of Heb 12:22–24 is the basis for the exhortation to not "reject the one who warns from heaven!" (v. 25). This warning of punishment for those who reject God suggests that positive and negative rewards still lie in the future. Thus, v. 28 reminds the believers that they "are receiving [παραλαμβάνοντες] a kingdom that cannot be shaken," which recognizes that though the believers have begun to enjoy the promise (of a "heavenly city"; cf. 11:10–16) in the present they are still waiting for its consummation in the future.[542] In fact, the author plainly recognizes that they had not yet arrived at

---

Ἐκκλεσία has here, probably, the ordinary sense of an assembly of the city, i.e., its legislative body. Cf. 1 Macc 3:13; Sir 26:5; Acts 19:32, 39, 40; Josephus, *Ant.* 12.164; 19.332; BDAG, 303–304; L&N 11.78. See Bruce, *The Epistle to the Hebrews*; deSilva, *Perseverance in Gratitude*, 466–467; Koester, *Hebrews*, 550–551; Johnson, *Hebrews*, 332.

541 The meaning of the phrase "the spirits of the righteous made perfect" is debated. The image of souls or spirits of departed human beings in the presence of God was common in the apocalypses and other Jewish literature. E.g., *1 En.* 22:3–9; 39:4; 70:4; 103:3, 4; Pr Azar 1:64 (Add Dan 3:86 [LXX]); *2 Bar.* 3:2; *3 Bar.* 10:5; 4 Ezra 7:99; Rev 6:9; Wis 3:1; Philo, *Alleg. Interp.* 3.74; *3 En.* 43:1; Sifre 40. See Attridge, *The Epistle to the Hebrews*, 376, nn. 82–83. Here, however, the phrase has a different sense. It is parallel to "the assembly of the firstborn" who has in mind the believers who are not yet dead (see also previous note). Thus, it seems that this phrase should be understood in the context of Hebrews' understanding that "human hearts, minds, and spirits have been 'perfected' and granted access to God's own realm by the cleansing sacrifice of Christ" (Attridge, *The Epistle to the Hebrews*, 376).

542 Bruce, *The Epistle to the Hebrews*, 383, n. 199; Koester, *Hebrews*, 557; Michel, *die Hebräer*, 475–476; Spicq, *L'épître aux Hébreux*, 2:413. Esp. Laub, *Bekenntnis und Auslegung*, 253; Attridge, *The Epistle to the Hebrews*, 382; Ellingworth, *The Epistle to the Hebrews*, 690. (They emphasize correctly the "already/not yet" character of salvation expressed in this passage.) Contra, Cody, *Heavenly Sanctuary and Liturgy*, 141. The idea that the place from which God rules is unshakable is an OT motif (Pss 93:1; 96:10; 125:1; Isa 33:20, Lane, *Hebrews 9–13*, 484–486).

their heavenly destination when he says—a little later—"we are looking for the city that is to come" (13:14).[543]

On the other hand, the fact that the author characterizes the experience of Israel at Mount Sinai as something that could be "touched" (ψηλαφωμένῳ; 12:18–21) may suggest that what the author describes as its opposite in 12:22–24 (i.e., the festal gathering at Mount Zion) was incorporeal or spiritual in nature.[544]

On the basis of these two observations, scholars have understood the readers' participation in the festal gathering at the "heavenly Jerusalem" as being complex in nature. On the one hand, it takes place in the present "in principle and in their imagination."[545] That is to say, Heb 12:22–24 describes the future consummation of the promises as "already present *in faith*" (emphasis mine):[546] "Der Glaubende hat jetzt schon Zutritt zur himmlisch-transzendenten Wirklichkeit als den ἐλπιζόμενα und οὐ βλεπόμενα."[547] In this sense,

---

543 Cf. the exhortation to enter the rest (Heb 4:1–11). Similarly, the description of the patriarchs as looking for the heavenly city (Heb 11:10–16) and the realization that neither they nor the readers have obtained the promises (11:39–40); therefore, they need to endure in the race (12:1–13).

544 James W. Thompson considers this passage an evidence of the metaphysical dualism of the author: "That which is "heavenly" (ἐπουράνιος) is set over against that which is ψηλαφημένος. This contrast indicates that ψηλαφημένος is used by the author as a code-word for 'earthly' in a metaphysical sense. The Sinai event is evaluated and interpreted with the assumptions which indicate the author's metaphysical dualism…. Thus, by the use of ψηλαφημένος, the author indicates that he does not think merely in typological terms of old event and new event, as his tradition probably did. His intention is not to point to the correspondence between Sinai and Zion; rather Sinai becomes merely an event in the created order. This reinterpretation of the tradition is made in the context of a cosmological dualism" (*Beginnings*, 45–46). Against him, I believe the perspective of the author is mainly eschatological (or typological, to use Thompson's term). The participle ψηλαφημένος reminds us, instead, of the palpable darkness of Egypt (Exod 10:21). See, Koester, *Hebrews*, 543; Lane, *Hebrews 9–13*, 461. Also, Dunnill, *Covenant and Sacrifice*, 144–145. For a critique of the use of Platonism as the background of thought of Hebrews, see Hurst, *The Epistle to the Hebrews*, 7–43; Adams, , "The Cosmology of Hebrews"; Williamson, *Philo and Hebrews*.

545 Johnson, *Hebrews*, 328.

546 Koester, *Hebrews*, 544. Cf. Hofius, *Katapausis*, 147–149; Lane, *Hebrews 9–13*, 466.

547 (The believer even now has access to the heavenly-transcendental reality as the ἐλπιζόμενα [hoped for] and οὐ βλεπόμενα [not yet seen; cf. Heb 11:1]) Gräßer, *An die Hebräer*, 3:310. See also, Weiß, *Der Brief an die Hebräer*, 674–675.

Similarly, "Man „naht" sich den Heilsgütern, indem man das Wort Gottes ernst nimmt, das durch den Neuen Bund eine besondere Dringlichkeit empfängt. Dies „Nahen" ist einerseits eschatologisch: wir stehen unmittelbar vor der endzeitlichen Vollendung; andererseits gegenwärtig: wir sind im Glauben an das Wort gebunden" (One draws near to the good things of salvation when one first grasps the word of God, which receives through the new covenant a particular urgency. This "drawing near" is on the one hand eschatological: we stand immediately before the final perfection. On the other hand, it is present: we are bound by faith to the word) (Michel, *die Hebräer*, 460, n. 2).

then, the event transcends sensual experience in the present and is "proleptic" in nature, that is, it anticipates the future.[548]

This position implies that the use of the perfect tense (προσεληλύθατε [vv. 18, 22], "you have come") has a rhetorical purpose. The author refers to a *future event* as having already occurred in order to add "vividness" and "forcefulness" to his exhortation and give listeners "incentive to persevere in the *earthly* city where they live" (emphasis mine).[549] Similarly, Demetrius (2nd century BCE) argued: "Furthermore, the following words, 'I am dead' instead of 'I am dying,' add yet more vividness by the use of an actual past tense, since *what has already happened is more forceful than what will happen or is still happening*" (Demetrius, *Eloc.*, 214 [Innes, LCL]; emphasis mine).

This understanding of Heb 12:22–24 is correct as far as it goes but neglects the historical dimension of this passage. While it is clear that in Hebrews the consummation of salvation is future,[550] the author also argues that believers "*have tasted* the heavenly gift, and *have shared* in the Holy Spirit, and *have tasted* the goodness of the word of God and the powers of the age to come" (Heb 6:4–5, emphasis mine). Thus, I argue that the use of the perfect "you have come" is more than a rhetorical strategy on the part of the author, and that the "present" experience described in 12:22–24 is more than a prolepsis, an act of the imagination, or an act of faith in the future.[551] Instead, it is the historical dimension of this passage (as opposed to its eschatological dimension) that provides the hortatory argument of Hebrews with its compelling force. It is not that the future becomes present through their faith (cf. 11:1) or that the certainty of the future should make them feel *as if* they were already there. The argument is, instead, that they have already been there and, therefore, should act accordingly (cf. 6:4–6). Let me explain.

This passage consists of a contrast which the author develops into an *a fortiori* argument ("from the lesser to the greater").[552] The author compares here—once again—the experience of the ancient Israelites before Sinai at the inauguration of the first covenant to the experience of believers at Mount

---

548 Johnson, *Hebrews*, 328.
549 Koester, *Hebrews*, 550.
550 "Hebrews most often uses the terms 'save' (σῴζω) and 'salvation' (σωτηρία) for the final deliverance that will take place in the future, when God's designs are completed at the time of Christ's return. Salvation is the share in the world to come that the faithful hope to inherit (1:14; 2:5; 6:10), and it means deliverance from divine judgment and everlasting glory in the presence of God (2:3, 10; 5:9; 7:25; [9:28])" (Koester, "God's Purposes," 362–363).
551 "The perfect tense [προσεληλύθατε "you have come"] indicates that the action, and the relationship it symbolizes, has begun and is still in effect" (Attridge, *The Epistle to the Hebrews*, 372).
552 Johnson, *Hebrews*, 326. Contra, Ellingworth, *The Epistle to the Hebrews*, 669.

Zion on the occasion of the inauguration of the new covenant (2:1–4; cf. 3:7–4:11; 9:15–23).[553]

On the one hand stands Sinai.[554] The mountain is enshrouded in the numinous phenomena of the blazing fire, the darkness, the gloom, the tempest, and the sound of the trumpet. These were all-powerful physical events that produced fear even in Moses, the mediator of the covenant. This formidable scene climaxes in a "voice" that "made the hearers beg that not another word be spoken to them" (v. 19).[555]

On the other hand stands Zion where a "festal gathering" stands in contrast to the dreadful scene of Mount Sinai. No phenomena or barriers prevent access to God; instead, believers blend with angels in the celebration that takes place. The description culminates with the "sprinkled blood" of Jesus that "*speaks* a better word than the blood of Abel" (v. 24, emphasis mine).

The main point of the contrast is that at the climax of each event both Israel and the believers have "heard" a voice. This is the pivot on which the hortatory argument of the passage turns. On this basis the author warns the readers:

> See that you do not refuse *the one who is speaking*; for if they did not escape [ἐξέφυγον] when they refused the one who warned them on earth, how much less will we escape if we reject the one who warns from heaven! (Heb 12:25, emphasis mine)

This warning repeats, in essence, the first warning of the Letter:

> Therefore we must pay greater attention to what we have heard, so that we do not drift away from it. For if the message declared through angels was valid, and every transgression or disobedience received a just penalty, how can we escape [ἐκφευξόμεθα] if we neglect so great a salvation? (2:1–3a)[556]

---

553 There is no close parallel between items in each list. Harold W. Attridge counts 7 in the first and 12 in the second (*The Epistle to the Hebrews*, 372, n. 6). Otto Michel notes that attempts to count the characteristics of the new (22–24) as only 7 (e.g., Hughes, *Hebrews*, 545) are "künstlich" (artificial) and therefore should be rejected (Michel, *die Hebräer*, 462–463).

554 The mountain itself is not referred to by name. The description assumes that the readers are familiar with Deut 4:11–12. Hebrews 12:21 quotes Deut 9:19 which refers to Moses's fear to approach God after the golden calf incident.

555 Ironically, "the physical phenomena, which might seem to manifest divine power, do more to conceal God than to reveal him" (Koester, *Hebrews*, 549).

556 For the relationship of this passage to Heb 1–2 see Vanhoye, *La structure littéraire*, 233–234.

This passage, then, culminates the extended argument of Hebrews that Jesus's achievements—especially the new covenant he has mediated—are superior to all that the first covenant was able to offer.[557] It is the "word" spoken at the foundation of each covenant, however, that embraces the whole exhortation of the Letter: "Long ago God spoke to our ancestors in many and various ways by the prophets, but in these last days he has spoken to us by a Son [ἐν υἱῷ]" (Heb 1:1–2a). Therefore, after showing what was spoken ἐν υἱῷ to be superior throughout the Letter, the author warns the readers towards the end: "See that you do not refuse the one who is speaking; for if they did not escape when they refused the one who warned them on earth, how much less will we escape if we reject the one who warns from heaven!" (12:25).

I will argue that a correct understanding of the nature of God's speech referred to in the Letter is the key to understanding the nature of the presence of the believers at Mount Zion in 12:18–27. This is also what provides the hortatory argument of the work its compelling force.

---

557 Several consider this passage the rhetorical climax of Hebrews. E.g., Ellingworth, *The Epistle to the Hebrews*, 669; Gräßer, 3:302; Isaacs, *Sacred Space*, 87; Koester, *Hebrews*, 548; Barnabas Lindars, "The Rhetorical Structure of Hebrews," *NTS* 35 (1989): 402. Kiwoong Son considers Heb 12:18–24 "the hermeneutical key to the Epistle" to the Hebrews (*Zion Symbolism in Hebrews: Hebrews 12:18–24 as a Hermeneutical Key to the Epistle*).

Craig R. Koester explains how the three main series of arguments culminate in Heb 12:18–27. The first series traced Israel's journey through the wilderness where the faithless perished (3:7–19); yet, the author held the hope that the promise of the celebration of a "Sabbath rest" remains for the people of God (4:1–11). This argument culminates in our passage in the transition from the gloom of Sinai in the wilderness to the joyous celebration of the righteous. The second series of arguments announces the superiority of the new covenant inaugurated with Jesus's blood to the first covenant that was inaugurated with the blood of animals (chs. 7–10). The superiority of the new covenant consists in the fact that Jesus's sacrifice perfects the consciences of believers and provides access to the presence of God. The first covenant, on the other hand, cleansed only the body and did not provide access to God. This argument culminates in the fearful description of the inauguration of the first covenant where the phenomena conceals God, access to him is forbidden, and his voice is unbearable. On the other hand, believers stand purified in the presence of God and the "sprinkled blood" of the new covenant "speaks a better word."

The third series of arguments follows the pilgrimage of the righteous who endure in the midst of trials waiting "to be made complete" (or "to be perfected") through the realization of God's promises of a "better country" and a "city" built by God (11:10–16, 39–40; cf. 10:36–39). This series culminates with the "spirits of the righteous made perfect" in "the city of the living God, the heavenly Jerusalem" (Koester, *Hebrews*, 548–549).

Hebrews' Use of the Old Testament Creates a World in Which the Readers Stand in the Presence of God

No other document of the NT quotes the OT as often as Hebrews does.[558] Beyond the number of quotations, however, there is something unique to Hebrews' use of Scripture: the oral nature of the word of God and its immediacy.[559]

Pamela Michelle Eisenbaum has noted—and I will follow her argument here—that almost all the quotations from the OT "are quotations of *direct speech*" (emphasis hers).[560] The significant thing is that whether he quotes the oracles of the prophets or the meditations of the psalmist, the author of Hebrews understands and presents them as instances of divine utterance.[561] In some cases, Hebrews quotes God's *ipssissima verba* from the LXX; for example, "I will surely bless you and multiply you" in Heb 6:14 (quoting Gen 22:17). In other cases, when Hebrews quotes a person inspired by God such

---

558 See George H. Guthrie, "Old Testament in Hebrews," *DLNT* 841–842. Pamela Michelle Eisenbaum has identified 31 such quotations. She identifies as quotations only those places where the OT material is formally introduced and the original OT text is largely intact (*The Jewish Heroes of Christian History: Hebrews 11 in Literary Context*, SBLDS 156 [Scholars Press, 1997], 90–91). Hebrews' scholars do not agree, however, on the number of quotations of, and allusions to, the OT in Hebrews largely because they use different criteria to identify them. For an overview of the different lists and criteria, see Kistemaker, *Psalm Citations*, 16. George Guthrie, for example, counts 36 quotations and 37 allusions ("Old Testament in Hebrews," 846–849).

559 Eisenbaum, *The Jewish Heroes of Christian History*, 89–133. Richard B. Hays argues convincingly that there was a hermeneutical tradition in early Christianity to understand the Psalms as *having been spoken by Jesus* and that this phenomenon is the matrix from which early Christology arose ("Christ Prays the Psalms: Israel's Psalter as Matrix of Early Christology," in *The Conversion of the Imagination: Paul as Interpreter of Israel's Scripture* [Eerdmans, 2005], 101–118). The difference with Hebrews is that Hebrews emphasizes this aspect in the introduction to its quotations from the OT, while placing the Psalms in the mouth of Jesus elsewhere in the NT is implicit.

560 Eisenbaum, *The Jewish Heroes of Christian History*, 92. She identifies the following quotations as being of "direct speech" (the numbers in parenthesis refer to OT passages quoted from the LXX): Heb 1:5a (Ps 2:7); 1:5b (2 Sam 7:14); 1:6b (Deut 32:43); 1:7 (Ps 103:4); 1:8–9 (Ps 44:7–8); 1:10–12 (Ps 101:26–28); 1:13 (Ps 109:1); 2:12 (Ps 21:23); 2:13a (Isa 8:17=2 Sam 22:3); 2:13b (Isa 8:18); 3:7–11 (and several times in the section; Ps 94:7–8); 5:5 (Ps 2:7); 5:6 (Ps 109:4); 6:14 (Gen 22:17); 7:21 (Ps 109:4); 8:5 (Exod 25:40); 8:8–12 (Jer 38:31–34); 9:20 (Exod 24:8); 10:5–7 (Ps 39:7–9); 10:16–17 (Jer 38:31–34); 10:30a (Deut 32:35); 10:30b (Deut 32:36); 10:37a (Isa 26:20–21); 10:37b (Hab 2:3–4); 11:18 (Gen 21:12); 12:5–6 (Prov 3:11–12); 12:21 (Deut 9:19); 12:26 (Hag 2:6); 12:29 (Deut 4:24); 13:5 (Deut 31:8); 13:6 (Ps 117:6).

There are two exceptions: Heb 4:4 (Gen 2:2) and 11:5 (Gen 5:24). There are, as well, two that are of an intermediate nature (neither direct nor indirect speech). These are introduced by the verbs διαμαρτύρομαι and μαρτυρέω: 2:6–8a (Ps 8:5–7); 7:17 (Ps 109:4). Both of them imply the written nature of the word of God. See Eisenbaum, *The Jewish Heroes of Christian History*, 98–100.

For the several functions of quotations of direct speech and a brief history of its research, see George W. Savran, *Telling and Retelling: Quotation in Biblical Narrative*, Indiana Studies in Biblical Literature (Indiana University Press, 1988), 7–12.

561 Eisenbaum, *The Jewish Heroes of Christian History*, 92.

as a prophet or a psalmist, it makes no mention of the human agent.[562] Sometimes, the quotation itself makes clear that God is speaking; for example, "The days are surely coming, *says the Lord*, when I will establish a new covenant with the house of Israel ..." (Heb 8:8, quoting LXX Jer 38:31, emphasis mine). Other times, the use of the first person in the quotation itself identifies God as the speaker; for example, "*I* will be his Father, and he will be my Son" (Heb 1:5, quoting LXX 2 Sam 7:14, emphasis mine). Finally, in the vast majority of cases, Hebrews introduces the quotation with a verb of saying in which God is the subject.[563]

Thus, implicitly or explicitly, the author of Hebrews describes God as speaking directly to the audience of the Letter in the words of the Scriptures. Note that the "word of God" is spoken, not written.[564] It is a striking fact that the author of Hebrews does not use the common formula "as it is written." Many other ancient authors—including Qumran and the Mishnah—use verbs of saying to introduce OT quotations; however, "no other author uses

---

562   There are three exceptions: David is mentioned in Heb 4:7 and Moses in 9:19–20; 12:21. In both cases, however, the mention of the human agent is necessary for the argument of the letter. The mention of David in 4:7 makes clear that the promise to the wilderness generation to enter the rest was repeated centuries later. This is important for two points. One, it proves that Joshua did not lead them into the rest. Two, the promise is still available for the readers of the psalm.

The mention of Moses in 9:19–20 is important because it serves as the basis for a typological relationship between Jesus and Moses which explains the nature of Jesus's sacrifice as the inauguration of the new covenant.

Heb 12:21 is a unique quotation because it is the only example of direct speech in which God is not the speaker. The purpose of the quotation is clearly to make the scene more vivid.

There are two quotations which are of an intermediary nature, 2:6–8a (Ps 8:5–7); 7:17 (Ps 109:4). See page 292, n. 560.

563   There are cases in which Jesus (2:12; 10:5) or the Holy Spirit (3:7) are identified as the speakers.

Verbs of saying are common in introductory formulas for the quotation of Scripture in Qumran, the NT, and the Mishnah; see Joseph A. Fitzmyer, "The Use of Explicit Old Testament Quotations in Qumran Literature and in the New Testament," in *Essays on the Semitic Background of the New Testament*, SBLSBS, no. 5 (Society of Biblical Literature and Scholars Press, 1974), 7–17; Bruce M. Metzger, "The Formulas Introducing Quotations of Scripture in the NT and the Mishna," *JBL* 70 (1951): 297–307. Note, however, that only in a few cases is God the subject of the verb in the Qumran and the NT. Fitzmyer, "The Use of Explicit Old Testament Quotations," 10–12. In the Mishnah, the great majority of cases use the Niphal form of the verb—implying its written nature. In the minority of cases where the active form is used, the Scriptures or God are the implied subject (Metzger, "Formulas," 298–299).

564   This does not negate that the author of Hebrews recognizes that God has spoken through human agents. Hebrews 1:1 makes clear that he understands this (Attridge, *The Epistle to the Hebrews*, 24). He, however, has chosen to present Scripture as spoken immediately by God in the presence of or to the audience (see Eisenbaum, *The Jewish Heroes of Christian History*, 97; Luke Timothy Johnson, "The Scriptural World of Hebrews," *Int* 57 [2003]: 239–240).

them to the complete exclusion of writing verbs or references to scripture *qua* scripture, i.e., as written text."[565]

This leads us to the second peculiar characteristic of Hebrews' use of Scripture: its immediacy. Note that a quotation of direct speech—as the vast majority of Hebrews' quotations are—is in fact a subcategory of the more general term "quotation" and has unique characteristics.[566] A quotation evokes the past and therefore is bound to the original context and meaning.[567] As George W. Savran affirms: "Repetition [i.e., quotation] ... de-emphasizes the present moment by *supplying the perspective of an earlier time*" (emphasis mine)."[568] A quotation of direct speech has a different force, however. It "*speaks directly to and within the new context*, with as much immediate impact as it had in its original context" (emphasis mine).[569] In other words, a quotation refers the hearer to a time and context different from his, but the quotation of direct speech *reuses* the past to speak to the hearer in the present. In this sense, the "quotations in Hebrews are reused prophetic oracles" which retain their original oracular force.[570]

---

565 Eisenbaum, *The Jewish Heroes of Christian History*, 97. "The author never uses the word 'written' in any form in connection with biblical material" (ibid). Hebrews 2:6 and 7:17, however, seem to imply or at least to point toward the written nature of the word of God. Kenneth Schenck suggests that the author considered the scriptures as "instantiations" of the word of God ("God Has Spoken: Hebrews' Theology of the Scriptures," *The Epistle to the Hebrews and Christian Theology*, ed. Richard Bauckham et al. [Eerdmans, 2009], 321–336).

566 Savran, *Telling and Retelling*, 7.

567 A quotation is a speech act and, as such, not only informs or describes something, but is itself an act. Speech acts comprise (1) locution (what is actually said), (2) illocution (what is done or accomplished in an utterance), and (3) perlocution (the effect on the hearer). See, J. L. Austin, *How to Do Things with Words* (Clarendon, 1962). See also the development and refinement of his ideas in John R. Searle, *Speech Acts: An Essay in the Philosophy of Language* (Cambridge University Press, 1969). We are interested here with the illocutionary force of quotations, that is, with what they accomplish or do.

A quotation may "accomplish" or "do" several things. For example, a quotation may lend an "air of objectivity" to the argument of the author who quotes the words of another as independent witness of his point of view. If that independent witness is a recognized authority, it gives the "illusion of external evidence." A quotation may demonstrate the fulfillment of a past idea in the present. Also, the repetition of something said in the past suggests a comparison between the past and the present. See Eisenbaum, *The Jewish Heroes of Christian History*, 110. On the illocutionary force of Hebrews' description of God's speech, see also Dunnill, *Covenant and Sacrifice*, 245–248. Cf. Harold W. Attridge, "God in Hebrews: Urging Children to Heavenly Glory," *The Forgotten God: Perspectives in Biblical Theology*, ed. A. Andrew Das and Frank J. Matera (Westminster John Knox, 2002), 203–208.

568 Savran, *Telling and Retelling*, 12.

569 Eisenbaum, *The Jewish Heroes of Christian History*, 109. Also, Schenck, "God Has Spoken: Hebrews' Theology of the Scriptures."

570 Eisenbaum, *The Jewish Heroes of Christian History*, 111. Her discussion of the function of prophetic biblical oracles in Hebrews in contrast to their function in Matthew and John, for example, is illuminating.

The effect of the use of direct speech in Hebrews is, then, that quotations in Hebrews are not used to refer to or evoke something God said in the past but to "re-present" God's words to the audience in the present.[571] They speak "directly to and within the new context" of the audience. In this sense, they are a new speech-act of God.[572] Accordingly, Hebrews not only uses verbs of saying to introduce its quotations from Scripture but also, in most of the cases, the verb form introducing the quotation is indicative or present participle.[573] In those cases in which it uses a perfect or an aorist verb, it uses it to refer to a text quoted earlier in the argument or to introduce a promise given in the past but which is still valid.[574] Therefore, the author of Hebrews either

---

She argues that biblical prophetic oracles have two essential characteristics: they had to be proclaimed and the proclamation itself was causative, that is, it triggered the realization of its own prophecy. (For the nature of biblical prophetic oracles, see Michael Fishbane, *Biblical Interpretation in Ancient Israel* [Clarendon, 1988], 458–469. For the nature of oracles in the Mediterranean world, see David E. Aune, *Prophecy in Early Christianity and the Ancient Mediterranean World* [Eerdmans, 1983]).

Matthew and John quote prophetic oracles from the Hebrew Bible but in a different way from Hebrews. The oracles they quote, however, have lost their original force; that is, they are not a re-proclamation of the word of God and do not *set off* the fulfillment of their own proclamation. Instead, they refer to them as belonging to the past and emphasize their fulfillment in the present. Matthew often concludes that such-and-such event happened "in order that" a certain oracle "be fulfilled." E.g., Matt 1:23 (Isa 7:14 LXX); 2:6 (Mic 5:2); 2:15 (Hos 11:1); 2:18 (Jer 31:15); 2:23 (prob. Isa 11:1); 4:15–16 (Isa 9:1–2); 8:17 (Isa 53:4); 12:17–21 (Isa 42:1–3 and 42:4 [LXX]); 13:35 (Ps 78:2); 21:4–5 (Isa 62:11 and Zech 9:9); 26:15 and 27:9–10 (Zech 11:12–13 and Jer 18–19). (See Craig A. Evans, "Old Testament in the Gospels," *Dictionary of Jesus and the Gospels*, ed. Joel B. Green and Scot McKnight [Downers Grove, Ill.: InterVarsity, 1992], 585.) Similarly, John invariably introduces in the second half biblical prophetic oracles with "in order that it be fulfilled (12:38, 39–40; 13:18; 15:25; 19:24, 28, 36, 37). See Evans, "Old Testament in the Gospels," 587.

Hebrews, instead, does not focus on the fulfillment of the biblical oracles it quotes (though this is not contradicted or ignored) but on the "current" force those oracles have. Thus, when it says, for example, "today, if you hear his voice, do not harden your hearts as in the rebellion ... ," the author does not emphasize that this was true for the wilderness generation, or even the generation of the psalmist, but that this applies to his audience "today." See her further analysis of other biblical oracles in Hebrews in Eisenbaum, *The Jewish Heroes of Christian History*, 111–119.

571 They refer to or evoke the past only *indirectly* because the readers know that the author is using the words of Scripture. So Luke Timothy Johnson concludes: "But by constantly citing the LXX and by introducing such citations with verbs of speaking, Hebrews in effect treats texts as words from 'the prophets' through whom God spoke in the past. And because many of the verbs of introduction are in the present tense, the reader learns that God's speech through these prophetic words is not only past but also present.... Scripture, in other words, is not simply a collection of ancient texts that can throw light on the present through analogy; it is the voice of the living God who speaks through the text directly and urgently to people in the present. The word of God is therefore living and active (4:12)" ("Scriptural World," 240–241).

572 Savran, *Telling and Retelling*, 14.

573 I am referring here to the large majority of verses in which God is implicitly or explicitly understood as the subject. See page 292, n. 560.

574 Hebrews 1:13; 5:5 refer to a text already quoted. Hebrews 2:6; 10:30ab; 12:26; 13:5 refer to a promise issued in the past which is still valid.

presents the word of God as addressing the audience now, or as repeating promises spoken in the past which remain valid, that is, continue to speak to the audience in the present.[575]

This immediacy of the word of God in Hebrews is very important for the argument. By means of the quotation of the word of God as direct speech, Hebrews has made a "theological redescription of time and space."[576] In other words, it has constructed through Scripture a world where the readers—or, hearers—stand in the presence of God and hear him speak.

God Performs the Events at Mount Zion through His Word

Now, what happens in this Scriptural world? How are space and time re-described? How should we define the event in which the readers are participating at Mount Zion?

Hebrews 12:22 defines the space as "Mount Zion and ... the city of the living God, the heavenly Jerusalem." The priority in the structure of the sentence and the contrast to Mount Sinai in vv. 18–21 suggest that Mount Zion is the chief definition of the place in this passage. This is the only place where Mount Zion is explicitly referred to in Hebrews; nonetheless, Mount Zion is the scriptural background to the events referred to through scriptural quotations in the Epistle.[577]

First, Mount Zion is the place where the Son of God is enthroned. Three of the Psalms Hebrews uses to describe the enthronement of the Son in chap. 1 have Mount Zion as their context. Hebrews 1:5 (also 5:5) quotes Ps 2:7 which refers to an event happening at Mount Zion: " 'I have set my king *on Zion*, my holy hill.' I will tell of the decree of the LORD: He said to me, 'You are my son; today I have begotten you' " (Ps 2:6–7, emphasis mine). Likewise, Ps 110:1, quoted in Heb 1:3, 13 (passim), refers to an event in Zion: "The LORD says to my lord, 'Sit at my right hand until I make your enemies your footstool.' The LORD sends out *from Zion* your mighty scepter. Rule in the midst of your foes"

The exceptions are Heb 1:5 that refers to what God has not said *in the past* to angels as a contrast to what God is saying to the Son *in the present* and 8:5 that refers to the erection of the Mosaic tabernacle.

575 Schenck, "God Has Spoken: Hebrews' Theology of the Scriptures." In this context it is interesting to note that "the author never follows a prophesy and fulfillment formula as in Matthew or John" (Eisenbaum, *The Jewish Heroes of Christian History*, 97).

576 Dunnill, *Covenant and Sacrifice*, 134. Luke Timothy Johnson shows that Hebrews' *allusions* to the Hebrew Bible (especially to the laws of Hebrew ritual in Heb 9–10) are also an important part of this theological redescription of the world ("Scriptural World," 239–247).

577 For an introduction to Zion traditions in the Hebrew Bible, see Jon D. Levenson, *Sinai and Zion: An Entry into the Jewish Bible*, New Voices in Biblical Studies (Winston, 1985). For the study of Zion traditions in Hebrews, see Son, "Zion Symbolism in Hebrews."

(Ps 110:1–2, emphasis mine). Finally, the acclamation of Jesus's eternal rule in Heb 1:10–12 uses the words of Ps 102:21–25 that again have Zion as their context (cf. vv. 13, 16, 21).

Thus, the "assembly of the firstborn" at Mount Zion in Heb 12:22–24 evokes—beyond Esau's forfeiture of his "birthright for a single meal" (12:16)—the enthronement scene at Mount Zion where God introduces the "firstborn" into the heavenly world to enthrone him as Son (1:6).[578]

Second, Mount Zion is the place where the Son is appointed as "priest forever, according to the order of Melchizedek" (Heb 5:6). As I have argued above (see above section "When Did Jesus Become a High Priest?" on page 213), the introduction of Jesus's appointment as priest (5:6) with a reference to his adoption as Son of God (5:5), links the appointment of Jesus as high priest with his enthronement as king. Likewise, the scriptural context of Ps 110:4—the scriptural basis for Jesus's appointment as high priest—is, again, Mount Zion (cf. Ps 110:2).

Finally, the argument of Hebrews implies that Zion is also the place where the covenant is inaugurated. Hebrews 7:12 argued that a change in the priesthood implies a change in the law (cf. 7:11–19). From this, the author develops the notion that a new covenant has been inaugurated with the appointment of Jesus as high priest (chs. 8–10). This is confirmed in Heb 12:24 where at the center of the "festal gathering" at Mount Zion stand "Jesus, the mediator of a new covenant, and ... the sprinkled blood that speaks a better word than the blood of Abel."

These three events—Jesus's enthronement, his appointment as high priest, and the inauguration of the new covenant—constitute the backbone of the structure of Hebrews' expository sections and all of them are performed through God's speech—or what contemporary philosophers would call God's "illocution."[579] God enthrones Jesus above the angels (Heb 1–2) with the words of a catena of Psalms (Heb 1:5–14)—especially Pss 2:7 and 110:1. God appoints Jesus as high priest (Heb 5–7) with the oath of Ps 110:4. God creates a new covenant (Heb 8–10) with the words of Jer 31:31–34. Therefore, by referring to and using Scripture as God's *own speech* in his exposition, the author of Hebrews has constructed a world in which the audience stands at

---

578 For the relationship between Heb 1 and 12, see Vanhoye, *La structure littéraire*.

579 Hebrews' exposition follows a logical order that develops step by step from Jesus's enthronement (Heb 1–4), through his appointment as high priest (Heb 5–7), to the inauguration of the new covenant (Heb 8–10). For a description of this linear development of the exposition of Hebrews, see George Guthrie, *The Structure of Hebrews*, 116–127.

For a fuller analysis of God's speech and a description of its role in the argument of Hebrews, see Attridge, "God in Hebrews," 203–208.

Mount Zion where they hear God speak and, hence, witness the enthronement of the Son, his appointment as high priest, and the inauguration of the new covenant.

As Harold W. Attridge notes, "Hebrews ... operates with the conceit that readers and hearers of Scripture can listen to God speaking to the Son and ultimately to all God's children. In this conceit, the character of God and of his scriptural speech provides the raw material for both reflection and parenesis.... In the development of this conceit resides the most creative theological work of this complex text."[580]

Now, though the author has discussed these three events in sequence throughout his exposition, they all are in fact constitutive of a single complex event. The enthronement of the Son "at the right hand of the majesty" (1:3, 13; quoting Ps 109:1 LXX) *implies* his appointment as high priest "according to the order of Melchizedek (5:6; quoting Ps 109:4 LXX).[581] The appointment of Jesus as high priest "according to the order of Melchizedek" *implies*, as well, the abrogation of the commandment of Levitical descent and, therefore, the obsolescence and removal of the first covenant (7:11–19)[582] and the inauguration of a new covenant with better promises (7:20–22). The author, then, has collapsed several events into one.

The Audience's Participation at Mount Zion Is What Provides Compelling Force to the Exhortation of Hebrews

Now, what is the role of Hebrews' description of the readers' participation at Mount Zion's events in the argument of Hebrews?

The notion that the readers have heard God speaking to them through Scripture and, therefore, have stood in God's presence at Mount Zion and witnessed the enthronement of the Son, his appointment as high priest, and the inauguration of the new covenant is extremely important for the hortatory argument of Hebrews.

The hortatory argument of Hebrews contains five warning passages in which the readers are alerted against behavior that will lead them to disas-

---

580 Attridge, "God in Hebrews," 203–204.
581 Note, again, that Hebrews explicitly connects Jesus's appointment as high priest with his enthronement by referring to Jesus's adoption as preliminary to his appointment as high priest (Heb 5:5–6; cf. 7:28). See section "When Did Jesus Become a High Priest" on page 213.
582 This is so because Hebrews considers that the people received "the law"—i.e., the first covenant—under the Levitical priesthood. See Haber, "From Priestly Torah to Christ Cultus," 105–124.

trous results (2:1–4; 4:12–13; 6:4–8; 10:26–31; 12:25–29).[583] They have a common element: "Each of these warnings concerns the hearers' relationship to the word of God."[584] They advise the readers in the clearest terms against rejecting the "word of God."[585] It is noteworthy that three of them are built around an *a fortiori* argument (2:1–4; 10:26–31; 12:25–29) in which the rejection of the law of Moses is the lesser situation and the rejection of God's word to the hearers is the greater situation. The logic is simple. If those who rejected the law of Moses received "a just penalty" (2:2) *how much more* those who reject "the one who warns from heaven!" (12:25). Thus, the readers need to pay "greater attention" to what they have heard "so that they do not drift away from it" (2:1–4) and "do not refuse the one who is speaking; ... the one who warns from heaven!" (12:25).[586]

The hortatory argument has a positive aspect as well. Just as rejecting the "word of God" will result in punishment, hearing the "word of God" entails the inheritance of its promises. Mainly, two positive actions may secure the blessings for the readers: faithfulness (esp. 3:7–4:11) and endurance (esp. 10:32–12:24).[587] Those who do this will be able to inherit the promises of God which are referred to as entering God's "rest" or the heavenly city.[588] In this sense, the

---

583 For an analysis of the hortatory argument of Hebrews, see George Guthrie, *The Structure of Hebrews*, 127–39. He has suggested that the hortatory units of Hebrews may be grouped in four main sections (3:1–4:11; 5:11–9:12; 10:32–12:24; chap. 13). He has bracketed, however, the transitional sections (4:14–16; 10:19–25)—which also belong to the hortatory units—and treats them in a special section, George Guthrie, *The Structure of Hebrews*, 105–111.

584 Ibid., 135.

585 Hebrews 4:12–13 does not warn expressly against rejecting God's Word (all the other warnings do) but achieves the same effect by describing the Word of God as a formidable judge to whom readers "must render an account."

586 Similarly, the readers need someone to teach them "again the basic elements of the oracles of God" (Heb 5:12) so that they may make the correct decisions.
The plural "oracles" (λόγια) is used commonly to refer to the Law (Deut 33:9–10; Acts 7:38; Philo, *Moses* 2.56; *Decalogue* 36; cf. Ps 119:10–11, 102–103, 162–163) or Jewish Scriptures (Philo, *Moses* 2.188; *Let. Aris.* 176–177; Rom 3:2; 1 Clem. 53:1; 62:3). Most consider that Hebrews here refers to the OT or God's revelation in general; e.g., Attridge, *The Epistle to the Hebrews*, 159; Hughes, *Hebrews*; Koester, *Hebrews*, 301; Spicq, *L'épître aux Hébreux*; Westcott, *The Epistle to the Hebrews*.
I suggest, however, that the expression "the basic elements of the oracles of God" refers here specifically to the utterances of God to which the author refers throughout the document (1:5–13; 2:6–8; 3:7–11; 5:5–6). These oracles concern the dignity and office of Christ. The neglect of these oracles by the readers will lead them to "fall away" from the "Son of God" (6:4–8). The "oracles of God" of 5:12 are, then, intimately related to "the basic teaching about Christ" of 6:1. Thus, the author is probably referring to the basic elements of the Old Testament on which early Christians based their belief that Jesus was the Messiah promised by God. See Ellingworth, *The Epistle to the Hebrews*, 304; Lane, *Hebrews 1–8*, 137.

587 George Guthrie, *The Structure of Hebrews*, 137.

588 Similarly, those who "hold fast to the confession" (4:14; 10:23) will be able to enter into God's presence "within the veil" (6:19–20; 10:19–22).

readers need to "look" to Jesus, the pioneer and perfecter of their faith, and run with perseverance the race set before them (12:1–3; cf. 10:35–39).

The force of the hortatory argument, however, resides in two facts. First, past experience shows that those who have disobeyed the "word of God" have endured a punishment as well. The author mentions as negative examples those who disobeyed the law of Moses (2:1–4; 10:26–31; 12:18–29) and those who disobeyed the command to enter Canaan (3:7–4:11). Second, Jesus's exaltation in heaven shows, on the other hand, that God's promises are real as well. In fact, the readers are considered witnesses that God's purpose of "honor and glory" for humanity has been accomplished in Jesus who has been enthroned in heaven (2:5–10). This, however, does not exhaust the promises of God. Jesus has been exalted as their forerunner and leader into God's glory (cf. 2:10; 4:14–16; 6:19–20; 12:1–3).[589] Therefore, this is the time not to "shrink back" and be "lost" but to have "faith" and be "saved" (10:39).

The clinching argument is, however, that they "have heard" God themselves and participated through Scripture in the exaltation of the Son at Mount Zion. They are, therefore, witnesses of the reality of "God's word" (cf. 6:5) so that they cannot elude their responsibility.[590] It is on this fact that their liability to punishment resides (12:25). That is why their responsibility toward the "word of God" is so serious.

The argument is compelling, then, because readers are not exhorted to be faithful and endure on the basis of a promise of salvation that God intends to fulfill for them in the future, but on the present reality of that salvation in the exaltation of Jesus of which the readers have been witnesses.[591]

---

589 See section "The Son and the Sons in the Argument of Hebrews" on page 180.

590 The author had also mentioned that the message of "great salvation"—which includes the notion of Jesus's exaltation in heaven—had been attested to the readers by two witnesses (2:1–4): the testimony of those who heard Jesus and the testimony of God himself through "signs and wonders" and the distribution of gifts from the Holy Spirit (2:3–4).

The author also includes as corroborating evidence the Scriptures (Heb 2:6–8). Finally, the author notes that the readers themselves are witnesses of the truth of the word of God: they "have tasted the goodness of the word of God and the powers of the age to come" (6:5; cf. 12:18–29).

For a study of the notion of witness in Hebrews, see Allison A. Trites, *The New Testament Concept of Witness*, SNTSMS 31 (Cambridge University Press, 1977), 217–221.

591 Similarly, the inauguration of the Mosaic sanctuary and its priesthood included a theophany (Lev 8–9). This theophany was followed by the judgment with fire upon Nadab and Abihu, new priests, who had been on the mountain to witness God and saw the fire from heaven (Exod 24:1, 9, 17); thus, God's warning regarding those who come near him (Lev 10:3).

Hebrews refers to the moment of Jesus's exaltation as "today" (Heb 1:5; 5:5). He also refers to "today" as the moment of decision for the believers (3:7–4:11). For an analysis of the concept of "today" in the argument of Hebrews, see Anderson, "Who Are the Heirs?" 255–257; Dunnill, *Covenant and Sacrifice*, 135–136.

Conclusion

In this chapter I have analyzed in order the six passages in which the ascension of Jesus is explicitly referred to in the Letter to the Hebrews. These passages are Heb 1:6; 4:14–16; 6:19–20; 9:11–14; 9:24; 10:19–25.[592] The analysis included two steps. The first step concerned the imagery of the passage and its logic. In other words, I tried to understand "how" the ascension is described in each passage and what that implies. The second step analyzed the rhetorical function of the ascension in the argument of the section of Hebrews to which that passage belongs. In other words, I tried to understand "why" the author of Hebrews explicitly referred to the ascension at that particular place.

These are the results of my study.

Hebrews 1:6 refers to the ascension of Jesus into heaven as an act of God in which he introduces the Son to the heavenly court as their ruler. Hebrews 1:6 is part of a catena of OT passages (Heb 1:5–14) that describe the enthronement of Jesus as Son at the right hand of God. This description fulfills an important function in the argument of chs. 1–2. God has fulfilled in Jesus his purpose of crowning humanity with "glory and honor" (Heb 2:6–9). At the same time he has provided Jesus as leader and pioneer (ἀρχηγός) for taking human beings into heavenly glory (2:10–18). Therefore, the author exhorts believers to "pay greater attention" to the Son and not "drift away" and "disobey" (2:1–4). (This hortatory argument is developed in new ways in the following sections of Hebrews.) Thus, the ascension in Heb 1:6 is part of Jesus's enthronement ceremony as ruler over the universe.

Hebrews 4:14 describes the ascension as a journey through the heavens towards the throne of God. It has the purpose of explaining why Jesus is "a great high priest" able to help those who are journeying toward the heavenly rest. The description of Jesus's passage "through the heavens" and his "tested" faithfulness make him an exceptional "helper" for those who are exhorted to enter into God's rest but are being fiercely tempted on the journey. Thus, the ascension in 4:14 implies that Jesus has entered into God's rest and as a result is able to help us in our journey.

Hebrews 6:13–20 describes Jesus's ascension as an entrance "within the veil," that is, into the immediate presence of God as the consummation of his appointment as heavenly high priest. This image is part of the author's explanation of how believers may "realize the full assurance of hope to the very

---

[592] Multiple passages in which Jesus's ascension is assumed but not directly referred to were not studied (e.g., 8:1, etc.). In the end, the argument of the Letter as a whole assumes Jesus's ascension.

end" (6:11) and become "imitators of those who through faith and patience inherit the promises" (6:12). The author explains both elements in reverse order. Verses 13–16 present Abraham as one who through patient endurance inherited the promises and vv. 17–20 present Jesus as the full assurance of the hope of the believers. He argues, then, that God's oath to Jesus by which he becomes the believers' high priest (6:17 referring to 5:5–6) is one of the "two immutable things" on which their certainty of salvation is established (cf. 6:9). Jesus's entrance into heaven is considered in this passage, then, the attainment of salvation (6:9) or the inheritance of the promises (v. 12). In this sense Jesus is the "forerunner" who confirms that God's purpose for humanity (i.e., to bring them to "honor and glory") is for real. Thus, the ascension in Heb 6:19 is the consummation of Jesus's appointment as heavenly high priest that confirms the certainty of God's promises for us.

Hebrews 9:11–14 describes Jesus's ascension to heaven as an entrance into the heavenly sanctuary. Against the majority position, I suggest that Hebrews does not describe this entrance as part of an eschatological or transcendental Day of Atonement, but as constitutive of the inauguration of Jesus's ministry in heaven and—therefore—of the new covenant. I argued that Heb 9:11–14 does not refer to Jesus's entrance specifically to the heavenly holy of holies but to the heavenly sanctuary in general.[593] I suggested that the Day of Atonement in Heb 9:1–10 illustrates this transition between covenants and not specifically Jesus's entrance into the heavenly sanctuary. Therefore, the contrast developed between 9:1–10 and 9:11–14 is a contrast between covenants—including a contrast of their sanctuaries and ministries—and not of specific rituals. In summary, Jesus's ascension to heaven implies a transition from the earthly sanctuary of the first covenant to the heavenly sanctuary of the new covenant and, therefore, the inauguration of the new covenant. This is confirmed by the fact that the immediately following section (9:15–23) interprets Jesus's death and ascension as the inauguration of the new covenant—which, in the argument of Hebrews, implies the inauguration of the heavenly sanctuary. This agrees, as well, with the fact that the overruling concern of chs. 8–10 is the inauguration of the new covenant.

---

593 Heb 6:19–20 and 10:19–23 refer specifically to Jesus's entrance "within the veil," an expression that denotes the holy of holies (see page 203, n. 230). This image is used in 6:19 in the context of the inauguration of Jesus's priesthood to refer to the total access he enjoys to the presence of God. The image of entering "through the courtain" in 10:20 (referring to the holy of holies again) refers again to the total access believers enjoy by virtue of Jesus's sacrifice. I will suggest below that the imagery of 10:19–22 describes the privileges of believers as the inauguration of a priestly function of access.

Hebrews 9:24 describes Jesus's ascension as an act of appearance in the presence of God on our behalf. According to this passage, Jesus has ascended in order to "remove sin" by the sacrifice of himself. This not only refers to the forgiveness of sin but implies a change in the human condition so as to bring about righteousness in their lives. This refers to the fulfillment of God's new covenant promise: "I will put my laws in their minds, and write them on their hearts ... for they shall all know me" (Heb 8:10–11; 10:16). Thus, Jesus's ascension inaugurates the fulfillment of God's new covenant promises.

Finally, Heb 10:19–25 describes Jesus's ascension as the opening of "a new and living way" "through the curtain," that is, into the immediate presence of God. The "new" path Jesus has opened is the new covenant that cleanses believers and gives them "confidence" (παρρησία) to approach God. The ascension, then, is conceived as the inauguration of the "full access" believers enjoy in Jesus Christ.

Hebrews 12:18–25 does not refer to Jesus's ascension but to the believers' ascension, through Scriptures, to the heavenly Mount Zion. This passage integrates the different aspects of Jesus's ascension into a coherent image and forcefully concludes the hortatory argument of the Letter. The author argues that, through Scriptures, the believers have witnessed the event that transpired at Mount Zion. They have heard the voice of God speaking to them in Jesus. Through his speech God has accomplished two things: he has adopted Jesus as royal son and enthroned him as ruler over the universe (1:5–14) and has appointed him as high priest forever (5:1–10). In this way God has made Jesus the mediator of the new covenant. Thus, the author concludes, believers should be careful not to disregard the One who speaks to them, lest they incur the wrath of God. Instead, the implicit argument is that they should "hold fast to the confession."

CHAPTER 4

CONCLUSION: JESUS'S ASCENSION INAUGURATES HIS RULE AS THE ESCHATOLOGICAL "SON" OF GOD, FULFILLING THE EXPECTATIONS OF A DAVIDIC RIGHTEOUS RULER IN THE OT

After concluding those passages in which Jesus's ascension is explicitly referred to, we are ready to evaluate the suggestion I made at the end of the second chapter. I suggested there that Jesus's exaltation in heaven embodies the achievements of righteous Davidic rulers. The difference is that Jesus's achievements have an eschatological significance.

I concluded in chap. 2 that the analysis of the rule of righteous Davidic kings in biblical history showed a pattern of their actions that reached its most perfect expression in the reigns of Hezekiah and Josiah. Seven main elements—not always in the same order—comprised this pattern. After ascending the throne, the king would (1) renew the covenant between God and the nation, (2) cleanse the land from spurious forms of worship, (3) build or repair the temple, (4) reform the cult by ordinances that secured a better service for the worshipers and reorganize or reestablish the cultic function of the priests and Levites, (5) promote the reunification of Israel, and (6) achieve "rest" by defeating their enemies. Finally, in several cases, the rise to power of the Davidic king coincides with (7) the emergence of a faithful priest. After the failure of the Davidic dynasty, the prophets projected the fulfillment of the Davidic covenant into the future and elevated the 7 elements of the pattern to eschatological proportions. Later on, early Judaism reacted in diverse fashion to these hopes. Many gave up hope of the restoration of Davidic rule; some sectors, however, continued to hold a belief in the future coming of a Davidic ruler as political liberator and religious reformer.

I have argued that Hebrews describes Jesus's ascension to heaven as part of a complex event that includes several aspects or facets. Hebrews emphasizes three main aspects of this event.

First, Jesus's exaltation in heaven involves his enthronement as king (Heb 1:5–14; cf. 8:1, passim). The author of Hebrews considers this enthronement the fulfillment of the Davidic dynastic promises to which he refers explicitly in Heb 1:5 (quoting 2 Sam 7:14). The Davidic dynastic promises included (1) cutting off the enemies of the king, (2) a great name, (3) "rest" from enemies, (4) the building of a house for God by the Davidic scion, (5) the adoption of the Davidic scion as son of God, and (6) the establishment of the Davidic throne forever (2 Sam 7:5–16).[1] Hebrews relates most of these elements to the enthronement of Jesus. God (1) promised to subdue Jesus's enemies under his feet (Heb 1:13; 10:13), (2) gave Jesus a more excellent name than that of the angels (1:4), (3) has offered the people entrance into his "rest" (4:1–11), (4) adopted Jesus as his Son (Heb 1:5; 5:5), and (5) established Jesus's throne forever (Heb 1:8–10; 12:28). Finally, Jesus is also considered the builder of a "house" (3:3, 6; cf. 1:2, 10),[2] which is identified as consisting of people who "hold firm the confidence and the pride that belong to hope".[3]

As I mentioned above, this identification of Jesus as the Davidic heir is the basis of the author's exposition throughout the Letter. On this basis he identifies Jesus as the heavenly high priest according to the order of Melchizedek, something that in turn implies the inauguration of a new covenant. It is important to note, however, that Hebrews does not argue this point but assumes it. This was an essential belief of early Christianity and he does not feel the need to elaborate on it.[4]

Second, Jesus's exaltation involves his appointment as a faithful high priest over the house of God (3:1–6, chs. 5–7). The books of Chronicles often refer to the ministry of a faithful priest in relation to the enthronement of a righteous Davidic king.[5] The prophet Jeremiah related the raising of a "righteous branch" for David with the perpetuation of the Levitical priesthood (Jer

---

1 For the role that the belief in the permanence of the Davidic dynasty played in the blossoming of messianism in pre-Christian Judaism, see Joseph A. Fitzmyer, *The One Who Is to Come* (Eerdmans, 2007), 33–55.

2 The assertion in Heb 3:4 that "the builder of all things is God" does not deny this. Hebrews 1:2, 10, and elsewhere in the NT (cf. John 1:3), notes that God created all things "through" Jesus.

3 The comparison with Moses in this context suggests that there is a connotation that the building of the believers implies the building of a sanctuary similar to the Pauline idea that the church is the temple of God (1 Cor 3:16; 2 Cor 6:16; Eph 2:21).

4 The belief that Jesus was the Son of David is clear in the NT. It is part of early Christian confessions (Rom 1:3; 2 Tim 2:8) and affirmed throughout the NT (e.g., Mark 12:35–37 [par. Matt 22:41–46; Luke 20:41–44]; Luke 1:32, 69; Acts 2:29–36). See Lohse, 484–488. See also Fitzmyer, *The One Who Is to Come*, 134–145.

5 Note that according to 1 Chr 29:22 the assembly anointed both Solomon as king *and* Zadok as priest together. This dual anointing brings to mind God's commission of Joshua and Branch in Zech 6:9–13.

33:14–22). Similarly, Zech 6:9–13 seems to refer to the joint anointment of a king and a priest. Jesus's appointment as priest, however, has important differences from the OT pattern. The OT has in mind a *Levitical* priesthood and does not foresee the combination of the two offices in one person.[6] Hebrews, however, combines both offices in the person of Jesus and argues for the cessation of the Levitical priesthood.

Third, Jesus's exaltation implies the inauguration of a new covenant (Heb 8–10). Righteous Davidic kings normally renewed the covenant between God and the people (Solomon, 1 Kgs 8:22–26, 56–58; Asa, 2 Chr 15:8–15; Joash, 2 Kgs 11:17; 2 Chr 23:16; Hezekiah, 2 Chr 29:10; Josiah, 2 Kgs 23:1–3; 2 Chr 34:29–33). Therefore, they acted throughout the history of monarchic Israel as the mediators of the covenant between God and the people. It is noteworthy, however, that Ezek 37:24–26 identified the raising of a new David with the inauguration of a new covenant between God and the nation (cf. Ezek 37:22–28; cf. 36:24–28; see above section "Ezekiel" on page 95). Similarly, Jeremiah relates the restoration of Davidic rule over Israel in Jer 33:14–22 to the inauguration of the new covenant of Jer 31:31–34 (see above section "Jeremiah" on page 88).

Moreover, these three main aspects—the exaltation as enthronement, appointment to priesthood, and inauguration of the new covenant—subsume additional aspects (or, sub-aspects) of Jesus's exaltation.

First, Jesus's enthronement as king makes it possible for believers to enter into God's "rest" (Heb 3:11–4:16). This is the result of Jesus's defeat of the devil that resulted in the deliverance of those who were under his dominion (2:10–18). Likewise, God's promises to David included the defeat of his enemies and the provision of "rest" for the people (2 Sam 7:10–11). This implied that Israel's entrance into Canaan under the leadership of Joshua had not really achieved God's promised rest to Israel (see above section "The Davidic King as Reformer of the Cult ..." on page 46). In fact, it could not have achieved it because the permanent place of the sanctuary/temple was not yet established. The book of Deuteronomy had instructed the nation that when they crossed "over the Jordan," lived in the "land," and God had given them "rest from ... enemies all around" (12:10), God would choose "a place ... out of all your tribes as his habitation to put his name there" (12:5, 11, 14, etc.). Thus, the rest under these conditions was achieved only when Solomon built the temple (2 Kgs 8:56; cf.

Similarly, several pairs of kings and priests are noteworthy in the story of Chronicles; for example, Jehoshaphat and Amariah (2 Chr 19:11), Joash and Jehoiada (chs. 23–24), Uzziah and Azariah (26:16–21); Hezekiah and Azariah (31:13); Josiah and Hilkiah (chs. 34–35).

6 Though this is a possible meaning for Zech 6:9–13. See above section "Zechariah" on page 102.

1 Chr 22:9; 23:5).[7] In the same way, the author of Hebrews argues that Joshua did not give the people rest (Heb 4:8); instead, it is Jesus who has given Israel the true rest.

Second, Jesus, the heavenly king-priest, is the mediator of a new covenant and, as such, he implements a major reorganization of the cult.[8] The cultic order of the first covenant that included multiple Levitical priests and multiple sacrifices has been replaced by one eternal high priest according to the order of Melchizedek and the "once for all" sacrifice of Jesus Christ. Similarly, righteous Davidic kings were described as reformers of the cult. The building of the temple by Solomon fulfilled the conditions necessary for the cultic changes foreseen in Deuteronomy (see 12:1–12, passim; see above section "The Davidic King as Reformer of the Cult" on page 46). The most conspicuous element of this reform was a change concerning the law of sacrifices, which centralized the sacrifices at the place that would be chosen by God (cf. Deut 12). God also revealed to David new stipulations regarding the priestly and Levitical courses and their service for the temple (1 Chr 28:13). The reform of the sacrifices began with but was not totally implemented by Solomon. A full reform was achieved until the time of Hezekiah and Josiah.[9] Other Davidic kings also implemented the Davidic stipulations regarding the priestly and Levitical courses and, in fact, several of them implemented additional changes in the cultic roles of the priests and Levites (e.g., Joash, 2 Chr 23:18; Hezekiah, 2 Chr 29–30; and Josiah, 2 Chr 35:1–9).

Third, Jesus's sacrifice cleanses believers from the transgressions committed under the old covenant. This cleansing, however, denotes not only forgiveness (Heb 9:22) but also the removal of sin through the interiorization of the law in the believers (9:25–10:10) as promised in the new covenant (8:8–12). In other words, by inaugurating the new covenant, Jesus's sacrifice makes possible a new era of righteousness for the people of God. Similarly, righteous Davidic kings tried to enforce faithfulness to Yahweh by cleansing the land from idolatry. Their reforms were short lived, however. Therefore, the prophets

---

[7] Later on, Davidic kings are also described as receiving rest from God (e.g., Asa, 2 Chr 14:6; Jehoshaphat, 2 Chr 20:30; Hezekiah, 2 Chr 32:22).

[8] Jesus, like the Davidic king, is mediator of the covenant in a special sense. First, Jesus represents humanity in general and as such God fulfills in him his saving purposes for them (2:5–10). (Similarly, as I showed in pp. 43–46, God assigns to David and his descendants the promises he had made to Israel.) Second, Jesus mediates the blessings to believers. Jesus has been enthroned in order to lead "many children [υἱοί] to glory." He is their leader (ἀρχηγός) and forerunner and guarantees the fulfillment of God's promises to them (7:22). (Similarly, the Davidic king is a channel of God's promises for the people. See above section "The Davidic King as Covenant Mediator: He Renews the Mosaic Covenant under 'Better Promises' on page 43.")

[9] Hezekiah and Josiah finally removed the high places (since Manasseh had rebuilt them; 2 Kgs 18:22; 23:5–9; 2 Chr 31:1; 32:12; 34:3).

told of the coming of a righteous Davidic king who would bring about a new era of righteousness (e.g., Hos 3:4–5; Isa 9:6–7; 11:1–10; Jer 23:5–6; Zech 12:10–14; cf. *Pss. Sol.* 17).

Finally, Jesus's inauguration of the covenant implies the consecration of a heavenly sanctuary with his "better" sacrifice (9:23). Similarly, the renewal of the covenant by righteous Davidic kings included either the inauguration of a new temple (Solomon), the reparation of the temple (Asa, 2 Chr 15:8; cf. 1 Kgs 15:15; Joash, 2 Kgs 12:1–16; 2 Chr 24:4–14; Josiah, 2 Chr 34:8–13; 2 Kgs 22:3–7) or, plainly, its re-consecration (Hezekiah, 2 Chr 29:5–19). Ezekiel prophesied as well that the restoration of Davidic rule would include the construction of a new temple (Ezek 37:26–28; cf. Zech 6:9–15).

The only aspect in which Hebrews does not show any interest is the reunification of Israel. A summary of this relationship is shown in table 11.

Hebrews' purpose, however, is not to prove that Jesus's exaltation fulfills the expectations for an eschatological Davidic ruler; instead, it assumes that the readers know this and establishes this notion as the foundation for his exhortation to the readers to hold on to their faith. In other words, these Davidic traditions function as an essential subtext of the Letter that provide the necessary force to its hortatory argument. Thus, the author of Hebrews argues that Jesus's exaltation in heaven as the eschatological Davidic king and faithful high priest—which the readers have witnessed through the Scriptures (pp. 287–298)—demands their allegiance to him; otherwise, they will suffer the judgment of God.[10] As members of Jesus's household, they are to enter before God, as "priests" who therefore are bound to God and have greater accountability to holiness. He exhorts them, then, to "hold fast the confession" of their faith and "persevere" in the race so they may inherit the promises of God.

Achievements of the Davidic Righteous Rulers	Implications of the Enthronement of Jesus as Son
Renewal of the covenant between God and the nation	Mediation of a new covenant (Heb 8–10)
Cleansing of the land from spurious forms of worship	Cleansing of the conscience (9:14) and removal of sin by the interiorization of God's law in the believers (9:24–10:10)
The building or repair of the temple is followed by its consecration through cleansing	God builds the temple (3:3–4; 8:2) Jesus consecrates the heavenly sanctuary with better sacrifices (9:23)

Reform of the Cult. This includes: (1) the centralization of the sacrifices at Jerusalem as disposed in Deuteronomy (2) new stipulations regarding the priestly and Levitical courses as revealed to David (1 Chr 28:11–19)	Substitution of the Levitical priesthood with a new high priest according to the order of Melchizedek (Heb 5–7) Substitution of animal sacrifices with the "once for all" sacrifice of Christ (10:18) Inauguration of a new spiritual worship for the believers (12:28–29; 13:10–16)
Reunification of Israel	Implied in the "new covenant with the house of Israel and the house of Judah" that Jesus mediates [Heb 8:8]. This is not developed, however, in the argument of the Letter.[11]
"Rest" from the enemies	Availability of God's rest (3:7–4:16)
The emergence of a faithful priest	Jesus is a faithful high priest over the house of God (3:1–6)

Table 11. The Enthronement of the "Son" in Hebrews as an Eschatological Amplification of the Achievements of Righteous Davidic Rulers

---

11 This aspect of the argument of Hebrews was brought to my attention by George H. Guthrie and David Moffitt at the Hebrews Section of the Annual Meeting of the Society of Biblical Literature (San Diego, Calif., November 17–20, 2007).

Bibliography

Abegg, Martin G., Jr. "Messianic Hope and 4Q285: A Reassesment." *JBL* 113 (1994): 81–91.

Aberbach, Moses, and Bernard Grossfeld. *Targum Onkelos: A Critical Analysis Together With An English Translation of the Text*. Ktav, 1982.

Achtemeier, Elizabeth. *Nahum–Malachi*. IBC. John Knox, 1986.

Adams, Edward. "The Cosmology of Hebrews." Pages 122–139 in *The Epistle to the Hebrews and Christian Theology*. Edited by Richard Bauckham et al. Eerdmans, 2009.

Aitken, Ellen Bradshaw. "The Hero in the Epistle to the Hebrews: Jesus as an Ascetic Model." Pages 179–188 in *Early Christian Voices: In Texts, Traditions, and Symbols: Essays in Honor of François Bovon*, edited by David H. Warren, Ann Graham Brock, and David W. Pao. BibInt 66. Brill Academic, 2003.

———. "Portraying the Temple in Stone and Text: The Arch of Titus and the Epistle to the Hebrews." Pages 131–148 in *Hebrews: Contemporary Methods—New Insights*. Edited by Gabriella Gelardini. BibInt 75. Brill, 2005.

Alexander, Philip S. "Targum, Targumim." *ABD* 6:320–631.

Alexandre, Manuel, Jr. "The Art of Periodic Composition in Philo of Alexandria." Pages 135–150 in *Studia Philonica Annual: Studies in Hellenistic Judaism*. Vol. 3. BJS. Scholars Press, 1991.

Allegro, John M., and with the collaboration of Arnold A. Anderson. *Qumrân Cave 4: I (4Q158–4Q186)*. DJD 5. Clarendon, 1968.

Allen, David L. *Hebrews*. NAC. Broadman & Holman, 2010.

Allen, Leslie C. *Ezekiel 20–48*. WBC 29. Word, 1990.

———. *Psalms 101–150: Revised*. WBC 21. Thomas Nelson, 2002.

Allenbach, J., and others. *Des origines à Clément d'Alexandrie et Tertullien*. BiPa 1. Éditions du centre national de la recherche scientifique, 1975.

———. *Philon d'Alexandrie. Biblia Patristica: Supplément*. Éditions du centre national de la recherche scientifique, 1982.

Allison, Dale C., Jr. "Melchizedek." *DLNT* 729–731.

Aloisi, John. "Who Is David's Lord? Another Look at Psalm 110:1." *Detroit Baptist Seminary Journal* 10 (2005): 103–123.

Alomía B., Merling. "La singularidad de Jesús en la Epístola a los Hebreos." *Theo* 4 (1989): 2–33.

Althann, Robert. "Gedaliah (Person)." *ABD* 2:923–925.

Álvarez Cineira, D. "Los Sacrificios en la Carta a los Hebreos 10,1–18." *EstAg* 30 (1995): 5–58, 207–237.

Andersen, Francis I., and David Noel Freedman. *Amos: A New Translation with Introduction and Commentary*. AB 24A. Doubleday, 1989.

———. *Hosea: A New Translation with Introduction and Commentary*. AB 24. Doubleday, 1980.

———. *Micah: A New Translation with Introduction and Commentary*. AB 24E. Doubleday, 2000.

Anderson, A. A. *2 Samuel*. WBC 11. Word, 1989.

Anderson, C. P. "The Epistle to the Hebrews and the Pauline Letter Collection." *HTR* 59 (1966): 429–438.

———. "Hebrews among the Letters of Paul." *SR* 5 (1976): 258–266.

———. "Who Are the Heirs of the New Age in the Epistle to the Hebrews?" Pages 255–277 in *Apocalyptic and the New Testament*. Edited by Joel Marcus and Marion L. Soards. JSNTSup 24. JSOT Press, 1989.

Anderson, David R. *The King-Priest of Psalm 110 in Hebrews*. StuBibLit 21. Lang, 2001.

Anderson, H. "The Jewish Antecedents of the Christology in Hebrews." Pages 536–568 in *The Messiah: Developments in Earliest Judaism and Christianity*. Edited by James H. Charlesworth. Fortress, 1992.

Anderson, R. Dean, Jr. *Ancient Rhetorical Theory and Paul*. Rev. ed. CBET 18. Peeters, 1999.

———. *Glossary of Greek Rhetorical Terms Connected to Methods of Argumentation, Figures and Tropes from Anaximenes to Quintilian*. CBET 24. Peeters, 2000.

Anderson, Robert. *Types in Hebrews*. Kregel, 1978.

Andriessen, Paul C. B. "Das größere und vollkommenere Zelt (Hebr 9, 11)." *BZ* 15 (1971): 76–92.

———. "La Teneur Judéo-Chrétienne de HE I 6 et II 14B–III 2." *NovT* 18 (1976): 293–313.

Andriessen, Paul C. B., and A. Lenglet. "Quelques passages difficiles de l'Épître aux Hébreux (5,7.11; 10,20; 12,2)." *Bib* 51 (1970): 207–220.

Andross, E. E. *A More Excellent Ministry*. Pacific Press, 1912.

The Ante-Nicene Fathers. Edited by Alexander Roberts and James Donaldson. 10 vols., 1885–1887. Reprint, Hendrickson, 1994.

Aquinas, St. Thomas. *The Resurrection of the Lord (3a. 53–59)*. Translated by C. Thomas Moore. Summa Theologiae 55. Blackfriars, 1976.

Argyle, A. W. "The Ascension." *ExpTim* 66 (1955): 240–242.

Aristotle. *The "Art" of Rhetoric*. Translated by John Henry Freese. LCL. Harvard University Press, 1947.

Arnold, Bill T. *1 & Samuel*. NIVAC. Zondervan, 2003.

Aschim, Anders. "Melchizedek and Jesus: 11QMelchizedek and the Epistle to the Hebrews." Pages 129–147 in *Jewish Roots of Christological Monotheism: Papers from the St. Andrews Conference on the Historical Origins of the Worship of Jesus*. Edited by Carey C. Newman, James R. Davila, and Gladys S. Lewis. JSJSup 63. Brill, 1999.

Ashley, Timothy R. *The Book of Numbers*. NICOT. Eerdmans, 1993.

Atkins, Peter. *Ascension Now: Implications of Christ's Ascension for Today's Church*. Liturgical, 2001.

Attridge, Harold W. *The Epistle to the Hebrews*. Edited by Helmut Koester. Hermeneia. Fortress, 1989.

———. "God in Hebrews: Urging Children to Heavenly Glory." Pages 197–209 in *The Forgotten God: Perspectives in Biblical Theology*. Edited by A. Andrew Das and Frank J. Matera. Westminster John Knox, 2002.

———. "Historiography." Pages 157–184 in *Jewish Writings of the Second Temple Period: Apocrypha, Pseudepigrapha, Qumran Sectarian Writings, Philo, Josephus*. Edited by Michael E. Stone. CRINT Van Gorcum; Fortress, 1984.

———. "Josephus and His Works." Pages 185–232 in *Jewish Writings of the Second Temple Period: Apocrypha, Pseudepigrapha, Qumran Sectarian Writings, Philo, Josephus*, edited by Michael E. Stone. CRINT. Van Gorcum; Fortress, 1984.

———. "'Let Us Strive to Enter That Rest': The Logic of Heb 4:1–11." *HTR* 73 (1980): 279–288.

———. "New Covenant Christology in an Early Christian Homily." *Quarterly Review* 8, no. 3 (1988): 89–108.

———. Review of *Sohn und Hoherpriester: Eine traditionsgeschichtliche Untersuchung zur Christologie des Hebräerbriefes*, by William R. G. Loader. *JBL* 103 (1984): 303–305.

———. Review of *Theozentrik und Bekenntnis: Untersuchungen zur Theologie des Redens Gottes im Hebräerbrief*, by David Wider. *CBQ* 62 (2000): 378–379.

———. "The Uses of Antithesis in Hebrews 8–10." *HTR* 79 (1986): 1–9.

Auffret, Pierre. "Il est seigneur sur les nations: Etude structurelle du psaume 110." *BN* 123 (2004): 65–74.

Auld, A. Graeme. *Kings without Privilege: David and Moses in the Story of the Bible's Kings*. T&T Clark, 1994.

Aulén, Gustaf. *Christus Victor: An Historical Study of the Three Main Types of the Idea of Atonement*. Translated by A. G. Hebert. Macmillan, 1958.

Aune, David E. "Heracles and Christ: Heracles Imagery in the Christology of Early Christianity." Pages 1–19 in *Greeks, Romans, and Christians: Essays in Honor of Abraham Malherbe*. Edited by D. L. Balch, Everett Ferguson, and W. A. Meeks. Fortress, 1990.

———. *Prophecy in Early Christianity and the Ancient Mediterranean World*. Eerdmans, 1983.

———. *Revelation 6–16*. WBC 52B. Word, 1998.

———. *The Westminster Dictionary of New Testament and Early Christian Literature and Rhetoric*. Westminster John Knox, 2003.

Austin, J. L. *How to Do Things with Words*. Clarendon, 1962.

Avalos, Hector. "Daniel 9:24–25 and Mesopotamian Temple Rededications." *JBL* 117 (1998): 507–511.

Averbeck, R. E. "Sacrifices and Offerings." *DOTP* 185–232.

Avis, Paul. *God and the Creative Imagination: Metaphor, Symbol and Myth in Religion and Theology*. Routledge, 1999.

Backhaus, Knut. "Die Hebräerbrief und die Paulus-Schule." *BZ* 37 (1993): 183–208.

———. "Das Land der Verheißung: Die Heimat der Glaubenden im Hebräerbrief." *NTS* 47 (2001): 171–188.

Bailey, Daniel P. Review of *Der Tod Jesu als Heiligtumsweihe: Eine Untersuchung zum Umfeld der Sühnevorstellung in Römer 3, 25–26a*, by Wolfgang Kraus. *JTS* 45 (1994): 247–252.

Baillet, Maurice. *Qumran grotte 4: III (4Q482–4Q520)*. DJD 7. Clarendon, 1982.

Baker, David W. *Joel, Obadiah, Malachi*. NIVAC. Zondervan, 2006.

Baldick, Chris. *The Concise Oxford Dictionary of Literary Terms*. Oxford University Press, 1990.

Balla, Peter. *The Melchizedekian Priesthood*. Károli Gáspár Reformed University Faculty of Theology, 1995.

Ballard, Harold Wayne, Jr. *The Divine Warrior Motif in the Psalms*. BIBAL Dissertation Series 6. BIBAL, 1999.

Barker, Kenneth L., and Waylon Bailey. *Micah, Nahum, Habakkuk, Zephaniah*. NAC 20. Broadman & Holman, 1998.

Barker, Margaret. *The Gate of Heaven: The History and Symbolism of the Temple in Jerusalem*. SPCK, 1991.

_____. *The Great High Priest: The Temple Roots of Christian Liturgy*. T&T Clark, 2003.

_____. *On Earth as It Is in Heaven: Temple Symbolism in the New Testament*. T&T Clark, 1995.

_____. "Temple Imagery in Philo: An Indication of the Origin of the Logos?" Pages 70–102 in *Templum amicitiae: Essays on the Second Temple Presented to Ernst Bammel*. Edited by William Horbury. JSNTSup 48. JSOT Press, 1991.

_____. *Temple Theology: An Introduction*. SPCK, 2004.

Barnett, Albert E. *Paul Becomes a Literary Influence*. University of Chicago Press, 1941.

Barrett, C. K. "Attitudes to the Temple in the Acts of the Apostles." Pages 345–367 in *Templum amicitiae: Essays on the Second Temple Presented to Ernst Bammel*. Edited by William Horbury. JSNTSup 48. JSOT Press, 1991.

_____. "The Christology of Hebrews." Pages 110–127 in *Who Do You Say That I Am: Essays on Christology*. Edited by Mark Allan Powell and David R. Bauer. Westminster John Knox, 1999.

_____. *A Critical and Exegetical Commentary on The Acts of the Apostles*. 2 vols. ICC. T&T Clark, 1994.

_____. "The Eschatology of the Epistle to the Hebrews." Pages 363–393 in *The Background of the New Testament and Its Eschatology*. Edited by William David Davies and David Daube. Cambridge University Press, 1956.

Barth, Karl. *Doctrine of Creation*. Edited by Geoffrey W. Bromiley and Thomas F. Torrance. *Church Dogmatics* 3/2. T&T Clark, 1960.

Bateman IV, Herbert W. *Early Jewish Hermeneutics and Hebrews 1:5–13: The Impact of Early Jewish Exegesis on the Interpretation of a Significant New Testament Passage*. AUSTR 193. Lang, 1997.

Bauer, Walter. *A Greek-English Lexicon of the New Testament and other Christian Literature*. Edited and revised by F. W. Danker, W. F. Arndt, and F. W. Gingrich. 3d ed. The University of Chicago Press, 2000.

Baumgarten, Joseph M. "Yom Kippur in the Qumran Scrolls and Second Temple Sources." *DSD* 6 (1999): 184–191.

Beale, Gregory K. "The Descent of the Eschatological Temple in the Form of the Spirit at Pentecost (Part 1): The Clearest Evidence." *TynBul* 56 (2005): 73–102.

_____. "Eden, the Temple, and the Church's Mission in the New Creation." *JETS* 48 (2005): 5–31.

_____. *The Temple and the Church's Mission: A Biblical Theology of the Dwelling Place of God*. NSBT 17. Apollos, InterVarsity, 2004.

Beavis, Mary Ann. "The New Covenant and Judaism." *TBT* 22 (1984): 24–30.

Becker, O. "μεσίτης." *NIDNTT* 1:372–375.

Beckman, Gary. *Hittite Diplomatic Texts*. Edited by Harry A. Hoffner, Jr. 2d ed. SBLWAW 7. Scholars, 1999.

Behm, Johannes. "διαθήκη." *TDNT* 2:124–134.

———. "Ἐγκαινίζω." *TDNT* 3:453–454.

Bénétreau, Samuel. "Le repos du pèlerin (Hébreux 3,7–4:11)." *ETR* 78 (2003): 203–223.

———. *L'épître aux Hébreux*. 2 vols. CEB 10. Édifac, 1989.

———. "La mort du Christ selon L'épître aux Hébreux." *Hok* 39 (1989): 25–47.

———. "La mort de Jésus et le sacrifice dans l'épître aux Hébreux." *FoiVie* 95/4 (1996): 33–145.

Berényi, Gabriella. "La portée de δια τουτο en He 9, 15." *Bib* 69 (1988): 108–112.

Bergen, Robert D. *1, 2 Samuel*. NAC 7. Broadman & Holman, 1996.

Bietenhard, Hans. *Die himmlische Welt im Urchristentum un Spätjudentum*. WUNT I/2. Mohr Siebeck, 1951.

Birch, Bruce C. "The First and Second Books of Samuel." *NIB* 2:947–1383.

Birnbaum, Ellen. "Two Millennia Later: General Resources and Particular Perspectives on Philo the Jew." *CurBR* 4 (2006): 241–276.

Black, David Alan. "Hebrews 1:1–4: A Study in Discourse Analysis." *WTJ* 49 (1987): 175–194.

———. "Literary Artistry in the Epistle to the Hebrews." *Filología Neotestamentaria* 7/13 (1994): 43–52.

———. "On the Pauline Authorship of Hebrews (Part 1): Overlooked Affinities between Hebrews and Paul." *Faith & Mission* 16/2 (1999): 32–51.

———. "On the Pauline Authorship of Hebrews (Part 2): The External Evidence Reconsidered." *Faith & Mission* 16/3 (1999): 78–86.

———. "The Problem of the Literary Structure of Hebrews: An Evaluation and a Proposal." *Grace Theological Journal* 7 (1986): 163–177.

Blass, F., A. Debrunner, and Robert W. Funk. *A Greek Grammar of the New Testament and Other Early Christian Literature*. University of Chicago Press, 1961.

Blenkinsopp, Joseph. *Ezra–Nehemiah: A Commentary*. OTL. Westminster, 1988.

———. *Isaiah 1–39: A New Translation with Introduction and Commentary*. AB 19. Doubleday, 2000.

———. *Isaiah 40–55: A New Translation with Introduction and Commentary*. AB 19A. Doubleday, 2002.

Block, Daniel I. *The Book of Ezekiel: Chapters 1–24*. NICOT. Eerdmans, 1997.

———. *The Book of Ezekiel: Chapters 25–48*. NICOT. Eerdmans, 1998.

Boda, Mark J. *Haggai, Zechariah*. NIVAC. Zondervan, 2004.

Borgen, Peder. "Moses, Jesus, and the Roman Emperor: Observations in Philo's Writings and the Revelation of John." *NovT* 38 (1996): 145–159.

———. *Philo, John, and Paul: New Perspectives on Judaism and Early Christianity*. BJS 131. Scholars, 1987.

———. "Philo of Alexandria." *ABD* 5:333–342.

———. *Philo of Alexandria: An Exegete for His Time*. NovTSup 86. Brill, 1997.

Borgen, Peder, Kåre Sigvald Fuglseth, and Roald Skarsten. *The Philo Index: A Complete Greek Word Index to the Writings of Philo of Alexandria*. Eerdmans, 2000.

Bosman, Philip. *Conscience in Philo and Paul: A Conceptual History of the Synoida Word Group.* WUNT I/166. Mohr (Siebeck), 2003.

Botterweck, G. Johannes, and Helmer Ringgren, eds. *Theological Dictionary of the Old Testament.* Translated by John T. Willis et al. 14 vols. Eerdmans, 1974–2006.

Boustan, Ra'anan S., and Annette Yoshiko Reed, eds. *Heavenly Realms and Earthly Realities in Late Antique Religions.* Cambridge University Press, 2004.

Bräumer, Hansjörg. *Das erste Buch Mose.* Wuppertaler Studienbibel: Altes Testament. Brockhaus, 1983.

Braun, Herbert. *An die Hebräer.* HNT 14. Mohr Siebeck, 1984.

———. "Qumran und das Neue Testament: ein Bericht über 10 Jahre Forschung (1950–1959): Hebräer." *TRu* 30 (1964): 1–38.

Bray, G. L. "Ascension and Heavenly Session of Christ." Pages 46–47 in *New Dictionary of Theology.* Edited by Sinclair B. Ferguson and David F. Wright. InterVarsity, 1988.

Brege, Daniel J. "Eucharistic Overtones Created by Sacrificial Concepts in the Epistle to the Hebrews." *CTQ* 66 (2002): 61–81.

———. *Brill's New Pauly: Encyclopaedia of the Ancient World.* Edited by Hubert Cancik. 22 vols. Brill, 2002–2011.

Bronstein, Herbert. "Yom Kippur Worship: A Missing Center." *CCAR Journal* 51/3 (2004): 7–15.

Brooke, Alan England, Norman McLean, and Henry St John Thackeray, eds. *The Old Testament in Greek: According to the Text of Codex Vaticanus, Supplemented from Other Uncial Manuscripts, with a Critical Apparatus Containing the Variants of the Chief Ancient Authorities for the Text of the Septuagint.* The Later Historical Books 1. Cambridge University Press, 1927.

Brooke, George J., ed. "4Q252 as Early Jewish Commentary." *RevQ* 17 (1996): 385–402.

———. *The Dead Sea Scrolls and the New Testament.* Fortress, 2005.

———. "Florilegium (4Q174)." *DNTB* 378–380.

———. "Pesharim." *DNTB* 778–782.

———. *Temple Scroll Studies.* JSPSup 7. JSOT Press, 1989.

———. "The Ten Temples in the Dead Sea Scrolls." Pages 417–434 in *Temple and Worship in Biblical Israel.* Edited by John Day. LHBOTS 422. T&T Clark, 2005.

Brooks, Walter Edward. "The Perpetuity of Christ's Sacrifice." *JBL* 89 (1970): 205–214.

Brown, Raymond. *Christ Above All: The Message of Hebrews.* The Bible Speaks Today. InterVarsity, 1982.

Brown, Raymond E. *The Birth of the Messiah: A Commentary on the Infancy Narratives in the Gospels of Matthew and Luke.* New upd. ed. ABRL. Doubleday, 1993.

Brown, Stephen J. *Image and Truth: Studies in the Imagery of the Bible.* Catholic Book Agency, 1955.

Bruce, F. F. *The Epistle to the Hebrews.* Rev. ed. NICNT. Eerdmans, 1990.

———. "A Shadow of Good Things to Come." Pages 75–94 in *The Time Is Fulfilled: Five Aspects of the Fulfilment of the Old Testament in the New.* Eerdmans, 1978.

———. " 'To the Hebrews' or 'To the Essenes'." *NTS* 9 (1963): 217–232.

Brueggemann, Walter. *First and Second Samuel.* IBC. John Knox, 1990.

Bryan, Steven M. "The Eschatological Temple in John 14." *BBR* 15 (2005): 187–198.

―――――. *Jesus and Israel's Traditions of Judgement and Restoration.* SNTSMS 117. Cambridge University Press, 2002.

Buchanan, George Wesley. "The Present State of Scholarship on Hebrews." Pages 299–330 in volume 1 of *Christianity, Judaism and Other Greco-Roman Cults.* Edited by Jacob Neusner. SJLA 12. Brill, 1975.

―――――. *To the Hebrews: Translation, Comment and Conclusions.* AB 36. Doubleday, 1972.

Burger, Christoph. *Jesus Als Davidssohn: Eine traditionsgeschichtliche Untersuchung.* FRLANT 98. Vandenhoeck & Ruprecht, 1970.

Burgess, Andrew. *The Ascension in Karl Barth.* Barth Studies. Ashgate, 2004.

Burtness, James H. "Plato, Philo and Hebrews." *Lutheran Quarterly* 10 (1958): 54–64.

Busch, Peter. "Der mitleidende Hoherpriester: Zur Rezeption der mittelplatonischen Dämonologie in Hebr 4,14f." Pages 19–30 in *Religionsgeschichte des Neuen Testaments.* Edited by Axel von Dobbeler, Kurt Erlemann, and Roman Heiligenthal. Francke, 2000.

Caird, G. B. "The Exegetical Method of the Epistle to the Hebrews." *CJT* 5 (1959): 44–51.

―――――. *The Revelation of Saint John.* BNTC. Black, 1966. Reprint, Hendrickson.

―――――. "Son by Appointment." Pages 73–82 in volume 1 of *The New Testament Age,* edited by William C. Weinrich. Mercer University Press, 1984.

Camacho, Harold S. "The Altar of Incense in Hebrews 9:3–4." *AUSS* 24 (1986): 5–12.

Cameron, Alan. *Circus Factions: Blues and Greens at Rome and Byzantium.* Clarendon, 1976.

Campbell, Jonathan G. *The Exegetical Texts.* Companion to the Qumran Scrolls 4. T&T Clark, 2004.

Campbell, Kenneth M. "Covenant or Testament?" *EvQ* 44 (1972): 107–111.

Canivet, P. "Theodoret of Cyr." *NCE* 13:878–879.

Cantalamessa, Raniero. "Il papiro Chester Beatty III (P^{46}) e la tradizione indiretta di Hebr. 10,1." *Aegyptus* 45 (1965): 194–215.

Carey, Gary, and Mary Ellen Snodgrass. *A Multicultural Dictionary of Literary Terms.* McFarland, 1999.

Carlston, Charles. "The Vocabulary of Perfection in Philo and Hebrews." Pages 133–160 in *Unity and Diversity in New Testament Theology.* Edited by Robert A. Guelich,. Eerdmans, 1978.

Carroll, John T., and Joel B. Green. *The Death of Jesus in Early Christianity.* Hendrickson, 1995.

Carroll, Robert P. *Jeremiah: A Commentary.* OTL. Westminster, 1986.

Casalini, Nello. *Agli Ebrei: Discorso di esortazione.* SBFA 34. Franciscan, 1992.

―――――. *Dal simbolo alla realta': L'expiazione dall'Antica alla Nuova Allenaza secondo Ebr 9,1–14: Una proposta esegetica.* SBFA 26. Franciscan, 1989.

―――――. "Ebr 9,11: La tenda più grande e più perfetta: Una proposta per la soluzione del problema." *Liber annuus Studii biblici franciscani* 36 (1986): 111–170.

―――――. "I sacrifici dell'antica alleanza nel piano salvifico di Dio secondo la Lettera agli ebrei." *Rivista biblica italiana* 35 (1987): 443–464.

―――――. "Per un commento a Ebrei." *Liber annuus Studii biblici franciscani* 41 (1991): 125–128.

_____. "Per un commento a Ebrei (II) Eb 7,1–10,18." *Liber annuus Studii biblici franciscani* 44 (1994): 111–214.

Casey, Juliana. *Hebrews*. NTM 18. Glazier, 1980.

Caudill, R. Paul. *Hebrews: A Translation with Notes*. Broadman, 1985.

Chae, Young S. *Jesus as the Eschatological Davidic Shepherd*. WUNT II/216. Mohr Siebeck, 2006.

Champlin, Edward. *Nero*. Belknap, 2003.

Charles, J. Daryl. "The Angels, Sonship and Birthright in the Letter to the Hebrews." *JETS* 33 (1990): 171–178.

Charlesworth, James H. "From Jewish Messianology to Christian Christology: Some Caveats and Perspectives." Pages 225–264 in *Judaisms and Their Messiahs at the Turn of the Christian Era*, edited by Jacob Neusner, William Scott Green, and Ernest S. Frerichs. Cambridge University Press, 1987.

_____. "From Messianology to Christology: Problems and Prospects." Pages 3–35 in *The Messiah: Developments in Earliest Judaism and Christianity*. Edited by James H. Charlesworth. Fortress, 1992.

Chester, Andrew. "The Sibyl and the Temple." Pages 37–69 in *Templum amicitiae: Essays on the Second Temple Presented to Ernst Bammel*. Edited by William Horbury. JSNTSup 48. JSOT Press, 1991.

Childs, Brevard S. *Isaiah*. OTL. Westminster John Knox, 2001.

Christensen, Duane L. *Deuteronomy 1:1–21:9*. Rev. ed. WBC 6A. Word, 2001.

_____. *Deuteronomy 21:10–34:12*. WBC 6b. Word, 2002.

Clarke, A. D. "Alexandria." *DNTB* 23–25.

Classicae, Lexicon Iconographicum Mythologiae, and J. Paul Getty Museum. *Thesaurus cultus et rituum antiquorum*. 5 vols. J. Paul Getty Museum, 2004.

Clifford, Richard J. "The Roots of Apocalypticism in Near Eastern Myth." Pages 3–38 in *The Origins of Apocalypticism in Judaism and Christianity*. Edited by John J. Collins. Vol. 1 of *The Encyclopedia of Apocalypticism*. Edited by Bernard McGinn, John J. Collins, and Stephen J. Stein. Continuum, 1998.

_____. "Second Isaiah." *ABD* 3:490–501.

_____. "The Temple and the Holy Mountain." Pages 107–124 in *The Temple in Antiquity: Ancient Records and Modern Perspectives*. Edited by Truman G. Madsen. Religious Studies Monograph Series 9. Religious Studies Center Brighan Young University, 1984.

Coats, George W. *Moses: Heroic Man, Man of God*. JSOTSup 57. JSOT Press, 1988.

Cockerill, Gareth Lee. "The Better Resurrection (Heb 11:35): A Key to the Structure and Rhetorical Purpose of Hebrews 11." *TynBul* 51 (2000): 215–234.

_____. "Heb 1:1–4, *1 Clem.* 36:1–6 and the High Priest Title." *JBL* 97 (1978): 437–440.

_____. "Hebrews 1:6: Source and Significance." *BBR* 9 (1999): 51–64.

_____. "Melchizedek or 'King of Righteousness.' " *EvQ* 63 (1991): 305–312.

_____. "Structure and Interpretation in Hebrews 8:1–10:18: A Symphony in Three Movements." *BBR* 11 (2001): 179–201.

Cody, Aelred. *Heavenly Sanctuary and Liturgy in the Epistle to the Hebrews: The Achievement of Salvation in the Epistle's Perspective*. Grail, 1960.

Cogan, Mordechai. *1 Kings: A New Translation with Introduction and Commentary*. AB 10. Doubleday, 2001.

Coggins, R. J. "Commentary on 1 Esdras." Pages 4–75 in *The First and Second Books of Esdras*. Edited by P. R. Ackroyd, A. R. C. Leaney, and J. W. Packer. CBC. Cambridge University Press, 1979.

Coleman, Kathleen. Review of *Nero*, by Edward Champlin. *Roman Archaeology* 18 (2005): 545–550.

Colijn, Brenda B. " 'Let Us Approach': Soteriology in the Epistle to the Hebrews." *JETS* 39 (1996): 571–586.

Collins, Adela Yarbro. *The Combat Myth in the Book of Revelation*. HDR 9. Scholars Press, 1976.

———. "Pergamon in Early Christian Literature." Pages 163–184 in *Pergamon, Citadel of the Gods: Archaeological Record, Literary Description, and Religious Development*. Edited by Helmut Koester. HTS 46. Trinity, 1998.

———. "The Seven Heavens in Jewish and Christian Apocalypses." Pages 57–92 in *Death, Ecstasy, and Other Worldly Journeys*. Edited by John J. Collins and Michael Fishbane. State University of New York Press, 1995.

Collins, John J. "Dead Sea Scrolls." *ABD* 2:85–101.

———. "Messianism in the Maccabean Period." Pages 97–110 in *Judaisms and Their Messiahs at the Turn of the Christian Era*. Edited by Jacob Neusner, William Scott Green, and Ernest S. Frerichs. Cambridge University Press, 1987.

———. *The Scepter and the Star: The Messiahs of the Dead Sea Scrolls and Other Ancient Literature*. ABRL. Doubleday, 1995.

———. "The *Son of God* Text from Qumran." Pages 65–82 in *From Jesus to John: Essays on Jesus and New Testament Christology in Honour of Marinus de Jonge*. Edited by Martinus C. De Boer. JSNTSup 84. JSOT Press, 1993.

———. "The Testamentary Literature in Recent Scholarship." Pages 268–285 in *Early Judaism and Its Modern Interpreters*. Edited by Robert A. Kraft and George W. E. Nickelsburg. SBLBMI 2. Fortress; Scholars Press, 1986.

———. "A Throne in the Heavens: Apotheosis in Pre-Christian Judaism." Pages 43–58 in *Death, Ecstasy, and Other Worldly Journeys*. Edited by John J. Collins and Michael Fishbane. State University of New York Press, 1995.

Collins, John J., and Michael Fishbane, eds. *Death, Ecstasy, and Other Worldly Journeys*. State University of New York Press, 1995.

Collins, Raymond F. *Letters That Paul Did Not Write*. Good News Studies. Glazier, 1988.

Combs, Allen Eugene. "The Creation Motif in the 'Enthronement Psalms'." Ph.D. diss., Columbia University, 1963; University Microfilms International, 1988.

Comfort, Philip W., and David P. Barrett, eds. *The Text of the Earliest New Testament Greek Manuscripts*. Tyndale, 2001.

Cook, Edwin. " 'Conscience' in the New Testament." *JATS* 15 (2004): 142–158.

Cook, Gerald. "The Israelite King as Son of God." *ZAW* 73 (1961): 202–225.

Coppens, J. "Les affinités qumrâniennes de L'Épître aux Hebreux." *La nouvelle revue théologique* 84 (1962): 128–143; 257–282.

Cortez, Félix H. "From the Holy to the Most Holy Place: The Period of Heb 9:6–10 and the Day of Atonement as a Metaphor of Transition." *JBL* 125 (2006): 527–547.

———. *The Letter to the Hebrews*. Seventh-day Adventist International Bible Commentary. Pacific Press, forthcoming.

———. "The Son as Representative of the Children in the Letter to the Hebrews." Pages 31–42 in *Son, Sacrifice, and Great Shepherd: Studies on the Epistle to the Hebrews*. Edited by David Moffitt and Eric Mason. WUNT II/510. Mohr Siebeck, 2020.

Cosaert, Carl P. "The Use of ἅγιος for the Sanctuary in the Old Testament Pseudepigrapha, Philo, and Josephus." *AUSS* 42 (2004): 91–103.

Cosby, Michael R. *The Rhetorical Composition and Function of Hebrews 11: In Light of Example Lists in Antiquity*. Mercer University Press, 1988.

Cowdery, Ann Hoch. "Hebrews 4:1–13." *Int* 48 (1994): 282–286.

Craddock, Fred B. "The Letter to the Hebrews." *NIB* 12:1–173.

Craigie, Peter C. *Psalms 1–50*. WBC 19. Word, 1983.

Craigie, Peter C., Page H. Kelley, and Joel F. Drinkard, Jr. *Jeremiah 1–25*. WBC 26. Word, 1991.

Crawford, Sidnie White. *The Temple Scroll and Related Texts*. Companion to the Qumran Scrolls 2. Sheffield Academic, 2000.

Crenshaw, James L. "Sirach." *NIB* 5:601–868.

Cross, Frank Moore. *Cannanite Myth and Hebrew Epic: Essays in the History of the Religion of Israel*. Harvard University Press, 1973.

———. "Notes on the Doctrine of the Two Messiahs at Qumran and the Extracanonical *Daniel Apocalypse* (4Q246)." Pages 1–13 in *Current Research and Technological Developments on the Dead Sea Scrolls: Conference on the Texts from the Judean Desert, Jerusalem, 30 April 1995*. Edited by Donald W. Parry and Stephen D. Ricks. STDJ 20. Brill, 1996.

———. "The Structure of the Apocalypse of 'Son of God' (4Q246)." Pages 151–158 in *Emanuel: Studies in Hebrew Bible Septuagint and Dead Sea Scrolls in Honor of Emanuel Tov*. Edited by Shalom M. Paul and others. VTSup 94. Brill, 2003.

Croy, N. Clayton. "A Note on Hebrews 12:2." *JBL* 114 (1995): 117–119.

Cuddon, J. A. *A Dictionary of Literary Terms and Literary Theory*. 3d ed. Blackwell, 1991.

Cullmann, Oscar. *The Christology of the New Testament*. Translated by Shirley C. Guthrie and Charles A. M. Hall. Rev. ed. Westminster, 1963.

———. *The Earliest Christian Confessions*. Translated by J. K. S. Reid. Lutterworth, 1949.

Culpepper, Robert H. "The High Priesthood and Sacrifice of Christ in the Epistle to the Hebrews." *The Theological Educator* 32 (1985): 46–62.

Dahl, Nils A. "A New and Living Way: The Approach to God According to Hebrews 10:19–25." *Int* 5 (1951): 401–412.

Dahood, Mitchell. *Psalm 1–50: Introduction, Translation, and Notes*. AB 16. Doubleday, 1965.

Daly, Robert J. *Christian Sacrifice: The Judaeo-Christian Background before Origen*. Catholic University of America Studies in Christian Antiquity 18. Catholic University of America Press, 1978.

———. *The Origins of the Christian Doctrine of Sacrifice*. Fortress, 1978.

Dan, Joseph. "Mysticism in Jewish History, Religion and Literature." Page 1–14 in *Studies in Jewish Mysticism*, edited by Joseph Dan and Frank Talmage. Association for Jewish Studies, 1982.

D'Angelo, Mary Rose. "Hebrews." Pages 455–459 in *Women's Bible Commentary*. Edited by Carol A. Newsom and Sharon H. Ringe. Expanded ed. Westminster John Knox, 1998.

─────────. *Moses in the Letter to the Hebrews*. SBLDS 42. Scholars Press, 1979.

Daniels, Richard. "How Does the Church Relate to the New Covenant? or, Whose New Covenant Is It, Anyway?" *Faith & Mission* 16/2 (1999): 64–98.

Davenport, Gene L. "The 'Anointed of the Lord' in Psalms of Solomon 17." Pages 67–92 in *Ideal Figures in Ancient Judaism: Profiles and Paradigms*. Edited by John J. Collins and George W. E. Nickelsburg. SBLSCS 12. Scholars, 1980.

Davidson, Richard M. "Christ's Entry 'Within the Veil' in Hebrews 6:19–20: The Old Testament Background." *AUSS* 39 (2001): 175–190.

─────────. "Inauguration or Day of Atonement? A Response to Norman Young's 'Old Testament Background to Hebrews 6:19–20 Revisited.'" *AUSS* 40 (2002): 69–88.

─────────. "A Natureza [e Identidade] da Tipologia Bíblica — Questôes Cruciais." *Hermenêutica* 4 (2004): 61–99.

─────────. *Typology in Scripture: A Study of Hermeneutical Τυπος Structures*. Andrews University Seminary Doctoral Dissertation Series 2. Andrews University Press, 1981.

Davies, J. G. *He Ascended into Heaven: A Study in the History of Doctrine*. Bampton Lectures 1958. Association, 1958.

Davies, J. H. *A Letter to Hebrews*. CBC. Cambridge University Press, 1967.

Dawson, Gerrit Scott. *Jesus Ascended: The Meaning of Christ's Continuing Incarnation*. P&R; T&T Clark, 2004.

Day, John. *God's Conflict with the Dragon and the Sea: Echoes of a Canaanite Myth in the Old Testament*. UCOP 35. Cambridge University Press, 1985.

de Jonge, M. "The Future of Israel in the Testaments of the Twelve Patriarchs." *Journal for the Study of Judaism in the Persian, Hellenistic, and Roman Periods* 17 (1986): 196–211.

─────────. "The Psalms of Solomon." Pages 159–77 in *Outside the Old Testament*. Edited by M. de Jonge. Cambridge Commentaries on Writings of the Jewish and Christian World 200 BC to AD 200 4. Cambridge University Press, 1985.

─────────. "Testaments of the Twelve Patriarchs." *ABD* 5:181–186.

de Souza, Elias Brasil. "The Heavenly Sanctuary/Temple Motif in the Hebrew Bible: Function and Relationship to the Earthly Counterparts." Ph.D. diss., Andrews University, 2005.

de Vries, Simon J. *1 Kings*. WBC 12. Thomas Nelson, 2003.

─────────. "Moses and David as Cult Founders in Chronicles." *JBL* 107 (1988): 619–639.

Dean-Otting, Mary. *Heavenly Journeys: A Study of the Motif in Hellenistic Jewish Literature*. Judentum und Umwelt 8. Lang, 1984.

Dearman, J. Andrew. *Jeremiah and Lamentations*. NIVAC. Zondervan, 2002.

Deissmann, Adolf. *Light from the Ancient East: The New Testament Illustrated by Recently Discovered Texts of the Graeco-Roman World*. Translated by Lionel R. M. Strachan. New and completely revised ed. Hodder & Stoughton, 1927.

Delitzsch, Franz. *Commentary on the Epistle to the Hebrews*. Translated by Thomas L. Kingsbury. 2 vols. Eerdmans, 1952.

Delling, Gerhard. "στάσις." *TDNT* 7:568–571.

———. "τελειόω." *TDNT* 8:79–84.

Demetrius. "On Style." Pages 309–525 in *Aristotle XXIII*. Edited and translated by Doreen C. Innes. LCL 199. Harvard University Press, 1995.

deSilva, David A. *Despising Shame: Honor Discourse and Community Maintenance in the Epistle to the Hebrews*. SBLDS 152. Scholars Press, 1995.

———. "Entering God's Rest: Eschatology and the Socio-Rhetorical Strategy of Hebrews." *TJ* 21 (2000): 25–43.

———. *Perseverance in Gratitude: A Socio-Rhetorical Commentary on the Epistle "to the Hebrews."* Eerdmans, 2000.

Dey, Lala Kalyan Kumar. *The Intermediary World and Patterns of Perfection in Philo and Hebrews*. SBLDS 25. Scholars Press for Society of Biblical Literature, 1975.

Di Giovambattista, Fulvio. "Eb 9,2–5: la Tenda del Convegno nel Giorno dell'Expiazione. La *crux interpretum* di χρυσοῦν θυμιατήριον (9,4)." *Lugano Theological Review* 4 (1999): 29–52.

———. *Il Giorno dell'Espiazione nella Lettera agli Ebrei*. Tesi Gregoriana Serie Teologia. Pontificio Istituto Biblico, 2000.

Di Lella, Alexander A. *The Hebrew Text of Sirach: A Text-Critical and Historical Study*. Studies in Classical Literature 1. Moulton, 1966.

Dillard, Raymond B. *2 Chronicles*. WBC 15. Word, 1987.

Dio. *Roman History*. Translated by Earnest Cary. LCL. Heinemann, 1925.

Docherty, Susan E. "The Use of the Old Testament in the New Testament: Reflections on Current Trends and Future Prospects with Reference to the Letter to the Hebrews." *Scripture Bulletin* 34 (2004): 60–70.

Donne, Brian K. "The Significance of the Ascension of Jesus Christ in the New Testament." *SJT* 30 (1977): 555–568.

Drane, J. W. "Son of God." *DLNT* 1111–1115.

Drazin, Israel. *Targum Onkelos to Exodus: An English Translation of the Text with Analysis and Commentary*. Center for Judaic Studies University of Denver and Society for Targumic Studies, 1990.

Du Plessis, Paul Johannes. *Teleios: The Idea of Perfection in the New Testament*. J. H. Kok, [1959].

Duguid, Iain M. *Ezekiel*. NIVAC. Zondervan, 1999.

Dumbrell, W. J. *Covenant and Creation: A Theology of Old Testament Covenants*. Thomas Nelson, 1984.

Dunkel, F. "Expiation et Jour des Expiations dans L'épître aux Hebreux." *La revue réformée* 33, no. 2 (1982): 63–71.

Dunn, James D. G. "The Ascension of Jesus: A Test Case for Hermeneutics." Pages 301–22 in *Auferstehung—Resurrection*. Edited by Friedrich Avemarie and Hermann Lichtenberger. WUNT I/135. Mohr Siebeck, 2001.

———. *Christology in the Making: A New Testament Inquiry into the Origins of the Doctrine of the Incarnation*. Westminster, 1980.

———. *Romans 1–8*. WBC 38A. Word, 1988.

———. *Unity and Diversity in the New Testament: An Inquiry into the Character of Earliest Christianity*. Westminster, 1977.

Dunnill, John. *Covenant and Sacrifice in the Letter to the Hebrews.* SNTSMS 75. Cambridge University Press, 1992.

Dussaut, Louis. *Synopse structurelle de L'épître aux Hébreux.* Cerf, 1981.

Eberhart, Christian A. "Characteristics of Sacrificial Metaphors in Hebrews." Pages 37–64 in *Hebrews: Contemporary Methods—New Insights.* Edited by Gabriella Gelardini. BibInt 75. Brill, 2005.

Ebrard, John H. A. *Biblical Commentary on the Epistle to the Hebrews.* Translated by John Fulton. Clark's Foreign Theological Library 32. T&T Clark, 1853.

Edwards, David Darnell. "Jesus and the Temple: A Historico-Theological Study of Temple Motifs in the Ministry of Jesus." Ph.D. diss., Southwestern Baptist Theological Seminary, 1992; UMI Dissertation Services, 1993.

Eichrodt, Walther. *Ezekiel: A Commentary.* OTL. Westminster, 1970.

Eisenbaum, Pamela Michelle. *The Jewish Heroes of Christian History: Hebrews 11 in Literary Context.* SBLDS 156. Scholars Press, 1997.

Eissfeldt, Otto. "The Promises of Grace to David in Isaiah 55:1–5." Pages 196–207 in *Israel's Prophetic Heritage.* Edited by Bernhard W. Anderson and Walter Harrelson. Harper, 1962.

Ellingworth, Paul. *The Epistle to the Hebrews: A Commentary on the Greek Text.* NIGTC. Eerdmans, 1993.

_____. "Hebrews and the Anticipation of Completion." *Themelios* 14 (1988): 6–11.

_____. "Jesus and the Universe in Hebrews." *EvQ* 58 (1986): 337–350.

_____. "Hebrews in the Eighties." *Bible Translator* 39 (1988): 131–138.

Emmrich, Martin. "Amtscharisma: Through the Eternal Spirit (Hebrews 9:14)." *BBR* 12 (2002): 17–32.

_____. *Pneumatological Concepts in the Epistle to the Hebrews.* University Press of America, 2003.

Encyclopaedia Judaica. 16 vols. 1972.

Engnell, Ivan. *Studies in Divine Kingship in the Ancient Near East.* Blackwell, 1967.

Enns, Peter E. "Creation and Re-Creation: Psalm 95 and Its Interpretation in Hebrews 3:1–4:13." *WTJ* 55 (1993): 255–280.

Eskola, Timo. *Messiah and the Throne: Jewish Merkabah Mysticism and Early Christian Exaltation Discourse.* WUNT II/142. Mohr Siebeck, 2001.

Eslinger, Lyle. *House of God or House of David: The Rhetoric of 2 Samuel 7.* JSOTSup 164. JSOT Press, 1994.

_____. *Kingship of God in Crisis: A Close Reading of 1 Samuel 1–12.* BLS 10. JSOT Press, 1985.

Evans, Craig A. "Are the 'Son' Texts at Qumran Messianic? Reflections on 4Q369 and Related Scrolls." Pages 135–153 in *Qumran-Messianism: Studies on the Messianic Expectations in the Dead Sea Scrolls.* Edited by James H. Charlesworth, Hermann Lichtenberger, and Gerbern S. Oegema. Mohr Siebeck, 1998.

_____. "Inaugurating the Kingdom of God and Defeating the Kingdom of Satan." *BBR* 15 (2005): 49–75.

_____. "Old Testament in the Gospels." *DJG* 579–590.

_____. "Son of God Text (4Q246)." *DNTB* 1134–1137.

Evans, C. F. *The Theology of Rhetoric: The Epistle to the Hebrews*. Friends of Dr. Williams's Library Forty-second Lecture. Dr. Williams's Trust, 1988.

Falk, Daniel K. *Daily, Sabbath, and Festival Prayers in the Dead Sea Scrolls*. STDJ 27. Brill, 1998.

Farrow, Douglas. "Ascension and Atonement." Pages 67–92 in *The Theology of Reconciliation*. Edited by Colin E. Gunton. T&T Clark, 2003.

_____. *Ascension and Ecclesia: On the Significance of the Doctrine of the Ascension for Ecclesiology and Christian Cosmology*. Eerdmans, 1999.

Fears, J. Rufus. *Princeps a diis electus: The Divine Election of the Emperor as a Political Concept at Rome*. Papers and Monographs of the American Academy in Rome 26. American Academy in Rome, 1977.

Feld, Helmut. *Der Hebräerbrief*. EdF 228. Wissenschaftliche, 1985.

Ferguson, Everett. "Selection and Installation to Office in Roman, Greek, Jewish and Christian Antiquity." *TZ* 30 (1974): 273–284.

Field, Fridericus, ed. *Origens hexaplorum: Quae supersunt sive veterum interpretum graecorum in totum vetus testamentum*. 2 vols. Georg Olms, 1964.

Finley, Thomas J. *Joel, Amos, Obadiah*. Wycliffe Exegetical Commentary. Moody, 1990.

Fischer, John. "Covenant, Fulfilment and Judaism in Hebrews." *Evangelical Review of Theology* 13 (1989): 175–187.

Fischer, Thomas. "First and Second Maccabees." *ABD* 4:439–450.

Fishbane, Michael. *Biblical Interpretation in Ancient Israel*. Clarendon, 1988.

Fitzgerald, John T. "Last Wills and Testaments in Greco-Roman Perspective." Pages 637–72 in *Early Christianity and Classical Culture: Comparative Studies in Honor of Abraham J. Malherbe*. Edited by John T. Fitzgerald, Thomas H. Olbricht, and L. Michael White. NovTSup 110. Brill, 2003.

Fitzmyer, Joseph A. "4Q246: The 'Son of God' Document from Qumran." *Bib* 74 (1993): 153–174.

_____. *The Acts of the Apostles: A New Translation with Introduction and Commentary*. AB 31. Doubleday, 1998.

_____. "The Ascension of Christ and Pentecost." *TS* 45 (1984): 409–440.

_____. *The One Who Is to Come*. Eerdmans, 2007.

_____. "The Son of David Tradition in Mt 22:41–46 and Parallels." Pages 113–126 in *Essays on the Semitic Background of the New Testament*. SBLSBS 5. Society of Biblical Literature; Scholars Press, 1974.

_____. "The Use of Explicit Old Testament Quotations in Qumran Literature and in the New Testament." Pages 3–58 in *Essays on the Semitic Background of the New Testament*. SBLSBS 5. Society of Biblical Literature; Scholars Press, 1974.

Flender, O. "Οἰκουμένη." *NIDNTT* 1:518–519.

Flusser, D. "The Hubris of the Antichrist in a Fragment from Qumran." *Imm* 10 (1980): 31–37.

_____. "Psalms, Hymns and Prayers." Pages 551–578 in *Jewish Writings of the Second Temple Period: Apocrypha, Pseudepigrapha, Qumran Sectarian Writings, Philo, Josephus*, edited by Michael E. Stone. CRINT. Van Gorcum; Fortress, 1984.

Fontenrose, Joseph. *Python: A Study of Delphic Myth and Its Origins*. University of California Press, 1959.
Forsyth, Neil. *The Old Enemy: Satan and the Combath Myth*. Princeton University Press, 1987.
Fossum, Jarl. "Son of God." *ABD* 6:128–137.
Franco Martínez, César Augusto. *Jesucristo, su persona y su obra, en la Carta a los Hebreos: Lengua y cristología en Heb 2, 9–10; 5, 1–10; 4, 14 y 9, 27–28*. Studia Semitica Novi Testamenti 1. Ciudad Nueva, 1992.
Frankfort, Henri. *Kingship and the Gods: A Study of Ancient Near Eastern Religion as the Integration of Society and Nature*. University of Chicago Press, 1948.
Fredenburg, Brandon L. *Ezekiel*. College Press NIV Commentary. College Press, 2002.
Freedman, William. "The Literary Motif: A Definition and Evaluation." *Novel: A Forum on Fiction* 4 (1971): 123–131.
Fretheim, Terence E. *Jeremiah*. Smyth & Helwys Bible Commentary. Smyth & Helwys, 2002.
Fritsch, C. T. "Το Ἀντίτυπον." Pages 100–107 in *Studia Biblica et Semitica*. Veenman & Zonen, 1966.
Fuller, Reginald H. "Hebrews." Pages 1–23 in *The General Letters: Hebrews, James, 1–2 Peter, Jude, 1–2–3 John*. Edited by Gerhard Krodel. Rev. and enl. ed. Proclamation Commentaries. Fortress, 1995.
Gäbel, Georg. *Die Kulttheologie des Hebräerbriefes: Ein exegetisch-religionsgeschichtliche Studie*. WUNT II/212. Mohr Siebeck, 2006.
Gager, John G. *Moses in Greco-Roman Paganism*. SBLMS 16. Abingdon, 1972.
Gakuru, Griphus. *An Inner-Biblical Exegetical Study of the Davidic Covenant and the Dynastic Oracle*. Mellen Biblical Press Series 58. Mellen, 2000.
Gane, Roy E. *Altar Call*. Diadem, 1999.
_____. *Cult and Character: Purification Offerings, Day of Atonement, and Theodicy*. Eisenbrauns, 2005.
_____. *Heroes imperfectos de Dios*. Translated by Félix Cortés A. APIA, 1995.
_____. "Judgment as Covenant Review." *JATS* 8 (1997): 181–194.
_____. *Leviticus, Numbers*. NIVAC. Zondervan, 2004.
_____. "Re-Opening *Katapetasma* ('Veil') in Hebrews 6:19." *AUSS* 38 (2000): 5–8.
_____. *Ritual Dynamic Structure*. Gorgias Dissertations 14, Religion 2. Gorgias, 2004.
_____. Review of *Sin, Impurity, Sacrifice, Atonement: The Priestly Conceptions*, by Jay Sklar. *RBL* [http://www.bookreviews.org] (2006).
Gane, Roy E., and Jacob Milgrom. "פָּרֹכֶת." *TDOT* 12:95–97.
García Martínez, Florentino. *Qumran and Apocalyptic: Studies on the Aramaic Texts from Qumran*. STDJ 9. Brill, 1992.
García Martínez, Florentino, and Eibert J. C. Tigchelaar, eds. *The Dead Sea Scrolls Study Edition*. 2 vols. Brill, 1997–1998.
Garuti, Paolo. *Alle origini dell'omiletica cristiana La Lettera agli Ebrei: Note di analisi retorica*. SBFA 38. Franciscan, 1995.
_____. "Due cristologie nella Lettera agli Ebrei?" *Liber annuus Studii biblici franciscani* 49 (1999): 237–258.

Gaston, Lloyd. *No Stone on Another: Studies in the Significance of the Fall of Jerusalem in the Synoptic Gospels*. NovTSup 23. Brill, 1970.

Gehman, Henry S. "Ἅγιος in the Septuagint, and Its Relation to the Hebrew Original." *VT* 4 (1954): 337–348.

Gelardini, Gabriella. "Hebrews, an Ancient Synagogue Homily for *Tisha be-Av*: Its Function, Its Basis, Its Theological Interpretation." Pages 107–127 in *Hebrews: Contemporary Methods—New Insights*. Edited by Gabriella Gelardini. BibInt 75. Brill, 2005.

Gench, Frances Taylor. *Hebrews and James*. Westminster Bible Companion. Westminster John Knox, 1996.

Gerbrandt, Gerald Eddie. *Kingship according to the Deuteronomistic History*. SBLDS 87. Scholars, 1986.

Gheorghita, Radu. *The Role of the Septuagint in Hebrews: An Investigation of Its Influence with Special Consideration to the Use of Hab 2:3–4 in Heb 10:37–38*. WUNT II/160. Mohr Siebeck, 2003.

Gianotto, Claudio. "Il sacrificio nell'*Epistola agli Ebrei*." *Annali di storia dell'esegesi* 18 (2001): 169–179.

Gieschen, Charles A. *Angelomorphic Christology: Antecedents and Early Evidence*. Arbeiten zur Geschichte des antiken Judentums und des Urchristentums 42. Brill, 1998.

Gileadi, Avraham. "The Davidic Covenant: A Theological Basis for Corporate Protection." Pages 157–164 in *Israel's Apostasy and Restoration*. Edited by Avraham Gileadi. Baker, 1988.

Girdwood, Jim, and Peter Verkruyse. *Hebrews*. College Press NIV Commentary. College Press, 1997.

Gleason, Randall C. "The Old Testament Background of Rest in Hebrews 3:7–4:11." *Bibliotheca Sacra* 157 (2000): 281–303.

⸻. "The Eschatology of the Warning in Hebrews 10:26–31." *TynBul* 53 (2002): 97–120.

Goldstein, Jonathan A. *I Maccabees: A New Translation with Introduction and Commentary*. AB 41. Doubleday, 1976.

⸻. "How the Authors of 1 and 2 Maccabees Treated the 'Messianic' Promises." Pages 69–96 in *Judaisms and Their Messiahs at the Turn of the Christian Era*. Edited by Jacob Neusner, William Scott Green, and Ernest S. Frerichs. Cambridge University Press, 1987.

Gombis, Timothy G. "Ephesians 2 as a Narrative of Divine Warfare." *JSNT* 26 (2004): 403–418.

Gooding, David. *An Unshakeable Kingdom: The Letter to the Hebrews for Today*. Eerdmans, 1989.

Goodman, William R. "First Book of Esdras." *ABD* 2:609–611.

Goppelt, Leonhard. *Typos: The Typological Interpretation of the Old Testament in the New*. Translated by Donald H. Madvig. Eerdmans, 1982.

Gordon, Robert P. "Better Promises: Two Passages in Hebrews against the Background of the Old Testament Cultus." Pages 434–449 in *Templum amicitiae: Essays on the Second Temple Presented to Ernst Bammel*. Edited by William Horbury. JSNTSup 48. JSOT Press, 1991.

_____. *Hebrews*. Readings: A New Biblical Commentary. Sheffield Academic, 2000.

Gorman, Frank H., Jr. *The Ideology of Ritual*. JSOTSup 91. JSOT Press, 1990.

Goulder, Michael. "Hebrews and the Ebionites." *NTS* 49 (2003): 393–406.

Gourgues, M. *A la droite de Dieu: Résurrection de Jésus et actualisation du Psaume 110:1 dans le Nouveau Testament*. EBib. Gabalda, 1978.

Graham, M. Patrick. Review of *Josiah and David Redivivus: The Historical Josiah and the Messianic Expectations of Exilic and Postexilic Times*, by Antti Laato. *CBQ* 56 (1994): 334–336.

Grant, Robert M. "Justin Martyr." *ABD* 3:1133–1134.

Gräßer, Erich. *An die Hebräer*. 3 vols. EKKNT 17. Benziger Neukirchener, 1990–1997.

_____. *Aufbruch und Verheissung: Gesammelte Aufsätze zum Hebräerbrief*. Edited by Martin Evang and Otto Merk. BZNW 65. Walter de Gruyter, 1992.

_____. *Der Glaube im Hebräerbrief*. Marburger Theologische Studien 2. Elwert, 1965.

_____. "Das Heil als Wort: Exegetische Erwägungen zu Hebr 2,1–4." Pages 261–274 in *Neues Testament und Geschichte: Historisches Geschehen und Deutung im Neuen Testament*. Edited by Heinrich Baltensweiler and Bo Reicke. Mohr Siebeck, 1972.

_____. "Neue Kommentare zum Hebräerbrief." *TRu* 56 (1991): 113–139.

_____. " 'Viele Male und auf vielerlei Weise …': Kommentare zum Hebräerbrief 1968 bis 1991." *Bibel und Kirche* 48 (1993): 206–215.

Gray, John. *I & II Kings: A Commentary*. OTL. Westminster, 1963.

Gray, Patrick. "Brotherly Love and the High Priest Christology of Hebrews." *JBL* 122 (2003): 335–351.

_____. *Godly Fear: The Epistle to the Hebrews and Greco-Roman Critiques of Superstition*. SBLAB 16. Society of Biblical Literature, 2003.

Grayston, Kenneth. "Salvation Proclaimed: III Hebrews 9:11–14." *ExpTim* 93/6 (1982): 164–168.

Greenberg, Moshe. *Ezekiel 21–37: A New Translation with Introduction and Commentary*. AB 22A. Doubleday, 1997.

Greer, Rowan A. *The Captain of Our Salvation: A Study in the Patristic Exegesis of Hebrews*. BGBE 15. Mohr Siebeck, 1973.

Grelot, Pierre. *Une lecture de l'épître aux Hébreux*. Cerf, 2003.

Grogan, G. W. "The Old Testament Concept of Solidarity in Hebrews." *TynBul* 49 (1998): 159–173.

Gudorf, Michael E. "Through a Classical Lens: Hebrews 2:16." *JBL* 119 (2000): 105–108.

Guinan, Michael D. "Davidic Covenant." *ABD* 2:69–72.

Gulley, Norman R. "Ascension of Christ." *ABD* 1:472–474.

Gurtner, Daniel M. "Καταπέτασμα: Lexicographical and Etymological Considerations on the Biblical 'Veil'." *AUSS* 42 (2004): 105–111.

Guthrie, Donald. *The Letter to the Hebrews: An Introduction and Commentary*. TNTC. Inter-Varsity, 1983.

_____. *New Testament Introduction*. 4th ed. InterVarsity, 1990.

Guthrie, George H. *Hebrews*. NIVAC. Zondervan, 1998.

———. "Hebrews in Its First Century Contexts: Recent Research." Pages 414–443 in *The Face of New Testament Studies: A Survey of Recent Research*. Edited by Scot McKnight and Grant R. Osborne. Baker, 2004.

———. "Hebrews' Use of the Old Testament: Recent Trends in Research." *CBR* (2003): 271–294.

———. "Old Testament in Hebrews." *DLNT* 841–850.

———. *The Structure of Hebrews: A Text-Linguistic Analysis*. NovTSup 73. Brill, 1994.

Haber, Susan. "From Priestly Torah to Christ Cultus: The Re-Vision of Covenant and Cult in Hebrews." *JSNT* 28 (2005): 105–124.

Habermann, Jürgen. *Präexistenzaussagen im Neuen Testament*. Europäische Hochschulschriften, Series 23, no. 362. Lang, 1990.

Haddock, Robert. "A History of the Doctrine of the Sanctuary in the Advent Movement." B.Div. Thesis, Andrews University, 1970.

Hagen, Kenneth. *Hebrews Commenting from Erasmus to Bèze: 1516–1598*. BGBE 23. Mohr Siebeck, 1981.

Hagner, Donald A. *Encountering the Book of Hebrews: An Exposition*. Encountering Biblical Studies. Baker Academic, 2002.

———. *Hebrews*. NIBC 14. Hendrickson, 1990.

———. "The Son of God as Unique High Priest: The Christology of the Epistle to the Hebrews." Pages 247–267 in *Contours of Christology in the New Testament*, edited by Richard N. Longenecker. McMaster New Testament Studies. Eerdmans, 2005.

Hahn, Ferdinand. *Christologische Hoheitstitel: Ihre Geschichte im Frühen Christentum*. 3d ed. FRLANT 83. Vandenhoeck & Ruprecht, 1966.

Hahn, Scott W. "A Broken Covenant and the Curse of Death: A Study of Hebrews 9:15–22." *CBQ* 66 (2004): 416–436.

———. "Covenant in the Old and New Testaments: Some Current Research (1994–2004)." *CBR* 3 (2005): 263–292.

———. "Covenant, Cult, and the Curse of Death: Διαθήκη in Heb 9:15–22." Pages 65–88 in *Hebrews: Contemporary Methods—New Insights*. Edited by Gabriella Gelardini. BibInt 75. Brill, 2005.

Halpern, Baruch. *The Constitution of the Monarchy in Israel*. HSM 25. Scholars, 1981.

Hamilton, Mark W. *The Body Royal: The Social Poetics of Kingship in Ancient Israel*. BibInt 78. Brill, 2005.

Hanhart, Robert. *Esdrae liber I*. Septuaginta: Vetus Testamentum Graecum 8/1. Vandenhoeck & Ruprecht, 1974.

Hanson, Anthony Tyrrell. *Jesus Christ in the Old Testament*. SPCK, 1965.

Hanson, Paul D. *The Dawn of Apocalyptic: The Historical and Sociological Roots of Jewish Apocalyptic Eschatology*. Rev. ed. Fortress, 1979.

———. *Isaiah 40–66*. IBC. John Knox, 1995.

Hanson, R. P. C. *Allegory and Event: A Study of the Sources and Significance of Origen's Interpretation of Scripture*. John Knox, 1959.

Haran, Menahem. *Temples and Temple-Service in Ancient Israel: An Inquiry into the Character of Cult Phenomena and the Historical Setting of the Priestly School*. Clarendon, 1978.

Harkins, P. W. "St. John Chrysostom." *NCE* 7:945–9.
Haroutunian, Joseph. "The Doctrine of the Ascension." *Int* 10 (1956): 270–281.
Harrington, Daniel J. *What Are They Saying about the Letter to the Hebrews?* Paulist, 2005.
Harvanek, R. F., and K. B. Steinhauser. "St. Gregory of Nyssa." *NCE* 6:517–521.
Hasel, Gerhard F. "The Meaning of the Animal Rite in Genesis 15." *JSOT* (1981): 61–78.
_____. *Understanding the Book of Amos: Bassic Issues in Current Interpretations.* Baker, 1991.
Hauck, Friedrich. "παραβολή." *TDNT* 5:744–761.
Hay, David M. *Glory at the Right Hand: Psalm 110 in Early Christianity.* SBLMS 18. Abingdon, 1973.
Hayes, John H. "The Resurrection as Enthronement and the Earliest Church Christology." *Int* 22 (1968): 333–345.
Hays, Richard B. *The Conversion of the Imagination: Paul as Interpreter of Israel's Scripture.* Eerdmans, 2005.
Heen, Erik M., and Philip D. W. Krey, eds. *Hebrews.* ACCS 10. InterVarsity, 2005.
Hegermann, Harald. *Der Brief an die Hebräer.* THKNT 16. Evangelische, 1988.
Heim, K. M. "Kings and Kingship." *DOTHB* 610–623.
Heininger, Bernhard. "Sündenreinigung (Heb 1,3): Christologische Anmerkungen zum Exordium des Hebräerbriefs." *BZ* 41 (1997): 54–68.
Hengel, Martin. *Judaism and Hellenism: Studies in Their Encounter in Palestine During the Early Hellenistic Period.* Translated by John Bowden. 2 vols. Wipf and Stock, 1974.
_____. *The Son of God: The Origin of Christology and the History of Jewish–Hellenistic Religion.* Translated by John Bowden. SCM, 1976.
_____. *Studies in Early Christology.* T&T Clark, 1995.
Hengel, Martin, James H. Charlesworth, and D. Mendels. "The Polemical Character of 'On Kingship' in the Temple Scroll: An Attempt at Dating 11QTemple." *JJS* 37 (1986): 28–38.
Heppenstall, Edward. *Our High Priest: Jesus Christ in the Heavenly Sanctuary.* Review & Herald, 1972.
Héring, Jean. *The Epistle to the Hebrews.* Translated by A. W. Heathcote and P. J. Allcock. Epworth, 1970.
Hill, Andrew E. *1 & 2 Chronicles.* NIVAC. Zondervan, 2003.
_____. *Malachi.* AB 25D. Doubleday, 1998.
Hill, Craig C. *Hellenists and Hebrews: Reappraising Division within the Earliest Church.* Fortress, 1992.
Himmelfarb, Martha. "Apocalyptic Ascent and the Heavenly Temple." Pages 210–217 in *Society of Biblical Literature 1987 Seminar Papers.* SBLSPS 26. Scholars Press, 1987.
_____. *Ascent to Heaven in Jewish and Christian Apocalypses.* Oxford University Press, 1993.
_____. "Das 'erste' und das 'zweite' Zelt: Ein Beitrag zur Auslegung von Hebr 9,1–10." Pages 203–209 in *Neutestamentliche Studien.* WUNT I/132. Mohr Siebeck, 2000.

———. *Katapausis: Die Vorstellung vom endzeitlichen Ruheort im Hebräerbrief.* WUNT I/11. Mohr Siebeck, 1970.

———. *Der Vorhang vor dem Thron Gottes: Eine exegetisch-religionsgeschichtliche Untersuchung zu Hebräer 6,19 un 10,19 f.* WUNT I/14. Mohr Siebeck, 1972.

Holbrook, Frank B. "Christ's Inauguration as King-Priest." *JATS* 5 (1994): 136–152.

Holladay, William L. *Jeremiah 1: A Commentary on the Book of the Prophet Jeremiah Chapters 1–25.* Edited by Paul D. Hanson. Hermeneia. Fortress, 1986.

Hollander, Harm W. "Hebrews 7.11 and 8.6: A Suggestion for the Translation of *nenomothetêtai epi.*" *The Bible Translator* 30 (1979): 244–247.

Holman, C. Hugh. "Imagery." *Encyclopedia Americana.* International ed., 2005.

Hooker, Morna D. *Not Ashamed of the Gospel: New Testament Interpretations of the Death of Christ.* Eerdmans, 1994.

Horbury, William. "Aaronic Priesthood in Hebrews." *JSNT* 19 (1983): 43–71.

———. "Herod's Temple and 'Herod's Days'." Pages 103–149 in *Templum amicitiae: Essays on the Second Temple Presented to Ernst Bammel.* Edited by William Horbury. JSNTSup 48. JSOT Press, 1991.

———. "New Wine in Old Wine-Skins (IX): The Temple." *ExpTim* 86 (1974): 36–42.

Horgan, Maurya P. *Pesharim: Qumran Interpretations of Biblical Books.* CBQMS 8. Catholic Biblical Association of America, 1979.

House, Paul R. *1, 2 Kings.* NAC 8. Broadman & Holman, 1995.

Hughes, Graham. *Hebrews and Hermeneutics: The Epistle to the Hebrews as a New Testament Example of Biblical Interpretation.* SNTSMS 36. Cambridge University Press, 1979.

Hughes, John J. "Hebrews IX 15ff. and Galatians III 15 ff.: A Study in Covenant Practice and Procedure." *NovT* 21 (1979): 27–96.

Hughes, Philip Edgcumbe. "The Blood of Jesus and His Heavenly Priesthood in Hebrews (Part II): The High-Priestly Sacrifice of Christ." *BSac* 130 (1973): 195–212.

———. "The Blood of Jesus and His Heavenly Priesthood in Hebrews: (Part IV) The Present Work of Christ in Heaven." *BSac* 131 (1974): 26–33.

———. "The Christology of Hebrews." *SwJT* 28 (1985): 19–27.

———. *A Commentary on the Epistle to the Hebrews.* Eerdmans, 1977.

Huie-Jolly, Mary R. "Threats Answered by Enthronement: Death/Resurrection and the Divine Warrior Myth in John 5.17–29 and Daniel 7." Pages 191–217 in *Early Christian Interpretation of the Scriptures of Israel: Investigations and Proposals.* Edited by Craig A. Evans and James A. Sanders. JSNTSup 148; SSEJC 5. Sheffield Academic, 1997.

Hume, C. R. *Reading through Hebrews.* SCM, 1997.

Hurst, Lincoln D. "The Christology of Hebrews 1 and 2." Pages 151–164 in *The Glory of Christ in the New Testament: Studies in Christology.* Edited by Lincoln D. Hurst and N. T. Wright. Clarendon, 1987.

———. "Did Qumran Expect Two Messiahs?" *BBR* 9 (1999): 157–180.

———. *The Epistle to the Hebrews: Its Background of Thought.* SNTSMS 65. Cambridge University Press, 1990.

———. "How 'Platonic' Are Heb. viii. 5 and ix. 23 f.?" *JTS* 34 (1983): 156–168.

———. "Qumran." *DLNT* 997–1000.

_____. Review of *Sacred Space: An Approach to the Theology of the Epistle to the Hebrews*, by Marie E. Isaacs. *CRBR* 7 (1994): 207–209.

Hurtado, L. W. "Christology." *DLNT* 170–184.

Hvalvik, Reidar. *The Struggle for Scripture and Covenant: The Purpose of the Epistle of Barnabas and Jewish-Christian Competition in the Second Century.* WUNT II/82. Mohr Siebeck, 1996.

Innes, Doreen C. "Period and Colon: Theory and Example in Demetrius and Longinus." Pages 36–53 in *Peripatetic Rhetoric after Aristotle*. Edited by William W. Fortenbaugh and David C. Mirhady. Rutgers University Studies in Classical Humanities 4. Transaction, 1994.

Isaacs, Marie E. "Hebrews." Pages 145–159 in *Early Christian Thought in Its Jewish Context*. Edited by John Barclay and John Sweet. Cambridge University Press, 1996.

_____. "Hebrews 13:9–16 Revisited." *NTS* 43 (1997): 268–284.

_____. "Priesthood and the Epistle to the Hebrews." *HeyJ* 38 (1997): 51–62.

_____. *Reading Hebrews and James*. Reading the New Testament. Smyth & Helwys, 2002.

_____. *Sacred Space: An Approach to the Theology of the Epistle to the Hebrews*. JSNTSup 73. JSOT Press, 1992.

_____. "Why Bother with Hebrews?" *HeyJ* 43 (2002): 60–72.

Jacobsen, Thorkild. *The Sumerian King List*. AS 11. The University of Chicago Press, 1939.

James, Nicholas. "Edith Stein and the Day of Atonement." *ScrB* 34 (2004): 24–32.

Jansen, John F. "The Ascension, the Church, and Theology." *ThTo* 16 (1959): 17–29.

Janzen, J. Gerald. *Studies in the Text of Jeremiah*. HSM 6. Harvard University Press, 1973.

Japhet, Sara. *I & II Chronicles: A Commentary*. OTL. SCM, 1993.

Jeremias, Joachim. *Die Briefe an Timotheus und Titus*. NTD 9. Vandenhoeck & Ruprecht, 1975.

_____. "Hebräer 10 20: τοῦτ' ἔστιν τῆς σαρκὸς αὐτοῦ." *ZNW* 62 (1971): 131.

Jewett, Robert. *Letter to Pilgrims: A Commentary on the Epistle to the Hebrews*. Pilgrim, 1981.

Jobes, Karen H., and Moisés Silva. *Invitation to the Septuagint*. Baker Academic, 2000.

Johnson, Aubrey. *Sacral Kingship in Ancient Israel*. 2d ed. University of Wales Press, 1967.

Johnson, Luke Timothy. *Hebrews: A Commentary*. NTL. Westminster John Knox, 2006.

_____. "The Scriptural World of Hebrews." *Int* 57 (2003): 237–250.

Johnson, Marshall D. *The Purpose of Biblical Genealogies: With Special Reference to the Setting of the Genealogies of Jesus*. SNTSMS 8. Cambridge University Press, 1969.

Johnson, M. D. "Life of Adam and Eve: A New Translation and Introduction." *OTP* 2:249–257.

Johnsson, William G. "The Cultus of Hebrews in Twentieth-Century Scholarship." *ExpTim* 89 (1977–1978): 104–108.

_____. "Day of Atonement Allusions." Pages 105–120 in *Issues in the Book of Hebrews*, edited by Frank B. Holbrook. DARCOM 4. Biblical Research Institute General Conference of Seventh-day Adventists, 1989.

———. "Defilement and Purgation in the Book of Hebrews." Ph.D. diss., Vanderbilt University, 1973; Xerox University Microfilms, 1974.

———. "Defilement/Purification and Hebrews 9:23." Pages 79–103 in *Issues in the Book of Hebrews*, edited by Frank B. Holbrook. DARCOM 4. Biblical Research Institute General Conference of Seventh-day Adventists, 1989.

———. *Hebrews: Full Assurance for Christians Today*. The Abundant Life Bible Amplifier. Pacific Press, 1994.

———. *In Absolute Confidence: The Book of Hebrews Speaks to Our Day*. Southern Publishing Association, 1979.

———. "Pilgrimage Motif in the Book of Hebrews." *JBL* 97 (1978): 239–251.

Johnston, George. "Christ as Archegos." *NTS* 27 (1981): 381–384.

———. "Οἰκουμένη and κόσμος in the New Testament." *NTS* 10 (1963–1964): 352–360.

Johnstone, William. *2 Chronicles 10–36: Guilt and Atonement*. Vol. 2 of *1 and 2 Chronicles*. JSOTSup 254. Sheffield Academic, 1997.

Jones, Ivor H. *The Apocrypha*. Epworth Commentaries. Epworth, 2003.

Josephus. Translated by Henry St John Thackeray and others. 10 vols. LCL. Harvard University Press, 1926–1965.

———. "The Promise Theme and the Theology of Rest." *BSac* 130 (1973): 135–150.

Kappler, Werner. *Maccabaeorum libri I–IV*. Septuaginta: Vetus Testamentum Graecum 9/1. Vandenhoeck & Ruprecht, 1936.

Karrer, Martin. *Der Brief an die Hebräer: Kapitel 1,1–5,10*. Ökumenischer Taschenbuchkommentar zum Neuen Testament 20/1. Gütersloher Verlag, 2002.

———. "The Epistle to the Hebrews and the Septuagint." Pages 335–354 in *Septuagint Research: Issues and Challenges in the Study of the Greek Jewish Scriptures*. Edited by Wolfgang Kraus and R. Glenn Wooden. SBLSCS 53. Society of Biblical Literature, 2006.

———. *Der Gesalbte: Die Grundlagen des Christustitels*. FRLANT 151. Vandenhoeck & Ruprecht, 1991.

Käsemann, Ernst. *The Wandering People of God: An Investigation of the Letter to the Hebrews*. Translated by Roy A. Harrisville and Irving L. Sandberg. Augsburg, 1984.

Kaylor, Robert David. "The Ascension Motif in Luke-Acts, the Epistle to the Hebrews, and the Fourth Gospel." Ph.D. diss., Duke University, 1964.

Kealy, Seán P. Review of *Il Giorno dell'Espiazione nella lettera agli Ebrei*, by Fulvio Di Giovambattista. *CBQ* 63 (2001): 740–741.

Kee, Howard Clark. Introduction to "Testaments of the Twelve Patriarchs." *OTP* 1:775–781.

Keel, Othmar. *The Symbolism of the Biblical World: Ancient Near Eastern Iconography and the Book of Psalms*. Translated by Timothy J. Hallett. Seabury, 1978.

Kelly, Brian, E. *Retribution and Eschatology in Chronicles*. JSOTSup 211. Sheffield: Sheffield Academic, 1996.

Kelly, J. N. D. *Early Christian Creeds*. 3d ed. David McKay, 1972.

Kennedy, George A. *Classical Rhetoric and Its Christian and Secular Tradition from Ancient to Modern Times*. University of North Carolina Press, 1980.

Keown, Gerald L., Pamela J. Scalise, and Thomas G. Smothers. *Jeremiah 26–52*. WBC 27. Word, 1995.

Kertzer, David I. *Ritual, Politics, and Power*. Yale University Press, 1988.

Kilpatrick, G. D. "Διαθήκη in Hebrews." *ZNW* 68 (1977): 263–265.

King, Karen L. *What Is Gnosticism?* Belknap, 2003.

Kistemaker, S. *The Psalm Citations in the Epistle to the Hebrews*. van Soest, 1961.

Kistemaker, Simon J. "Atonement in Hebrews." Pages 163–175 in *The Glory of the Atonement: Biblical, Historical & Practical Perspectives*. Edited by Charles E. Hill and Frank A. James. InterVarsity, 2004.

_____. *Exposition of the Epistle to the Hebrews*. Baker, 1984.

_____. "Exposition of the Epistle to the Hebrews." In *Exposition of Thessalonians, the Pastorals, and Hebrews*. New Testament Commentary. Baker, 1995.

Klausner, Joseph. *The Messianic Idea in Israel: From Its Beginning to the Completion of the Mishnah*. Translated by W. F. Stinespring. Macmillan, 1955.

Klawans, Jonathan. *Impurity and Sin in Ancient Judaism*. Oxford University Press, 2000.

Klein, Ralph W. "The Books of Ezra & Nehemiah." *NIB* 3:661–851.

Kleinig, John W. "The Blood for Sprinkling: Atoning Blood in Leviticus and Hebrews." *Lutheran Theological Journal* 33 (1999): 124–135.

Klingbeil, Gerald A. *A Comparative Study of the Ritual of Ordination as Found in Leviticus 8 and Emar 369*. Mellen, 1998.

Knibb, M. A. "Martyrdom and Ascension of Isaiah: A New Translation and Introduction." *OTP* 2:143–155.

Knight, J. M. "Alexandria, Alexandrian Christianity." *DLNT* 34–37.

Knoppers, Gary N. *1 Chronicles 1–9: A New Translation with Introduction and Commentary*. AB 12. Doubleday, 2003.

_____. *I Chronicles 10–29: A New Translation with Introduction and Commentary*. AB 12A. Doubleday, 2004.

Knöppler, Thomas. *Sühne im Neuen Testament*. WMANT 88. Neukirchener Verlag, 2001.

Knox, E. "The Samaritans and the Epistle to the Hebrews." *Churchman* (1927): 184–193.

Koehler, Ludwig, Walter Baumgartner, and Johann Jakob Stamm. *The Hebrew and Aramaic Lexicon of the Old Testament*. Translated and edited under the supervision of M. E. J. Richardson. 4 vols. Leiden: Brill, 1994–1999.

Koester, Craig R. *The Dwelling of God: The Tabernacle in the Old Testament, Intertestamental Jewish Literature, and the New Testament*. CBQMS 22. Catholic Biblical Association of America, 1989.

_____. "The Epistle to the Hebrews in Recent Study." *CurBR* 2 (1994): 123–145.

_____. "God's Purposes and Christ's Saving Work According to Hebrews." Pages 361–387 in *Salvation in the New Testament: Perspectives on Soteriology*. Edited by Jan G. van der Watt. NovTSup 121. Brill, 2005.

_____. Review of *Hebrews: A Commentary*, by Luke Timothy Johnson. *RBL* [http://www.bookreviews.org] (2007).

_____. *Hebrews: A New Translation with Introduction and Commentary*. AB 36. Doubleday, 2001.

_____. "Hebrews, Rhetoric, and the Future of Humanity." *CBQ* 64 (2002): 103–123.

Koester, Helmut. *History and Literature of Early Christianity.* Vol. 2 of *Introduction to the New Testament.* 2d ed. Walter de Gruyter, 2000.

_____. "Outside the Camp: Hebrews 13:9–14." *HTR* 55 (1962): 299–315.

Kooten, Robert Van. "Guarding the Entrance to the Place of Rest." *Kerux* 11/3 (1996): 29–33.

Kooy, V. H. "Image, Imagery." Pages 681–682 in vol. 2 of *Interpreter's Dictionary of the Bible.* Edited by George Arthur Buttrick. Abingdon, 1962.

Kosmala, Hans. *Hebräer, Essener, Christen: Studien zur Vorgeschichte der frühchristlichen Verkündigung.* Studia post-biblica 1. Brill, 1959.

Kovelman, Arkady. *Between Alexandria and Jerusalem: The Dynamic of Jewish and Hellenistic Culture.* BRLA 21. Brill, 2005.

Kraus, Hans-Joachim. *Theology of the Psalms.* Translated by Keith Crim. Augsburg, 1986.

Kraus, Wolfgang. "Der Jom Kippur, der Tod Jesu un die 'Biblische Theologie': Ein Versuch, die jüdische Tradition in die Auslegung von Röm 3,25f einzubeziehen." *Jahrbuch für Biblische Theologie* 6 (1991): 155–172.

_____. *Der Tod Jesu als Heiligtumsweihe: Eine Untersuchung zum Umfeld der Sühnevorstellung in Römer 3,25–26a.* WMANT 66. Neukirchener Verlag, 1991.

Kreitzer, Larry J. "The Messianic Man of Peace as Temple Builder: Solomonic Imagery in Ephesians 2.13–22." Pages 484–512 in *Temple and Worship in Biblical Israel.* Edited by John Day. LHBOTS 422. T&T Clark, 2005.

Kubo, Sakae. "Hebrews 9:11–12: Christ's Body, Heavenly Region, or …?" Pages 97–109 in *Scribes and Scripture: New Testament Essays in Honor of J. Harold Greenlee.* Edited by David Alan Black. Eisenbrauns, 1992.

Kügler, J. *Pharao und Christus? Religionsgeschichtliche Untersuchung zur Frage einer Verbindung zwischen altägyptischer Königstheologie und neutestamentlicher Christologie im Lukasevangelium.* BBB 113. Philo, 1997.

Kuhn, Karl A. "The 'One Like a Son of Man' Becomes the 'Son of God'." *CBQ* 69 (2007): 22–42.

Kuhn, Karl Georg. "The Two Messiahs of Aaron and Israel." Pages 54–64 in *The Scrolls and the New Testament.* Edited by Krister Stendahl. Harper, 1957. Reprint, with a new Introduction by James H. Charlesworth. Crossroad, 1992.

Laansma, Jon. *"I Will Give You Rest": The Rest Motif in the New Testament with Special Reference to Mt 11 and Heb 3–4.* WUNT II/98. Mohr (Siebeck), 1997.

Laato, Antti. "The Eschatological Act of Kipper in the Damascus Document." Pages 91–108 in *Intertestamental Essays in Honour of Józef Tadeusz Milik.* Edited by Zdzislaw J. Kapera. Qumranica Mogilanensia 6. Enigma, 1992.

_____. *Josiah and David Redivivus: The Historical Josiah and the Messianic Expectations of Exilic and Postexilic Times.* ConBOT 33. Almqvist & Wiksell, 1992.

Labat, René. *Le caractère religieux de la royauté assyro-babylonienne.* Librairie d'Amerique et d'Orient, 1939.

Lackenbacher, Sylvie. *Le Roi Bâtisseur: Les recits de construction assyriens des origines à Teglatphalasar III.* Éditions Recherche sur les civilisations, 1982.

Landes, George M. Review of *Josiah and David Redivivus: The Historical Josiah and the Messianic Expectations of Exilic and Postexilic Times,* by Antti Laato. *JBL* 113 (1994): 519–521.

Lane, William L. "Hebrews." *DLNT* 443–58.

———. *Hebrews 1–8*. WBC 47a. Word, 1991.

———. *Hebrews 9–13*. WBC 47b. Word, 1991.

———. Review of *Moses in the Letter to the Hebrews*, by Mary Rose D'Angelo. *JBL* 101 (1982): 151–153.

———. "Social Perspectives on Roman Christianity during the Formative Years from Nero to Nerva: Romans, Hebrews, *1 Clement*." Pages 196–244 in *Judaism and Christianity in First-Century Rome*. Edited by Karl P. Donfried and Peter Richardson. Eerdmans, 1998.

Larkin, William J., Jr. "Ascension." *DLNT* 95–102.

LaRondelle, Hans K. *Our Creator Redeemer: An Introduction to Biblical Covenant Theology*. Andrews University Press, 2005.

Larrañaga, Victorien. *L'ascension de Notre-Seigneur dans le Nouveau Testament*. Scripta pontificii instituti biblici. Pontifical Biblical Institute, 1938.

Laub, Franz. *Bekenntnis und Auslegung: Die paränetische Funktion der Christologie im Hebräerbrief*. Biblische Untersuchungen 15. Pustet, 1980.

———. " 'Ein für allemal hineingegangen in das Allerheiligste' (Heb 9,12)—Zum Verständnis des Kreuzestodes im Hebräerbrief." *BZ* 35 (1991): 65–85.

Launderville, Dale. *Piety and Politics: The Dynamics of Royal Authority in Homeric Greece, Biblical Israel, and Old Babylonian Mesopotamia*. Eerdmans, 2003.

Lausberg, Heinrich. *Handbook of Literary Rhetoric: A Foundation for Literary Study*. Edited by David E. Orton and R. Dean Anderson. Translated by Matthew Bliss, Annemiek Jansen, and David E. Orton. Brill, 1998.

Lea, Thomas D. *Hebrews & James*. Holman New Testament Commentary. Holman Reference, 1999.

Lee, Thomas R. *Studies in the Form of Sirach 44–50*. SBLDS 75. Scholars, 1986.

Lehmann, M. R. "A Re-interpretation of 4 Q Dibrê Ham-me'oroth." *RevQ* 17 (1964): 106–110.

Lehne, Susanne. *The New Covenant in Hebrews*. JSNTSup 44. JSOT Press, 1990.

Leithart, Peter J. "Womb of the World: Baptism and the Priesthood of the New Covenant in Hebrews 10.19–22." *JSNT* 78 (2000): 49–65.

Leschert, Dale Frederick. *Hermeneutical Foundations of Hebrews: A Study in the Validity of the Epistle's Interpretation of Some Core Citations from the Psalms*. National Association of Baptist Professrs of Religion Dissertation Serie 10. Mellen, 1994.

Levenson, Jon D. *Sinai and Zion: An Entry into the Jewish Bible*. New Voices in Biblical Studies. Winston, 1985.

———. *Theology of the Program of Restoration of Ezekiel 40–48*. HSM 10. Scholars Press for Harvard Semitic Museum, 1976.

Lévi, Israel, ed. *The Hebrew Text of the Book of Ecclesiasticus*. 3d ed. SSS 3. Brill, 1969.

Levin, Yigal. "Jesus, 'Son of God' and 'Son of David': The 'Adoption' of Jesus into the Davidic Line." *JSNT* 28 (2006): 415–442.

Levine, Baruch A. *Numbers 21–36: A New Translation with Introduction and Commentary*. AB 4A. Doubleday, 2000.

Levoratti, Armando J. " 'Tu no has querido sacrificio ni oblación' Salmo 40, 7; Hebreos 10:5." *RevistB* 48 (1986): 1–30, 65–87, 141–52, 193–237.

Lewis, Naphtali, and Meyer Reinhold, eds. *Roman Civilization: Selected Readings*. 2 vols. 3d ed. Columbia University Press, 1990.

Liddell, H. G., R. Scott, and H. S. Jones. *A Greek-English Lexicon*. 9th ed. with revised supplement. Oxford University Press, 1996.

Lierman, John. *The New Testament Moses: Christian Perceptions of Moses and Israel in the Setting of Jewish Religion*. WUNT II/173. Mohr Siebeck, 2004.

Limburg, James. *Hosea–Micah*. IBC. John Knox, 1988.

Lincoln, Andrew T. *Hebrews: A Guide*. T&T Clark, 2006.

―――――. *Paradise Now and Not Yet: Studies in the Role of the Heavenly Dimension in Paul's Thought with Special Reference to His Eschatology*. SNTSMS 43. Cambridge University Press, 1981.

―――――. "Sabbath, Rest, and Eschatology in the New Testament." Pages 197–220 in *From Sabbath to Lord's Day: A Biblical, Historical, and Theological Investigation*. Edited by D. A. Carson. Zondervan, 1982.

Lincoln, Lucy. "Translating Hebrews 9:15–22 in Its Hebraic Context." *JOTT* 12 (1999): 1–29.

Lindars, Barnabas. "Hebrews and the Second Temple." Pages 410–433 in *Templum amicitiae: Essays on the Second Temple Presented to Ernst Bammel*. Edited by William Horbury. JSNTSup 48. JSOT Press, 1991.

―――――. "The Rhetorical Structure of Hebrews." *NTS* 35 (1989): 382–406.

―――――. *The Theology of the Letter to the Hebrews*. New Testament Theology. Cambridge University Press, 1991.

Linnemann, Eta. "A Call for a Retrial in the Case of the Epistle to the Hebrews." *Faith & Mission* 19/2 (2002): 19–59.

Loader, William R. G. "Christ at the Right Hand—Ps. cx.1 in the New Testament." *NTS* 24 (1978): 199–217.

―――――. "Hughes on Hebrews and Hermeneutics." *Colloquium* 13 (1981): 50–60.

―――――. *Sohn und Hoherpriester: Eine traditionsgeschichtliche Untersuchung zur Christologie des Hebräerbriefes*. WMANT 53. Neukirchener Verlag, 1981.

Lohfink, Gerhard. *Die Himmelfahrt Jesu: Untersuchungen zu den Himmelfahrts- und Erhöhungstexten bei Lukas*. SANT 26. Kösel, 1971.

Lohmann, Theodor. "Zur Heilsgeschichte des Hebräerbriefes." *OLZ* 79 (1984): 118–125.

Lohse, Eduard. "υἱὸς Δαυίδ." *TDNT* 8:478–488.

Long, Thomas G. "Bold in the Presence of God: Atonement in Hebrews." *Int* 52 (1998): 53–69.

―――――. *Hebrews*. IBC. John Knox, 1997.

Long Westfall, Cynthia. *A Discourse Analysis of the Letter to the Hebrews: The Relationship between Form and Meaning*. LNTS 297. London: T&T Clark, 2005.

Longinus. "On the Sublime." Pages 143–308 in *Aristotle XXIII*. Edited by Donald Russell. Translated by W. H. Fyfe. LCL 199. Harvard University Press, 1995.

Longman, Tremper, III, and Raymond B. Dillard. *An Introduction to the Old Testament*. 2d ed. Zondervan, 2006.

Longman, Tremper, III, and Daniel G. Reid. *God Is a Warrior*. Studies in Old Testament Biblical Theology. Zondervan, 1995.

Löning, Karl. "Kultmetaphorik im Neuen Testament." Pages 229–267 in *Kult, Konflikt und Versöhnung: Beiträge zur kultischen Sühne in religiösen, sozialen und politischen Auseinandersetzungen des antiken Mittelmeerraumes*. Edited by Rainer Albertz. AOAT 285. Ugarit, 2001.

Louw, Johannes P. *Semantics of New Testament Greek*. Fortress; Scholars Press, 1982.

Louw, Johannes P., and Eugene A. Nida, eds. *Greek-English Lexicon of the New Testament: Based on Semantic Domains*. 2 vols. 2d ed. United Bible Societies, 1989.

Lundbom, Jack R. *Jeremiah 21–36: A New Translation with Introduction and Commentary*. AB 21B. Doubleday, 2004.

Lundquist, John M. "Temple, Covenant, and Law in the Ancient Near East and in the Old Testament." Pages 293–305 in *Israel's Apostasy and Restoration: Essays in Honor of Roland K. Harrison*. Edited by Avraham Gileadi. Baker, 1988.

Lust, Johan. "The Diverse Text Forms of Jeremiah and History Writing with Jer 33 as a Text Case." *JNSL* 20 (1994): 31–48.

Lust, J., E. Eynikel, and K. Hauspie, comps. *A Greek-English Lexicon of the Septuagint*. 2 vols. Deutsche Bibelgesellschaft, 1992–1996.

Lux, Rüdiger. "Der König als Tempelbauer: Anmerkungen zur sakralen Legitimation von Herrschaft im Alten Testament." Pages 99–122 in *Die Sakralität von Herrschaft: Herrschaftslegitimierung im Wechsel der Zeiten und Räume: Fünfzehn interdisziplinäre Beiträge zu einem weltweiten und epochenübergreifenden Phänomen*. Edited by Franz-Reiner Erkens. Akademie, 2002.

MacArthur, John. *Hebrews*. The MacArthur New Testament Commentary. Moody, 1983.

MacCarty, Skip. *In Granite or Ingrained? What the Old and New Covenants Reveal about the Gospel, the Law, and the Sabbath*. Andrews University Press, 2007.

Macdonald, John, ed. and trans. *Memar Marqah: The Teaching of Marqah*. 2 vols. BZAW 84. Töpelmann, 1963.

Macdonald, John. *The Theology of the Samaritans*. NTL. SCM, 1964.

Mack, Burton L. *Wisdom and the Hebrew Epic: Ben Sira's Hymn in Praise of the Fathers*. CSHJ. University of Chicago Press, 1985.

Mackie, Scott D. "Confession of the Son of God in Hebrews." *NTS* 53 (2007): 114–129.

_____. *Eschatology and Exhortation in the Epistle to the Hebrews*. WUNT II/223. Mohr Siebeck, 2007.

Macky, Peter W. *St. Paul's Cosmic War Myth: A Military Version of the Gospel*. The Westminster College Library of Biblical Symbolism 2. Lang, 1998.

MacLeod, David J. "The Cleansing of the True Tabernacle." *BSac* 152 (1995): 60–71.

_____. "The Doctrinal Center of the Book of Hebrews." *BSac* 146 (1989): 291–300.

_____. "The Literary Structure of the Book of Hebrews." *BSac* 146 (1989): 185–97.

_____. "The Present Work of Christ in Hebrews." *BSac* 148 (1991): 184–200.

MacRae, George W. "Apocalyptic Eschatology in Gnosticism." Pages 317–25 in *Apocalypticism in the Mediterranean World and the Near East: Proceedings of the International Colloquium on Apocalypticism Uppsala, August 12–17, 1979*. Edited by David Hellholm. Mohr Siebeck, 1983.

_____. "Heavenly Temple and Eschatology in the Letter to the Hebrews." *Semeia* 12 (1978): 179–200.

Majercik, Ruth. "Dialogue." *ABD* 2:185–188.

――――. "Rhetoric and Rhetorical Criticism." *ABD* 5:710–712.

Manson, William. *The Epistle to the Hebrews: An Historical and Theological Reconsideration*. Hodder & Stoughton, 1951.

Manzi, Franco. Review of *Il giorno dell'Espiazione nella Lettera agli Ebrei*, by Fulvio Di Giovambattista. *RivB* 50 (2002): 106–111.

――――. "Metodo retorico ed Epistola agli Ebrei: A proposito di un commentario recente." *RivB* 53 (2005): 469–477.

March, W. Eugene. "Haggai." *NIB* 7:705–732.

Margolis, Max L. "Day of Atonement." Pages 284–289 in vol. 2 of *The Jewish Encyclopedia*. Edited by Isidore Singer. Funk and Wagnalls, 1902.

Marshall, I. Howard. *The Origins of New Testament Christology*. Issues in Contemporary Theology. InterVarsity, 1976.

Martin, D. M. "Philo." *DLNT* 931–934.

Martínez de Pisón Liébanas, Ramón. "Acción Salvífica de Jesucristo y Lenguaje Sacrificial-Sacerdotal: ¿Continuidad o Ruptura en la Epístola a los Hebreos?" *Cmio* 25 (1992): 333–358.

Martitz, Peter Wülfing von. "υἱός." *TDNT* 8:335–340.

März, Claus-Peter. *Hebräerbrief*. NEchtB 16. Echter, 1989.

Massonnet, Jean. "Note sur la fête juive de Kippour." *LumView* 43/2 (1994): 77–86.

Mays, James L. *Amos: A Commentary*. OTL. Westminster, 1969.

――――. *Psalms*. IBC. John Knox, 1994.

McCann, J. Clinton, Jr. "The Book of Psalms: Introduction, Commentary, and Reflections." *NIB* 4:639–1280.

McCarter, P. Kyle, Jr. *II Samuel: A New Translation with Introduction, Notes and Commentary*. AB 9. Doubleday, 1984.

McCarthy, Dennis J. "Compact and Kingship: Stimuli for Hebrew Covenant Thinking." Pages 75–92 in *Studies in the Period of David and Solomon and Other Essays*. Edited by Tomoo Ishida. Eisenbrauns, 1982.

McCruden, Kevin. "Christ's Perfection in Hebrews: Divine Beneficence as an Exegetical Key to Hebrews 2:10." *BR* 47 (2002): 40–62.

McCullough, J. C. "Hebrews in Recent Scholarship." *IBS* 16 (1994): 66–86.

――――. "Hebrews in Recent Scholarship (Part 2)." *IBS* 16 (1994): 108–120.

――――. "The Old Testament Quotations in Hebrews." *NTS* 26 (1980): 363–379.

McCurley, Foster R. *Ancient Myths and Biblical Faith: Scriptural Transformations*. Fortress, 1983.

McKane, William. *A Critical and Exegetical Commentary on Jeremiah: Commentary on Jeremiah XXVI–LII*. ICC. T&T Clark, 1996.

McKelvey, R. J. *The New Temple: The Church in the New Testament*. Oxford Theological Monographs. Oxford University Press, 1969.

McKenzie, Steven L. "The Typology of the Davidic Covenant." Pages 152–178 in *The Land That I Will Show You: Essays on the History and Archaeology of the Ancient Near East in Honour of J. Maxwell Miller*. Edited by J. Andrew Dearman and M. Patrick Graham. JSOTSup 343. Sheffield Academic, 2001.

McKnight, Edgar V., and Christopher Church. *Hebrews–James*. Smyth & Helwys Bible Commentary. Smyth & Helwys, 2004.

McKnight, Scot. *Jesus and His Death: Historiography, the Historical Jesus, and Atonement Theory*. Baylor University Press, 2005.

McRay, John. "Atonement and Apocalyptic in the Book of Hebrews." *ResQ* 23 (1980): 1–9.

Meeter, H. H. *The Heavenly High Priesthood of Christ: An Exegetico-Dogmatic Study*. Eerdmans, n.d.

Meier, John P. "Structure and Theology in Heb 1,1–14." *Bib* 66 (1985): 168–189.

──────. "Symmetry and Theology in the Old Testament Citations of Heb 1,5–14." *Bib* 66 (1985): 504–533.

Ménégoz, Eugène. *La théologie de L'Epitre aux Hébreux*. Fischbacher, 1894.

Merrill, Eugene H. *An Exegetical Commentary: Haggai, Zechariah, Malachi*. Moody, 1994.

──────. "Royal Priesthood: An Old Testament Messianic Motif." *BSac* 150 (1993): 50–61.

Mettinger, Tryggve N. D. *King and Messiah: The Civil and Sacral Legitimation of the Israelite Kings*. ConBOT 8. Gleerup, 1976.

Metzger, Bruce M. "The Formulas Introducing Quotations of Scripture in the NT and the Mishna." *JBL* 70 (1951): 297–307.

──────. "The Fourth Book of Ezra: A New Translation and Introduction." *OTP* 1:516–559.

──────. *A Textual Commentary on the Greek New Testament*. 2d ed. Deutsche Bibelgesellschaft, 2002.

Meyers, Carol L. "David as Temple Builder." Pages 357–376 in *Ancient Israelity Religion: Essays in Honor of Frank Moore Cross*. Edited by Patrick D. Miller, Jr., Paul D. Hanson, and S. Dean McBride. Fortress, 1987.

Meyers, Carol L., and Eric M. Meyers. *Haggai, Zechariah 1–8: A New Translation with Introduction and Commentary*. AB 25B. Doubleday, 1987.

──────. *Zechariah 9–14: A New Translation with Introduction and Commentary*. AB 25C. Doubleday, 1993.

Meyers, Jacob M. *II Chronicles: Introduction, Translation, and Notes*. AB 13. Doubleday, 1965.

Michaud, Jean-Paul. " 'Parabolê' dans L'épître aux Hébreux et Typologie." *Semiotique et Bible* 46 (1987): 19–34.

──────. "Le passage de l'ancien au nouveau, selon L'épître aux hébreux." *ScEs* 35 (1983): 33–52.

Michel, Otto. *Der Brief and die Hebräer*. KEK 13. Vandenhoeck & Ruprecht, 1966.

──────. "ἡ οἰκουμένη." *TDNT* 5:157–159.

Milgrom, Jacob. "Israel's Sanctuary: The Priestly 'Picture of Dorian Gray'." *RB* 83 (1976): 390–399.

──────. *Leviticus 1–16: A New Translation with Commentary*. AB 3. Doubleday, 1991.

──────. "New Temple Festivals in the Temple Scroll." Pages 125–133 in *The Temple in Antiquity: Ancient Readers and Modern Perspectives*. Edited by Truman G. Madsen. Religious Studies Monograph Series 9. Religious Studies Center Brighan Young University, 1984.

──────. *Numbers: The Traditional Hebrew Text with the New JPS Translation*. JPS Torah Commentary. Jewish Publication Society, 1990.

_____. "The Paradox of the Red Cow (Num. XIX)." *VT* 31 (1981): 62–72.

Milik, J. T. "Les modèles Aramèens du livre d'Esther dans la grotte 4 de Qumran." *RevQ* 15 (1992): 321–406.

Miller, Patrick D., Jr. *The Divine Warrior in Early Israel*. HSM 5. Harvard University Press, 1973.

Miller, Patrick D. "The Book of Jeremiah." *NIB* 6:553–926.

Milligan, George. *The Theology of the Epistle to the Hebrews*. T&T Clark, 1899.

Milligan, William. *The Ascension and Heavenly Priesthood of Our Lord*. Mcmillan, 1892.

Minear, Paul S. "An Early Christian Theopoetic?" *Semeia* 12 (1978): 201–214.

Mish, Frederick C., ed. *Merriam-Webster's Collegiate Dictionary*. 11th ed. Merriam-Webster, 2003.

Moffatt, James. *A Critical and Exegetical Commentary on the Epistle to the Hebrews*. ICC. T&T Clark, 1924.

Moingt, Joseph. "La fin du sacrifice." *LumVie* 43, no. 2 (1994): 15–32.

Montefiore, Hugh. *A Commentary on the Epistle to the Hebrews*. HNTC. Harper & Row, 1964.

Moore, George Foot. *Judaism in the First Centuries of the Christian Era: The Age of the Tannaim*. 3 vols. Harvard University Press, 1932.

Morgen, Michèle. "Christ venu une fois pour toutes." *LumVie* 43/2 (1994): 33–45.

Morris, Leon. *Hebrews*. Bible Study Commentary. Zondervan, 1983.

Mosser, Carl. "No Lasting City: Rome, Jerusalem and the Place of Hebrews in the History of Earliest 'Christianity.'" PhD diss., The University of St Andrews, 2005.

Motyer, Stephen. "The Psalm Quotations of Hebrews 1: A Hermeneutic-Free Zone?" *TynBul* 50 (1999): 3–22.

Moule, C. F. D. *The Birth of the New Testament*. 3d rev. and rewritten ed. HNT. Harper & Row, 1982.

_____. *An Idiom Book of New Testament Greek*. 2d ed. Cambridge University Press, 1959.

Moulton, James Hope. *Prolegomena*. Vol. 1 of *A Grammar of New Testament Greek*. 3d ed. T&T Clark, 1908.

Mueller, Ekkhardt. *Come Boldly to the Throne: Sanctuary Themes in Hebrews*. Pacific Press, 2003.

Müller, Paul-Gerhard. *ΧΡΙΣΤΟΣ ΑΡΧΗΓΟΣ: Der religionsgeschichtliche und theologische Hintergrund einer neutestamentlichen Christusprädikation*. Europäische Hochschulschriften, Series 23, no. 28. Lang, 1973.

Muraoka, T. *A Greek-English Lexicon of the Septuagint: Twelve Prophets*. Peeters, 1993.

Nairne, Alexander. *The Epistle of Priesthood*. T&T Clark, 1913.

_____. *The Epistle to the Hebrews*. The Cambridge Bible for Schools and Colleges. Cambridge University Press, 1921.

Nardoni, Enrique. "Partakers in Christ (Hebrews 3.14)." *NTS* 37 (1991): 456–472.

Nash, Ronald H. "The Notion of Mediator in Alexandrian Judaism and the Epistle to the Hebrews." *WTJ* 40 (1977): 89–115.

Nauck, Wolfgang. "Zum Aufbau des Hebräerbriefes." Pages 199–208 in *Judentum, Urchristentum, Kirche*. Edited by Walther Eltester. BZNW 26. Töpelmann, 1964.

Nelson, Milward Douglas. *The Syriac Version of the Wisdom of Ben Sira Compared to the Greek and Hebrew Materials.* SBLDS 107. Scholars, 1988.
Nelson, Richard D. *Deuteronomy: A Commentary.* OTL. Westminster John Knox, 2002.
⸻. *First and Second Kings.* IBC. John Knox, 1987.
⸻. " 'He Offered Himself': Sacrifice in Hebrews." *Int* 57 (2003): 251–65.
⸻. *Raising Up a Faithful Priest.* Westminster John Knox, 1993.
Neufeld, Vernon H. *The Earliest Christian Confessions.* NTTS 5. Eerdmans, 1963.
Neusner, Jacob. *The Idea of Purity in Ancient Judaism.* SJLA 1. Brill, 1973.
⸻. *The Mishnah: A New Translation.* Yale University Press, 1988.
⸻. *Purity in Rabbinic Judaism: A Systematic Account: The Sources, Media, Effects, and Removal of Uncleanness.* South Florida Studies in the History of Judaism 95. Scholars Press, 1994.
Neusner, Jacob, and William Scott Green, eds. *Dictionary of Judaism in the Biblical Period: 450 BCE to 600 CE.* Hendrickson, 1999.
Neusner, Jacob, William Scott Green, and Ernest S. Frerichs, eds. *Judaisms and Their Messiahs at the Turn of the Christian Era.* Cambridge University Press, 1987.
Newsom, Carol. *Songs of the Sabbath Sacrifice: A Critical Edition.* HSM 27. Scholars Press, 1985.
The Nicene and Post-Nicene Fathers. Series 2. Edited by Philip Schaff and Henry Wace. 14 vols., 1890–1899. Reprint, T&T Clark, 1988.
Nicholson, E. W. "The Covenant Ritual in Exodus xxiv 3–8." *VT* 32 (1982): 74–86.
Nickelsburg, George W. E. *Jewish Literature between the Bible and the Mishnah: A Historical and Literary Introduction.* 2d ed. Fortress, 2005.
Nickelsburg, George W. E., and Robert A. Kraft. "Introduction: The Modern Study of Early Judaism." Pages 1–30 in *Early Judaism and Its Modern Interpreteters.* Edited by Robert A. Kraft and George W. E. Nickelsburg. SBLBMI 2. Fortress; Atlanta, Ga.: Scholars Press, 1986.
Nida, Eugene A., Johannes P. Louw, A. H. Snyman, and J. v W. Cronje. *Style and Discourse: With Special Reference to the text of the Greek New Testament.* Bible Society, 1983.
Nitzan, Bilhah. *Qumran Prayer and Religious Poetry.* Translated by Jonathan Chipman. STDJ 12. Brill, 1994.
Norden, Eduard. *Die Geburt des Kindes: Geschichte einer religiösen Idee*, 1924. Reprint, Teubner, 1969.
Noth, Martin. "David and Israel in II Samuel VII." Pages 250–259 in *The Laws in the Pentateuch and Other Studies.* Translated by D. R. Ap-Thomas. Fortress, 1967.
Novakovic, Lidija. *Messiah, the Healer of the Sick: A Study of Jesus as the Son of David in the Gospel of Matthew.* WUNT II/170. Mohr Siebeck, 2003.
Oberholtzer, Thomas Kem. "The Kingdom Rest in Hebrews 3:1–4:13." *BSac* 145 (1988): 185–196.
O'Brien, Julia M. *Nahum, Habakkuk, Zephaniah, Haggai, Zechariah, Malachi.* AOTC. Abingdon, 2004.
Oegema, Gerbern S. *The Anointed and His People: Messianic Expectations from the Maccabees to Bar Kochba.* JSPSup 27. Sheffield Academic, 1998.
Oepke, A. "μεσίτης." *TDNT* 4:598–624.

Olafsson, Gudmundur. "The Use of NS' in the Pentateuch and Its Contribution to the Concept of Forgiveness." Ph.D. diss., Andrews University, 1992.

Olbricht, Thomas H. "Analogy and Allegory in Classical Rhetoric." Pages 371–390 in *Early Christianity and Classical Culture: Comparative Studies in Honor of Abraham J. Malherbe*. Edited by John T. Fitzgerald, Thomas H. Olbricht, and L. Michael White. NovTSup 110. Brill, 2003.

———. "Anticipating and Presenting the Case for Christ as High Priest in Hebrews." Pages 355–372 in *Rhetorical Argumentation in Biblical Texts: Essays from the Lund 2000 Conference*. Edited by Anders Eriksson, Thomas H. Olbricht, and Walter G. Übelacker. Emory Studies in Early Christianity 8. Trinity, 2002.

———. "Delivery and Memory." Pages 159–167 in *Handbook of Classical Rhetoric in the Hellenistic Period: 330 B.C.–A.D. 400*. Edited by Stanley E. Porter. Brill Academic, 2001.

———. "Hebrews as Amplification." Pages 375–387 in *Rhetoric and the New Testament: Essays from the 1992 Heidelberg Conference*. Edited by Stanley E. Porter and Thomas H. Olbricht. JSNTSup 90. JSOT Press, 1993.

Ollenburger, Ben C. "Zechariah." *NIB* 7:733–840.

O'Neill, J. C. "The Death of the Teacher of Righteousness in Hebrews 13:12–13." *Journal of Higher Criticism* 7 (2000): 286–288.

———. "Jesus in Hebrews." *Journal of Higher Criticism* 6 (1999): 64–82.

Oswalt, John N. *The Book of Isaiah: Chapters 1–39*. NICOT. Eerdmans, 1986.

———. *The Book of Isaiah: Chapters 40–66*. NICOT. Eerdmans, 1998.

Otto, Eckart. "The Judean Legitimation of Royal Rulers in Its Ancient Near Eastern Contexts." Pages 131–139 in *Psalms and Liturgy*. Edited by Dirk J. Human and Cas J. A. Vos. JSOTSup 410. T&T Clark, 2004.

The Oxford Dictionary of the Classical World. Oxford University Press, 2005.

Paget, James Carleton. *The Epistle of Barnabas: Outlook and Background*. WUNT II/64. Mohr Siebeck, 1994.

Pannenberg, Wolfhart. *The Apostle's Creed: In the Light of Today's Questions*. Translated by Margaret Kohl. Westminster, 1972.

———. *Jesus: God and Man*. Translated by Lewis L. Wilkins and Duane A. Priebe. 2d ed. Westminster, 1977.

Parke-Taylor, Geoffrey H. *The Formation of the Book of Jeremiah: Doublets and Recurring Phrases*. SBLMS 51. Society of Biblical Literature, 2000.

Parsons, Mikeal C. *The Departure of Jesus in Luke-Acts*. JSNTSup 21. JSOT Press, 1987.

———. "Son and High Priest: A Study in the Christology of Hebrews." *EvQ* 60 (1988): 195–216.

Patrologia Graeca. Edited by J.-P. Migne. 162 vols. Paris, 1857–1886.

Paul, Shalom M. *Amos: A Commentary on the Book of Amos*. Edited by Frank Moore Cross. Hermeneia. Fortress, 1991.

Paulien, Jon. "The Role of the Hebrew Cultus, Sanctuary, and Temple in the Plot and Structure of the Book of Revelation." *AUSS* 33 (1995): 245–264.

Pauly, A. F. *Paulys Realencyclopädie der Classischen Altertumswissenschaft*. Edited by Georg Wissowa. 49 vols. New ed. Stuttgart: Metzler, 1901.

Penna, Romano. Review of *Der Tod Jesu als Heiligtumsweihe: Eine Untersuchung zum Umfeld der Sühnevorstellung in Römer 3,25–26a*, by Wolfgang Kraus. *Bib* 75 (1994): 428–431.

Penner, Erwin. "The Enthronement Motif in Ephesians." Ph.D. diss., Fuller Theological Seminary, 1983. University Microfilms, 1987.

Pérez Fernández, Miguel, trans. *Los capítulos de Rabbí Eliezer*. Biblioteca Midrásica 1. Institución S. Jerónimo para la Investigación Biblica, 1984.

Pesce, Mauro. "Gesù e il sacrificio ebraico." *Annali di storia dell'esegesi* 18 (2001): 129–168.

Petersen, David L. *Zechariah 9–14 and Malachi*. OTL. Westminster John Knox, 1995.

Peterson, David. *Hebrews and Perfection: An Examination of the Concept of Perfection in the "Epistle to the Hebrews."* SNTSMS 47. Cambridge University Press, 1982.

―――. "The Prophecy of the New Covenant in the Argument of Hebrews." *RTR* 38 (1979): 74–81.

Pfann, Stephen J., and others. *Qumran Cave 4: XXVI Criptic Texts and Miscellanea*. DJD 36. Clarendon, 2000.

Pfeiffer, Robert H. *History of New Testament Times: With an Introduction to the Apocrypha*. Harper, 1949.

Pfister, Friedrich. "Herakles und Christus." *AR* 34 (1937): 42–60.

Pfitzner, Victor C. *Hebrews*. ANTC. Abingdon, 1997.

Philo. Translated by F. H. Colson and G. H. Whitaker. 10 vols. LCL. Heinemann, 1929–1962.

Pilhofer, Peter. "Κρειττονος Διαθηκης Εγγυος: Die Bedeutung der Präexistenzchristologie für die Theologie des Hebräerbrief." *TLZ* 121 (1996): 319–328.

Pirke de Rabbi Eliezer: (The Chapters of Rabbi Eliezer the Great) According to the Text of the Manuscript of the Manuscript Belonging to Abraham Epstein of Vienna. Translated and annotated by Gerald Friedlander. Blom, 1971.

Plato. *The Republic*. 2 vols. LCL. Harvard University Press, 1935.

Plutarch. "Anthony." Pages 137–332 in vol. 9 of *Lives*. Translated by Bernadotte Perrin. LCL. Harvard University Press, 1959.

Pokorný, Petr. *Der Gottessohn: Literarisch Übersicht und Fragestellung*. ThSt 109. Theologischer Verlag, 1917.

Pomykala, Kenneth E. *The Davidic Dynasty Tradition in Early Judaism: Its History and Significance for Messianism*. SBLEJL 7. Scholars, 1995.

―――. "Images of David in Early Judaism." Pages 33–46 in vol. 1 of *Of Scribes and Sages: Early Jewish Interpretation and Transmission of Scripture: Ancient Versions and Traditions*. Edited by Craig A. Evans. SSEJC 5; LSTS 50. T&T Clark, 2004.

Porter, Stanley E. *Idioms of the Greek New Testament*. Biblical Languages: Greek 2. JSOT Press, 1992.

―――. "Septuagint/Greek Old Testament." *DNTB* 1099–1106.

―――. *Verbal Aspect in the Greek of the New Testament*. Studies in Biblical Greek 1. Lang, 1989.

Preuss, H. D. "עוֹלָם." *TDOT* 10:530–545.

Prigent, Pierre, and Robert A. Kraft. *Épître de Barnabé*. SC 172. Cerf, 1971.
Pritchard, James B., ed. *Ancient Near Eastern Texts Relation to the Old Testament*. 3d ed. Princeton University Press, 1969.
Propp, William H. C. *Exodus 19–40*. AB 2A. Doubleday, 2006.
Prostmeier, Ferdinand R. *Der Barnabasbrief*. Kommentar zu den Apostolischen Vätern 8. Vandenhoeck & Ruprecht, 1999.
Pryor, John W. "Hebrews and Incarnational Christology." *RTR* 40 (1981): 44–50.
Puech, Émile. "4QApocryphe de Daniel ar (Pl. XI)." Pages 165–184 in *Qumran Cave 4 XVII: Parabiblical Texts, Part 3*. Edited by James C. VanderKam. DJD 22. Clarendon, 1996.
———. "Fragment d'une Apocalypse en Araméen (4Q246=pseudo Dan[d]) et le 'Royaume de Dieu'." *RB* 99 (1992): 98–131.
Punt, Jeremy. "Hebrews, Thought-patterns and Context: Aspects of the Background of Hebrews." *Neot* 31 (1997): 119–158.
Pursiful, Darrell J. *The Cultic Motif in the Spirituality of the Book of Hebrews*. Mellen Biblical, 1993.
Quinn, Edward. *A Dictionary of Literary and Thematic Terms*. Facts on File, 1999.
Quintilian. *The Orator's Education*. Edited and translated by Donald Russell. 5 vols. Loeb Classical Library. Harvard University Press, 2001.
Rad, Gerhard von. "The Royal Ritual in Judah." Pages 222–231 in *The Problem of the Hexateuch and Other Essays*. Translated by E. W. Trueman Dicken. McGraw-Hill, 1966.
———. "There Remains Still a Rest for the People of God: An Investigation of a Biblical Conception." Pages 94–102 in *The Problem of the Hexateuch and Other Essays*. Translated by E. W. Trueman Dicken. McGraw-Hill, 1966.
Rahlfs, Alfred. *Psalmi cum Odis*. Septuaginta: Societatis Scientiarum Gottingensis 10. Vandenhoeck & Ruprecht, 1931.
———, ed. *Septuaginta: Id est Vetus Testamentum graece iuxta LXX interpretes*. Deutsche Bibelgesellschaft, 1979.
Rappaport, Uriel. "Onias (Person)." *ABD* 5:23–24.
Reid, Richard. "The Use of the Old Testament in the Epistle to the Hebrews." Ph.D. diss., Union Theological Seminary, 1964. University Microfilms International, 1978.
Reiterer, Friedrich Vinzenz. *"Urtext" und Übersetzungen: Sprachstudie über Sir 44,16–45,26 als Beitrag zur Siraforschung*. Arbeiten zu Text und Sprache im Alten Testament 12. EOS, 1980.
Rhackahm, H., trans. "Rhetorica ad Alexandrum." Pages 257–449 in *Aristotle Problems II*. LCL. Harvard University Press, 1952.
Rice, George E. "Apostasy as a Motif and Its Effect on the Structure of Hebrews." *AUSS* 23 (1985): 29–35.
———. "The Chiastic Structure of the Central Section of the Epistle to the Hebrews." *AUSS* 19 (1981): 243–246.
———. "Hebrews 6:19: Analysis of Some Assumptions Concerning *Katapetasma*." *AUSS* 25 (1987): 65–71.
Riggenbach, Eduard. *Der Brief and die Hebräer*. Deichertsche, 1922. Reprint, Brockhaus, 1987.

Riley, William. *King and Cultus in Chronicles: Worship and the Reinterpretation of History.* JSOTSup 160. JSOT Press, 1993.

Rissi, Mathias. *Die Theologie des Hebräerbriefs: Ihre Verankerung in der Situation des Verfassers und seiner Leser.* WUNT I/41. Mohr Siebeck, 1987.

Roberts, J. J. M. "Davidic Covenant." *DOTHB* 206–211.

Robertson, A. T. *A Grammar of the Greek New Testament in the Light of Historical Research.* Broadman, 1934.

Rogers, Cleon L., Jr. "The Davidic Covenant in Acts–Revelation." *BSac* 151 (1994): 71–84.

———. "The Davidic Covenant in the Gospels." *BSac* 150 (1993): 458–4–78.

———. "The Promises to David in Early Judaism." *BSac* 150 (1993): 285–302.

Rooke, Deborah W. "Jesus as Royal Priest: Reflections on the Interpretation of the Melchizedek Tradition in Heb 7." *Bib* 81 (2000): 81–94.

Rose, Christian. "Verheißung und Erfüllung: Zum Verständnis von ἐπαγγελία im Hebräerbrief." *BZ* 33 (1989): 60–80, 178–91.

Rose, Herbert Jennings. "Herakles and the Gospels." *HTR* 31 (1938): 113–142.

Rowe, Galen O. "Style." *Handbook of Classical Rhetoric in the Hellenistic Period: 330 B.C.–A.D. 400.* Edited by Stanley E. Porter. Brill Academic, 2001. 121–157.

Rowland, C. C. "The Second Temple: Focus of Ideological Struggle?" Pages 175–198 in *Templum amicitiae: Essays on the Second Temple Presented to Ernst Bammel.* Edited by William Horbury. JSNTSup 48. JSOT Press, 1991.

Royster, Dmitri. *The Epistle to the Hebrews: A Commentary.* St. Vladimir's Seminary Press, 2003.

Runia, David T. *Exegesis and Philosophy: Studies on Philo of Alexandria.* Collected Studies 332. Variorum, 1990.

———. *Philo in Early Christian Literature: A Survey.* Edited by Y. Aschkenasy and others. Vol. 3 of *Jewish Traditions in Early Christian Literature.* CRINT. Fortress, 1993.

Russell, Donald A., ed. and trans. *Quintilian: The Orator's Education Books 9–10.* LCL 127. Harvard University Press, 2001.

Ryken, Leland, James C. Wilhoit, and Tremper Longman III, eds. *Dictionary of Biblical Imagery.* InterVarsity, 1988.

Rylaarsdam, J. Coert. "Day of Atonement." *IDB* 1:313–316.

Sabourin, Leopold. *Priesthood: A Comparative Study.* SHR 25. Brill, 1973.

Sailhamer, John H. *The Pentateuch as Narrative: A Biblico-Theological Commentary.* Zondervan, 1992.

Salom, Alwyn P. "*Ta Hagia* in the Epistle to the Hebrews." Pages 219–227 in *Issues in the Book of Hebrews.* Edited by Frank B. Holbrook. DARCOM 4. Biblical Research Institute General Conference of Seventh-day Adventists, 1989.

Salvesen, Alison. *The Books of Samuel in the Syriac Version of Jacob of Edessa.* Monographs of the Peshitta Institute Leiden 10. Brill, 1999.

Sanders, E. P. *Jesus and Judaism.* Fortress, 1985.

Sandmel, Samuel. *Philo of Alexandria: An Introduction.* Oxford University Press, 1979.

Sarna, Nahum M. *Exodus: The Traditional Hebrew Text with the New JPS Translation.* JPS Torah Commentary. Jewish Publication Society, 1991.

Saucy, Mark. "Exaltation Christology in Hebrews: What Kind of Reign?" *TJ* 14 (1993): 41–62.

Savran, George W. *Telling and Retelling: Quotation in Biblical Narrative*. ISBL. Indiana University Press, 1988.

Schaefer, James R. "The Relationship between Priestly and Servant Messianism in the Epistle to the Hebrews." *CBQ* 30 (1968): 359–385.

Scharlemann, Martin H. *Stephen: A Singular Saint*. AnBib 34. Pontifical Biblical Institute, 1968.

Schenck, Kenneth L. "A Celebration of the Enthroned Son: The Catena of Hebrews 1." *JBL* 120 (2001): 469–485.

―――. "Keeping His Appointment: Creation and Enthronement in Hebrews." *JSNT* 66 (1997): 91–117.

―――. "Philo and the Epistle to the Hebrews: Ronald Williamson's Study after Thirty Years." Pages 112–135 in vol. 14 of *Studia Philonica Annual: Studies in Hellenistic Judaism*. BJS 335. [Brown University], 2002.

―――. *Understanding the Book of Hebrews: The Story Behind the Sermon*. Westminster John Knox, 2003.

―――. "God Has Spoken: Hebrews' Theology of the Scriptures." Pages 321–336 in *The Epistle to the Hebrews and Christian Theology*. Edited by Richard Bauckham et al. Eerdmans, 2009.

Schenke, Hans-Martin. "Erwägungen zum Rätsel des Hebräerbriefes." Pages 421–438 in *Neues Testament und christliche Existenz*. Edited by Hans Dieter Betz and Luise Schottroff. Mohr Siebeck, 1973.

Schenker, Adrian. "Sacrifices anciens, sacrifice nouveau dans l'Epître aux Hébreux." *LumVie* 43 (1994): 71–76.

Schierse, F. J. *The Epistle to the Hebrews*. Translated by Benen Fahy. New Testament for Spiritual Reading. Herder & Herder, 1969.

Schleiermacher, Friedrich. *The Christian Faith*. Edited by H. R. Mackintosh and J. S. Stewart. T&T Clark, 1928.

Schlosser, Jacques. "La médiation du Christ d'après l'épître aux Hébreux." *RevScRel* 63 (1989): 169–181.

Schmid, H. H. "לקח." *TDOT* 2:648–651.

Schneiders, Sandra M. "The Raising of the New Temple: John 20.19–23 and Johannine Ecclesiology." *NTS* 52 (2006): 337–355.

Schniedewind, William M. "King and Priest in the Book of Chronicles and the Duality of Qumran Messianism." *JJS* 45 (1994): 71–78.

―――. *Society and the Promise to David: A Reception History of 2 Samuel 7:1–17*. Oxford University Press, 1999.

―――. "Traditions of Melchizedek." *DNTB* 693–695.

Scholem, Gershom G. *Major Trends in Jewish Mysticism*. Paperback ed. Schocken, 1961.

Scholer, John M. *Proleptic Priests: Priesthood in the Epistle to the Hebrews*. JSNTSup 49. JSOT Press, 1991.

Schröger, Friedrich. *Der Verfasser des Hebräerbriefes als Schriftausleger*. Biblische Untersuchungen 4. Pustet, 1968.

Schunack, Gerd. *Der Habräerbrief*. Zürcher Bibelkommentare 14. Theologischer Verlag, 2002.

Schürer, Emil. *The History of the Jewish People in the Age of Jesus Christ*. Edited and revised by Geza Vermes, Fergus Millar, and Matthew Black. 3 vols. Revised English ed. T&T Clark, 1979.

Schwartz, M. J. "L'Égypte de Philon." In *Philon d'Alexandrie: Lyon, 11–15 Septembre 1966*, 35–44. Centre national de la recherche scientifique, 1967.

──────. "Note sur la famille de Philon d'Alexandrie." *AIPHOS* 13 (1953): 591–602.

Scobie, Charles H. H. "Origins and development of Samaritan Christianity." *NTS* 19 (1973): 390–414.

Scott, Brett R. "Jesus's Superiority over Moses in Hebrews 3:1–6." *BSac* 155 (1998): 201–10.

Scott, Ernest Findlay. *The Epistle to the Hebrews: Its Doctrine and Significance*. T&T Clark, 1922.

Scott, J. M. "Heavenly Ascent in Jewish and Pagan Traditions." *DNTB* 447–452.

Scott, J. Julius, Jr. "*Archegos* in the Salvation History of the Epistle to the Hebrews." *JETS* 29 (1986): 47–54.

Scullion, James Patrick. "A Traditio-Historical Study of the Day of Atonement." Ph.D. diss., Catholic University of America, 1990; UMI, 1991.

Searle, John R. *Speech Acts: An Essay in the Philosophy of Language*. Cambridge University Press, 1969.

Seebass, Horst. "לָקַח לֶקַח." *TDOT* 8:16–21.

Segal, A. F. "Heavenly Ascent in Hellenistic Judaism, Early Christianity and Their Environment." *ANRW* 23.2:1333–1394. Part 2, *Principat*, 23.2. Edited by H. Temporini and W. Haase. de Gruyter, 1980.

Segraves, Daniel L. *Hebrews: Better Things*. 2 vols. Word Aflame, 1997.

Seid, Timothy W. "Synkrisis in Hebrews 7: The Rhetorical Structure and Strategy." Pages 322–347 in *The Rhetorical Interpretation of Scripture: Essays from the 1996 Malibu Conference*. Edited by Stanley E. Porter and Dennis L. Stamps. JSNTSup 180. Sheffield Academic, 1999.

Seitz, Christopher R. "The Book of Isaiah 40–66." *NIB* 6:307–552.

──────. *Figured Out: Typology and Providence in Christian Scripture*. Westminster John Knox, 2001.

──────. *Isaiah 1–39*. IBC. John Knox, 1993.

Selby, Gary S. "The Meaning and Function of Συνείδησις in Hebrews 9 and 10." *ResQ* 28 (1985–1986): 145–154.

Selwyn, Edward Gordon. *The First Epistle of St. Peter*. Macmillan, 1946.

Seneca. *Tragedies*. Edited and translated by John G. Fitch. 2 vols. LCL. Harvard University Press, 2004.

Seow, Choon-Leong. "Ark of the Covenant." *ABD* 1:386–393.

──────. "The First and Second Books of Kings." *NIB* 3:1–296.

Sherlock, Charles. *The God Who Fights: The War Tradition in Holy Scripture*. Rutherford Studies in Contemporary Theology 6. Rutherford, 1993.

Sherman, Robert. *King, Priest, and Prophet: A Trinitarian Theology of Atonement*. Theology for the Twenty-first Century. T&T Clark, 2004.

Silva, Moises. "Perfection and Eschatology in Hebrews." *WTJ* 39 (1976): 60–71.

Simian-Yofre, H. "פָּנִים." *TDOT* 11:589–615.

Simon, Marcel. *St. Stephen and the Hellenists in the Primitive Church*. Longmans Green, 1958.
Simundson, Daniel J. "Micah." *NIB* 7:531–590.
Skehan, Patrick W., Translation and Notes, and Alexander A. Di Lella, Introduction and Commentary. *The Wisdom of Ben Sira*. AB 39. Doubleday, 1987.
Sklar, Jay. *Sin, Impurity, Sacrifice, Atonement: The Priestly Conceptions*. Hebrew Bible Monographs 2. Sheffield Phoenix, 2005.
Sloane, Thomas O., ed. *Encyclopedia of Rhetoric*. Oxford University Press, 2001.
Smith, Billy K., and Frank S. Page. *Amos, Obadiah, Jonah*. NAC 19B. Broadman & Holman, 1995.
Smith, Gary V. *Hosea, Amos, Micah*. NIVAC. Zondervan, 2001.
Smith, Morton. "Ascent to the Heavens and Deification in 4QM^a." Pages 181–188 in *Archaeology and History in the Dead Sea Scrolls: The New York University Conference in Memory of Yigael Yadin*. Edited by Lawrence H. Schiffman. JSOT/ASOR Monograph Series 2; JSPSup 8. JSOT Press, 1990.
Smith, Mark S. *The Pilgrimage Pattern in Exodus*. JSOTSup 239. Sheffield Academic, 1997.
———. "'Seeing God in the Psalms': The Background of the Beatific Vision in the Hebrew Bible." *CBQ* 50 (1988): 171–183.
Smith, Robert H. *Hebrews*. ACNT. Augsburg, 1984.
Smith, Ralph L. *Micah–Malachi*. WBC 32. Word, 1984.
Snijders, L. A. "מָלֵא." *TDOT* 8:297–307.
Soderlund, Sven. *The Greek Text of Jeremiah: A Revised Hypothesis*. JSOTSup 47. JSOT Press, 1985.
Son, Kiwoong. *Zion Symbolism in Hebrews: Hebrews 12:18–24 as a Hermeneutical Key to the Epistle*. Paternoster Biblical Monographs. Paternoster, 2005.
Songer, Harold S. "A Superior Priesthood: Hebrews 4:14–7:28." *RevExp* 82 (1985): 345–359.
Sowers, Sidney G. *The Hermeneutics of Philo and Hebrews: A Comparison of the Interpretation of the Old Testament in Philo Judaeus and the Epistle to the Hebrews*. Basel Studies of Theology 1. John Knox, 1965.
Spencer, William David. "Christ's Sacrifice as Apologetic: An Application of Heb 10:1–18." *JETS* 40 (1997): 189–197.
Spicq, Ceslas. *L'épître aux Hébreux*. 2 vols. EBib. Gabalda, 1952.
———. "L'Épître aux Hébreux, Apollos, Jean-Baptiste, les Hellénistes et Qumrân." *RevQ* 1 (1959): 365–390.
———. *Theological Lexicon of the New Testament*. Translated and edited by James D. Ernest. 3 vols. Hendrickson, 1994.
Stanley, Steve. "Hebrews 9:6–10: The 'Parable' of the Tabernacle." *NovT* 37 (1995): 385–399.
Stanley, Steven K. "A New Covenant Hermeneutic: The Use of Scripture in Hebrews 8–10." *TynBul* 46 (1995): 204–206.
Starbuck, Scott R. A. *Court Oracles in the Psalms: The So-Called Royal Psalms in Their Ancient Near Eastern Context*. SBLDS 172. Society of Biblical Literature, 1999.
Stedman, Ray C. *Hebrews*. IVP New Testament Commentary Series. InterVarsity, 1992.

Stegemann, Ekkehard W., and Wolfgang Stegemann. "Does the Cultic Language in Hebrews Represent Sacrificial Metaphors? Reflections on Some Basic Problems." Pages 13–23 in *Hebrews: Contemporary Methods—New Insights*. Edited by Gabriella Gelardini. BibInt 75. Brill, 2005.

Sterling, Gregory E. "Ontology versus Eschatology: Tensions between Author and Community in Hebrews." Pages 190–211 in *In the Spirit of Faith: Studies in Philo and Early Christianity in Honor of David Hay*. Edited by David T. Runia and Gregory E. Sterling. Vol. 13 of *Studia Philonica Annual Studies in Hellenistic Judaism*. BJS 331. [Brown University], 2001.

⸻⸻⸻. "Philo." *DNTB* 789–793.

Stökl Ben Ezra, Daniel. "The Christian Exegesis of the Scapegoat Between Jews and Pagans." Pages 207–232 in *Sacrifice in Religious Experience*. Edited by Albert I. Baumgarten. SHR 93. Brill, 2002.

⸻⸻⸻. *The Impact of Yom Kippur on Early Christianity: The Day of Atonement from Second Temple Judaism to the Fifth Century*. WUNT I/163. Mohr Siebeck, 2003.

⸻⸻⸻. "Yom Kippur in the Apocalyptic *imaginaire* and the Roots of Jesus's High Priesthood: Yom Kippur in Zechariah 3, 1 Enoch 10, 11QMelchizedeq, Hebrews and the Apocalypse of Abraham 13." Pages 349–366 in *Transformations of the Inner Self in Ancient Religions*. Edited by Jan Assmann and Guy G. Stroumsa. SHR 83. Brill, 1999.

Stone, Michael E. *Fourth Ezra: A Commentary on the Book of Fourth Ezra*. Edited by Frank Moore Cross. Hermeneia. Fortress, 1990.

Strack, Hermann L., and Paul Billerbeck. *Kommentar zum Neuen Testament aus Talmud und Midrasch*. 6 vols. C. H. Beck, 1922–1961.

Strathmann, Hermann. *Der Brief an die Hebräer*. 9th ed. NTD 9. Vandenhoeck & Ruprecht, 1968.

Strobel, August. *Der Brief an die Hebräer*. NTD 9. Vandenhoeck & Ruprecht, 1975.

Stuart, Douglas. *Hosea–Jonah*. WBC 31. Word, 1987.

Stuart, Douglas K. *Exodus*. NAC 2. Broadman & Holman, 2006.

Stuckenbruck, Loren T. *Angel Veneration and Christology: A Study in Early Judaism and in the Christology of the Apocalypse of John*. WUNT II/70. Mohr Siebeck, 1995.

Suetonius. "Nero." Pages 82–179 in vol. 2 of *Suetonius*. Translated by J. C. Rolfe. LCL. Harvard University Press, 1997.

Swanson, Dwight D. *The Temple Scroll and the Bible: The Methodology of 11QT*. STDJ 14. Brill, 1995.

Sweet, J. P. M. "A House Not Made with Hands." Pages 368–390 in *Templum amicitiae: Essays on the Second Temple Presented to Ernst Bammel*. Edited by William Horbury. JSNTSup 48. JSOT Press, 1991.

Swete, A. B. *The Ascended Christ*. 1910.

Swetnam, James. Review of *Bekenntnis und Auslegung: Die paränetische Funktion der Christologie im Hebräerbrief*, by Franz Laub. *CBQ* 44 (1982): 336–338.

⸻⸻⸻. Review of *Der Brief and die Hebräer*, by Otto Kuss. *CBQ* 29 (1967): 155–157.

⸻⸻⸻. "Christology and the Eucharist in the Epistle to the Hebrews." *Bib* 70 (1989): 74–95.

———. "'The Greater and More Perfect Tent': A Contribution to the Discussion of Heb 9:11." *Bib* 47 (1966): 91–106.

———. *Jesus and Isaac: A Study of the Epistle to the Hebrews in the Light of the Aqedah.* AnBib 94. Biblical Institute Press, 1981.

———. "A Merciful and Trustworthy High Priest." *Pacific Journal of Theology* 21 (1999): 6–27.

———. "Sacrifice and Revelation in the Epistle to the Hebrews: Observations and Surmises on Hebrews 9,26." *CBQ* 30 (1968): 227–234.

———. Review of *Sohn und Hoherpriester: Eine traditionsgeschichtliche Untersuchung zur Christologie des Hebräerbriefes*, by William R. G. Loader. *CBQ* 45 (1983): 496–498.

Synge, F. C. *Hebrews and the Scriptures.* SPCK, 1959.

Tabor, James D. "Ascent to Heaven." *ABD* 3:91–94.

———. *Things Unutterable: Paul's Ascent to Paradise in Its Greco-Roman, Judaic, and Early Christian Contexts.* Studies in Judaism. University Press of America, 1986.

Talbert, Charles H. "Myth of a Ascending-Descending Redeemer in Mediterranean Antiquity." *NTS* 22 (1976): 418–440.

Talmon, Shemaryahou. "Waiting for the Messiah: The Spiritual Universe of the Qumran Covenanteers." Pages 123–131 in *Judaisms and Their Messiahs at the Turn of the Christian Era.* Edited by Jacob Neusner, William Scott Green, and Ernest S. Frerichs. Cambridge University Press, 1987.

Tate, Marvin E. *Psalms 51–100.* WBC 20. Word, 1990.

Taubenschlag, Raphael. *The Law of Greco-Roman Egypt in the Light of the Papyri: 332 B.C.–640 A.D.* 2d ed. Panstwowe Wydawnictwo Naukowe, 1955.

Taylor, Richard A., and E. Ray Clendenen. *Haggai, Malachi.* NAC 21A. Broadman & Holman, 2004.

Theißen, Gerd. *Untersuchungen zum Hebräerbrief.* SNT 2. Gütersloher Verlag, 1969.

Theobald, Michael. "Zwei Bünde und ein Gottesvolk: Die Bundestheologie des Hebräerbriefs im Horizont des christlich-jüdischen Gesprächs." *TQ* 176 (1996): 309–25.

Thompson, J. A. *1, 2 Chronicles.* NAC 9. Broadman & Holman, 1994.

Thompson, James W. "The Appropriate, The Necessary, and the Impossible: Faith and Reason in Hebrews." Pages 302–317 in *The Early Church in Its Context: Essays in Honor of Everett Ferguson.* Edited by A. J. Malherbe, Frederick W. Norris, and James W. Thompson. NovTSup 90. Brill, 1998.

———. *The Beginnings of Christian Philosophy: The Epistle to the Hebrews.* CBQMS 13. Catholic Biblical Association of America, 1982.

———. "Hebrews 9 and Hellenistic Concepts of Sacrifice." *JBL* 98 (1979): 567–78.

Throntveit, Mark A. *Ezra–Nehemiah.* IBC. John Knox, 1992.

Tigay, Jeffrey H. *Deuteronomy: The Traditional Hebrew Text with the New JPS Translation.* JPS Torah Commentary. Jewish Publication Society, 1996.

Tobin, Thomas H. *The Creation of Man: Philo and the History of Interpretation.* CBQMS 14. Catholic Biblical Association of America, 1983.

Tommasi, Chiara Ombretta. "Ascension." *ER* 1:518–526.

Toon, Peter. *The Ascension of Our Lord*. Thomas Nelson, 1984.

Torrance, Thomas F. *Space, Time and Resurrection*. Handsel, 1976.

Toussaint, Stanley D. "The Eschatology of the Warning Passages in the Book of Hebrews." *Grace Theological Journal* 3 (1982): 67–80.

Tov, Emanuel. "4QJer^c (4Q72)." Pages 249–276 in *Tradition of the Text: Studies Offered to Dominique Barthélemy in Celebration of His 70th Birthday*. Edited by Gerard J. Norton and Stephen Pisano. OBO 109. Vandenhoeck & Ruprecht, 1991.

Treat, Jay Curry. "Epistle of Barnabas." *ABD* 1:611–614.

Treiyer, Alberto. "The Priest-King Role of the Messiah." *JATS* 7 (1996): 64–80.

Trites, Allison A. *The New Testament Concept of Witness*. SNTSMS 31. Cambridge University Press, 1977.

Trotter, Andrew H., Jr. *Interpreting the Epistle to the Hebrews*. Guides to New Testament Exegesis. Baker, 1997.

Tucker, Gene M. "The Book of Isaiah 1–39." *NIB* 6:25–306.

Tuell, Steven Shawn. *First and Second Chronicles*. IBC. John Knox, 2001.

_____. *The Law of the Temple in Ezekiel 40–48*. HSM 49. Scholars Press, 1992.

Tye, Michael. "Imagery." Pages 703–705 in vol. 4. of *Routledge Encyclopedia of Philosophy*. Edited by Edward Craig. Routledge, 1998.

Übelacker, Walter G. *Der Hebräerbrief als Appell: Untersuchungen zu exordium, narratio und postscriptum (Hebr 1–2 und 13,22–25)*. ConBNT 21. Almqvist & Wiksell, 1989.

Urbach, Ephraim E. *The Sages: Their Concepts and Beliefs*. Translated by Israel Abrahams. 2 vols. Publications of the Perry Foundation in the Hebrew University of Jerusalem. Magnes Hebrew University, 1975.

VanderKam, James C. Review of *Ascent to Heaven in Jewish and Christian Apocalypses*, by Martha Himmelfarb. *JBL* 114 (1995): 323–324.

_____. *Enoch and the Growth of an Apocalyptic Tradition*. CBQMS 16. Catholic Biblical Association of America, 1984.

_____. "Feast of Dedication." *ABD* 2:123–125.

_____. *From Joshua to Caiaphas: High Priests after the Exile*. Fortress; Van Gorcum, 2004.

_____. "Hanukkah: Its Timing and Significance According to 1 and 2 Maccabees." Pages 128–144 in *From Revelation to Canon: Studies in the Hebrew Bible and Second Temple Literature*. JSJSup 62. Brill, 2000.

_____. "John 10 and the Feast of Dedication." Pages 145–156 in *From Revelation to Canon: Studies in the Hebrew Bible and Second Temple Literature*. JSJSup 62. Brill, 2000.

_____. "John 10 and the Feast of the Dedication." Pages 203–214 in *Of Scribes and Scrolls: Studies on the Hebrew Bible, Intertestamental Judaism, and Christian Origins*. Edited by Harold W. Attridge, John J. Collins, and Thomas H. Tobin. College Theology Society Resources in Religion 5. University Press of America, 1990.

_____. "Joshua the High Priest." Pages 157–176 in *From Revelation to Canon: Studies in the Hebrew Bible and Second Temple Literature*. JSJSup 62. Brill, 2000.

VanderKam, James C., and Peter W. Flint. *The Meaning of the Dead Sea Scrolls: Their Significance for Understanding the Bible, Judaism, Jesus, and Christianity*. HarperSanFrancisco, 2002.

Vanhoye, Albert. "L'épître aux Hébreux." In *Les dernières épîtres: Hébreux—Jacques—Pierre—Jean—Jude*. Commentaires "Évangile et Vie". Bayard/Centurion, 1997.

———. *La lettre aux Hébreux: Jésus-Christ, médiateur d'une nouvelle alliance*. Jésus et Jésus-Christ. Desclée, 2002.

———. "L'οἰκουμένη dans l'épître aux Hébreux." *Bib* 45 (1964): 248–253.

———. *Old Testament Priests and the New Priest: According to the New Testament*. Translated by J. Bernard Orchard. Studies in Scripture. St. Bede's, 1986.

———. "Par la tente plus grande et plus parfaite (He 9:11)." *Bib* 46 (1965): 1–28.

———. *Situation du Christ: Hébreux 1–2*. LD 58. Paris: Cerf, 1969.

———. *Structure and Message of the Epistle to the Hebrews*. Vol. 12 of *Subsidia biblica*. Editrice Pontificio Istituto Biblico, 1989.

———. *La structure littéraire de l'Épitre aux Hébreux*. 2nd ed. Desclée De Brouwer, 1976.

———. "La '*teleiôsis*' du Christ: point capital de la Christologie sacerdotale d'Hébreux." *NTS* 42 (1996): 321–338.

Vaux, Roland de. *Les institutions de L'Ancien Testament*. 2 vols. 2d rev. ed. Cerf, 1961.

Verhoef, Pieter A. *The Books of Haggai and Malachi*. NICOT. Eerdmans, 1987.

Verrecchia, Jean-Claude. "Le sanctuaire dans L'épître aux Hébreux: Etude exegetique de la section centrale." Ph.D. diss., Universite de Sciences Humaines de Strasbourg, 1981.

Versnel, H. S. *Triumphus: An Inquiry into the Origin, Development and Meaning of the Roman Triumph*. Brill, 1970.

Via, Dan Otto, Jr. "Revelation, Atonement and the Scope of Faith in the Epistle to the Hebrews: A Deconstructive and Reader-response Interpretation." *BibInt* 11 (2003): 515–530.

Vicent Cernuda, Antonio. "La introducción del primogénito según Hebr. 1,6." *EstBib* 39 (1981): 107–153.

Voegelin, Eric. *Israel and Revelation*. Vol. 1 of *Order and History*. Louisiana State University Press, 1956.

Wallace, Daniel B. *Greek Grammar Beyond the Basics: An Exegetical Syntax of the New Testament*. Zondervan, 1996.

Wallenkampf, Arnold V. "Challengers to the Doctrine of the Sanctuary." Pages 197–216 in *Doctrine of the Sanctuary: A Historical Survey (1845–1863)*. Edited by Frank B. Holbrook. DARCOM 5. Biblical Research Institute General Conference of Seventh-day Adventists, 1989.

Waltke, Bruce K. "The Phenomenon of Conditionality within Unconditional Covenants." Pages 123–140 in *Israel's Apostasy and Restoration*. Edited by Avraham Gileadi. Baker, 1988.

Waltke, Bruce K., and M. O'Connor. *An Introduction to Biblical Hebrew Syntax*. Eisenbrauns, 1990.

Watson, Duane F. "Rhetorical Criticism of Hebrews and the Catholic Epistles since 1978." *CurBr* 5 (1997): 175–207.

Watson, Duane F., and Alan J. Hauser. *Rhetorical Criticism of the Bible: A Comprehensive Bibliography with Notes on History and Method*. BibInt 4. Brill, 1994.

Watson, Rebecca S. *Chaos Uncreated: A Reassessment of the Theme of "Chaos" in the Hebrew Bible*. BZAW 341. Walter de Gruyter, 2005.

Watts, John D. W. *Isaiah 1–33*. WBC 24. Word, 1985.

_____. *Isaiah 34–66*. WBC 25. Word, 1987.

Wedderburn, A. J. M. "The 'Letter' to the Hebrews and Its Thirteenth Chapter." *NTS* 50 (2004): 390–405.

Weinberg, Joel. *The Citizen-Temple Community*. Translated by Daniel L. Smith-Christopher. JSOTSup 151. JSOT Press, 1992.

Weinfeld, M. "בְּרִית." *TDOT* 2:253–278.

_____. "The Covenant of Grant in the Old Testament and in the Ancient Near East." *JAOS* 90 (1970): 184–203.

Weiser, Artur. *The Psalms: A Commentary*. OTL. Westminster, 1962.

Weiss, Herold. "*Sabbatismos* in the Epistle to the Hebrews." *CBQ* 58 (1996): 674–689.

Weiß, Hans-Friedrich. *Der Brief and die Hebräer*. KEK 13. Vandenhoeck & Ruprecht, 1991.

Werman, Cana. "The Concept of Holiness and the Requirements of Purity in Second Temple and Tannaic Literature." Pages 163–180 in *Purity and Holiness: The Heritage of Leviticus*. Edited by Marcel J. H. M. Poorthuis and Joshua Schwartz. Jewish and Christian Perspectives Series 2. Brill, 2000.

Westcott, Brooke Foss. *The Epistle to the Hebrews: The Greek Text with Notes and Essays*. Mcmillan, 1892. Reprint, Eerdmans, 1984.

Wevers, John William. *Notes on the Greek Text of Leviticus*. SBLSCS 44. Scholars Press, 1997.

Whiston, William. *The Works of Josephus: Complete and Unabridged*. New updated ed. Hendrickson, 1987.

White, L. Michael, and John T. Fitzgerald. "Quod est comparandum: The Problem of Parallels." Pages 13–39 in *Early Christianity and Classical Culture: Comparative Studies in Honof of Abraham J. Malherbe*. Edited by John T. Fitzgerald, Thomas H. Olbricht, and L. Michael White. NovTSup 110. Brill, 2003.

Whitelam, Keith W. "King and Kingship." *ABD* 4:40–48.

Whitney, K. William. *Two Strange Beasts: Leviathan and Behemoth in Second Temple and Early Rabbinic Judaism*. HSM 63. Eisenbrauns, 2006.

Wider, David. *Theozentrik und Bekenntnis: Untersuchungen zur Theologie des Redens Gottes im Hebräerbrief*. BZNW 87. Walter de Gruyter, 1997.

Wiid, J. S. "The Testamental Significance of διαθήκη in Hebrews 9:15–22." *Neot* 26 (1992): 149–56.

Wilder, Amos Niven. *Theopoetic: Theology and the Religious Imagination*. Fortress, 1976.

Williams, Michael A. *Rethinking "Gnosticism": An Argument for Dismantling a Dubious Category*. Princeton University Press, 1996.

Williamson, Ronald. "Background of the Epistle to the Hebrews." *ExpTim* 87 (1976): 232–237.

_____. "The Incarnation of the Logos in Hebrews." *ExpTim* 95 (1983): 4–8.

_____. *Jews in the Hellenistic World: Philo*. Cambridge Commentaries on Writings of the Jewish and Christian World 200 BC to AD 200, no. 1, part 2. Cambridge University Press, 1989.

_____. *Philo and the Epistle to the Hebrews*. ALGHJ 4. Brill, 1970.

———. "The Sinlessness of Jesus." *ExpTim* 86 (1974): 4–8.
Willi-Plein, Ina. "Some Remarks on Hebrews from the Viewpoint of Old Testament Exegesis." Pages 25–35 in *Hebrews: Contemporary Methods—New Insights*. Edited by Gabriella Gelardini. BibInt 75. Brill, 2005.
Wilson, Joseph P. *The Hero and the City: An Interpretation of Sophocles' Oedipus at Colonus*. University of Michigan Press, 1997.
Wilson, R. McL. *Gnosis and the New Testament*. Fortress, 1968.
———. *Hebrews*. NCBCom. Eerdmans, 1987.
Wilson, W. T. "Hellenistic Judaism." *DNTB* 477–482.
Windisch, Hans. *Der Hebräerbrief*. 2d ed. HNT 14. Mohr Siebeck, 1931.
Wise, Michael Owen. "4QFlorilegium and the Temple of Adam." *RevQ* 15 (1991): 103–132.
———. *A Critical Study of the Temple Scroll from Qumran Cave 11*. SAOC 49. Oriental Institute of the University of Chicago, 1990.
———. "Dead Sea Scrolls: General Introduction." *DNTB* 252–266.
Witherington, Ben. "The Influence of Galatians on Hebrews." *NTS* 37 (1991): 146–152.
———. *Jesus the Sage: The Pilgrimage of Wisdom*. Fortress, 1994.
Wolff, H. J. "Hellenistic Private Law." Pages 534–560 in *The Jewish People in the First Century: Historical Geography, Political History, Social, Cultural, and Religious Life and Institutions*. Edited by S. Safrai and others. CRINT. Van Gorcum, 1974.
Worley, David R. "Fleeing to Two Immutable Things—God's Oath-Taking and Oath-Witnessing: The Use of Litigant Oath in Hebrews 6:19–20." *ResQ* 36 (1994): 223–236.
Wray, Judith Hoch. *Rest as a Theological Metaphor in the Epistle to the Hebrews and the Gospel of Truth: Early Christian Homiletics of Rest*. SBLDS 166. Scholars Press, 1998.
Wright, David P. "Day of Atonement." *ABD* 2:72–76.
Wright, J. Edward. *The Early History of Heaven*. Oxford University Press, 2000.
Wright, John W. "The Legacy of David in Chronicles: The Narrative Function of 1 Chronicles 23–27." *JBL* 110 (1991): 229–242.
Wright, N. T. *Hebrews for Everyone*. 2d ed. SPCK and Westminster John Knox, 2004.
Wright, R. B. "Psalms of Solomon: A New Translation and Introduction." *OTP* 2:639–670.
Wyatt, Nicolas. " 'Jedidiah' and Cognate Forms as a Title of Royal Legitimation." *Bib* 66 (1985): 112–125.
———. *Space and Time in the Religious Life of the Near East*. BibSem 85. Sheffield: Sheffield Academic, 2001.
Yadin, Yigael. "The Dead Sea Scrolls and the Epistle to the Hebrews." Pages 36–55 in *Aspects of the Dead Sea Scrolls*. Edited by Chaim Rabin and Yigael Yadin. 2d ed. ScrHier 4. Magnes, 1965.
———. *The Temple Scroll: The Hidden Law of the Dead Sea Sect*. Random, 1985.
———, ed. *The Temple Scroll*. 3 vols. English ed. The Israel Exploration Society; the Institute of Archaeology of the Hebrew University of Jerusalem; the Shrine of the Book; 1983.
Yee, Gale A. "The Book of Hosea." *NIB* 7:195–298.
Yeo, Khiok-Khng. "The Meaning and Usage of the Theology of 'Rest.' " *AsJT* 5 (1991): 2–33.

Yoder Neufeld, Thomas R. *"Put on the Armour of God": The Divine Warrior from Isaiah to Ephesians.* JSNTSup 140. Sheffield Academic, 1997.
Yonge, Charles Duke. *The Works of Philo: Complete and Unabridged.* New updated ed. Hendrickson, 1993.
Young, Frances M. *Sacrifice and the Death of Christ.* SPCK, 1975.
Young, Norman H. " 'Bearing His Reproach' (Heb 13:9–14)." *NTS* 48 (2002): 243–261.
_____. "The Day of Dedication or the Day of Atonement? The Old Testament Background to Hebrews 6:19–20 Revisited." *AUSS* 40 (2002): 61–68.
_____. "The Gospel according to Hebrews 9." *NTS* 27 (1981): 198–210.
_____. "Τοῦτ᾽ ἔστιν τῆς σαρκός αὐτοῦ (Heb. X. 20): Apposition, Dependent or Explicative?" *NTS* 20 (1974): 100–104.
_____. " 'Where Jesus Has Gone as a Forerunner on Our Behalf' (Hebrews 6:20)." *AUSS* 39 (2001): 165–173.
Zanker, Paul. *The Power of Images in the Age of Augustus.* Translated by Alan Shapiro. Jerome Lectures. University of Michigan Press, 1988.
Ziegler, Joseph, ed. *Duodecim prophetae.* Septuaginta: Vetus Testamentum Graecum 12. Vandenhoeck & Ruprecht, 1943.
_____, ed. *Ieremias, Baruch, Threni, Epistula Ieremiae.* Septuaginta: Vetus Testamentum Graecum 15. Vandenhoeck & Ruprecht, 1957.
_____, ed. *Sapientia Iesu Filii Sirach.* Septuaginta: Vetus Testamentum Graecum 12/2. Vandenhoeck & Ruprecht, 1965.
Zimmerli, Walther. *Ezekiel 1: A Commentary on the Book of the Prophet Ezekiel Chapters 1–24.* Edited by Frank Moore Cross, Klaus Baltzer, and Leonard Jay Greenspoon. Translated by Ronald E. Clements. Hermeneia. Fortress, 1979.
_____. *Ezekiel 2: A Commentary on the Book of the Prophet Ezekiel Chapters 25–48.* Edited by Paul D. Hanson and Leonard Jay Greenspoon. Translated by James D. Martin. Hermeneia. Fortress, 1983.
Zimmermann, Johannes. "Observations on 4Q246—The 'Son of God'." Pages 175–190 in *Qumran-Messianism: Studies on the Messianic Expectations in the Dead Sea Scrolls.* Edited by James H. Charlesworth, Hermann Lichtenberger, and Gerbern S. Oegema. Mohr Siebeck, 1998.
Zwiep, A. W. *The Ascension of the Messiah in Lukan Christology.* NovTSup 87. Brill, 1997.

Index

Old Testament

Genesis
1:1	189 n. 175
2:2	292 n. 560
5:24	1, 292 n. 560
8:22	94
15	298 n. 403
15:5	94 n. 222
15:9–21	244 n. 390
15:18	47 n. 41
21:12	292 n. 560
22:16–18	247 n. 399
22:17	94 n. 222, 207, 208, 292
26:4	94 n. 222
28:1–11	242
28:11–22	186–187 n. 164, 259 n. 444
28:15	197 n. 208
30:35	238 n. 359
31:10	238 n. 359
31:12	238 n. 359
32:12	94 n. 222
32:15	238 n. 359
49:5–7	93 n. 216
49:9–10	137
49:10	126

Exodus
2:11	163
3:8	218–219 n. 283, 241
3:13–14	163
3:16–17	198 n. 211
4:18	163
4:22–23	43, 151 n. 22, 169 n. 104, 174 n. 123, 286 n. 540
10:21	281 n. 544
12	249
13:3	163
14:13–14	163
14:21–31	163
15	166
16:35	151 n. 22, 152 n. 29
17:7	195 n. 197
19:1	56 n. 68
19:5–6	65
19:22	65
20–24	245 n. 394
20:2	163
20:12	218–219 n. 283
20:24	46 n. 40,
23:15–17	260
24	19, 247, 248, 249
24:1	300 n. 591
24:1–11	245, 250
24:8	292 n. 560
24:9	300 n. 591
24:9–11	1, 242
24:17	300 n. 591
25	251 n. 410
25:8, 9	43, 48, 187 n. 164, 249, 250 n. 407, 251 n. 410, 259 n. 444
25:22	188
25:23–40	222 n. 292
25:40	23, 48, 187 n. 164, 251 n. 410, 259 n. 444, 292 n. 560
26:31–36	203 n. 230
26:33	22, 203, 204
26:37	203 n. 230
28–29	93

28:36–38	113 n. 297	8	25, 62 n. 102, 252, 256 n. 434
29	62, 252		
29:1–37	23	8–9	23, 62, 64, 284, 300 n. 591
29:6	113 n. 297	8:6	253 n. 419
29:9	65, 93	8:6–13	252
29:10	256	8:9	113 n. 297
29:14	7–8 n. 27, 11 n. 36, 232	8:10–12	22, 204, 250, 253 n. 420
29:28–29	93	8:14–29	62
29:36–37	253, 254, 274	8:15	26 n. 100, 62 n. 101, 253, 254, 256, 274
29:44	62		
30:6	222 n. 292	8:17	11, 232
30:17–21	223 n. 298	8:24–30	63 n. 108
30:22–33	23	8:30	253
31:18	58	8:33	65
32–34	242	8:34	253 n. 419
32:1–14	247 n. 399	9:7	26 n. 100, 64
32:25–34	247 n. 399	9:11	11, 232
32:32	212 n. 268	9:23–24	251 n. 410
32:26–29	93	10:3	300 n. 591
32:29	65	10:17	246 n. 396
32:32	286 n. 540	12	62 n. 104
33:12–23	43	13–14	62 n. 104
34:7	246 n. 396	16	9, 20, 25, 218, 230, 231 n. 320, 238, 254
34:23	260 n. 447		
34:29	58	16 (LXX)	231
36:37	203 n. 230	16:1–3	204, 223 n. 298
37:10–24	222 n. 292	16:2	7–8 n. 27, 203
38:18	203 n. 230	16:3	239, 278 n. 500
39:30	113 n. 297	16:5	20, 238, 268 n. 476
39:36–37	63	16:6	7–8 n. 27, 15
40	25, 62, 252, 256 n. 437, 284	16:7–10	15, 20, 238
40:2	254–255 n. 429	16:9	15
40:5	222 n. 292	16:11	7–8 n. 27
40:1–9	22, 204	16:11–14	274
40:1–15	23	16:12	203
40:2	61	16:15	9 n. 31, 203
40:9–10	250	16:15–16	17 n. 59
40:12–13	104 n. 253	16:17	7–8 n. 27, 225, 226
40:12–16	62	16:18–19	253 n. 420, 274
40:17	61	16:19	7–8 n. 27, 63
40:33	23	16:20–22	15
		16:27	11 n. 36, 230, 231, 232
Leviticus		16:29	13
1:10–13	25	16:31	13
4:1–21	268 n. 476	17	46 n. 40
4:3–12	62 n. 104	20:9	62 n. 104
4:5–7	232	20:30	62
4:12	11, 232	21:10	278
4:13–26	64	21:10 (LXX)	214–215 n. 273
4:16–21	232	23:26–32	218
4:26	62 n. 104	23:27	13
6:23 (LXX)	232	23:29	13
6:30	232	23:32	13
7:19–21	66	25:39–41	43
		26	99, 244 n. 389

Index 359

Numbers
1:3	68
4:2	198 n. 211
6:1–10	198 n. 211
7	20, 22, 25, 238, 252
7–8	22, 62
7:1	22, 23, 204, 251, 255 n. 433
7:10, 11	22 n. 75, 283
7:84	22 n. 75
7:88	22 n. 75, 63
7:89	251 n. 410
10:35–36	278 n. 499
13	202–203 n. 229
13:1–16	196 n. 206
13:30	198
14	195
14:1–10	198 n. 211
14:4	198 n. 211
14:7	218–219 n. 283, 241
14:7–9	198
14:22	195 n. 198
14:43–45	196
15:22–26	232 n. 325
18:7	203–204 n. 230
18:25–32	46 n. 40
19	239 n. 364, 239 n. 366
20:13	195 n. 197
24:16	207 n. 239
25	44 n. 32, 164 n. 77
25:4	61
25:11–13	93, 112
25:12	93
29:7–11	218
31	164 n. 77
35:25	278 n. 500

Deuteronomy
1:25	218–219 n. 283, 241
3:20	195 n. 197
4	78
4:11–12	290
4:20	58
4:24	292 n. 560
4:25–26	244 n. 389
5:2–4	249
5:6	163
6:5	56, 68
6:10	151 n. 22
7:5	55, 58
7:14–20	42
8:1	241
8:7	218–219 n. 283
9:19	290 n. 554, 292 n. 560
9:29	58
10:8	93
10:12	56
11:24	47
11:29	151 n. 22
12	308
12:1–4	58
12:2	55
12:5	43, 54, 67
12:6	46 n. 40
12:8–10	43, 46 n. 40, 195 n. 197
12:10–11	96 n. 228
12:11	46 n. 40
12:15	46 n. 40
12:18	46 n. 40
13:6–10	56
14:2	58
14:22–27	46 n. 40, 54 n. 62
15:19–23	54 n. 62
16:1–8	65
16:1–17	54 n. 62
16:16	260
16:21	54 n. 62
17:2–7	56, 244 n. 389
17:8–10	46 n. 40, 54 n. 62, 57
17:9	93 n. 215
17:18	58, 93 n. 215, 158
18:1	93 n. 215
18:1–8	54 n. 62
18:5	79 n. 168
18:18	97
18:20	79 n. 168
19:1–13	54 n. 62
20:5	283
24:8	93 n. 215
25:19	195 n. 197
26:1–25	54 n. 62
26:12	46 n. 40
26:18	58
27:9	58, 93 n. 215
28	99, 244 n. 389
28:15–68	69 n. 137
28:36	42
29–30	245 n. 394
29–31	19
29:11	190 n. 180
29:13–14	249
30	78
31:8	197 n. 208, 292 n. 560
31:11	54 n. 62, 260
31:16–17	244 n. 389
32:8	169 n. 104
32:15	238 n. 359
32:35	292 n. 560
32:36	292 n. 560
32:43	149 n. 14, 155 n. 42, 292 n. 560

33:8–11	93	16:1	79, 159 n. 59
33:9–10	207 n. 239, 299 n. 586	16:7	42
		16:12	159 n. 59
Joshua		16:13	159 n. 59
1:5	197 n. 208	17:2	79
1:13	43 n. 31, 195 n. 197	17:45	79
3:3	93 n. 215	19:11	107 n. 272
7	44	20:16	107 n. 272
7:10–15	244 n. 389	24:6	159 n. 59
7:24–8:1	44	24:12 (LXX)	263 n. 464
8:33	93 n. 215	26:9	159 n. 59
11:23	47		
14:15	47	**2 Samuel**	
18:1	53	2:27	187 n. 164
19:9	93 n. 216	3:1	107 n. 272
21:43–45	43 n. 31, 195 n. 197, 197 n. 207	3:18	119
		5:3	58 n. 83
22:4	43 n. 31, 47, 195 n. 197, 197 n. 207	6:1	107 n. 272
		7	37, 39, 40, 49, 76, 79 n. 167, 85, 87 n. 201, 96 n. 228, 98, 99, 101 n. 244, 107, 108, 129, 142
22:10–34	44		
23:1	43 n. 31, 47		
23:16	244 n. 389		
		7:1	42, 47
Judges		7:1–17	58
1–2	47	7:4–7	42
5:10	158 n. 58	7:5–16	306
5:15 (LXX)	202–203 n. 229	7:8–11a	38, 43, 75
9:8	159 n. 59	7:8–16	35
10:4	158 n. 58	7:9	42, 79, 157–158 n. 52
12:14	158 n. 58	7:9–11	43, 44, 123
		7:10–11	88, 307
Ruth		7:10–14	128
4:11	79	7:11	67, 74, 75, 80, 107 n. 272
		7:11–14	77
1 Samuel		7:11b–16	38, 79 n. 167, 120 n. 324, 127, 135
2:17 (LXX)	263 n. 464		
2:27–36	53	7:12	35, 76
2:39–35	93	7:12–16	38
2:30	39 n. 14	7:13	38 n. 8, 74, 80, 98, 104
2:35	53	7:14	28, 39, 42, 43, 45, 75, 135, 149 n. 14, 151, 155 n. 42, 168–169 n. 101, 169 n. 104, 172, 174 n. 123, 292 n. 560, 293, 306
4:2–9	278 n. 499		
4:4	210 n. 253, 278 n. 499		
8:6	42 n. 24		
9:6	103		
9:7	81	7:14–16	88, 115, 117
9:12–27	46–47 n. 40, 66–67 n. 124	7:15–16	84 n. 185, 115 n. 304
9:16	159 n. 59	7:16	49, 53, 79, 105
9:17	103	7:27	76
10:5	46–47 n. 40, 66–67 n. 124	8	47, 77, 82
10:10	159 n. 59	8:13	38
10:16	46 n. 39	10	47
10:24	159 n. 59	12:24–25	157–158 n. 52
10:26	46 n. 39	12:30	113
11:15	46 n. 39	16:16	159 n. 59
13:14	42	16:21	89–90 n. 208

Index 361

18:26	103	9:3–9	40
21:1	261	9:4	42
21:19	157–158 n. 52	9:4–7	43
21:15–22	47	9:4–9	44, 139
22:3	292 n. 560	9:6–9	42
22:7	259 n. 444	10:24	261 n. 453
23:1–7	39	11:4	51, 52
23:5	38, 84, 127	11:12–13	39 n. 14
24:1	45 n. 34	11:32–36	39 n. 14
		12:19	107 n. 272

1 Kings

1:25	159 n. 59	12:20	107 n. 272
1:32–40	159 n. 59	12:26	107 n. 272
1:33	158 n. 58	13:2	107 n. 272
1:33–53	156	14:8	42, 107 n. 272
1:35	159	14:14	97
1:38	158 n. 58	14:23	46–47 n. 40, 66–67 n. 124
1:46–47	159	15:4	39 n. 14
1:46–48	158 n. 58	15:11–13	55
1:47	159 n. 59	15:12	55 n. 65
2	73	15:12–13	73
2:1–4	40, 139	15:13	56
2:1–9	53	15:14	46–47 n. 40, 66–67 n. 124
2:13–46	53	15:15	56, 73, 309
2:26–27	73, 93	19:15–16	159 n. 59
2:35	93	22:19–23	1
3:1–15	173	22:43	46–47 n. 40, 52 n. 54, 66–67 n. 124
3:3	51, 52		
3:3–4	46–47 n. 40, 66–67 n. 124		
3:6	42	2 Kings	
3:14	40	2:1–12	1
4:1	73	8:19	39 n. 14
4:21–24	47 n. 42	8:56	307
5–8	73	11:4	57, 57 n. 77
5:3	38, 47 n. 42	11:4–21	156
5:4	38, 47, 73	11:12	58, 157, 158, 159 n. 159
6:12–13	40, 41, 43	11:13–14	59
6:19–22	222 n. 292	11:17	57, 58 n. 81, 307
8:9	42, 55	11:17–20	58
8:10–13	55	11:19	159
8:12–13	42	12:1–16	59, 309
8:14–26	73	12:2	51, 57, 60
8:15–21	47	12:3	46–47 n. 40, 66–67 n. 124
8:21	42, 55,	12:7	59
8:22–26	54, 307	12:10	59
8:25	40	12:11	278 n. 500
8:29	42	12:18	52 n. 54
8:51–53	55	14:3	51, 52 n. 54, 57
8:56	47, 73	14:4	46–47 n. 40, 66–67 n. 124
8:56–58	55, 73, 307	15:4	46–47 n. 40, 66–67 n. 124
8:61	55, 73	15:34	52 n. 54
8:63	283	16:7–8	45
8:66	47	17:2	57 n. 77
9:1–14	55	18–20	67
9:3	42, 54	18:3	52, 60
		18:5	60

18:22	46–47 n. 40, 66–67 n. 124, 67, 308 n. 9	21:19	79 n. 168
19:15	188	21:29	46–47 n. 40, 48 n. 44, 66–67 n. 124
20:12–19	60 n. 95	22:3	56
21:3–8	71 n. 144	22:8	47 n. 42
22:2	52, 67	22:9	57, 308
22:3	68 n. 127	22:10	139, 169 n. 104
22:3–7	69 n. 135, 73, 309	22:12–13	48
22:3–20	69	22:14	56
22:8	278 n. 500	23–26	48 n. 45, 53
23:1–3	70, 73, 307	23–27	53
23:1–27	54	23:5	308
23:4–20	68, 68 n. 127, 73	23:24	68
23:5–9	46–47 n. 40, 66–67 n. 124, 308 n. 9	23:25	47
23:10	62	24:1–5	93 n. 219
23:22	70	25–26	69
23:25	68	28	38
23:34	157–158 n. 52	28:2	210 n. 253, 278 n. 499
24:17	89 n. 207, 157–158 n. 52	28:3	47 n. 42
25:18–21	105 n. 258	28:6	169 n. 104
25:22	89–90 n. 208	28:11–19	48, 310
25:25	89–90 n. 208	28:13	48, 308
		29:1–5	56
		29:5	65

1 Chronicles

		29:22	50, 73, 306 n. 5
2–3	47–48 n. 43	30:24	70 n. 139
2:1	139	33:18	79 n. 168
3:16–19	100 n. 242, 101	35:7–9	70 n. 139
3:19	104 n. 254		
5:39–40	105 n. 258		

2 Chronicles

6:13–14	105 n. 258	1:2–3	73
6:31	47–48 n. 43	1:3	48 n. 44
6:49	48 n. 44	1:4	47–48 n. 43
7:14	66 n. 122	2–7	73
9:22	47–48 n. 43	2:1	49 n. 48
11:3	58	2:7	47–48 n. 43
12:38	68 n. 130	2:12	49 n. 48
13	55	3–7	60 n. 95
15:15	48 n. 44	3:1	47–48 n. 43
16:39	46–47 n. 40, 66–67 n. 124	3:19	101
17	37, 49, 142	5:1	47–48 n. 43
17:7–8	52 n. 54	5:7	204
17:7–10	44	5:7–10	73
17:7–14	38	5:10	42, 48 n. 44, 55
17:8	157–158 n. 52	6:1–2	42
17:10b–14	39 n.14	6:4–11	47
17:11	35	6:7	47–48 n. 43
17:12	39 n. 14	6:11	42
17:13	28, 151, 155 n. 42, 157, 169 n. 104, 172	6:14	55
17:14	39 n. 14, 49	6:20	42
17:24	107 n. 272	6:41–42	42
18–20	47, 47 n. 42	6:42	47–48 n. 43
18:11	56	7:1–4	55
19:8–10	52 n.54	7:5	283
		7:6	47–48 n. 43, 53, 54

Index

7:8–10	66, 254–255 n. 429	23:18	47–48 n. 43, 48, 59, 308
7:9	22 n. 75	23:18–19	67
7:12	42, 54	23:20–21	58
7:12–21	55	23:25–26	60 n. 95
7:14	261	24:2	60
7:16	42	24:4–14	59, 73, 283, 309
7:17–22	43, 44	24:5	59
7:19–22	42	24:6	48 n. 44
8:12–15	48	24:9	48 n. 44
8:13	48 n. 44, 66 n. 123	24:14	59
8:14	54	24:16	60
8:14–15	53, 67, 73	25:2	52 n. 54
9:23	261 n. 423	25:4	48 n. 44
13:5	38	26:5	50 n. 51
14:1	56, 57	26:16–21	50, 306–307 n. 5
14:1–7	73	26:18	50 n. 51
14:2	55	27:2	52 n. 54
14:3	55, 73	28:3	62
14:5	55	28:24	61, 67
14:6, 7	56, 308	28:24–25	62
15:3–7	57	28:29–33	70
15:7	56 n. 69	29	254–255 n. 429
15:8	55, 56, 73, 283, 309	29–30	308
15:8–15	55, 307	29:2	52, 60
15:9	56	29:3	73
15:10	56 n. 68	29:3–11	61
15:10–14	73	29:5–19	309
15:12	46, 190 n. 180	29:6–8	62
15:15	56, 73	29:10	46, 61, 73, 307
15:16	56	29:12–19	61
15:17	46–47 n. 40, 66–67 n. 124	29:12–36	73
15:18	56, 73	29:15	24
15:19	56, 73	29:15–16	63
17:3	52 n. 54	29:16–19	62
17:6	52 n. 54	29:17	61
17:9	52 n.54	29:20–24	63
17:10	52 n. 54	29:20–30	61
18:18–21	1	29:23	64
19:3	52 n. 54	29:25–27	47–48 n. 43
19:4	52 n. 54	29:30	47–48 n. 43
19:11	50, 52 n. 54, 306–307 n. 5	29:31–36	61
20:1–30	52 n. 54	29:35	65
20:30	308	29:36	66, 70
20:33	46, 66–67 n. 124	30	65, 254–255 n. 429
21:7	38, 107 n. 272	30:5–18	73
21:12	52 n. 54	30:8	65
23–24	50, 306–307 n. 5	30:15	62
23:1	57	30:16	48 n. 44
23:3	58	30:17	65 n. 118
23:8–21	156	30:18	66
23:9	47–48 n. 43	30:21–26	66
23:11	58	31:1	46–47 n. 40, 66–67 n. 124, 73, 308
23:12	67		
23:16	46, 57, 73, 307	31:2	67, 73
23:17–19	58, 73	31:3	66

31:13	50, 306–307 n. 5	9	125 n. 347
31:20–21	60	9:6–37	125
32:10–11	67	12:45	48 n. 45
32:12	46–47 n. 40, 66–67 n. 124, 308	13:9	24
		13:29	92, 93
32:22	67, 308	13:30	24
33:6	62		
33:7	47–48 n. 43	Esther	
33:8	48 n. 44	6:7–11	158 n. 58
33:15–16	69 n. 133		
34–35	50, 254–255 n. 429, 306–307 n. 5	Job	
		1:6–12	169 n. 104
34:1–7	54	2:1–6	169 n. 104
34:2	67	10:17	283
34:3	46–47 n. 40, 66–67 n. 124, 68, 308	26	166 n. 87
		31:36	105 n. 257
34:3–7	68 n. 127, 73		
34:8	68 n. 127	Psalms	
34:8–13	69, 73, 309	2	75, 75 n. 148, 108, 157 n. 51
34:9–14	73	2:1	129
34:10	69	2:1–3	75 n. 149
34:12	52	2:6–7	43, 296
34:14	48 n. 44	2:7	28, 149 n. 14, 151, 155 n. 42, 157, 168–169 n. 101, 169 n. 104, 172, 174 n. 123, 214, 292 n. 560, 297
34:14–28	69		
34:27–28	70		
34:29–33	73, 307		
34:30–33	46, 70	2:7–8	135
34:33	68 n. 127	2:8	79, 135, 171, 180
35:1–10	70, 308	2:9	122, 123
35:1–16	73	8	147 n. 5, 175, 181 n. 147, n. 148, 182 n. 150, 183, 185, 211, 270, 270 n. 484
35:1–19	54		
35:3	71, 204 n. 231		
35:4	47–48 n. 43, 48 n. 45, 71	8:4–6	181, 182, 183
35:6	48 n. 44	8:5–6	175
35:7–9	71	8:5–7	292 n. 560, 293 n. 562
35:12	48 n. 44	12:6	207 n. 239
35:15	47–48 n. 43	17:15	261
35:16	72	18	75, 108
35:18	70	18:6	186–187 n. 164, 259 n. 444
35:20	47 n. 43	18:30	207 n. 239
		20	157 n. 51
Ezra		21	157 n. 51
3:8	103 n. 249, 106 n. 266	21:4	113
6:6–12	66	21:23 (LXX)	292 n. 560
6:14–15	106 n. 267	27:8	261
6:14–22	255	29:1	169 n. 104
6:15	255 n. 430	29:9	186–187 n. 164, 259 n. 444
6:16, 17	22 n. 75	30:1, 2	22 n. 75
6:19	255 n. 430	39:7–9 (LXX)	292 n. 560
6:20	71	41:3 (LXX)	260 n. 447
7:1–7	93 n. 219	42:2	260
		42:3	261
Nehemiah		44	125 n. 347
2:9	202–203 n. 229	44:7–8 (LXX)	292 n. 560
3:1	278 n. 500	45:6–7	155 n. 42, 174 n. 123

47	159 n. 59	98:9	159 n. 59
50	248–249 n. 403	99:1	188
50:13	239	99:4	159 n. 59
51:12	283	99:5	210 n. 253, 278 n. 499
51:12–13 (LXX)	117 n. 313	99:6	22 n. 73
51:19	239 n. 363	101	157 n. 51
69:28	286 n. 540	101:24–29 (LXX)	174
79:31	239 n. 363	101:26–68 (LXX)	159 n. 59, 292 n. 560
72	83 n. 182, 157 n. 51	102:21–25	297
72:1	159 n. 59	102:23	175 n. 124
72:6	159 n. 59	102:25–27	168–169 n. 101
72:8	79	103:4 (LXX)	292 n. 560
72:16	159 n. 59	104:4	155 n. 42
74	125 n. 347	104:30	283
74:12–17	159 n. 59, 166 n. 87	106:28–31	112
78:2	294–295 n. 570	107:11	207 n. 239
78:71	172	109:1 (LXX)	292 n. 560, 298
80:1	188	109:3 (LXX)	157
89	74, 79 n. 167, 84, 108, 125 n. 347	109:4 (LXX)	292 n. 560, 293 n. 562, 298
		110	75, 75 n. 150, 108, 157 n. 51, 171 n. 109, 181 n. 148
89:3–4	120 n. 324		
89:4–5	127	110:1	28, 155 n. 42, 170 n. 106, 171, 174 n. 123, 214, 296
89:6	169 n. 104		
89:9–14	167 n. 96	110:1–2	297
89:10–12	159 n. 59	110:4	28, 171 n. 109, 209, 209 n. 250, 213, 213 n. 270, 216 n. 278, 247 n. 399, 297
89:10–15	166 n. 87		
89:18	114 n. 300		
89:19–37	39, 120 n. 324	117:6	292 n. 560
89:20–30	157	119:10–11	299 n. 586
89:20–35	127	119:102–103	299 n. 586
89:25	114 n. 300, 159 n. 59	119:162–163	299 n. 586
89:26–27	135, 169 n. 104	125:1	287 n. 542
89:27	43, 151	132	74, 108
89:28	38, 174 n. 123	132:7	210 n. 253, 278 n. 499
89:30–32	42	132:11–12	40
89:36–37	94	132:11–14	43
89:39	84	132:17	114 n.300, 117 n. 313
93	159 n. 59	150:1	186–187 n. 164, 259 n. 444
93:1	152 n. 28, 159 n. 59, 287 n. 542		

Proverbs

3:11–12	292 n. 560
8:27–31	173
29:26	261 n. 453

93:3–4	159 n. 59		
94:7–8 (LXX)	292 n. 560		
95	159 n. 59, 195, 195 n. 197, 228, 229		

Isaiah

95:9	200 n. 221	1–39	83 n. 183, 84–85 n. 190, 86
96–99	159 n. 59	1:1	80 n. 171, 83 n. 183
96:5	159 n. 59	1:8	76
96:7 (LXX)	155 n. 42	1:11	239
96:9–11	152 n. 28	1:12	260
96:10	287 n. 542	1:18	15
96:10–13	159 n. 59	4:2	104 n. 254
97:2	159 n. 59	4:3	286 n. 540
97:7	149 n. 14	6:1	188
97:8	159 n. 59	6:1–3	1
98:1	159 n. 59		

6:1–8	186–187 n. 164, 259 n. 444
6:10	83 n. 183
7:1–12	45
7:2	107 n. 272
7:10–14	80 n. 172
7:13	107 n. 272
7:14 (LXX)	294–295 n. 570
8:11	129
8:17–18	292 n. 560
9:1–2	294–295 n. 570
9:5–7	109
9:6	80 n. 172
9:6–7	80, 81, 309
9:7	82 n. 177, 86, 109
10:21–11:5	130, 131
10:34	132, 133 n. 372
11	131
11:1	97, 132, 133, 294–295 n. 570
11:1–5	137
11:1–10	80 n. 171, 81–83
11:2	122
11:2–9	109
11:4–5	86
11:10	86
11:10–13	109
11:10–16	82
14:10–15	166 n. 88
16:5	76 n. 155, 80 n. 171, 86
20:2–4	105 n. 260
22:19	77 n. 158
22:22	107 n. 272
24:14	79
26:20–21	292 n. 560
32:1–8	80 n. 171, 80 n. 171
33:8–12	244 n. 389
33:20	287 n. 542
36–38	67
37:35	80 n. 171
38:5	80 n. 171
40–55	83 n. 183, 84, 84 n. 190, 86, 86 n. 199, 87 n. 200
40–66	83
41:9	198 n. 213
42:1–4	86, 294–295 n. 570
42:6	86 n. 199, 198 n. 213
42:13	163
43:10	86 n. 198
43:12	86 n. 198
44:8	86 n. 198
49:1–13	86
49:8	86 n. 199
49:24–26	163
51:9–11	166 n. 88
52:7	218–219 n. 283, 241
53	246
53:1	83 n. 183
53:4	246 n. 396, 294–295 n. 570
53:7–8	83 n. 183
54:13	87 n. 202
55:3	80 n. 171, 83–87, 84–85 n. 185, n. 188, 87 n. 201, 109
55:3–4	84, 85
55:3–5	86 n. 195
55:4–5	86 n. 198
55:1–6	86
55:6–7	87 n. 202
55:7	109
55:10–11	87, 87 n. 201
58:12	76
59:15–20	163
62:4	152 n. 28
62:11	294–295 n. 570
63	125 n. 347
66:1	168 n. 99

Jeremiah

3:19	43
7:1–15	53
7:2	107 n. 272
11:10–16	244 n. 389
13:18	113
17:12–14	188
17:24–30	100 n. 242, 101 n. 243
17:25	88
18–19	294–295 n. 570
19:22	91
21–23	89–90 n. 208
21:11–23:8	89 n. 206
22	88–90
22:8–12	244 n. 389
22:24–30	41, 45 n. 35, 100 n. 242, 101
23	90, 91
23:1–8	89
23:4–5	97
23:5	104 n. 254, 122, 129, 131 n. 364, 133
23:5–6	41, 90, 91 n. 210, 127, 309
23:5–8	85 n. 194, 88
25:26	203–204 n. 230
26:1–9	53
27:2–7	105 n. 260
29:15	97
30–33	90–91 n. 209, 94
30:2	90–91 n. 209
30:8–9	85 n. 194, 88, 90
30:9	78, 94, 96, 102, 124 n. 344
30:18	94
30:19	94
30:21	94
31:4	94

Index 367

31:6	56 n. 69, 94	34–37	96
31:9	43, 169 n. 104	34:23	172
31:14	94	34:23–24	78, 85 n. 194, 96, 102, 124 n. 344
31:15	294–295 n. 570		
31:31–34	83, 87, 91, 94, 109, 227, 257, 270, 297, 307	34:23–31	83
		36	98, 99
31:31–37	95	36:16–21	99
31:35–37	91 n. 210	36:22–28	98
32:28–41	91	36:24–28	270, 307
33:4–6	94	36:25	107 n. 268
33:11	94	36:25–28	83, 87
33:14–18	90	36:27	99
33:14–22	306, 307	37	98, 99
33:14–26	85 n. 194, 90–91 n. 209, 91–95, 91 n. 210	37:15–27	98
		37:15–28	99
33:15	97, 104, 104 n. 254, 105, 129, 131, 131 n. 364, 133	37:16–24	109
		37:22–28	307
33:15–26	109	37:24	172
33:15–17	127	37:24–25	78, 124 n. 344
33:17	120 n. 324	37:24–28	85 n. 194, 96
33:17–18	105	37:25	97
33:19–22	91 n. 210, 106	37:26	83
34:8–10	42	37:26–28	109, 309
34:17–22	43	38–39	96
34:18–20	244 n. 390	40–48	66, 96, 99, 99 n. 239, 286 n. 539
34:18–21	244 n. 389		
36:30	89	40:46	93
38:31 (LXX)	293	41:21	229 n. 313, 230 n. 317, 231
38:31–34	292 n. 560	41:15–26	231, 231 n. 321
40–41	88, 89–90 n. 208	43:18–27	63
40:5	89–90 n. 208	43:19	93, 93 n. 215
41:1	89–90 n. 208	43:18–27	254
41:10	89–90 n. 208	43:20	253 n. 421
48:24	203–204 n. 230	44:10–11	71
51:34	166 n. 88	44:5–16	93
		44:10	129
Lamentations		44:15	93 n. 215, 106
5:21	283	44:27	62 n. 104
		45	72 n. 146, 254–255 n. 429
Ezekiel		45:8	123
1	1	45:17	66
1–37	99 n. 239	45:18–20	254
10	1	45:18–21	63
12:1–2	105 n. 260	45:20	254 n. 427
16:59–63	248–249 n. 403	45:21–24	254–255 n. 429
17:1–24	97	45:22	66
17:13–19	244 n. 387	46:4	66
17:23	97 n. 232	47:13	123
21:26–27	45	47:21	123
21:31	113	48:11	93, 106
22:26	265 n. 464		
28:1–9	166 n. 88	**Daniel**	
29:3–5	166 n. 88	3:25	169 n. 104
29:21	117 n. 313	3:86 (LXX)	287 n. 541
32:2–8	166 n. 88	7:7	136

7:7–14	16	Haggai	
7:14 (LXX)	265–266 n. 472	1:12	278 n. 500
7:18 (LXX)	265–266 n. 472	1:12–14	49
9	125 n. 347	2:4	278 n. 500
9:3	125 n. 347	2:6	24, 292 n. 560
9:17	125 n. 347	2:20–23	85 n. 194, 100–102
9:24	265 n. 471	2:23	100 n. 242, 101 n. 244, 116 n. 312
9:24–28	265–266 n. 472		
9:25–27	87 n. 202		
9:27	55 n. 65, 261 n. 456	Zechariah	
11:35	261 n. 456	1:7	103 n. 249, 106 n. 266
12:1	286 n. 540	3:5–10	103, 104
12:11	136	3:8	85 n. 194, 97, 105
12:13	261 n. 456	4:6–10	103, 104
		4:8–10	103 n. 249
Hosea		4:14	105 n. 257
1:1	77 n. 161	6:10	104 n. 252, 105 n. 257
1:11	77	6:12	85 n. 194, 97
2:18	83	6:12–13	103 n. 249
3:4	78 n. 162	6:12–14	49
3:4–5	77, 78, 109, 309	6:9–13	50
3:5	96, 102, 124 n. 344	6:9–15	102–106
5:15	261	6:14	104 n. 252, 106 n. 263
6:7	244 n. 389	8:9–13	56 n. 69
7:13	244 n. 389	12:2–13:1	106–108
11:1	169 n. 104, 294–295 n. 570	13:2–6	107

Joel		Malachi	
4:17	190 n. 180	2	93–94 n. 221
		2:1–9	93, 93 n. 217
Amos		2:4	92
1:1	76 n. 153	2:8	82
1:2–2:3	77		
5:26	76 n. 155		
9:11	77, 77 n. 158, 128, 129		
9:11–12	76, 109		
9:11–15	76 n. 154		

Ancient Near Eastern Texts

Enuma Elish   165

Deuterocanonical Books

Micah		Judith	
1:1–2	78 n. 165	4:3–14	282 n. 525
1:2–3	242	4:6	278 n. 500
5:1–5	78–80, 79 n. 167	15:8	278 n. 500
5:2	294–295 n. 570		
5:3–5	109	Wisdom of Solomon	
5:4	79 n. 168	3:1	287 n. 541
		7–9	173
Nahum		7:26	172, 173
2:1	190 n. 180	9:1–4	173, 173 n. 115
		9:7	169 n. 104
Habakkuk		18:13	169 n. 104
2:3–4	292 n. 560		

Zephaniah
3:16   56 n. 69

Index

Sirach
- 26:5 — 286–287 n. 540
- 29:15–17 — 212 n. 268
- 36:5 — 283
- 36:17 — 286 n. 540
- 39:27–44:17 — 111 n. 285
- 44–45 — 113
- 44–50 — 116
- 44:1–50:24 — 111
- 45:12 — 113
- 45:23–25 — 94
- 45:23–26 — 93, 112
- 45:25 — 140
- 45:25–26 — 110, 111, 113 n. 293
- 47:1–22 — 113
- 47:2–11 — 113. N293
- 47:5, 7 — 114
- 47:11–22 — 110, 114
- 47:12–22 — 140
- 47:12–23 — 115
- 47:22 — 110, 115 n. 308, 116
- 47:25 — 115 n. 308
- 48:17–25 — 113
- 48:24–25 — 83 n. 183
- 49:4–5 — 110, 115, 116, 140
- 49:5 — 114
- 49:11–12 — 116 n. 312
- 50 — 111 n. 184, 113, 140
- 50:1–4 — 140
- 50:5–21 — 14
- 50:8 — 278 n. 500
- 51:12–13 — 117 n. 313

Additions to Daniel
Prayer of Azariah
- 1:64 — 287 n. 541

1 Maccabees
- 2:49–68 — 119, 140
- 2:57 — 117, 118, 141
- 3:13 — 286–287 n. 540
- 4:30 — 119 n. 321
- 4:36 — 22 n. 75, 283
- 4:36–59 — 24, 255
- 4:36–61 — 24 n. 84
- 4:54 — 283
- 4:56 — 22 n. 75
- 4:57 — 283
- 4:59 — 22 n. 75, 268 n. 474
- 5:62 — 118, 119
- 7:49 — 268 n. 474
- 10:8 — 268 n. 474
- 13:52 — 268 n. 474
- 14:4–15 — 119 n. 321
- 14:41 — 118 n. 316, 171 n. 109
- 14:41–49 — 118 n. 315, 119 n. 321

2 Maccabees
- 1:18 — 24 n. 84
- 2:9 — 22 n. 75
- 2:16 — 24 n. 84
- 2:19 — 22 n. 75, 24
- 3:1–4 — 112
- 4:7 — 112
- 10:3–7 — 24 n. 84
- 14:36 — 282 n. 525

1 Esdras
- 3:1–5:6 — 101 n. 244
- 4:55 — 251 n. 410
- 5:5 — 100 n. 242, 101, 101 n. 244, 104 n. 254
- 7:7 — 22 n. 75

Psalm 151
- 151 — 78 n. 165

3 Maccabees
- 1:11 — 268 n. 474

2 Esdras
- 3:1 — 136 n. 382
- 6:58 — 286 n. 540
- 7:28 — 169 n. 104
- 7:28–29 — 137
- 7:99 — 287 n. 541
- 10:44 — 259 n. 444
- 10:48–50 — 259 n. 444
- 11–12 — 136 n. 382
- 11:1–12:3 — 136
- 11:36–12:3 — 137
- 12:11 — 136
- 12:31–34 — 136
- 13:1 — 162 n. 69
- 13:32 — 169 n. 104
- 13:37 — 169 n. 104
- 13:52 — 169 n. 104
- 14:9 — 169 n. 104

Pseudepigrapha

Apocalypse of Abraham
- 10:8 — 188 n. 167
- 13:14 — 187
- 19:4 — 188 n. 167

Apocalypse of Zephaniah
- 8:3–4 — 187

Assumption of Moses

10:1	162 n. 69	Letter of Aristeas	
2 Baruch		176–177	299 n. 586
3:2–3	287 n. 541	Life of Adam and Eve	
4:2–6	259 n. 444	13–16	147
		35:2	188 n. 167
3 Baruch			
10:5	287 n. 541	Martyrdom and Ascension of Isaiah	
11–17	188 n. 167	6–9	187
		6–11	188 n. 167
1 Enoch		9:1–2	187
1–36	186–187 n. 164	10:7–16	152
6–11	166	11:22–33	151–152
10.13	162 n. 69		
12:4	187	Odes of Solomon	
14	188 n. 167	2:43	149 n. 14, 155 n. 42
14:9–17	186–187 n. 164	15:9	162
14:9–15:2	187	29:4	162
14:16–18	259 n. 444		
14:20	259 n. 444	Psalms of Solomon	
22:3–9	287 n. 541	3:8	13
26:1–2	259 n. 444	17	119–123, 140, 141, 143, 309
37–71	186–187 n. 164	17:1–21	120
39:4	287 n. 541	17:4	119
45:1, 3	171 n. 109	17:5	122
48:2	178	17:5–6	120 n. 325
51:3	171 n. 109	17:5–10	141
52:1–7	171 n. 109	17:8	123
55:4	171 n. 109	17:9	122
61:8	171 n. 109	17:19–20	120 n. 325
62:15–16	187	17:20–30	122
70:4	287 n. 541	17:22–42	121
71	187 n. 165	17:27	169 n. 104
71:1–5	188 n. 167	17:28	123
71:5–7	259 n. 444	17:31	122 n. 336
71:14–17	178	17:32–34	123
90:28–36	259 n. 444	17:32–37	122
91:13	259 n. 444	17:36	123, 264
103:3–4	287 n. 541	17:40	122
		17:41	264
2 Enoch		17:43	122
3–22	188 n. 167	23–24	123
22:8–10	187		
31:2	148 n. 7	Sibylline Oracles	
		3:63–74	162 n. 69
3 Enoch		3:652–656	110 n. 283
4	187, 187 n. 165		
43:1	287 n. 541	Testament of Twelve Patriarchs	
		Testament of Benjamin	
Jubilees		11:3	261 n. 456
1:24–25	169 n. 104		
4:25	187	Testament of Dan	
5:6–11	166 n. 89	5:10	162 n. 69
17:17–18	207 n. 243	11:3	261 n. 456

Index

Testament of Judah
- 21:1–5 — 213 n. 270
- 24 — 110 n. 283
- 25:3 — 162 n. 69

Testament of Levi
- 2–3 — 188 n. 167
- 2–5 — 187
- 2:5–3:4 — 188 n. 167
- 3:4 — 188
- 3:4–6 — 259 n. 444
- 4:2 — 213 n. 270
- 5:1 — 188 n. 167, 259 n. 444
- 5:2 — 187
- 8 — 187
- 8:1–4 — 110 n. 283
- 10:2 — 261 n. 456
- 18 — 110 n. 283
- 18:1–2 — 162 n. 69
- 18:2–12 — 164 n. 78
- 18:3 — 213 n. 270
- 18:9 — 264
- 18:10–12 — 163 n. 76, 164

Testament of Reuben
- 6:7 — 110 n. 283

Testament of Simon
- 7:1–2 — 110 n. 283

Testament of Zebulun
- 9:8 — 163 n. 76

Testament of Job
- 33:3 — 171 n. 109

Testament of Moses
- 10.1–10 — 163 n. 76

Dead Sea Scrolls

1Q28a
- I, 2 — 131, 135 n. 379

1QM
- I, 5 — 261 n. 456
- I, 11, 13, 15 — 162 n. 69
- XII, 1–4 — 286 n. 540

4Q161 — 130–131, 133
- 2–6, II, 15 — 131
- 8–10, III, 11–25 — 130
- 8–10, III, 18 — 131

4Q174 — 77, 127–129, 153 n. 32
- I, 1–13 — 127
- I, 1–19 — 129
- I, 6–13 — 136
- I, 10–13 — 169 n. 104
- I, 10–19 — 128
- I, 2, 12, 15, 19 — 127 n. 358
- I, 11 — 131

4Q175 — 153 n. 32

4Q246 — 133–135
- II, 1–3 — 169 n. 104

4Q252 — 126–127, 132
- V, 1–7 — 126–127
- V, 3 — 127 n. 355

4Q285 — 131–133
- 7, 1–6 — 132
- 7, 2–6 — 133

4Q369 — 378

4Q504 — 123–126
- 1–2 IV, 1–3 — 124
- 1–2 IV, 5–6 — 125
- 1–2 IV, 5–8 — 123
- 1–2 V, 5–14 — 126

4QDeut
- 32:43 — 149 n. 14, 155 n. 42

4QJer^b — 91 n. 211, 91–92 n. 212

4QJer^c — 91, 91 n. 211, 92 n. 213

4QJer^d — 91 n. 211

11Q13
- II, 13 — 163 n. 76

11Q19
- XV, 3–XVI, 4 — 256 n. 434
- XV, 16–18 — 256
- LIX, 13–21 — 41 n. 19

11Q Melchizedek — 171 n. 109

Ancient Jewish Writers

Josephus

Jewish Antiquities
- 3.8.6 — 250

3.123	233 n. 330
3.179–181	233 n. 330
3.239–240	25–26 n. 96
4.78–81	239 n. 364
5.336	138
6.165	138
7.93–95	139
7.337	139
7.384–385	139
8.126–127	140
10.143	138
11.112	138
12.164	286–287 n. 540
17.271–274	110 n. 283
17.278–281	110 n. 283
19.332	286–287 n. 540

Jewish War

2.434	110 n. 283
4.507–508	110 n. 283
5.211–214	233 n. 330
7.29	110 n. 283
236	13

Philo

Allegorical Interpretation

2.52	13, 25 n. 96
3.74	287 n. 541
3.96	174 n. 119

On Dreams

1.215	173 n. 117, 233 n. 330

On Drunkenness

207, 208, 210	149 n. 14

On Flight and Finding

108	173 n. 117

On the Confusion of Tongues

28	173
41	173 n. 117, 174
62–63	174
146	173 n. 117

On the Decalogue

36	299 n. 586

On the Embassy to Gaius

306	13

On the Life of Moses

1.158	259 n. 444
2.3	25 n. 91

2.23–24	13
2.56	299 n. 586
2.74–76	259 n. 444
2.101–108	233 n. 330
2.146	25 n. 90
2.152–154	25 n. 90
2.153	256 n. 437
2.188	299 n. 586
231–236	251 n. 410
247	256 n. 437

On the Migration of Abraham

130	174
173–175	173

On the Posterity of Cain

70	25–26 n. 96

On the Special Laws

1.66	233 n. 330
1.188	13, 25–26 n. 96
1.262–272	239 n. 364
2.193–201	13

Questions and Answers on Exodus

2.52–82	259 n. 444
2.91	233 n. 330

Who Is the Heir?

179	25–26 n. 96
205	173 n. 117
205–207	174
230–231	174 n. 119

New Testament

Matthew

1:7–13	100 n. 242
1:12–13	101, 104 n. 254
1:23	294–295 n. 570
2:6	172, 294–295 n. 570
2:15	294–295 n. 570
2:18	294–295 n. 570
2:23	294–295 n. 570
4:15–16	294–295 n. 570
5:11	149 n. 15
8:4	62 n. 104
8:17	294–295 n. 570
10:19	149 n. 15
12:17–21	294–295 n. 570
12:25–30	162 n. 69
12:29	163
13:3	146
13:10–17	223 n. 299

Index 373

13:35	294–295 n. 570	John	
13:39–40	261 n. 456	1:3	306 n. 2
13:49	261 n. 456	1:14	235–236 n. 345
18:10	260 n. 448	1:29	8 n. 28
21:4–5	294–295 n. 570	1:51	259 n. 444
22:41–45	170 n. 106	2:21	235–236 n. 345
22:41–46	306 n. 4	3:14	5
22:42–45	171 n. 109	4:15	190 n. 181
24:3	261 n. 456	4:26	259 n. 444
26:15	294–295 n. 570	5	167 n. 93
26:31	172	7:18	201 n. 224
26:64	171 n. 109	8:46	201 n. 224
27:9–10	294–295 n. 570	10:11–16	172
27:15–23	8 n. 28	10:22	22 n. 75, 235–236 n. 345, 283, 283 n. 530
28:18–20	156		
28:20	261 n. 456	10:22–39	255–256 n. 433
		12:31	162 n. 69, 235–236 n. 345
Mark		12:32, 34	5
1:44	62 n. 104	12:38–40	294–295 n. 570
3:27	163	12:38–41	83 n. 183
4:15	149 n. 15	13:18	294–295 n. 570
4:35–41	166	14:2–3	259 n. 444
7:10	62 n. 104	14:30	162 n. 69
12:35–37	170 n. 106, 171 n. 109, 306 n. 4	15:25	294–295 n. 570
		16:11	162 n. 69
14:27	172	16:28	146
14:62	171 n. 109	17:19	8 n. 28
16:19	3, 171 n. 109	19:24	294–295 n. 570
		19:28	294–295 n. 570
Luke		19:36–37	294–295 n. 570
1:69	114 n. 300, 176–177 n. 132		
1:30–33	45 n. 37	Acts	
1:31–33	39	1:9	1, 3
1:32	178, 306 n. 4	2:17	261 n. 456
1:32–33	35 n. 1	2:22–36	176–177 n. 132
1:35	178	2:29–36	39, 45 n. 37, 306 n. 4
2:1	152	2:31–36	170 n. 106
2:13	147 n. 6	2:32–33	5
2:15	190 n. 181	3:20	200 n. 219
2:22	62 n. 104	3:22	176–177 n. 132
2:32	86 n. 199	3:26	176–177 n. 132
2:49	178	2:34–35	171 n. 109
3:22–8	178	5:30–31	5
3:27	100 n. 242, 101, 104 n. 254	7:38	207 n. 239, 299 n. 586
5:14	62 n. 104	8:28	83 n. 183
6:22	149 n. 15	9:20	198 n. 212
10:18	162 n. 69, 252 n. 415	9:20–22	177
10:20	286 n. 540	13:6	190 n. 179
11:21–22	163	13:32–34	176–177 n. 132
20:41–44	170 n. 106, 171 n. 109, 306 n. 4	13:33	151 n. 23, 178, 178 n. 137
		13:34	87 n. 201
22:69	171 n. 109	14:2	197 n. 210
24:51	1, 3	14:9	197 n. 210
		16:1–3	32–33 n. 119
		17:3–4	177

18:2	32–33 n. 119	2 Corinthians	
18:5	177	1:19	198 n. 212
18:23	190 n. 179	2:4	237 n. 352
19:32	286–287 n. 540	5:1–5	259 n. 444
19:39	286–287 n. 540	5:16	279
19:40	286–287 n. 540	5:21	201 n. 224
24:24	177	6:16	306 n. 3
26:23	86 n. 199	12:2–4	1, 188 n. 167
27:9	7, 13		
		Galatians	
Romans		1:4	162
1:3	178, 306 n. 4	2:20	180
1:3–4	151, 176, 176 n. 131, 180	3:6–18	207 n. 243
1:3–5	45 n. 37	3:10	8 n. 28
1:4	198 n. 212	3:13	8 n. 28
2:27	237 n. 352	4:14	261 n. 456
3:2	207 n. 239, 299 n. 586		
3:10–18	153–154 n. 32	Ephesians	
3:21	262	1:18	198 n. 213
3:21–26	262 n. 461	1:20	171 n. 109
3:25–26	8 n. 28	1:20–22	151, 181 n. 148
4	207 n. 243	1:20–2:22	167
4:11	237 n. 352	2:18	200 n. 219
5:2	200 n. 219	2:21	306 n. 3
5:12	190 n. 181	3:12	200 n. 219
6:10	262	4:8–10	151, 162, 167
8:10	180	4:10	189 n. 172
8:25	237 n. 352	6:12	252 n. 415
8:34	171 n. 109		
8:38–39	162, 167	Philippians	
10:7	218–219 n. 283	2:6–11	160, 160–161 n. 64
10:15	241	2:8–11	5
11:29	198 n. 213	2:9–10	151
11:30–32	197 n. 210	2:9–11	156, 170 n. 106
14	32–33 n. 119	2:10	162, 167
14:20	237 n. 352	3:14	198 n. 213
16:26	262	3:20	286 n. 540
1 Corinthians		Colossians	
1:9	198 n. 212	1:1	32–33 n. 119
1:26	198 n. 213	1:5	190 n. 178
3:3–4	245 n. 395	1:16	190 n. 178
3:16	306 n. 3	1:20	190 n. 178, 252 n. 415
6:16–18	153 n. 32	1:23	190 n. 178
8:6	178	2:6–7	180
10:4	197 n. 207	2:15	162, 167
15:24	162, 167	2:18	154, 154 n. 37
15:24–28	176–177 n. 132	3:1	171 n. 109
15:25	171 n. 109	4:1	190 n. 178
15:26	162		
15:26–27	181 n. 148	1 Thessalonians	
15:27	150	1:9–10	176 n. 129, 198 n. 212
15:45	180	1:10	5, 190
15:55	162	4:16	5, 190

Index 375

1 Timothy
  3:16   151 n. 24, 156, 262

2 Timothy
  1:10   162
  2:8   306 n. 4

Philemon
  1   32–33 n. 119

Hebrews
  1   179
  1–2   168, 175, 176 n. 128, 181, 185, 198–199 n. 214, 199, 200, 297, 301
  1–4   167, 199, 297 n. 579
  1–7   184
  1:1–2   218–219 n. 283, 291
  1:1–4   34 n. 122, 153–154 n. 32, 154, 171, 198–199 n. 214, 200
  1:1–14   150, 170, 270
  1:2   35, 152, 169 n. 103, 169 n. 104, 170 n. 106, 171, 172, 173, 175 n. 127, 179, 180, 182, 261 n. 456, 262, 306, 306 n. 2
  1:2–3   174, 272
  1:3   7–8 n. 27, 27, 28, 35, 143, 147 n. 5, 160, 162 n. 67, 168 n. 100, 171, 172, 173, 174 n. 123, 176 n. 128, 184, 188 n. 168, 200 n. 219, 205 n. 235, 211, 214, 215, 226, 277–278 n. 498, 295 n. 574, 296, 298
  1:3–14   174
  1:4   157–158 n. 52, 168–169 n. 101, 170 n. 106, 175 n. 127, 306
  1:5   27, 28, 35, 39, 149, 151, 160 n. 62, 169 n. 104, 170 n. 106, 171, 174 n. 123, 175 n. 127, 181 n. 148, 214, 293, 296, 295–296 n. 574, 300 n.591
  1:5–6   143, 172, 179 n. 139
  1:5–13   155, 155 n. 42, 292 n. 560, 299 n. 586
  1:5–14   147 n. 5, 149 n. 14, 153, 153 n. 32, 156, 164 n. 78, 167, 168, 168 n. 100, 168–169 n. 101, 181, 181 nn. 147–148, 182, 183, 184, 199, 200, 297, 301, 302, 306
  1:6   27, 34, 145, 147, 149, 152, 153, 169 n. 103, 174 n. 123, 185, 286 n. 540, 297, 301
  1:6–8   146
  1:6–12   158
  1:7–8   159 n. 59, 235 n. 344, 272 27, 169 n. 103, 169 n. 104, 171, 188 n. 168, 200 n. 219
  1:8
  1:8–9   174 n. 123
  1:8–11   170 n. 106
  1:8–13   159
  1:9   171, 172, 199 n. 215
  1:10   169 n. 103, 172, 189 n. 176, 272, 306 n. 2
  1:10–12   159 n. 59, 297
  1:13   15 n. 54, 27, 28, 34 n. 122, 35, 171, 174 n. 123, 175 n. 127, 181 n. 148, 182, 188 n. 168, 200 n. 219, 214, 272, 296, 298
  1:14   181, 181 n. 148, 183, 198–199 n. 214, 272, 289 n. 550
  2   181 n. 147, 211
  2:1   182, 186 n. 162
  2:1–2   246
  2:1–3   290
  2:1–4   28, 35, 154, 181 n. 148, 185, 199, 290, 299, 300, 300 n.590, 301
  2:3   169 n. 103, 182, 289 n. 550
  2:4   198–199 n. 214
  2:5   152, 152 n. 27, 156, 181 n. 148, 183, 289 n. 550
  2:5–9   168 n. 100, 181, 182, 184, 200
  2:5–10   201, 270, 300, 308 n. 8
  2:5–18   181 n. 148, 198, 199, 199 n. 215, 212
  2:6   295 n. 574
  2:6–8   181, 292 n. 560, 293 n. 562, 299 n. 586, 300 n.590
  2:6–9   301
  2:6–10   174 n. 123, 185, 211
  2:7   148
  2:7–8   175
  2:8   150
  2:9   34 n. 122, 35, 148, 160, 167, 168, 171, 172 n. 111, 173, 175 n. 127, 176 n. 128, 183, 184, 185, 190, 190 n. 182, 200 n. 222, 201 n. 225, 208, 216 n. 277, 234 n. 338
  2:9–11   169 n. 103
  2:9–18   200, 210 n. 257
  2:10   162 n. 67, 169 n. 103, 172 n. 111, 175, 175 n. 127, 176 n. 128, 198–199 n. 214, 200 n. 222, 202–203 n. 229, 237, 260, 270, 271, 273, 286 n. 539, 289 n. 550

2:10–18	183, 200, 301, 307	3:14	199, 199 n. 215, 199 n. 216, 200
2:10–3:6	244		
2:11	7–8 n. 27, 169 n. 103, 184	3:15	195, 195 n. 196
2:11–13	178, 179	3:17	195 n. 197
2:12	293 n. 563	3:17–19	197, 275 n. 494
2:12–13	292 n. 560	3:18	197 n. 210
2:12–15	163	3:18–19	195, 283 n. 534
2:13	149, 200 n. 222	4:1–3	198
2:13–14	184	4:1–10	28, 143
2:14	216, 279	4:1–11	151 n. 22, 152 n. 29, 197, 286, 288 n. 543, 291 n. 557, 306
2:14–15	7, 280 n. 513		
2:14–16	28, 143, 161, 163 n. 71, 167, 168, 176 n. 128, 185	4:2	198 n. 212
		4:3	152
2:14–18	164, 215, 216 n. 277	4:4	292 n. 560
2:16	208, 216, 247 n. 399	4:5	149
2:16–18	184	4:5	197 n. 210
2:17	161, 169 n. 103, 205 n. 235	4:6	198, 198 n. 212
2:17–18	200, 202–203 n. 229, 211 n. 259, 212 n. 263	4:7	149, 195 n. 196, 293 n. 562
		4:8	153, 195, 197 n. 205, 308
2:17–3:1	181	4:11	181, 194 n. 193, 197 n. 210
2:18	176 n. 128, 200 n. 221, 200 n. 222, 201, 205 n. 235, 217, 261	4:11–13	192 n. 189, 196
		4:12	295 n. 571
		4:12–13	202, 299, 299 n. 585
3–4	198, 199, 202–203 n. 229, 275 n. 494	4:14	7–8 n. 27, 35, 169 n. 103, 169 n. 104, 170, 183 n. 151, 189 n. 176, 190 n. 182, 191 n. 186, 198 n. 212, 199 n. 216, 214, 286, 286 n. 539, 299 n. 588, 309 n. 10
3–7	176 n. 128		
3:1	169 n. 103, 183 n. 151, 192 n. 189, 194, 198, 199 n. 215, 202, 309 n. 10		
3:1–2	201		
3:1–6	22, 25 n. 93, 28, 143, 163 n. 73, 170, 194, 199, 216, 246, 271 n. 485, 306, 310	4:14–16	4, 6, 26, 27, 28, 34, 35, 145, 162 n. 67, 181, 185–202, 192 n. 189, 194 n. 193, 202–203 n. 229, 210 n. 257, 215, 216, 226, 234, 234 n. 338, 277–278 n. 498, 299 n. 583, 300, 301
3:1–4:11	299 n. 583		
3:1–4:16	195		
3:2	7–8 n. 27, 171, 175 n. 127		
3:3	167, 169 n. 103, 306	4:15	169 n. 103, 176 n. 128, 200 n. 221, 216 n. 277, 246
3:3–4	310		
3:4	306 n. 2	4:15–16	205 n. 235, 211 n. 259, 212 n. 263, 217, 261
3:5–6	7–8 n. 27, 194		
3:6	35, 169 n. 103, 169 n. 104, 176 n. 128, 178, 179, 186 n. 162, 199, 199 n. 216, 200, 236 n. 351, 269 n. 479, 284, 306	4:16	168 n. 99, 181, 269 n. 479, 277
		5–7	28, 144, 297, 297 n. 579, 306, 310
		5–10	192–194
3:7	293 n. 563	5–10:18	164, 202, 281
3:7–8	195 n. 196	5:1	205 n. 235, 235 n. 344
3:7–11	292 n. 560, 299 n. 586	5:1–7:28	193, 281
3:7–19	291 n. 557	5:1–10	5 n. 20, 184, 205, 206, 210, 210 n. 257, 302
3:7–4:11	168, 168 n. 99, 196 n. 200, 197, 199, 208 n. 247, 228, 290, 299, 300, 300 n.591		
		5:3	7–8 n. 27
3:7–4:13	163, 195	5:4–6	170
3:9	200 n. 221	5:5	27, 168 n. 100, 169 n. 104, 170, 171, 175 n. 127, 179 n. 139, 295 n. 574, 296, 300
3:11–4:16	307		

Index

	n. 591, 306	6:17–20	209 n. 250, 302
5:5–6	35, 179, 209 n. 250, 211, 213, 214, 216 n. 278, 217, 292 n. 560, 297, 298 n. 581, 299 n. 586, 302	6:18	186 n. 162
		6:19	6, 25, 34, 189 n. 173, 226, 234, 302
		6:19–20	7–8 n. 27, 22, 23, 26, 27, 145, 170, 186 n. 161, 188, 190, 190 n. 182, 202–17, 234 n. 338, 235, 258 n. 443, 260, 277, 278, 280, 282, 286 n. 539, 299 n. 588, 300, 301, 302 n. 593
5:5–10	213 n. 270		
5:6	28, 209, 298		
5:7	216 n. 276, 279		
5:7–8	160 n. 62, 168–169 n. 101, 177, 178, 216 n. 277, 280 n. 513		
5:7–10	169 n. 103, 216	6:20	169 n. 103, 171, 175 n. 127
5:8	27, 35, 169 n. 104, 170, 179	7–10	291 n. 557
5:8–9	162 n. 67, 172 n. 111, 176 n. 128, 200, 200 n. 222	7:1–28	205, 228
		7:2	273
5:8–10	214	7:3	169 n. 104, 170, 214, 273
5:9	169 n. 103, 175 n. 127, 237, 270, 271, 273, 289 n. 550	7:5	279, 279 n. 508, 280
		7:8	273
5:9–10	214–215 n. 273	7:11	214–215 n. 273, 237, 247 n. 399, 268, 269, 271, 287
5:10	175 n. 127		
5:11	182, 206	7:11–12	193
5:11–6:3	206	7:11–19	297, 298
5:11–6:12	205	7:11–28	271
5:11–6:20	192 n. 191, 206	7:13–14	273
5:11–9:12	299 n. 583	7:14	28, 169 n. 103
5:11–10:39	192 n. 190	7:16	175 n. 127, 216, 273
5:12	149, 207, 299 n. 586, 299 n. 586	7:17	28, 264, 292 n. 560, 293 n. 562
5:14	214–215 n. 273	7:18	247 n. 399, 263
6–9	7 n. 26	7:19	6, 172 n. 111, 186 n. 161, 237, 241 n. 374, 268, 269, 270, 271, 273, 277, 287
6:1	149, 214–215 n. 273, 286, 299 n. 586		
		7:20–22	209 n. 250, 213, 273, 298
6:1–2	198 n. 212	7:21	28, 175–176 n. 127, 292 n. 560
6:4–5	208		
6:4–6	289	7:22	18, 20, 169 n. 103, 175–176 n. 127, 212, 241 n. 374, 246 n. 396, 267, 308 n. 8
6:4–8	181, 206, 299, 299 n. 586		
6:4–12	202 n. 228		
6:5	207, 286 n. 539, 300, 300 n. 590	7:23–25	225, 273
		7:25	14 n. 49, 188 n. 168, 212 n. 263, 215, 235 n. 344, 261, 265, 277, 286, 289 n. 550
6:6	27, 149, 169 n. 104, 170		
6:9	217, 302		
6:9–20	207	7:26	188, 189 n. 176, 190, 190 n. 179, 190 n. 182, 191, 201, 216, 234 n. 338, 269, 271, 273
6:10	32–33 n. 119, 289 n. 550		
6:11	209, 213, 302		
6:11–20	217	7:26–27	7–8 n. 27, 246
6:12	182, 209 n. 250, 302	7:26–28	176 n. 128, 273
6:13–14	209	7:27	19, 262, 268, 268 n. 476, 269, 271, 276
6:13–15	247 n. 399		
6:13–17	213	7:28	27, 35, 168 n. 100, 169 n. 104, 170, 171, 175–176 n. 127, 213 n. 270, 214, 237, 270, 271, 273, 298 n. 581
6:13–20	206, 210, 301		
6:14	292, 292 n. 560		
6:15	208 n. 248		
6:15–20	208		
6:17	208 n. 245	8–9	273 n. 487
6:17–18	209, 211	8–10	20, 184, 205, 206, 243, 269,

	282, 284, 297, 297 n. 579, 302, 307, 309		229, 230, 261, 262, 276, 278, 284
8:1	4, 27, 35, 145 n. 1, 171, 188, 189 n. 176, 200 n. 219, 226, 234, 301 n. 592, 306	9:8–10	224, 240, 241
		9:9	223–224 n. 299, 247 n. 399, 252, 268, 268 n. 477, 269, 287
8:1–2	4, 34 n. 122, 153, 168 n. 100, 189, 190, 190 n. 182, 191, 234 n. 338	9:9–10	264, 275
		9:9–10:18	144, 223
8:1–5	28, 143, 277–278 n. 498	9:10	268
8:1–6	235, 240–241 n. 370	9:10–13	280 n. 513
8:1–10:18	193–194, 219, 219 n. 284, 237, 281	9:11	5 n. 20, 14, 24, 214–215 n. 273, 262, 279, 279 n. 508
8:2	168 n. 98, 169 n. 103, 229, 232, 237 n. 354, 310	9:11–12	9, 12, 189, 263, 277–278 n. 498
8:4	216	9:11–14	6, 11, 14, 22, 23, 24, 26, 27, 34, 145, 189 n. 173, 202–203 n. 229, 215, 216, 218–258, 284, 301, 302
8:5	23, 153, 168 n. 98, 198–199 n. 214, 225 n. 304, 233, 251 n. 410, 259 n. 445, 292 n. 560, 295–296 n. 574		
		9:11–18	229
8:6	18, 20, 169 n. 103, 175–176 n. 127, 211, 212, 241 n. 374, 251 n. 410, 267	9:11–23	24
		9:11–10:18	224
		9:12	5 n. 22, 15, 19, 20, 22, 25, 26, 186 n. 161, 204, 262, 268, 268 n. 477, 269, 271, 273, 276
8:7	227 n. 310, 228 n. 311		
8:7–13	227		
8:8	293, 310		
8:8–12	241, 257, 292 n. 560, 308	9:12–14	279
8:10–11	277, 302	9:13	268, 268 n. 477, 269, 271
8:10–12	265	9:13–14	9
8:12	212 n. 263	9:14	15, 19, 201, 252, 269, 270, 271, 310
8:13	219, 226, 227 n. 310, 228, 283		
		9:15	17, 18, 20, 211, 247 n. 400, 265, 265–266 n. 472
9–10	204, 223, 265–266 n. 472		
9:1	228 n. 311, 235, 257	9:15–18	19
9:1–5	11	9:15–22	17, 19, 20, 23, 24, 212
9:1–10	11, 180, 220, 221, 222, 228, 233, 258, 267 n. 473, 276 n. 495, 302	9:15–23	7–8 n. 27, 17, 17–18 n. 63, 218, 218–219 n.283, 219, 242–250, 256–259, 265–266 n. 472, 267, 275, 283, 285, 290, 302
9:1–14	190, 190 n. 182, 240–241 n. 370		
9:1–10:18	18, 205–206 n. 236	9:15–24	22
9:2	205 n. 234, 225 n. 304, 229, 280	9:16	17, 273
		9:18	22, 273 n. 487, 283
9:3	229, 230	9:18–19	20
9:3–4	222 n. 292	9:18–21	23
9:3–5	278	9:18–22	248 n. 401
9:5	7–8 n. 27, 188	9:18–23	273, 278 n. 500
9:6	251 n. 410	9:19	20, 23, 219, 239, 240, 268, 268 n. 477, 269, 271, 273
9:6–7	7		
9:6–8	225 n. 304	9:19–20	293 n. 562
9:6–10	11, 223, 223 n. 297, 224 n. 300, 225, 226, 232, 267, 276, 278 n. 500, 284	9:19–21	22, 26
		9:20	264, 292 n. 560
		9:21	18, 233, 252, 259 n. 445
9:7	12, 17, 18, 19 n. 68, 218, 219, 230, 276–277 n. 497	9:22	20, 26, 263, 308
		9:23	7, 9, 15, 18, 24, 26, 168 n. 98, 189 n. 176, 198–199 n.
9:8	19, 224–225 n. 301, 226,		

Index 379

	214, 241 n. 374, 252, 260, 265–266 n. 472, 268 n. 477, 269, 273 n. 487, 309, 310
9:23–24	190, 276
9:23–26	216, 263
9:24	6, 22, 23, 24, 27, 34, 145, 186 n. 161, 189, 189 n. 176, 190 n. 182, 202–203 n. 229, 204, 225, 230, 234 n. 338–339, 252, 277–278 n. 498, 286 n. 539, 301, 302
9:24–25	7, 11, 229
9:24–26	215
9:24–28	26, 258–277
9:24–10:10	310
9:24–10:18	28, 257
9:25	12, 18, 19, 23, 221, 230, 276–277 n. 497, 278 n. 500
9:25–28	225, 257, 265 n. 471, 268 n. 477, 271
9:25–10:4	276
9:25–10:10	308
9:26	19, 152, 186 n. 161, 200 n. 222
9:28	7–8 n. 27, 11, 14, 15, 15 n. 54, 19, 186 n. 161, 241 n. 372, 246 n. 396, 289 n. 550
10:1	239 n. 365, 241, 241 n. 372, 247 n. 399, 267, 268 n. 477, 269, 276–277 n. 497, 286, 287
10:1–2	264, 269
10:1–4	7, 11, 19, 239, 240, 271, 273, 275, 276
10:2	225, 265 n. 471, 268, 276
10:2–3	267
10:3	19, 247 n. 399, 269, 276–277 n. 497
10:3–4	238, 239 n. 365
10:4	25, 239, 265 n. 471, 268 n. 477, 269
10:5	152, 293 n. 563
10:5–7	292 n. 560
10:5–10	11, 179, 200, 200 n. 222, 201, 215, 269, 270, 271, 273
10:9–10	268 n. 477
10:10	19, 216, 262, 268, 276
10:10–13	15
10:11	268 n. 476, 269
10:11–12	268 n. 477
10:11–13	225, 268
10:12	27, 175 n. 127, 188 n. 168, 200 n. 219, 215, 276
10:12–13	34 n. 122, 35, 168 n. 100, 171, 265–266 n. 472
10:12–14	216
10:13	15 n. 54, 28, 306
10:14	268, 270, 271, 273, 276, 287
10:16	264, 302
10:16–17	265, 277, 292 n. 560
10:17	212 n. 263
10:18	15, 262, 263, 265–266 n. 472, 310
10:19	17, 198–199 n. 214, 204, 229, 230, 269 n. 479
10:19–20	189, 234 n. 338, 236, 236 n. 348
10:19–21	189 n. 173, 190, 190 n. 182, 202–203 n. 229, 225, 235, 278 n. 500
10:19–22	19, 20, 22, 23, 26, 27, 34, 186 n. 161, 226
10:19–23	6, 181, 192, 192 n. 189, 193, 194 n. 193, 251, 258 n. 443, 262, 282 n. 525, 299 n. 588, 302 n. 593
10:19–25	28, 35, 145, 186 n. 163, 194 n. 193, 277–285, 299 n. 583, 301, 302
10:19–31	202 n. 228
10:20	25, 234, 235 n. 344, 262, 262 n. 461
10:22	23, 181, 225, 264 n. 470, 265 n. 471, 269, 270, 271, 283 n. 534
10:22–23	286
10:23	183 n. 151, 186 n. 162, 199 n. 216
10:24–31	192 n. 189
10:26–31	181, 299, 300
10:29	17, 18, 20, 35, 169 n. 104, 170, 212, 247 n. 400, 267
10:30	149, 292 n. 560, 295 n. 574
10:32	32–33 n. 119, 32–33 n. 119, 199 n. 215
10:32–34	182, 200, 200 n. 221
10:32–39	15
10:32–12:24	299, 299 n. 583
10:34	241 n. 374
10:35	186 n. 162, 269 n. 479
10:35–36	161
10:35–39	28, 181, 208, 300
10:36	208 n. 248
10:36–39	291 n. 557
10:37	292 n. 560
10:38–11:40	184
10:39	300
11–13	184, 282
11:1	288 n. 547
11:3	262 n. 457

11:4	275	12:22–29	28, 144, 185
11:5	1, 292 n. 560	12:23	189 n. 176, 234, 287
11:6	188 n. 168, 264, 275, 286	12:24	17, 18, 20, 169 n. 103, 211, 212, 241 n. 374, 244, 247 n. 400, 267
11:7	152		
11:9	223–224 n. 299, 286		
11:10	260, 286 n. 539	12:25	181, 189 n. 176, 234, 287, 291, 300
11:10–16	288 n. 543, 291 n. 557		
11:12	189 n. 176	12:25–26	190
11:13	208, 208 n. 248, 286	12:25–29	154, 299
11:13–15	153	12:26	189 n. 176, 292 n. 560, 295 n. 574
11:13–16	260		
11:14	286, 286 n. 539	12:26–27	24, 286 n. 539
11:16	198–199 n. 214, 241 n. 374, 279, 286, 286 n. 539	12:26–29	265–266 n. 472
		12:26–28	15 n. 54
		12:28	14 n. 49, 153, 185, 265–266 n. 472, 284, 287, 306
11:17	200 n. 221		
11:18	292 n. 560		
11:19	208 n. 248, 247 n. 399	12:28–29	310
11:24–26	163	12:29	181, 292 n. 560
11:26	197 n. 205	13	299 n. 583
11:29	235 n. 344	13:2	154
11:31	197 n. 210	13:3	182
11:33	208 n. 248	13:5	197 n. 208, 292 n. 560, 295 n. 574
11:35	241 n. 374		
11:38	152	13:6	292 n. 560
		13:7	32–33 n. 119, 202–203 n. 229
11:39	208		
11:39–40	201, 208 n. 248, 288 n. 543, 291 n. 557	13:9	32–33 n. 119
		13:9–16	7–8 n. 27
11:40	241 n. 374, 287	13:10–13	232, 233
12:1–3	161, 168 n. 100, 181, 184, 260, 300	13:10–16	28, 144, 310
		13:11	16, 229, 230, 231, 231 n. 323
12:1–4	4 n. 17, 15, 28	13:12	200 n. 222, 215, 246
12:2	27, 28, 34 n. 122, 35, 160, 162 n. 67, 169 n. 103, 171, 175 n. 127, 188, 200 n. 219, 214–215 n. 273, 270	13:12–15	181
		13:13	16, 246
		13:13–14	15, 161
		13:14	153, 288
12:2–3	201, 216, 216 n. 275		
12:3	186 n. 162	13:15	183 n. 151, 186 n. 162, 279, 280, 309 n. 10
12:4	32–33 n. 119		
12:5–6	292 n. 560	13:15–16	284
12:5–13	185	13:16	264
12:10–11	161	13:17	32–33 n. 119, 202–203 n. 229
12:16	286 n. 540, 297		
12:18	264	13:18	264 n. 470, 269 n. 479, 270, 271
12:18–21	288, 296		
12:18–24	202 n. 228	13:20	17, 18, 20, 168 n. 100, 169 n. 103, 172, 191 n. 185, 210 n. 257, 212, 247 n. 400, 267
12:18–29	35, 145, 285–300, 300, 300 n.590		
12:21	262 n. 457, 292 n. 560, 293 n. 562	13:21	241, 264
		13:23	32–33 n. 119
12:22	154, 198–199 n. 214, 286, 296	13:24	32–33 n. 119
12:22–24	14 n. 46, 168, 287, 288, 289, 297	James	
		1:2	149 n. 15
12:22–25	277–278 n. 498	2:18–24	207 n. 243

Index

1 Peter
- 1:4 — 190 n. 178
- 1:12 — 190 n. 178
- 1:19 — 201 n. 224
- 1:20 — 262
- 2:8 — 197 n. 210
- 2:22 — 201 n. 224
- 2:22–24 — 8 n. 28
- 3:1 — 197 n. 210
- 3:18 — 201 n. 224, 262
- 3:18–22 — 162, 167
- 3:22 — 151, 190 n. 178
- 4:11 — 207 n. 239
- 4:17 — 197 n. 210
- 5:4 — 262

2 Peter
- 1:3 — 237 n. 352
- 1:10 — 198 n. 213

1 John
- 2:2 — 8 n. 28
- 4:10 — 8 n. 28

Revelation
- 3:21 — 5
- 4–20 — 259 n. 444
- 4:1 — 1, 262 n. 461
- 5:5–14 — 156
- 6:1–7 — 5
- 6:9 — 287 n. 541
- 7:17 — 5
- 8:1–5 — 8 n. 28
- 11:15–19 — 8 n. 28
- 12 — 166
- 12:7–9 — 252 n. 415
- 12:7–10 — 162 n. 69
- 13:8 — 286 n. 540
- 15:1–8 — 8 n. 28
- 17:8 — 286 n. 540
- 21:4 — 162
- 22:4 — 260 n. 448

Rabbinic Works

Mishnah

Horayot
- 1:4 — 232 n. 325

Yoma
- 6:4 — 16 n. 55
- 6:8 — 15
- 7:4 — 14
- 8:1 — 13
- 8:9 — 14

Ta'an.
- 2:1 — 13
- 4:8 — 14

Babylonian Talmud

Yoma
- 19b — 13

Sanhedrin
- 59b — 148 n. 7
- 110b — 195 n. 197

Tosefta

Sanhedrin
- 13:10 — 195 n. 197

Jerusalem Talmud

Sanhedrin
- 9.29c — 195 n. 197

Other Rabbinic Works

Pirqe Rabbi Eliezer
- 29, 31, 46 — 272 n. 486

Sifre
- 40 — 287 n. 541

Early Christian Writings

Barnabas
- 4:4 — 16 n. 56
- 5:6 — 162
- 7 — 16
- 7:3 — 13
- 7:3–11 — 7
- 7:4–10 — 25–26 n. 96
- 7:8 — 16 n. 55
- 12:8 — 197 n. 205
- 14:5 — 162
- 15:9 — 3
- 16:3 — 16 n. 56

1 Clement
- 1:3 — 32–33 n. 119
- 21:6 — 32–33 n. 119
- 36 — 153–154 n. 32
- 36:1–5 — 32–33 n. 119
- 53:1 — 299 n. 586
- 62:3 — 299 n. 586

Gregory of Nyssa
Against Eunomius
    4.3   148

John Chrysostom
On the Epistle to the Hebrews
    3.1   146

Justin Martyr
First Apology
    12.9   202–203 n. 229
    21.1   161 n. 66
    63.5   202–203 n. 229

Dialogue with Trypho
    40   16
    69.3   161 n. 66
    75   197 n. 205

Origen
Against Celsus
    3.22, 42   161 n. 66

Greco–Roman Literature

Aeschylus
Seven Against Thebes
    43–47   248

Anaximenes of Lampascus
Rhetorica ad Alexandrum
    3   276–277 n. 497

Aristotle
Rhetoric
    1.9.38–40   276–277 n. 497

Arrian
Anabasis
    7.8.3   158

Cornutus
Summary of the Traditions concerning Greek Mythology
    31   162 n. 67

Demetrius
Style
    214   289

Dio
    61.11.3–4   29 n. 108
    62.9.4–10.1   30

Dio Chrysostom
First Tarsic Discourse
    47   162 n. 67
Kingship 4
    29–32   162 n. 67

Epictetus
    3.22.56–67   162 n. 67

Herodotus
    3.8   248

Lucius Annaeus Florus
Epitome
    1.14.3   282 n. 523

Pindar
Nemean Odes
    7.94–97   162 n. 67

Plato
Republic
    9.592   259 n. 444

Pliny the Younger
Epistulae ad Trajanum
    10.52–53   309 n. 10

Plutarch
Alexander
    27–28   158
Antonius
    24.3   32

Quintilian
Institutio oratoria
    9.4.124   222 n.294
    9.4.128   223

Seneca
Hercules Otaeus
    889–892   162
    1434–1440   162
    1557–1559   162
    1940–1988   162

Suetonius
Nero
    21.3   30
    28.2   29 n. 108

Tacitus
Annals
    1.7.3   309

14.2	29 n. 108
15.44.6	32–33 n. 119

History
2.79–81	309

Xenophon
Anabasis
2.2.9	248

www.ingramcontent.com/pod-product-compliance
Lightning Source LLC
Chambersburg PA
CBHW071951110526
44592CB00012B/1056